HISTORY OF URBAN FORM

Prehistory to the Renaissance

HISTORY OF URBAN FORM

Prehistory to the
Renaissance

A. E. J. MORRIS
Dip Arch (UCL), Dip TP (Lond), ARIBA

A HALSTED PRESS BOOK

JOHN WILEY & SONS
New York

First published in Great Britain by
George Godwin Limited, London 1972

This edition published in the USA by
Halsted Press, a Division of
John Wiley & Sons Inc, New York 1974

Library of Congress Cataloging in Publication Data

Morris, Anthony Edwin James.
    History of urban form: prehistory to the Renaissance.

    'A Halsted Press book.'
    Bibliography: p.
    1. Cities and towns–Planning–History. 2. Cities
and towns, Ancient. 3. Cities and towns, Medieval.
I. Title.
HT166.M59 1974   309.2'62'09   73-22099
    ISBN 0-470-61584-2

Printed and bound in Great Britain by Tonbridge Printers Ltd
Peach Hall Works, Shipbourne Road, Tonbridge, Kent

Foreword
by
Professor J. W. Reps

This book is the best single-volume general history of urban planning and development that has yet appeared, and I think it unlikely that a better one will be written. Skilfully drawing on more specialised studies by others of individual countries or periods, Mr Morris has incorporated the results of his own research and observations. He has accomplished the seemingly impossible in being both complete and concise.

Carefully chosen quotations from other authorities placed alongside the admirably clear and straightforward text provide additional or contrasting commentary on the topics selected for discussion. Equally helpful to the reader are the numerous illustrations – many of them drawn especially for this book – which facilitate understanding of the text.

History of Urban Form is the ideal book for those seeking an introductory treatment of the history of urban planning and physical growth. The more advanced student can also read it with profit because of the author's fresh interpretations of familiar themes and his insights gained through first-hand explorations of the cities about which he writes.

A projected second volume tracing the development of cities to our own time is now under preparation. It will provide a companionpiece to this splendid study which it is my privilege to introduce and recommend to American readers.

Department of Urban Planning and Development
College of Architecture, Art and Planning
Cornell University

TO MY PARENTS

and to

PAT, SARAH, JOANNA AND JONATHAN

Contents

This book would not have been possible without the direct assistance of many people and my sincere apologies, as well as my grateful thanks, are due to those whose names are excluded from the necessarily brief list which follows.

Professional colleagues to whom I owe a particular debt include Sean McConnell, Head of the Department of Town Planning at the Polytechnic of the South Bank and formerly of Brixton School of Building, whose consistent interest and support during the years of preparation were invaluable; Peter Inch, a fellow planning lecturer, who gave the firm criticism which was frequently needed and removed inconsistencies from the typescript; and the South Bank Polytechnic authorities for a generous allowance of research time over the past two years.

Librarians deserving special thanks for their tolerance of my use of their facilities include those of the Royal Institute of British Architects, the Architectural Association, the Polytechnic of the South Bank (Chesterton Annexe), and the Gordon Square library of University College, London.

I should also like to thank Robert McKown of George Godwin Limited, for his sympathetic treatment of a sometimes distracted author, and his colleagues Julia Burden and George Mockridge; Anthony Davis and Cornelius Murphy, two former editors of *Official Architecture and Planning* (now *Built Environment*) for permission to re-use material from my articles on aspects of urban history first published in that journal; Valerie Wood, who typed most of the text drafts (producing order out of corrections and additions) as well as the final manuscript; and finally my wife Pat (a history graduate of University College, London) who has lived through the preparation of this book and who – latterly with Sarah, Joanna and Jonathan – has perforce shared with me the fascination of visiting places both old and new.

Acknowledgements are made to Aerofilms Limited for the aerial photographs of Bath (p. 207), Caernarvon (p. 92), Edinburgh (p. 210), Erbil (p. 9), Nancy (p. 150), Palma Nova (p. 118), Regent's Park (p. 201), Siena (p. 74), and Washington (p. 235); to the Institut Géographique National, Paris for Aigues-Mortes (p. 85) and Neuf Brisach (p. 161 and jacket); and to KLM Aerocarto for Naarden (p. 113). The picture maps of Caernarvon and Flint on page 91 are by courtesy of the British Museum and the engraving of Kingston-upon-Hull on page 89 is from a photograph kindly supplied by the City Librarian. Many of the maps and plans were drawn by the author specially for this book; others were previously used in *Official Architecture and Planning*. The source of other material is indicated in the appropriate sections of the text.

Introduction

This book has been written for students of urban history in the widest sense, and not merely those who are concerned with the subject as a formal professional pre-requisite. The wider public envisaged comprises those ordinary citizens in many walks of life, throughout the urbanised world, who are becoming more and more aware of the vital rôles which are open to them to play in the processes of planning. Accordingly, although my primary concern as an architect and urban planner has been to describe in detail the most significant international examples of urban form, I have established as simply as possible those factors, in particular the politics of planning, which have had the greatest determining effect on this form and must be understood if urban history is not to be just an academic luxury.

This book deals only with that main period of urban history which can be regarded as essentially historical: from the origins of urban settlement through to the end of the Renaissance in Europe in the early nineteenth century, and the Civil War of 1861 as a comparable date in the USA. Subsequently the advent of mass-production, factory-system industry brought about the continuing modern period, a record of which must be reserved for a later volume.

As a long-term literary project this urban history dates from around 1963 when an interest in the history of places, which had developed as a result of my own student involvement, first came to be transposed into notes for a lecture series on the subject. Existing general urban histories were found to be lacking in a number of important plans, and frequently failed to relate examples of detail design to their contemporary urban context. Gradually a concept evolved of a fully international urban history which would include as many significant plans as possible, whilst taking into account availability of information and admitting my own personal preferences. In particular, plans of individual parts of towns would be carefully related to the whole. My background as an architect and urban planner determined an emphasis on the physical form of towns. The title of the book logically reflects the fact that the great majority of urban places during the period covered were not 'planned' and that to have written of the history of urban *planning* would have been inaccurate.

The book follows the traditional sequence of historical periods: the origins of urban settlement; Greek city states; Rome and the Empire;

If you can face the prospect of no more public games
Purchase a freehold house in the country. What it will cost you
Is no more than you pay in annual rent for some shabby
And ill-lit garret here. A garden plot's thrown in
With the house itself, and a well with a shallow basin –
No rope-and-bucket work when your seedlings need some water!...
Insomnia causes more deaths amongst Roman invalids
Than any other factor (the most common complaints, of course,
Are heartburn and ulcers, brought on by over-eating.)
How much sleep, I ask you, can one get in lodgings here?
Unbroken nights – and this is the root of the trouble –
Are a rich man's privilege. The wagons thundering past
Through those narrow twisting streets, the oaths of draymen
Caught in a traffic jam – these alone would suffice
To jolt the doziest sea-cow of an Emperor into
Permanent wakefulness. If a business appointment
Summons the tycoon, he gets there fast, by litter,
Tacking above the crowd. There's plenty of room inside:
He can read, or take notes, or snooze as he jogs along–
Those blinds drawn down are most soperific. Even so
He outstrips us; however fast we pedestrians hurry
We're blocked by the crowds ahead, while those behind us
Tread on our heels. Sharp elbows buffet my ribs,
Poles poke into me; one lout swings a crossbeam
Down on my skull, another with a barrel.
My legs are mud-encrusted, big feet kick me, a hobnailed.
Soldier's boot lands squarely on my toes...
(Juvenal, 'The Sixteen Satires')

the mediaeval period; the Renaissance in Italy, France, Europe generally and Britain; and a chapter dealing with the early history of urban development in the USA. Japan and various other parts of the world are less extensively covered in the appendices.

A wide-ranging, general history of a complex subject must inevitably draw from specialist works of others. This urban history is no exception and special recognition is due of my debt to the following works: R. E. Wycherley, *How the Greeks Built Cities*; Jerome Carcopino, *Daily Life in Ancient Rome*; John Summerson, *Georgian London*; and J. W. Reps, *The Making of Urban America*. Each of these books was invaluable in laying the basis of individual chapters; indeed without the availability of Reps' masterly work Chapter Nine would not have been possible in its present form. His is the specialist urban history I would most like to have written. Numerous other works have been a source of reference for parts of chapters and are acknowledged as such in a select bibliography on page 259. Other general urban histories that I have found of great value include: Paul Zucker, *Town and Square*; Lewis Mumford, *The City in History* – a generally admirable work lacking only the necessary illustrations for it to have made this book unnecessary; and Patrick Abercrombie, *Town and Country Planning* – a miniscule heavyweight book with an excellent historical summary based on his prolific article writings which, had they been properly put into book form, might also have made subsequent efforts superfluous.

A primary concern has been to draw the reader's attention to specialist works in the hope that this book will stimulate wider and deeper interest in the subject. Advantage has been taken of the two-column major and minor text sections to quote widely from related historical sources as well as from general and specialist urban histories. The extracts accompanying this introduction illustrate this use of supplementary text items and offer a variety of outside angles on the subject.

It is customary for the author to give the locality where the book was written. If readers should be intrigued as to why a history of urban form should have been written in a village in Hampshire, the answer is simple: my kind of ideal city no longer exists, if indeed it ever did, and I, with my family, have been able to opt for a rural base from which to observe the urban world.

A. E. J. MORRIS

Lower Froyle

Hampshire, England

Summer 1972

Is the city a natural triumph of the herd instinct over humanity, and therefore a temporal necessity as a hangover from the infancy of the race, to be outgrown as humanity grows?

Or is the city only a persistent form of social disease eventuating in the fate all cities have met? Civilization always seemed to need the city. The city expressed, contained, and tried to conserve what the flower of the civilization that built it most cherished, although it was always infested with the worst elements of society as a wharf is infested with rats. So the city may be said to have served civilization. But the civilizations that built the city invariably died with it. Did the civilizations themselves die of it?

Acceleration invariably preceded such decay.

Acceleration in some form usually occurs just before decline and while this acceleration may not be the cause of death it is a dangerous symptom. A temperature of 104 in the veins and arteries of any human being would be regarded as acceleration dangerous to life . . .

I believe the city, as we know it today, is to die.

We are witnessing the acceleration that precedes dissolution.

(Frank Lloyd Wright, 'The Future of Architecture')

What is to be the future development of the great city? . . . On this question the division is clear and sharp, especially in the United States, where mechanization is so much more advanced than in Europe. One opinion is that the metropolis cannot be saved and must be broken up; the other that, instead of being destroyed, the city must be transformed in accordance with the structure and genius of our time . . .

(This point of view) holds likewise that men cannot be separated from nature, and consequently that the city cannot continue to exist in its present form. But it immediately points out that the city is more than a contemporary and passing phenomenon. It is a product of many differentiated cultures, in many different periods. Thus the question of its life or death cannot be settled simply on the basis of present-day experience or conditions. The city cannot be damned to extinction merely because it has been misused since industrialization or because its whole structure has been rendered impotent by the intrusion of a technical innovation, the motorcar. The question has to be considered from a broader view and extended into other queries: Are cities connected with every sort of society and civilization? . . . Or are they eternal phenomenon based on the contact of man with man despite the interference of any mechanization? For myself, I believe that the institution of the city is one native to every cultural life and every period.

(Sigfried Giedion, 'Space, Time and Architecture')

1—The Early Cities

In the historical evolution of the first urban civilisations and their cities it is possible to discern three main phases. Each of these involved '...radical and indeed revolutionary innovations in the economic sphere in the methods whereby the most progressive societies secure a livelihood, each followed by such increases in population that, were reliable statistics available, each would be reflected by a conspicuous kink in the population graph'[1].

The first of these phases covers the whole of the Palaeolithic Age, from its origins, at least half a million years ago, until 10,000 BC, followed by the proto-Neolithic and Neolithic Ages. These in turn lead to the fourth phase, the Bronze Age, starting between 3500 and 3000 BC and lasting for some 2,000 years. During this last period the first urban civilisations were firmly established.

In his excellent book *The First Civilisations: the Archaeology of their Origins*, Dr Glyn Daniel states that 'we now believe that we know from archaeology the whereabouts and the whenabouts of the first civilisations of man – in southern Mesopotamia, in Egypt, in the Indus Valley, in the Yellow River in China, in the Valley of Mexico, in the jungles of Guatemala and Honduras, and the coastlands and highlands of Peru. We will not call them primary civilisations because this makes it difficult to refer to Crete, Mycenae, the Hittites, and Greece and Rome as other than secondary civilisations and this term secondary seems to have a pejorative meaning. We shall talk rather of the first, the earliest civilisations, and of later civilisations'. Figure 1.3 gives the locations of these seven original urban civilisations and relates them to the earliest known, or assumed, agricultural regions[2].

As shown in the accompanying time chart, the seven civilisations first occurred at markedly different times. The first three, in assumed order of origin – Mesopotamia, Egypt and India – are the so-called 'dead' cultures, from which Western civilisation developed. Although originating much more recently than Chinese civilisation, which was the next oldest, the three American cultures – Mexican, Central American and Peruvian – are also all dead: brutally destroyed, in their respective stages of development, or decline, by Spanish Conquistadors in the fifteen years between 1519 and 1533. Here in the sixteenth century, 'Europe met, if not its own past, at least a form of

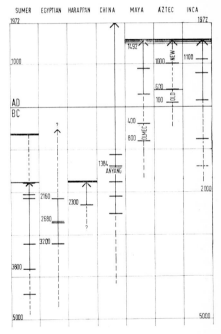

Figure 1.1 – Time chart showing the comparative dates of the seven first civilisations.

---

1. Gordon Childe, *What Happened in History*.
2. It is essential to keep in mind that archaeologists are continuing to rewrite the pages of mankind's early history. Minor re-assessments are continually occurring; major ones regarding 'first' civilisations and cities cannot be discounted (eg Jane Jacobs' New Obsidian theory, mentioned on page 2 and discussed more fully in Appendix G).

its own past'[3], where, for example, metal technology was either strictly limited, or yet to be discovered.

China is the fascinating exception. From its origins in the Yellow River basin during the late third millenium BC, its culture has lasted to the twentieth century without permanent interruption. Furthermore, during the eighth century AD – one of its peaks of power and influence – Chinese urban civilisation was introduced into Japan, where until then only essentially agricultural settlements had existed.

The present chapter will deal with the origins of urban settlement in Mesopotamia, Egypt and India. Briefer descriptions of urban origins in China, Mexico, Central America and Peru, are given in Appendices A, C, D, and E between pages 243 and 254. Appendix B summarises the history of urban Japan, from earliest city origins to its own industrial revolution commencing in the last half of the nineteenth century. (Urban beginnings in Europe generally, and the British Isles in particular, are dealt with in Chapter Four as part of the background to the mediaeval period.)

In some parts of the world, notably North America and Australasia, an urban culture was either introduced into uninhabited territory or imposed on essentially primitive peoples. There are still isolated societies which are no further advanced than the Palaeolithic phase.

This chapter is based on the view that the development of agriculture was an essential prerequisite for the birth of urban settlements. Until recently this view was not seriously challenged. However Jane Jacobs' *Economy of Cities*, written in 1969, contains the contrary proposition that 'the dogma of agricultural primacy is as quaint as the theory of spontaneous generation' and that in reality 'agriculture and animal husbandry arose in cities'. It is thus inferred that 'cities must have preceded agriculture'. It is probable that Jane Jacobs devised her theory to fit recent archaeological findings in Anatolia, which show that in several respects Çatal Hüyük was seemingly qualified for 'city' status by the seventh millenium BC or even earlier – three thousand or more years before the beginnings of Sumerian urban civilisation. (Jericho has also occasioned controversy as to its early status and is described with Çatal Hüyük in a separate section of this chapter.)

Detailed criticism of this persuasively presented yet decidedly suspect premise is not of immediate relevance to this chapter; our main concern is to show the form of early 'cities' or 'towns'. As archaeological fact, urban form itself is unaffected by the argument. Nevertheless, the Neolithic revolution and the urban revolution are both of such great importance in the development of civilisation that we cannot merely dismiss Jane Jacobs' proposition and a case against it is included as Appendix G.

Early settlements

Manlike creatures first appear on the earth perhaps as long ago as a million years, and become '. . . dispersed from England to China, and from Germany to the Transvaal'[4]. By about 25,000 BC the physical and organic evolution of Homo sapiens is considered to have come to an end and the modern processes of cultural evolution start.

From his first appearance, down to the beginning of the Neolithic

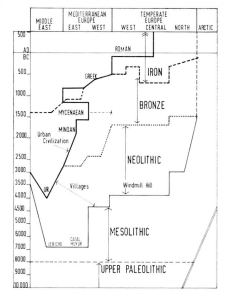

Figure 1.2 – Time chart showing the comparative dates of Neolithic and other early cultures in the Middle East and Europe.

It is impossible to make an exact determination of the world's population in remote ages because firm data cannot be established. Nevertheless, scientists have done their best. Here is a recent estimate, rough as it necessarily is (E. S. Deevey, Human Population, 'Scientific American', September 1960, pp 195–196):
Prehistoric world population
Lower Paleolithic (1,000,000 years ago)
125,000
Middle Paleolithic (300,000 years ago)
1,000,000
Upper Paleolithic (25,000 years ago)
3,340,000
Mesolithic (before 10,000 years ago)
5,320,000
If these figures are even fairly correct, there were little more than five million human beings when the hunting and food-gathering phase of mankind's existence reached its full development. The long, slow increase in population was brought about by improved weapons, better hunting techniques, and more capable methods of dealing with cold weather, predatory beasts, and other natural threats to existence. Getting more food made it possible for more people to stay alive and breed even more people.
(Philip van Doren Stern, 'Prehistoric Europe')

---

3. Glyn Daniel, *The First Civilisations.*
4. Lewis Mumford, *The City in History.*

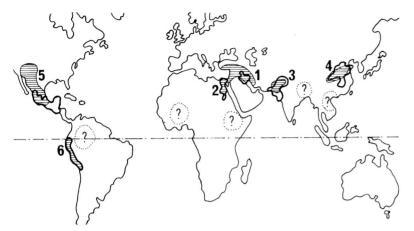

Figure 1.3 – The location of the first civilisations (in heavy outline) related to the location of the earliest known agricultural communities (the hatched areas) and possible other early agricultural centres. Key: 1, Southern Mesopotamia (Sumerian civilisation); 2, Nile valley (Egyptian); 3, Indus valley (Harappan); 4, Yellow River (Shang); 5, Mesoamerica (Aztec and Maya); 6, Peru (Inca).

Age, man existed on much the same basis as any of the other animals, by gathering naturally occurring foodstuffs in the form of berries, fruits, roots and nuts and, somewhat later, by preying on other animals and by fishing. The social unit was the family, but the society was of necessity a mobile one, always having to move to fresh sources of food, carrying its few possessions from one crudely-fashioned temporary shelter to another. There was no permanent physical unit until about 140,000 BC when '... as the last great ice age was approaching men were sufficiently well equipped to evict other denizens and themselves to find shelter in caves. There we find true homes'[5]. Permanence of residence was however determined by the continuing availability of food within reach of the 'home'.

Professor Childe notes that this gathering economy corresponds to what Morgan[6] calls savagery and that it '... provided the sole source of livelihood open to human society during nearly 98 per cent of humanity's sojourn on this planet'[7]. Such an economy imposed a limit on population with a direct relationship to the prevailing climatic and geological conditions. The entire population of the British Isles around 2000 BC has been put by Childe at no more than 20,000, with an increase to a maximum of 40,000 during the Bronze Age. In France the Magdalenian culture between 15,000 to 8,000 BC, with at first exceptionally favourable food resources, had a maximum population density of one person per square mile, with the general figure around 0.1 to 0.2[8]. Other examples given by Childe are that '... in the whole continent of Australia the aboriginal population is believed never to have exceeded 200,000 – a density of only 0.03 per square mile'[9], whilst on the prairies of North America he quotes Kroeber's estimate that 'the hunting population would not have exceeded 0.11 per square mile'[10].

Somewhere around 8,000 to 10,000 years ago mankind started to exercise some measure of control over the supply of food by systematic cultivation of certain forms of plants, notably the edible wild grass seed, ancestors of barley and wheat, and by the domestication of animals. 'The escape from the impasse of savagery was an economic and scientific revolution that made the participants active partners with nature instead of parasites on nature'[11]. This Neolithic agricultural revolution transformed the economy into one with an increasing food producing basis, enabling the social unit to expand, if only marginally so, to that of the clan.

5. Gordon Childe, *What Happened in History.*
6. Lewis H. Morgan, *Ancient Society: or Researches in the Lines of Human Progress from Savagery through Barbarism to Civilisation* (1877). (Republished as *Ancient Societies,* Harvard University Press, 1964.) Morgan defined these terms more exactly according to the enlargements of man's sources of subsistence. He distinguished seven periods – seven ethnic periods as he called them. The first six were: Lower Savagery, from the emergence of man to the discovery of fire; Middle Savagery, from the discovery of fire to the discovery of the bow and arrow; Upper Savagery, from the discovery of the bow and arrow to the discovery of pottery; Lower Barbarism. which began with the discovery of pottery (which, to Morgan, was the dividing line between Savagery and Barbarism) and ended with the domestication of animals; Middle Barbarism, from the domestication of animals to the smelting of iron ore; and Upper Barbarism, from the discovery of iron to the invention of the phonetic alphabet. Finally, the seventh period was civilisation with writing and the alphabet. (Quoted Daniel, *The First Civilisations.*)
7. Gordon Childe, *What Happened in History.*
8. Gordon Childe, *The Dawn of European Civilisation.*
9. Gordon Childe, *What Happened in History.*
10. A. L. Kroeber, *A Roster of Civilisations and Culture.*
11. Gordon Childe, *What Happened in History.*

Permanence of residence in one place was now far more possible, with the physical unit becoming that of the village, although the earliest settlements would have amounted to no more than a cluster of rudimentary huts. Morgan terms this stage in the development of civilisation, barbarism.

Neolithic man did not bring about controlled food production solely by his own efforts. On the contrary, evidence perhaps points to the fact that left to his own devices 'Homo sapiens would have remained a rare animal – as the savage in fact is'[12]. The decisive step forward towards eventual urban civilisation had to await the external stimulus provided by the climatic changes resulting from the ending of the last of the ice ages around 7000 BC. This melting of the vast northern ice sheets 'not only converted the steppes and tundras of Europe into temperate forest, but also initiated the transformation of the prairies south of the Mediterranean, and in Hither Asia, into deserts interrupted by oases'[13].

On these prairies '... when Northern Europe was tundra or ice sheet ... grew the wild grasses that under cultivation became our wheats and barleys; sheep and cattle fit for domestication roamed wild. In such an environment human societies could successfully adopt an aggressive attitude to surrounding nature and proceed to the active exploitation of the organic world. Stock breeding and the cultivation of plants were the first revolutionary step in man's emancipation from dependence on the external environment'[14].

The Neolithic, although often referred to as a period for the sake of convenience, was not confined to a particular period of time, but its duration varied in different areas. In some cases people continued to depend on hunting, fishing and gathering while their more progressive neighbours practised a Neolithic economy. Similarly, Neolithic peoples in certain areas continued to use stone tools long after others were making tools and weapons of bronze or iron. The word Neolithic, in fact, simply implies food production based on crops and domesticated stock, without metals.

Although there is no doubt that the Neolithic was a 'revolution' in man's way of life, it has been suggested that the word 'evolution' is more appropriate since the transformation was so gradual. Recent research has shown that there were semi-settled communities, from about 8900 BC onwards, among peoples formerly known as Mesolithic but now generally referred to as proto-Neolithic. The development of full food production was an evolution rather than a sudden revolution; yet there is no doubt that the consequences of this change were revolutionary in the fullest sense of the word.
(Sonia Cole, 'The Neolithic Revolution')

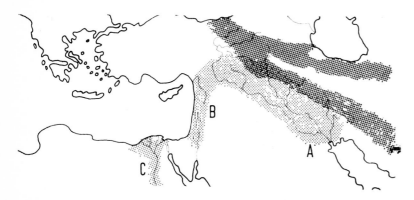

Figure 1.4 – Map of the Near East showing the 'Fertile Crescent' in light tint, and ancient sources of copper in dark tint. Key: A, Southern Mesopotamia, the valleys of the Tigris and the Euphrates; B, Palestine; C, Egypt, the valley and delta of the Nile.

It is generally accepted that favourable conditions for the agricultural revolution first occurred south and east of the Mediterranean, around what is known as the 'Fertile Crescent' – a term introduced by Professor Breasted[15] and synonymous with the phrase 'the Cradle of Civilisation'. This fertile zone, related to which were all the village and later urban civilisations of the Near and Middle East, is shown in the light tint on Fig. 1.4. The zone is shaped, appropriately enough, in the form of a sickle, starting at the head of the Persian Gulf and extending northwards towards the mountain sources of the Tigris before turning westwards across to the Euphrates. From here the zone curves out through Syria and the valleys and plains of Palestine. It is interrupted by the Sinai desert but the broad delta and narrow valley of the Nile form a substantial continuation further south into the Egyptian hinterland.

In Mesopotamia the record of Neolithic settlement '... begins in small oases on steppes and plateaux. Despite the threat of drought

12, 13. Gordon Childe, *What Happened in History*.
14. Lewis Mumford, *The City in History*.
15. James Breasted, *Ancient Times*.

the difficulties of taming the soil were less formidable there than on the flood plains of the major rivers[16]. By 5500 BC, following at least three thousand years of slow development, farming communities were firmly established on the higher ground and were gradually moving down the valleys of the Tigris and Euphrates as the alluvial deposits dried out, and as techniques, especially irrigation, were improved.

In Egypt at Merimde, in the north-west delta area, Professor Fairman records that 'perhaps as early as 4000 BC the settlement occupied an area of at least 600 by 400 yards, and in one part some of the huts are arranged in two definite rows with a lane between'[17]. Other Egyptian Neolithic village sites are recorded at Fayum, beside a lake west of the Nile Valley, as being firmly established during the first half of the fifth millenium.

Bronze Age

Before describing the transformation between 3500 and 3000 BC of Neolithic folk society villages into the first cities – Professor Childe's 'urban revolution' – a definition of the term city is needed. This has been concisely provided by Gideon Sjoberg as 'a community of substantial size and population density that shelters a variety of non-agricultural specialists, including a literate élite'[18].

Two requirements for the urban revolution are implicit in this definition : first, the production of a surplus of storable food, and other primary materials, by a section of the society, in order to support the activities of the specialists; second, the existence of a form of writing, without which permanent records cannot be kept and the development of mathematics, astronomy and other sciences is not possible.

There are other requirements which must be considered, the most important of which are : third, social organisation to ensure continuity of supplies to the urban specialists and to control labour forces for large scale communal works; fourth, technological expertise, providing the means for transporting materials in bulk, and significant improvements in the nature and quality of tools.

As Childe has said, 'the possibility of producing the requisite surplus was inherent in the very nature of the Neolithic economy; its realisation, however, required additions to the stock of applied science at the disposal of all barbarians, as well as modification in social and economic relations'[19].

Throughout the fourth millenium BC sufficient technological requirements for the urban revolution were met, either by invention or discovery. To quote Mumford again, 'as far as the present record stands, grain cultivation, the plough, the potter's wheel, the sail boat, the draw-loom, metallurgy, abstract mathematics, exact astronomical observations, the calendar, writing and other modes of intelligible discourse in permanent form, all came into existence around 3000 BC, give or take a few centuries'[20].

The critical requirement for the urban revolution is the production of a food surplus. So far as is known this first became a possibility on the alluvial plains of the Tigris/Euphrates[21]. Between 4000 and 3000 BC – perhaps earlier – some of the village communities in the lower Tigris/Euphrates region not only increased greatly in size but changed in structure. These processes culminated

Most of the major technological innovations of antiquity were made within the limited area of the Near East and the eastern end of the Mediterranean, and little could be more fatal than imagining that those regions were in antiquity as we know them today. Even in the past ten thousand years enormous changes have taken place which owe nothing to population changes (either migrations or explosions), nor to the recent development of cities, roads and railways. Far more fundamental is that fact that the entire ecology of the region has undergone drastic changes. What we know today as open, dusty plains or rich farmlands were, ten thousand years ago, more or less thickly forested, and within the forest lived a wide variety of wild animals. This is not to say that deserts did not exist, but rather that many hills that we know of today as barren ranges of rock were then at least lightly covered with trees, while the river valleys probably carried very dense forest cover.
(Henry Hodges, 'Technology in the Ancient World')

16. James Breasted, *Ancient Times*.
17. H. W. Fairman, *Town Planning in Pharaonic Egypt*, Town Planning Review, April 1949.
18. Gideon Sjoberg, *The Origin and Evolution of Cities*, Scientific American, September 1965, (also in *Cities*, a Scientific American book 1967). Other definitions of civilisation include:
'A society to be called civilised must have two of the following : towns of upwards of 5,000 people; a written language; and monumental ceremonial centres.' (Professor Clyde Kluckhohn)
'Writing is of such importance that civilisation cannot exist without it, and, conversely, that writing cannot exist except in a civilisation.' (I. J. Gelb, *A Study of Writing: the Foundations of Grammatology*)
'A civilisation was a society with a functionally inter-related set of social institutions as : (i) class stratification marked by highly different degrees of ownership of control of the main productivity resources; (ii) political and religious hierarchies complementing each other in the administration of territorially organised states; and (iii) complex division of labour with full-time craftsmen, servants, soldiers and officials alongside the great mass of primary peasant producers.' (Professor Robert Adam.) These quotations are given by Daniel, as set out in Carl H. Kraeling and Robert C. Adams (eds), *City Invincible: A Symposium on Urbanisation and Cultural Development in the Ancient Near East*.
19. Gordon Childe, *What Happened in History*.
20. Lewis Mumford, *The City in History*.
21. The reader is referred to Jane Jacobs, *The Economy of Cities*; (as discussed in Appendix F of this book) for a contrary proposition that towns preceded agriculture, and that this first took place in locations away from river valleys.

in the Sumerian city states of 3000 BC onwards, with their tens of thousands of inhabitants, elaborate religions, political and military class structures, advanced technology and extensive trading contracts.

Agriculture on the alluvium depended on irrigation, at first only in localised, rudimentary forms but later utilising large-scale canal and embankment works associated with the advent of fully established cities. 'The land that was to become Sumer lacked building-stone or even timber (apart from palm-stems), let alone minerals; its climate was arid and its rivers did not give rise to annual inundations like those provided by the Nile. Yet it was a land of opportunity'[22].

It is not certain when the first settlements on the alluvium were founded. Grahame Clark records that 'the first inhabitants well known to us are those named after al 'Ubaid, a humble village set on a low mound or island of river silt in the Euphrates valley. These people first appear in the archaeological record in the latter part of the fifth millenium . . .'[23]. Through to about 2750 BC, when Sargon founded the city of Agade near Babylon as the capital of a united Sumerian state, the major urban settlements were effectively autonomous city-states with 'at least eleven of these, including Ur, Erech, Larsa, Kish and Nippur at one time supporting independent and sometimes warring dynasties'[24]. In turn the Akkadian dynasty was overthrown and the city of Ur assumed control of the Sumerian empire during the period of the Third Dynasty – about 2110 to 2015 BC. Ur is the most revealing example of a Sumerian city both on account of its importance as the capital of one of the dynasties and the greater extent of excavations there. Its location is about half way between the present-day head of the Persian Gulf and Baghdad. During the Third Dynasty it was alongside the Euphrates (which now flows 10 miles away to the west) only a few miles from the sea.

Figure 1.5 – Urban centres in Mesopotamia, mountain foothills shown tinted. Key 1, Eridu; 2, Ur; 3, Erech (all Sumerian cities); 4, Babylon; 5, Assur; 6, Arbela (Erbil); 7, Ninevah. The dotted coastline is that of the period around 2000 BC.

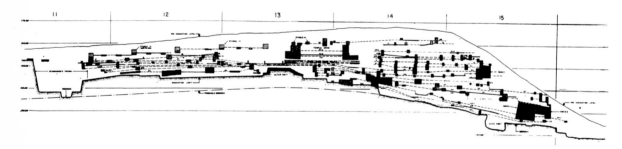

Figure 1.6 – Megiddo, in Palestine; cross-section through the *tell*, looking north.

Before describing the city of Ur, a brief explanation is needed of the formation of *tells*, both in early Mesopotamia and in subsequent urban history. The word *tell* is of pre-Islamic origin and refers to those clearly defined man-made settlement mounds which are such an archaeological feature of Iran, Iraq, Palestine, Turkey, southern Russia and a few places in Europe. In recent times these mounds have generally been inhabited; nevertheless they are the result of site occupation over several millenia. Indeed Erbil (ancient Arbela – Fig. 1.11) and Kirkuk are still lived in, or following Glyn Daniel 'perhaps one should say lived on; they have been more or less continuously occupied from very early times to the present day – perhaps for six to eight thousand years'[25].

A *tell* was created from a city's new buildings being constructed on the ruins of old ones. In Mesopotamia, and other river valley

22, 23. Grahame Clark, *World Prehistory – an Outline.*
24. Leonard Woolley, *Ur of the Chaldees.*
25. Glyn Daniel, *The First Civilisations.*

locations, most buildings were made of sun-dried mud-brick; kiln-fired bricks were used only for facing city walls or for palaces and temples. The life of a mud-brick house in Mesopotamia was probably limited to about 75 years, by which time weathering brought about collapse. The rubble was levelled to provide foundations for the new house, thereby raising the effective ground level. This process was normally continuous, the city regenerating itself cell by cell. Complete rebuilding, perhaps after destruction and an unoccupied period, sometimes also occurred.

Analogous processes, it may be noted, have raised present day ground levels in other cities to considerable heights above their original levels; London and Rome, amongst many other old established cities, are characterised by historic buildings with ground floors well below adjoining street levels. Sir Leonard Woolley records that 'the mosaic pavements of Roman Londinium lie 25 to 30 feet below the streets of the modern City'[26]. The hilly topography of Rome itself, as described by Professor Lanciani, was totally changed even before the end of the ancient period; the Palatine Hill, for example, became covered 'with a layer of rubbish from 6 to 67 feet thick'[27]. Where occupation has been continuous, streets have risen because new surfaces have been laid on old levels, often necessitating the incorporation of steps. Where cities have been deserted for lengthy periods, dust accumulates naturally. Lanciani notes that 'if the Forum of Trajan, excavated by Pius VII (1800–1823), was not cleaned or swept once a week, at the end of each year it would be covered by an inch of dust, by one hundred inches at the end of a century'[28].

The Sumerian civilisation

UR OF THE CHALDEES

The most consistently preserved level of ruins is that of the Isin-Larsa period of around 1700 BC, the excavation of which is described in Sir Leonard Woolley's fascinating book *Ur of the Chaldees*. In this later period the layout retained the basic form of the Third Dynasty city 'and work upon other sites makes it clear that Ur was, in all essentials, typical of the Sumerian state capitals from the Persian Gulf right up to Mari on the middle Euphrates'[29].

There are three basic parts of Third Dynasty Ur: the old walled city, the *temenos* or religious precinct, and the outer town. The walled city was an irregular oval shape, about three-quarters of a mile long by half a mile wide. It stood on the mound formed by the ruins of the preceding buildings with the Euphrates flowing along the western side and a wide navigable canal to the north and east. Two harbours to the north and west provided protected anchorages and it is possible that a minor canal ran through the city area.

The defensive wall was essentially that constructed during the 18-year reign of Ur-Nammu – the founder of the Third Dynasty. Sir Leonard Woolley describes it as 'rising 26 feet or more above the plain and acting as retaining-wall to the platform on which the town buildings were raised. There was a rampart constructed of unbaked brick throughout, which at its base was no less than 77 feet thick. The wall proper, built of baked brick, which ran along the top of the rampart, has disappeared at the point where the trial

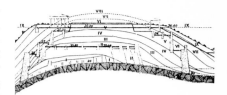

Figure 1.7 – Cross-section through the *tell* at Troy showing the various stages whereby 'ground' level within the successive defensive walls was gradually raised above bedrock.

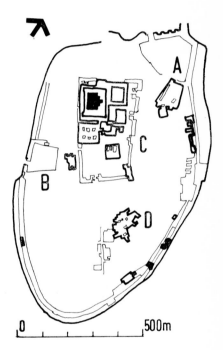

Figure 1.8 – Ur; general layout plan of the period 2100–1900 BC (as excavated by Sir Leonard Woolley). The city area within the wall was 89 hectares and its possible maximum population was 35,000. A figure of 250,000 has been estimated for the total city-state population. Key: A, North harbour; B, West harbour; C, the *temenos* (as Figure 1.9); D, housing area of the period around 1900 BC (as Figure 1.10). The main stream of the Euphrates flowed alongside the western side.

26. Leonard Woolley, *Digging up the Past.*
27, 28. Rodolfo Lanciani, *The Ruins and Excavations of Ancient Rome.*
29. Leonard Woolley, *Ur of the Chaldees.*

excavations were made but, judging from the unusually large size of the bricks employed for it, it must have been a very solid structure'[30].

The *temenos* occupied most of the north-western quarter of the city. With the exception of the harbours, it contained the only significant open spaces in the city, even though their use was essentially reserved for the priests and members of the royal household. The *temenos* layout (see Figure 1.9 and the general city plan) dates from Nebuchadnezzar's reign (c 600 BC) when the generally unplanned arrangement of the area was reorganised along rectilinear lines. The remainder of the city within the walls was densely built up as residential quarters. A considerable part of one such district has been excavated to the south-east of the *temenos*. This housing area seems to have been one of the oldest parts of the city, 'where for many hundreds of years houses had been built, and had fallen into decay, only to pile up a platform for fresh building, so that by 1900 BC it was a hill rising high above the plain'[31].

The houses appear to have been occupied by the middle class rather than by the wealthy. Their size varied, as did their ground plan, depending upon the availability of space and the owner's means. But on the whole the houses were built according to a general plan.

The construction of these houses proved far more sophisticated and their proportions more ambitious than Woolley had expected. He had thought to find buildings of only one storey, built in mud brick, and with a mere three or four rooms. Instead he discovered houses of two stories, built with walls of burnt brick below and rising in mud brick above – plaster and whitewash hiding the change in material. There were as many as 13 or 14 rooms round a central paved court, which gave light and air to the house. In Woolley's words, this was obviously a great city, whose sophisticated living conditions proved that it had inherited the traditions of an ancient and highly organised civilisation.

The development of courtyard housing in response to an assumed need for domestic privacy in densely built-up urban conditions, where the narrow streets would have been noisy, dirty and potentially dangerous, has a present-day parallel in the adoption of inward-looking 'patio' house types. These combine privacy with conditions of high density in a way that could not be achieved with conventional outward-looking house types. In addition to the above reason, courtyard housing in Mesopotamia, Egypt and the Indus valley, and subsequently in Greece and the warmer parts of the Roman Empire, would have encouraged natural air convection giving cooler internal environmental conditions.

These houses, with their highly civilised room arrangements and adequate servicing, clearly represent the results of a long evolutionary process but they are grouped together in layouts which have 'grown out of the conditions of the primitive village and are not laid out on any system of town planning'[32]. This natural unplanned evolution of a town, usually from village origins, is termed 'organic growth' and it represents by far the broadest of two directly opposed continuing streams of activity whereby mankind, throughout history, has created and expanded his urban settlements. The second stream, which by comparison has produced only a very small number of towns and, relatively, is of much more recent origin, is the planned, predetermined approach. Organic growth, at least until recent times, denotes uncontrolled expansion. It is possible to have such organic

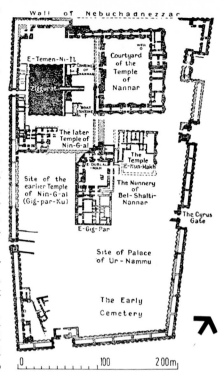

Figure 1.9 – Ur; plan of the *temenos*, the city's religious citadel, enclosed by massive walls and dominated by the multi-stage Ziggurat in the western corner. The arrangement of Ziggurat, temples, palaces and associated government buildings is as organised along *planned* lines under Nebuchadnezzar. Woolley believes that the form of the *temenos* at the beginning of the second millenium BC (ie contemporary with the housing area shown below) would also have been the result of *organic growth* processes, although individual *temenos* buildings of that date would have had rectilinear plans.

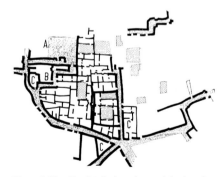

Figure 1.10 – Ur, detail plan of part of the housing area of the period 1900–1674 BC, excavated by Sir Leonard Woolley south-east of the *temenos* (as Figure 1.8, D).
Key: A, Baker's Square, a small market space; B, Bazaar Alley leading to it from the main street; C, small local shrines. Streets are in random tint; house courtyards in dotted tint.

30, 31, 32. Leonard Woolley, *Ur of the Chaldees*.

growth from a planned origin with urban status resulting from, for example, the decision to build on a chosen site. Throughout history there are many towns which originated in this way.

Organic growth produced townscape of picturesque variety– perhaps best illustrated by mediaeval urban form. Despite their meandering and seemingly illogical route-structures, these town plans nevertheless clearly conform to some indefinable natural pattern. The detail plan of typical housing at Ur clearly shows this result of organic growth. Further consideration of the evolution of urban settlements from village origins is given in Chapter Four, page 80. Planned urban form, with predetermined street patterns generally based on a simple rectilinear gridiron, must, for reasons given later in this chapter (in connection with the earliest known examples), have appeared after the first settlements acquired urban status through organic growth processes.

Figure 1.11 – Erbil (ancient Arbela) in north-east Iraq, some 200 miles north of Baghdad at the foot of the Kurdistan mountains. The *tell*, in the centre of the photograph, has been more or less continuously occupied for perhaps 6,000–8,000 years. The close-knit, cellular grain epitomises *organic growth* urban form throughout mankind's civilised history. Narrow streets, private house courtyards and probably the market place provide the only open space within the city. Erbil will not have undergone significant physical change since the fourth and fifth millenia BC; the housing area at Ur (Figure 1.10) would have appeared very much the same from the air. The recent 'suburban' housing, top left, also composed of courtyard dwellings but laid out to a gridiron pattern, can be taken as an equivalent aerial view of the *planned* Egyptian 'villages' of Tel-el-Amarna (Figure 1.18) and Kahun (Figure 1.19) and also the housing areas of Harappan cities in the Indus Valley (pages 14 to 18).

HISTORY OF URBAN FORM

JERICHO AND ÇATAL HÜYÜK

Ancient Jericho, which has been known about for several decades, and Çatal Hüyük, which has been excavated comparatively recently, are two of the most powerful challenges to the thesis that civilisation first emerged in Mesopotamia. Jericho is known to have been a densely developed settlement, with formidable defences and an evolved administration as early as 8000 BC. Kathleen Kenyon, who directed excavations at Jericho, notes in the third edition of her *Archaeology in the Holy Land* that 'after the settlement had expanded to its full size, it was surrounded by massive defences, and assumes an urban character'. Çatal Hüyük (which is illustrated and in greater detail later in this book in Appendix G) also had certain urban characteristics by 7000 BC. However neither Sir Mortimer Wheeler, in *Civilisations of the Indus Valley*, nor Dr Glyn Daniel, in *The First Civilisations*, is convinced by these claims. Wheeler writes that 'in common usage civilisation is held to imply certain qualities in excess of the attainment ascribable to Jericho', and 'an approach to this condition is represented by a substantial town at Çatal Hüyük'. Daniel is even more forthright: 'neither Jericho nor Çatal Hüyük were civilisations: they were large settlements that could be called towns or proto-towns. They did not have the other requirements of the Kluckhohn formula. They may have been unsuccessful experiments towards civilisation, a synoecism that did not succeed; or we might label them just as very overgrown peasant villages'. (See note 18, page 5.)

JERUSALEM

Jerusalem's long urban history has been traced back for nearly 4,000 years but fortunately for the archaeologist the area of the modern city does not include the site of the earliest settlements which lies to the south-east. Kathleen Kenyon in *Jerusalem: Excavating 3000 Years of History*, describes how the importance of the city from probably the third millenium onwards lies in the fact that its location enabled it to control the vital north-south route through the central highland of Palestine.

The first settlement occupied the southern end of a ridge bounded to the east by the valley called Siloam (ancient Kedron) and on the west by the valley called the Tyropoeon. The city's written history predates the extensive Biblical records by several centuries in that it is mentioned in letters of c 1390 to 1360 BC sent by local governors to Akhenaten's officials in Egypt. The present record shows that the earliest settlement occupied an area of some 10.87 acres and that the first defensive wall dated from around 1800 BC. The line of this wall was followed by that of Jebusite Jerusalem, captured by David in around 996 BC. David, and his son and successor Solomon, established Jerusalem as the religious centre uniting the tribes of Judah and Israel. Solomon built the first temple on an extensive artificial terrace north of the old city area, most probably combined with his palace complex. However nothing is known of these buildings: whatever remained by the time of Herod the Great (37–4 BC) was buried within the vast platform constructed for a new temple.

Herod's temple has also completely disappeared but the great platform, bounded by massive retaining walls, has survived as the most striking feature of the modern city.

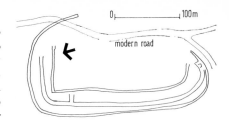

Figure 1.12 — Jericho, outline of the walls and excavated areas (after Kathleen Kenyon). The earliest carbon-14 dating so far obtained is of approximately 9000 BC for what is assumed to have been a form of sanctuary established by Mesolithic hunters beside a spring, which was later to make cultivation by irrigation possible in the Jordan Valley, which at Jericho is some 900 ft below sea level. The descendants of these hunters must have made remarkable progress to have achieved 'full transition from a wandering to a settled existence in what must have been a community of considerable complexity' in about one thousand years.

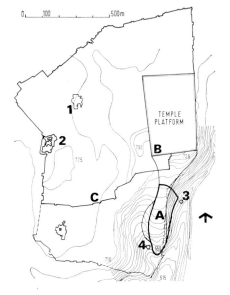

Figure 1.13 — Jerusalem, a general plan relating the site of the first settlement to the area of mediaeval Jerusalem within the line of Suleiman the Magnificent's walls of AD 1538–41.

BABYLON

Babylon was originally located on the left bank of the central arm of the old Euphrates at a junction of trading routes between the Persian Gulf and the Mediterranean. The city had an ancient history and was fought over on numerous occasions before being rebuilt for the last time under Essarhaddon from 680 BC. As excavated the plan is essentially that of the city of Nebuchadnezzar who reigned from 605 to 561 BC, succeeding shortly after the Babylonians had destroyed the Assyrian Empire. Following Nebuchadnezzar's capture of Jerusalem in 587 BC, it was the city to which Johoakim, King of Judah, and thousands of his tribesmen were taken in exile. From 680 BC Babylon was a gridiron-based city, divided into two parts by the stone-embanked Euphrates, and with a permanent bridge.

URUK

Uruk, known also as Warka, and the Erech of the Old Testament, was situated near the Euphrates some 60 miles upstream from Ur. It was the largest of the known Sumerian cities with an area of 1,235 acres within the third-millenium BC ramparts. This defensive perimeter has been traced in its entirety and consisted of a double wall some 6 miles in length strengthened by nearly a thousand semi-circular bastions. Uruk flourished from about 3500 to 2300 BC.

Figure 1.14 — Babylon, general plan of Nebuchadnezzar's city. The total area of about 90 acres was enclosed within a double wall. Greater Babylon was surrounded by an outer wall some 11 miles in length; estimates of the total population thus enclosed range as high as 500,000.

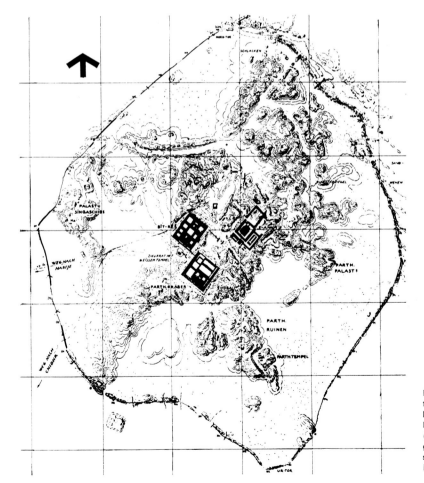

Figure 1.15 — Uruk, general plan of the city showing the line of the third millenium BC wall and the location of the centre which was occupied by the Eanna temple complex. During the Uruk period (c 3500 to 3000 BC) this consisted of the usual group of temples, palaces and administrative and storage buildings. The impressive Ziggurat of Ur Nammu dated from around 2100 BC.

Egypt

Although superficially closely comparable with Mesopotamia, in that both countries contained great rivers flowing through immensely fertile valleys and plains and offering parallel opportunities to early man, the evolution of urban settlements in Egypt took place along totally opposed lines. Jacquetta Hawkes and Sir Leonard Woolley say that 'nothing could be more unlike the mosaic of city states, that divided between them the valley of the Euphrates and the Tigris, than the unified kingdom of Egypt, in which the city was really non-existent'[33]. The absence of urban remains of any significance earlier than around 2600 BC had encouraged the false impression that civilisation in Egypt has much more recent origins than in Mesopotamia. This must be far from the truth, as evidenced by the technological advancement needed to carry through the Great Pyramid of Cheops (c 2600 BC). That there were 'cities' in Egypt at least as early as the Sumerian examples is now generally agreed, but for a number of reasons they took a completely different form, resulting in the absence of identifiable early remains.

The principal, perhaps determining, reason for this is the internal peace which existed in Egypt from earliest times; there was no economic necessity, as in Mesopotamia, continually to occupy the same site in order to take advantage of the enormous capital investment represented by the defensive walls. A second reason directly relates to the first – given urban mobility each successive pharaoh was free to spend his reigning life on earth preparing his tomb for the life after death (the basis of Egyptian religion) in a different location to that of his predecessor.

A further related reason for the paucity of urban remains, as compared with the many surviving religious buildings, is that almost all of the resources of the building industry, together with all the durable materials, were made available for the process of tomb and temple construction. The Egyptian urban areas were built of mud-brick, as in Mesopotamia, but failing the creation of a recognisable *tell*, resulting from long-term site occupation, there is no way of locating the ancient cities, even if worthwhile remains could have survived unprotected by later layers of buildings. As Henri Frankfort aptly explains, 'each pharaoh took up residence near the site chosen for his tomb, where, during the best part of his lifetime, the work on the pyramid and temple was carried out whilst government was based on the nearest town. After the death of the pharaoh the place was abandoned to the priests, who maintained his cult and managed his mortuary estate unless the successor also decided to build his tomb in the area'[34].

So as not to delay the mortuary work, city building under the pharaohs was generally a quick one-stage process. This is illustrated by the still only partially excavated ancient Egyptian city of Tel-el-Amarna. This settlement, situated about half way between Cairo and Luxor, was occupied for the space of only 40 years. The city was built on the eastern bank of the Nile 'at a spot where the cliffs recede to form a huge semi-circle some seven miles long by two and a half to three miles wide'[35]. The reason for starting the new city was that the Pharaoh Akhenaten found it difficult to institute religious reforms in the existing capital of Thebes and moved down river to the new site. Two years after his death, in 1356 BC, his suc-

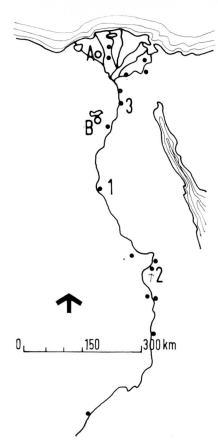

Figure 1.16 – Urban centres in Egypt. Key: 1, Akhetaten (Tel-el-Amarna); 2, Thebes; 3, Memphis. (A, Neolithic villages at Merimde; B, at Fayum.)

33. Jacquetta Hawkes and Leonard Woolley, *Prehistory and the Beginnings of Civilisation.*
34. Henri Frankfort, *The Birth of Civilisation in the Near East.*
35. H. W. Fairman, *Town Building in Pharaonic Egypt,* Town Planning Review, April 1949.

cessor returned to Thebes and the old faith. Amarna was abandoned and never occupied again.

The plan of the city shows a form of linear development alongside the Nile, with three main routes parallel to each other and to the river, linking the various areas together. Its maximum length is about five miles, with a width in from the bank varying from half a mile to one mile. There is little evidence of deliberate and controlled town planning in its layout. The religious and other public buildings are not formed into a single zone so that, as Henri Frankfort puts it, 'while there is a main central group which includes the vast Temple of the Sun's Disk, the official palace, the Hall of Foreign Tribute and the Secretariat, the Northern Palace is a mile and a half away in one direction and the main pleasure park is three and a half miles to the south'[36].

In the housing districts, says Professor Fairman, 'there were no defined blocks or *insulae*, no standardised sizes of estates. What appears to have happened is that the wealthiest people selected their own house sites, and built along the main streets, to whose line in general they adhered. Less wealthy people then built in vacant spaces behind the houses of the rich and finally the houses of the poor were squeezed in, with little attempt at order, wherever space could be found. The houses of all types were found in a single quarter, and though there are slum areas it is evident that there was no zoning'[37]. To the east of the city centre there is the workmen's village which, by contrast, was clearly built to a predetermined plan (Fig. 1.18).

The significance of this Tel-el-Amarna example of gridiron planning, and its similar, even earlier, application at Kahun (Fig. 1.19) in 2670 BC, has been widely misinterpreted. Neither Tel-el-Amarna nor Kahun amounts to more than contractors' hutments used for the more important workmen, engaged respectively in building the new city and the pyramid at Illahun for the Pharaoh Usertesen II. There is no indication that use of the gridiron at either Tel-el-Amarna or Kahun is more than the means to an end of housing the key workmen as quickly as possible – the vast army of ordinary labourers having to make do with rudimentary shelter.

Use of the gridiron for only a small and relatively insignificant part of Tel-el-Amarna would seem to be a clear example of mid-14th century BC political expediency – alternatively expressed as town planning being the art of the practical. In this way it is possible to resolve the apparent anomaly whereby the main urban area of the city was allowed to develop along *laissez-faire* organic growth lines – even though the value of the gridiron in laying out a new town was understood. The implementation of any town plan implies political control, either autocratic or democratic, to ensure that the inhabitants conform to its requirements. Clearly it was possible to impose a plan on the workmen; unfortunately, we may never know whether or not Akhenaten would have preferred to impose a similar planning control on his wealthy powerful relatives and his political and religious officials.

The earlier workmen's village at Kahun covered less than 20 acres. It was contained by a wall, also intended to prevent people getting out, and seems to have been occupied for only 21 years. Sir Flinders Petrie has observed that 'each street was of a uniform type of house; there were no gardens but each house, no matter

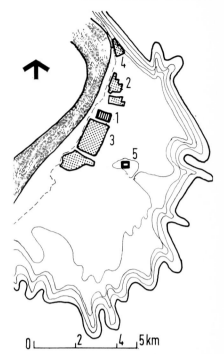

Figure 1.17–Layout of Akhetaten (Tel-el-Amarna). 1, central area; 2, north suburb; 3, south city; 4, customs house; 5, workers village (Figure 1.18)

Figure 1.18 – Detail arrangement of the workers village at Tel-el-Amarna. Sir Leonard Woolley, who excavated this city wrote, 'We dug out a model village put up for the labourers who excavated the rock-cut-out tombs made in the desert hills. A square walled enclosure was entirely filled with rows of small houses divided by narrow streets; except for the foreman's quarters near the gate they were all monotonously alike, each with its kitchen-parlour in front, its bedrooms and cupboard behind, the very pattern of mechanically devised industrial dwellings.' (*Digging up the Past*)

36. Henri Frankfort, *The Birth of Civilisation in the Near East*.

37. H. W. Fairman, *Town Building in Pharaonic Egypt*, Town Planning Review, April 1949.

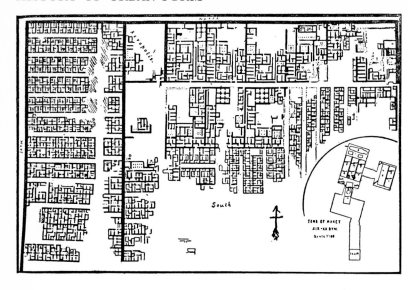

Figure 1.19 — Kahun, detail arrangement of the workers camp of 2670 BC.

how small, had its own open court just as the present-day Egyptian houses have. The ordinary workman had at least three rooms, plus the courtyard, and the other houses – depending on the status of the occupants – had four, five and six rooms, with some of the larger houses being on two floors'[38].

India: Harappan cities

The Indian sub-continent's two major river systems, those of the Indus and Ganges basins, in the west and east respectively (Fig. 1.20), have markedly different climatic regions. The Indus plains have low rainfall but, when irrigated, the alluvial soil is fertile. The Ganges basin is much wetter, with over 80 inches of rain per annum in Bengal. Archaeological records seem to indicate that urban settlement began in the western Indus basin, where conditions would have been much the same as in the Tigris/Euphrates region, and later spread across to the Ganges. Annual natural inundation, probably with simple irrigation control, allowed relatively large communities to become established on the Indus plains by the third millenium BC, but, in contrast, the rich damp soils of the Ganges basin 'must originally have consisted of forests and marshes, which would have needed a considerable labour force, equipped with effective tools, to bring them under cultivation'[39]. Bridget and Raymond Allchin in their *Birth of Indian Civilisation*, give the sixth century BC, at the earliest, for the origins of urban settlement along the Ganges, observing that the situation is probably analogous to that found in many parts of Europe where heavier and richer soils could not be, or were not, utilised until well into the Iron Age.

Development of settlement in the Indus basin seems to have paralleled that in Mesopotamia, with Neolithic farming communities establishing villages on the higher plains away from the actual river courses during the fifth millenium BC, before becoming sufficiently well organised socially and technically to take on the challenge of farming the flood-plains. The civilisation which produced the principal known urban centres is the Harappan, named after

On the other hand the general configuration of the Indus civilisation was quite distinct. The leading characteristics betrayed by the excavated remains include a high degree of civic discipline and organisation, uniformity over an extensive area and stability over long periods of time. The rectangular grid of the street plan, differing so notably from the cramped irregularity prevalent in ancient Mesopotamia, the elaborate system of sewers and rubbish shoots, the carefully maintained walls, the great communal granaries and the standardised systems of weights and measures all reflect an ordered and settled society. What was the basis of this discipline maintained over so long a period of time? There is no indication that military authority was at all prominent: weapons were relatively inconspicuous and defences were apparently confined to the citadels, a reflection no doubt of the comparative isolation of the Indus people from neighbours at a comparable level of technology. Nor has any obvious sign of royal authority been found, whether in the form of palaces, outstanding tombs or regalia. A likely alternative is that the sanctions behind this ordered way of life were religious and that the Indus Valley civilisation, like that of modern Tibet, was essentially theocratic.
(Grahame Clark, 'World Prehistory – An Outline')

38. W. M. Flinders Petrie, *Some Sources of Human History*.

39. Bridget and Raymond Allchin, *Birth of Indian Civilisation*.

Harappa, one of its two most important examples. Harappa itself existed between 2150 and 1750 BC, allowing a tolerance of 100 years at the beginning and the Allchins quote radio-carbon dates obtained by G. F. Dales[40] from Mohenjo-daro (the other most important Harappan city) which give the mature Harappan civilisation a span of 2154–1864 BC. Although the origins of this culture are only vaguely known, it is clear that around 1750 BC it came to a sudden end. Archaeologists are divided as to whether the cause was natural – possibly extreme long-term flooding, or desiccation – or of human origin, resulting from the Aryan invasion of India.

THE ORIGINS OF TOWN PLANNING

Before concentrating on Mohenjo-daro as the most important Harappan city example – Harappa, Kalibangan and Lothal are discussed more briefly later in the section – the remarkable consistency of Harappan urban form and the intriguing questions this poses must first be considered. There is a basic form to these three examples and others of lesser significance. Each has an imposing citadel sited to the west of, and completely separate from, the main 'lower city' urban area. These citadels are raised on high mud-brick platforms and are surrounded by massive walls – probably as much for protection against river flooding as against military assault. Although the lower cities were similarly protected, the higher stronger citadels provided refuge when, as excavations reveal, they suffered periodic inundation.

The isolation of citadel from lower city, and the assumptions which have to be made concerning its function, present problems which archaeologists have yet to answer. If Harappan cities had developed along the same organic growth lines as in Mesopotamia we should expect to find the citadel *within* the urban area, most probably at its highest levels. This is partly because the citadel would probably have been established on the mound formed by preceding occupation, and partly because of the subsequent massive walls with which it would have been surrounded; for the citadel to be located in one instance *outside* the main urban area could be regarded as an exception to this rule – the result of some chance growth determinant. However this cannot be the case with the Harappan cities, separated as they are by hundreds of miles and with the major examples all following the same basic plan form. We must look for reasons other than chance.

The answer is perhaps to be found in the evidence of a second fascinating aspect of Harappan urban form. The lower cities have more or less regular gridiron layouts: main north-south street lines and east-west cross routes lead to the citadel. A gridiron layout cannot just happen – in direct contrast to organic growth it must be consciously determined and applied to the chosen site. This action does not necessarily amount to town planning, with all the implications of this crucial term[41]; we have already seen how the 2670 BC gridiron street system of Kahun should be dismissed as being 'planned' only in the sense that the gridiron was used as an end in itself – that of easily and quickly laying out a construction workers' camp[42].

Nevertheless there is enough evidence in the carefully organised relationships between the parts of these Harappan cities to accept that they were the result of very early, if not the earliest, deliberate

Figure 1.20 – Outline map of the Indus valley locating the (assumed) three main cities of the Harappan civilisation and minor urban settlements. Running parallel to the Indus, to the south-east, is the dried-up bed of the river Sutlej (Ghaggar).

More than one archaeologist writing about these early cities in the Indus valley has commented upon the dreariness, the repetitiveness and the dead-level nature of the various objects produced by the Indus craftsmen. Looking at the way in which the cities were planned, with their rows of mean huts for the workers, grouped close to furnaces for metal production or to pottery kilns, one has the uncomfortable feeling that here were city states in which production was ruthlessly organised but in which the techniques employed were probably not very efficient. One gets, in fact, the feeling that here again the dead hand of the civil servant was in operation, such as was surmised during the declining years of Rome.

(Henry Hodges, 'Technology in the Ancient World')

40. Bridget and Raymond Allchin, *Birth of Indian Civilisation*.

41. See also discussion of urban origins in mediaeval Europe, in Chapter Four.

42. See also description of uses of the gridiron in the USA, in Chapter Nine.

town planning processes. It could well be that the irregularities in the plan of the Mohenjo-daro lower city are the result of continual rebuilding, over several centuries, gradually modifying the street lines, with periodic flooding necessitating more or less complete new starts. This view is supported by what happened to the rigid grid-irons of Roman towns following their complete or partial destruction, after the end of the Empire, and their rebuilding six or more centuries later. (See examples on pages 75–6 in Chapter Four). Urban history, perhaps more so than history in general, has a habit of repeating itself. This is only one of its attractions.

Urban historians have traditionally assumed that the gridiron is used as the *means* to the end of organising *complete* urban entities only with Greek cities of the middle part of the first millenium BC – for the reconstruction of Miletus from 479 BC, and certain earlier applications. (See page 26.) This view was formulated before the still incomplete information on the Harappan cities became available. It now seems certain that, far from Hippodamus of Miletus[43] being 'the father of town planning', it was not a Greek at all who first consciously put together the component parts of a city in a planned relationship. If it was any one person, it was more likely to have been an anonymous Harappan priest, of as yet unknown date.

As has now happened to claims that the Greeks originated the art (or science) of town planning, such supposition could well be invalidated by archaeologists proving theories that urban civilisation was introduced into the Indus basin by an already advanced people. The Allchins suggest that if the Harappan civilisation came into existence only around 2150 BC, it is necessary to admit that not only the end of the cities, but even their initial impetus, may have been due to the Indo-European speaking peoples[44]. If this is indeed the case then we have the answer to the remaining problem of the consistency of Harappan urban form. The cities are variants of a standard plan, already developed by newcomers to the Indus basin, who established their urban culture in much the same way as the Romans did throughout their Empire and as Europeans later did in their 'new world' colonies. Where, when, and by whom were the earlier versions of the Harappan cities built?

MOHENJO-DARO

The best documented centre of the Harappan civilisation is Mohenjo-daro, located on the right bank of the Indus some 5 km from the present river course. Little is known of the early history of the city. Continuing alluvial deposition has, according to the Allchins, 'raised the whole land surface in this area more than 30 feet since Harappan times, and as the water table has risen correspondingly archaeologists have so far been unable to plumb the lower levels of this vast site'[45].

The citadel mound at Mohenjo-daro was raised above the level of the flood-plain and surrounded by a burnt brick embankment some 43 feet in height. It would seem to have included neither the palace of an absolute ruler nor a dominating religious symbol – like the ziggurat at Ur – but rather a number of buildings for various civic-religious purposes. These include granaries for the protected storage of the food-surplus; what are taken to be administrative offices, with possibly a large assembly hall; and, the most intriguing find of all, the Great Bath – 8 ft deep and 39 ft by 23 ft on plan. The bath

Figure 1.21 – Mohenjo-daro; general layout relating the citadel to the west of the lower city, with contours at 10-metre intervals on an otherwise flat plain location. The present course of the Indus is some 5 km to the west.

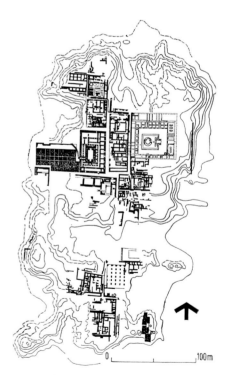

Figure 1.22 – Mohenjo-daro; detail plan of the citadel mound, as excavated.

43. See further discussion of the position in urban history of Hippodamus of Miletus in Chapter Two, page 27.

44, 45, 46. Bridget and Raymond Allchin, *Birth of Indian Civilisation*.

was surrounded by a portico and other rooms on more than one floor; bitumen was used as a waterproofing membrane between the outer and foundation brick layers, with water supplied from an adjoining well and overflowing through a corbelled drain. 'The significance of the extraordinary structure can only be guessed. It has been generally agreed that it must be linked with some sort of ritual bathing such as has played so important a part in later Indian life.[46]'

The nature of the houses in the lower city is seen to be equally advanced. The street pattern is the modified gridiron already discussed, with the entrances to the houses being from minor lanes at right angles to the main routes. There is evidence of a wide range of house types, from small single-room 'tenements' to large houses, with several dozen rooms and several courtyards. The larger houses were all inward-looking, with no openings on to the main streets. In many cases brick stairways led up to upper floors, or usable flat roofs. Most houses had bathrooms, connected by drainage channels to main drains with access manholes running under the streets. Some of the bathrooms may have been on upper floors. In his work, *Civilisation of the Indus and Beyond*, Sir Mortimer Wheeler includes two intriguing photographs of elaborate sanitary installations and observes that 'the high quality of the sanitary arrangements at Mohenjo-daro could well be envied in many parts of the world today. They reflect decent standards of living coupled with an obviously zealous municipal supervision. Houses sometimes had a privy on the ground or upper floor connected with the attendant drains and water-chutes which in their turn gave onto the main sewers.' It is possible that a branch of the main stream of the Indus may have been taken through the lower town to flush the sewers and serve as a 'sanitary' canal. Water supply was on the basis of both private and public wells and climate and the high water-table in the porous alluvial soil must have required some form of downstream sewage disposal system.

Shops have been identified along main streets in Mohenjo-daro; one such building, which could perhaps have been a restaurant, measured 87 by 64½ ft on plan and had separate living quarters arranged around a courtyard. Wheeler notes that 'temples have not been clearly identified, but further examination would probebly reveal two or three in the areas already excavated'. In *Birth of Indian Civilisation* the Allchins endorse an estimate of 35,000 as a probable population figure for Mohenjo-daro and believe that this figure would also apply to Harappa.

HARAPPA

Harappa was situated some 4,000 miles away to the north-east, in the Punjab alongside the Ravi, a tributary of the Indus. Its ancient remains were plundered for brick rubble by railway constructors around the middle of the nineteenth century but the general outline of the citadel has been identified and enough disclosed of the lower-town layout to confirm its essential similarity to Mohenjo-daro. The citadel was enclosed by a revetted mud-brick rampart or embankment, constructed on a 40 foot-wide base and faced with burnt brick. Within this wall a mud-filled platform carried the citadel buildings, the remains of which were unfortunately too badly damaged for the interior layout to be established. Outside the citadel, in the 300 yard-wide space between it and the river, Wheeler records the existence of

Figure 1.23 – Mohenjo-daro; detail plan of the excavated housing area in the south-west corner of the lower city, with one of the main north-south city streets at the top. 'The lower town must also have contained a wide range of shops and craft workshops: among these potters' kilns, dyers' vats, metal-workers', shell-ornament-makers' and bead-makers' shops have been recognised, and it is probable that had the earlier excavators approached their task more thoughtfully much more information would have been obtained about the way in which these specialists' shops were distributed through the settlement. Another class of building to be expected in the lower city is the temple.' (*Birth of Indian Civilisation*)

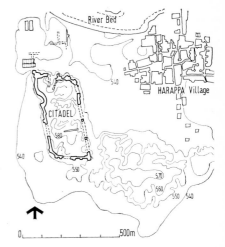

Figure 1.24 – Harappa; general layout. Less extensively excavated than Mohenjo-daro and more disturbed by subsequent site occupation, the city of Harappa closely resembles Mohenjo-daro in most important respects.

'barrack-like blocks of workmen's quarters, serried lines of circular brick floors, formerly with central wooden mortars for pounding grain, and two rows of ventilated granaries, twelve in all, marshalled on a podium. The total floorspace of the granaries was something over 9,000 square feet, approximating closely to that of the Mohenjo-daro granary before enlargement. The whole layout, in the shadow of the citadel, suggests close administrative control of the municipal food-stocks within convenient proximity to the river-highway.'

LOTHAL

This smaller Harappan town was an important trading centre on the coast south-east from the Indus delta and 450 miles from Mohenjo-daro. Lothal was approximately rectilinear in outline, with its long axis running north-south. It was surrounded by a massive embankment and a level platform some 12 ft in height, which formed the south-eastern quarter of the town, is believed to have served similar functions to the separate citadels of other Harappan cities. Alongside this platform and running north for almost the entire length of the eastern wall, a rectilinear enclosure some 239 by 40 yards in area has been identified as a dock for shipping; its high baked-brick revetments, 15 ft high, are still perfectly preserved. In their *Birth of Indian Civilisation*, the Allchins note that at one end of this dock 'a spillway and locking device were installed to control the inflow of tidal water and permit the automatic desilting of the channels'.

A POSTSCRIPT TO HARAPPAN CIVILISATION

After the fall of the Harappan civilisation at the hands of savage, nomadic, light-skinned Aryans who did not know what to do with the urban centres they found on the Indus plain, Wheeler writes in his *Civilisation of the Indus and Beyond* of a 'long phase of cultural fragmentation, not altogether unlike that from which it sprang, but including, perhaps, remoter exotic elements'. The new-comers gradually became settled agriculturalists, and as Andreas Volwahsen notes in his *Living Architecture: Indian*, 'gradually the villages of their tribal chiefs developed into towns, the centres of small principalities and republics. The ancestors of these new city-builders had completely destroyed the urban civilisation of the Indus valley and their otherwise very detailed legends contain hardly any mention of them . . . for this reason the transformation of their simple village culture into an urban civilisation of far greater complexity took place without any connection with, and even without any recollection of, the skilful town planning of their predecessors.'

One highly significant aspect of this new civilisation is the evolution of a theoretical and practical basis of urban planning, according to strictly applied religious principles, which involved the selection and application of a suitable predetermined plan-form, the term for which is *mandala*. A brief description of the rôle of the *mandala* in Indian town planning, based on an excellent section of Volwahsen's book, is given as Appendix F.

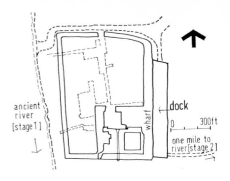

Figure 1.25 — Lothal, general layout. The 'citadel' occupies the south-eastern quarter, with an impressive wharf between it and the dock basin. The Allchins describe how 'an important part of the raised platform contained further brick platforms intersected by ventilating channels, representing no doubt the foundations of warehouses or granaries comparable to those of the other sites. The overall dimensions of this block were 48.5 by 42.5 m. Evidently there were no other buildings on the platform, for a row of 12 bathrooms and drains were discovered there. The remaining three-quarters of the town seem to have been the principal living area, divided by streets of 4 to 6 m in width and narrower lanes of 2 to 3 m. The main street ran from north to south. In this area numerous traces of specialists workshops were found, including copper and goldsmiths' shops, a bead factory, etc.' (*Birth of Indian Civilisation*).

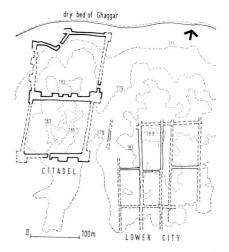

Figure 1.26 — Kalibangan, general layout of this typical Harappan town situated overlooking the dry valley of the Ghaggar some 100 miles south-east of Harappa.

2 — Greek City States

Townscape, writes Professor Anthony Kriesis in his book *Greek Town Building*, is the true reflection of the way of living and the attitude to life of its inhabitants. Although this observation holds true throughout urban history, including the 29th century, at no time is it more clearly exemplified than by the Greek cities of the sixth to third centuries BC. In addition, seldom in history has this attitude been so clearly determined by factors inherent in its geographical situation.

The first of these factors was topography. This determined Greek territorial organisation on the basis of clearly defined, separate city states, rather than through a single unified nation. The two main foci of the city states, Greece itself and the Ionian coastline of Asia Minor, are mountainous, with only limited fertile areas in the form of isolated valleys, plains and plateaux (Fig. 2.1). Such conditions favoured the existence of small and independent states, each of which generally came to consist of an urban nucleus, surrounded by countryside and subordinate agricultural village communities[1].

Two more or less synonymous terms are given to this wholly typical urban/rural entity – 'city state' and 'polis'. Kitto explains these terms by saying: 'polis is the Greek word which we translate as city state; it is a bad translation, because the normal polis was not much like a city and was very much more than a state ... since we have not got the thing the Greeks called the polis, we do not possess an equivalent word'[2]. For the purposes of his general history, *The Greeks*, Kitto elects to avoid 'the misleading term city state, and use the Greek word instead.'

In urban history however there were other comparable distinct urban/rural entities, both in theory and practice, during subsequent periods. For Kitto's reason that polis is specifically a Greek word, this history of urban form will use the more generally applicable term city state. On occasions the Greek city states joined together to face a common enemy, notably the Persians, but they were also intermittently in conflict with each other.

The Greek city (the urban nucleus of the city state) with its clearly defined limits, compact urban form and – superficially at least – integrated social life, often represents unparalleled achievements to modern planners. Caught up in the intricacies of today's situation they tend to look back nostalgically across the centuries

There are a few plains – not large ones, but extremely important in the economy and the history of the country. Of these, some are coastal, like the narrow and fertile plain of Achaea that runs along the southern coast of the Gulf: others lie inland, like Lacedaemon (Sparta), perhaps almost entirely barred from the sea by mountains, like the plains of Thessaly and Boeotia. The Boeotian plain is particularly lush, and with a heavy atmosphere; 'Boeotian pig' the more nimble witted Athenians used to call their neighbours.
(H. D. F. Kitto, 'The Greeks')

1. Glyn Daniel in his *The First Civilisations; the Archaeology of their Origins*, writes that 'the trouble with the word Urban, and with referring as Childe did to the Urban Revolution, is that this word is to most people overlaid with ideas of conurbations, skyscrapers, factories, underground railways and double-decker buses, with commuters and big business. I would prefer to use the English version of the Greek word 'synoecismus' which was used by Thucydides and meant the union of several towns and villages under one capital city. Garner in 1902 spoke of the time 'when the town was first formed by the synoecism of the neighbouring villages.'
2. H. D. F. Kitto, *The Greeks*.

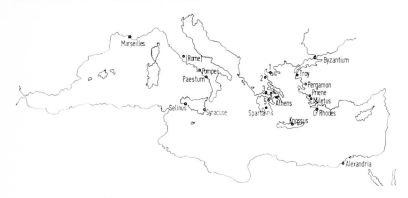

Figure 2.1 – General map of the central and eastern Mediterranean showing the Greek sphere of influence. (Miletus, Priene, Pergamon and Troy are on the Ionian coastline of Asia Minor.) Key: 1, Olynthus; 2, Olympia; 3, Delphi; 4. Thebes; 5, Corinth.

to what they believe was a veritable golden age of cities. Greek culture however was far from being exclusively urban. Professor Kitto stresses this: 'Town and country were closely knit – except in those remoter parts, like Arcadia and western Greece, which had no towns at all. City life, where it developed, was always conscious of its background of country, mountains and sea, and country life knew the usages of the city. This encouraged a sane and balanced outlook; classical Greece did not know at all the resigned immobility of the steppe-mind, and very little the short-sighted follies of the urban mob'[3]. Similarly, Wycherley notes that 'the life of the Greek city state was founded upon agriculture and remained dependent on it; city state and city were not necessarily the same even though the former was most visibly embodied in the latter'[4].

Climate had a beneficial determining influence on the basis of everyday life in ancient Greece – throughout the year it was generally both agreeable and reliable. As Kitto puts it, 'Greece is one of those countries which have a climate and not merely weather. Winter is severe in the mountains; elsewhere moderate and sunny. Summer sets in early, and is hot, but, except in the land-locked plains, the heat is not enervating for the atmosphere is dry, and the heat is tempered with the daily alternation of land and sea breezes. Rain in summer is almost unknown; late winter and autumn are the rainy seasons'[5]. This attractive situation encouraged an open-air, communally orientated attitude to life, which in turn assisted the development of Greek democracy.

In theory, at least, all citizens had a voice in the affairs of their city state. Here numbers were never large: only three cases of more than 20,000 citizens are known – Athens (the city state occupying the plain of Attica and in most respects a non-typical example), Syracuse and Acragas (Girgenti) both in Sicily. Many never exceeded 5,000 citizens. Those which did invariably developed from humble origins. The possibility for all citizens to gather throughout the year in one place, at one time, made feasible the Greek self-governing innovation. Meetings had to take place in the open air; only late in Greek history were construction techniques sufficiently advanced to enable the, by then, representative assemblies to take place indoors, in the bouleuterion. Similarly, large-scale open-air theatrical ceremonies were performed initially at the foot of conveniently sloping natural auditoria. Later these were frequently laid out as beautifully conceived architectural and landscape entities.

... when the reader has calculated how much of his working time is consumed in helping him to pay for things which the Greeks simply did without – things like settees. collars and ties, bedclothes, laid-on water, tobacco, tea and the Civil Service – let him reflect on the time-using occupations that we follow and he did not – reading books and newspapers, travelling daily to work. pottering about the house, mowing the lawn – grass being. in our climate, one of the bitterest enemies of social and intellectual life. Again. the daily round was ordered not by the clock but by the sun, since there was no effective artificial light. Activity began at dawn. In Plato's 'Protagoras' an eager young man wants to see Socrates in a hurry. and calls on him so early that Socrates is still in bed (or rather, 'on' bed, wrapped presumably in his cloak) and the young man has to feel his way to the bed because it is not yet light. Plato obviously thinks that this call was indeed made on the early side, but it was nothing outrageous. We envy, perhaps, the ordinary Athenians who seem to be able to spend a couple of hours in the afternoon at the baths or a gymnasium (a spacious athletic and cultural centre provided by the public for itself). We cannot afford to take time off in the middle of the day like this. No: but we get up at seven, and what with shaving, having breakfast, and putting on the complicated panoply which we wear, we are not ready for anything until 8.30. The Greek got up as soon as it was light, shook out the blanket in which he had slept, draped it elegantly around himself as a suit, had a beard and no breakfast, and was ready to face the world in five minutes. The afternoon, in fact, was not the middle of his day. but very near the end of it.
(H. D. F. Kitto, 'The Greeks')

3. H. D. F. Kitto, The Greeks.
4. R. E. Wycherley, How the Greeks Built Cities.
5. H. D. F. Kitto, The Greeks.

Climate also gave Greek citizens the leisure to enjoy these and other civic privileges. Greek living standards were low, certainly as compared with Roman and more recent ones. Few of the city states had particularly fertile agricultural situations, even if relatively little effort was needed to produce the basic essentials of life. The availability of slave labour must be taken into account, but its rôle should not be exaggerated. Whilst the Greeks were slave-owners 'like all civilized peoples in antiquity, and many since'[6] it is certainly false to believe that Athenian culture was dependent on slavery. The average small farm produced little more than the proprietor's domestic requirements and although larger farms could support a few slaves there is no comparison with the rural depopulation situation in Italy which produced the Roman *latifundia* – large estates worked by slaves. Professor A. W. Gomme estimates, in Volume One of his *History of Greece*, that before the Peloponnesian War Attica alone had about 125,000 slaves – approximately 65,000 as domestic servants, 50,000 in industry and 10,000, by far the worst off, in the mines. (At the same time there were about 45,000 male adult citizens, giving a total population in excess of 100,000.) Industrial slavery was on a small scale; hardly any concern is likely to have employed more than twenty slaves. Kitto describes how the buildings on the Acropolis were built through thousands of separate contracts: 'one citizen with one slave contracts to bring ten cartloads of marble ... (another) employing two Athenians and owning three slaves contracts for the fluting of one column'[7]. Slaves could hold responsible positions as, for example, 'policemen', without either the obligation or the honour of serving in the Athenian army or navy. Slave labour did not force wages down to a subsistence level. On the contrary, as Childe notes, working at the minimum wage an Athenian day labourer in the fifth century would earn in a hundred and fifty days enough to provide the subsistence minimum of food and clothing for the whole year[8]. General acceptance of this minimum is a basic reason why the Greeks had so much 'spare time' to spend on their civic activities.

Another factor, with a more immediate impact on the character of Greek cities, was the ready availability of high quality marble. Worked to fine details, marble was the medium by which Greek architecture attained standards of perfection seldom reached in later history. The important civic buildings were conceived as three-dimensional, free-standing sculptural *objets d'art*, in whose construction neither expense nor effort were spared. Some care was given to the organisation of spatial relationships between these buildings – notably the group on the Acropolis in Athens (Fig. 2.18). If rivalled by a few isolated Roman and Renaissance examples, the attention that the Greeks gave to detail when they fashioned civic spaces was neither understood nor relevant during the Middle Ages and although vitally needed in the twentieth century is neither appreciated nor, seemingly, attainable today.

Yet, and this is entirely in keeping with Greek values, there was only minimal concern for domestic comforts. Homes, in direct contrast to civic buildings, were but rudimentary structures, either grouped together by chance, in organic growth districts, or rigidly organised along basic gridiron lines. Such marked contrast between the splendour of civic areas and the squalor of housing is entirely typical of Greek cities.

Democracy in the age of Pericles produced that inherent dignity of the individual born of free speech, a sense of unity with one's fellow men, and a full opportunity for participation in affairs of the community. The Athenian citizen experienced the exhilaration of freedom and accepted the challenge of responsibility it thrust upon him with honour and with pride. The discovery of freedom gave impetus to the search for truth as honest men desire it. Philosophy was nurtured, and there were no depths which the wise and intelligent were afraid to plumb. Reason was encouraged, logic invited and science investigated. There was no truth which might be covered and remain undisclosed. Inspired by this atmosphere it was no wonder that great philosophy was born; only in freedom can such greatness be cultivated, not freedom from care but freedom of the spirit. This was the environment of culture which produced Socrates, Plato and Aristotle.
(R. D. Gallion, 'The Urban Pattern')

The year 500 BC represents in antiquity almost the end of one aspect of technological development in the Near East and indeed in the whole of the western world. It is true to say that virtually no new raw material was to be exploited for the next thousand years and that no really novel method of production was to be introduced. What new advances were made were to be almost entirely in the field of engineering, and most of the principles involved had themselves already been discovered and applied, although usually on a smaller scale.

Historians reviewing this state of affairs ... have tended to attribute it to a number of causes, the first of which was the widespread use of slave labour. The dirty end of production, it is argued, was put entirely into the hands of slaves, and increased output could be achieved only by one of two means: either by acquiring more slaves or making those that one had work the harder. Since it is not in the nature of slaves either to invent new means of production or to exploit new materials, the possibility of any further technological development came to an abrupt end.
(Henry Hodges, 'Technology in the Ancient World')

6, 7. H. D. F. Kitto, *The Greeks*.
8. Gordon Childe, *The Dawn of European Civilisation*.

Emergence of Greek civilisation

Greek civilisation emerged by way of direct antecedents in the Mycenaean and Minoan cultures which were established respectively on the Greek mainland and on the island of Crete. In this way Greece is known to have had direct links with at least the Sumerian and Egyptian civilisations. The Minoan civilisation 'emerges into literacy about 2000 BC'[9], following more than 1,000 years of inter-action between Cretan Neolithic villagers, functioning in a mixed farming and fishing subsistence economy, and immigrants from the Nile delta and the mainland of Asia Minor. Initially Minoan culture developed in eastern Crete, under the continuing influence of immigrants from Asia Minor, before spreading to the Messara Plain where it was cross-fertilized by Egyptian contacts and 'the richer culture of Early Minoan II–III developed'[10]. From around 2000 BC, during the Middle Minoan period (which lasted until 1580 BC), a combination of wealth gained by trade and of inspiration derived by contact with the civilised peoples to the south and east made possible the first distinctively European civilisation.

Civilisation in Crete was at its peak during Late Minoan I–II times. The beginning of this period is marked by the reconstruction of the Palace of Knossos after earthquake devastation; its end comes probably at the hands of the Mycenaeans. The typical Minoan city was concentrated around a centre formed by the palace and a kind of agora – an open space for festal and possibly political gatherings[11]. The most important example of such a palace-town is Knossos, situated some three and a half miles inland from the northern coast of the island (Fig. 2.2).

In mainland Greece the Early Helladic people were conquered, about 1800 BC, by more war-like farmers, probably Greek-speaking Indo-Europeans. Their civilisation – the Late Helladic, better known as Mycenaean – grew to strength in the 16th century BC. Although there were obvious Minoan influences, Clark stresses that the Mycenaeans and their culture were firmly rooted in mainland Greece[12]. Culminating with the destruction of Knossos around 1400 BC the Mycenaeans conquered Crete and established their dominion throughout the Aegean world. Childe writes disparagingly about their civilisation, calling it semi-barbarous, barely literate and highly militarist[13]. Their 'cities', notably Mycenae itself (Fig. 2.4) and Tiryns (Fig. 2.5), were like their Cretan precursors, little more than fortified castle-towns. Mycenae covered only 11 acres; Tiryns, as it stood within its walls 26 ft thick and 60 ft high, stretched over a mere 4.94 acres, 2 of which were taken by the palace. Troy illustrated in cross-section on page 7, did not exceed 4 acres.

During the 13th century Mycenaean power declined. 'Other conquerors, the Dorians, came down from north-central Greece, making a sudden end of a long civilisation and beginning a Dark Age, three centuries of chaos, after which Classical Greece began to emerge'[14]. It is now thought most likely that European Greece, rather than Ionia, recovered first from this setback and, following the re-establishment of urban culture, took the lead in the colonising movement after 750 BC. Between 900 and 600 BC city states were evolving both in Greece and Ionia, with Sparta 'asserting her primacy in the Peloponnese and becoming the acknowledged leader of the Hellenic race'[15]. Athens, although at this time only a second- or third-

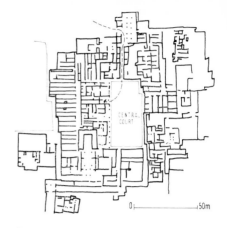

Figure 2.2 – Knossos was one of a number of palace-towns built in central Crete by Minoan rulers. It was notable for the waterborne sewage disposal system serving part of the domestic quarter of the palace.

Figure 2.3 – Gournia in eastern Crete, near the large Bay of Hierapetra, consisted of about 60 houses, mostly two-storied, crowded together on a lime-stone ridge. The site area was about 6½ acres. On the summit, the palace faced onto a large public space which may have been used as a market.

9. Gordon Childe *What Happened in History.*
10. Grahame Clark, *World Prehistory.*
11. R. W. Hutchinson, *Prehistoric Town Planning in and around the Aegean,* 'Town Planning Review', 1953. Vol. XXIII, No. 4.
12. Grahame Clark, *World Prehistory.*
13. Gordon Childe, *What Happened in History.*
14, 15. H. D. F. Kitto, *The Greeks.*

class power, succeeded in carrying through the unification of Attica. Her power was slow to develop and not until the twenty years of beneficient administration under Pisistratus (546–527) did she become a city of international significance. By the 6th century BC Greek cities generally had attained high levels of civilisation.

The contribution made by fifth-century Athens to Greek and European culture is held by Kitto to be quite astonishing; he says that, unless our standards of civilisation are comfort and contraptions, Athens from (say) 480 to 380 was clearly the most civilised society that has yet existed. Under the leadership initially of Sparta, and latterly of Athens, the Greeks defeated the Persians between 499–479 although many cities were destroyed by the invaders, including Miletus in 494 and Athens itself in 480. (The totally different ways with which these two opportunities to reconstruct were followed up are described later.)

Victory inspired the Athenians. During the fifty years between the Persian and Peloponnesian wars they 'aimed at, and for a short time held, an empire which comprised or controlled not only the whole Aegean, but also the Corinthian Gulf and Boetia: and there were those who dreamed, and continued to dream, of conquering distant Sicily'[16]. This supreme period in Athenian history is known as the Periclean Age, after their most famous leader, Pericles, who dominated the Assembly from 461 until his death in 429. His policy made Athens the undisputed artistic centre of Greece: architects created the incomparable new buildings of the Acropolis; her sculptors, painters and potters were unequalled; and, 'the most Athenian art of all, tragic drama, was growing more assured every year'[17].

However, as Professor W. B. Dinsmoor observes, 'the supremacy of Athens in the Aegean portion of the Greek world was but short-lived; for a succession of long wars, the Peloponnesian (431–404 BC) and the Corinthian (395–387 BC), drained all her energies and deprived her of political leadership. Thus the fall of Athens in 404 BC may justly be taken as the beginning of a new epoch; humiliated and impoverished she was in no condition to maintain the high artistic excellence which she had reached under Pericles'[18]. Subsequently, first Sparta (404–371 BC), then Thebes (371–362 BC), became dominant powers, until, as a result of the battle of Chaeronea in 338 BC, the Greeks were forced to surrender their independence to the Macedonians under King Philip II. His celebrated son – Alexander the Great (336–323 BC) – consolidated their victory before turning his attentions eastward to conquer the Persians. Alexander sought to maintain power throughout his huge empire by founding new Greek cities – notably Alexandra (331 BC). As such he anticipated the policy adopted by imperial Rome.

The term 'Hellenic' is usually applied to Greek civilisation prior to the Macedonian conquest. Afterwards, 'the Greek cities lost something vital, though not without certain gains, and some of the finer qualities of Greek art and architecture evaporated; and the modified form of Greek culture which is found in the succeeding centuries can be conveniently distinguished as Hellenistic, though the lower limit of the age to which the name is applicable is not clear; from the first century BC onwards, when Roman power had supplanted that of the Hellenistic monarchs in the eastern Mediterranean, one usually speaks of Roman times in Greece'[19]. This chapter limits itself to the Hellenic city states of the sixth and fifth centuries BC.

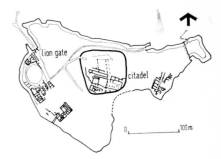

Figure 2.4 – The citadel at Mycenae was first occupied around 3000 BC and the 'city' which had grown up around it reached a peak of prosperity from 2200 to 1600 BC. During this time it is believed that the citadel was occupied by the ruling clan and possibly special craftsmen. Old Mycenae was destroyed around 1100 BC but was re-established for a period, sending troops to fight against the Persians in 480 and 479 BC before eventual final destruction in 468 BC.

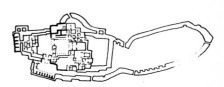

Figure 2.5 – Tiryns is regarded as a second, smaller 'capital' of the Mycenaean rulers. The area within the citadel was only 4.94 acres, but outside the walls the settlement spread for some distance over the plain to the east of the hills. The citadel, as illustrated, was in two parts: the palace, at the southern higher end and an area within the wall which served as a refuge for the neighbouring population.

16, 17. H. D. F. Kitto, *The Greeks.*
18. W. B. Dinsmoor, *The Architecture of Ancient Greece.*
19. R. E. Wycherley, *How the Greeks Built Cities.*

The Greek contribution

The Greeks made quite a few immensely significant contributions to urban history. In this chapter these are described on the basis of historical sequence rather than comparative importance. First came the colonising movement, whereby urban growth pressures were contained by sending out emigrant expeditionary parties to found new cities in other parts of the Mediterranean. More or less contemporary with this movement was the evolution of the twin foci of Greek cities – the acropolis as the religious centre and the agora as the multi-purpose everyday heart; these are described with other Greek urban form components. Lastly there was the use made of the gridiron by Greek town planners from the early part of the 5th century BC as the basis of a systematic approach to the organisation of cities. Chapter One has shown how, contrary to accepted opinion, it is more than likely that the Greeks were not the first to plan cities, the honour probably going to Harappan priests if not to their antecedents of as yet undetected origin outside the Indus basin. (See page 16.)

The Greek period is also notable for the clear contrasts revealed between the two streams of urban development: planned urban form, either as new towns or redeveloped city districts, and organic growth pattern, of which the city of Athens is by far the most important example.

COLONISING MOVEMENT

Beginning around 750 BC and lasting for something over 200 years, Greek city states were involved in a process of urban growth control the value of which was appreciated only intermittently over the succeeding centuries until taken by Ebenezer Howard as the basis of his revolutionary garden-city movement. This process involved the Greeks in the creation of new city states – colonies – one major reason for which was to take excess population from the parent city.

It was a process forced on the Greeks in that, as Wycherley says, 'they have usually been a fertile race and the nature of the country imposes a very definite limit on the population'[20], rather than as the result of any intellectual reasoning concerning the ideal size of cities. In addition, but probably secondary to growth pressures, the Greeks were quick to develop trading contacts which their colonies established for them throughout virtually the length and breadth of the Mediterranean. In this they were following the examples of the Phoenicians, who also had substantial trade in the area.

By 734 BC Corinth founded Syracuse in Sicily. Marseilles also has early Greek colonial origins dating from the seventh century BC, with 'the site of the ancient Phoenician-Greek agora remaining the site of the later Roman forum and even of the mediaeval market square'[21]. Naples and Pompeii are other distant examples of early Greek foundations. Miletus, later to become a planning byword coupled with the name of Hippodamus, was the starting point of a gigantic colonisation, and at least sixty colonies originated from there[22].

Each of the colonies was a city state organised along the social and economic lines of its parent, but in contrast to the generally unplanned, uncontrolled organic growth patterns of the parents the majority of the offspring were developed along planned lines.

The Athenians occupied a territory, Attica, which is slightly smaller than Gloucestershire, and in their greatest period were about as numerous as the inhabitants of Bristol – perhaps rather less. Such was the size of the state which, within two centuries and a half, gave birth to Solon, Pisistratus, Themistocles, Aristeides and Pericles among statesmen, to Aeschylus, Sophocles, Euripides, Aristophanes and Menander among dramatists, to Thucydides, the most impressive of all historians, and to Demosthenes, the most impressive of orators, to Mnesicles and Ictinus, architects of the Acropolis, and to Phidias and Praxiteles the sculptors, to Phormio, one of the most brilliant of naval commanders, to Socrates and to Plato – and this list takes no account of mere men of talent. During the same period she beat off Persia, with the sole aid of 1,000 at Plataeans, at Marathon; did more than the rest of Greece together to win the still more crucial victory of Salamis; and built up the only truly Greek empire that ever existed.
(H. D. F. Kitto, 'The Greeks')

Ever since Neolithic times the coasts and islands of the Aegean had been the subject of exploration by mariners eager for trade or new areas for colonisation; at the height of their power the Mycenaeans has posts as far west as South Italy, Sicily and the Lipari Islands and trade connections over broad tracts of Europe from Iberia and southern Britain in the west to the Ukraine and even Transcaucasia in the east.
Already during the eighth century Ionian Greeks had begun to explore the northern shore of Asia Minor and in due course trading stations were established at Trebizond and Sinope, the first for loading iron, copper and gold from Transcaucasia and the latter perhaps for transhipment into larger craft. Doubtless it was the adventures of these pioneers which nourished the myth of the Argonauts in search of the Golden Fleece that we find incorporated in the 'Odyssey'. During the following century exploration was extended to the western and northern shores and here no doubt the leading attractions were the fish that abounded in the great rivers of South Russia, the Bosporus and the Sea of Azov, and which were traded dried or preserved in jars; the salt that could so conveniently be prepared in the great estuaries; and the honey and wax, known to have abounded in medieval Russia and of which the importance was already implied by Herodotus.
(Grahame Clark, 'World Prehistory – An Outline')

20. R. E. Wycherley, *How the Greeks Built Cities.*
21. P. Zucker, *Town and Square.*
22. S. E. Rasmussen, *Towns and Buildings.*

GREEK URBAN COMPONENTS

The basic elements of the typical Greek city plan comprise the acropolis, the enclosing city wall, the agora, residential districts, one or more leisure and cultural areas, a religious precinct (if separate from the acropolis), the harbour and port, and possibly an industrial district. The organisation of these parts – with the exception of the last two – into a city is best illustrated by the example of Priene (Fig. 2.10).

The acropolis is the general term for the original defensive hill-top nucleus of the older Greek cities and the fortified citadel of many of the colonial foundations. From being the site of the total urban area, the acropolis either gradually evolved into the religious sanctuary of the city, as with the most famous example at Athens, or became deserted and left outside the city limits, as at Miletus. As long as the city remained of limited size, centred directly on the acropolis, there was no need for a perimeter defensive wall. When attacked the citizens withdrew on to the acropolis until either they capitulated or their enemies gave up. With all the important buildings located on the acropolis, only a proportion of the relatively expendable housing would be lost.

From about the sixth and fifth centuries, however, starting in Ionia, the real and sentimental value of investment outside the acropolis was great enough for it to require protection. Democratic Greek society of this time also required security for the whole community; separate fortification of the acropolis was felt to be anti-democratic and a symbol of tyranny[23]. It was Aristotle, on the subject of town walls, who said that an acropolis was suitable for oligarchy and monarchy and level ground for democracy[24].

Not all Greek cities were fortified. The typical arrangement is at Athens, Miletus and Priene, where the walls are loosely spread around both unplanned and planned urban areas taking maximum advantage of the terrain. The wall is more of an afterthought – in contrast to the initial, rigidly rectilinear perimeter of the average Roman Empire foundation. (See page 39.) Two reasons why Greek city walls are more flexible than the urban form constrictors of later ages are a balance of population between urban and rural parts of city states, and the policy of limiting population by founding new cities.

'The word agora', as Wycherley observes, 'is quite untranslatable, since it stands for something as peculiarly Hellenic as polis, or sophrosyne. One may doubt whether the public places of any other city have ever seen such an intense and sustained concentration of varied activities. The agora was in fact no mere public place, but the central zone of the city – its living heart. In spite of an inevitable diffusion and specialisation of functions, it retained a real share of its own miscellaneous functions. It remained essentially a single whole, or at least strongly resisted division. It was the constant resort of all citizens, and it did not spring to life on occasions but was the daily scene of social life, business and politics'[25]. As the focal point of a planned city, the agora was as near the middle as possible, or in the harbour cities alongside the port. With unplanned cities a natural place for the agora was between the main gate and the entrance to the acropolis. Athens clearly illustrates this.

To the Greeks, preoccupied with intellectual matters, home life was secondary to communal activity. As a result – to quote Wycherley

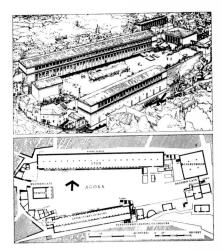

Figure 2.6 – Assos; restored plan of the Agora, and a conjectural perspective view. The trapezoidal shape, wide at the western end, was determined by the shape of the narrow natural terrace on which the Agora was located.

Only after 500 BC did genuine squares develop in Greece. City planning as such, conscious collective and integrated action beyond the mere construction of individual houses, existed already in India and Egypt in the third millenium BC, but never the impulse to shape a void within the town into a three-dimensional area which we call a 'square'. This may be explained sociologically: only within a civilisation where the anonymous human being had become a 'citizen', where democracy had unfolded to some extent could the gathering place become important enough to take on a specific shape. This sociological development was paralleled by an aesthetic phenomenon: only when a full consciousness of space evolved and at least a certain sensitive perception of spatial expansion began to spread – one may compare the essentially frontal sculpture of Egypt and Mesopotamia with the roundness of Greek classical sculpture – only then could the void before, around, and within a structure become more than a mere counterpart to articulated volume. (P. Zucker, 'Town and Square')

23. R. E. Wycherley, *How the Greeks Built Cities.*
24. Aristotle, *Politics* vii 10.4.
25. R. E. Wycherley, *How the Greeks Built Cities.*

again – 'the Greeks of the fifth century put their best, architecturally, into temples and public buildings; in the scheme of the Greek city the houses were subordinate. The agora, shrines, the theatre, gymnasia and so forth occupied sites determined by traditoal sanctity or convenience. The houses filled in the rest'[26].

Home comforts were minimal. Drainage and refuse disposal were more or less non-existent and the resulting contrast between the magnificence of the civic areas and the squalor of the housing districts was probably as marked as at any time in urban history. In both planned and unplanned cities the invariable form taken by the houses is that of a number of rooms grouped around a courtyard (Fig. 2.7). There are, however, no standard room arrangements. Even at Miletus and Priene, with their repetitive housing block modules, individual dwellings are of different sizes and plans.

The economy of the Greek city states, being based to a considerable extent on slave labour, gave the citizens ample leisure time to be employed on either intellectual discussion or collective activities. For these latter communal requirements, specialised building types were developed including the theatre, gymnasium and stadium, each of which was regarded as essential in every city. The theatre required a suitable natural auditorium slope and in many cities it is to be found on the southern side of the acropolis. Often, these leisure and cultural functions are grouped together.

Systematic city planning

By coincidence the two most important planned Greek cities – Miletus and Priene – are located within a short distance of each other on the Ionian coastline of Asia Minor. Priene is the clearer example, described by Wycherley as 'containing everything which makes a polis, all very neatly and ingeniously arranged and subordinated to the Hippodamian plan'[27]. Compared to Miletus, which in Roman times during the first century AD acquired 80,000 to 100,000 inhabitants, Priene contained only some four hundred houses, with at most 4,000 population. Miletus will be described first because its rebuilding predates that of its neighbour by over a century; it moreover introduces here the systematic Hippodamian method of planning cities.

MILETUS AND HIPPODAMUS
Miletus had played a major rôle in the gradual establishment of Greek commercial and military power between the tenth and sixth centuries BC, founding, as described earlier, a large number of colonies and becoming as a result the head of a powerful confederacy of city states. But early in the fifth century Ionia was overrun by the Persians and in 494 BC Miletus was captured, sacked and destroyed. It can safely be assumed that the old city was the product of centuries of haphazard, organic growth– in contrast to the planned forms of at least some of its more recent colonies. In rebuilding Miletus from 479 BC onwards the opportunity was taken to plan 'an entirely new and modern city unlike the Athenians, who also returned to find their city destroyed, but gradually restored the *status quo ante* with the addition of more magnificent temples'[28].

The master plan for the reconstruction of the city was prepared by a Milesan architect, Hippodamus of Miletus, concerning whose

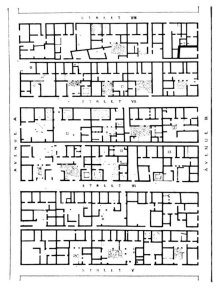

Figure 2.7 – Detail of north hill housing at Olynthus, built after 432 BC to a gridiron layout based on main streets running the length of the ridge (as Avenues A and B) with numerous cross-streets alternating with back alleys which divide the housing blocks into two parts. The tinted areas within the houses mark the internal courtyard around which the rooms are planned. As in the preceding historical periods, courtyard housing was the general pattern of Greek urban housing. This layout could well be part of a present-day housing scheme, perhaps designed in accordance with ideas put forward by Alexander and Chermayeff in their *Community and Privacy*, but note the variety of room arrangements within the standard house areas, indicative perhaps, of do-it-yourself building within a tightly controlled planned framework. Surely this is one of the directions in which twentieth-century urban housing should be moving?

26 27, 28. R. E. Wycherley, *How the Greeks Built Cities.*

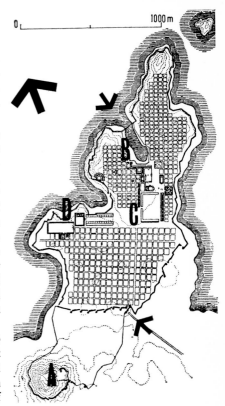

planning work, at Miletus and elsewhere, one of the more insidious myths of urban history has been perpetrated. Traditionally Hippodamus has been revered as the 'father of town planning' and the inventor of the gridiron. In these respects commentators have misrepresented his achievements, rather in the same way that Sir Christopher Wren's admirers have claimed unwarranted planning expertise on his behalf and critics of Baron Haussmann have distorted his rôle in renewing mid-nineteenth century Paris.

Clearly Hippodamus was not the inventor of the gridiron: its application to the layout of planned *parts* of cities as early as 2670 BC, and its probable general rôle as the urban form regulator of the early third millenium BC Harappan cities have been described in the preceding chapter. The claim that he was the 'father of town planning' may, however, still retain a measure of truth. If the Harappan cities are recognised as the first known planned urban settlements then Hippodamus has been anticipated by at least 2,000 years. (Caution is necessary because of the continuing archaeological work in the Indus basin, with always the added possibility of significant finds elsewhere.) But if Mohenjo-daro, Harappa and other contemporary Indus basin cities are not accorded planned urban status, then Hippodamus might still conceivably have set a significant precedent with his plan for Miletus.

The key consideration is whether or not it was Hippodamus who first, at a given moment in time, organised all of the component parts of a new town, central area, housing, commerce, cultural and leisure facilities and defensive wall, to make an integrated urban entity. It may seem improbable on the basis of scanty knowledge of what actually happened at Miletus, but we do have extensively documented modern examples of individuals forcing a change of direction in accepted urban growth trends – Ebenezer Howard as the recognised instigator of the garden-city/new-town movement, and Constantine Doxiadis as the *éminence-grise* behind many mid-twentieth century developments, are but two examples.

For all his significance in the history of town planning, Hippodamus remains a mysterious personality concerning whom there is little information of value. Aristotle, no less, has much to answer for in creating the myth with his observation that Hippodamus was 'the son of Euryphon, a native of Miletus, the same who invented the art of planning cities, and who also laid out the Piraeus – a strange man, whose fondness of distinction led him into a general eccentricity of life, which made some think him affected ... besides aspiring to be an adept in the knowledge of nature, he was the first person not a statesman who made inquiries about the best form of government'[29].

Various city planning schemes have been attributed to him. He can certainly be regarded as responsible for Miletus, his first work; he then moved on to Athens with a commission from Pericles to lay out the new harbour town of Piraeus about 450 BC. Piraeus was followed by the colonisation of Thurii, in Southern Italy, from 443 BC onwards: this was described by Kriesis as a progressive community which believed in planning and employed Hippodamus to build them a model town[30]. Claims that he was responsible for planning the new city of Rhodes in 408 BC are now discounted. Zucker eliminates these as highly improbable, since by then he would have reached an age unusual even for city planners[31].

Figure 2.8 – Miletus; the general plan as excavated by von Gerkan. The original peninsular situation on the southern side of the estuary of the River Meander, facing across to Priene, has long since disappeared as a result of silting-up of the bay. (A similar fate to that experienced by Winchelsea in the fourteenth and fifteenth centuries – see page 88.) Key: A, early fortified hilltop settlement, a form of acropolis; B, the main harbour; C, the Agora complex; D, theatre and other cultural/leisure activity facilities.

The plan of Miletus in Ionia of c470 BC, as reconstructed by A. von Gerkan. Urban historians have conceived a violent affectation for this exercise in modular coercion which – if it had ever been executed – would have looked like a nightmare to anyone who could think three-dimensionally. It would have been a rat's maze of blank walls, since all Greek houses were walled, bare of any compass orientation or ornamental identification features, and indifferent to a spectacularly beautiful location. View and access to the sea cliffs were barred by a wall that followed the cliff's contours, as if to be certain that the inhabitants of a divinely inspired theorem were not distracted by the irregularities of nature.
(Sibyl Moholy-Nagy. 'Matrix of Man')

29. Aristotle, quoted, A. Kriesis, *Greek Town Building.*
30. A. Kriesis, *Greek Town Building.*
31. P. Zucker, *Town and Square.*

MILETUS : THE PLAN

Of even greater significance than the detailed form of the plan of Miletus is the far-sighted attitude of the Milesians, who seem to have had visions of their city regaining much of its former greatness, and to have planned accordingly[32]. Although there must have been every reason for the returning survivors to restart on a small scale along reinstated organic lines (as with the rebuilding of the City of London after 1666), the citizens decided instead to adopt a plan which not only served for the initial rebuilding phases but was later able to serve as a basis for the vastly increased area of the first century AD Roman city. There was no loss of form resulting from this unanticipated expansion, nor was demolition of houses needed to accommodate the greatly enlarged agora area with its eventual complex of spaces and buildings.

As rebuilt from 479 BC, Miletus occupied the whole of a rocky, indented peninsula to the north of the original acropolis (Fig. 2.8). At first the new walls included this hill, but in the course of time a new wall was built excluding it. The agora area is centrally placed in the form of a rectangle with the long side leading from the defended harbour inlet. Of the three distinct residential groups, the southernmost with its considerably larger house blocks dates from Roman times. West of the agora and grouped around a second inlet are the theatre gymnasium and stadium building. The area within the walls is about 220 acres and the maximum dimensions along and across the peninsular are 1,960 yards and 1,200 yards respectively. Rasmussen records that Miletus prospered even more under the Romans and grew to be a city of 80,000 to 100,000 inhabitants[33]. Its final decay dates from the second century AD.

PRIENE

Across the valley of the aptly named river Meander from Miletus, on a south-facing spur of Mount Mycale, Priene was constructed from about 350 BC onwards to replace an abandoned nearby settlement. The city is built on four broad terraces which descend some 320 feet from the acropolis to the stadium and gymnasium on its southern edge (Fig. 2.10). The Temple of Athena Polias, the theatre, a second gymnasium, and the agora are located on the two intermediate terraces. The basis of the plan is formed by seven east-west streets following the contours, and a total of fifteen north-south stepped paths, giving access between them, up and down the hillside. The main streets are 23 feet wide and the remainder 13 feet wide. Streets and paths are orientated north/south and east/west : housing blocks so formed are of a regular 51.4 by 38.6 yards size and contains four dwellings on average[34]. It has been estimated that there were about four hundred houses in Priene, thus giving a total population not exceeding 4,000.

The agora is in the centre of the city occupying two complete housing blocks and parts of others, on both sides of the main street running from the western gate (Fig. 2.12). This street is widened to 10 yards across the agora. Along its northern side a continuous flight of six steps lead up 1.6 yards to the Sacred Stoa (127 yards in length) built in about 150 BC to replace an earlier building. At the rear of this stoa is a line of magistrates' offices. The Bouleuterion and Prytaneion are at the eastern end of the stoa. At the western end an access stairway lets on to the western portico

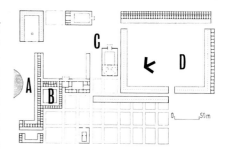

Figure 2.9 – Miletus, detail plan of the Agora area in the second century BC. (Note: harbour to the left.) Key: A, harbour and port facilities; B, large colonnaded courtyard, surrounded by shops and offices; C, Council House (175–164 BC) with a colonnaded court in front; D, South Agora (third century BC). Later additions to the Agora area were made in the first and second centuries AD under Roman rule. (See plan of second century AD in *How the Greeks Built Cities,* p 83.)

R. E. Wycherley notes that 'the harbour building was the first important architectural scheme of the new agora, and besides giving the town a fine waterfront, provided facilities for the merchants as Miletus' mercantile prosperity returned. The harbour zone was, naturally, developed first . . . The architects who succeeded one another in carrying out the great work maintained its unity and also its subordination to the general street-plan.'

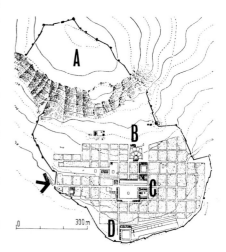

Figure 2.10 – Priene, general plan (north at the top). The contour lines, both solid and dotted, are at 25-metre intervals; the 50-metre contour passes through the main western gate into the city. The ancient course of the River Meander provided water access a short distance further down the slope to the south. Key: A, the Acropolis, rising to more than 375 m above sea level (some 300 m above the level of the Agora); B, Theatre; C, Agora complex; D, gymnasium and stadium.

32. R. E. Wycherley, *How the Greeks Built Cities.*
33. S. E. Rasmussen, *Towns and Buildings.*
34. A. Kriesis, *Greek Town Building.*

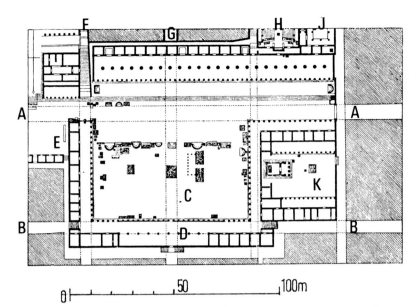

Figure 2.11 – Priene, detail plan of the Agora (north at the top). Key: A–A, main east-west street across city; B–B, grid street continued through the southern stoa with access up by way of steps; C, main Agora space; D, colonnaded hall; E, fish- and meat-market; F, stepped grid footpath on hillside; G, the north stoa; H, Bouleuterion; J, Prytaneion; K, Temple of Zeus.

of the main open southern section of the agora, a space some 82 by 50 yards in area originally containing only one altar in the middle but acquiring in the course of time a number of other monuments and statues. Directly to the west of this portico is the main food market. The portico continues around the southern and eastern sides of the space, and then eastward to face the Sacred Stoa across what is in effect a 46-yard-long colonnaded street. The Temple of Zeus is in its own religious precinct immediately to the east. The main civic buildings are most on the north side of the main street.

Figure 2.12 – An artist's impression of Priene, a clear example of the form of a small Greek city of the period. The close-knit but ordered urban grain can be contrasted with that of Erbil – an organic growth counterpart – as shown by the aerial photograph reproduced in Figure 1.11. Key: A, Agora; B, Temple of Zeus; C. Gymnasium; E, Temple of Athena; F, Stadium; G, on far left, main entrance into city. (Drawing after A. Zippelius)

Athens: organic growth

In direct contrast to Miletus and other systematically planned Greek cities of the 5th century BC, Athens was never planned as a whole. As with Miletus an opportunity for comprehensive reconstruction was offered, following devastation during the Persian wars but, perhaps, because of its greater size or the need for more immediate rebuilding, the Athenians preferred to reinstate their old city. The two main groups of civic buildings – the Acropolis and the agora – were rebuilt with great care and considerable attention to spatial relationships, but in each instance their layouts were determined by inherited constraints. Similarly later in history, the city of Rome did not lose its organic growth structure, although it also contained a number of methodically organised building groups.

The Athenian Acropolis, site of the Neolithic village nucleus of the city, must have been one of the best natural fortresses of the ancient world. At its highest point, north-east of the Parthenon, it rises some 300 feet above the general level of the plain with sheer rock faces on all sides except the west, where there is an accessible slope. It is of irregular shape, roughly 350 yards by 140 yards, with the long dimension orientated east-west. The Acropolis is situated some 4 miles from the Aegean sea, on the plain of Attica (Fig. 2.17). Including the Acropolis there were five hills within the ancient walls and the city, which now occupies the greater part of the Attic plain, is surrounded by an amphitheatre of mountains, nowhere far distant and to the east in Hymettos barely five miles from the centre[35].

From earliest times man had been attracted to the area by the presence of natural springs: it is known to have been occupied as early as 2800 BC, although the traditionally accepted date of the foundation of Athens is 1581 BC, when the worship of Athena was established on the Acropolis[36]. At first the city was confined to its hilltop site, with the main approach path winding its way up the western slope.

Following the unification of Attica under the leadership of Athens during the 8th century BC, the city grew steadily in authority and extent. New housing districts were added by haphazard growth on the plain, around the lower slopes of the Acropolis, which gradually assumed the religious precinct function which it was to keep throughout the city's ancient history. The agora area developed from a market and meeting place which had long been established where the Panathenaic Way started its ascent up the western Acropolis slope (Fig. 2.14).

At first the Athenian fleet was based on the Bay of Phaleron, which by its gently shelving sands was admirably adapted for beaching ships in accordance with the customs of early times[37]. When the city became a major naval power, with a fleet of two hundred ships, a more permanent anchorage was required and in 493 BC the Piraeus peninsula was chosen as a new fortified naval base. To overcome the problem of ensuring access between Athens and its harbour in time of war Themistocles proposed moving the city to the Piraeus. Pericles in effect did this, in about 456 BC, when he built the 'Long Walls' linking the two. The northern and southern walls were respectively about $4\frac{1}{2}$ and 4 miles in length. It is known that Hippodamus planned Piraeus, towards the middle of the 5th

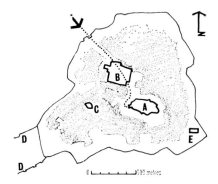

Figure 2.13 – Athens, general plan of the fifth century BC showing the relationship of the main parts of the city. Key: A, the Acropolis; B, the Agora; C, the Pnyx; D, the Long Walls to Piraeus; E, the Olympieion Temple. The dotted line through the north-western part of the city, leading to the Acropolis, shows the route of the Panathenaic Way.

This closeness to rural ways no doubt partly accounts for the primitive housing accommodations and sanitary facilities that characterised the Greek cities right into the fourth century and even later. The houses were lightly built of wood and sun-dried clay; so flimsy were the walls that the quickest way for a burglar to enter a house was by digging through the wall. Residentially speaking the biggest cities were little better at first than overgrown villages; indeed. precisely because of their overgrowth and density of site occupation, they were certainly much worse, because they lacked the open spaces of the farmyard and neighbouring field.

Thus the highest culture of the ancient world, that o. Athens, reached its apex in what was, from the standpoint of town planning and hygiene, a deplorably backward municipality. The varied sanitary facilities that Ur and Harappa had boasted two thousand years before hardly existed even in vestigial form in fifth-century Athens. The streets of any Greek city, down to Hellenistic times, were little more than alleys. and many of these alleys were only passageways, a few feet wide. Refuse and ordure accumulated at the city's outskirts, inviting disease and multiplying victims of the plague. The stereo-typed, largely false image of the 'medieval town'. which many people who should know better still retain, would in fact be a true image for the growing cities of sixth- and fifth-century Greece, particularly in Attica and the Peloponnese. Certainly it applies with far more justice to these cities than to many towns in Western Europe in the thirteenth century AD.

(Lewis Mumford. 'The City in History')

35. L. Russell Muirhead, *Athens and Environs*.
36. The date 1581 BC is that of Greek legend: it has as little real meaning as 753 BC, when Romulus and Remus reputedly founded Rome or the 25 March, 421 AD, at midday exactly, when Venice is supposed to have been established.
37. E. A. Gardner, *Greece and the Aegean*.

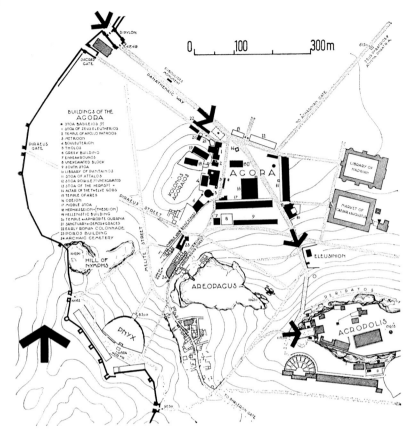

BUILDINGS OF THE
AGORA
◆ STOA BASILEIOS (?)
1 STOA OF ZEUS ELEUTHERIOS
2 TEMPLE OF APOLLO PATROOS
3 METROON
4 BOULEUTERION
5 THOLOS
6 GREEK BUILDING
7 ENNEAKROUNOS
8 UNEXCAVATED BLOCK
9 SOUTH STOA
10 LIBRARY OF PANTAINOS
11 STOA OF ATTALOS
12 STOA POIKILE (UNEXCAVATED)
13 STOA OF THE HEPHSII
14 ALTAR OF THE TWELVE GODS
15 TEMPLE OF ARES
16 ODEION
17 MIDDLE STOA
18 HEPHAISTEION (THESEION)
19 HELLENISTIC BUILDING
20 TEMPLE of APHRODITE OURANIA
21 SANCTUARY of DEMOS & GRACES
22 EARLY ROMAN COLONNADE
23 POROS BUILDING
24 ARCHAIC CEMETERY

Figure 2.14 – Detail plan of the north-western part of Athens in the second century AD. The Agora is shown in its final form with the 'huge, clumsy structure of the Odeion' (Bacon) and that of the Middle Stoa, inserted into the central space. The line of the Panathenaic Way is shown by a sequence of arrows. East of the Agora, two important Roman buildings are shown; the library of Hadrian and the market of Caesar Augustus. A typical linear group of organic growth housing is shown south of Areopagus hill. This was the general pattern of housing in Athens.

. . . somewhere between the second and the first century BC, Dicaearchus could observe: 'The road to Athens is a pleasant one, running between cultivated fields the whole way. The city is dry and ill-supplied with water. The streets are nothing but miserable old lanes, the houses mean, with a few better ones among them. On his first arrival a stranger would hardly believe that this is the Athens of which he has heard so much.' The best one can say of the housing situation in Athens is that the quarters of the rich and the poor were side by side, and that except perhaps in size and inner furnishings. were scarcely distinguishable: in the fifth century. noble poverty was more esteemed than ignoble riches, and public honours and family repute counted for more than private wealth.
(Lewis Mumford, 'The City in History')

century, giving it his gridiron structure and, apparently, an unusual arrangement of one agora near the sea and another inland.

As it approached the Acropolis, the Panathenaic Way was deflected towards the north-east by a spur of higher ground running north from the Areopagus hill. Along the eastern slope of this spur were situated the first civic buildings, thereby establishing the basis of a north/south, east/west orientated agora space, traversed diagonally by the ceremonial route. The earliest known remains are possibly of the seventh century BC, but most monuments of the archaic agora date from the sixth. The later history of the agora can be divided into three separate phases: Classical 5th century; Hellenistic 2nd century BC; and Roman 2nd century AD.

The first agora buildings were largely destroyed by the Persians; subsequent rebuilding was slow but by the end of the 5th century the classical Athenian agora was completed (Fig. 2.16). Most of the buildings were on previously occupied sites. The western side comprised the Tholos (a circular committee-room in the south-western corner); the old Bouleuterion, with the new one behind, further up the slope; and the site of the Metroön (a special temple) not built on until later and forming the greater part of the open area in front of the Hephaisteion. This imposing Doric temple (c 428 BC) still survives, almost intact, on top of the spur, opposite and dominating the centre of the agora. The Temple of Apollo, north of the Hephaisteion axis, was not rebuilt until the 4th century. The last building on this side was the Stoa of Zeus. In front of it, along-

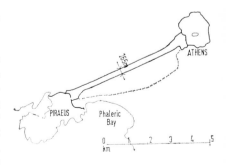

Figure 2.15 – Diagrammatic plan of Athens and Piraeus showing the line of the Long Walls and (dotted) that of a possible earlier wall. The Long Walls enclosed a protected corridor some 6 km in length, averaging 165 m in width.

31

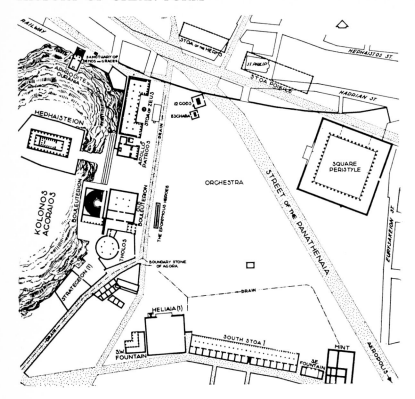

Figure 2.16 – Athens, the Agora area in the third century BC (compare with Figure 2.14 which gives the final form of the ancient Agora in the second century AD). The route of the Panathenaic Way, leading up to the western end of the Acropolis, was deflected north and east by a spur of high ground (to the left of the plan) along the eastern side of which the earliest Agora buildings were located. The precise nature of the buildings along the northern and eastern sides of the Agora of this period have not been determined. The Stoa of Attalus which formed the eastern side of the final arrangement of the Agora was not built until the second century AD. (See Edmund Bacon, *Design of Cities*, for a series of plans showing the growth of the Athenian Agora.)

side the Panathenaic Way, a late 6th-century altar was dedicated as a central milestone of the Attic road system, showing that the spot was thought of as the centre not only of Athens but of all Attica[38].

Little is known of the buildings along the northern and eastern sides. There is evidence of a square peristyle at their intersection – possibly a law court – but it was not completed. To the south was a sequence of buildings – the central south stoa of the late 5th century, flanked by a mint to the east and possibly a law court to the west. 'Not before the 2nd century BC was the agora framed by the Stoa of Attalus (to the east), one more proof that nothing was less in the mind of archaic and classical Athens than the creation of a regularised, closed or half-closed square . . .'[39]. It seems that buildings were not permitted in the classical agora. Part of the area was used for theatrical performances, up to the time when a specialist theatre was built on the southern Acropolis slopes, with spectators perhaps sitting on the broad flight of steps leading up to the Hephaisteion.

During the Hellenistic period a number of improvements were made to the agora. A new south stoa was added in front of the old one, and its colonnade, together with that of the Stoa of Attalus, must have provided a highly effective and simple repetitive foil to the important individual buildings along the western side – where the old Bouleuterion had been replaced by a new, larger Metroön. This latter building also had a colonnaded front, complementing the Stoa of Zeus on each side of the Hephaisteion axis. Subsequent developments were of retrograde quality: 'symptomatic of the architectural disaster to come is the huge, clumsy structure of the Odeion, an indoor meeting hall . . . its ungainly mass throws the sensitive and delicate buildings of the earlier periods out of scale'[40]. A second

At Athens, the single-handed victory over the Persian hosts at Marathon on 11 October, 490 BC, supplied the motive for an architectural renaissance. Another factor was the opening, at about the same time, of the Pentelic marble quarries just outside Athens; hitherto very little material had been extracted from this source, and for architectural and sculptural purposes it had been necessary to import marble at considerable expense from the islands, especially Paros, so that it had been employed very sparingly. The conjunction of these events led to a scheme, presumably sponsored by Aristeides, for the rebuilding of the Acropolis in a material unrivalled in the Greek world.
(W. B. Dinsmoor, 'The Architecture of Ancient Greece')

38. R. E. Wycherley, *How the Greeks Built Cities.*
39. P. Zucker, *Town and Square.*
40. Edmund Bacon, *Design of Cities.*

building – the Temple of Ares – was also allowed in the agora, which became increasingly cluttered by statues, fountains and shrines. The destruction of the agora occurred near the end of the 3rd century AD.

As for the Acropolis, in the course of time the original rocky outcrop was terraced up with massive retaining walls in order to form a number of inter-connected platforms. The most important phase in its history was the second half of the 5th century BC when, as the culmination of the city's reconstruction after the Persian sack[41], four world-famous buildings were completed – the incomparable Parthenon (447–432); the Propylaea (437–432); the beauti-

Figure 2.17 – Athens, aerial view of the Acropolis from the south-west, looking across the partially restored ruins of the Roman Theatre of Herodes.

41. E. A. Gutkind, *Urban Development in Southern Europe: Italy and Greece.* writes that 'the devastation of Athens by the Persians in 480 BC was so great that, as the story goes, Themistocles considered the transfer of the city to Piraeus. Yet in 479 BC Athens was surrounded by walls. This was the first fortification of a city on mainland Greece . . . (and) finally ended the rôle of the acropolis as the citadel of Athens.'

ful little Temple of Nike Apteros (426) and the three-part Erechtheion (420–393).

The Parthenon – officially the temple of Athena Polias – was built on a magnificent limestone platform 237 ft long by 110 ft wide, centrally located on the southern side of the Acropolis. This platform is some 35 ft above bedrock in one corner. It was previously intended for an earlier temple – itself the second on the site – started after the defeat of the Persians in 490, only to be destroyed at an early construction stage when the city had to be abandoned ten years later. The Erechtheum was built to the north of the Parthenon, separated from it by the site of the Peisistratid Temple of Athena also destroyed by the Persians. The main central space on the Acropolis between these buildings and the Propylaea was dominated by the colossal bronze statue of Athena Promachos. The Propylaea, which stood on the site of earlier gateways to the Acropolis, remained incomplete at the outbreak of the Peloponnesian War. The Temple of Nike Apteros stands on a separate bastion to the right of the Propylaea, as viewed from the outside.

Greek attitudes to urban space are assessed below, when further reference is made to the Athenian Acropolis. Here it remains only to stress that it was topography and respect for traditional siting which effectively determined the location of these four buildings, even though the axis of the Propylaea is parallel to that of the Parthenon and also points approximately toward the statue of Athena Promachos, thus constituting one of the rare instances of formal relations between buildings antedating Hellenestic times[42].

Greek urbanism: minor examples

SELINUS

Selinus in western Sicily was founded around 630 BC by local tribesmen. It was situated on two flattish hills, the southern of which, alongside the sea, formed the original site. Early expansion took place on to the second, northern hill and adjoining slopes. The original hilltop gradually lost its predominantly residential character and became from 580 BC onwards an acropolis with about $7\frac{1}{2}$ acres of its total area of nearly 22 acres forming a religious precinct containing several extremely important examples of Greek temple architecture. Unplanned housing groups however continued to occupy the easier slopes of the hill. It has been estimated that the total area of the city in the late fifth century BC amounted to some 70 acres, with a population of around 30,000, excluding slaves. In 409 BC the city was completely destroyed by the Carthaginians. It was then rebuilt on the original southern hilltop, the layout being based on the gridiron, incorporating the temple in its south-eastern quarter.

DURA-EUROPOS

Dura-Europos is believed to have been founded about 280 BC as one of several fortress colonies safeguarding the Euphrates river-crossings and trade route. It was laid out on the right bank of the river with a straightforward gridiron plan and, anticipating Roman imperial policy, was populated with Greek soldiers. Around 100 BC the town became part of the Parthian Empire and enjoyed a period of great prosperity as its northernmost garrison town, well situated on the main caravan route west to Palmyra.

Figure 2.18 – Athens; plan of the Acropolis, north at the top. (See Figure 2.14 for relationship of the Acropolis with the Agora, to the north-west.) Key: A, Athena Temple (Parthenon); B, Archaic Athena Temple site; C, Erechtheum; D, Propylaea; E, Nike Temple.

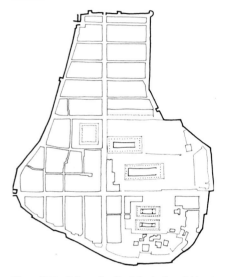

Figure 2.19 – Selinus (north at the top), as laid out from 409 BC with the temple group in the south-eastern corner. The main cross-axes are a departure from usual Greek practice.

Figure 2.20 – Dura Europos, general plan (north at the top); the Euphrates ran north-east of the town.

42. W. B. Dinsmoor, *The Architecture of Ancient Greece*.

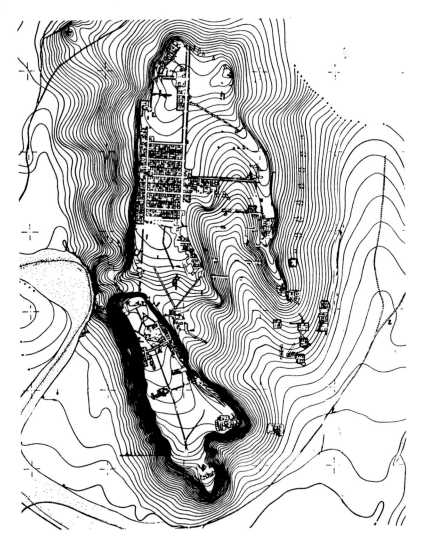

Figure 2.21 – Olynthus, general plan of the city as built from 430 BC (north at the top), locating the gridiron housing area shown in detail in Figure 2.7. New Olynthus was laid out on the gentle slopes of the plateau north of the original site and covered an area of approximately 3,600 feet from north to south, by 600 feet wide. The gridiron formed the basis of the plan : four main north-south streets between 21 and 15 feet wide were intersected by minor cross-streets 15 feet wide. (Figure 2.7 shows only the western section of Olynthus. There were three further rows of less regular grid blocks to the east.) The main entrance was in the north-west corner; the agora area was probably located between the western grid section of New Olynthus and the original site, which remained in more or less unplanned occupation.

OLYNTHUS

Olynthus was located on the northern Aegean coastline, alongside the Toronaic Gulf. The original village settlement had occupied the southern spur of two hills from about 1000 BC before being destroyed during the Persian invasion of 479 BC, following which the site was redeveloped as one of several Chalcidian towns. Olynthus soon became the dominant one of these centres and from around 430 BC the Chalcidians abandoned their other settlements to concentrate around Olynthus. From 379 BC the city grew rapidly until 348 BC when, at the time of its final destruction by Philip of Macedonia, its population including many slaves may have exceeded 15,000.

Greek urbanism, theory and practice

The planned Greek city, for all its regularity and formal building relationships, was never the result of academic urban planning rules. Indeed Wycherley, in *How the Greeks Build Cities*, comments that 'as far as we can tell there was no recognised body of theory'. This is illustrated by the various views on 'ideal city' populations. Aristotle perceptively argues that 'ten citizens do not make a polis, whereas with ten thousand it is a polis no longer'. Plato, basing his estimate on mathematical theory, writes of 5,040 shares in the land; whilst Hippodamus divides his preferred total of 10,000 into three parts: artisans, husbandmen and armed defenders of the state. (He also divided the land into three zones: sacred, private and public.) More generally, Aristotle wanted city-state populations to be 'self-sufficient for the purpose of living the good life after the manner of a political community', and argued that 'to decide questions of justice and in order to distribute the offices according to merit it is necessary for the citizens to know each other's personal characters'. Aristotle also made several deceptively simple general pronouncements including: 'a town should be built so as to give its inhabitants security and happiness' and, 'the difficulty with such things is not so much in the matter of theory but in that of practice'.

Greek urban form of the Hellenic period was therefore essentially the result of applying uncomplicated planning principles to the site in question and of accepting, seemingly without question, that town planning is indeed the art of the practical. Paul Zucker in *Town and Square* regards this overriding concern with practicalities as 'all the more astonishing since after all Aristotle was the first philosopher to deal with aesthetic problems in general ... yet he never discusses the city planning from an aesthetic point of view'. Urban space as such had no aesthetic meaning: it existed only as a by-product of placing two or more buildings together on the same site, even if, as happened frequently in Hellenistic times, buildings around a space are 'no longer spatially isolated but are anchored in some system of mutual reference, as are the stoas and porticos'. Greek architects and artists alike were preoccupied with volume – the physical mass of individual buildings or sculpture. Interest in spatial modelling, as it developed slowly from the fifth century, was centred on the agora and hardly ever applied to the arrangements of temples, monuments and statues on an acropolis.

The Greek approach to urban planning was then essentially a practical one. Yet several urban historians make the mistake of applying contemporary values in decrying the assumed quality of Greek urban environment – notably Sibyl Moholy-Nagy who, in the generally admirable *Matrix of Man*, writes of Miletus as 'a nightmare to anyone who would think three-dimensionally. It would have been a rat's maze of blank walls ...' (See the section on Miletus on page 27.) In the absence of contemporary Greek observations on their cities it is pointless to pursue the argument further except to note that if the Greeks had not found their surroundings acceptable then they, of all people, surely had the ability to change them.

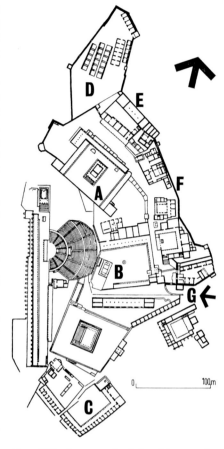

Figure 2.22 – Pergamon, detail plan of the acropolis complex. Key: A, Temple of Trajan; B, precinct with Temple of Athena; C, the upper agora with the Great Altar of Zeus on the terrace to the north; D, store-houses; E, barracks; F, palace complex; G, main gateway.

Pergamon had poor communications inland but combined a strong acropolis site with a fertile coastal plain giving easy sea access. Little is known of the plan and buildings of the lower town: archaeological interest has been centred on the acropolis and its remarkable group of buildings and civic spaces. The extravagance of their layout on extremely difficult, steeply sloping ground is typically Hellenistic in character, compared with the simple approach adopted by Hellenic planners at, for example, Priene. Nevertheless the skill with which the great crescent of buildings was arranged around the central natural theatre (each on its own terraced platform) has seldom been equalled.

3 — Rome and the Empire

The legendary date for the foundation of the city of Rome is 753 BC[1]. Subsequent Roman history is usually divided into three phases: the Kings, 753–510 BC; the Republic 509–27 BC; and the Empire (imperial Rome) 27 BC–AD 330. Before about 270 BC the Romans were fully committed, establishing their mastery of the Italian peninsular, after which the Punic Wars against the Carthaginians, from 264–146 BC, further decided that Rome should become a world power, and that the lands of the west should be ruled by an Aryan, not a Semitic race[2]. For the next 300 years the imperial boundaries were extended ever further from Rome, reaching their maximum extent under the Emperor Trajan (AD 98–117); in conquering Mesopotamia and Assyria he made the Tigris instead of the Euphrates the eastern boundary (see Fig. 3.2). His successor, Hadrian (AD 117–138), abandoned these territories, and Armenia, but successfully consolidated the frontier defences for an uneasy but peaceful period. However, under Marcus Aurelius (161–180), the tide began to turn. From then on Rome was always on the defensive; the period of the decline and fall of the Empire begins.

Dacia was lost to the Goths in AD 270. They also invaded east Germany, Transylvania, Illyricum, and Greece as far as Athens and Sparta. The Juthungi reached North Italy; the Alemanni, who first appear about AD 210, thrust into Gaul and Italy, and for a moment appeared before Rome[3]. Gradually the centre of gravity of the Empire moved to the east, Rome becoming increasingly unsuited to the strategic requirements of military government. Diocletian (284–305) ruled mainly from Nicomedia, on the eastern shore of the Sea of Marmora, and his successor, Constantine (306–337), finally deserted Rome for the new eastern capital of Constantinople, founded in 330 on the site of Byzantium (see page 61). The decline and fall of Rome itself will be outlined in the introduction to the chapter on the Renaissance in Italy.

In the past it has been fashionable to dismiss the artistic, architectural and urban design work of the Romans as at best mediocre copies of Greek originals. Whilst the Greeks were recognised as 'artists' in the fullest sense, the Romans were discounted as 'practical engineers' without any significant aesthetic ideas of their own. Lewis Mumford is strongly anti-Roman; his book *The City in*

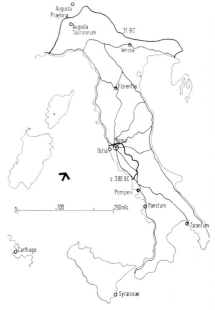

Figure 3.1 – Italy showing the extent of Roman territory around 300 BC and latterly the Alpine frontier as existing before the reign of Augustus (29 BC – 14 AD). The main roads are also shown. (Augusta Praetoria is modern Aosta; Augusta Taurinorum is Turin.)

---

1. Rome, with her Romulus and Remus legend— twin baby brothers set adrift in a basket on the Tiber, washed ashore beneath the Palatine Hill, suckled by a she-wolf, adopted by shepherds and founders of Rome – is one of several cities with mystical, and mythical, birthdays. See also the legends concerning Athens and Venice.

2, 3. R. H. Barrow, *The Romans.*

History will be quoted later in this chapter for its critique of the city of Rome. In general he has this to say, 'the special Roman contribution to planning was chiefly a matter of sturdy engineering and flatulent exhibitionism: the taste of *nouveaux riches*, proud of their pillaged bric-à-brac, their numerous statues and obelisks, stolen or meticulously copied, their imitative acquisitions, their expensive newly commissioned decorations'. Such criticism is unduly harsh. There were of course pronounced negative aspects to the Roman way of life, particularly in Rome itself, but for a more balanced assessment we need only turn to the contemporaneous conclusions of a fellow-American author Paul Zucker in his book *Town and Square*; he observes that 'in architecture as well as in sculpture the Romans created entirely new and original artistic values, although taking over the artistic vocabulary of the Greeks'[4].

Artistic attainment apart, the main achievement of the Romans was surely the creation and administration of their vast Empire during the course of which they introduced urban civilisation into all of Europe east of the Rhine and Danube. With more recent situations coming readily to mind as analogies, it may perhaps be argued that many recipients of Roman civilisation would rather have been left alone in their furs and mud huts. Certainly exploitation of mineral and agricultural resources to supply the city of Rome's population of one and a quarter million played an ever-increasing rôle but this side to Roman activities is directly comparable to those of the British in many parts of their Empire, and if native societies were dragged, protesting, into the nineteenth and twentieth centuries, are the long term benefits really to be doubted? Accepting the Empire as a fact it must be recognised that the Romans had undoubted organising genius. Merely to keep their capital functioning at all, with its grossly inflated population, is proof of the devoted, efficient labours of a host of anonymous bureaucrats able to deploy the talents of gifted, resourceful civil engineers. Mumford, it seems, finds pleasure in drawing comparisons between Roman society and its eventual breakdown, and present-day situations, particularly in the USA, as quoted below, but he neglects to stress that Rome's unimaginative acceptance of its urban circumstances is in no way different from twentieth century society's inability to break out of its urban impasse, for all its technological advantages. We are, as the Romans were, enmeshed in our own bureaucratic webs.

The main problem in writing about ancient Rome is that of selection. Compressing the results of over 1,000 years of rapid change into a section – albeit a major one – of this general study has inevitably resulted in some aspects of the subject being omitted, and others only too briefly mentioned. Rome has been described in great detail in a multitude of archaeological studies. The present work relies in the main on three outstanding books: two from the later 19th century – Professor Lanciani's *The Ruins and Excavations of Ancient Rome* and J. H. Parker's *Archaeology of Rome* – are not ordinarily available[5]; the third – Jerome Carcopino's *Daily Life in Ancient Rome*, first published in 1941, has been made available in paperback by Penguin Books[6]. The method adopted here for presenting an ordered description of such a disorganised subject is to first give a brief introductory general history of Rome, and to follow this by a more detailed description of the most important elements of urban form both in Rome itself and throughout the Empire.

Despite the fact that the Romans were quite capable of indulging in gigantic undertakings, their technologies remained at the small-equipment level. Thus, for example, if it was required to increase the output of iron the number of furnaces was multiplied, but the furnaces themselves remained the same size. Whatever the cause, the idea of building a larger furnace and devising machinery to work it seems to have been beyond the Roman mind. As a result, the last few centuries of Roman domination produced very little that was technologically new. No new raw materials were discovered, no new processes invented, and one can indeed say that long before Rome fell all technological innovation had ceased. (Henry Hodges, 'Technology in the Ancient World')

A great deal of nonsense has been talked about the luxury of the Romans as one of the causes of their decline. Even Mommsen relates with shocked emotion that they imported anchovies from the Black Sea and wine from Greece. Two hot meals a day they had and 'frivolous articles' including bronze-mounted couches. There were professional cooks, and actually baker's shops began to appear about 171 BC. It is true that all this luxury would pale into insignificance before the modern worker's breakfast-table with bacon from Canada, tea from Ceylon or coffee from Brazil, sugar from Jamaica, eggs from Denmark, and marmalade from South Africa. Cato would have swooned at the sight of our picture frames coated with real gold, for he taxed table-ware worth more than 1,000 'denarii'. The truth is that Rome, having grown rich, was just beginning to grow civilised. It is the everlasting misfortune of Rome that events occurred in that order. (Richard Mansfield Haywood, 'Ancient Rome')

4. The reader is referred to Gilbert Picard, *Living Architecture: Roman*, for a general illustrated description of Roman architecture; and to Fritz Baumgart, *A History of Architectural Styles*, for the relationship of Roman architecture to the preceding and succeeding styles.

5. *The Ruins and Excavations of Ancient Rome* was published by Macmillan and Co, London, in 1897; *The Archaeology of Rome* was published in 1874, from which an abridged version entitled *The Architectural History of Rome* was published by Parker and Co, London, in 1881.

6. Jerome Carcopino was Director of the Ecole Française de Rome; his *Daily Life in Ancient Rome* was first published in 1941 and was published in Penguin Books in 1956. *Daily Life in Ancient Rome* (on the daily round of business appointments, social calls, amusements amid the tumult and power of Rome in the second century AD) is unquestionably one of the most informative and easy to read amongst specialist works on urban history.

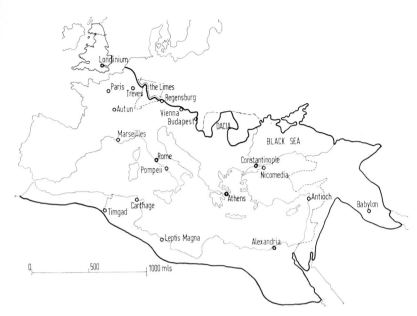

Polybius, a Greek statesman and historian of the second century BC, who spent many years among the Romans, left a careful account of the camps in his discussion of the Roman army. Every camp was constructed according to the same master plan; although natural features were sometimes made a part of it, ordinarily it was pitched on reasonably flat land and constituted a fort without rivers or cliffs to aid in its defense. It was square; each side was 2,150 feet long and had a gate. Inside each wall there was an empty space in which the soldiers could form and which could keep the tents of the soldiers from being reached by any missiles sent over the wall from outside. The commander's quarters were always in the same place, as were a little forum and the headquarters of the 'quaestor' who served as paymaster. The troops always had a specified location, so that a given maniple would know that when the camp had been constructed it would find its quarters, as it were, on the corner of 4th Street and Second Avenue.
(Richard Mansfield Haywood, 'Ancient Rome')

ROMAN URBAN PLANNING

The total contrast between the chaotic organic growth of Rome itself and the regulated formality of the great majority of Roman provincial towns is even more marked than that between Athens and the numerous systematically planned Greek cities of the post-Hippodamian period. This is due partly to the extreme size and population of the city of Rome – estimated to have been at least 1,200,000 in the second century AD – and its complexity of building relationships and partly to the direct simplicity of layout adopted by the Roman engineers for smaller, planned, provincial urban settlements.

Rome was perhaps ancient history's most fascinating and most complex urban agglomeration, but before describing significant aspects of it, the general principles and practice of Roman town planning must be established. In imposing and maintaining their authority throughout their vast empire, the Romans built thousands of fortified legionary camps known as *castra*; many of these existed only as temporary centres for local military activities. Such camps had to be operational in the shortest time and, following strictly applied rules of castremetation[7], they were invariably laid out according to the gridiron, within predetermined rectilinear defensive perimeters (Fig. 3.3). Though many *castra* were only temporary, a large number of them did form the basis of permanent towns. In addition, many other towns were founded for economic and political reasons.

Permanent urban settlements, whether developed from the *castra* or of special origin, were given equally simple standardised plans. Venta Silurum (Caerwent), a Romano-British town (Fig. 3.30), and Timgad in North Africa (Fig. 3.21) are good examples although, as described later, they differ considerably in the way the housing blocks are developed. The perimeter is usually square or rectangular; within this two main cross streets form the basis of the street structure – the *decumanus*, through the centre of the town, and the *cardo*, usually bisecting the *decumanus* at right angles, towards one end.

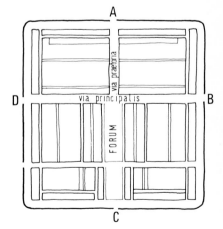

Figure 3.3 – Typical Roman *castra* plan.

7. Castrametation – the art of laying out military camps.

Secondary streets complete the grid layout, and form the building blocks, known as *insulae*. The forum area – the Roman equivalent of the Greek agora – is usually located in one of the angles formed by the intersection of the *decumanus* and the *cardo*; it normally consists of a colonnaded courtyard with a meeting hall built across one end. The main temple, the theatre, and the public baths – the latter made the Roman occupation of foggy, damp Britain tolerable in part – were also located near the forum in the centre of the town. The amphitheatre, a large spatial unit requiring sloping ground for seating, was normally located outside the town. Fortifications were sometimes omitted at first because of the strong imperial frontier defences, but proved necessary at later, insecure stages in the history of these towns.

The Romans fully appreciated that to attempt to hold newly acquired territories by military force alone could result in continuing guerilla warfare which would distract the legions from their task of extending and maintaining the imperial frontiers, and could prejudice the development of commerce. Native tribesmen therefore had to be brought into the Empire on advantageous terms; this was achieved, explains R. G. Collingwood, by equating Romanisation with urbanisation[8]. Tribal centres, which usually amounted to little more than crudely assembled villages, were redeveloped as Roman towns of varying status and leading tribesmen, with varying degrees of enthusiasm, were invited to share the advantages of Roman urban culture and trading prospects. Other towns were also founded for economic and political reasons, their populations provided by time-expired legionaires, or emigrant settlers from Rome and other older towns. The most important imperial towns were directly connected by the magnificent system of main roads which facilitated strategic military and trading communications. Less important towns were linked to it by minor roads.

The three main classes of imperial towns were: *coloniae* – either newly founded settlements or native towns, allied to Rome with full Roman status and privileges; *municipia* – usually important tribal centres, taken over with formal chartered status but only partial Roman citizenship for their inhabitants; and *civitates* – market and administrative centres for tribal districts which were retained in a Romanised form. Throughout the Empire status was not necessarily reflected by size. London with a walled area of 326 acres was more than half as big again as York, which, with a total area of some 200 acres, was the largest of the four *coloniae* whilst St Albans, the only known *municipium,* was rebuilt on 203 acres in 150 AD. But its exact status remains unknown, except that it was not in the category of *colonia, municipium* or *civitas* (see page 58). Cirencester, at 240 acres the second largest Romano-British city, was apparently an important and prosperous *civitas*. Neither did status have any significant effect on urban form. Roman urbanisation invariably implied gridiron structures for new and rebuilt towns alike although, as explained at the end of this chapter, local topographical features usually determined the details of the layout of the individual towns.

The function of the Roman camps, writes C. T. Smith, was more often offensive than defensive; they were the supply bases and troop headquarters of armies that depended greatly on movement[9]. Accessibility was therefore a main siting requirement and in place of the comparatively isolated but more readily defended hilltop sites preferred

The Romans definitely preferred the urban type of local government. The absence of a fully developed civil service obliged them to use a system of local self-government. In other words. the central government at Rome allowed its subjects to manage their own affairs, while it devoted its attention chiefly to safeguarding the Pax Romana. which alone rendered such local self-government possible. The Roman language, Roman religion and Roman customs were not imposed upon the subject peoples, although – thanks in no small measure to Rome's magnificent road system – they made their way over increasingly large areas. Trade within the Empire was not indeed free, but it attained a considerable volume, and it inevitably encouraged Romanisation. The widespread use of Latin as a 'lingua franca' must have contributed to the same end: the ex-soldiers settled in the provinces helped to disseminate it. The institutions of Rome also exercised a great attraction. at any rate in the west; this helped to Romanise many areas.
(E. T. Salmon, 'A History of the Roman World')

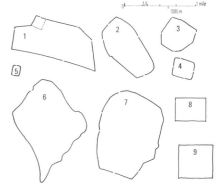

Figure 3.4 – Imperial towns, some comparative sizes. Key: 1, Londinium (London); 2, Corinium Dobunnorum (Cirencester); 3, Calleva Atrebatum (Silchester); 4, Venta Silurum (Caerwent); 5, Viroconium (Wroxeter); 6, Augustodunum (Autun); 7, Augusta Treverorum (Trier); 8, Augusta Praetoria (Aosta); 9, Thamugadi (Timgad).
(See also Appendix H relating Londinium and Timgad to the sizes of other cities in history.)

8. R. G. Collingwood, Chapter VIII – Britain – contributed to Volume 12 of *The Cambridge Ancient History.*
9. C. T. Smith, *An Historical Geography of Western Europe before 1800.*

by their Celtic predecessors and German successors, the Romans opted for river crossings and route intersections. Towns developed from such favourably located *castra* most frequently survived the Dark Ages, or, if they were abandoned, stood the best chance of resuscitation, stimulated by the early mediaeval commercial revival. Similarly many Celtic *oppida* were moved from their hilltops on being taken over as Roman *civitates*. Autun, laid out below Bibracte, and Dorchester, by the Frome, replacing Maiden Castle are but two of many examples.

Rome

THE FIRST SETTLEMENT

Rome, City of the Seven Hills, had its origins in the several villages built by Latin tribes when they moved down to the Tiber plain from mountains to the south-east. Six of the seven hills – in reality only low but steep-sided mounds rising above the flood plain on the Tiber's left bank – are the Palatine, Capitoline, Caelian, Esquiline, Viminal and Quirinal. They are ranged around a small depression or valley which in earliest times must have been a swamp[10], and this land subsequently became the centre of Rome. The seventh hill, the Aventine, is to the south of this group.

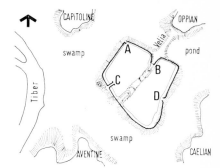

Figure 3.5 – Rome outline plan of the Kingly Palatine Hill related to the adjoining hills and the Tiber and showing the lower ground conditions prior to the construction of the surface water drainage system. Key: A, Porta Romanula; B, Porta Mugonia; C, Steps of Cacius; D, possible gateway (after Lanciani).

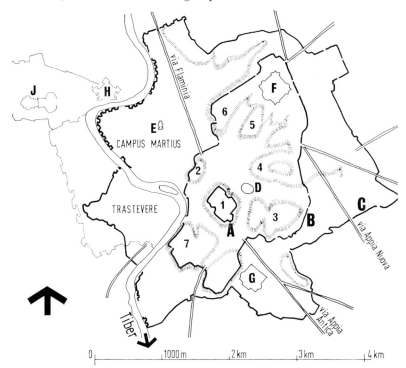

Figure 3.6 – Rome, diagrammatic plan of the city at its greatest extent. The figures indicate the seven hills – 1, Palatine; 2, Capitoline; 3, Caelian; 4, Esquiline; 5, Viminal; 6, Quirinal; 7, Aventine. The three defensive perimeters are indicated by letters A to C:

A, The Palatine, site of the dominant of the original village settlements (see Figure 3.5);
B, The Republican Wall of 378-352 BC;
C, The Aurelian Wall of 272-280 AD, hurriedly constructed in response to the Barbarian invasions of 271. This wall did not enclose the entire area of the city but followed the line of an existing customs barrier (see description, page 44). It has been estimated that the total area of 1,386 hectares (3,465 acres) within the Aurelian Wall was used as follows: streets, 138 ha; public buildings, 84 ha; warehouses, 24 ha; gardens, 98 ha; Campus Martius, 60 ha; river Tiber, 22 ha; residential (all classes), 970 ha. (J. C. Russell, *Late Ancient and Mediaeval Population*)

West of the Tiber, later defences including those for the Vatican, are shown in light line.

Letters from D onward represent major buildings: D, the Colosseum, at the south-eastern end of the Forum area; E, the Pantheon; F, Baths of Diocletian; G, Baths of Caracalla; H, Mausoleum of Hadrian; J, St Peter's, built 1506-1626 on the site of the ancient basilican church of St Peter.

It is believed that each of the hills had its village settlement, with origins dating back well before 753 BC. The two most important of these were the Palatine, traditionally the home of the early Romans, and the Capitoline, that of the Sabine tribe. The Palatine was approximately square, with an area of about 65 acres. Each side was about 490 yards in length and for this reason Roman writers refer to the hilltop village as Roma Quadrata (Fig. 3.5)[11]. Lanciani

10. F. R. Cowell, *Everyday Life in Ancient Rome*.
11. There is no general agreement on the form taken by the ancient layout of the Palatine Hill; various authorities give differing assumed plans. It seems certain however that whatever shape Roma Quadrata did take, it was not that of a regular rectangle. (Figure 3.5 shows the plan assumed by Lanciani in *The Ruins and Excavations of Ancient Rome*.)

argues against the traditional view that this first settlement had a regular plan based on *cardo* and *decumanus* cross-axes, believing that the shepherds who occupied the hill in 753 BC had no idea whatever of grammatical or astronomical rules of their own[12]. The Palatine, in common with the other hills, was admirably suited for early defensive settlement, with its steeply sloping sides rising above lower ground which was marshy at all times and under water whenever the Tiber was in flood. The location had a further strategic advantage in its central position on the Italian peninsular, where routes converged to cross the river Tiber.

The basic requirements of early hill-village communities are, however, very different from those of a great metropolis. From the time when the first three settlements (those on the Palatine, Capitoline and Quirinal) expanded down their hill slopes on to the lower ground to coalesce into one continuous urban area, through to the present-day Roman planners, the architects and engineers have been engaged in a continuing struggle to overcome the intrinsic deficiencies of the site. Flooding, disease – in particular malaria – river pollution and the related drinking water problem, poor bearing capacity, and the hilly topography have been ever-present hazards. Add to these natural problems the planning constraints that resulted from preceding generations' attempts to overcome them – in particular the large scale sewer and aqueduct systems – and it is by no means surprising that ancient Rome, like so many large modern urban centres, was incapable of being comprehensively restructured. At best there could only be piecemeal 'town-patching' measures.

SEWERS AND WATER SUPPLY

A description of the component parts of ancient Rome is given later in this chapter. The rôle of the sewer and aqueduct systems as urban form determinants warrants, however, their separate consideration now. The numerous shallow-depth culverted streams and surface water sewers constructed to drain the marshes, and Rome's magnificent system of elevated aqueducts and associated fresh-water reservoirs, created impediments to subsequent redevelopment similar to those presented by railway viaducts and other such barriers in modern cities – notably in South London. In both ancient and modern examples the resource investment has been such that, although planning considerations would imply re-routing, economic constraints all too frequently dictate their retention.

The centre of Rome enclosed by the 5½-mile long Servian Wall was the Forum Romanum. Here stood the traditional market and public gathering area in the valley between the Palatine, Capitol and Quirinal Hills, and overlooked by the Temple of Jupiter on the Capitol. The Cloaca Maxima, the first of the great sewers of Rome, was constructed in about 578 BC as an open drain (Fig. 3.7). In 184 BC it was roofed with a magnificent 11-foot diameter semicircular stone vault, and is still in use as part of central Rome's present-day surface water drainage system. For most of its length it ran at or near surface level, as did many of the less famous sewers.

In addition to draining the lower-lying parts of the city and taking surface water from the streets, the system served to collect the sewage of the *rez-de-chausée* and of the public latrines which stood directly along the route, but no effort was made to connect the *cloacae* with the private latrines of the separate *cenacula* (upper

Sanitary reform was accomplished. first, by the draining of marshes and ponds; secondly, by an elaborate system of sewers, thirdly, by the substitution of spring water for that of polluted wells fourthly, by the paving and multiplication of roads; fifthly, by the cultivation of land; sixthly, by sanitary engineering, applied to human dwellings; seventhly, by substituting cremation for burial; eighthly, by the drainage of the Campagna; and lastly, by the organisation of medical help. The results were truly wonderful. Pliny says that his 'villegiatura' at Laurentum was equally delightful in winter and summer, while the place is now a hotbed of malaria. Antoninus Pius and M. Aurelius preferred their villa at Lorium (Castel di Guido) to all other imperial residences. and the correspondence of Fronto proves their presence there in midsummer. No one would try the experiment now. The same can be said of Hadrian's villa below Tivoli. of the Villa Quinctiiorum on the Appian Way. of that of Lucius Versus at Acqua Traversa etc. The Campagna must have looked in those happy days like a great park, studded with villages, farms, lordly residences, temples, fountains and tombs.

The cutting of the aqueducts by the barbarians, the consequent abandonment of suburban villas, the permanent insecurity, the migration of the few survivors under cover of the city walls, and the choking up of drains, caused a revival of malaria. Mediaeval Romans found themselves in a condition worse than that of the first builders of the city.

(R. Lanciani. 'The Ruins and Excavations of Ancient Rome')

Figure 3.7 – Rome, the line of the Cloaca Maxima across the north-western end of the Forum area to the Tiber. Lanciani describes how the hills of the left bank made three valleys, each drained originally by its own river, and that 'the first step towards the regulation of these three rivers was taken before the advent of the Tarquins. Their banks were then lined with great square blocks of stone, leaving a channel about five feet wide, so as to prevent the spreading and the wandering of flood-water, and provide the swampy valleys with a permanent drainage; but, strange to say, the course of the streams was not straightened nor shortened. If the reader looks at the map above, representing the course of the Cloaca Maxima through the Argiletum and the Velabrum, he will find it so twisted and irregular as to resemble an Alpine torrent more than a drain built by skilful Etruscan engineers. The same thing may be repeated for the other main lines of drainage in the valleys Sallustiana, Murcia etc. When the increase of the population and the extension of the city beyond the boundaries of the Palatine made it necessary to cover those channels and make them run underground, it was too late to think of straightening their course, because their banks were already fixed and built over.'

12. R. Lanciani, *The Ruins and Excavations of Ancient Rome*.

storey flats)[13]. The great majority of ordinary people in Rome had to rely on the public latrines. This network of underground services, although not as great a planning constraint as the aqueduct system, certainly inhibited large scale redevelopment.

Rome's water supply, in common with all riverside settlements, was originally taken mainly from its river. This source met demand until the end of the fourth century BC, by which time the volume of sewage discharged into the Tiber had resulted in an unacceptable pollution level. Drinking water was having to be laboriously brought in from outside the city area. On a grand civil engineering scale, typical of the Romans, this problem was solved by constructing the system of aqueducts and reservoirs which eventually attained a total length of 509 km. The first aqueduct was the Aqua Appia of 312 BC; the longest was the Aqua Marcia at just over 91 km – built between 144–140 BC when increase of the population had diminished the distribution of water from 116 gallons to 94 gallons per head daily[14]. The largest volume of water was supplied by the Anio Novus; this was supported on arches 105 ft in height for 8 miles of its length. Most aqueducts reached Rome at considerable heights above the level of the valley, in order to supply the prestigious hilltop districts. (The wealthy had their own private reservoirs and paid the State for the water supplied; about one third of supplies was expended under this head.) Where the aqueducts, the Anio Novus and the Claudia, entered Rome massive structures were necessary, and these formed barriers to any subsequent redevelopment proposals.

The total volume of water carried by the aqueducts was $1\frac{3}{4}$ million cubic metres per day, but, as Carcopino notes, very little of this immense supply found its way to private houses[15], and that which did had to be carried from distribution fountains to the upper level dwellings. During the latter part of the third century AD there were in Rome 11 great *thermae*, 926 public baths, 1,212 public fountains, 247 reservoirs, and a 'stagnum Agrippae'[16]. During the Empire, 'planning consent' for the construction of new baths for public use was granted only if the applicant could prove that he had arranged for a special supply of water.

DEVELOPMENT UNDER THE CAESARS

After the first century BC, civil wars inside Italy and the collapse of the Republic, attributed in part by some historians to the extremes of wealth and squalor and poverty prevailing in the city, Augustus reconstituted the State, and reorganised the city between 27 BC and AD 14. Augustus boasted that he had found Rome a city of brick and left it one of marble – a claim which could have been only partially true, but which has inspired numerous subsequent planning programmes. Augustus in 7 BC completed the reorganisation of Rome into the fourteen regions which lasted as long as the Empire; five were contained within the ancient circuit of the city, five others were partly within, and four were completely outside. The regions were divided into *vici* – quarters separated from each other by the streets which bounded them; Augustus had granted each *vicus* a special administration presided over by its own *magister*[17]. In AD 73 the elder Pliny records that Rome was divided into 265 such *vici*.

Several years before this census, Nero's famous fire of AD 64 had left only four of the regions untouched; 'three had been completely

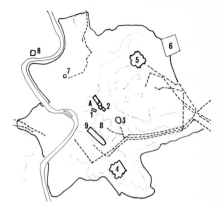

Figure 3.8 – Rome, the aqueduct system. Key: A Capitoline Hill; B, Palatine Hill; 1, Forum Romanum Magnum; 2, sequence of imperial fora; 3, Colosseum; 4, Baths of Caracalla; 5, Baths of Diocletian; 6, Praetorium barracks; 7, Pantheon; 8, Mausoleum of Hadrian; 9, Circus Maximus.

The majority of the aqueducts entered the city at its eastern corner. Identified from north to south these were: Aqua Appia, which runs through to the Aventine Hill; Aqua Marcia and, on the same aqueduct into the city, the combined Aqua Tepula and Aqua Julia; Anio Vetus; Aqua Claudia and Anio Novus, both carried on the same arches for the last seven miles into the city. The Aqua Virgo entered Rome from the north and served the low-lying Campus Martius district; Aqua Traiana and Aqua Aurelia served the Trastevere district from the west and water was also carried to this part of the city by service aqueducts crossing the Tiber on the bridges. The Aqua Marcia Antoniniana served the Baths of Caracalla from the south-east (not shown on map).

13. Jerome Carcopino, *Daily Life in Ancient Rome*.
14. R. Lanciani, *The Ruins and Excavations of Ancient Rome*.
15. Jerome Carcopino, *Daily Life in Ancient Rome*.
16. R. Lanciani, *The Ruins and Excavations of Ancient Rome*.
17. Jerome Carcopino, *Daily Life in Ancient Rome*.

obliterated and seven others hopelessly damaged'[18]. Premeditated or not, this fire was needed to remove the worst excesses of high density, shoddy buildings and grossly inadequate streets, in order to give an opportunity for comprehensive rebuilding, which the Romans would not otherwise have accepted.

In succession to Nero, three emperors – Vespasian, Titus and Domitian (AD 69–96) – established an era of peace and prosperity through the Empire which made possible the second century AD 'Golden Age' of Rome under the Emperors Nerva, Trajan, Hadrian, Antonius Pius and Marcus Aurelius (AD 96–180). During this age, according to F. R. Cowell, 'grand and glorious edifices were then added to the city, so that buildings, markets, baths, temples, statues and other monuments accumulated in Rome, until it had attained a splendour and a magnificence which made it truly a wonder of the world. Perhaps no city before or since has ever so captured the admiration and the imagination of mankind'[19]. This quotation shows however only one side of the picture, that of the magnificence of Rome's civic areas. As a contrasting view, Lewis Mumford in *The City in History* has argued that, 'from the standpoint of both politics and urbanism, Rome remains a significant lesson of what to avoid : its history presents a series of classic danger signals to warn one when life is moving in the wrong direction. Wherever crowds gather in suffocating numbers, wherever rents rise steeply and housing conditions deteriorate, wherever a one-sided exploitation of distant territories removes the pressures to achieve balance and harmony nearer at hand, there the precedents of Roman building almost automatically revive, as they have come back today : the arena, the tall tenement, the mass contests and exhibitions, the football matches, the international beauty contests, the strip-tease made ubiquitous by advertisement, the constant titillation of the senses by sex, liquor and violence – all in true Roman style.'

URBAN FORM COMPONENTS

Lanciani notes that Rome has been fortified seven times, within seven lines of walls : by the first king, by Servius Tullius, by Aurelian, by Honorius, by Leo IV, by Urban VIII, and by the Italian Government (Fig. 3.6)[20]. The first fortifications were those around the Palatine Hill. The second wall, attributed to Servius Tullius of 550 BC, is, according to Carcopino[21], that of the Republic of two centuries later, constructed between 378–352 BC. As already described, the need for defences gradually diminished and it is not until 650 years later that a new system was required.

The Aurelian Wall was constructed between AD 272 and about 280, in response to the barbarian invasion of 271. It was $11\frac{1}{2}$ miles in length, enclosed an area of $5\frac{1}{3}$ square miles, and required a strip of land some 62 ft wide – 16 ft for the inner perimeter route, 13 ft for the wall itself, and 33 ft for the external cleared defensive zone[22]. The wall had projecting towers at intervals of 100 Roman feet (32 yds) which after the restoration of the defences by Honorius in 402, totalled 381 in number. The Aurelian Wall did not enclose the entire city but, as recorded by Lanciani[23], followed the line of the existing octroi – the customs barrier encircling the city proper within the surrounding surburban areas. One sixth of this barrier was formed by natural features and substantial engineering works – including retaining walls to hillside developments, the wall of the

Whether it was accidental or caused by the emperor's criminal act is uncertain – both versions have supporters. Now started the most terrible and destructive fire which Rome had ever experienced. It began in the Circus, where it adjoins the hills. Breaking out in shops selling inflammable goods, and fanned by the wind, the conflagration instantly grew and swept the whole length of the Circus. There were no walled mansions or temples, or any other obstructions which could arrest it. Nero was in Antium. He only returned to the city when the fire was approaching the mansion he had built to link the Gardens of Maecenas to the Palatine. The flames could not be prevented from overwhelming the whole of the Palatine, including his palace. Nevertheless, for the relief of the homeless, fugitive masses he threw open the Field of Mars, including Agrippa's public buildings, and even his own Gardens. Nero also constructed emergency accommodation for the destitute multitude. Food was brought from Ostia and neighbouring towns, and the price of corn was cut. Yet these measures, for all their popular character, earned no gratitude. For a rumour had spread that, while the city was burning, Nero had gone to his private stage and, comparing modern calamities with ancient, had sung of the destruction of Troy . . . Nero profited by his country's ruin to build a new palace. Its wonders were not so much customary and commonplace luxuries like gold and jewels, but lawns and lakes and faked rusticity – woods here, open spaces and views there. With their cunning, impudent artificialities, Nero's architects and contractors outbid Nature . . . In parts of Rome unfiled by Nero's palace construction was not – as after the burning by the Gauls – without plan or demarcation. Street-fronts were of regulated dimensions and alignment, streets were broad and houses spacious. Their height was restricted, and their frontages protected by colonnades. . . A fixed proportion of every building had to be massive, untimbered stone from Gabii or Alba (these stones being fireproof). Furthermore, guards were to ensure a more abundant and extensive public water-supply, hitherto diminished by irregular private enterprise. Householders were obliged to keep fire-fighting apparatus in an accessible place; and semi-detached houses were forbidden – they must have their own walls. These measures were welcomed for their practicality, and they beautified the new city. Some, however, believed that the old town's configuration had been healthier, since its narrow streets and high houses had provided protection against the burning sun, whereas now the shadowless open spaces radiated a fiercer heat.
(Tacitus, 'The Annals of Imperial Rome', translated by Michael Grant)

18, 19. F. R. Cowell, *Everyday Life in Ancient Rome.*

20. R. Lanciani, *The Ruins and Excavations of Ancient Rome.*

21. Carcopino cites G. Saeflund's masterly work on the Servian Wall, *Le Mura di Roma Republicana* (Lund, 1932), as superseding all previous discussions and establishing the date 378-352 BC for this wall. Lanciani would seem to be one of the authorities accepting the earlier, 550 BC date: he was, however, writing of archaeological work of the second part of the nineteenth century.

22, 23. R. Lanciani, *The Ruins and Excavations of Ancient Rome.*

Praetorian camp and lengths of the Marcian and Claudian aqueducts. For those sections of the octroi which required strengthening, Aurelian expropriated an area of about 80 acres of private property[24] of private property involving the demolition, or incorporation into the defences, of innumerable houses, garden walls and tombs. The succeeding fortifications of Rome, down to those of the nineteenth century, all follow in the main the lines of the Aurelian Wall.

The functional zones were linked together by a route system of streets, which always smacked of their ancient origin and maintained the old distinctions which had prevailed at the time of their rustic development: the *itinera*, which were tracks only for men on foot; the *actus*, which permitted the passage of only one cart at a time; and finally the *viae* proper, which permitted two carts to pass each other, or to drive abreast[25]. Within the Republican Wall only the Sacra Via, which ran through the original forum area between the Colosseum and the Capitoline Hill, and the Via Nova, parallel to it against the Palatine Hill to the south-west, are considered by Carcopino as of *via* status. Leading out from the limits of Republican Rome, through the subsequent built-up areas, 'not more than a score of others deserved the title: the roads which led out of Rome to Italy, the Via Appia, the Via Latina ... etc. They varied in width from 15 ft to 21 ft, a proof that they had not been greatly enlarged since the day when the Twelve Tables had prescribed a maximum width of 15 ft'[26]. Few of the *vici* which formed the general route network were of this width. They were not only inconveniently narrow but also extremely tortuous. By the time of Julius Caesar the street system was grossly overloaded, with continual conflict between pedestrian and vehicle traffic. As a result Caesar was forced to ban transport carts from the city during the hours of daylight, with the exceptions of builders' carts and a few categories of official chariots. During the daytime Rome was therefore largely free from wheeled traffic, but at night, as observed by Juvenal, the crossing of wagons in the narrow winding streets and the swearing of the drivers brought to a standstill would snatch sleep from a sea-calf or the Emperor Claudius himself[27]. These regulations were not of temporary effect. Subsequent emperors extended them first to other Italian municipalities and then generally throughout the Empire. Hadrian further controlled traffic by limiting the teams and load of the carts allowed to enter the city[28].

HOUSING

There were two basic types of housing found in the city: the *domus* for privileged single-family occupation and the *insula* (building block) divided up into a number of flats or *cenacula*. In the middle of the fourth century AD, 1,797 *domus* were recorded; this compared with 46,602 *insulae* each, according to Caropino, with an average of five flats whose average occupancy was at least five or six persons. (Taking these figures Carcopino deduces a population of 1,200,000 in the early second century AD, the period of his *Daily Life in Ancient Rome*.) Rome was therefore predominantly a city of flat-dwellers, living in buildings which as early as the third century BC had reached up three floors. As the population increased still further so did the height of buildings: Julius Caesar in his *Lex Julia de Mode Aedificorum* had to impose a limit of 70 ft in order to minimise the ever present dangers of structural collapse. Augustus reaffirmed

The great dictator had realised that in alleyways so steep, so narrow, and so traffic-ridden as the 'vici' of Rome the circulation by day of vehicles serving the needs of the population of so many hundreds of thousands caused an immediate congestion and constituted a permanent danger. He therefore took the radical and decisive step which his law proclaimed. From sunrise until nearly dusk no transport cart was henceforward to be allowed within the precincts of the 'urbs'. Those which had entered during the night and had been over-taken by the dawn must halt and stay empty. To this inflexible rule four exceptions alone were permitted: on days of solemn ceremony, the chariots of the Vestals, of the Rex Sacrorum, and of the Flamines; on days of triumph, the chariot necessary to the triumphal procession; on days of public games those which the official celebration required. Lastly one perpetual exception was made for every day of the year in favour of the carts of the contractors who were engaged in wrecking a building to reconstruct it on better and hygienic lines.

(Jerome Carcopino, 'Daily Life in Ancient Rome')

24. There is a modern parallel here with the construction of the Berlin Wall – dividing the city into its Eastern and Western sectors – which also includes numerous buildings and other existing structures.

25, 26. Jerome Carcopino, *Daily Life in Ancient Rome*.

27. Juvenal, *The Sixteen Satires*, Satire III, translated by Peter Green, Penguin Books, 1967.

28. See Chapter Eight, page 188, for a description of the closely similar traffic situation in London of the century and a half before the Fire of 1666.

this limit and Trajan later reduced it to 60 feet. Carcopino remarks that necessity knows no laws and in the fourth century the sights of the city included that giant apartment house, the Insula of Felicula[29]. Only the very rich could afford a *domus*, which in plan was generally a sequence of rooms facing into courtyards (as at Pompeii, illustrated on page 53). By turning blind unbroken walls to the street a *domus* afforded a degree of privacy to its fortunate occupants, in direct contrast to the *insula* which always opened to the outside and, when it formed a quadrilateral around a central courtyard, had doors, windows and staircases opening both to the outside and to the inside[30]. Either way there was no escaping noise and dust. Fire was obviously an ever-present hazard; construction relied to a great extent on timber and lighting was by naked flames. Such heating as there was took the form of movable, mainly charcoal-fuelled stoves. Running water was not supplied to the upper floors.

Julius Caesar's legislation required the use of tiles as an incombustible roof material and stipulated that between buildings an open space – the *ambitus* – 28.75 inches wide, had to be maintained. This 'fire-break' was lost when the legislation was amended to permit party-wall construction. Augustus created a corps of fire-fighting night watchmen, or *vigiles*, but dread of fire was such an obsession among rich and poor alike that Juvenal was prepared to quit Rome to escape it saying, 'No, No, I must live where there is no fire and the night is free from alarms'[31].

Topographically Rome was essentially an egalitarian city. With the exception of the emperors' palaces built on the Palatine Hill and possibly separate working-class districts on the downstream banks of the Tiber and the slopes of the Aventine, 'high and low, patricians and plebeian, everywhere rubbed shoulders without coming into conflict'. On the subject of workers' housing Carcopino states that 'they did not live congregated in dense, compact, exclusive masses; their living quarters were scattered about in almost every corner of the city but nowhere did they form a town within a town'[32].

MARKETS

Economically Rome was sustained only by imports on a vast scale. She had three ports: Ostia (Figs. 3.9 and 3.20), Portus and, within the city, the pool of the Tiber. The latter began with the last of the city bridges (Pons Sublicius) and extended as far as the reach of the Vicus Alexandri, $1\frac{1}{2}$ miles below the Porta Ostiensis. Here larger sea-going vessels were obliged to take to moorings to avoid sandbanks and the exceedingly sharp turns of the upper channel. Between these limits the left bank of the river was divided into wharves, called *porti* or harbours. Each was used for a particular kind of trade – marble, wine, oil, lead, pottery, etc. Associated with the *porti* and occupying the left-bank area between the Aventine and the city walls, as well as a considerable right-bank area, were the warehouses, or *horrea*. Some of these, notably the grain stores, which were government property, specialised in one commodity, most however comprised a sort of general store where all kinds of wares lay cheek by jowl[33]. Lanciani records that there were 290 of these public warehouses, named either after their contents or their owner or builder. He notes that the Horrea Galbana alone occupied a space of 218 yds by 169[34]. Carcopino, in the light of more recent excava-

The *via Portuensis* became important on the construction of Portus Augusti, the new harbour and city, now Porto, at the Tiber's mouth, and on the northern or right bank. These works were projected by Augustus, and carried out by Claudius, for the double purpose of remedying the silted-up condition of the natural port of Ostia, and of providing a straighter and deeper course for the waters of the river, which, being held back by the bar at its mouth, aggravated the frequent floods at Rome. The process of silting, however, proceeds so rapidly in the Tiber, owing to the quantity of sand washed down from the hills, that by the time of Trajan it was necessary to form both a new harbour and a new channel. The site of the Claudian works has become completely solid land, while the Port of Trajan, which is hexagonal in form and about 2,400 yards in circuit still exists, with a depth of about ten feet of water. The canal communicating with this port is still open and is the only navigable channel into the river. Porto itself is now two miles from the sea.
(J. H. Parker, 'The Architectural History of the City of Rome')

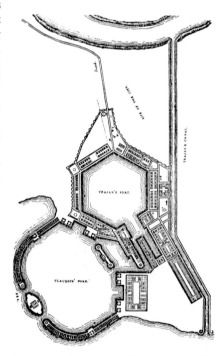

Figure 3.9 – Ostia (Port of Rome), the artificial harbours constructed under Claudius (42-54 AD) and Trajan (100-106) to augment the capacity of the original facilities alongside the Tiber.

29, 30. Jerome Carcopino, *Daily Life in Ancient Rome*.
31. Juvenal, *The Sixteen Satires, Satire XIV*, translated by Peter Green.
32. Jerome Carcopino, *Daily Life in Ancient Rome*.
33, 34. R. Lanciani, *The Ruins and Excavations of Ancient Rome*.

tions, describes how their foundations went back to the end of the second century BC, and states that they were enlarged under the Empire and possessed rows of *tabernae* ranged around three large intermediate courtyards which covered more than 8 acres[35]. In addition to the *horrea* – the 'supermarkets' of their day – Rome was a city of small shopkeepers, the great majority trading from ground-floor *insulae* premises but with major concentrations in and around the fora area, notably the Forum of Trajan.

Supplies needed for daily consumption were brought into specialist wholesale trade markets, eg, the *holitorium* for vegetables, *boarium* for horned cattle, *suarium* for pigs, *vinarium* for wine-merchants, and *piscarium* for fishmongers. Other trades gradually established themselves in their own districts and streets. The *holitorium* was centrally located between the Capitoline Hill and the Tiber, with the *boarium* some distance downstream between the Palatine and the river. Near the latter, again centrally located, was the *suarium*. A third meat market, the Campus Pecuarius for sheep, has not been located. Lanciani describes how these three markets were all used for actual trade, on the spot, and suggests that to avoid yet further congestion in the streets the oxen came to the *boarium* by the river, by barge-loads[36]. However, cattle once bought were driven down city streets to the individual butcher's shops for slaughter.

CITY CENTRE

The original centre of the city, on the valley floor between the Palatine and Capitoline Hills and the end of the Quirinal ridge, responded to population increase in two contrasting ways. First it was extended towards the south-east by 'controlled' organic growth which was ultimately to be halted in AD 82 against the massive walls of the Colosseum, some 600 yards distant from its origins under the Capitoline (Fig. 3.12). The second response was the construction of a carefully planned sequence of linked imperial fora between 50 BC and AD 114, with a main axis at an angle to the north, between the Capitoline and the Quirinal (Fig. 3.12). The original centre formed part of Regio VIII and is properly termed the Forum Romanum Magnum. The title Forum Romanum is generally applied to the sequence of buildings and spaces extending to the south-east.

The linearity of the Forum Romanum was determined mainly by topography. The valley between the Palatine and the Oppian was not only the logical direction for growth but already contained in addition the immensely important Sacra Via – 'Queen of Streets' as a further reason for locating there the city's new civic buildings, both religious and secular. The Forum Romanum Magnum had commercial origins: Lanciani records that at the time of the foundation of Rome the bartering trade between the various tribes settled on the heights of the left bank of the Tiber was concentrated in the hollow ground between the Palatine, Capitoline and Quirinal[37]. This was the marshy area subsequently drained, from around 509 BC, by the Cloaca Maxima.

During the 'Kingly' period in the city's history, ie, to 509 BC, the embryonic forum gradually took on the regular shape of a parallelogram – which it retained down to the end of the Empire. At first it would have had a multi-purpose function, combining market and civic activities with political business. This simple situa-

The student wishing to survey the ground formerly occupied by these great establishments connected with the harbour of Rome, must make the ascent of the Monte Testaccio, which rises to the height of 115 feet in the very heart of the region of Horrea. The hill itself may be called a monument of the greatness and activity of the harbour of Rome. The investigations of Reiffersheid and Bruzza, completed in 1878 by Heinrich Dressel, prove that the mound is exclusively formed of fragments of earthen jars (amphorae, diotae), used in ancient times for conveying to the capital the agricultural products of the provinces, especially of Baetica and Mauretania. Baetica supplied not only Rome but many parts of the western Empire with oil, wine, wax, pitch, linseed, salt, honey, sauces and olives prepared in a manner greatly praised by Pliny. Potters' stamps and painted or scratched inscriptions of Spanish origin, identical with those of Monte Testaccio, have been discovered in France, Germany and the British Islands. It appears that the harbour regulations obliged the owners of vessels or the keepers of warehouses to dump in a space marked by the Commissioners the earthen jars which happened to be broken in the act of unloading or while on their way to the sheds. The space was at first very limited; in progress of time part of a public cemetery, containing among others the tomb of Rusticelii, was added to it. At the beginning of the fourth century the rubbish heap had gained a circumference of half a mile, and a height of over a hundred feet. (R. Lanciani, 'The Ruins and Excavations of Ancient Rome')

---

35. Jerome Carcopino, *Daily Life in Ancient Rome.*
36, 37. R. Lanciani, *The Ruins and Excavations of Ancient Rome*

tion could not last for long however: the beaten earth and rudimentary huts were the nucleus of history's most complex city centre. From serving a population numbered in hundreds it grew to meet the demands of considerably over one million[38]. Exemplifying Rome's general organic growth character the centre was never planned in its entirety: new facilities were added as need arose. Development was controlled to a considerable extent by inherited constraints: regions, sites and routes, sacrosanct for various reasons; topographical limitations beyond even Roman engineering capabilities; and perhaps the major reason, the need to maintain adequate open space for movement by foot and wheel, and for civic assemblies. In describing the Forum Romanum Magnum and its enclosing buildings, where 'for so many centuries the destinies of the ancient world were swayed',[39] it is most convenient to take the Rostra at its north-western end (under the Capitoline) as a viewpoint and looking south-east refer to right and left-hand sides. (The detailed plan as Fig. 3.10.)

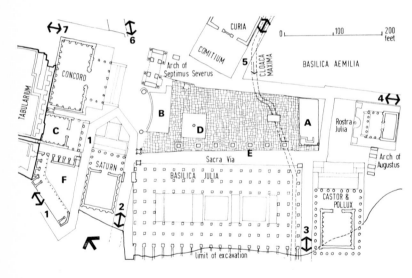

By the first century BC the gross overcrowding in the forum area, and its multifarious activities, forced the start of an extension and redevelopment programme which was to last for some 150 years. As a first measure, fishmongers were removed from the steps of the basilicae to their own specialist market – the *forum piscatorium*. New civic buildings were required and in 54 BC work started on the Basilica Aemilia, to the south-east of the Curia, on a site acquired at great expense from a number of owners. It was completed in 34 BC, during the construction period of the new Forum Julium on the other side of the Curia. This latter consisted of a sacred enclosure around the Temple of Venus Genetrix, consecrated by its founder, Julius Caesar, in 45 BC. Pliny, obviously impressed, wrote 'we wonder at the Egyptian pyramids, when Caesar as dictator spent one hundred millions of sesterces merely for the land on which to build his forum'[40]. (Lanciani writing at the end of the nineteenth century calculated that this was equivalent to 44.5 dollars per square foot.) The Forum Julium was especially intended for legal business.

Figure 3.10 – The Forum Romanum Magnum, detail plan. (For the view as reconstructed, from the direction shown top right, see Figure 3.11.) The forum contains too many buildings for individual descriptions; the two most important basilicae – Aemilia and Julia – and the Temple of Caesar have been described in the main text. Brief notes on some of the other major buildings are as follows:

Right-hand side (looking from the Rostra. B) Temple of Saturn (rebuilt in 42 BC) on a raised platform, reached by an impressive flight of stairs up from the Clivus Capitolinus. Between this temple and the Basilica Julia the Vicus Jugarius led from the forum, against the Capitoline Hill to the Forum Olitorium.

Temple of Castor and Pollux (AD 6), across the Vicus Tuscus from the Basilica Julia. This street rivalled the Sacra Via in importance and linked the forum with the Circus Maximus.

Within the forum at its eastern end, in front of the Temple of Caesar, nineteenth-century archaeologists mistakenly demolished a multi-cell building (keyed A) possibly of the late fourth century AD. Opinions have varied as to whether this was a wine shop or, more likely, a public office building.

Left-hand side

The Comitium, across the Argiletum – the main street leading from the forum to the Subura – from the Basilica Aemilia, was the centre of civil and political business during Rome's early days, while the forum functioned solely as a market-place. The Comitium itself served as a semi-private forecourt to the Curia, the Senate House, 'politically speaking,' observes Lanciani, 'the most important building in the Roman world'.

The Arch of Septimus Severus (AD 204) was erected on the edge of the Rostra platform, some six or seven feet above the level of the forum and the Comitium, and could not therefore have been across the main street bordering the forum, as incorrectly shown on some plans.

Behind the Rostra, against the Capitoline Hill, there were two important temples – the Temple of Concord, reconstructed for a second time in AD 10, and the Temple of Vespasian (AD 94) – and the Tabularium, the Roman public records office, rebuilt in 78 BC after the fire of 83 BC, on the steep slope of the Capitoline facing the forum. The upper part of this building coincides almost exactly with the area of the mediaeval Palazzo del Senatore which formed the south-eastern side of the Renaissance Capitoline Piazza (page 128).

Key: A, unknown multi-cell building; B, Rostra; C, Temple of Vespasian; D, Column of Phocas; E, the eight monumental columns; 1, Clivus Capitolinus; 2, Vicus Jugarius; 3, Vicus Tuscus; 4, Sacra Via; 5, the Argiletum; 6, link to the imperial fora; 7, slope up to the Capitoline Hill.

38. It is reasonable to assume that whatever the population of the city proper, the administrative and commercial centre must have served well over one million people.

39. R. Lanciani, *The Ruins and Excavations of Ancient Rome.*

40. Quoted by J. H. Middleton in *The Remains of Ancient Rome.*

TEMPLE OF JUPITER CAPITOLINUS

TEMPLE OF JUNO MONETA

A

THE FORUM ROMANUM (RESTORED) LOOKING TOWARDS THE CAPITOL

Figure 3.11 – The Forum Romanum, an artist's impression of the buildings and spaces of the later Empire period. The direction of this view is given in Figure 3.10. In the distance can be seen the temples on the twin eminences of the Capitoline Hill. The hollow on top of the Capitoline Hill was to become the location of Michelangelo's incomparable sixteenth century Capitoline Piazza in front of the mediaeval Palazzo del Senatore which, in turn, was built in part on ruins of the ancient Tabularium. (After Banister Fletcher, *History of Architecture on the Comparative Method*.)

On the far, right-hand side of the Forum Romanum Magnum and occupying almost its entire length, Caesar, in about 54 BC, also laid out his magnificent Basilica Julia. Dedicated whilst still in an unfinished state in 46 BC, it was completed, after fire damage, by Augustus in 12 BC. About 350 ft by 185 ft this basilica was one of Rome's largest buildings. It was used for the court of the *centumviri*. The younger Pliny has described an important trial day : eighty judges sat on their benches, while on either side of them stood the eminent lawyers who had to conduct the prosecution and to defend the accused. The great hall could hardly contain the mass of spectators; the upper galleries were occupied by men on one side, by women on the other, all anxious to hear, which was very difficult, and to see, which was easier[41]. At ground level on the right-hand side of the forum there were the shops of bankers and money-lenders. At the far, south-eastern end, on the spot where he was murdered on 15 March 44 BC, the Temple of Julius Caesar was erected (33–29 BC) to his memory. The site of this building was taken out of the Forum Romanum, thereby reducing its length to 110 yards and necessitating a change in the line of the Sacra Via.

The Forum Julium was the first of the imperial fora, constructed to the left (north-east) of the Forum Romanum. It was not on the new south-north axis but was to constitute in effect a link between that and the Forum Romanum. The second of the new fora was built by Augustus in 42–2 BC, beyond the Forum Julium, between it and the Quirinal. The layout of the Forum Augusti is basically that of a forecourt to the magnificent Temple of Mars Ultor, with flanking hemicycles to north and south. The most remarkable feature of the place, noted Carcopino, was a wall of blocks of peperino raised to a great height to screen the view of the mean houses on the Quirinal[42]. This forum also had a mainly legal function.

South of the Forum Augusti and separate from it by a wide street – the Argiletum – which led from the Subura to the Forum Romanum Magnum, Vespasian built the Temple of Peace (dedicated in AD 75) around which he laid out the third forum, named after him. It is believed that it functioned as a public library and was the venue for literary discussion. The route space of the Argiletum, some 127 yards by 43, was shortly afterwards converted by Domitian and his successor Nerva (96–98) into the Forum Transitorium (later the Forum of Nerva).

PALATINE

CAPITOL

Figure 3.12 – The imperial fora, related to the buildings and spaces of the Forum Romanum and the Palatine and Capitoline Hills. Key: 1, Forum Romanum Magnum (as Figure 3.10); 2, Basilica Julia; 3, House of the Vestal Virgins; 4, Temple of Venus and Rome; 5, Colosseum; 6, Basilica of Constantine; 7, Forum of Vespasian; 8, Forum of Nerva; 9, Forum of Augustus; 10, Forum of Trajan; 11, Forum of Caesar.

41. Quoted by J. H. Middleton in *The Remains of Ancient Rome*.
42. Jerome Carcopino, *Daily Life in Ancient Rome*.

The last and most magnificent of the imperial fora was built by Trajan between 112–114 from designs of Apollodorus of Damascus. It is the outstanding example of Roman civic design, both for its intrinsic architectural qualities and for the immense engineering works it required. To Zucker the Forum Traiani represents the definite triumph of the Roman spatial concept based on absolute axiality and symmetry[43]. In addition to doubling the area of the five existing fora, its construction on ground immediately to the north of the Forum Augusti enabled the problem of traffic circulation around the Capitoline to be resolved. Originally the Capitoline was not a completely isolated hill but was connected to the main Quirinal spur by a lower ridge. Access to the fora from the north was either across this ridge, by the steep and narrow Clivus Argentarius, or around the three sides of the Capitoline. Trajan and his architect-planner took the bold step of removing the ridge to create a level area about 200 yards in width between the hills, with a total length of about 720 feet. Private property covering nearly 10 acres was acquired for the site, from which about a million cubic yards of earth and rock were excavated and spread outside the Porta Collina. The Column of Trajan, which was 124 feet in height without the statue, was erected 'to show posterity how high rose the mountain levelled to make room for the forum'[44].

Figure 3.13 – Detail plan of the sequence of imperial fora; the relationship to the Forum Romanum is given in Figure 3.12.
Key: A, the Temple of Trajan, which closed the monumental group at its north-western end; B, Trajan's Column, completed in 113 AD and traditionally taken as marking the depth of the excavation necessary to construct the forum; C, two libraries – the Bibliotheca Ulpia and the Templi Traiani; D, the Basilica Ulpia (also known as Trajan's Basilica), a magnificent hall 288 by 177 ft in area, surrounded by a double row of columns and with hemicycles at each end; E, the Forum of Trajan; F, hemicycles on each side of Trajan's forum serving as retaining walls against the Capitoline Hill to the south-west and the Quirinal Hill to the north-east; G, the Forum of Augustus; H, the Temple of Mars Ultor, behind which was raised a high stone wall to screen the view of mean houses clustered on the slopes of the Quirinal (Lanciani records that 'the irregular form of the wall at the back of the temple is accounted for by the circumstance that Augustus was unable to obtain a symmetrical area, as the owners of the nearest houses could not be induced to part with their property'); J, the Forum of Nerva, or Forum Transitorium, so called because it was traversed by the main thoroughfare of the Argiletum. Its long and narrow shape (400 by 128 ft) made it more like a handsomely decorated street than a formal public space; the small Temple of Minerva was located at its north-eastern end; K, the Forum of Caesar (also known as the Forum Julium) containing L, the Temple of Venus Genetrix, which was dedicated in 45 BC; M, the Curia; N, the Comitium; and O, the thoroughfare of the Argiletum. (These latter three parts of the plan are also located on the detail plan of the Forum Romanum Magnum shown in Figure 3.10.)

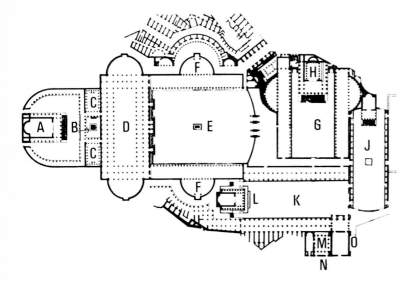

Trajan's forum comprised five main parts: first, the propylaia – an entrance gateway in the form of a triumphal arch – which gave access from the adjoining Forum Augusti into the second part, the main forum area, 125 yards long by 110 wide, with double colonnades in front of twin hemicycles excavated into the hillsides and third, the Basilica Ulpia facing the forum on its longest side (also with hemicycles at each end). The fourth part, entered from the basilica, was a small court, only 76 feet wide by 52 long, in which still stands the 124-feet high Trajan's column, flanked at each end by library buildings. Fifth and last was the Temple of Trajan which stood in its own colonnaded space and closed the monumental group at its north-western end.

43. Paul Zucker, *Town and Square*.
44. R. Lanciani, *The Ruins and Excavations of Ancient Rome*

RECREATION

One of the major preoccupations facing the Roman emperors was to divert the anti-establishment potential of the urban mob which the handouts of food and money sustained. In the second century AD, 175,000 persons received public assistance from the city. If one accepts a figure of only three persons per family it is likely that, directly or indirectly, at least one third and possibly one half of the population of the city lived on public charity[45]. In addition to feeding the plebs, the authorities also had to amuse them during their holidays, which numbered 159 annually during the time of Claudius, rising to about 200 in the third century AD. A high proportion of the holidays were devoted to games staged at state expense and involving elaborate organisation and building facilities. The largest recreation centre was the Circus Maximus, located in the valley between the Palatine and Aventine Hills. It eventually attained dimensions of 654 by 218 yards and provided at least 255,000 seats – possibly as many as 385,000. The best known centre was the Colosseum (the Flavian Amphitheatre), completed in AD 80 on an imposing site at the south-east end of the Forum Romanum complex; here there were some 45,000 seats and 5,000 standing places. The three major theatres in Rome could accommodate about 50,000 spectators : in addition there were many smaller theatres.

Providing for perhaps more wholesome pastimes, a number of enormous baths were constructed in the city. They included those of Caracalla (officially designated the Thermae of Antonius) over 27 acres in extent, and those of Diocletian, 32 acres in area. In addition to every possible type of bath, these establishments included shops, stadia, rest rooms, libraries, museums, and numerous other facilities. As Carcopino put it, the Caesars had in fact shouldered the dual task of feeding and amusing Rome[46]. Here we have a restatement of Juvenal's famous indictment that the populace, who once bestowed commands, consulships, legions, and all else, now meddled no more and longed eagerly for just two things – bread and circuses[47].

With this appropriate contemporary Roman conclusion we must leave the city itself for a description of a number of the most important provincial examples of imperial urban planning. The decline, fall and eventual resurgence of the city of Rome, which continued through to the end of the Renaissance period, is described later as part of Chapter Five.

Roman imperial urbanism

AOSTA

Aosta was founded in 25 BC, following the defeat of the local tribesmen, the Salassi, by a Roman force under Terentius Varro Murena. The first Roman settlement took the form of a military camp on the site of the Salassi village in the valley of the Dora Baltea, strategically situated at the foot of the Great and Little St Bernard Passes, some 25 miles north-west of Ivrea which had been founded as a *colonia* before 100 BC. In 22 BC Augustus upgraded the camp into a strongly fortified *colonia* with the full title Augusta Praetoria Salassorum. It was used for the settlement of 3,000 time-expired legionaires from the *cohortes praetoria*, and their families. Figure 3.15 shows the rectangular Roman grid which covered an area of approximately 100 acres.

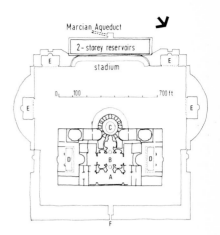

Figure 3.14 – Rome, outline of the Baths of Caracalla, built between 211-217 AD, in the southern part of the city (see Figure 3.6). Accommodation was provided for more than 1,600 bathers. The main central building contained the various bathing halls as keyed: A, Frigidarium; B, Tepidarium; C, Calidarium; D, open colonnaded courtyards; E, lecture halls, libraries etc.

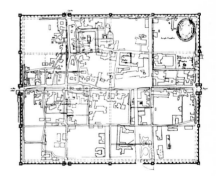

Figure 3.15 – Aosta (Augusta Praetoria), plan of the town showing the mediaeval modification of the underlying Roman grid. Six streets divided the town in sixteen main grid blocks which were further sub-divided into *insulae* of about 90 by 70 yards. The arena is in the top righthand (north-east) corner.

45 46. Jerome Carcopino, *Daily Life in Ancient Rome*.
47. Juvenal, *The Sixteen Satires. Satire X*, translated by Peter Green.

POMPEII

Uniquely preserved beneath the ash and dust from Vesuvius (AD 79), Pompeii has provided archaeologists with a complete cross-section of urban form and social life of the time. Whereas, in so many other examples of Roman planning, continued site occupation throughout centuries has made comprehensive excavation impossible, at Pompeii life was abruptly suspended and the site subsequently unoccupied.

Pompeii was originally founded as a Greek colonial city in the early sixth century BC. In form it is essentially late Hellenistic, having been rebuilt about 200–100 BC, during which period Greek city building practice was gradually being superseded by Roman methods. Apart from the ultimate deficiency of its location Pompeii was well situated in an area alongside the Bay of Naples which was both beautiful and richly fertile.

The city in AD 79 was roughly oval in shape, about four-fifths of a mile long by two-fifths wide with an area of some 160 acres enclosed within a double wall. Population estimates vary between 25,000 and 30,000. The original Greek settlement centred on its old triangular forum (agora), was in the south-east corner; the final area of the city, based on a freely interpreted gridiron form, was extended from here. There were eight gates into the city leading to well-paved main streets provided with raised pavements. Mercurio Street at 32 ft was the widest. Other main streets had widths of about 26 ft; whilst the minor ones, which served only to give access to the houses, varied between 18 and 12 ft wide.

The new forum was located roughly in the centre of the city, near to the harbour front. Enclosing a civic space of some 500 by 160 ft, it displayed carefully composed building relationships and unifying colonnades (Fig. 3.17). Anticipating modern practice by almost 2,000 years, and illustrating the traffic conditions in many Roman towns, the forum at Pompeii constituted a pedestrian precinct with gateways preventing vehicular access. The city had two

Figure 3.16 – Pompeii, general plan of the city, as revealed by the continuing excavation programme. Key: A, the main forum (Figure 3.17); B, the triangular forum, centre of the original Greek settlement; C, location of the two theatres; D, the arena. The detail housing district plan, as Figure 3.18, occupies ten major *insulae* in the western corner of the city (top left-hand corner). The House of Sallust (plan shown as Figure 3.19) is indicated in heavy outline at the southern end of the rectangular *insula* in this western corner (Region VI; Insula 2; Number 4).

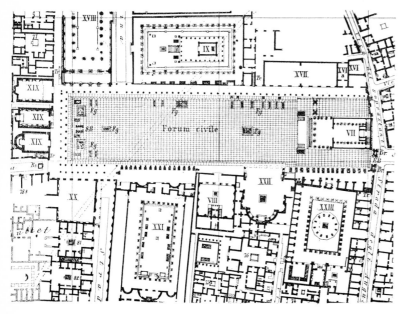

Figure 3.17 – Pompeii, detail plan of the forum and surrounding buildings (north to the bottom right: the orientation of the forum has been moved in this plan clockwise through 90° from its position in Figure 3.16). Note how the two streets which approach the forum at its southern end (left) are discontinuous across the main central pedestrian space. Key (as Roman numerals): VII, Temple of Jupiter; seriously damaged during the earthquake of 62 AD, it was still partially ruined in 79 AD; IX, Temple of Apollo; XVI, public conveniences; XVII, market; XVIII, the basilica centre of Pompeii's commercial life; XIX, three civic halls, the central one probably the Tabularium (Public Archives Office); XX, Comitium, the location of public elections; XXI, Building of Eumachia, the most impressive construction of the forum, after the basilica; XXII, Temple of Lares; XXIII, covered market.

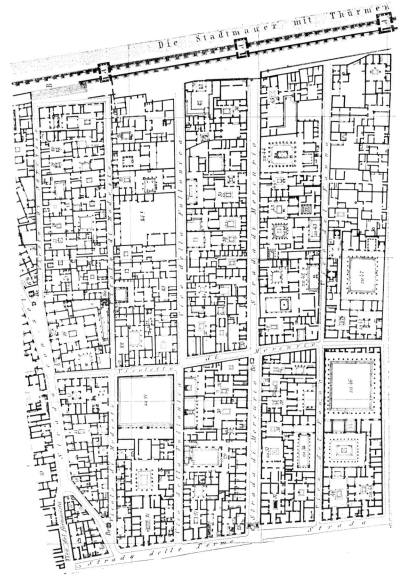

theatres seating 5,000 and 1,500 persons, located near the old forum, and a magnificent oval amphitheatre, some 450 ft in length and capable of holding some 20,000 persons, in the eastern corner. With these three buildings alone able to accommodate almost the total population of the city, it is reasonable to assume that Pompeii functioned as a regional leisure and cultural centre. Near the forum to the north there were the two main public baths.

The forum area provided the main shopping and commercial facilities but flanking the main streets were many smaller shops and workshops. Although these uses formed part of the housing blocks, they generally stayed completely distinct from the dwellings themselves. The houses invariably followed the pattern whereby rooms faced into a central courtyard with only the entrance doors opening into the street. These houses were on two, three and as many as five or six floors in the undulating southern part of the city.

Figure 3.19 – Pompeii, plan of the House of Sallust. (The orientation of this house in the north-west corner of the city, has been moved anti-clockwise through 90° from its position in Figure 3.18). 'This house', writes Amedo Maiuri, 'notwithstanding the presence of *tabernae* on either side of its entrance and the changes wrought by the addition of a *viridarium* in the peristyle and of a small *pistrinum* in the west wing, is one of the noblest examples of a pre-Roman habitation of the Samnite period. The spacious Tuscan *atrium* with a large *impluvium* basin and great characteristic doorways narrowing towards the top, the walls of the airy *tablinum*, of an *oecus* looking upon the portico and of a *cubiculum*, all preserve to a great extent their stucco revetments.' (Amedo Maiuri, *Pompeii*)

53

OSTIA

The traditional date for the foundation of Ostia, at the mouth of the Tiber, is during the reign of Ancus Marcius, fourth king of Rome. However, the earliest remains so far discovered are of a $5\frac{1}{2}$-acre *castra* built about 330 BC, in the angle formed by the Tiber and the Mediterranean. Ostia played an important rôle as a naval base during the Carthaginian Wars and became a busy commercial port from the third century BC when its growth and prosperity directly reflected the rise of Rome itself. Expansion required a new defensive perimeter in 80 BC, enclosing an area of approximately 160 acres, about the same as Pompeii. The main route of the east-west *decumanus* formed the basis of development to the east; immediately west of the original *castra* area this route divided into two branches. Most of the buildings between the *decumanus* and the river were warehouses.

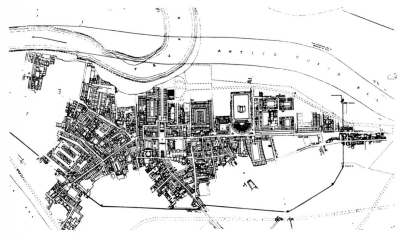

Figure 3.20 – Ostia, general plan of the port (north at the top). The ancient bed of the Tiber ran from east to west along the northern side of the town (Antico Corso, as plan); the modern bed approaches from the north before rejoining the ancient line. Lanciani, writing in 1897, noted that, 'Ficana, the oldest human station near the bar of the river, is now 12,000 metres inland and kingly Ostia 6,600 metres The Torre di S. Michele, built in 1567 by Michelangelo on the edge of the sands, stands 2,000 metres away from the present shore. The average yearly increase of the coast at the Ostia mouth is 9.02 metres.'(*Ruins and Excavations of Ancient Rome*).
The original *castra* is directly opposite the modern bend in the Tiber (immediately right of the fork in the *decumanus*, the main east-west street); the forum was the centrally located open space.

TIMGAD

Timgad (Thamugadi) is a well preserved North African example of a Roman legionary town. Situated some 24 miles east of the modern town of Batna in Algeria, on flattish ground just south of the hills, it has been possible to excavate comprehensively the original town free from the complications of later, overlaying buildings. Originally in a well-watered, fertile part of the Roman 'granary', the area today is only sparsely cultivated. Timgad was founded in AD 100 by the Emperor Trajan for time-expired veterans of the Third Legion which garrisoned the nearby fortress of Lambeisis. As first completed the town was almost square on plan, with sides of about 380 yards enclosing an area of about 30 acres (Fig. 3.21). Later suburban additions were added, mainly to the western side. The plan has a rigid gridiron pattern, formed by eleven streets in each direction which intersect to give square *insulae* with sides of 23 yards. There were originally four gates, three of which have been identified. The forum, about 160 by 145 ft, and the theatre, were both formed out of several *insulae*, and other public buildings occupied one *insula* each. Main streets were widened and flanked by colonnades and were well paved and drained.

Mumford considers Timgad to be 'an example of the Roman planning art in all its latter-day graces. Being a small town, like

48. Lewis Mumford, *The City in History*.

Priene, planned and built within a limited period, it has the same diagrammatic simplicity, unmarred by later displacements and renovations that busier towns subject to the pressures of growth would show'[48]. But the formal built-up pattern of Timgad, with virtually no incidental open space within its limits other than streets and public spaces, should be compared with the contemporary situation at Calleva Atrebatum (Silchester) in Britain. Here the native predeliction for informal groups of buildings in space had completely modified the imperial norm.

Figure 3.21 – Timgad, general plan of the settlement as excavated by the Direction des Antiquités, Gouvernement Général de l'Algerié. (Orientation is somewhat away from the cardinal points: the upper side faces north north-west. The scale as reproduced is approximately 1:3500.) Timgad is possibly the most regular example of imperial gridiron-based urban planning, which makes more strange the inconsistant alignment of the central forum space (13). The plan departs from general imperial practice in that there are no continuous cross-axes. Outside the original perimeter organic growth suburban accretion can be seen.

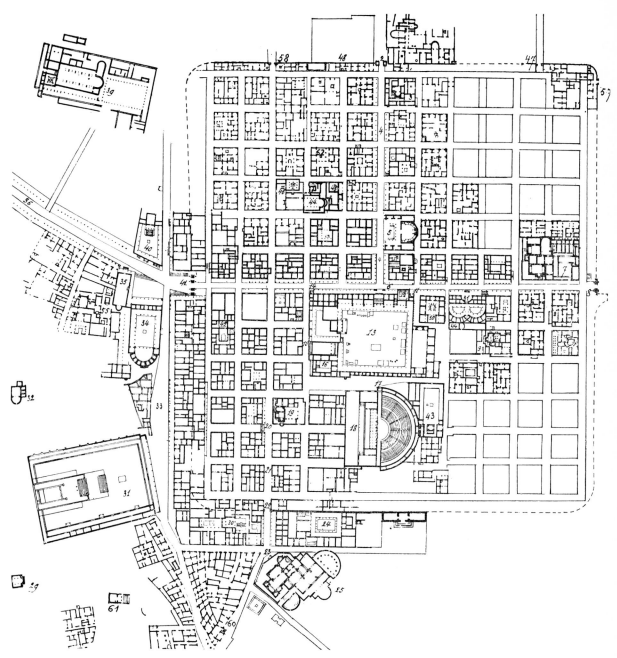

AUGUSTA TREVERORUM

Augusta Treverorum (Trier) was situated on the river Moselle in north-east Gaul. It was founded in the territory of the Treveri by Augustus in about 14 BC and achieved *colonia* status in AD 50. Although at first possibly only 120 or 130 acres in extent, it steadily expanded until, as fortified by Diocletian (AD 285–305), it had become perhaps the largest city in Western Europe, with an area of 704 acres. Moreover, as Haverfield has pointed out in *Ancient Town Planning*, Diocletian made it the capital of Gaul and built the magnificent imperial palace for his occupation. Constantine subsequently governed from there between 306 and 331, before moving the capital of the Empire to Constantinople. Trier managed to survive the fall of the Empire and, following occupation by the Franks in 455, it became the seat of the Merovingian king, Clovis.

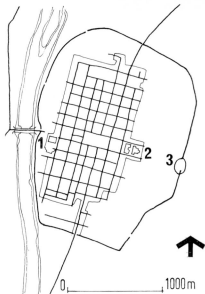

Figure 3.22 – Augusta Treverorum (Trier). Key: 1, baths; 2, emperor's palace; 3, the arena.

Figure 3.23 (Left) – Aventicum (Avanche) showing the gridiron structure of the Roman settlement related to the outer earthworks, the *ager*, protecting the immediate landholdings. This plan shows a clear contrast between the orthogonal formality of the Roman plan and the organic growth pattern of the modern Swiss village to the west.

AUGUSTODUNUM

Augustodunum (Autun) was established about 12 BC when Augustus, in the process of organising the new territories in northern and central Gaul which had been conquered by Caesar, moved the Celtic tribesmen of the Eduens from their hilltop village of Bibracte, some 12 miles away, to a new location alongside the river Arroux, some 100 miles north-north-west of Lyons. Augustodunum covered an area possibly as great as 490 acres and became renowned as the sister and rival of Rome'.

Figure 3.24 – Augustodunum (Autun), general plan.

Roman Britain

The first invasion of Britain by Julius Caesar in 55 BC followed a five-year expansion period of the Roman Empire during which its frontier had been advanced from the Alps and the Cevennes to the shores of the Channel. Troubles inside the Empire prevented first Julius, then Augustus from following up this reconnaissance, but contact between Rome and Britain had been established. In AD 43 Claudius invaded Britain and Roman legions methodically conquered England, Wales and southern Scotland. Before the conquest systematic town planning was unknown in Britain; the largest tribal capitals were probably no more than informal groupings of crude huts clustered together within earthwork defences[49].

Following normal procedure Roman power lodged and consolidated itself by the building of towns, often on the sites of existing tribal villages. Four *coloniae* were recognised: three founded for demobilised veterans – Camulodunum (Colchester), Lindum (Lincoln) and Glevum (Gloucester); and Eburacum (York), subsequently granted *colonia* status[50]. Verulamium (St Albans) is believed to have been the only *municipium*. Organisation of the native Britons was on the basis of local authorities, *civitates*, which followed existing tribal divisions as far as possible, with a third class of town, the *civitas*, acting as cantonal capitals.

However as A. L. F. Rivet observes in his *Town and Country in Roman Britain*, whereas '*colonia* and *municipium* are precise Latin terms, and as applied to a town they defined its rank and the status of its citizens, the term "cantonal capital" is not precise, for it has no Latin equivalent. The reason for this is that to the Roman, reared in the traditions of the Mediterranean city state, the country was an adjunct of the town, not the town of the country. *Coloniae* and *municipia* had territory attributed to them, but the significant unit was the *colonia* and *municipium* itself, not the territory by which it was surrounded.' Outside the new towns, Celtic village communities were affected mainly in so far as any surplus of corn production was exported to Europe. The native Briton, even when Romanised, remained a countryman at heart[51], with the tribal aristocracy preferring to live in Romanised villas established as country estates, generally within easy reach of the towns.

One of the first towns was started in AD 49–50 on the site of Camulodunum (Colchester); the intention was to establish the new provincial capital here. After ten years completed buildings included a senate house, theatre, private dwellings, and the Temple of Claudius. The latter was the religious centre for Romans in Britain, and a considerable part of the available building resources had been devoted to it. But no defences were constructed by AD 60, an omission which proved disastrous when Camulodunum was destroyed during the short-lived uprising under Boadicea.

LONDINIUM

Londinium (London) already established as a military base and trading centre, was also burnt in AD 60 but during the following 25 years it rapidly assumed the functions of provincial capital. 'No question of status', notes Professor Richmond, 'could prevent Londinium from becoming the natural centre for British trade and administration once the Roman engineer picked it. If the first inten-

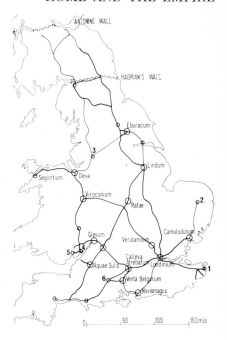

Figure 3.25 – Roman Britain, outline map relating major towns to the main Roman roads. Key: 1, Rutupiae (Richborough) one of three ports nearest to Gaul; 2, Venta Icenorum, tribal capital of the Iceni; 3, Mamueium (Manchester); 4, Venta Silurum (Caerwent); 5, Isca (Caerlin); 6, Sorviodunum (Old Sarum).
Roman place name equivalents: Londinium (London); Camulodunum (Colchester); Verulamium (St Albans); Ratae (Leicester); Lindum (Lincoln); Eburacum (York); Deva (Chester); Segontium (near Caernarvon); Viroconium (Wroxeter); Glevum (Gloucester); Aquae Sulis (Bath); Calleva Atrebatum (Silchester); Venta Belgarum (Winchester); Noviomagus (Chichester).

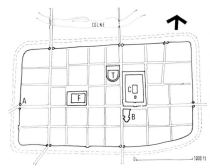

Figure 3.26 – Camulodunum (Colchester) one of the earliest, and most rectilinear Romano-British towns. Key: A, main gateway (from Londinium); F, forum; T, theatre; C, Temple of Claudius; B, baths.

49. This is the traditional view held by A. L. F. Rivet, R. G. Collingwood and J. N. L. Myres. Current archaeological work may however modify it.
50. I. A. Richmond, *Roman Britain*.
51. R. G. Collingwood and J. N. L. Myres, *Roman Britain*.

tion was to govern the province from Camulodunum it is clear that within a generation the financial administration was using Londinium as its headquarters; whilst in the fourth century AD it was not only the seat of the provincial treasury but the residence of the civil governor who presided over the four divisions into which the province was then broken'[52].

The importance of Londinium was due to its siting at the lowest point at which the Thames could be crossed. Here the tidal river was contained within hard gravel banks which made possible the construction of a bridge, where land traffic and sea traffic of the whole island met. As Richmond puts it, the roads radiated from the bridge-head, the sea lanes converged upon it from the Rhine, the Gallic coastal ports, and the North Sea, or by the Channel route from Bordeaux, Spain, and the Mediterranean[53]. It is also believed that in those days the Thames was tidal only as far as Chelsea Reach where there was virtually a non-tidal ford. Despite all these advantages there is no proof that the site of London was occupied before Roman times. A factor which was to encourage Roman London's growth – its location at the boundary intersection of several powerful Celtic tribes – may well have discouraged earlier settlement.

Londinium was probably established in AD 43 as the base on the north bank of the Thames for further military operations in the direction of Colchester, following the Roman success in crossing the river. Two low gravel mounds on either side of the Walbrook – a small north-bank tributary – provided an ample and well-drained building space, with the Walbrook itself developed as the Roman port of London. A second small stream, the Fleet river, formed a natural western defensive barrier and low-lying ground to the north and east could be easily fortified. The exact position of the Roman bridge over the Thames, linking Londinium with the south-bank Southwark suburb, is still unknown. Towards the top of the eastern hill (the present-day Cornhill) there was a magnificent basilica, or town hall, over 400 feet in length and forming the northern side of the forum. Towards the end of the first century AD a military depot was constructed in the northern corner of the city, in the present-day Cripplegate area. Little is known of the street pattern of Londinium and the grid shown on reconstructed maps is largely conjecture.

Londinium steadily expanded and had an area of some 325 acres when the Roman wall was built in the third century AD. This was more than most other Roman cities north of the Alps. In the ninth century the walls were reconstructed for use against the Danes by King Alfred and again in the mediaeval period they formed the city limits. (See pages 181–2.)

CALLEVA ATREBATUM

Calleva Atrebatum (Silchester), sited in Hampshire between Basingstoke and Reading, has been completely excavated (although each section of the town was returned to farmland after the findings were recorded). Originally intended to have an ambitious area of around 200 acres, it was reduced to its irregular polygonal shape of about half that size. This was when defensive expediency required that a wall of economic length should be built. Richmond says that the town wall was an impressive structure, with a large fosse outside it and imposing semi-monumental gates. The main street was lined

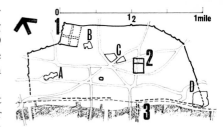

Figure 3.27 – Londinium, the outline of Roman London superimposed on the present day road pattern. Key: A, St Paul's; B, Guildhall; C, Bank of England; D, Tower of London. 1, Cripplegate Fort; 2, forum and basilica; 3, Roman bridge over the Thames (the river bank during the Roman period is shown dotted).

The Walbrook, the sheltered stream used as the first port of London, divided the city into two more or less equal halves, and entered the Thames just upstream of modern Cannon Street Station. Like the Fleet, which formed the western 'moat', it still flows in a culvert as part of the present-day surface water drainage system.

Figure 3.28 – Calleva Atrebatum (Silchester) – the 'Woodland Town' of the Atrebates – general plan, north at the top. (The greatest east-west width is almost exactly half a mile; from north to south the greatest width is 800 yards.) The diagonal route across the town, north-east of the forum, is a modern farm lane – 'the Drove' – superimposed on the Roman plan.

52, 53. I. A. Richmond, *Roman Britain*.

58

fairly thickly with shops and workshops. There were about twenty-five really large houses and something like the same number of small ones. To estimate accurately the population of such a place is difficult; surely at not less than 2,500 on the showing of the plan. But if, as seems very probable, many timber structures were missed this number may have been doubled or even trebled[54]. The most significant aspect of Silchester, in contrast to Timgad, is the difference between the formal street pattern and the informality of the low-density building groupings: here the large proportion of open space within the town has gained for Silchester the title of the 'Romano-British Garden City'.

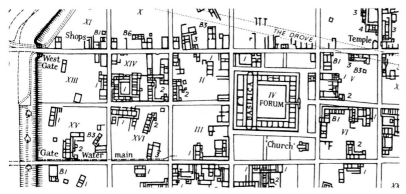

Figure 3.29 – Calleva Atrebatum, detail plan of the forum area, and six *insulae;* Nos V, VI, II, III, XIV, XVI, XIII, XV. The forum occupied the major part of a double *insula.* 130 yards (east/west) by 200 yards in size; the minor *insulae* are approximately 90 yards square. The forum and adjoining basilica together covered nearly two acres. The forum was an open square, 143 by 130 feet, lined by colonnades, shops and offices on three sides. The fourth side was closed by the basilica with a central hall 234 feet long by 58 feet wide. The baths were south-east of the forum on the side of a small valley in which 'the stream that flushed its drains still runs'. (George C. Boon, *Calleva Atrebatum; A New Guide,* Reading Museum in conjunction with the Calleva Museum Committee, 1967.) An intriguing, unexplained occurrence at Calleva Atrebatum was that the forum, baths and three temples were erected *before* the road system was established; the portico of the baths actually being removed to make way for the street. (Boon)

VENTA SILURUM

Venta Silurum (Caerwent) was in South Wales, ten miles from Newport and five miles from Chepstow. It dates from AD 75 and was founded to replace the Silurian tribal hill-fort situated on high ground a mile to the north-west.

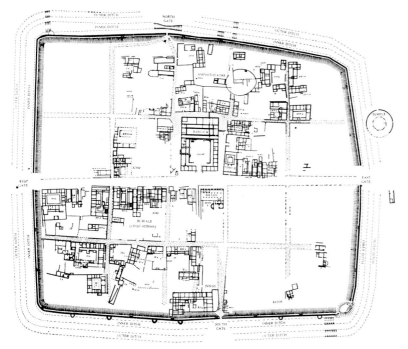

Figure 3.30 – Venta Silurum (Caerwent), general plan as excavated (north at the top). Scale: 1 inch to 450 feet (approx.). O. E. Craster has described how the new town had the customary rectangular Roman layout and covered an area of forty-four acres. It was divided in half by the main street running through it from east to west; two other roads running east and west and four running north and south further divided it into twenty blocks, or *insulae.* Although in no sense a military fort it had defences which consisted of an earth bank probably revetted by a wooded palisade and fronted from the first by double ditches. There was a gate in the centre of each side.' (*Caerwent Roman City,* HM Stationery Office, 1951) The central colonnaded forum, with the basilica along the northern side, is a good example of this Roman urban form component. Small 'strip' houses with shop fronts line the main east-west street. Caerwent was developed at a higher density than Calleva Atrebatum and included several large 'patio' houses but some parts of the interior of the town appear not to have been built on. Evidence of a decline in Caerwent's economic life during the third century is given by the fact that an arena, north-east of the forum, was built at that time over the ruins of houses and on top of a road. It has been estimated that there were around 100 houses in Caerwent with a population not exceeding 2,000.

54. I. A. Richmond, *Roman Britain.*

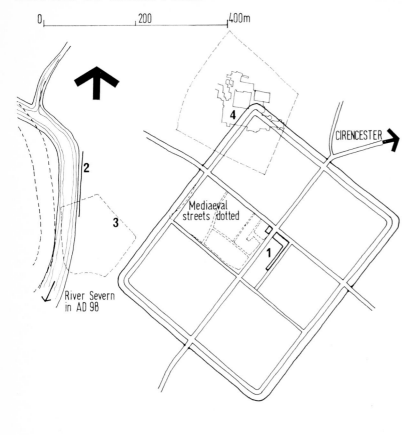

Mediaeval
streets dotted

CIRENCESTER

River Severn
in AD 98

Figure 3.31 (Left) – Glevum (Gloucester) on the right bank of the Severn, had as its full title Colonia Nervia Glevensium and is therefore known to have been founded for veterans during the reign of Nerva (96-8 AD) on a new site about half a mile downstream of an earlier legionary fortress of 50 AD, probably that of the Twentieth Legion. Collingwood and Myres in their *Roman Britain* consider that in order for the Romans to take the offensive in South Wales it was necessary to establish 'a legionary fortress on the left bank of the Severn at some point where it could be easily crossed, threatening the hostile right bank as Cologne or Mainz threatened the right bank of the Rhine. The obvious position for such a fortress was Gloucester, which is still the lowest bridge on the Severn . . .' Glevum covered an area of about 46 acres within a rectangular perimeter some 630 yards long by 440 yards wide.

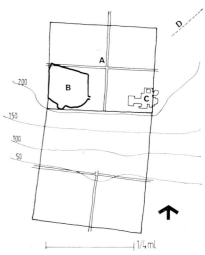

Figure 3.32 – Lindum (Lincoln). Key: A, the forum location; B, the mediaeval castle; C, the cathedral; D, an aqueduct. Contours at 50-foot intervals.

LINDUM

Lindum (Lincoln) was converted from *castra* to *colonia* status for veterans of the ninth legion in about AD 92. Writing about Lindum in his book *Town and Country in Roman Britain*, A. L. F. Rivet notes that 'in its earliest form the *colonia* occupied the actual site of the legionary fortress . . . and covered an area of 41 acres'. Subsequently the town expanded down the slope towards the river and a later defensive perimeter enclosed a total of 97 acres. Little is known of Lindum's detail plan or its buildings; continuous site occupation, following what was at most only a brief desertion after the breakdown of Roman Britain, has left few remains even where excavations have been possible. It is known however that there was a partial system of sewers, and that water was brought in by an aqueduct.

VERULAMIUM

Verulamium (St Albans) is generally assumed to have been the only *municipium* in Roman Britain and as such was established for the Catuvellauni, near to their own tribal centre. As first built, Verulamium seems to have been largely unplanned. However it was a thriving commercial centre when burnt down by Boadicea's men in AD 60. The rebuilt Verulamium was considerably bigger than before, with an enclosed area of 140 acres, and included a great monumental forum and basilica of AD 79. Hadrian however seems to have been dissatisfied with the town, which was entirely rebuilt from about 129–30, partly on and partly off the old site.

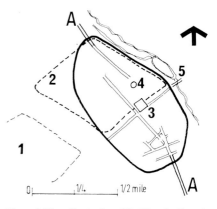

Figure 3.33 – Verulamium (St Albans). Key: 1 location of earlier tribal hill village; 2, first Romano-British city as rebuilt AD 60 (dotted); 3, the forum; 4, theatre; 5, river ford; A, Watling Street. The perimeter of the second city is in heavy outline.

Epilogue: Constantinople

The Emperor Diocletian, who ruled between 284 and 305 AD, before eventually retiring to tend his garden at Split[55], reimposed order on third century imperial chaos but was forced to recognise that with all its problems the Empire had become too unwieldy for individual rule. Accordingly he divided the Empire into four parts, each with its own Caesar. Diocletian himself became emperor in the East, ruling the Balkan peninsular, Asia Minor, Syria and Egypt from Nicomedia (modern Izmit) on the southern shore of the Sea of Marmora[56]. Rome could still claim to be the western capital although Milan, Trier and Ravenna periodically usurped much of its authority.

Constantius had ruled as Western Emperor until his death in 306, but, from the time of being proclaimed as his successor by the army at York, Constantine took six years to consolidate his authority in the West, defeating Maxentius in 312 outside Rome, and a further eleven years to become absolute emperor when in 323 and 324 he routed his eastern rival. Constantine assumed a formidable weight of imperial responsibility: prosperity and population were declining, barbarian pressures along the western frontiers were continually increasing, and, above all, there was the problem of Rome itself. The city's way of life had for a long time imposed an intolerable economic burden, sustained only at great and increasingly disproportionate expense, and after 313, when Christianity was partially recognised as the state religion, the city's essentially pagan associations hindered a union of the State and its new Church. Accordingly Constantine resolved to create a new capital away from the threats of the present and the distasteful reminders of the past. He recognised that if a new Empire were to be founded out of the crumbling fabric of the old order, then its centre should be located at the eastern end of the Mediterranean. Numerous possible locations were considered, including Troy, Chalcedon and Sardica (modern Sofia), until in the latter part of 324 Constantine decided to base his new capital on the ancient city of Byzantium. This location was admirably situated on the land route between Europe and Asia; it also controlled the western entrance to the Bosphorus, linking the Mediterranean to the Black Sea by way of the Sea of Marmora (Fig. 3.34).

Byzantium had an eventful early history, allied with one Greek power after another before becoming, from about 150 BC, a free, tribute-paying city on the fringe of the Roman Empire. This status was withdrawn by Vespasian who incorporated Byzantium into the Empire in AD 73. At the end of the second century AD Byzantium paid the penalty for supporting an unsuccessful contender for imperial power: the victor, Septimus Severus, captured the city in 196 after nearly three years of siege and razed it to the ground. However the site was far too important to be left unoccupied; accordingly Severus refortified an enlarged area giving it the name of Antoninia (Fig. 3.36). The citizens of Antoninia also backed an imperial loser, this time in Licinius, Constantine's pagan eastern rival; and it was when he captured Antoninia that Constantine realised the potential strength of the site.

The Emperor was in no doubt as to the required size of his new capital, shrugging off incredulous courtiers' objections with the legendary remark – 'I shall still advance till He, the invisible guide who marches before me, thinks proper to stop' – before, with cere-

Figure 3.34 – The location of Constantinople (on the site of earlier Byzantium) at the south-western end of the Bosphorus, which links the Sea of Marmora to the Black Sea and separates Europe from Asia. Not only was this position of immense stategic importance but the site of Constantinople itself, on the tip of a peninsular surrounded on three sides by water, was also one of history's best defensive locations.

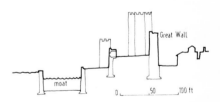

Figure 3.35 – Constantinople, section through the land walls. As completed by 413 the Great Wall ran for 4½ miles from the Sea of Marmora, taking in the Golden Gate, to the Golden Horn. It was some 40 ft high on the outside, 16 ft thick at the bottom and strengthened by 96 surviving towers about 60 ft high – there may have been a total of 100 before the reconstruction of the northern end.

55. Diocletian's palace at Spalato (modern Split) on the Jugoslavian coast of the Adriatic was more than a palace, it was a town in itself, which is what it became after the fall of the Empire when it was occupied by numerous 'squatter' families.

56. The other Caesars and their parts of the Empire were: Maximian – Italy and Africa; Galerius – Illyricum and the Danube; Constantius – Britain, Gaul and Spain.

monial spear in hand, he traced out the boundary line all of two miles west of the Severus Wall (Fig. 3.36). Divine guidance or not, Constantine held temporal purse-string power to populate the area[57]. As Cecil Stewart observes, 'the presence of the Emperor and government meant that a large part of the revenue of the Empire would automatically come to the new city. Many were attracted by a sense of duty; some came at the invitation of Constantine itself, an invitation which could not be distinguished from a command. The favourites were given palaces, replicas of their Roman villas, and others were encouraged to build in the city by the offers of estates outside the walls, which were granted on the tenure of maintaining a residence in the capital. The wheat which had hitherto been sent from Egypt to Rome was diverted to the new capital, and provided for the daily free distribution of 80,000 loaves'[58]. First, however, he had to deal with a shortage of architects by commanding the immediate institution of new imperial schools of architecture.

Constantine's ramparts were completed by 330 and on 11 May he dedicated the city as the Christian capital of the East and the declared rival of Rome in the West. From this moment on their fortunes were in marked contrast: Constantinople prospered whilst Rome declined. By 410, the year in which Rome fell to Alaric and the Goths, Constantine's optimism was justified; the area within his perimeter was fully prescribed such that Themistius could write, 'no longer is the vacant ground in the city more extensive than that occupied by buildings; nor are we cultivating more territory within our walls than we inhabit; the beauty of the city is not as heretofore, scattered over it in patches but covers its whole area like a robe woven to the very fringe . . . its former extremity is not its centre'[59].

Under Theodosius II (408–450) the city was expanded within a new defensive system which was constructed about one mile further to the west of Constantine's wall. This system, which eventually took the form of three walls and a wide moat, as shown in Figure 3.35, is known after the emperor and the regent, Anthemius, who held the office of prefect. The Walls of Anthemius (or Theodosius) remained unrivalled and impregnable through to 1453 when they finally succumbed to Turkish cannon[60]. Ironically these revolutionary weapons were designed and manufactured by one of the earliest cannon-founders, a Hungarian called Urban, who had previously offered his services to the beleaguered Constantine XI without being offered his stipulated price. In breaching Arthemius's walls artillery opened up a new era in urban fortification. This is described in Chapter Five in so far as it concerned Renaissance Europe generally and Italian cities in particular, and in Chapters Six and Seven its effects on individual European cities in other countries are discussed.

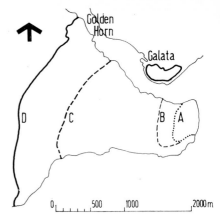

Figure 3.36 – Constantinople, an outline plan showing the city related to the Golden Horn, which provided water defences along its northern side, and the Sea of Marmora to the south. Key: A, the extent of Byzantium before its destruction in 196 AD; B, the Wall of Septimus Severus; C, Constantine's fortifications of 330 AD; D, the Walls of Anthemius (or Thecdosius). See Figure 3.35 for a cross-section of these.

Very little is known of the detailed layout of Constantine's city. The line of its walls has been determined, and it is known that it comprised fourteen districts and covered seven hills, as did Rome, with the main street system in the form of a 'Y' traversing five main fora, the most important of which was the circular Forum of Constantine located at what had been the main gateway in the Severus wall. It is most likely that Constantinople followed the general pattern of Rome with carefully organised civic spaces and public buildings interspersed with more or less uncontrolled organic growth residential districts. Constantinople also had a water supply problem and an aqueduct system was required to bring supplies into the city where numerous reservoirs, some of enormous size, provided for periods of drought and lengthy sieges.

57. Brazilia is a close modern parallel to Constantinople with the decision to move a national capital; its host of civil servants and government dependants also had little choice but to move.
58. Cecil Stewart, *A Prospect of Cities*.
59. Themistius, *Oratio XVIII*.
60. The Crusaders in capturing Constantinople in 1204 broke into the city across the Golden Horn, through the comparatively weaker sea-ward defences. Walls, no matter how impressive, require adequate manning and in 1453 Constantine XI had a garrison of perhaps only 7,000 to set against 80,000 Turks and their cannon.

4 — Mediaeval towns

Classified on the basis of their origins there can be said to be five broad categories of towns in mediaeval Europe of the eleventh to fifteenth centuries. Three categories are of *organic growth towns*:

(1) towns of Roman origin – both those which may have retained urban status throughout the Dark Ages, albeit considerably reduced in size, and those which were deserted after the fall of the Empire, but which were re-established on their original sites;

(2) burgs (borough, burk, bourg, burgo), built as fortified military bases and acquiring commercial functions later;

(3) organic growth towns developed mostly from village settlements. The remaining categories are of *new towns* which were established formally at a given moment in time, with full urban status, and with or without a predetermined plan;

(4) bastide towns, founded in France, England and Wales;

(5) planted towns, founded throughout Europe generally.

The sequence is in approximate chronological order. Before the Romans, urban settlements in Europe are believed to have been few and far between. Chapter Three has established that many of them were taken over by the Romans and redeveloped along planned lines. After the collapse of the Empire in the fifth century, urban life in Europe was greatly curtailed (in Britain it effectively disappeared) until, beginning in the tenth and eleventh centuries, political stability and resurging trade gave renewed life to many Roman foundations, converted burgs to commercially orientated towns, and instigated the slow process whereby a number of villages were transmuted into towns. New towns were founded throughout the Middle Ages but the rate of creations was slow at each end of the period; the pronounced peak came during the thirteenth century.

Although the mediaeval period shows a two-dimensional contrast between organic growth and planned urban form as marked as at any other time, classification in terms of plans on the simple basis of either of these extremes is no longer possible. The route structures of the great majority of rebuilt Roman towns, and of many of those which had continued in being were as much the result of organic processes as determined by their original gridiron layouts. Similarly, numerous mediaeval new towns which started out from a plan subsequently underwent uncontrolled expansion and change. There are

Figure 4.1 – Western Europe, showing the locations of six groups of planned new towns described in this chapter: 1, the French bastides (detail map, Figure 4.19); 2, the Welsh bastides (detail map, Figure 4.29); 3, the Zähringer towns (detail map, Figure 4.38); 4, towns in East Germany and Poland, east of the Elbe; 5, towns founded by the Florentine Republic in the valley of the Arno (detail map, Figure 4.42); 6, towns in South Bohemia (Czechoslovakia).
The two English bastides, Winchelsea and Kingston-upon-Hull are located individually. Londonderry, an English planted town in Ulster, is also shown.

also a few examples of planned additions to organic growth towns. This chapter does not attempt to present a complete description of mediaeval urban form and its determining background factors for all European countries. The mediaeval period was the formative era of town development in Europe: in many ways it is the most important part of this volume. Not only is the political, economic and social context extremely complex, but the towns themselves present an almost infinite variety of forms. But there are a number of similarities in the context of urban development in European countries, which makes possible a general consideration of a number of key factors: feudalism; the early mediaeval revival of commerce, related to the rôle played by the Church; the mediaeval industrial situation, and common features of urban form which are found in most parts of Europe. This shared background will comprise the introductory section to this chapter and will be followed by a description of towns in the five groups.

The origins of Rome and London are described in Chapter Three, and Paris in Chapter Six. To enable *continuity* of development to be properly established, the histories of these cities during the mediaeval period are included in their respective national Renaissance chapters[1]. Similarly Chapter Seven includes the mediaeval periods of most of its city examples in other European countries.

RELIGION AND REVIVAL OF COMMERCE

In AD 395 the Roman Empire was divided into two parts. With Constantinople as its capital, the Eastern Empire prospered (as described in the previous chapter), but the already disintegrating Western Empire, under its capital Rome, lasted only until the beginning of the fifth century, by which date, writes Pirenne, 'all was over. The whole West was invaded. Roman provinces were transformed into Germanic kingdoms. The Vandals were installed in Aquitaine and in Spain, the Burgundians in the valley of the Rhône, the Ostrogoths in Italy'[2].

Contrary to popular misconception the fall of the Empire in the West did not immediately result in a more or less complete breakdown of the Roman economic system. (The question of the varying fates of individual Roman towns is discussed later in this chapter.) Although there was a continued commercial *raison d'être* for many Roman towns – in particular those in southern Gaul – the effect of this factor must not be exaggerated. The economic order of fifth to eighth century Gaul remained, as it always had been, founded on agriculture. Neither must we underestimate the rôle played by the Church in maintaining the continuity of urban life in many parts of Western Europe (although Britain was a notable exception to this). In general the Church had taken imperial administrative districts as the basis of its ecclesiastical organisation, each diocese corresponding to a *civitas*. These districts were unaffected by the setting up of the new Germanic kingdoms such that 'from the beginning of the sixth century the word *civitas* took the special meaning of "episcopal city", the centre of the diocese'[3]. These cities also retained trading functions, varying from simple local produce markets to comparatively highly developed commercial activities.

Imperial economic unity, and the urban life it supported, survived the Germanic invasions largely because the Mediterranean remained open for trade. From early in the seventh century however the vital

In the fourteenth century the English town was still a rural and agricultural community, as well as a centre of industry and commerce. It had its stone wall or earth mound to protect it, distinguishing it from an open village. But outside lay the 'town field' unenclosed by hedges, where each citizen-farmer cultivated his own strips of cornland; and each grazed his cattle or sheep on the common pasture of the town, which usually lay along the river side as at Oxford and Cambridge. In 1388 it was laid down by Parliamentary Statute that in harvest time journeymen and apprentices should be called on to lay aside their crafts and should be compelled 'to cut, gather and bring in the corn'; mayors, bailiffs and constables of towns were to see this done (Stats. of Realm II, 56.). In Norwich, the second city of the kingdom, the weavers, till long after this period, were conscripted every year to fetch home the harvest. Even London was no exception to the rule of a half rustic life. There was none of the rigid division between rural and urban which has prevailed since the Industrial Revolution. No Englishman then was ignorant of all country things, as the great majority of Englishmen are today.

(G. M. Trevelyan. 'English Social History')

---

1. Rome, Chapter Five, pages 120–132; Paris, Chapter Six, pages 138–149; London, Chapter Eight, pages 181–205.
2. Henri Pirenne, *Mediaeval Cities*.
3. C. T. Smith, *An Historical Geography of Western Europe before 1800*.

link was first constricted, then closed, by the rapid growth of Islam. Syria was taken from the Byzantines in 634–36 and progressive advances westward along the African coast brought Islam into Spain by 711. Its growth was contained only by the successful defence of Constantinople (713) and Martel's victory in Spain (732).

Moslem control of the Mediterranean extended to continual piracy along its northern shores. Trade was completely disrupted; by the middle of the eighth century 'solitude reigned in the port of Marseilles. Her foster-mother, the sea, was shut off from her and the economic life of the inland regions which had been nourished through her intermediary was definitely extinguished. By the ninth century Provence, once the richest country of Gaul, had become the poorest'[4]. Already under sustained pressure from the south, the northern and western coasts of the Carolingian Empire and areas reaching for a considerable distance inland along navigable rivers also suffered increasingly from Danish and Norwegian raids. Their attention, writes Robert-Henri Bautier, 'was directed alternately towards the Continent and England. Plunder was the essential if not the sole object : only the ports, the main economic centres and the salt-works were affected. Every year from 834 to 837 Duurstede, the principal port for Frisian trade, was pillaged, as well as neighbouring ports, and also the island of Noirmoutier and the Thames estuary. Rouen was taken in 841, Quentovic (the chief Frankish port) and London in 842, Nantes was sacked in 843, Paris in 845, Bordeaux in 848'[5].

Commerce of any significance, and certainly of a kind that had previously supported professional international merchant bodies, was impossible in these unsettled conditions. As a direct result urban life in Western Europe declined to its nadir by the end of the ninth century. Pirenne observes that 'an economy of exchange was substituted for an economy of consumption. Each demesne [great estate] in place of continuing to deal with the outside constituted from this time on a little world of its own . . . the ninth century is the golden age of what we have called the closed domestic economy and which we might call, with more exactitude, the economy of no markets'[6].

However, a commercial revival took root and steadily gained in strength as soon as the political climate became only relatively more stable during the early decades of the tenth century. Throughout Western Europe long-distance trading routes were reopened, notably those connecting with Venice and the north Italian trading communities, and by mid-century Flanders had become a comparable north-western focus. The resurgence of trade had a particularly early origin in Germany where, in 918, Conrad I granted market rights to Würzburg and, as Bautier notes, 'twenty-nine Acts granting market concessions have come down to us mainly dating from the third quarter of the tenth century'[7].

The Church, which had preserved for Europe a semblance of civilised life during the Dark Ages, not only provided nuclei for many early mediaeval towns but also used its 'ubiquitous and persuasive influence to restrain the quick impulses which were at all times so close to the surface'[8]. In addition to the protection afforded by the bishops' walled cities and strongly defended monasteries, numerous burgs established in all parts of Europe as heavily fortified military and administrative centres also served to promote the tenth century resurgence of trade. Again referring to Germany, C. T. Smith notes that, 'of about 120 towns identified in Germany in the eleventh

In the Middle Ages the inhabitants of each town regarded themselves as a separate community, almost a separate race, at commercial war with the rest of the world. Only a freeman of the city could be bound apprentice; and the freedom of the city was but grudgingly bestowed on 'foreigners' or 'aliens', as the people of the neighbouring towns and villages were called. This idea of the civic community was now gradually yielding to the idea of the national community, and to the broader aspects of economic and racial policy introduced by the discovery of America and the struggle with Spain. But the old ideas still lingered.
(G. M. Trevelyan, 'England under the Stuarts')

4. Henri Pirenne, *Mediaeval Cities.*
5. Robert-Henri Bautier, *The Economic Development of Mediaeval Europe.*
6. Henri Pirenne, *Mediaeval Cities.*
7. Robert-Henri Bautier, *The Economic Development of Mediaeval Europe.*
8. J. W. Thompson and E. N. Johnson, *An Introduction to Mediaeval Europe: 300–1500.*

century, about 40 were on the sites of bishops' seats, 20 were near monasteries, and no less than 60 grew around royal foundations, including some 12 near the sites of royal palaces'[9]. Throughout Europe these towns, stimulated by long-distance trade, encouraged local trade through systems of market towns which developed naturally from village origins or were 'planted' in favourable new locations (see below for a further discussion of both cases).

By the eleventh century commerce was generally re-established but, to quote Pirenne, 'it was only in the twelfth century that, gradually but definitely, Western Europe was transformed. The economic development freed her from the traditional immobility to which a social organisation, depending solely on the relations of man to the soil, had condemned her'[10]. Urban expansion continued apace during the twelfth and thirteenth centuries and even the Black Death, which hit Europe generally between 1348–78, did no more than produce temporary setbacks. Paradoxically its effect was greatest on rural populations. Chances of survival were greater in the country, but on the other hand the commercial advantages of living in towns were still very attractive. Thus there was a tendency to move towards the towns, so accelerating the problems of rural depopulation.

FEUDALISM

During the twelfth and thirteenth centuries, throughout Europe, feudalism was 'the basis of local government, of justice, of legislation, of the army and of all executive power. In this period . . . all land is held from the kind either mediately or directly. The king himself is a great landowner with demesnes (estates) scattered over the length and breadth of the realm; the revenues of these supply him with the larger part of his permanent income. The king is surrounded by a circle of tenants-in-chief, some of whom are bishops and abbots and ecclesiastical dignitaries of other kinds; the remainder are dukes, counts, barons, knights. All of these, laymen and churchmen alike, are bound to perform more or less specific services in return for their lands . . . These tenants-in-chief have on their estates a number of sub-tenants who are bound to them by similar contracts'. In a typical feudal state all members are grouped voluntarily or forcibly under the rule of persons higher up the feudal heirarchy, either as 'servile village-communities who give up perforce a large proportion of their working days to the cultivation of the lord's demesne, (or) . . . the small freeholders who pay to this or that lord a rent in money, kind or services'[11].

The feudal system encouraged slight, but highly significant improvements in agricultural techniques, making an increase in the rural food surplus available to urban settlements with their steadily growing proportions of non-agricultural specialists. (For a comparison with the 'urban revolutions' in Mesopotamia and the other first civilisations see Chapter One, page 5.) In the emerging towns the inhabitants are also subject to a lord or the king, but whilst '. . . some are only half-emancipated communities of serfs . . . in others the burgesses have the status of small freeholders and in a minority, but a growing minority, of cases the burgesses have established the right to deal collectively with the lord, to be regarded as communes, or free cities'[12]. This latter factor was to be of profound importance in the rise of European urban society and the corresponding decline of mediaeval feudalism.

While the Greek and Roman thought that the happy life could only be lived in the city, the nascent civilisation of the Middle Ages was of the country not of the town. Its unit was the court and manor of the feudal landlord, the homesteads and farm buildings of his humbler tenants. There was neither the good government necessary for ordered town life, nor the commerce which made it economically possible for great hordes of men to dwell together in an urban area.
(T. F. Tout, 'Mediaeval Town Planning')

9. C. T. Smith, *An Historical Geography of Western Europe before 1800.*
10. Henri Pirenne, *Mediaeval Cities.*
11, 12. H. W. C. Davis, *Mediaeval Europe.*

MEDIAEVAL INDUSTRY IN ENGLAND

The two principal industries of mediaeval England seem to have been the production of woollen cloth and the smelting and working of iron. Timber, a most important raw material, was used both for general purpose construction and as the source of the pure charcoal fuel required for the iron industry. Coal was widely used only for domestic purposes.

Neither the location of mediaeval towns nor their form was significantly affected by industry. The appalling condition of roads, totally neglected since the Romans' departure, meant that the only way of transporting bulk materials for any distance was by water. As a result such 'heavy' industry as existed was decentralised, on a largely rural basis, in those districts where raw materials, eg iron ore and timber, were readily available. Production levels remained low until the end of the period when, with demand increasing, some small towns, notably Birmingham, started to become urban industrial centres. Long-established boroughs with vested guild interests, such as Coventry, frequently reacted against the introduction of new techniques thereby prejudicing their futures[13].

Within towns and manufacturing villages there would have been no separate industrial premises of any great size. Industry would have been of a predominantly secondary nature, converting bar-iron, for instance, into a limited range of products, with the same premises serving as a workshop, shop and the home of the proprietor. Furthermore, there is, as such, no separate Renaissance industrial context for urban growth. The mediaeval industrial situation, with its steady expansion of trade and production, leads directly to the eighteenth-century phases of the Industrial Revolution.

Wool – 'From the twelfth to the nineteenth centuries the woollen industry was the premier English industry, and as such was largely responsible for the growth of the country's wealth'[14]. The history of the cloth industry goes back well before the Roman occupation. Although a uniform-producing centre for the Roman army is recorded at Winchester[15], this is an exception to the rule that the spinning of wool fibre into yarn, to be woven into cloth, was a part-time rural 'cottage-industry' occupation.

Cloth production initially paralleled agricultural production, being for subsistence rather than for marketing. Most parts of the country were reasonably suited for sheep, and the wool industry was very widely scattered. From the twelfth century there was a surplus of raw wool and finished cloth and exports of both were being made to the Continent. Specialist cloth workers set themselves up in the market-town centres of the main wool producing districts, and by the reign of Henry I (1100–1135) weavers' guilds are recorded in London, Lincoln, Oxford and Winchester.

Coal – The Romans recognised some of the valuable properties of coal and organised its production from surface and shallow excavation workings in several parts of the country. During the Dark Ages there was hardly any demand for coal but within a few decades of the Norman Conquest several of the coalfields were again being worked. At first this was from shallow quarries, along the exposed surfaces of the coal seams, but later there were 'adit' mines following the seams underground on easy slopes. Shaft mining was also in

In 1427 there were 180 wool shops in Florence, and nearly twice this number 50 years later; but each one might produce on average less than 100 bolts of cloth a year. A 'shop' was more like an office, with a manager and his assistant, and perhaps a book-keeper and one or two errand boys. Most of the operations – and there were 26 different stages in the production of wool cloth – were put out to pieceworkers whose status varied according to their job. At the bottom were the humble carders and combers, characterised by Archbishop Antonino as rowdy and foul-mouthed, who never saw their employer in person, and whose names never appeared on the company books. Forming a sort of aristocracy at the top were the dyers who sometimes even became partners in industrial ventures. In Genoa the silk dyers were the best organised working groups because they were not outworkers, but gathered together in shops; and it was a dyer, Paolo da Novi, whom the popular party elected as Doge in 1507. (John Gage, 'Life in Italy at the Time of the Medici')

13. Birmingham, which steadily overtook Coventry during the seventeenth and eighteenth centuries, had a population of 71,000 at the time of the first census of 1801 (compared to Coventry's 16,000). In 1831, when its population had doubled to 144,000, Birmingham was still in effect a feudal village, not receiving its Municipal Charter until 1838. Coventry over the same period increased to 27,000.

14, 15. L. Dudley Stamp and S. H. Beaver, *The British Isles.*

early use, but depths were limited by the lack of pumping facilities until the Industrial Revolution.

Coal was used basically for domestic heating purposes; London in particular constituted a growing market for the Northumberland and Durham coalfields, with coal being transported by sea down the east coast. Elsewhere only those towns with good navigable water links to coalfields could obtain it at economic prices. As workable faces were exploited further inland from water-fronts, expediency resulted in the earliest crude wooden tracks and 'railways'; along these, carts were hauled from the fifteenth century onwards. However, the use of coal for manufacturing purposes was strictly limited by the impurities it contained – until the Industrial Revolution found ways of converting it into a usable form.

Iron – The essential prerequisite for the production of workable iron from naturally occurring iron ore was the availability of wood; this needed to be converted into charcoal for the smelting process. For this reason the fairly widespread, but relatively small-scale, Celtic ironworking industry of the Iron Age and Roman occupation had concentrated by the Middle Ages in two zones of the country where ore was available in extensively wooded surroundings – the Forest of Dean and the Weald of Sussex and Kent. As early as 1282 there were sixty forges in the forest using the local ore and the industry continued to flourish for many centuries[16]. By the sixteenth and seventeenth centuries the Weald was the leading centre of production, with the first cast-iron guns made at Buxted in 1543. An acre of woodland provided charcoal for three tons of iron. In one week a sixteenth century furnace could produce 20 tons of iron and the resulting demand on the nation's timber resources, both for ship-building and iron production, led to crisis legislation being put into effect under Elizabeth I to conserve the woodlands and secure supplies for the navy. This legislation forced the iron masters to develop alternative sources of iron ore along the wooded valleys of the Welsh borders, in Staffordshire, south Yorkshire and a few other areas[17]. Nevertheless shortage of fuel for smelting in the years before coal could be used resulted, by the early eighteenth century, in a situation whereby almost twice as much iron was being imported into this country, mainly from Sweden and Russia, as was being produced in our own furnaces. The marriage of coal and iron, from 1730 onwards, and the subsequent growth of their offspring, steel, made possible the major growth phase of the Industrial Revolution.

Mediaeval urban form

Whatever their origin, mediaeval towns in the five groups have similar social, economic and political contexts in most European countries. They are also alike as regards most visual details : the same kind of local vernacular buildings make up both the formal gridirons of planned new towns and the informal uncontrolled layouts of their unplanned contemporaries. The component parts of the mediaeval town are normally the wall, with its towers and gates; streets and related circulation spaces; the market place, probably with a market hall and other commercial buildings; the church, usually standing in its own space; and the great mass of general town buildings and related private garden spaces.

The latter half of the seventeenth century had seen a decline in the manufacture of iron, and particularly of iron bar, in this country and the beginnings of a revival of this trade were associated with a migration of the iron-making centres from the Sussex Weald and the Forest of Dean, to the thick woodlands of the Welsh borders, the South Yorkshire and Derbyshire valleys, and to Furness. The search in all cases was for an abundant charcoal supply within reasonable reach of reserves of iron ore, and water power. All these new areas had an ancient if modest tradition of ironworking in monastic forges, and many of the bloomery sites of the early sixteenth century became, in the seventeenth century, small furnace units. In the Midlands and the Welsh borders there were many men who described themselves as ironmongers, lock and nail makers, smiths and workers in small ironware, and from these many of the early Friends were drawn. The family of Lloyd of Dolobran had small forges which they leased from the landlord to whom they had been appropriated at the Dissolution of the Monasteries, and these lay in rich woodlands within reasonable reach of Welshpool and other centres on the Severn. For some years, into the early part of the eighteenth century, their pig iron or ore was purchased and brought up the river from Shropshire or Gloucestershire, but later they built a small furnace of their own. Other Friends had furnaces in many parts of the Midlands, and in the other new areas of Yorkshire and Furness. These furnaces were subservient to the forges where the iron was refined and converted to rod and bar iron, and so in the end were dependent upon the vagaries of the bar iron trade. This trade suffered many checks in the eighteenth century, due to our changing relations with Sweden, and the incidence of taxation and protective tariffs, and the fortunes of the forges and furnaces fluctuated in sympathy.
(Arthur Raistrick, 'Dynasty of Iron Founders')

16. G. W. Southgate, *English Economic History*.
17. Arthur Raistrick, *Dynasty of Iron Founders: The Darbys and Coalbrookdale*.

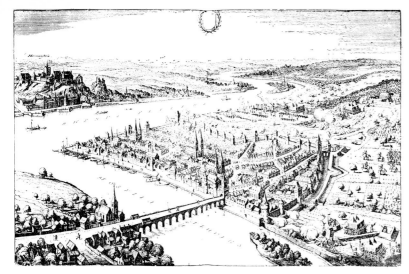

Figure 4.2 – Coblenz, an early seventeenth-century view of the city under siege. At this comparatively late date (many cities had already acquired complex Renaissance-period defensive systems) Coblenz has only its mediaeval wall and towers augmented by the beginnings of exterior earthworks. Note the clearly defined contrast between town and country – a mediaeval characteristic – and the bridgehead settlement which has become established across the Moselle. A typical hilltop castle can be seen on the far side of the Rhine.

THE WALL

From the list of England's largest towns in the poll tax of 1377, it appears that 'only Boston, among the first ten, lacked substantial defences and even then there was a ditch. All but three of the forty largest towns and cities were defended'[18]. A town wall became necessary when the fixed wealth of a settlement required protection, and perhaps only then.

One clear distinction, at least, can be drawn between English and continental European town defences. By the fourteenth century the military significance of the English town wall became greatly reduced because of the state of peace within the island. As a result the wall subsequently served mainly as a customs barrier, protecting trading interests of the townsmen and enabling tolls to be levied on all goods passing through the gates. Norwich is an instance of this diminished military significance. Given its charter by Richard I in 1194 (100 years after the foundation of the cathedral) its city wall, 'which replaced the original ditch and bank, was commenced towards the end of the thirteenth century and finished in 1343. . . . It was built of flint and, in comparison with examples elsewhere, had no great strength and was probably not intended as a major fortification'[19]. Nevertheless, over 2 miles in length, 20 feet high and 5 feet thick, it was no mean undertaking.

On the Continent however, the wall did retain its primary military function (in addition to its use as a customs barrier). As Chapters Five to Seven will show, it was to assume extremely complex and costly characteristics during the Renaissance period – so much so that city defences became probably the main determinant of urban form. Because larger, prosperous continental cities found it essential to maintain strong defences, horizontal growth could not be a continuous process; it had to take place in stages, each of which was normally preceded by the construction of a new wall, although previously undefended 'suburbs' were also frequently included. Typically, the new wall completely surrounded the city, the distance out from the previous perimeter representing a careful compromise between short-term investment considerations and the need to enclose enough land for future expansion. Walls were also sometimes built to enclose dis-

M. Pirenne. writing more particularly of the Low Countries, tells us that up to the close of the Middle Ages a sum never falling short of five-eighths of the communal budget was expended on purposes connected with the maintenance of the walls and the provision of instruments of war. In Italy, despite the fact that she was now fast securing for herself the leadership of the world in craftsmanship and international commerce, the warfare of city with city was almost perpetual. Cities would fight about diocesan boundaries and feudal rights, over tolls and markets, for the extension of their powers over the 'contado' or surrounding country, or in pursuance of the long-inherited feuds of the nobles within their walls.
(H. A. L. Fisher, 'A History of Europe')

A wall girding a town was an earlier method of defence than a castle, and a much more popular one; while the hated castle was the visible symbol of subjection, the wall around the town reminded the burgesses of their rights as citizens and their community of interests; they looked on their allotted share in its defence as a privilege, no less than a duty, and the townsmen of the open towns eagerly applied for and warmly welcomed, the right to protect themselves with a wall.
(Alfred Harvey, 'The Castles and Walled Towns of England', 1911)

18. M. W. Beresford and J. K. S. St Joseph, *Mediaeval England: an Aerial Survey.*
19. *City of Norwich Plan: 1945.*

continuous new suburbs. Either way this is in direct contrast to the situation in England where there are very few instances of post-mediaeval defence work. Exceptions are the generally rudimentary Civil War fortifications, and 'Palmerston's Folly' – the extremely costly, and, as it turned out, totally pointless system of forts constructed between 1857 and 1868 to defend Portsmouth against the French[20]. In neither case was there any significant effect on the growth of urban areas involved.

Florence is a clear example of the European concentric-ring type of growth, her two mediaeval walls of the late twelfth and early fourteenth centuries enclosed the original Roman nucleus (Fig. 4.3). The tremendous growth of this city between 1172 and about 1340 involved an increase in area from 197 acres to 1,556 acres. The second mediaeval circle 'cost about 6,000 L a year in the first years of the fourteenth century and in 1324 nearly 20,000 L was spent on it in five months, which represented roughly a quarter of the commune's total expenditure'[21]. The growth of Paris required perhaps the greatest number of walls: that of AD 360, probably enclosing the Ile de la Cité; the second, of 1180, on both banks of the Seine; the wall of 1370, built on the right bank only (extended 1610–43); the one of 1784–91 (essentially a customs barrier); and lastly that of 1841–45, now the line of the outer ring of boulevards (Fig. 6.13, page 146). Cologne (Fig. 5.6) is one of the best illustrations of a town combining suburban accretion with concentric ring addition (the latter was on the west bank only of the Rhine).

STREETS

All mediaeval towns contained a space, if not several, which acted as a market – this is explained below. However, as Howard Saalman stresses, 'the existence of these specialised spaces dedicated to trade should not blind us to a basic fact: the *entire* mediaeval city was a market. Trade and production went on in all parts of the city: in open spaces and closed spaces; public spaces and private spaces'[22]. As a result, although frequently little more than narrow, irregular lanes in organic growth towns, main thoroughfares leading to the gates from the centre were as much linear extensions of the market place as communication routes, and the notion of a 'traffic network' was as absent as constant wheeled traffic itself[23]. Street frontage was therefore a valuable commercial asset, especially near the gates and market place, and its continuous development was normal. Later it also became usual for narrow passageways to be formed off the streets, providing access to new minor street and court development of back gardens. The City of London is one of the best examples of this type of internal elaboration.

Movement in mediaeval towns was very largely on foot; wheeled traffic reached significant proportions only late in the period and transport of goods was mainly by pack-animal. Street paving commenced early in the period; Paris 1185, Florence 1235, Lübeck 1310 – indeed by 1339 all of Florence was paved[24]. Throughout the Middle Ages there was a tendency for buildings to encroach even further on to streets (including bridges) and into public open spaces. Attempts to regulate this gradual strangulation met with little success. Upper floors projected still further out over the street until eventually it was literally possible to shake hands between opposite windows. Thus the mediaeval city acquired its traditional street scene – here was

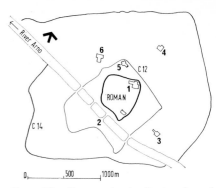

Figure 4.3 – Florence, showing the two rings of mediaeval defences around the Roman nucleus. Key: 1, Cathedral; 2, Ponte Vecchio; 3, S. Croce; 4, S. Marco; 5, S. Lorenzo; 6, S. Maria Novella; C12, twelfth century fortifications; C14, fourteenth century fortifications.

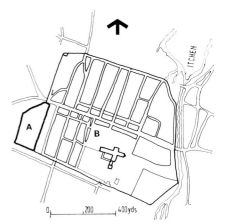

Figure 4.4 – Winchester, the mediaeval plan. The influence of the original gridiron structure of Roman Venta Belgarum has resulted in an uncharacteristically regular mediaeval street pattern. Key: A, the castle; B, the market place.

20. See Alan Balfour, *Portsmouth*.
21. Daniel Waley, *The Italian City-Republics*.
22. Howard Saalman, *Mediaeval Cities*.
23. Lewis Mumford, *The City in History*.
24. Daniel Waley, *The Italian City-Republics*.

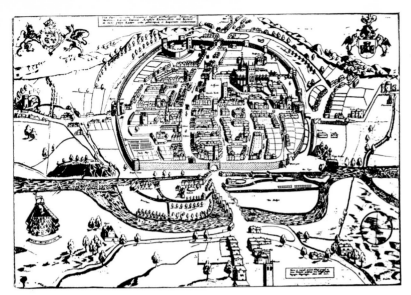

Figure 4.5 – Exeter, the city depicted in Hooker's plan of 1587. Even allowing for artistic licence, the wall, strengthened only by infrequent towers, can be seen to be of negligible military significance; there is also no sign of urban overcrowding at this late sixteenth-century date.

informality, 'romance', repeated visual surprise. Above all it was *apparently* accidental – although there was collective action more frequently than might be supposed.

One of the popular misconceptions concerning mediaeval towns is that inside the wall the usual situation was one of 'over-crowding and muddle – picturesque owing to architectural treatment, but insanitary'[25]. Possibly because of the accepted image of narrow, continuously built-up streets, it is assumed that away from the two main public spaces – those containing the market and the church – there was only strictly limited private open space, and that development was uniformly dense throughout. In a small number of instances this may well have been the case, but, as Mumford points out, 'the typical mediaeval town was nearer to what we should now call a village or a country town than to a crowded modern trading centre. Many of the mediaeval towns that were arrested in their growth before the nineteenth century still show gardens and orchards in the heart of the community'[26]. To Sir Patrick Abercrombie, the little town of Furnes, in Flanders, epitomised 'the mediaeval conception of a business town, with its noble central place, its range of public buildings, including a cathedral, a great town church, town hall, law courts, etc, its houses continuously lining the streets, economically making use of every foot of frontage, but backed by ample gardens'[27] (Fig. 4.6).

Overcrowding in continental towns more generally occurred in the late mediaeval and Renaissance periods – from growth constrained by inflexible fortification systems. In Britain it particularly accompanied the Industrial Revolution: existing gardens were developed for the new working class housing which, in the absence of mass transit systems, had to be as near the workplace as possible. Sanitary conditions are closely related to density. Although mediaeval towns had only rudimentary refuse disposal arrangements and water supply was a continual problem – particularly in hill-towns – it must not be assumed that disease was necessarily an everyday accompaniment to urban life. Mumford neatly disposes of this misconception: 'we must remember that practices that are quite innocuous in a small population surrounded by plenty of open land, become filthy when the same

Figure 4.6 – Furnes, in Flanders, a view of about 1590. Sir Patrick Abercrombie observed that 'the planning is not quite so regular as that of a Roman town, but its buildings are much more effectively placed; the whole might be called a garden city, completely realised, yet a community of frank urbanity'. *(Town and Country Planning)*

25. Sir Patrick Abercrombie, *Town and Country Planning*.
26. Lewis Mumford, *The City in History*.
27. Sir Patrick Abercrombie, *Town and Country Planning*.

number of people crowd together on a single street ... in all probability the early mediaeval village or town enjoyed healthier conditions, for all the crudeness of sanitary accommodation inside and outside the house, than its more prosperous sixteenth-century successor'[28].

THE MARKET PLACE

Marketing – the *raison d'être* of mediaeval towns – was accommodated in a number of basic ways. Two types are common in both planned and organic growth towns: first, where the market occupies a square to itself, normally located at or near the centre; second, where it is located at a widening of the main street. Paul Zucker defines two further types of market place in organic growth towns: as lateral expansions of the main street; and as squares at the town gate[29]. In planned towns laid out with a regular gridiron structure the market square is the most frequent type. Its general form here is that of a void within the grid, bounded by streets on all four sides. (Important exceptions are some of the Welsh castle-town bastides, where the market is located in front of the castle.) On the Continent it was usual for the surrounding buildings to be of the same height, and unified at ground level by arcades under which the streets frequently continued alongside the square; Monpazier – a typical French bastide – New Brandenburg and Ceske Budejovice (see Fig. 4.46) exemplify this type of square. Although arcades would have mitigated the climate, they do not seem to have been built in British examples. Typically, however, most squares contain market halls, sometimes on two floors but instances of the town church facing into the market place are rare. The market street was much less frequently incorporated into planned towns, and never in bastides. Its most important deliberate use was probably in the Zähringer new towns of Switzerland and southern Germany, where it usually ran the length of the town between the gates. Both Rottweil and Berne (the latter illustrated in Figure 4.39) demonstrate this use.

In unplanned towns both the market square and the market street defy precise description: no two layouts were alike, each had its own distinct spatial character. Many are still outstanding in Europe's cultural heritage. There are a few instances in Roman foundations of the market occupying the site of the old forum area, but usually a central position resulted from an original location within the village

Figure 4.7 – Munich, north at top; the market – Marienplatz – a lateral expansion of the main street.

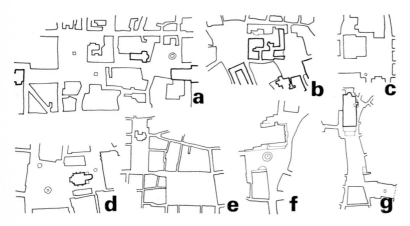

Figure 4.8 – Examples of mediaeval civic spaces in seven cities; in several instances two or more squares form a sequence of spaces. (In addition a number of these spaces were remodelled during the Renaissance period.) Key: a, Lucca, a complex sequence of spaces, reading from left to right; Piazza Grande (Napoleone), Piazza del Giglio, Piazza S. Giovanni, Piazza S. Martino, Piazza Antelminelli; b, Bruges, left the Grand'Place, right, Place du Bourg; c, Rothenburg, the market place in front of the Rathaus; d, Nuremburg, the Hauptmarkt in front of the Frauenkirche; e, Arras, Petite Place (top left) and the Grande Place; f, Perugia; g, Todi, the square in front of the cathedral.
See Paul Zucker, *Town and Squares* and Camillo Sitte, *City Planning According to Artistic Principles* (translated by George R. Collins and Christiane C. Collins), for detailed consideration of mediaeval civic space.

28. Lewis Mumford, *The City in History*.
29. Paul Zucker, *Town and Square*.

from which the town had gradually developed. 'More often than not ... the market place would be an irregular figure, sometimes triangular, sometimes many-sided or oval, now saw-toothed, now curved, seemingly arbitrary in shape because the needs of the surrounding buildings came first and determined the disposition of the open space'[30]. Several squares are shown in outline in Figure 4.8. In addition to their commercial function many squares were large enough for public gatherings.

'In towns which have evolved naturally from former villages, trading posts, etc, the main thoroughfare automatically becomes the market square since traffic is the vital element in the growth of the town'[31]. The street market is common to all European countries; the best examples are perhaps those in Germany, Austria and Switzerland.

Market places might have developed here as lateral extensions of the main street in order to free their activities from pedestrian and vehicle movement through the town. Corporate action would usually have been necessary to clear away existing buildings. Immediately inside the town gate was another logical place for trade to develop. Here, 'a peasant with produce to market has at last reached his goal. He is inside the city, in the market ... his cart is heavy, why bother to move it further?'[32] The latter type of market, however, rarely became the most important in the town.

CHURCH SQUARE

The space before the church – the mediaeval *parvis* – should not be confused with the burial ground where the latter adjoins the church, as is usual in Britain. 'It was on the *parvis* that the faithful gathered before and after the service; here they listened to occasional outdoor sermons and here processions passed. Here in front of the west portals of the church, mystery plays were performed from the twelfth century on. Here people from out-of-town left their horses and soon stalls of various kinds were set up. Nonetheless, the *parvis* was never intended to compete with the market square'[33]. The *parvis* – or, in Britain, the burial ground – meant that churches were generally located within their own space. As this frequently adjoined the market square, a two-part nucleus is a typical characteristic of mediaeval towns, both planned and unplanned.

To conclude this general introduction to mediaeval urban form we must briefly consider the extent to which its development was subject to control: how far was it pursued as a conscious effort to achieve order and beauty? Whilst Zucker's statement that, except in the comparatively few planned towns, the organisation of a town as a whole was neither understood nor desired by the builders of the Middle Ages,[34] is a fair summary of the situation, we must be careful not to presuppose that there was absolutely no concern for spatial organisation or aesthetic unity. This is a neglected area of documentary research. We are not concerned with those collective decisions which had to be taken from time to time – width of streets, maintenance or extension of the wall, rudimentary health measures, etc. These are well enough documented; but unfortunately there are only a few recorded instances of aesthetic awareness. Most of these concern Italian cities. Daniel Waley in his *Italian City-Republics* notes that 'in the thirteenth century Bologna retained a series of architects whose task it was to supervise all public buildings and works' and

Market means little to the average citizen today, but in this period it was the centre of his week, the day he could take his goods to sell and buy himself what the market could provide. Retail trade was conducted very largely in the market, for a mediaeval shop was less a store than a workshop. Traders kept no stocks of made-up goods, but sat in their shops and made what was ordered of them. Shops were generally very small, often no more than 6 feet wide. Osney Abbey built the Golden Cross Inn towards the end of the twelfth century. It sold the inn. but kept the ground floor, consisting of 4 shops. each measuring about 6 by 15 feet.
(Doris Mary Stenton. 'English Society in the Early Middle Ages')

30. Lewis Mumford, *The City in History.*
31. Paul Zucker, *Town and Square.*
32. Howard Saalman, *Mediaeval Cities.*
33, 34. Paul Zucker, *Town and Square.*

that 'the Sienese in 1309 asked their Dominicans to remove a wall which partially hid the grandiose church of San Domenico and thus detracted from the dominant architectural feature of the western part of the city'. It is also known that following the completion of Siena's impressive Town Hall in 1310 (the tower was not finished until 1344) it was decreed that other buildings on the Piazza del Campo should have similar windows.

This fourteenth century concern for visual order would seem to be a specifically Italian trait, presaging the emergence of the Renaissance and with it four centuries of more disciplined urban design. It also provides evidence of the continuing influence from the Roman past - one which included the visual unification of the forum at Pompeii by the construction of a colonnaded arcade in front of the disparate individual buildings (see page 52).

Figure 4.9 – Siena, the Piazza del Campo, dominated by the Torre del Mangia (1338-49). Daniel Waley observes that 'this tower had to be particularly imposing so that it rose above the cathedral. The curious site of the Sienese *palazzo*, on low ground where huge foundations were required, was dictated by the wish to choose neutral territcry between the three hills on which the city lies. The result was a triumph and indeed Siena had benefited from post-poning for so long the erection of a palace.' *(The Italian City-Republics)*
The paving of the central space is regulated by radii marked out from in front of the town hall, facing which are the uniform-height mediaeval palaces.

Organic growth towns

Although when the Middle Ages opened towns were few and far between, the essential fact remains that by the eleventh and twelfth centuries practically all the settlements which were subsequently to develop into towns were established on their sites. Either they were the vestigial remains of Roman foundations, about to take on a new lease of life; or they were burgs, built in the ninth century as fortified bases and acquiring commercial functions later; or again they were agricultural, subsistence-economy village settlements, able to exploit geographical advantages and promote themselves from village to town status. These are the organic-growth towns of Europe and they constitute the great majority of mediaeval towns, although in some regions planned towns are in a local majority – notably in central Europe east of the Elbe.

ROMAN ORIGINS

Any apparent contradiction presented by such a classification, where surviving Roman *urbes* became mediaeval organic-growth towns, is explained by the fact that, with but a few exceptions, the original Roman gridiron structure was lost during the decades, often centuries, when the town was deserted, or reduced to occupying only a small part of its earlier area. When rebuilding eventually took place it usually constituted unplanned organic growth of the mediaeval norm, the gridiron being ineffective.

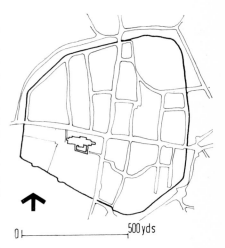

Figure 4.10 – Chichester, the mediaeval plan. Founded as Noviomagus Regensium, this site, in common with other Romano-British settlements, is believed to have been deserted for a considerable period of time following the Roman evacuation. As re-established however, the main axial crossing of the *cardo* and *decumanus* formed the basis of the layout; other minor streets have also followed the original gridiron to varying extents.

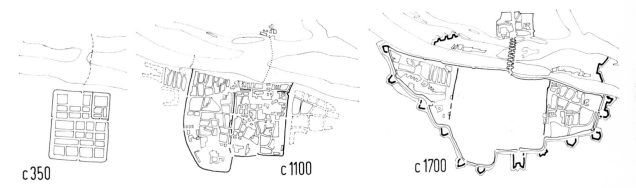

c 350   c 1100   c 1700

A distinction should be made between the fate suffered by Romano-British towns, following the final withdrawal of the Roman legions in AD 407, and the changed circumstances of their continental contemporaries after the fall of the Roman Empire. During their occupation of Britain the Romans had imposed only a thinly spread urban culture on the essentially rural civilisation of the native Celtic tribes. The Romano-British towns were small, and even if London could boast some 15,000 inhabitants most towns barely averaged a tenth of that number[35]. The invaders of the fifth century must have regarded the towns and villas as sources of plunder and objects of destruction. Celtic villagers had little to lose and for them the end of Roman rule was no overwhelming calamity[36]. Perhaps, too, it was no more than an enforced return to their old way of life for the urbanised population. Lacking organised military resistance, they would have to take to the woods in the face of invasion. The result was a temporary end to urban

Figure 4.11 – Regensburg, three stages in the development of the city from its Roman frontier *castra* origin on the southern bank of the Danube. Although not completely deserted following the withdrawal of the legions, the layout of 1100 within the *castra* perimeter shows little sign of the original gridiron. This sequence of stages in the growth of a strategically situated town also illustrates the effect of fortifications as an urban form determinant.

35, 36. M. Sayles, *Mediaeval Foundations of England.*

life in Britain. Some towns, notably Silchester, remained unoccupied long enough to disappear completely and it seems most probable that all the Roman towns, including London itself, were deserted for lengthy periods from 457 onwards. The advantages of their locations, and the existence of ruined buildings and defences which could be repaired, later attracted back a proportion of the old inhabitants and may have served as a ready-made base for immigrants into the district. But the original urban pattern, once disrupted, was never completely reinstated.

For a number of reasons the fate suffered by the Romano-British towns was worse than that endured by continental towns. Britain was the least Romanised of the provinces, it had been the last major acquisition and it was furthest from the origins of the imposed Mediterranean culture. The Barbarian invaders of Britain, in their turn, were much less affected by Roman influences than the new rulers of Western Europe generally. The latter had learned to appreciate the high civilisation into which they entered and sought in their clumsy way to copy it[37].

BURGS

The anarchy of the ninth century, which had compelled bishops to reinstate the walls of their Roman *civitates* and turned monasteries into religious citadels, also directly resulted in the emergence of a new class of town in Western Europe. On the Continent the Carolingian Empire, disintegrating in the face of continual Scandinavian invasions, 'was parcelled out, after the middle of the ninth century, into a number of territories subject to as many local dynasties, and attached to the Crown only by the fragile bond of feudal homage'[38]. Defences, as much against rival princes as against invading forces, were an essential requirement and castles were therefore built in many localities. As described by Thompson and Johnson 'these were not yet the great stone structures of the thirteenth century and later, but only rude, palisaded wooden blockhouses, often erected in a hurry to meet some crisis of invasion ... countless burgs were built by dukes, counts, and margraves in the ninth and early tenth centuries for protection against Norsemen, Magyars, Slavs and Saracens, especially in Saxony and on the eastern German frontier and in England, where many boroughs (burgs) served for defence against the Danes'[39].

David Wilson confirms, on the basis of archaeological and historical sources, that in England, even before the Viking invasion, 'some towns were flourishing centres of trade and mutual protection. Such towns were Rochester, Canterbury, Carlisle, Thetford, Winchester, and, of course, London ... nevertheless, the great development in English town life came in and after the reign of Alfred in the late ninth century. The need to protect the country against Danish attack led to the foundation of a series of fortified boroughs'[40].

The Danes first appeared in England in 793; the Anglo-Saxon Chronicle records that on 8 June the ravages of heathen men miserably destroyed God's church on Lindisfarne, with plunder and slaughter[41]. The essentially agricultural communities of England were not organised to resist these incursions, which by the middle of the ninth century had escalated into large-scale military operations. As a result Mercia and Northumbria were lost to the invaders and Wessex was seriously threatened. King Alfred (871–99) was responsible for

f towns on sites once Roman were richer and larger than towns on newer sites, as York was richer than Norwich and Lincoln than Ipswich, it was because of present circumstances, not an inheritance from their remote past. When William I became king there were in England boroughs which would never develop into towns in the modern sense, places little more in size than villages, and there were villages that would in time become towns. Bedwyn in Wiltshire cannot now be called anything but a village, but it was a borough in 1086 when Doomsday Book was compiled; so were Bruton and Langport in Somerset. It was not size or wealth that made a borough, but an act of royal will. The larger English boroughs at the beginning of this period had all grown up under royal protection and control as an integral part of the royal policy for the development of national resources and national defence. (Doris Mary Stenton, 'English Society in the Early Middle Ages')

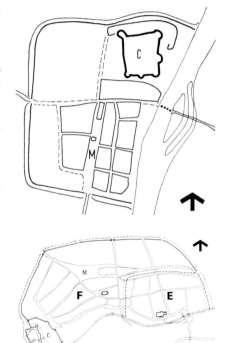

Figure 4.12 – Wallingford (top) and Nottingham, two examples of English burgs. Key: C, castle; M, marketplace.
At Nottingham, after the Norman Conquest a new French borough (F) was established adjoining the area of the original English burg (E).

37. E. A. Gutkind, *Urban Development in Central Europe*.
38. Henri Pirenne, *Mediaeval Cities*.
39. J. W. Thompson and E. N. Johnson, *An Introduction to Mediaeval Europe, 300–1500*.
40. David Wilson, *The Anglo-Saxons*.
41. Dorothy Whitelock, *The Beginnings of English Society*.

first containing the Danish advance and then defeating them in 878 at the battle of Edington. Dorothy Whitelock describes how the defensive strategy was based on his burghal system – the provision of fortified centres which could protect a tract of country against enemy attack, a policy continued under his son Edward from whose reign comes a document known as the Burghal Hidage, which gives the names of the boroughs thus formed under West Saxon rule[42]. According to Sir Frank Stenton there were thirty-one of these strongholds in Wessex during Alfred's reign, so located that no village was more than twenty miles away from safety[43].

Alfredian boroughs were of various origins. Many were based on existing settlements which had been given new or strengthened walls; others were new foundations. Oxford and Wallingford, each founded on eight yardlands of land, seem to belong to this class, and the account in Domesday Book suggests that population had been attracted to them by favourable conditions of tenure[44]. The boroughs created by the kings had their fates determined by economic circumstances. The borough of Sceaftesage is one of those that disappeared and it has only been tentatively identified as Sashes, on the Thames near Cookham. Many others prospered only to the extent of becoming well-established market and county towns.

The Danes also founded boroughs as bases for their offensive operations and after the treaty of 878, which recognised the Danelaw as their part of England, they settled peacefully around them as social, market and fortified centres. The five most important Danish boroughs – Derby, Lincoln, Leicester, Stamford and Nottingham – constituted a well-organised confederacy and the English counter-offensive under Edward the Elder (901-25) turned on their reduction. With the exception of Stamford these boroughs were confirmed as county towns in the eleventh century. Darby shows how the reconquest of the Danelaw was marked at every point by the creation of a stronghold. From the Anglo-Saxon Chronicle a list can be compiled of just over a score of boroughs established by Edward the Elder to secure his conquests in the Midlands[45].

Although the majority of burgs in Europe were essentially military and administrative centres, without significant commercial activities and therefore hardly to be accorded urban status, they constituted attractive 'pre-urban' nuclei around which many towns developed. The military presence generated immediate service industry activity and a produce market would have soon become established to provide for daily needs of both the military élite and the serf community. It is probable that an increasing proportion of local craft products became available for sale in the market before the general revival in European commerce brought confirmation of urban status – a revival encouraged first by the packs of itinerant pedlars and subsequently by the wagons of increasingly prosperous merchants.

Civil trading communities which grew up outside the walls of burgs were frequently called faubourgs (Latin foris burgum – 'outside the burg') or suburbs (Latin 'close to the urbs'). As they became established, perhaps even completely surrounding the burg, they required defensive walls of their own. There is no evidence that these simple two-part burgs which are found in all parts of Western Europe, were other than the result of organic growth. Some burgs, however, had more complex origins and were possibly planned in part. Magdeburg (Fig. 4.13) is taken by C. T. Smith as an example of a

The status of a borough was no assurance of prosperity and it was easy even for an ancient borough to lose ground to a new competitor. When late in the Middle Ages a bridge was built over the Thames at Abingdon it diverted the London to Gloucester road and drew trade from the borough of Wallingford, in early days the chief borough of Berkshire. But long before this, between Abingdon on the one hand and Reading on the other, Henry I's new abbey brought trade to the town, Wallingford was losing ground. Even today it has spread little beyond its Anglo-Saxon defences. Many of the boroughs founded by magnates did not prosper, either because of too close competition or because the site was unsuitable to a town. In Lancashire only 4 of the 23 boroughs founded there between 1066 and 1372 survived the Middle Ages as boroughs. Even Manchester and Warrington failed to keep their burghal status continuously into the modern age.
(Doris Mary Stenton, 'English Society in the Early Middle Ages')

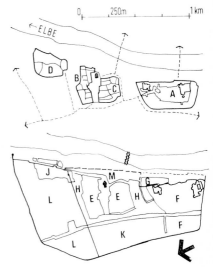

Figure 4.13 – Magdeburg, two stages in the development of this complex multi-nuclei settlement located on high ground on the west bank of the Elbe. Above (c 1000 AD). Key: A, Carolingian castle-site of 805 (on the probable site of a Saxon lord's house) and the monastery of St Moritz (937); B, cathedral of 968, and the early unplanned Ottonian town; C, planned Ottonian town of c 1200 with a market place; D, the count's burg.
Below (c 1250 AD). Key: E, Ottonian town; F, the immunity of the cathedral; G, monastic land; H, infilling development of the eleventh and twelfth centuries; J, part of the count's burg, used for church buildings from the thirteenth century; K, organic growth extension of 1152-1192; L, planned new district of 1213-1236; M, twelfth and thirteenth century riverside development.

42. Dorothy Whitelock, *The Beginnings of English Society.*
43. Sir Frank Stenton, *Anglo-Saxon England.*
44. Dorothy Whitelock, *The Beginnings of English Society.*
45. H. C. Darby, *An Historical Geography of England before 1800.*

multi-nuclear burg, comprising a Carolingian castle-site of 805 (with a monastery added in 937); the cathedral of 968 and its related buildings; the count's *burg*, further downstream; and, between cathedral and castle, a regularly laid-out market district of the early thirteenth century[46].

VILLAGE SETTLEMENT

By definition therefore organic growth towns of the Middle Ages developed from, or were based on, village settlements. Throughout Europe, the location of these towns and, to a very great extent, their urban form, were determined by the preceding slow, accumulative processes of village settlement. Thus it is first necessary to consider the circumstances of their village origins. England provides an instructive illustration of these processes.

With relatively few exceptions the thirteen thousand or so English villages were in existence on their present sites by the time of the Domesday Book survey of 1086, although in many instances these could have been only the embryonic nuclei of later mediaeval settlements. England became a country of villages as a result of the Anglo-Saxon settlement between the fifth and tenth centuries. By the time of the first Anglo-Saxon villages much of the earlier localised, cleared and tamed landscape had reverted to its natural state. W. G. Hoskins in his admirable *The Making of the English Landscape* records that in certain favoured regions, like the Cotswolds and north Oxfordshire, the Anglo-Saxons may have entered a fairly civilised landscape, but in general they had literally to start from scratch. The great majority of the English settlers faced a virgin country of damp oak/ash forest, or beech forest on or near the chalk; and what was not thickly wooded was likely to be cold, high, mist-wrapped moorland or water-logged, wet, heath, drowned marshes and estuary saltings, or sterile, thin-soiled, dry heath – hardly the sort of land that gave itself to cultivation.

This situation facing the Anglo-Saxon village settlers might be seen as the first of four distinct phases in the continuing evolution of the English landscape – first, more or less wild, inherited landscape; second, the result of village settlement, which, over most of the country, saw the forest largely cleared for the typical open-field farming system; third, the sub-division of the large fields into the 'traditional', small, hedgerow-enclosed fields during the enclosures of the sixteenth–eighteenth centuries; and lastly the continuing process of recent years whereby the small fields are being formed into larger areas suitable for mechanical cultivation, and the hedgerows uprooted.

At the time when a village was founded or inherited, one would expect the settlers to have only a vague conception of the ultimate extent of its fields and the quality of land which lay below still uncleared forest. The distance at which neighbours (or, for that matter, daughter settlements) came to be tolerated could not have been based on any calculation of 'adequate' agricultural territory. The field-area was but a tiny island in a sea of uncleared land, and future population requirements are unlikely to have concerned the small groups of settlers who lived hand to mouth. Yet, as W. F. Grimes has written of Northamptonshire villages, the whole has the semblance of a consciously planned and co-ordinated allocation of the land best suited for primary settlement[47]. In two sample areas

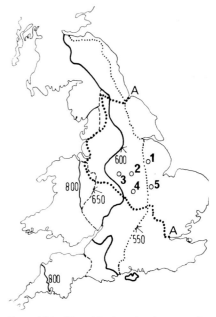

Figure 4.14 – Map of England showing successive stages in the extent of the Anglo-Saxon settlement at 550, 600, 650 and 800 AD. This map also shows in heavy dotted line (A-A) the extent of the Danelaw and locates the five boroughs referred to on page 77 as: 1, Lincoln; 2, Nottingham; 3 Derby; 4, Leicester; 5, Stamford.

46. C. T. Smith, *A Historical Geography of Western Europe before 1800.*
47. Quoted W. G. Hoskins, *The Making of the English Landscape.*

in England the distance from each village church to the nearest adjacent church has been measured. The uniformity is remarkable. In Northamptonshire 53 villages recorded in Domesday Book give an average distance between villages of 1.2 miles : 30 of the villages having their neighbours between 1.0 and 1.2 miles away. Similarly in an area of Huntingdonshire, 37 villages dating from at least Domesday Book are an average of 0.95 miles apart.

These two areas are of undulating open country without natural barriers to an even spread of colonisation in all directions. In a typical river valley, the Avon between Salisbury and Pewsey, there are 20 villages spaced on average 0.89 miles apart, although in several instances the distance over the ridge to the next village is considerably more. Beresford and St Joseph conclude therefore that where the physical conditions are uniform, or nearly uniform, settlements have been tolerated at about the same distance from each other with a strong preference, in the three districts examined, for having neighbours about a mile away[48].

Although our concern is not with the plans of mediaeval English villages as such, a brief consideration of their essential characteristics is necessary. Through to recent times the form of those towns which have developed from village origins has been effectively determined by the original route structures and property boundaries. Although each and every one of the English villages had a unique plan, uniquely formed to meet the requirements of its location, it is possible to classify their plans under three broad headings : first, enclosed villages (also known as nucleated or squared); second, linear villages (also known as street or roadside villages); third dispersed or disintegrated villages. The first two headings are generally accepted, notably by Thomas Sharp, author of *The Anatomy of the English Village*, and joint secretary of the 1942 *Report of the Scott Committee on Land Utilisation in Rural Areas*. A third group, not allowed for by other authorities, is the dispersed or disintegrated village, as referred to by W. G. Hoskins[49].

Illustrations of enclosed and linear villages are shown opposite on this page together with a further description in the captions. It must be stressed however that only a small minority of the total number of villages had such simple clarity of form; most combined one or other, perhaps even both characteristics, with other non-conforming elements. The dispersed village normally had no coherent form; houses were dotted about singly or in groups of two or three, linked by a network of paths and lines, but nevertheless they constituted recognisable social units. Such villages were generally off the main routes and few developed into towns. The conjectural form of a typical village in about AD 900 is shown in Figure 4.18; large open fields, collectively worked, surround the built-nucleus, within a progressively enlarged area of cleared woodland.

Even for the Anglo-Saxons, the open-field village was not the only form of human settlement. 'No single type of settlement' says Sir Frank Stenton, 'can ever have prevailed throughout the whole, or even most of southern England. On heavy lands and indeed wherever there was a prospect of a steady return to co-operative agriculture, ceorls tended to live together in villages. But as late as the eighth century life for perhaps a quarter of the English people was a struggle for existence against unprofitable soil and scrubland vegetation which would spread again over cultivated fields on any

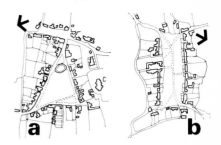

Figure 4.15 – Two enclosed villages with traditional, grassed village greens: a, Writtle in Essex, with a large triangular green with a pond in its eastern corner; b, Milburn in Westmorland.

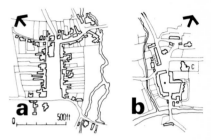

Figure 4.16 – Two enclosed villages with unusual, hard-surfaced 'urban' central spaces; a, Wickham in Hampshire between Southampton and Portsmouth; b, Blanchland in Northumberland.

Figure 4.17 – Wycombe in Buckinghamshire, a clear example of linear village form.

An essential characteristic of both types of village is the long back garden, frequently amounting in effect to a small-holding, which was attached to each dwelling, and which in many instances was approached from the rear by an access lane. The back lanes were generally upgraded into roads providing access to new houses during early stages in the expansion of a village. In small market towns to this day many of the back-gardens of the original cottages have yet to be developed. In towns which prospered and continued to expand this space was usually built over by the advent of the industrial revolution.

48. M. W. Beresford and J. K. S. St Joseph, *Mediaeval England: an Aerial Survey.*
49. W. G. Hoskins, *The Making of the English Landscape.*

slackening of effort. It was by individual enterprise that these poor lands had been brought into cultivation and innumerable isolated farmsteads bearing Anglo-Saxon names remain as memorials'[50].

The main phase of farmstead building, however, came much more recently. During the Parliamentary Enclosure Movement – the third phase in the creation of the landscape (c 1750–1850) – the remaining mediaeval open fields were converted into the modern chequer-board pattern of small, squarish fields enclosed by hedgerows of hawthorn[51]. Only in a relatively few instances could the enclosure commissioners establish the lines of the new fields such that direct access could be given for those owners whose original homestead was in the village itself.

As a result new farmsteads were required out in the fields away from the village, but according to Hoskins the total number built was very small; one would guess at not more than half a dozen in the average parish, often fewer than that. He adds that, whatever the actual figures, the number of Georgian farmers in any parish was generally only a fraction of the number there had been in the mediaeval or Tudor village[52].

URBAN ORIGINS

We must now consider two interrelated questions. When, during the Middle Ages, did a village attain town status? And why did only selected villages develop into towns, engulfing other villages, whilst their neighbours retained their original form and agricultural function through to the private-transit revolution of recent decades? To generalise in answering the first question we can say that a mediaeval village became a 'town' when it acquired the secondary function of a local trading centre, with probably also some small-scale specialist industry, with a proportion of its inhabitants spending some of their time on these non-agricultural pursuits. As the 'town' gains in strength, developing trade and meeting demands for its products, the proportion of non-agricultural specialists rises, and their involvement with agriculture diminishes. But – and this fact must be kept clearly in mind – only a small minority of the inhabitants would lose all contact with the land and a significant proportion of the day-to-day agricultural requirements of the town would be met by its own production. In addition, and this point is stressed, the great majority of towns were of very small size by modern standards, and until the later Middle Ages many were not much bigger than their village neighbours.

Certainly mere size, either of area or population, is not a safe criterion to apply in assessing town status. G. W. Southgate, in his *English Economic History*, notes that about 80 towns are mentioned in Domesday; only some 40 of these had, in 1377, populations of over 1,000. Doris Stenton in her *English Society in the Early Middle Ages*, also tries to estimate the size of Domesday Book towns, noting 'that it is possible to gather an impression of the immediate results of the Conquest on the thriving communities of Saxon days; most towns seem to have declined in population since the Conquest'. Neither London nor Winchester is described in Domesday but Lady Stenton attributes populations of 8,000 plus to York; more than 6,000 to Lincoln and around that figure to Norwich; to Thetford about 5,000 and Ipswich 3,000. These are the exceptionally large early mediaeval towns (see page 102).

The interdependence of city and countryside was not merely the consequence of landowning by citizens. The essential function of the great majority of towns was as the principal market centre for local commodities. Most towns were probably mainly dependent on their own rural territories for grain. wine. meat. cheese, vegetables and fruit, a majority even for their hides and wool, a great many too for their oil and fish. Those cities, such as Genoa and Florence, which became so large that they could not find sufficient cereals in their own vicinity, were quite exceptional. And the commodities that most towns had to import from further afield – salt. iron, perhaps building-stone – were also the exceptional ones. Its position as the centre of roads, and often waterways. for receiving and marketing wares is the key to the economic life of almost every city except the greatest nuclei of international commerce.
(Daniel Waley, 'The Italian City-Republics')

Tax lists and muster-rolls show that most Tudor towns were not only more densely populated but also wealthier than their village neighbours. The concentration of economic power had come through workshops and counters rather than by ploughs and animals. Fertility of soil may explain why one Elizabethan village was four times the size of another. but not why a town could be forty times the size of a village.
The protection afforded by walls and the freedom from feudal obligations had provided a climate in which trade and crafts could flourish more luxuriantly than in a village. and even when privilege hardened into jealous restriction of competition there were still enough advantages in town life to prevent every townsman and every occupation from fleeing countrywards.
(M. W. Beresford and J. St Joseph, 'Mediaeval England – an Aerial Survey')

50. Sir Frank Stenton, *Anglo-Saxon England*.
51. See W. G. Hoskins, *The Making of the English Landscape*.
52. W. G. Hoskins, *The Making of the English Landscape*.

Simple definitions of mediaeval urban status must be questioned, but attempts to cover all the criteria tend to become unwieldy like Professor Hofer's statement that 'a mediaeval town is the result of the inter-relationship of the following six aspects: economic structure (market handicrafts, trade); social structure (craftsmen, merchants, clergy, aristocracy); physical structure (town plan, public buildings, fortifications); legal personality (constitution, legal organs, districts); situation (land and waterways, bridge, halting places, reloading places); and political vitality'[53]. For Professor Hofer one or two of these aspects may be slight or absent but a vital strong town is created when all six are present and equally developed; if there are only two or three of these elements, the town remains small, reverts to village status or even disappears. Hofer rejects attempts at statistical definitions of a mediaeval town, dismissing as 'absurd' the suggestion that a dividing line between a village and a town could be placed at 10,000 inhabitants.

To generalise further it is safe to assume that if the trading activity was established, then the other aspects would most probably follow, given a favourable economic climate, but if there was no trade then there could be no town. The development of trading and industrial functions did not at first greatly affect the traditional relationship between the lord of the manor and the inhabitants of the town. 'The burgesses of a town, however, formed a larger and wealthier body of men than the serfs in the rural manor, and they were often able to extort privileges from the necessities of their lord'[54]. The ambition of the townsmen was to achieve as great a control of their interests as possible, and to ensure protection against competition in their trading activities. Towns therefore petitioned for a borough charter giving 'corporate' status (normally obtained by purchase) which would ensure significant privileges for the inhabitants. Although there was no consistently applied formula on which borough charters were drawn up, there was a common basis of rights which were conferred. One of the most sought after benefits was the right to hold a weekly market, supplemented if possible by one or more annual fairs. As implied by the definition of 'town' an informal, unrecognised market of some kind existed in all mediaeval towns, but the establishment of a market was not in itself sufficient to constitute a borough, and the distinction between 'corporate towns' and 'market towns' must be kept in mind[55].

The second question as to why only certain villages attained urban status becomes, in effect, a question as to how such villages acquired trading functions. Part of the answer has been given earlier when considering the general revival of European commerce; some villages became trading centres because they were conveniently located on through-routes, attracting custom to natural stopping places. Many others (and they most probably amount to a considerable majority of English market towns) became the dominant of the eight to twelve *vills* which together constituted a *hundred*, most probably adding commercial functions to their administrative rôles. As Stamp and Beaver explain[56], 'the market towns of mediaeval England were closely spaced. The visit to the market town had to be made on foot ... it is clear in the more settled rural parts of England that between seven and ten miles was regarded as the proper distance between marketing centres. Indeed there is an old law in existence which makes it illegal to establish a market within $6\frac{2}{3}$ miles of an existing legal market'[57].

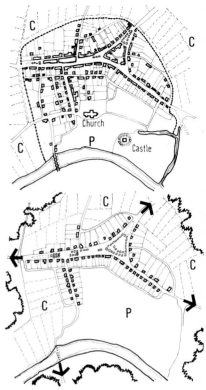

Figure 4.18 – Diagrammatic illustration of two stages in the transmutation of a village into a market town: below, c 900; above, c 1100. Key C, common fields; P, pasture.

These sketch plans are based on conjectural stages in the growth of Hereford, as illustrated in Cecil Stewart's *A Prospect of Cities*. But Stewart, in missing this town's vital growth phase as a burg (as revealed in volume one of *Historic Towns*, edited by Mrs Lobel), has compromised the validity of his argument that trade alone made Hereford. Nevertheless, as abstract diagrams they admirably illustrate the general process of organic growth change from a riverside trading village, conveniently located by a ford, with temporary market stalls set up alongside through-routes, to a fully fledged market town.

The plan of c 900 also shows the entirely typical relationship of the built-nucleus to its surrounding fields, enclosed in turn by as yet uncleared woodland. (By c 1100 the limit of cultivation had been pushed farther out.)

53. Paul Hofer, *The Zähringer New Towns*, Exhibition Catalogue, Department of Architecture, Swiss Federal Institute of Technology.

54, 55. G. W. Southgate, *English Economic History*.

56. L. Dudley Stamp and S. H. Beaver, *The British Isles*.

57. See also R. E. Dickinson, *Geography* XVII, March 1932. This offers another estimate, based on a study of East Anglia, of the maximum range of influence of the mediaeval market town as 6 miles.

New towns

The other category of mediaeval town – those settlements founded at a given moment in time with instant urban status – is, traditionally, divided into two sub-types: first, the 'bastides' which, as defined below, were built according to a predetermined plan; second, the various forms of 'planted towns', only a proportion of which were planned. The term 'bastide' has been misapplied by some urban historians to give this generic status to all the mediaeval new towns. Such a misuse of a valid and valuable term tends either to infer that all the new mediaeval towns, in all European countries, were bastides, or results in the completely erroneous impression that the *only* mediaeval new towns are those, in a limited number of countries, which are recognised as being bastides. Professor Beresford in his *New Towns of the Middle Ages* employs 'bastide' with reference to foundations in France, and 'new town' or 'planted town' for foundations in England and Wales. He notes that in France, 'bastida' in its Latin form occurs in almost every foundation charter, whereas in England the word was not employed.

Professor Beresford's limitation of 'bastide' to France seems unduly restricted, bearing in mind its traditional application to examples in England and Wales and the foundation by Edward I of towns in all three countries. A preferred definition is that bastides are the planned new towns of the thirteenth century, built in France – predominantly in the south-west of the country – by the French generally and by Edward I; and also those foundations of Edward I in England and Wales. With all these examples the term 'planned' is employed in its complete sense of the foundation, at a given moment in time, of a new settlement with full urban status and with a predetermined town plan.

'Planted town' is accepted as a term for all other mediaeval new towns, either with or without a predetermined plan. The thirteenth-century foundations of, for example, the Teutonic knights in the eastern part of Germany, cannot therefore, still be strictly classified as bastides[58].

THE BASTIDES

The French, English and Welsh bastides have much in common, nevertheless there are several significant differences in form and function which establish distinct national characteristics. The three main principles followed in the planning of all bastides were firstly that they were new urban foundations started with predetermined plan forms; secondly that the gridiron system of rectilinear plot subdivision formed the basis of their layout; and lastly that the main inducement to settle in a bastide was the grant of a house plot within the town together with farming land in the vicinity and other economic privileges.

These principles must be qualified however. Not all bastides were built on new sites; many were based on existing village settlements redeveloped along planned lines. Although a gridiron of streets, forming rectangular house plots, is present by definition in all bastides, there is no standard plan and in many examples the grid, often considerably distorted, is used only for a part of the town. As with the majority of applications in preceding historical periods it is a grid of convenience – the quickest and most equitable way of

During the Middle Ages, understood here as being the period from the ninth to the fifteenth century – in other words from the beginning of the Romanesque to the end of the Gothic style – the concept of a town was so entirely different from the Greek idea of a polis or the Roman concept of an urbs that the problem of town and square must be approached from new angles, both sociologically and visually. Except for the bastides in France and England and the foundations of the Teutonic Knights, the organisation of a town as a whole was neither understood nor desired by the builders of the Middle Ages. Even in those medieval towns which were of Roman origin, any changes or additions were interpolated without reference to the ancient general plan.
(Paul Zucker, 'Town and Square')

58. Salisbury (New Sarum), an English ecclesiastical foundation of 1220, widely referred to as a 'bastide', is the main British misapplication of the term.
It must be stressed however that many of the physical and socio-economic characteristics of bastides and planted towns are interchangeable; but whereas a bastide *must* have been given a predetermined plan, planted towns may, or may not, have been formally laid out.

laying out a town on a new site. The granting of farming land outside the town was essential in that in common with all early mediaeval towns, even the largest, bastides were primarily agricultural communities; only a small proportion of their inhabitants were exclusively involved in non-farming activities.

The great majority of bastides were built by the royal central authority, either to impose itself over dissident parts of its territory, or to extend its domain. It generally paid for and organised the town defences, present from the start in most bastides, and controlled the layout of the town. New tenants generally held their land direct from the Crown: in return for the valued status of freeman and other privileges they were usually committed to some form of part-time militia service[59].

Quite apart from its importance as a fortified militia garrison, the French bastide was also a source of primary agricultural production and the local market centre for trading. The Welsh bastides, on the other hand, were initially intended as impregnable bases for regular army garrisons and had only subsidiary trading functions. Despite their military function however, the French bastides and the two English examples, Winchelsea and Kingston-upon-Hull, were planned without any form of inner citadel.

As well as a contrast in the rôles played by the French and Welsh bastides, there was also a difference in the ways in which they were populated. Whereas the Welsh bastides contained a proportion of English immigrant families, brought in as part of a settlement policy, in the case of the French bastides, as C. T. Smith suggests in his work *An Historical Geography of Western Europe before 1800,* 'they often involved no more than a regrouping of population from hamlets to nucleated villages and small towns'.

With few exceptions bastides were fortified, but there is a marked contrast between the formidable castle towns of Edward I in North Wales, which could and did successfully resist organised military assault, and the town walls of most French examples, which gave their inhabitants little security other than from small-scale localised attack. Fortifying a gridiron town created planning problems around the perimeter. Combining the rectilinear street system with a circular wall – which enclosed maximum area for a given length and in addition offered the best means of defence against mediaeval assault tactics – created odd-shaped plots around the perimeter. Economic and military considerations frequently prevailed and a number of French examples have more or less circular walls – notably Monflanquin (Fig. 4.23) and Sauveterre-de-Guyenne. In east Germany, where strong fortifications were essential, the planted towns were normally enclosed within circular walls. New Brandenburg (Fig. 4.41) is a good example. Czeske Budejovice, further south in Bohemia (Fig. 4.45) also follows this pattern. Some other French examples, however, were given rectilinear walls, including Aigues-Mortes and Monpazier (Figs. 4.21 and 4.26). In England the two bastides are compromise solutions with only their corners rounded off. The later Welsh bastides, as the most advanced examples of military engineering of the time, had the emphasis placed on their massive castles, but the civil towns were also well protected within similar compromise defences[60]. Neither English nor French bastides were given castles, although the latter sometimes had strongly constructed churches which served as emergency citadels.

One of the most interesting aspects of the urban geography of mediaeval France is the creation of bastides in the south and particularly in the south-west. The recent study by Dr Deffontaines ('Les Hommes et leurs Travaux . . . Moyenne Garonne') of the historical geography of the middle Garonne region, where the building of the bastides in the thirteenth and fourteenth centuries was most actively undertaken. illustrates effectively this phase of French urban development. The middle Garonne region was a frontier district which included lands of the French king. of his vassal the Count of Toulouse and of the English king in Aquitaine, and it had suffered much depopulation in the course of Anglo-French wars and in the Albigensian religious war. The bastides were usually (though not invariably) newly created settlements and, what is more, as in the case of Roman cities, they were laid out according to a definite geometric plan. The plans were very often rectangular, but other shapes were adopted in conformity with the topography of the site, where, for example, the town was strung out along a valley or seated on the top of a spur of a plateau. Many of the bastides marked the advance of agriculture at the expense of the forest, as was the case in the molasse county south of the middle Garonne.

(W. G. East, 'An Historical Geography of Europe')

59. Land grants in return for military service made excellent economic sense: the king was spared the heavy expenses of permanent, regular garrison forces and yet, for a very reasonable capital investment, maintained an adequate local military presence.

60. See the various excellent illustrated guides prepared by the (late) Ministry of Public Building and Works – now part of the Department of the Environment – and obtainable from HM Stationery Office, London, and at other addresses. Notably, Beaumaris Castle; Harlech Castle; Caernarvon Castle; Conway Castle, Rhuddlan Castle and Flint Castle.

THE BASTIDES : FRANCE

In the early years of the thirteenth century, partly on the pretext of a religious crusade against the Albigensian heretics, the Languedoc region was conquered by the northern rulers after a bloody struggle which left it a land depopulated and exhausted by war, rich in resources, and sullenly hostile to its conquerors, ready for the victor to work his will on[61]. Like Edward I, later in the same century, the new rulers of the south relied on implanted bastide towns as a key factor in establishing their authority, building some hundreds of them strewn so thickly over the map that only a small proportion became real towns. St Louis, King of France, with his brother Alfonse, Count of Poitiers and son-in-law and successor to the last native Count of Toulouse, were the most active bastide builders and if the great king's bastides were the more enduring and important those of Alfonse were by far the more numerous[62].

Several general principles were followed in the design of the French bastides, which in some respects made them differ considerably from their Welsh counterparts. As far as possible a square or rectangular area, enclosed by a defensive wall, was laid out with generally equal-sized house-building plots. But although this was the standard approach there were bastides of all sorts of eccentric outlines, as for example the exceedingly irregular Sauveterre-de-Guyenne, shaped almost like a pear. The bastides were invariably protected by a wall and a ditch but, in direct contrast to the Welsh practice, only in a very few instances by a castle. Generally only the site and its defences were provided by the founder; tenants were responsible individually for their houses, and collectively for the town hall and the church – the two main public buildings in the town. The town hall often took the form of a two-storeyed building, with the ground floor used as covered market accommodation : it stood in the main square of the town, at the meeting point of the main streets leading from the entrance gates. Alongside the square the streets were frequently within arcades formed beneath the first floor of the buildings. The church, often strongly built so that it could function as an emergency inner citadel, was generally located in a separate but frequently adjoining square. Within the town each settler received a standard-sized house plot, although there is evidence that important people often got several allotments assigned to them. Each house plot carried with it the condition that it should be built on within a stipulated period and that the house was to cover the entire street frontage. However, it would be wrong to consider this as an aesthetic requirement. Rather, it seemed to stem from considerations of defence.

AIGUES-MORTES

As a result of the Albigensian crusade the territory of the king of France extended to the Mediterranean for the first time. Louis IX (St Louis) was now able to build himself a base for his first crusade to the Holy Land and in 1240 work was started on the new town and port of Aigues-Mortes. Progress by 1248 was such that this place was able to serve as the gathering point for the Seventh Crusade, led by Louis IX. In 1272 Phillipe le Hardi brought Simone Boccanegra from Genoa to add the massive defensive wall around the town. This wall, which still exists in its original form[63], is about 35 feet high and strengthened by fifteen engaged towers; it encloses

Figure 4.19 – South-western France, showing the location of Aigues-Mortes and Carcassone related to major towns and to a group of bastides of both English and French origin, situated between the Dordogne and Lot rivers, within a circle of 25 km radius centred on Villeréal.

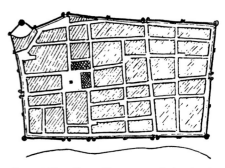

Figure 4.20 – Aigues-Mortes, general plan (north at top), alignment approximately as in Figure 4.21.

61, 62. T. F. Tout, *Mediaeval Town Planning*.
63. The wall and town of Aigues-Mortes, in happy contrast to Carcassone, have not suffered obvious restoration and, as yet, have not been unduly spoiled by the considerable numbers of tourists it attracts.

an area some 650 yards long by 300 yards wide. Inside the wall the town is laid out to a slightly distorted gridiron. The main town square is located about one-third of the way across from the western side; around it are grouped the main public buildings (Fig. 4.20). At the north-west corner of the town the Tour de Constance serves as an inner citadel, with a 'lighthouse' beacon on its roof. Aigues-Mortes suffered a similar fate to Winchelsea (see page 89): before the end of the fourteenth century the channel linking the port to the Mediterranean silted up, leaving it marooned inland with three miles of salt marsh between it and the sea.

Figure 4.21 – Aigues-Mortes, aerial plan view. The Mediterranean is south of the town, separated from it by salt marsh and industrial salt-pans, across which runs the canal, on the left of the picture, giving access for small coastal vessels. The original coastline runs diagonally from left to bottom right, marked by the edge of the vineyard field pattern.

CARCASSONE

There are two towns of Carcassone – the old original *cité* on its hilltop, east of the river Aude, and the *ville-basse* on the lower ground across the river. Despite being heavily restored by Viollet-le-Duc and others during the last century, the *cité* exists as a unique example of a mediaeval fortified town complete with two rows of ramparts, church and castle. The preservation of the *cité* is indirectly due to the action of Louis IX in expelling its inhabitants in 1240 and subsequently permitting them to found the new town across the Aude. From then on the *cité* was used mainly for military purposes, whilst the *ville-basse*, surviving destruction by the English in 1355, steadily grew in size and importance as the chief town of the department of the Aude – one of the very few bastide foundations to have flourished to such an extent.

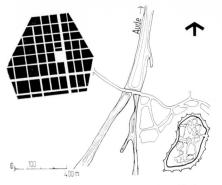

Figure 4.22 – Carcassone, the bastide *ville-basse* related to the original hilltop *cité*, on the other side of the Aude.

MONPAZIER

Monpazier is situated on the northern slopes of the valley of the upper Dropt. It was started in 1284 as a part of the system of defended towns which Edward I established to protect his territory in Gascony against French attack from the east, and to consolidate his authority over the district. Edward had been resident in Gascony since 1279, reorganising his administration there; in 1284 negotiations were completed for the site of Monpazier the landowner, the Duc de Biron, turning it over in return for an equal share in all revenues. Having selected the location Edward next wrote back to England asking for four men who knew how to arrange and order a new town 'in the manner most beneficial to us and the merchants'. It is not recorded how the request was answered, but the resulting layout is a classic of bastide planning in its regularity and relationships between the elements of the plan.

The town was laid out to the module of the standard house plot; these each had a frontage of 24 ft on to the 20 ft wide main streets, and a depth of 72 ft. Lanes 6 ft wide separated the plots at the rear. These house plots were grouped into twenty blocks, one of which was used for the market place, with part of a second (linked through at the corners) containing the fortified church. The market square contained the town hall and the well. Three streets ran through the town along the length of the ridge site, two of them being interrupted by the square; four further streets ran across the town, two of them forming the other sides of the arcaded central square. These streets passed through the ten gates in the wall. The latter had been completed by 1290; the church was added in the fourteenth century.

Each settler was given a house plot in the town, an 'allotment' close to the walls, and farmland in the vicinity. The house had to

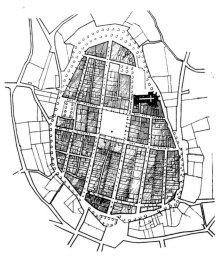

Figure 4.23 – Monflanquin, detail plan, giving modern plot boundaries within the area of the bastide and showing the surrounding suburban development.

Figure 4.24 – Eight French bastide plans illustrating their essential 'variations-on-a-theme' character. Key: a, Villeréal; b, Lalinde; c, Castillonnes; d, Eymet; e, Villefranche-du-Périgord; f, Domme; g, Beaumont; h, Monflanquin.

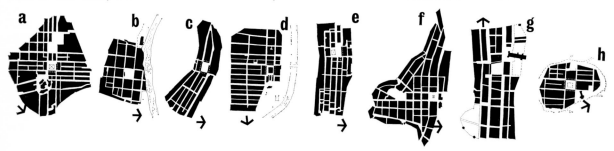

be completed within two years, to a building line along the main streets. A ten-inch gap between adjoining houses formed a fire-stop and contained the open sewer over which the latrines were corbelled. The sewers were taken down the ridge to the allotments.

In addition to these three French bastides, the plans of eight others are given in Figure 4.24. One reason why the French bastides are still left off the tourist itineraries and underplayed in the guide books is the misconception that, because of their planned origins, they are all alike. Professor Tout has much to answer for in this respect. In his authoritative if dated *Mediaeval Town Planning* he wrote, 'when you have sampled half-a-dozen or so, you have no real need to pursue your travels any further, since all are very much alike'. In fact their main attraction is precisely that they offer variations on a theme, and (to take the musical analogy further) it is essential to experience numerous variations to understand fully their individual forms and inter-relationships. Only when each one is appreciated in the context of a number of others can its essential *individuality* be understood. Quite apart from the rebuilding in the last 700 years, which has increased the superficial differences between each bastide, the limited vocabulary of planning components was, in any case, adapted to each site in such a way that individuality of form was established from the outset. Time has enhanced the variations, with many sympathetic relationships of mediaeval and minor Renaissance vernacular buildings.

THE BASTIDES : ENGLAND

Only two bastides were built in England – Winchelsea and Kingston-upon-Hull. Both were replacement harbours and present a fascinating difference in urban fortune – decline at Winchelsea when its *raison d'être* was removed and civic success at Hull, which today seems destined for yet greater development as a major east coast port and industrial centre. Salisbury, or New Sarum, which pre-dates them by half a century is not now regarded as a bastide and is described as a planted city, on page 93.

Only two others seem even to have been considered. In their fascinating *Mediaeval England: An Aerial Survey* Beresford and St Joseph describe the proposals by Edward I for the foundation of Newton on the shores of Poole Harbour, but there is no physical evidence of a start having been made. Berwick-on-Tweed came into Edward's possession at the end of the century and although there is ample evidence of the procedure he adopted for its rebuilding – including a 'conference' of town planners and others, held at Harwich in January 1297 – it is not known for certain what actually took place. Most probably Berwick, which was chartered in 1302, resembled Caernarvon as a castle town intended to control the key river crossing.

WINCHELSEA

Old Winchelsea, one of the Cinque Ports and a key defence station against French coastal incursions, had been seriously threatened by the sea since the beginning of the thirteenth century. It was located precariously on a crumbling low cliff line on the east bank of the estuary of the Brede. It had suffered extensive storm damage in 1244 and succumbed, inevitably, to inundation in 1287. Edward I had foreseen this disaster and planned accordingly. In 1280 he

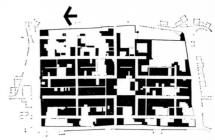

Figure 4.25 – Monpazier, present-day plan. There is reason to believe that the south-east quarter was never fully developed.

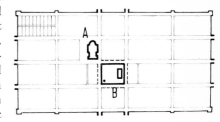

Figure 4.26 – Monpazier, stylised plan based on over-regularised versions of the actual layout, as appearing in other urban histories. Key: A, church; B, market square with market hall and pump.

Since his boyhood Edward I had been familiar with such town-planning as there was in his time in western Europe. The royal hunting-lodge or palace of Clarendon overlooked the new town of Salisbury, which had been laid out around the new cathedral and in 1227 was given the liberties of Winchester. Edward must have been there often. Later, as lord of the town and castle of Bristol, he would have been aware of the engineering feats done there between 1240 and 1250, when the Avon was diverted into its new cut to provide for town extension and Redcliffe and the manor of the Templars were enclosed by wall and ditch . . . As Duke of Aquitaine he knew all about the extensive foundations of bastides in Languedoc by Saint Louis, Alphonse of Poitiers, and other lords, and had encouraged the extension of the movement to Gascony in the time of his seneschal John de Grilly. (T. F. Tout, 'Mediaeval Town Planning') directed his steward to obtain, by purchase or exchange, land at Iham suitable for the new town[64]. The chosen location was a wooded plateau, some three miles north-west of Old Winchelsea, above the level of the marshes, with the river Brede forming two sides of the site. In the following year Edward nominated his three commissioners to develop the new town for 'the barons and good men of Winchelsea'. They were Stephen of Penshurst, a warden of the Cinque Ports; Henry le Waleys, a London merchant and sometime mayor of both London and Bordeaux; and Itier of Angoulême, an experienced Gascon bastide planner. Penshurst represented local political interest, le Waleys those of commerce, in particular the Bordeaux wine trade for which Winchelsea was the main port of entry. Itier of Angoulême was appointed to act as their professional adviser.

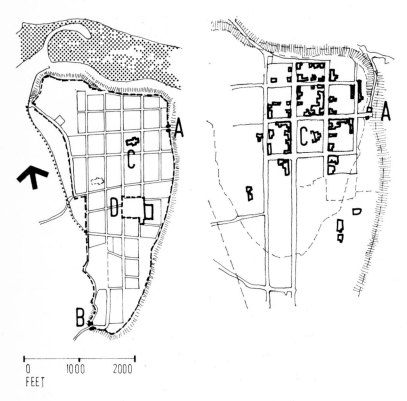

Figure 4.27 – Left, Winchelsea as originally laid out. The river Brede with its quayside at the bottom of the cliff was at the northern end of the town. The long eastern side was similarly protected by the cliff line. Key: A, the Strand Gate (still standing); B, the South (New) Gate, also still in existence but seemingly isolated from any urban function across a lane in the middle of fields; C, St Thomas's Church; D, the market place, long since disappeared. Right, Winchelsea, a tracing from an Ordnance Survey of the existing town which occupies only the north-eastern quarter of the thirteenth-century foundation. (Key as above.)

Progress was virtually non-existent at first. Prior to Old Winchelsea's final destruction the merchants were reluctant to leave the old town, even after the king had begun to lay out the new site to receive them.

In 1284 Gregory of Rokesley, Mayor of London, was added to a reconstituted commission which was to plan and give directions for the necessary streets and lanes, for places suitable for a market, and for two churches to be dedicated to St Thomas of Canterbury and St Giles, the patron saints of the two parishes in the old town[65]. In addition, building plots were to be assigned according to the requirements of the population of the old town. Still they refused to move, both from natural reluctance to break with their past and because of their misgivings at the absolute control which Edward I

64, 65. T. F. Tout, *Mediaeval Town Planning.*

would have over the new town. Edward at this time was in France; growing impatient at all this delay in implementing his desires, he instructed John Kirkby, Bishop of Ely, and his treasurer, to take personal charge of the work. At around the time of this appointment, there occurred the storms and coastal flooding which finally compelled the move to the new site. Advance knowledge of the decision taken in 1288 to hand over the site of the town to the 'barons of Winchelsea', with the King himself keeping only some 10 acres may perhaps have encouraged the move and may thus have facilitated the matter.

On the level plateau site the new town was laid out to the normal bastide/gridiron pattern, with streets forming a total of 39 quarters varying in size from one to three acres. Beresford and St Joseph record that $87\frac{1}{2}$ acres were available for the 611 houses. In addition to these there were also 79 houses on the slopes north and west of the town overlooking Iham marshes[66]. At first there were no proposals for a town wall but by 1297 New Winchelsea was so firmly established that it could accommodate the court and army which Edward I assembled there for transit to France. In 1295 permission was given to raise a tax on shipping to pay for defences, required because of French threats. Further works followed in 1321–28, although it is considered that the full perimeter was never completed. Later, in 1415, another wall was started for a portion only of the town but this again was not finished.

For a while the new town prospered but vacant holdings began to appear before the mid-fourteenth century. The drift away resulted in part from French coastal raids, and also from the clear signs of the silting-up process of the Brede, which eventually left New Winchelsea high and dry some distance inland. By 1369 there were at least 377 houses, but in 1575 the total was put at only around 60, and silting up of the harbour was complete; with its dual naval and commercial port function removed New Winchelsea had slowly faded away. Today, some 27 of the original 39 quarters are grass covered. The streets are recognisable, if at all, only as lines of hedges or depressions in the fields. One of the churches has long since disappeared and the remaining church exists only as a fragment of the original building. Quarter No. 15, where in 1292 twenty-five houses are recorded on two and eleven sixteenths acres, is now the local cricket ground. The Strand Gate still stands in the north-east corner of the remaining occupied area, on top of the slope down to the old harbour, but the South Gate, at the far end of the town, is now isolated in the middle of the fields. Defoe wrote of Winchelsea as rather the skeleton of an ancient city than a real town[67].

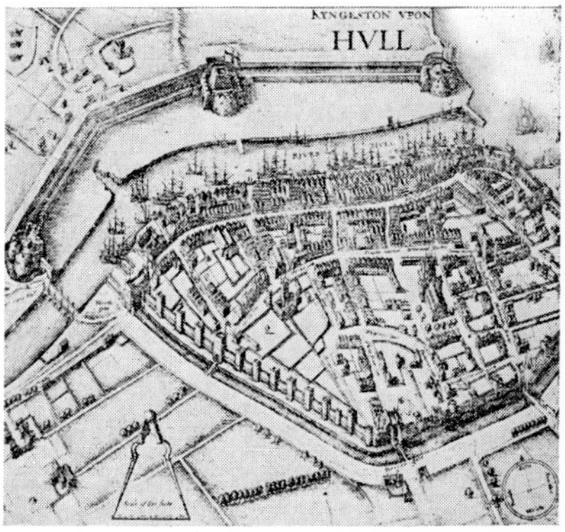

KINGSTON-UPON-HULL

Kingston-upon-Hull was developed from 1290 onwards as a replacement town and harbour for the old port of Ravenser, which, like Winchelsea some years earlier, was threatened by the sea. The site chosen for the new town was already occupied by a small township at the point where the river Hull enters the Humber estuary (Fig. 4.28). In contrast to Winchelsea the new Kingston-upon-Hull was strongly fortified from the start. It received its charter in 1299 and, unlike the great majority of bastides in France, England and Wales, it has steadily grown in importance and size.

Here I stayed [at Rye] till the 10th with no small impatience, when I walked over to survey the ruins of Winchelsea, that ancient cinq-port, which by the remains and ruins of ancient streets and public structures, discovers it to have been formerly a considerable and large city. There are to be seen vast caves and vaults, walls and towers, ruins of monastries and of a sumptuous church, in which are some handsome monuments, especially of the Templars, buried just in the manner of those in the Temple at London. This place being now all in rubbish, and a few despicable hovels and cottages only standing, hath yet a mayor. The sea, which formerly rendered it a rich and commodious port, has now forsaken it.
(John Evelyn, 'Diary')

Figure 4.28 – Kingston-upon-Hull, Wenceslaus Hollar's engraving of 1665 (the main stream of the river Humber is to the right).

66. M. W. Beresford and J. K. S. St Joseph, *Mediaeval England: an Aerial Survey.*
67. Daniel Defoe, *A Tour through the whole Island of Great Britain.*

THE BASTIDES : WALES

In Wales Edward I was responsible for a total of ten bastides, built in three phases following successive military campaigns against the Welsh. Three bastides resulted from the end of a period of hostilities in 1277 – Flint, Rhuddlan and Aberystwyth; five were under construction at the same time in 1282 after the defeat of Llewellyn – Caernarvon, Conway, Criccieth, Bere and Harlech; and the last two – Beaumaris and Bala – followed the uprisings of 1294. As with the earlier bastides in Aquitaine the military motif was supreme, and second to it was the economic motive emphasised by the desire of the Englishman, already rather a 'superior person', to teach 'civility' to the 'wild Welsh' and to direct them, not necessarily too gently, in the right way[68].

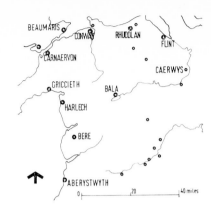

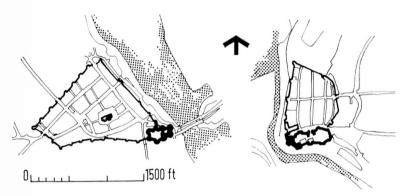

Each of these Welsh bastides had a castle attached to it as the base of a regular army garrison; this was in direct contrast to French examples where the military function was limited to the part-time performance of the citizen militia. All of the Welsh bastides were granted borough status, with the constable of the castle also serving as ex-officio mayor of the civil town. Applications for burgess-ship of the towns was considered only from free English-

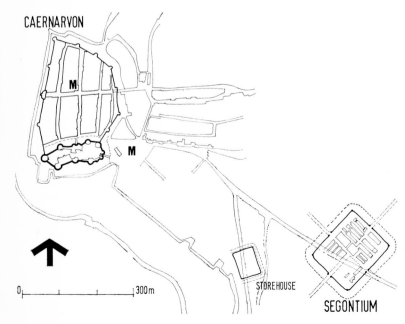

Figure 4.29 – North-west Wales, showing the locations of Edward I's bastides, as named individually, and other planted towns. (Caerwys was given its charter in 1290 but it was not military in character; Bala was not an Edwardian bastide as such.)

Figure 4.30 – Left, Conway, drawn to the same scale as Caernarvon (right). From a starting date in 1283 construction of the castle and town walls of Conway was urgently carried forward; it was garrisoned after only two years and effectively completed within five (accounts ceased by 1292). 'The spot selected for headquarters was a broad precipitous rock at the south-eastern angle of the existing hamlet, one side of it washed by the Conway river and another bounded by the Gyffin brook. Chief designer of the whole monument was James of St George, an international celebrity from Savoy, where Edward could have studied his methods. At the peak of activity, in the summer of 1285, the craft and labouring force employed reached 1,500. The bill is reckoned to have come close to £20,000, and to get a comparable figure for today it is fair to multiply by a hundred, making two million. This was the most costly of all Edwardian foundations in Wales.' (Alan Phillips, Conway Castle. HM Stationery Office, 1961)

Figure 4.31 – Caernarvon related to Segontium. G. C. Boon has written that 'the fort at Caernarvon was probably founded in AD 78, when the Romans conquered this part of Wales. It was an important bastion of imperial power in the west, and for the greater part of three centuries was garrisoned by a cohort of auxiliary troops.'
Segontium was some 710 yards south-east of Caernarvon and faced south-west towards Lleyn. 'Its ramparts, girt originally by a double ditch, were marked out – imperfectly – as a rectangle with rounded corners, like a playing-card, 550 feet by 470 feet. There were four gateways, one in the middle of either short side, and one just south-west of the central point of either long side. Within, the layout was of a standard pattern which the authorities diversified only as far as the needs of different types of regiment required. A clear space (intervallum) running round the foot of the rampart delimited the closely-packed buildings, which were arranged in three lateral blocks, with the administrative buildings in the middle. Like other forts of its date, Segontium was built at first in earth-work and timber; the stone structures which we see today are later'. (G. C. Boon, Segontium Roman Fort. HM Stationery Office, 1966)

68. T. F. Tout, Mediaeval Town Planning.

men – Welshmen and Jews were not admitted – with the usual inducements offered to the new settlers of a house plot within the walls and farmland outside, a monopoly of the commerce of the district and as many privileges as were compatible with the military unity of the borough. The success of Edward I's military campaigns in North Wales was due to his combined use of naval and military power to gain control of the coastal plains, leaving the Welsh insurgents to starve in the mountains. With two exceptions his ten Welsh bastides were concentrated at strategic locations along the coastline, controlling key river crossings and navigable inlets.

FLINT

The first of Edward's Welsh bastides was Flint, started in July 1277. It was an entirely new foundation, with the castle and the civil town planned separately, in marked contrast to the integrated form of later examples. The town was laid out to a regular gridiron plan with the main street connecting it to the castle gate.

The extreme importance given by Edward to the rapid establishment of the chain of castle towns is shown by the presence in his army, towards the end of July and throughout August 1277, of some 950 dykers, 330 carpenters, 200 masons and 320 woodcutters employed on the site work and construction of the castle and timber palisade of Flint[69]. This is a sizeable enough work-force by present-day standards and its advance organisation is clear proof of Edward's understanding of the strategic rôle of the castles and the associated towns. In subsequent centuries, however, as the military function diminished so did the town, and on Speed's map of 1610 Flint has almost disappeared, with a few houses shown dispersed within the town boundary. In 1652 a visitor could record that the town had no saddler, tailor, weaver, brewer, baker, butcher, button-maker; there was not so much as the sign of an ale-house[70].

Two hundred years later Flint was expanding again under the influence of the Industrial Revolution and the original gridiron street pattern became lined with standardised 'by-law' housing. In the convenient gap between the castle and the town the railway, the bringer of prosperity, had neatly slipped in.

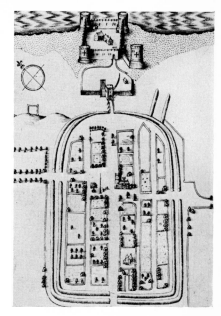

Figure 4.32 – Flint, as depicted in 1610 by John Speed in his *Theatre of the Empire of Great Britaine*. The castle, located on a sandstone outcrop about half way between Chester and Rhuddlan, commanded the estuary of the river Dee.

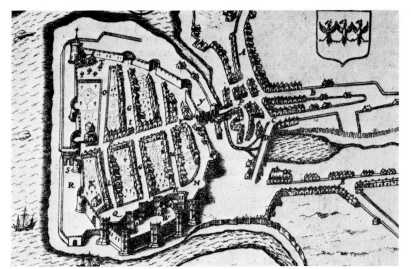

Figure 4.33 – Caernarvon in 1610, after Speed. The alignment is the same as Figure 4.31. The outer wall shown by Speed along the western side of the town has disappeared; now only a narrow quayside between the castle and the town's western gate, and a narrow seawalk further north remain.

69. H. W. Dove, *The Annals of Flint*.

70. See Cecil Stewart, *A Prospect of Cities*. Figure Survey Map Sheet IX. 4. This map shows the nineteenth century reinstatement of empty spaces within the town grid as revealed by Speed in 1610, but subsequent 'slum-clearance' redevelopment (over the most recent years to 1972) has replaced many of the terraced industrial cottages with anonymous tower flats and broken up the clarity of the ancient street pattern. However the massive textile mill shown by Ordnance Survey as adjoining the north-western wall of the castle has been demolished and sympathetic restoration of its towers and walls and the surrounding area is in progress.

RHUDDLAN AND CAERNARVON

Rhuddlan, controlling the line of the river Clwyd, followed Flint in August 1277. The castle still exists, but the small village shows no signs of systematic bastide planning and it is difficult to imagine that it was an important harbour during this period. Caernarvon, commenced in 1282, has an improved layout with a much closer integration of castle and town, than at Flint (Fig. 4.34). The town defences were ready by 1285 but the impressive castle was not completed until 1332. Guarding the harbour mouth and situated in a commanding position at the tip of the ridge between the rivers Seiont and Cadnant, the castle was of great strategic significance.

Figure 4.34 – Caernarvon, aerial view from the north-east looking across the clearly defined area of the bastide (the castle to the left) to the open country on the far side of the estuary of the river Seiont where it flows into the Menai Strait (right). The regularity of the bastide layout, within the surviving original town wall, is in marked contrast to subsequent uncontrolled 'suburban' additions.

Planted towns

ENGLAND

In addition to Winchelsea, Kingston-upon-Hull, and the nine Welsh castle towns, Professor Beresford lists a total of 120 other mediaeval urban foundations which he classes as planted towns[71]. Several of the planted towns have similar strategic, politico-military origins to the Edward I bastides, notably Portsmouth (1194) and Liverpool (1207). The great majority of the planted towns were, however, founded for a commercial function resulting from the general development of trading activity after the Dark Ages. It has been observed that during the Middle Ages it was the routes which made the towns and that subsequently, particularly during and after the Industrial Revolution, it is the towns which have made the routes. This is particularly relevant to the creation of planted towns. The essential prerequisite for a viable foundation was a roadside or a riverside location – assuming that the need for a town in that general locality had been established. Beresford points out that the choice of site for any particular *seigneur* (landowner) was correspondingly limited; if an important artery of road or water touched only the edge of his estate there was no choice at all but to lay out the town at the point of tangency[72]. Many old-established roads, notably the Roman system, were taken by the Anglo-Saxons as boundaries between villages (later parishes) and, as a result, a number of planted towns was formed out of two adjoining parishes – Professor Beresford lists Royston, Newmarket, Wokingham, Boscastle, Mitchell, and Maidenhead. Intersections of roads and river-crossing points were natural first choices, if the estate was so favoured. A number of landowners were hence able to establish new harbours for imports and exports – notably on the east and south coasts.

SALISBURY

The original settlement on the hill site of Old Sarum dates from the early Iron Age, though permanent occupation was possibly not earlier than the first century AD[73]. The earthworks of this period enclose an area of some 30 acres (Fig. 4.35). Within them the mediaeval town sheltered, in all probability preceded by Romano-British Sorviodunum. Actual evidence for Roman occupation of the hill fort is slight, but in the immediate vicinity of Old Sarum was the junction of four Roman roads– those to Winchester, Exeter (Ackling Dyke), Silchester and the Severn, by way of the lead mines in the Mendip Hills – and it is reasonable to presume that the Romans made use of the substantial existing defences.

The hilltop was probably deserted from the middle of the sixth century AD, when the Britons were forced to abandon the site, until the time of King Alfred, when it is recorded that the defences were strengthened. In 960 King Edgar held his court at Old Sarum and in 1003, whilst the nearby valley town of Wilton, was burned in a Viking raid, the strength of Old Sarum ensured its survival. (It also assumed the local mint function from Wilton.) William the Conqueror heightened and broadened the outer fortifications and levelled 6 acres in the centre for the 60-foot high motte of his new castle. By decree of the Council of London in 1075 the seat of the amalgamated sees of Sherborne and Ramsbury was transferred to Salisbury, and by 1092 a cathedral had been built[74].

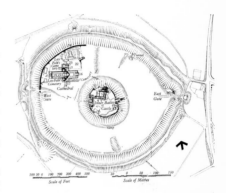

Figure 4.35 – Old Sarum as partially excavated showing the location of the cathedral (1092) in the north-west corner related to the 60-foot high central *motte* of William the Conqueror's castle. Within the impressive earthworks of the outer fortifications most of the remainder of the city would have consisted of tightly packed, organic-growth housing.

71, 72. M. W. Beresford, *New Towns of the Middle Ages.*

73. H. de S. Shortt, *Old Sarum* (HM Stationery Office, Illustrated Guide).

74. M. W. Beresford, *New Towns of The Middle Ages.*

During the next 120 years or so this crowding together of church, soldiers and townspeople led to much conflict, and probably led more than anything to Bishop Richard Poore's decision to remove his cathedral church down from the hilltop to a new location on the river plain. The power struggle between the governors of the castle and the bishops, who, in spite of a titular lordship of the manor, had little but spiritual authority and felt themselves to be prisoners in their own cathedral[75], was however only one of a number of reasons for moving. Certain others were noted by Pope Honorious in his consent to the bishop's proposals: 'Situated within a castle, the church is subject to such inconvenience that the clergy cannot stay there without danger to their persons. The church is exposed to such winds that those celebrating the divine offices can hardly hear each other speak. The fabric is so ruinous that it is a constant danger to the congregation, which has dwindled to the extent that it is hardly able to provide for the repair of the roofs, which are constantly damaged by the winds. Water is so scarce that it has to be brought at a high price, and access to it is not to be had without the governor's permission. People wishing to visit the cathedral are often prevented by guards from the garrison. Housing is insufficient for the clergy, who are therefore forced to buy houses from laymen. The whiteness of the chalk causes blindness'[76]. Beresford and St Joseph note that the abandonment of the mediaeval town between 1220 and 1227 is one of the most curious episodes in settlement history, so sudden that the chronicle story might be suspected of over-dramatisation to point the moral of a modern Sodom and Gomorrah. At the time of its desertion the earthwork contained a castle, a cathedral and the houses and streets of a great mediaeval town. Ruins of the castle remain, but the cathedral was buried until excavations conducted between 1909 and 1915 by the Society of Antiquarians laid its foundations bare. Very little of the houses and streets had yet been uncovered[77]. Before 1220, in which year the new Salisbury cathedral was commenced (it was to be the only English cathedral effectively started and finished in the same Gothic period), there is considerable evidence of a move away from Old Sarum. In 1187 a 'New Salisbury' is recorded in the pipe rolls being in existence on the bishop's rich meadow land alongside the Avon. In contrast to the English and Welsh bastides the foundation of New Salisbury was based on purely ecclesiastical and economic motives. It was necessary to find room and comfort for clergy and traders in a well-planned city of the plain. The unimportant castle could safely remain on the hill. Salisbury Cathedral was built on its magnificent close and stood, together with the Bishop's Palace, in the centre of a broad bend in the river Avon; the new city was laid out to a somewhat irregular gridiron to the north and north-east (Fig. 4.36). From its inception New Salisbury was intended to attract the remaining inhabitants of Old Sarum, and to take away the trade of the flourishing borough of Wilton some three miles to the west[78]. These objectives were finally achieved when the great western road was diverted to it from Old Sarum. The new city was not fortified, although walls had been authorised. A ditch fed by the Avon provided adequate defence for the inhabitants. The market square was located in the centre of the city with the town hall in the south-east corner and the main parish church in the south-west corner. By 1227 the city had received its charter and the

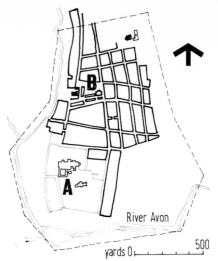

Figure 4.36 — New Sarum (Salisbury) as laid out from 1220 on the Bishop of Salisbury's meadows below the old hilltop location. Key: A, the cathedral; B, the market place. The line of the rudimentary defensive perimeter is shown dotted. New Sarum's grid structure is much less rigid than, for example, Winchelsea, but its comparative regularity has proved well suited to mid-twentieth century city centre regeneration.

Figure 4.37 — Londonderry, general plan of this planted town in Ulster (Northern Ireland). After the province of Ulster was acquired by the English Crown at the beginning of the seventeenth century, the plans drawn up for the creation of the six counties involved the foundation of 23 new towns. Two of these towns — Derry and Coleraine — were planned about 1611 by the Irish Society — a colonising company established by the City of London. Londonderry's plan was based on main cross-axes with a large building in the centre of the main square providing market, town hall and prison facilities. (For further reading see Gilbert Camblin, *The Town in Ulster*.)

75, 76. H. de S. Shortt, *Old Sarum* (HM Stationery Office, Illustrated Guide).

77. M. W. Beresford, *New Towns of the Middle Ages*.

78. T. F. Tout, *Mediaeval Town Planning*.

cathedral was in use. Old Sarum was deserted with the exception of the castle garrison and in 1331 a licence was granted for the use of the stone from the old cathedral for building purposes in the new city. The castle remained in use until the late fourteenth century, but the poll tax collectors of 1377 found only ten persons over sixteen years of age in Old Sarum. Nevertheless it continued to send its burghal representatives to Parliament until the Reform Bill of 1832.

PLANTED TOWNS : THE ZÄHRINGER FOUNDATIONS

In the twelfth century the Dukes of Zähringen created a dynastic state on both sides of the Rhine, in what is now Switzerland and southern Germany. Expansion of the Zähringer lands and the securing of their frontiers was based on the establishment of towns, castles and monasteries. Offenburg, as the first of the Zähringer towns, was followed by a group of towns founded after 1122, on the right bank of the Rhine – Freiburg in Breisgau, Villingen and Rottweil. In all twelve towns were created, with three others strongly influenced by the dukes. An excellent catalogue which accompanied a recent touring exhibition of the Zähringer new towns notes that 'the success of these twelfth-century foundations gave rise to a veritable new town boom in the thirteenth century, with every petty feudal lord gambling his financial future on new foundations... most of which failed, partly because of whimsical location and lack of hinterland, but primarily because of insufficient initial urban mass. What sufficed in the sparsely urbanised landscape of the twelfth century did not suffice in the relatively saturated urban region of the thirteenth, since the new creations now had to compete with the earlier foundations grown to maturity'[79]. Eight basic elements governed the layout of the Zähringer towns in their fully developed state at the end of the twelfth century: (1) a market thoroughfare, 75 to 100 ft wide running the full length of the town between the gates; (2) the absence of other interior spaces; (3) the use of the homestead (area) as a planning module and as (4) the taxation unit; (5) an orthogonal geometry (gridiron) basis of plan, in harmonic proportions of 2:3 and 3:5; (6) location of the public buildings away from the main market-street; (7) placing of the fortress at a corner or on a side wall; and (8) construction of a sewage system. Of these elemental 'laws' the most important by far was the market-street, not only the *raison d'être* of the town but also the point of departure for the entire plan. Contrary to what was usual in a mediaeval town, a strong encircling stone wall was not a component part of a Zähringer town; it probably had no more then a timber palisade and moat. Stone fortifications were added after the Zähringer period.

PLANTED TOWNS : EASTERN GERMANY

Around AD 1200 the Holy Roman Empire had about 250 towns west of the river Elbe and only 10 to the east. Two centuries later there were 1,500 to the west and the same number to the east : The result of eastern expansion of Germany brought about by land shortage and the crusading zeal of Teutonic Knights, seeking to establish Christianity in new areas. In the west most of the towns had developed by organic growth processes but in the east almost all were new foundations, generally established as 'colonies' by towns in the west.

Figure 4.38 – The Zähringer towns, locations related to the Rhine and Lake Geneva. Towns shown as solid circles were founded by four Dukes of Zähringen between 1122 and 1218; open circles denote other towns founded in the Zähringer conception.

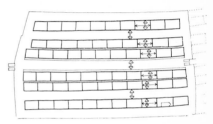

Figure 4.39 – Berne (north at the top); founded around 1190-91 by Duke Berthold V on an elevated site surrounded on three sides by the river Aare. The diagrammatic layout shows the arrangement of the 64 homesteads, each originally with a frontage of 100 feet and depth of 60 feet but later divided up into narrow-frontage strip lots, and the broad east-west market square.

Figure 4.40 – Breisach, founded in 1185 on a steep hill above the Rhine with a long but obscure history of pre-Roman and Roman settlement.

---

79. Paul Hofer, *The Zähringer New Towns*

The best known example of such a thirteenth century German colonial town is New Brandenburg. In his book *Towns and Buildings*, Rasmussen records that 'by letters patent, dated January 4th 1248, Markgraf Johann of Brandenburg authorised a certain knight, Sir Herbord, to build the town of New Brandenburg'. The purpose of the town was twofold. In addition to serving as part of the strategy of German expansion, it also followed the Greek city state precedent of founding a new town to take the overspill population from the over-crowded farmlands of the original town. As such there was no difficulty in attracting population to the settlements. 'At home in Brandenburg the younger sons of peasantry had no prospects of ever getting their own farms. They would have to be farmhands all their lives. In the new town they would be given land as such a colony was always started as a great agricultural undertaking. The newcomers settled in an untilled district thinly populated by a scarcely civilised people'[80]. New Brandenburg was laid out to a regular gridiron, each inhabitant being allocated land inside and outside the wall.

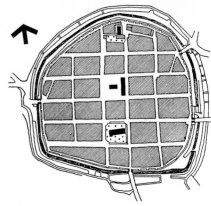

Figure 4.41 – New Brandenburg founded in January 1248 as a typical agricultural settlement in eastern Germany. The roughly circular form resulted from the fact that New Brandenburg's defensive requirements were greater than those of the generally more rectangular French bastides and Florentine new towns (see below).

PLANTED TOWNS : THE FLORENTINE REPUBLIC

The city of Florence has been briefly described earlier on in this chapter with reference to its mediaeval defensive systems; the city is also returned to in Chapter Five when its originating rôle in the Italian Renaisance is described together with an illustration of its Renaissance urban form. The Florentine Republic was also notable for a little-known town-building programme which was carried out around 1280 to 1310 in the main and tributary valleys of the river Arno. As Gutkind observes, 'this was not merely a political move directed against the feudal lords of the *contado* but an important step towards the unification of the city and surrounding country, one of the goals of every Italian major municipal administration'[81].

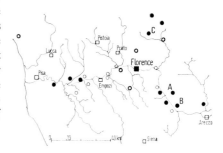

Figure 4.42 – Outline map of the valley of the Arno, showing the location of Florence and other major cities. *Terre murata* are denoted by solid circles; other towns as open circles. Key: A, Castelfranco di Sopra; B, Terranuova; C, Scarperia.

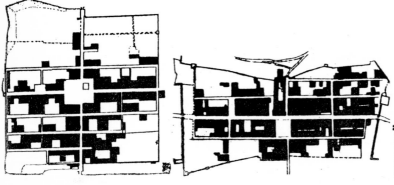

The policy of thirteenth century Florence was to control its territory with castles and citadels in subject communities; from 1284 however with the foundation of the first two *terra murata* (walled new towns), Santa Croce and Castelfranco di Sotto, the Republic's new policy involved the creation of upwards of twelve new towns and associated roads and bridge works (Fig. 4.42). From the point of view of their physical form and their socio-economic basis, *terre murata* can be said to be similar to French bastides.

Figure 4.43 – Three typical *terre murata*. From left to right: Castelfranco di Sopra; Scarperia, one of a group controlling the route to Bologna; Terranuova, guarding the valley leading to Arezzo.

80. S. E. Rasmussen, *Towns and Buildings*.
81. E. A. Gutkind, *Urban Development in Southern Europe: Italy and Greece*.

South Bohemia

This concluding section to Chapter Four is in the form of an illustrated supplement and presents four virtually unknown towns in South Bohemia. Recent history has served to keep this most beautiful part of Czechoslovakia off the tourist map (although it is nearer to Calais than the French Riviera) and except for a few minor effects of military and industrial action, these towns have come through from mediaeval to modern times virtually unscathed.

CESKE BUDEJOVICE

Ceske Budejovice has a present-day population of around 75,000 and is the main town of South Bohemia. It is located 146 km south of Prague, on the east bank of the Vltava, where it is joined by its tributary the Malse. Although it first felt the impact of the Industrial Revolution as early as the 1790s, Ceske Budejovice has expanded on the basis of new industrial suburbs, distinct from the old historic city, which has changed very little over the last 200 years. Ceske Budejovice was founded in 1265 as a royal town by the King of Bohemia, Premsyl Otakar II (1253–1278). Known as the gold and iron king by his contemporaries, Premsyl II greatly enhanced the already powerful position held by the Czech state in Central Europe, extending its territory in the south practically to the Adriatic, and in the north exerting pressure on Poland by building outposts on the

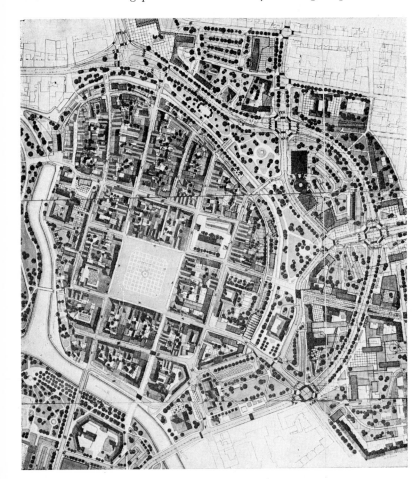

Figure 4.44 – Ceske Budejovice, the modern conservation, rehabilitation and development plan prepared with great sympathy and imagination by the Czechoslovakian Institute for Historic Buildings and Monuments, in Prague, and associated local architects and planners. The historic nucleus with its magnificent arcaded town square, is separated from the more recent suburban developments by the landscaped zone of the former fortifications containing main traffic routes around the core. A combination of historical accident and an enlightened modern planning programme has ensured the survival, largely unscathed, of the old town, although it is now surrounded by extensive housing districts and related industrial zones.

Baltic, including Königsberg (present-day Kaliningrad). The founding of Ceske Budejovice was the result of two strategic considerations – first, to enable the natural resources of the district to be more fully exploited; second, to consolidate the authority of the Czech crown over South Bohemia in the face of potential aggrandisement by the Austrians across the not very formidable mountain chain of Sumava and Nove Hrady to the south. Premsyl II organised two colonisation programmes in South Bohemia. The other was centred on a new monastery at Zlata Koruna, to which extensive lands were granted, some 23 km further south, just off the main road to Cesky Krumlov. Premsyl II selected as an agent for this work the Chevalier Hirzo, who was already a new settlement planner of some experience.

At Ceske Budejovice, Hirzo selected the site of the existing small village of Budejovice, situated among the marshes at the confluence of the multi-streamed Vltava and Malse. The main factor determining the plan of the new town was the need for it to be strongly fortified. For this purpose the site was ideal, and with relatively little effort an approximately oval-shaped area was raised above water level (Fig. 4.45). A new canal served as a moat around the eastern and northern sides of the town, where it was not protected by the rivers. The main regional routes approaching the town determined the location of the three gates – Prague and Pisek, to the north; Trebon and Vienna to the east; and Linz, via Cesky Krumlov, to the south. Within the town the plan was dominated by the central square; each side measured 650 ft with the streets and building plots arranged on a regular gridiron basis, modified only slightly in the northern corner. Work on draining and laying out the site started in 1263, and by 10 March 1265 Hirzo was able to report to the king that the town was effectively ready for occupation. Ceske Budejovice was populated from the surrounding countryside and further afield by extensive 'advertising'.

Figure 4.45 – Ceske Budejovice in the mid-eighteenth century (north at the top). After some 500 years of urban existence there are still only the beginnings of ribbon development along main routes from the gates. The Vltava and the Malse are immediately to the west and north.

Figure 4.46 — Ceske Budejovice, the magnificent arcaded square seen from the top of the Black Tower to the north-east. Although, perhaps inevitably, the square is used for car-parking, except on special occasions, this requirement has not unduly affected its appearance. The proposals for conservation and rehabilitation include provision of parking places outside the square.

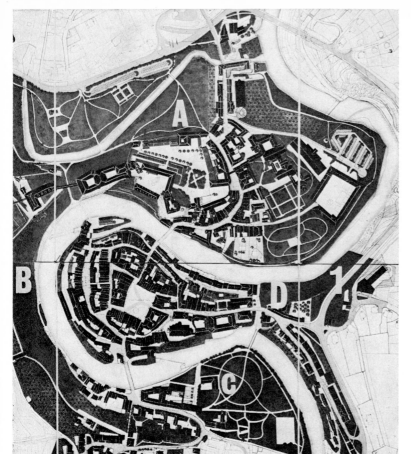

Figure 4.47 – Cesky Krumlov, north at the top, the river Vltava flowing from south to north. Key: A, the castle and its associated town; B, the lower, 'civil' town around its market square, surrounded almost on all sides by the Vltava; C, later development across the river; D, the artificial moat cut across the narrow land approach to the lower town

CESKY KRUMLOV

Cesky Krumlov is a three-part castle town intricately entwined with the river Vltava in a sharply defined valley, which is unexpectedly encountered in the otherwise gently undulating countryside that ascends to the mountains of the Austrian frontier. From its earliest history, dating back well before the first recorded mention of the castle in 1235, the site of Cesky Krumlov had great political signifi-cance, controlling the river route from the south through to the Elbe, which the Vltava joins north of Prague. Reference to the plan above is essential for and understanding of the fascinating organic growth structure of this town. The Vltava takes the form of a triple bend creating three well defined areas of land, the middle one of which is virtually a natural island. This area was in fact surrounded by water as a result of a moat excavated across it as part of the mediaeval defences. The artificial island so formed became the site of the lower civil market town of Cesky Krumlov developing, in the thirteenth century, from an earlier bridgehead settlement.

Immediately across the river to the north, on a high cliff, the powerful Rozmberk family consolidated, from the thirteenth century onwards, the earlier hill fortress as one of the most dramatically sited, urban-related castles of history. Below the castle and filling in the lower ground within the northernmost bend of the river, the castle town forms the third part of Cesky Krumlov. The existing development within the southern river bend is of more recent origin. The castle was largely rebuilt around the end of the sixteenth century, and further work was carried out in the eighteenth century in the Baroque and Rococo styles. Along the top of the cliff, to the west of the castle, formal gardens, now much overgrown, were laid out. The lower town comprised mediaeval and Renaissance buildings, intermixed with hardly a discordant note – either from the past or, fortunately, from more recent times.

Figure 4.48 – Tabor, general plan of the old Hussite town on its drammatic hilltop site (north at the top).

Figure 4.49 – Tabor, aerial view of the market square from the north-east, illustrating most of the characteristics of mediaeval organic growth form: the unevenly defined perimeter of the square which may have been regularly laid out but which tolerated gradual encroachment; the uneven roof lines and variety of building elevations which nonetheless add up to a consistent, harmonious ensemble; and the narrow meandering streets leading a way into the town. Although not clearly shown in this photograph, the square slopes markedly adding a further dimension to the scene.

TABOR

Tabor, on a magnificent hilltop location, is of relatively recent origin. It was founded at the beginning of the fifteenth century, around 1420, as a revolutionary centre of the Hussite movement. The Hussites, started by John Hus, the Rector of Charles University in Prague, were originally outspoken critics of the power of the Church in the Czech state before turning their attention to the repressive system of feudalism in general.

Hus himself was forced to leave Prague in 1412 to live at Kozi Hradek in South Bohemia, where he continued to preach against the Papacy, with the support of the local nobility. In 1415 Hus was burned at the stake, resolutely refusing to recant. After his death the movement gained strength throughout the Czech lands. Prague was taken, and 'revolutionary' authority was established in most Czech towns. Near to Kozi Hradek, where Hus had stayed, the new town of Tabor was created on the basis of a totally new kind of society: feudal privileges were abolished, all people were declared equal, property was held in common and both the administrative and military leaders were elected by popular vote.

Tabor can have changed little since the middle of the sixteenth century : those changes that have occurred have only resulted in the substitution of Renaissance elevations for earlier mediaeval ones. Although new housing districts have been added in recent years, they have not blurred the clearly defined outline of the old city on its hill above the broad expanse of the Jordan Lake.

TELC

This marvellous little town, set amongst lakes in typically undulating South Bohemian countryside some 90 Km east of Ceske Budejovice, is without doubt one of the most beautiful towns in all of Europe, although it still remains one of the least known. Telc had its origins in a moated fortress built towards the end of the thirteenth century and, during the succeeding one hundred years or so, the incomparable town square grew up either side of the approach route from the south-east. The unusual, elongated form of this square was determined by the narrowness of the neck of land in front of the fortress, bounded by lakes to the north-east and south-west, and the division of the approach route into two branches at its far end. The old town therefore took the form of a hollow shell, consisting only of the single row of burghers' houses fronting the square on each side.

The fortress was remodelled as a Renaissance palace in the latter part of the sixteenth century. The town itself was destroyed by fire on several occasions : a final rebuilding of the eighteenth century is essentially the Telc of today, although since 1945 a sympathetically conceived conservation programme has been carried out.

Figure 4.50 – Telc, general plan of the town (north at the top), with the palace and church occupying most of the north-western corner. The town was protected by a wall constructed across its south-eastern end, between the two lakes.

Figure 4.51 – Telc, view looking south-east from the palace, along the square, past the twin towers of St Mary's Church, and showing the lake to the north-east. The fifty or so burghers' houses around the square are connected by continuous arcades providing access to ground floor commercial premises. Each of the houses has an individual elevational design, notably the gable profiles, yet the total effect is that of entirely successful, subtly expressed variations on a theme.

Mediaeval urban populations

This chapter has established that during the Middle Ages in Western Europe the great majority of people lived in agricultural villages. Unfortunately, at neither end of the period is it possible to give accurate figures for the proportions of the total populations that lived in the country and in the towns. Reasons for this include the problem of defining urban status and the need to interpret such population records as are available. However J. C. Russell, in his detailed study *British Mediaeval Population* (Albuquerque, 1948), found it possible to arrive at reasonably convincing estimates, both for the English national population and for the numbers of inhabitants in boroughs, based respectively on Domesday Book and the poll tax.

Russell calculated total populations of 1,099,766 in 1086 and of 2,232,375 in 1377, based on an average 'household' figure of 3.5 (considerably less than assumptions made by other historians). He accepted for his purpose that settlements with more than 400 inhabitants could be classed as boroughs.

If there were eighty settlements with urban status in 1086 and if the average number of their inhabitants was 1,250, then the total 'urban' population of 100,000 would have been something under ten per cent of the national total. By 1377 this proportion would certainly have risen to between ten and fifteen per cent but, unfortunately, the poll tax evidence on borough populations was incomplete. Russell also concluded that it was probable that a smaller proportion lived in the boroughs in 1545 than in 1377. (See the conclusion to Chapter 8 for the effect on population location of the Industrial Revolution in the eighteenth and nineteenth centuries.)

The table below gives Russell's population figures for the ten largest boroughs in 1086 and their comparable 1377 totals, together with the factor of change (not percentage) and the corresponding factor for the counties in which they were situated.

The frightful wastage of mediaeval life, even omitting the toll taken by war, is not easily comprehended in these softer days. Many of the things we think most necessary to health were lacking. The normal modern safeguards against infection were unknown; the proper care of the sick was in a rudimentary state; the dangers of childbirth were immense, and the years of infancy a constant battle against plague and fevers which were endemic in mediaeval England. To all these must be added the limited rations which at times were all that were available.
(H.S. Bennett. 'Life in the English Manor')

In any closed population (that is where there is no migratory flow either in or out) changes in number can occur only through birth and death. The process may be compared to the flow of water into a bath through a tap and its removal down a plughole . . . the maximum rate of inflow is about 50 per 1000 per annum. Birth rates above this level are very exceptional and rates above 45 are uncommon . . . in large pre-industrial populations minima would rarely be less than 15 per 1000. In contrast to the comparatively narrow limits within which all variations in inflow must occur, the plughole in pre-industrial baths was very large in diameter. In bad years local populations sometimes experienced death-rates as high as 200, 300 and even 400 per 1000. The volume of water in the bath could quite clearly be reduced very markedly in a very short period of time if seasons of this severity occurred. National, indeed continental, populations were also subject to appalling setbacks in really bad years. The Black Death reduced European populations over areas measured in hundreds of thousands of square miles by up to a third in a single year.
(E. A. Wrigley, 'Population and History')

Town	Population		Factor of change	Factor of change for county	
	1086	1377			
London	17,850	34,971	1.96	Middlesex	2.02
Winchester	6,000	1,440	0.24	Hampshire	1.44
Norwich	4,445	5,928	1.33	Norfolk	1.54
York	4,134	10,872	2.63	Yorkshire	6.88
Lincoln	3,560	5,354	1.50	Lincolnshire	1.58
Bristol	2,310	9,518	4.12	Gloucestershire	2.01
Gloucester	2,146	3,358	1.56	Gloucestershire	2.01
Cambridge	1,960	2,853	1.46	Cambridgeshire	2.31
Hereford	1,689	2,854	1.69	Herefordshire	1.26
Canterbury	1,610	3,861	2.40	Kent	1.84

5 — The Renaissance: Italy sets a pattern

The Renaissance period in urban history is taken as extending from its commencement in Italy, at the beginning of the fifteenth century, until the end of the eighteenth century. 'Indeed', as Sir Patrick Abercrombie observes, 'it might be placed a little later at each end, for Bacon's dictum that men come to build stately, sooner than to garden finely, holds good also of site planning, which does not make its appearance until the Renaissance is well advanced...and continues to lap over into the nineteenth century'[1]. It is important to bear in mind that Renaissance urbanism spread slowly from Italy to other European countries, taking some seventy-five years to reach France and a further eighty-five years to become established in England. Renaissance architecture – the essential precursor of urbanism – takes over from Gothic as the momentum of that style wanes. Never strongly established in Italy, Gothic architecture was at its fifteenth-century peak in England at a time when the Renaissance was fully under way in both Florence and Rome. In turn the Renaissance flowered and died. In its final decadent phase it was to be overwhelmed, initially in Britain, by the irresistible, uncontrollable onslaught of the Industrial Revolution's urban expansion.

The term Renaissance means, literally, rebirth: a revival of interest in the classical art forms of ancient Rome and Greece, and their use as the inspiration of European painting, sculpture, architecture and urbanism. The competition-winning designs of Lorenzo Ghiberti for new bronze baptistery doors at Florence Cathedral in 1401 are generally taken as the first sign of the Renaissance in the plastic arts. The first architecture is similarly seen to be the Foundling Hospital designed by Filippo Brunelleschi, also in Florence, which was started in 1419. The earliest Renaissance urbanism – the conscious arrangement of buildings into a pre-determined form – is considered to be the Via Nuova in Genoa, of 1470[2]. The development of the Renaissance in the plastic arts is closely linked with the growth of literary and scientific humanism. In pre-dating them by about a century, this established an intellectual context favourable to a successful revolt against reactionary mediaeval mysticism. In this the leading writers are Dante (1265–1321), Petrarch (1304–74) and Boccaccio (1313–75). Following their lead came many scientists and voyagers whose work extended the knowledge of the physical world.

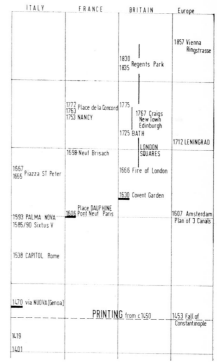

Figure. 5.1 – Time chart showing the duration of the Renaissance in Italy, France and Britain with dates of key buildings and examples of urbanism in these three countries and, as a fourth column, other European countries.

1. Sir Patrick Abercrombie, *Town and Country Planning*.
2. M. S. Briggs, *Architects of the Renaissance in Italy*.

H

The Renaissance originated in Florence where, as Nikolaus Pevsner observes, a particular social situation coincided with a particular nature of country and people, and a particular historical tradition[3]. The social situation is that of an immensely rich and powerful city state, in which leading families were active patrons of the arts. For these wealthy merchants the religious conventions of mediaevalism had little attraction, '...they tended to worldly ideals, not to the transcendental; to the active, not to meditation; to clarity not to the obscure'[4]. Furthermore Italy had never taken to the essentially northern, Gothic style of architecture with any enthusiasm, and it was a country with innumerable impressive, if ruined, Roman remains. It seems inevitable that in Florence 'the clear, proud and worldly spirit of Roman antiquity should be rediscovered...that its attitude to physical beauty in the fine arts and beauty of proportion in architecture found an echo'[5].

From Florence the new architectural style quickly spread throughout Italy and by the end of the fifteenth century it had become firmly established in Rome. Although the term Renaissance is used in this urban history for the entire period, architectural history usually divides it into phases – Early Renaissance (1420–1500); Late Renaissance (1500–1600); Baroque (1600–1750); and Rococo or Neo-classical (1750–1900). Of these phases, the Baroque is the only term with relevance to urban history, as explained below. (The time-chart on page 103 shows the key dates for Renaissance urbanism in Italy, France, Britain and elsewhere in Europe).

A key factor in the spread of the Renaissance was the development of printing, which following, it seems, some obscure preludes in the Netherlands, was used at Mainz for reproducing books around 1450 by John Gutenberg[6]. In architecture and urbanism two significant influences resulted from the 'discovery' in about 1412, and printed publication in 1521, of the writings of Vitruvius – an architect practising in the Rome of Augustus, and from the influx of Greek scholars and artists into Italy from Constantinople when it was captured by the Turks in 1453. At a time when architects were making detailed studies of the surviving Roman buildings, on which to base their designs, the *De Architectura* of Vitruvius had a mystical significance far beyond its real value to architects. The influence of the Constantinople émigrés has a modern parallel with that of the architects and designers who, forced to leave Nazi Germany in the 1930s, worked elsewhere in Europe and the USA[7].

Renaissance urbanism

The following section of this chapter also serves as an introduction to Renaissance urbanism in European countries generally, since as Abercrombie observes, during all this period, in spite of the marked changes of architectural style from Bramante to Adam, the planning continued to be practised on nearly similar lines[8]. The Renaissance coincided with marked increases in the extent and population of European cities. London's population grew from about 50,000 in 1530 to 225,000 by the early 1600s, although her boundaries were constrained until later on in that century. Berlin's population expanded fivefold between the mid-fifteenth and early seventeenth centuries. Rome – probably presenting the most marked change – grew from an estimated 17,000 in the 1370s to about 124,000 by 1650,

The historian Guicciardini, writing amid the troubles of the sixteenth century, thus describes the Florence of Lorenzo dei Medici in which his childhood was spent: 'The city was in perfect peace, the leading citizens were united, and their authority was so great that none dared to oppose them. The people were entertained daily with pageants and festivals; the food supply was abundant and all trades flourished. Talented and able men were assisted in their career by the recognition given to art and letters. While tranquillity reigned within her walls, externally the city enjoyed high honours and renown.' All the features upon which Guicciardini dwells – the internal peace and prosperity of Florence, her artistic and literary pre-eminence, and the prestige which she enjoyed throughout Italy – were due in large measure to the direction of her affairs by the Medici.
(A. Hearder & D. P. Waley, 'A Short History of Italy')

As part of his research Toscanelli wished to measure the sun's noon height. The higher he could place the upright of his gnomon, the longer the shadow, and the more accurate would be his calculations. In 1468 he obtained permission to construct a gnomon in the cathedral, using as his upright a column of the lantern of Brunelleschi's dome: it was typical of Florentine broad-mindedness to allow a scientist to conduct experiments in the house of God. Toscanelli installed a brass plate on the cathedral floor near the new sacristy. By measuring the shadow on this plate he was able to calculate the sun's meridian altitude, and thence plot its relation to the earth over the months. One of the discoveries he made was that the equinox fell twenty minutes earlier than would follow from tables based on the Ptolemaic system. This small discovery has an intrinsic and also symbolic importance. It shows a scientist, armed with Platonic hypotheses, finding that his observations disagree with Ptolemy, the accepted authority in the field; and this was to be the pattern of future developments.
(Vincent Cronin, 'The Florentine Renaissance')

3, 4, 5. Nikolaus Pevsner, *An Outline of European Architecture*.

6. C. W. Previte-Orton, *The Twelfth Century to the Renaissance*.

7. Notably Walter Gropius, Mies van der Rohe and Marcel Breuer, whose combined influence, with that of other expatriates, has had a continuing and widespread effect on the course of architecture in the United States.

8. Sir Patrick Abercrombie, *Town and Country Planning*.

yet this was still perhaps but one-tenth of her former maximum total.

Mainly because of size there were few opportunities for comprehensive redevelopment. Destruction by fire – the greatest scourge of pre-nineteenth century towns – or military action, as on the Continent, seldom necessitated complete rebuilding and when a chance was presented, as happened after the 1666 Fire of London, there was neither the will to rebuild to a new plan, nor the means to achieve such an end. Furthermore there was no demand for new commercially orientated urban settlements. Europe generally was adequately and in part even over-provided with such towns. Only in the closing decades of the Renaissance did industry become a significant generator of urban settlement. The relatively few new foundations of the fifteenth to eighteenth centuries were therefore primarily either of a strategic military origin, eg Palma Nova in Italy, Neuf Brisach as a Vauban example in France, and Christiansand in Norway – or the result of autocratic rule, eg Richelieu and Versailles in France and Karlsruhe in Germany. St Petersburg, the only example of a major city founded during the Renaissance period, combines both origins. Renaissance urbanism was therefore effectively limited either to the expansion of existing urban areas, or to their redevelopment in part. Furthermore, as explained below, there was only limited activity in other than the main cities.

For the purposes of this introductory study five broad areas of Renaissance urban planning can be distinguished: fortification systems; regeneration of parts of cities by the creation of new public spaces and related streets; restructuring of existing cities by the construction of new main-street systems which, extended as regional routes, frequently generated further growth; the addition of extensive new districts, normally for residential purposes; and the layout of a limited number of new towns. The design and construction of fortification systems had an extremely important effect on the form and social conditions of many continental cities (as also did the absence of this constraint in Britain). The rôle of fortifications is therefore considered separately, later in this chapter.

Renaissance urbanists can be seen to have had three main design components at their disposal: first, the primary straight street; second, gridiron-based districts; third, enclosed spaces (squares, piazzas and *places*). Writing about their use in general, Abercrombie remarks that these components 'were sometimes fused together to make a composite plan, but more often were found somewhat disjointedly used, as though the designer had now been under one influence, now under another'[9]. Before briefly describing the application of these components in general, and the related key examples or urban planning activity (regeneration, restructuring, expansion and new site layout), we must first establish the differences between early Renaissance and Baroque architecture (as defined earlier), the essential characteristics of Baroque urbanism, and briefly consider several significant social and political background factors.

RENAISSANCE AND BAROQUE

During the Renaissance period of urban history the principles of spacial design and those of the enveloping architecture were more closely integrated than at any other time. This holds true equally for the early and Baroque phases, when generally applied rules of proportion governing the plans, three-dimensional massing and de-

Pitirim Sorokin (in his work 'Society. Culture and Personality') traces the period of emergence of 355 great cities. those having more than 100.000 population.

Period of Emergence	Number	%
BC to 5th century AD	67	18.8
6th to 10th century	69	19.4
11th to 15th century	75	21.2
16th to 20th century	144	40.5
Total	355	99.9

Forty per cent of the cities he studied developed in the sixteenth to the twentieth centuries, and another twenty-one per cent in the eleventh to the sixteenth centuries. Sorokin's data indicate that great cultural changes had to take place before great cities could be built and before people could survive within them. Such changes also had to be made before the world's population could increase substantially and before it could have a somewhat steady rate of growth.

(William E. Cole, 'Urban Society')

In the old mediaeval scheme. the city grew horizontally: fortifications were vertical. In the baroque order. the city, confined by its fortifications, could only grow upward in tall tenements, after filling in its rear gardens: it was the fortifications that continued to expand. the more because the military engineers had discovered after a little experience that cannon fire with non-explosive projectiles can be countered best. not by stone or brick, but by a yielding substance like the earth: so the outworks counted for more than the traditional rampart, bastion, and moat. Whereas in earlier baroque fortifications, the distance from the bottom of the talus to the outside of the glacis was 260 feet, in Vauban's classic fort of Neuf-Brisach it was 702 feet. This unusable perimeter was not merely wasteful of precious urban land: it was a spatial obstacle to reaching the open country easily for a breath of fresh air. Thus this horizontal expansion was an organic expression of both the wastefulness and the indifference to health that characterized the whole regime.

(Lewis Mumford, 'The City in History')

---

9. Sir Patrick Abercrombie, *Town and Country Planning.*

tailed elevational design of buildings were extended outwards for the organisation of urban space. Contrasting Renaissance and mediaeval urbanism, Zucker writes that 'from the fifteenth century on, architectural design, aesthetic theory, and the principles of city planning are directed by identical ideas, foremost among them the desire for discipline and order, in contrast to the relative irregularity and dispersion of Gothic space'[10]. The characteristic informality of mediaeval (Gothic) space, even when developed from a regular plan, resulted in the picturesque effect of Gothic architecture's asymmetrical massing, punctuated skylines and frequently intricate detailing. Renaissance architecture on the other hand rejected asymmetrical informality for a classical sense of balance and regularity; emphasis was placed on the horizontal instead of the vertical. 'Gothic architecture', observes R. Furneaux Jordan, 'was born in France and, however many palaces or castles were built, was primarily ecclesiastical. The Renaissance was born in Italy and, however many churches were built, was primarily royal and mercantile – especially north of the Alps'[11], a distinction which is returned to below when considering the nature of Baroque urbanism.

For a simple, straightforward summary of the essential differences between early Renaissance and Baroque architecture we can do no better than to refer to an art-historian, Heinrich Wölfflin, who wrote : 'In contrast to Renaissance art, which sought permanence and repose in everything, the baroque had from the first a definite *sense of direction*'. Wölfflin adds that 'Renaissance art is the art of calm and beauty . . . its creations are perfect : they reveal nothing forced or inhibited, uneasy or agitated . . we are surely not mistaken in seeing in this heavenly calm and content the highest expression of the artistic spirit of that age. . . . Baroque aims at a different effect. It wants to carry us away with the force of its impact, immediate and overwhelming. Its impact on us is intended to be only momentary, while that of the Renaissance is slower and quieter, but more enduring, making us want to linger for ever in its presence. This momentary impact of baroque is powerful, but soon leaves us with a certain sense of desolation'[12].

Wölfflin's profound observations are directly applicable to urbanism. Early Renaissance spatial organisation aspired to a quiet, self-contained balance : the result is essentially *limited* space at rest. The Piazza Annunziata in Florence is perhaps the clearest example of this philosophy (see Figure 5.19). By comparison Baroque urbanism either strived for an illusion of *infinite* space, when contained within small-scale limits (eg the Piazza Navona in Rome – see Figure 5.22); or, for reasons explained below, was able to achieve effectively infinite perspectives. But what is more, although personal reactions will vary, experience of such vast urban perspectives can also readily engender 'a sense of desolation' once their grandiose impact was dispelled.

Where 'infinite' perspectives and the grand scale of the Baroque were achieved they were possible only as a result of the immense, centralised, autocratic powers which came to be vested in heads of certain European states. These were welded together out of the numerous mediaeval communities, founded on local authority, and personal aggrandisement came to replace collective interest in a number of instances. Absolute rulers acquired the political power and economic means to instigate and implement complex planning programmes on hitherto unheard-of scales : most notably those of Louis

The functional and aesthetic aims of the town planners were also becoming clear. In so far as they were not military, they were closely connected with each other. The city was meant to impress, firstly by its layout, in which its different parts and subordinate centres were to be connected by straight avenues, very much like the formal Italian gardens which were just beginning to be imitated beyond the Alps. Secondly, the city was meant to impress by the magnificent facades of its churches and palaces, and by elaborate fountains. Thirdly, and perhaps most important, it was meant to impress by monumental perspectives. The architects and town planners had learned this from the Renaissance and mannerist painters whose idealized architectural compositions they now began to translate from canvas into stone. To heighten the dramatic effect of perspective Sixtus V set up obelisks in front of St Peter's and in the Piazza del Popolo. Where the Renaissance statue had been related to a building – Verrocchio's Colleone in Venice, for example, or even much later Cellini's Perseus in Florence – the mannerist and the baroque statue was moved into the centre of a square, related no longer to a building but to a view. The possibilities of this new fashion for the glorification of the subject of such monuments were not lost on kings and princes. The baroque towns, as they began to be planned in the sixteenth century in Italy and developed over much of Europe in the seventeenth and eighteenth, became part of the deliberately dramatic and theatrical appeal of absolutist monarchy. Just as the new baroque style of church decoration developed a deliberate popular appeal by making the interior of the church, and especially the high altar, into a kind of stage where mass was celebrated almost as a theatrical performance for an audience-like congregation, so the baroque city became a huge theatrical setting for the display of the court, the princes of the church, the nobility and other rich and powerful persons. It was the visual aspect of the political and social change from the city state, with its free citizens, to the capital of the absolute monarch, with its court and its subject inhabitants.

(H. G. Koenigsberger and George L. Mosse, 'Europe in the Sixteenth Century')

---

10. Paul Zucker, *Town and Square*.

11. R. Furneaux Jordan, *A Concise History of Western Architecture*.

12. Heinrich Wölfflin, *Renaissance and Baroque*.

XIV and XV at Versailles, Peter the Great at St Petersburg, and with different objectives, Sixtus V in Rome. At a correspondingly reduced scale, other lesser rulers transformed their capitals to create an urban scenery appropriate to the grandeur of their activities and availability of resources. (Examples of such urbanism are described at appropriate places in the succeeding Renaissance chapters)

The British however were always careful to constrain their monarch's power over both their national capital and the country's purse strings. Accordingly Britain was effectively untouched by Baroque urbanism; and for this reason as much as any, it has remained a monarchy long after the halls of Versailles and St Petersburg echoed with new, revolutionary rulers[13]. It must be stressed that not only Baroque but also virtually all of Renaissance urbanism was created for minority sections of society, varying in extremes from Versailles to the unpretentious but none the less privileged squares and streets of Georgian London and other similar developments[14].

Throughout the Renaissance period several dominant design considerations determined general attitudes to urbanisation in all countries. Firstly, there was a preoccupation with symmetry, the organisation of parts of a planning programme to make a balanced composition about one or more axial lines. This was sometimes carried to ridiculous extremes as in the Piazza del Popolo in Rome, where the placing of identical churches on either side of the central street led Abercrombie to observe that 'churches are the last thing, ordinarily, to be produced in pairs, like china vases'[15].

Secondly, great importance was attached to the closing of vistas by the careful placing of monumental buildings, obelisks or suitably imposing statues, at the ends of long, straight streets. Thirdly, individual buildings were integrated into a single, coherent, architectural ensemble, preferably through repetition of a basic elevational design. Fourthly, perspective theory was 'one of the constituent facts in the history of art, the unchallenged canon to which every artistic representation had to conform'[16].

Before examining the practical results of these design considerations, as demonstrated by examples of Renaissance urbanism in various Italian cities, it is necessary to consider in general terms the main components of Renaissance planning: the primary straight street, gridiron based districts, and enclosed spaces.

THE PRIMARY STRAIGHT STREET

In the form of main routes 'emancipated from being mere access to a building plot on the one hand and an urban extension of the national highway on the other'[17], the primary straight street is a Renaissance innovation. In the majority of instances it still provided the approach to buildings, and frequently had direct connections with regional routes, but its main function was to facilitate movement, increasingly by carriage, between parts of the city. Rome and Paris are unique, certainly amongst major cities, in acquiring primary street systems as the result of comprehensive restructuring: Rome during the Renaissance proper, as described later in this chapter, and Paris during the 1850s and 60s. On the other hand such new streets as London did acquire were largely unrelated; the best example is Regent Street (Fig. 8.17), cut between Soho and Mayfair in the early nineteenth century, to link the St James's area with the Regent Park developments by means of a suitably imposing route.

The avenue is the most important symbol and the main fact about the baroque city. Not always was it possible to design a whole new city in the baroque mode; but in the layout of half a dozen new avenues, or in a new quarter, its character could be re-defined. In the linear evolution of the city plan, the movement of wheeled vehicles played a critical part; and the general geometrizing of space, so characteristic of the period, would have been altogether functionless had it not facilitated the movement of traffic and transport, at the same time that it served as an expression of the dominant sense of life. It was during the sixteenth century that carts and wagons came into more general use within cities. This was partly the result of technical improvements that replaced the old-fashioned solid wheel with one built of separate parts, hub, rim, spoke, and added a fifth wheel, to facilitate turning.

The introduction of wheeled vehicles was resisted, precisely as that of the railroad was resisted three centuries later. Plainly the streets of the medieval city were not adapted either in size or in articulation to such traffic. In England, Thomas tells us, vigorous protests were made, and it was asserted that if brewers' carts were permitted in the streets the pavement could not be maintained; while in France, parliament begged the king in 1563 to prohibit vehicles from the streets of Paris — and the same impulse even showed itself once more in the eighteenth century. Nevertheless, the new spirit in society was on the side of rapid transportation. The hastening of movement and the conquest of space, the feverish desire to 'get somewhere', were manifestations of the pervasive will-to-power.

(Lewis Mumford, 'The City in History')

13. The presidents of the United States are similarly constrained in their activities, such as they have been, in their capital (see the concluding section to Chapter Nine).

14. For illustration of the living conditions of Voltaire, a not so ordinary person living at Versailles, see an extract from Cobban's *A History of Modern France*, quoted on page 156.

15. Sir Patrick Abercrombie, *Era of Architectural Town Planning*, 'Town Planning Review', Vol V, 1914.

16. Sigfried Giedion, *Space, Time and Architecture*.

16, 17. Sir Patrick Abercrombie, *Town and Country Planning*.

The clearest examples of the primary straight street as a generative element, determining growth of existing cities, are the Champs Elysées and the avenue, Unter den Linden : both remarkably similar, royal routes west from palaces in Paris and Berlin respectively. New urban plans, either based on primary straight streets or incorporating them as major elements, include Versailles, Karlsruhe and St Petersburg in Europe; and Washington, most important amongst the examples in the USA. Sir Christopher Wren's unrealised proposals for rebuilding the City of London after the fire of 1666 were also based on use of such main streets.

In addition to effecting changes in its function, the Renaissance also introduced the concept of the street as an architectural whole. Although at first it is clear, from Alberti's contemporary writings, that streets could be considered to consist of individual building elevations – best appreciated from curved approaches – as the period progressed architectural uniformity became *de rigueur*. 'From the end of the fifteenth century,' Zucker observes, 'three-dimensional distinctness corresponded to structural clarity. Definite laws and rules directed the limits of space and volume. Purity of stereometric form was in itself considered beautiful'[18]. Perspective effects were emphasised by the location of terminal features, both architectural and sculptural, in the form of statues, fountains and obelisks (notably in Rome). 'The monument at the end is the recompense, as it were, for walking along a straight road (devoid of the surprises and romantic charm of the twisting streets) and economies are met by keeping the fronting buildings plain so as to enhance the climax – private simplicity and public magnificence'[19].

THE GRIDIRON

During the Renaissance period in Europe three main uses are made of the gridiron, history's oldest known urban form regulator : first, and by far the most widespread, as the basis of residential districts added to existing urban areas; second, for the entire layout of a limited number of new towns; third, in combination with a primary street system, for the layout of other new urban areas. (It should be noted that the gridiron was also used in these three ways – but to a far greater extent – in the USA. This is described in detail in Chapter Nine.) Because of the comparatively greater area that they covered, gridiron districts, in contrast to primary streets and enclosed-space components, are seldom found in redeveloped parts of Renaissance cities. In addition to being efficient and producing an equality of land subdivision – the same reasons for its use in preceding historical periods – the gridiron also conformed to the Renaissance ideal of aesthetic uniformity, even if the resulting townscape all too frequently reveals this to be mere monotony. Camillo Sitte, writing of Mannheim, a major new gridiron-based town (see page 172) refers to the rule that all streets intersect perpendicularly[20]. However, although its Renaissance applications may have been unimaginative, the results generally had urban qualities, notably spaciousness, which were to be sadly lacking in the inhuman gridiron 'by-law' housing of the Industrial Revolution[21].

New housing districts were most frequently either bounded by primary routes or divided into sections by their inclusion, with the gridiron streets themselves normally having only a minor, access nature. The districts which may have escaped Sitte's opprobrium

Similarly, the study of perspective demolished the closed vista. lengthened the distance towards the horizon, and centred attention on the receding planes, long before the wall was abolished as a feature of town planning. This was an aesthetic preface to the grand avenues of baroque design, which at most have an obelisk, an arch, or a single building to terminate the converging rays of the cornice lines and the pavement edges. The long approach and the vista into seemingly unbounded space – those typical marks of the baroque plan – were first discovered by the painter. The act of passage is more important than the object reached: there is keener interest in the foreground of the Farnese Palace than in the gawky facade that caps the hill. The new Renaissance window is definitely a picture frame. and the Renaissance painting is an imaginary window which, in the city makes one forget the dull courtyard that an actual opening would reveal.
(Lewis Mumford, 'The City in History')

18.   Paul Zucker, *Town and Square.*

19.   Sir Patrick Abercrombie, *Town and Country Planning.*

20.   Camillo Sitte, *City Planning According to Artistic Principles* (translated by George R. Collins and Christiane Collins.)

21.   The earliest 'working-class' housing in the emerging industrial towns usually consisted of organic growth, small-scale additions; later, but only in response to the dictates of ruthless construction economy, the gridiron was used as the basis of large housing areas. Gridiron 'by-law' housing layouts, giving minimum health standards of light, air, and drainage date from the mid-19th century. (See A. E. J. Morris, *Unplanned Towns.* 'Official Architecture and Planning,' April 1971 and *Philanthropic Housing.* 'Official Architecture and Planning,' August 1971.)

would most probably have done so only because their layouts embraced relieving natural landscape features, or were planned, usually in the form of squares, by the more sensitive urbanists. London's Mayfair, the area between Oxford Street and the New Road (Marylebone Road) (Fig. 8.12), and later Bloomsbury developments contain examples of landscaped squares which mitigate the effects of otherwise more or less straightforward gridiron planning. Craig's New Town, the major later eighteenth century addition to Edinburgh, was saved from mediocrity by its two squares, its (originally) limited extent, and the open-sided nature of the two long boundary streets – most famously Princes Street, with its incomparable views south across the valley to the old city. Berlin, as a third major example, added less interestingly planned districts on either side of the Unter den Linden in the late seventeenth century.

Figure 5.2 – Ystad, southern Sweden, a clear example of Renaissance gridiron-based expansion in a small organic-growth town.

ENCLOSED SPACE

There are semantic difficulties raised by this aspect of Renaissance urbanism. They have been resolved here by using the English word 'square' for enclosed spaces in Britain and other European countries, with the exceptions of Italy and France for which 'piazza' and 'place' respectively are used. On the basis of their traffic functions Renaissance urban spaces can be grouped under three broad headings : first, traffic space, forming part of the main urban route system and used by both pedestrians and horsedrawn vehicles; second, residential space, intended for local access traffic only and with a predominantly pedestrian recreational purpose; third, pedestrian space, from which wheeled traffic was normally excluded. In addition to the above physical uses, Renaissance spaces frequently served aesthetic and symbolic purposes, either as a setting for a statue or a monument, or as a forecourt in front of an important building.

Spatial enclosure was effected with three main types of buildings : first, civic or religious architecture; second, residential buildings, usually in terrace form; third, market and related commercial buildings. Renaissance urbanists also defined space by the use of architectural landscape elements, eg colonnades, screens and terraces, and by various forms of tree and shrub planting. These ways of enclosing space were often used in combination and in a number of instances existing buildings and natural features were incorporated into the design.

ENCLOSED SPACE : TRAFFIC SPACE

Before nineteenth-century increases in urban traffic there were few instances of formally designed spaces at intersections of main streets. Most were located on the urban perimeter – eg the Piazza del Popolo in Rome, and the three squares on the west side of Berlin : Potsdamer, Leipziger and Pariser Platz. The Place de la Concorde, which also performed this traffic function at the eastern end of the Champs Elysées on the edge of central Paris, was a unique form of space, combining civic buildings along its northern side and landscape elements on the other three sides. In addition to resolving the junction of routes, it also served as the setting for a statue of Louis XV. Westward along the Champs Elysées, the Place de l'Etoile around the Arc de Triomphe, the epitome of traffic space, was not completed until the middle of the nineteenth century. Paris also had the Place des Victoires, surrounded by impressive residences and containing a

In one place, however, baroque planning rose above its political and military premises; here it created a form independent of the purposes of the palace. This was in the conception of the residential square. The open square had never disappeared; but by the same token it had never, even in the Middle Ages, been used entirely for residential purposes, if only because the counting house and the shop were then part of the home. But in the seventeenth century, it reappeared in a new guise, or rather, it now performed a new urban purpose, that of bringing together, in full view of each other, a group of residences occupied by people of the same general calling and position. Dr Mario Labo is right in regarding the Strada Nuova in Genoa as more of a quarter than a street; but the new squares gave a fresh definition to this kind of class grouping.

In the older type of city, particularly on the Continent, the rich and the poor, the great and the humble had often mingled in the same quarter, and in Paris for instance, they long continued to occupy the same buildings, the wealthier on the ground floor, the poorest in the attic, five or six storeys above. But now, beginning, it would seem, with the establishment of Gray's Inn in London in 1600, a new kind of square was formed: an open space surrounded solely by dwelling-houses, without shops or public buildings, except perhaps a church. Gray's Inn indeed was a transitional form between the medieval walled enclosure, with inner gardens, dedicated to a convent or a great lord's mansion, and the square, walled in only by its own houses conceived as part of the new street pattern.
(Lewis Mumford, 'The City in History')

statue to Louis XIV. A number of theoretical traffic spaces for Paris were recorded on a map of the city published by Patte in 1765.

The main purpose of these proposals was to provide a setting for a statue of the king. London, and British cities generally, were in contrast hardly affected by this aspect of Renaissance urbanism: Nash's layout of Piccadilly Circus as a traffic space to accommodate a change in direction of Regent Street is an exceptional example.

ENCLOSED SPACE : RESIDENTIAL SPACE

The creation of an enclosure 'with no more monumental object than that of uniformity within itself, is perhaps the most attractive contribution of the whole Renaissance period'[22]. Such enclosures were almost all of a residential nature; wheeled traffic was limited to serving the individual dwellings. In Paris, where the residential space originated with the Place des Vosges (originally Place Royale, 1605–12) and elsewhere in France, such spaces were frequently used as the setting for a royal statue. The first of London's squares – probably the most famous examples of this kind of space – was Covent Garden (1630). London's expansion to the west was largely based on a combination of residential squares and gridiron streets. The squares – usually containing a planted central area – provided a basis for urban family life which is held in the highest esteem by mid-twentieth century planners, overwhelmed, seemingly, by mass housing problems. It must not be overlooked, however, that only a small minority of urban homes had such an advantageous situation. By the time nineteenth century London squares in Bloomsbury and Belgravia, and the comparable larger scaled development of Regent's Park (1810–30) were under way the Industrial Revolution had already created great tracts of effectively uncontrolled, high density housing in other parts of London and primary manufacturing centres, lacking almost all of even the minimum basic necessities of life. Residential spaces are a characteristic of *controlled* seventeenth and eighteenth century urban growth in Britain; few cities and towns of any size were without at least one pleasantly unpretentious square, those at Bath and Edinburgh being especially distinguished by unusual qualties of spatial organisation and architectural attention to detail.

ENCLOSED SPACE : PEDESTRIAN SPACE

A number of extremely important enclosed spaces were either completely closed to wheeled traffic, or arranged so that pedestrians were not unduly affected there – eg wheeled traffic was not continuous across the space or was restricted to one side only. The majority of these spaces served as forecourts or public assembly areas in front of important civic, religious and royal buildings. The most important examples are Italian, two of which are in Rome: the Piazza of St Peters, where the east front of the church dominates the colonnade-enclosed space; and Michelangelo's Capitoline Piazza where identically designed buildings form the sides of the forecourt to the Palace of the Senators, the fourth side consisting of a monumental flight of steps up the hillside. Venice has the incomparable Piazza of St Mark, where the enclosing buildings had civic, commercial and religious functions. Venice, as a unique water-orientated city with only pedestrian land traffic, contains several such spaces of great beauty. Elsewhere in Europe there were few opportunities to create forecourt spaces for pedestrians only.

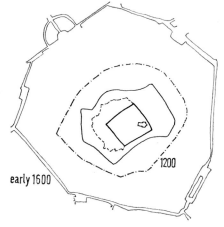

Figure 5.3 – Milan, concentric fortification rings around a Roman nucleus.

---

22. Paul Zucker, *Town and Square*.

Urban designers

By the time that such Renaissance attitudes and styles had been firmly established, the new technique of printing enabled new designs and theories to be communicated internationally; it was no longer necessary actually to turn ideas into buildings to demonstrate architectural intentions and to influence others. Urban designers of the Renaissance were presented, for the first time in history, with the possibilities of making their theories and experience available to others on a wide scale. This outlet came at a fortunate time. Italy had inherited from her imperial Roman past more towns than were needed, with the result that only two significant examples of new-site planning were actually built; however there are countless examples of military engineering theory applied to the fortifications of existing towns.

From the fifteenth century onwards a succession of published works dealing with the theory of architecture, urban design and military engineering came out. Before describing the ideas of individual theorists and main features of a major completed example, Palma Nova, a general description of the rôle of fortifications (a primary urban design determinant) must be given. This sets the context for the theoretical and practical work.

FORTIFICATIONS

The rôle of fortifications as an urban form determinant has been largely neglected by urban historians. In 1529, and again in 1683, Vienna's defences were all that stood between the Turks and the hinterland of Western Europe. As recently as 1914 the defences of the city of Paris, which had previously successfully resisted the Prussians in 1871, were put in readiness to withstand the German advances from the Marne. At both Vienna and Paris, as well as at countless other large and small continental European places, this need to ensure efficient defence against attack was a major reason for a tradition of high-density urban life based on relatively high-rise apartments; when successive rings of defences became obsolete, the land made available provided the opportunity to create the typical inner-ring boulevards. Crammed within their fortified girdles, for ever increasing in population and density, the typical continental European city of the fourteenth to mid-nineteenth centuries could expand only upwards. This is in direct contrast to Britain, whose island location with much more settled internal conditions, helped to encourage a tradition of horizontal growth. Where towns in Britain did keep their walls, this was more to maintain commercial interests than military necessity (in many cases they remained as such until the fifteenth and sixteenth centuries – see pages 68–70). The British therefore tended to evolve their own 'half-acre and a cow' philosophy – an essentially anti-urban attitude which has been maintained as the 'suburban-semi with a garden' preference, right up to the present day.

If European Renaissance cities, and those of later periods, could have been defended at lower cost, boundary expansion would have been more feasible and it is probable that growth would have been much more horizontal in character. With the military developments of the fourteenth and fifteenth centuries this was not possible. The factor which most upset the balance between defenders and attackers was the perfection of gunpowder and the cannon. Sir Reginald

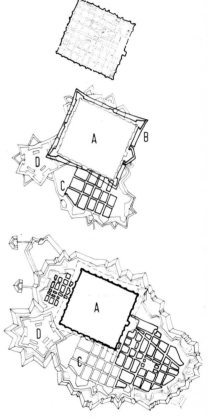

Figure 5.4 – Turin, three stages in the development of the city from its days as a Roman colony to the late seventeenth century, showing the extent and complexity of the Renaissance fortifications in marked contrast to the simple two-dimensional walled perimeter of Roman and mediaeval periods.
Above: The plan of the original Roman city of Augusta Taurinorum with the street pattern modified during the later Middle Ages.
Centre: Turin at the beginning of the seventeenth century with the Roman core (A) surrounded by an earlier wall of the sixteenth century (B); the new areas are (C), a Renaissance extension; and (D), the citadel.
Below: Turin at the end of the seventeenth century with further extensions to the north-west and south-east and a further ring of fortifications.

111

Blomfield, writing on Vauban, observes that in mediaeval days if the walls of the castle were strong enough and high enough, and there was a good moat around it filled with water, the castle was impregnable except by starvation or treachery[23]. Such defensive systems often drained resources but essentially they only had to follow one dimension – the vertical; and they could be extended to take in new districts, without compromising the overall strength of the system.

The cannon changed all this. Its use by the Turks when they overwhelmed the city of Constantinople in 1453 led to a new era in the history of military fortification. After resisting the power of Islam for over seven hundred years the city's triple defensive wall system succumbed to a monster cannon capable of firing projectiles exceeding 800 lb in weight. From this time on the creation of adequate defences required ever increasing *horizontal* distances to be left between the city perimeter and the outer edge of the fortifications. In addition to this extra space, fortifications themselves became increasingly complex, involving intricate systems of inter-dependent bastions and forts. Once established, these two-dimensional defences in depth could only be extended at enormous cost, thereby imposing ever higher densities on the city. The diagrams of Turin's growth based on originals in Rasmussen's *Towns and Buildings,* clearly show the effect of fortifications on its development. For the small town of Neuf Brisach, a Vauban example in eastern France, the width of the defensive zone exceed 700 ft. (See page 160.)

The end of Constantinople thus had two immediate effects on the development of town planning during the period of the Renaissance in Italy. The migration of classical scholars to Italy during the formative Renaissance era has been described earlier in this chapter. The second effect, encouragement of the science of military engineering, was exemplified in the majority of the 'ideal city' schemes produced by Italian Renaissance urbanists. These proposals are described separately, with reference to their designers.

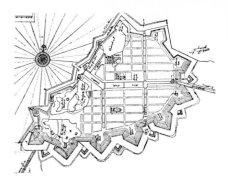

Figure 5.5 – Gothenburg, plan as founded in 1630 with a characteristically complex defensive perimeter. The city was laid out by a Dutch engineer as a 'Venice of the North.'

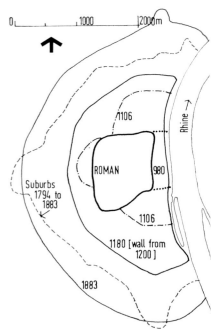

Figure 5.6 – Cologne, diagrammatic plan showing the city's growth from a Roman *colonia* to the nineteenth century as determined by successive defensive systems. The *colonia* was a defensive left-bank-only settlement: the river was too wide to be bridged before the nineteenth century. The first expansion of the Roman nucleus was the Rheinvorstadt of 980, between it and the river. In 1106 three suburban *faubourg* areas were included and in 1180 the line of the mediaeval wall was established.

Figure 5.7 – Cologne, view of 1646 within the defensive perimeter of 1180, as up-dated in part by Renaissance fortification works.

23. Sir Reginald Blomfield, *Sébastien le Prestre de Vauban 1633–1707.*

VITRUVIUS

Marcus Vitruvius Pollio, as mentioned briefly earlier in this chapter, was an architect working in Rome at the time of Augustus – the emperor who, it is claimed, found Rome a city of brick and left it one of marble. Towards the end of a seemingly uneventful life Vitruvius produced certain essays on the theory and techniques of architecture and on related aspects of town planning and civic engineering. These, in effect a textbook of classical Roman practice, are known collectively as the *De Architectura* of Vitruvius. Its 'discovery' as such about 1412–14 added considerably to the momentum of the Renaissance in architecture, urbanism, and the arts generally. Its influence was again increased when the first of numerous Italian editions came out in printed form in 1521.

De Architectura's early acclaim has not withstood the passage of time. Revered through much of the early Renaissance literally as a civic design gospel (an attitude not entirely dispelled), this work is now regarded only as that of an obscure and freely misinterpreted Roman authority on architecture[24]. The parts of the *De Architectura* of real significance to urban history are the fourth to the seventh chapters of the first book. In these chapters Vitruvius outlines fundamental considerations to be observed in designing towns and

Figure 5.8 – Naarden, east of Amsterdam on the southern shore of the Zuider Zee, the epitome of a small, strongly fortified town of the late seventeenth century. The original fishing village was destroyed by fire in 1350 and Naarden was rebuilt by Count Willem V as a *nieuwestad* some 1000 yards further inland, linked to the Zuider Zee by a canal.

During the seventeenth century Naarden became a vital strategic location and between 1673-85 earlier walls were replaced 'by mighty installations in the Vauban style, comprising six great bastions and ravelins set in wide moats, protected gun emplacements and enfilade firing points and a vast network of covered routes and passages connecting armouries and ammunition stores to firing positions. The super-structure was dismantled during the nineteenth century, but the outlines of rampart and moat, as seen from the air, still present a most formidable appearance.' (Gerald L. Burke, *The Making of Dutch Towns*)

See also Figures 5.17, Palma Nova, and 6.30, Neuf Brisach, for two other aerial views of fortress towns.

24. Nikolaus Pevsner, *An Outline of European Architecture*.

describes the features of a city designed on a circular plan. His ideas were not, however, illustrated by an actual plan. So far as is known this is a form never used in practice by the Romans for any of the countless military camps and towns they established throughout the empire. Vitruvius himself was therefore advocating a theoretical, ideal city plan[25].

The interpretations of Vitruvian theory are generally given a radial-concentric form, enclosed within an octagonal defensive wall; eight radial streets lead out to the angle towers rather than to the gateways in the centre of four of the sides (Fig. 5.9). Vitruvius advised this approach to avoid adverse winds. This was a curiously romantic idea which would not have worked as such in practice, but it would have had valuable defensive military advantages in that the gateways did not give direct access to the centre of the town. The main forum area was to be at the centre, enclosed within an octagonal space with eight secondary open spaces in the middle of each of the sectors. A primary consideration was the foundation of regularly shaped residential blocks. Vitruvius also wrote at length on the factors to be observed when siting towns.

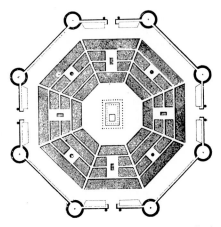

Figure 5.9 – Vitruvius, ideal city plan, as described but not drawn in his writings of the early first century AD.

ALBERTI

Leon Battista Alberti (1404–72) was born in Genoa, spent his childhood in Venice, and studied at the University of Bologna. Between 1432 and his retirement in 1464 he was employed as a secretary in the papal chancery, at first with general duties but subsequently concentrating on architectural and town-planning matters. In 1434 he accompanied the court of Eugenius IV to Florence, where he encountered Renaissance architecture for the first time and met, amongst other designers, Brunelleschi and Donatello. Systematic study of those buildings of ancient Rome still well preserved consolidated his special interests and led, in 1447, to Nicholas V appointing him as his architectural adviser. Together they undertook the first of the grand projects which were ultimately to restore the visual majesty of the eternal city[26]. Alberti put the Aqua Virgine back into operation, taking water to fountains in the Piazza del Trivio, and initiated reconstruction of the crumbling ancient fabric of St Peter's (eventually to be demolished in 1505, making way for the present church) and the Vatican Palace. He was also the architect of several extremely important early Renaissance buildings – notably the Rucellai Palace and S. Maria Novella at Florence and S. Andrea at Mantua.

In the urban planning field, however, his bold design for a new Borgo Leonino, the quarter that runs from St Peter's to the Castel Sant' Angelo, though significant as one of the earliest examples of the geometric spatial plans of the Renaissance, was only partially carried out. Here, 'Alberti wanted to have a plaza at both ends of the long rectangular area, connected by three broad avenues, and the entire scheme was to be given formal emphasis by the great obelisk which he wanted to set in the centre of one of the plazas, in front of St Peter's'[27]. This latter proposal was perhaps the inspiration of Sixtus V's programme to set up obelisks, one of which was erected in front of the still incomplete new St Peter's in 1589.

Important as were these completed and theoretical designs, Alberti's main contribution to the development of the Early Renaissance was his *De Re Aedificatoria* – twelve books on architecture and

25. Contrary to the impression given by some urban historians, the Vitruvian manuscript, in common with other ancient works, was never lost at all. What happened around 1412–14 was that Poggio Bracciolini—apostolic secretary at the Council of Constance—drew attention to its existence at the monastery of St Gallen. Sem Dresden has written of such texts that 'although they had been virtually ignored during the earlier Middle Ages, they had nevertheless been preserved during these hundreds of years . . . In our desire to credit the Renaissance with its due we should not completely strip the Middle Ages of theirs. The difference is rather that the humanists showed a fresh and, one might say, unprejudiced interest in ancient texts . . . the manuscript of the poems of Catullus, which came to light as early as 1295, could be considered to be the first of these.' (*Humanism in the Renaissance*.)

26, 27. Joan Gadol, *Leon Battista Alberti: Universal Man of the Early Renaissance*.

related matters, which he presented in manuscript to Nicholas V in 1452. This work was published posthumously in 1485, and established Alberti as the 'first theoretician of city planning in the Renaissance; with his treatises conscious city planning begins'[28]. Joan Gadol considers that his *De Re Aedificatoria* was prompted by deficiencies in Vitruvius's writings[29]. This is substantiated by Alberti's scathing denunciation of Vitruvius, accusing him of writing in such a manner that to the Latins he seemed to write Greek, and to the Greeks, Latin, though it was plain from the book itself that he wrote neither Greek nor Latin, and that he might almost as well never have written at all (*De Re Aedificatoria*, book six, chapter one).

Alberti recorded his architectural philosophy more completely than his urban design concepts. He included neither plans of ideal cities nor examples of urbanism, but he discussed at length many aspects of city planning which were to be more fully developed by later theoreticians, notably his concept of a centralised square with radiating streets which remained the crystallisation of theoretical thought and was not realised until more than one and a half centuries later[30]. To enhance the majesty of important cities and to facilitate movement, particularly of soldiers, Alberti preferred wide, straight streets. But although they were clearly out of keeping with early Renaissance planning principles, he also saw advantages in winding mediaeval streets; these minimised the effects of climatic extremes, assisted internal defence, and allowed each of a sequence of individual buildings to be clearly presented to view.

It was inevitable that Alberti's writings should reflect his rôle as a bridge between the Renaissance and the Middle Ages: he was, as Mumford observes, in many ways a typical mediaeval urbanist[31]. Nevertheless, in other respects he was well ahead of his time, notably in advocating that the front and whole body of the house should be perfectly well lighted, and that it be open to receive a great deal of light and sun, and a sufficient quantity of wholesome air. It is also possible to see the germ of twentieth-century suburbia in his observation that there is a great deal of satisfaction in a convenient retreat near the town, where a man is at liberty to do just what he pleases[32].

AVERLINO AND SOME OTHERS

Antonio Averlino (1404–72), known under his adopted name of Antonio Filarete, has the credit for producing the first fully planned ideal city of the Renaissance[33]. This was described, and illustrated by a plan, in his *Trattato d'Architettura*, written between 1457–64 but not published, and then only in part, until the nineteenth century. Its influence was, however, spread throughout Europe in numerous manuscript copies. Filarete's city was named Sforzinda, after his patron Francesco Sforza. The basis of the plan consists of two squares overlaid on each other to create an octagon within a circular perimeter (Fig. 5.11). From the centre of the city sixteen radial routes, one of which takes the form of an aqueduct, lead out to the perimeter. An intermediate ring road links secondary squares, sited at inter-sections with the radial routes; these have alternating market and church location functions. The central area of the city includes three separate squares, the most important of which contains the cathedral and the ruler's palace, the two lesser squares being provided for the market and the merchants. This arrangement is

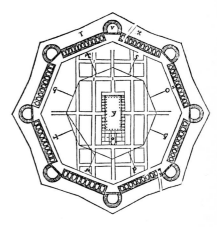

Figure 5.10 – Danieli Barbaro, ideal city plan from his *Commentary on Vitruvius* (1567).

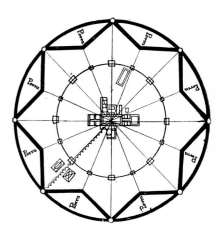

Figure 5.11 – Antonio Filarete, Sforzinda, the ideal city designed to illustrate points in his *Trattato d'Architettura* of 1457-64 (but not printed until the nineteenth century).

28. Paul Zucker, *Town and Square*.
29. Joan Gadol, *Leon Battista Alberti*.
30. Paul Zucker, *Town and Square*.
31, 32. Lewis Mumford, *The City in History*.
33. Paul Zucker, *Town and Square*.

much nearer to Roman forum-planning than to the highly centralised nuclei of the later Renaissance ideal cities. (Compare with the plan of Palma Nova on page 117.)

Francesco di Giorgio Martini (1439–1502) wrote his *Trattato d'Architettura* in 1495. In this work the fifth book is concerned with fortifications and some authorities regard it as marking the beginning of the new approach to military engineering required by rapid developments in offensive artillery. Sir Reginald Blomfield disagrees in no uncertain terms, however; he argues that, 'the true forerunner of Vauban was in fact Michele San-Michele of Verona (1484–1558) who was responsible, among many other works, for the fortifications of Verona and Padua'[34]. Martini was the most prolific designer of ideal cities; included in his work are examples of both formally centralised designs and those more freely adapted to sites.

Pietro Cataneo published his *Four Books on Architecture* in Venice in 1554. This work includes a large number of ideal city plans based on the regular polygon, including some with a separate citadel for the ruler of the city. This approach was to be used some fifty years later for the design of Mannheim in 1606. (See page 172.)

Buonaiuto Lorini's *Delle Fortificatione Libri Cinque*, also published in Venice, came out in 1592. It reflects the way in which, by this time, the depth of the defensive zone was steadily increasing to keep besieging artillery away from the edge of the city.

Not only did the ideal cities of the early Renaissance have little immediate influence on European urban form, other than perhaps improving the design of fortifications, but they also failed to have any effect on European town planning abroad, in particular in North America where it was the orthogonal grid geometry of the *colonia* and bastide which was favoured, not the stellar geometry of an ideal city. If the Indians had had artillery however, urban history could well have taken a different direction. (See Chapter Nine.) Meanwhile, back in Europe, E. A. Gutkind considers that 'it is characteristic that not a single plan of an ideal city contains even the slightest indication of the arrangement of the houses. Only streets, squares and walls are shown ... the designers had the doubtful privilege of being the unintentional originators of the cult of the street, which finally led to the empty plans of drawing-board architects'[35].

LEONARDO DA VINCI

Leonardo da Vinci (1452–1519) included among his theoretical work a wide range of proposals for architectural and planning schemes: this latter group involved both detailed town-planning considerations and regional development plans. There is, however, no conclusive evidence of completed work in this field, other than the addition of fortifications to several existing towns. Leonardo acted as consultant, on military engineering, road-making and canal building, to Ludovico Sforza, the ruler of Milan.

The plague in 1484–85, which resulted in the death of a large proportion of the population of Milan, was seen by Leonardo as a direct result of the overcrowded and insanitary conditions within the city. Leonardo advised the duke to rebuild the city at a lower density and accommodate the resulting 'overspill' population in a total of ten new towns, designed for populations of 30,000. Each of the new towns was to have 5,000 houses. (This figure of 30,000 is remarkably close to that of 32,000 recommended by Ebenezer

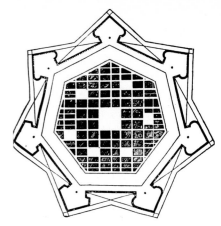

Figure 5.12 – Pietro Cataneo, ideal city plan from his *L'Architettura* of 1554, based on the gridiron with an oddly asymmetrical arrangement of the six minor squares.

Figure 5.13 – Buonaiuto Lorini, ideal city plan published in his *Delle Fortificatione Libri Cinque* (1592), an intricately devised defensive system with three most insignificant entrances (bottom, top left and top right). Shows radial street planning with the church facing onto the central piazza.

34. Sir Reginald Blomfield, *Sébastien le Prestre de Vauban 1633–1707*.

35. E. A. Gutkind, *International History of City Development – Southern Europe: Italy and Greece*.

Howard at the end of the nineteenth century as the basis for his garden city proposals.) In his ideal city Leonardo was also centuries in advance of his time when he advocated multi-level separation of vehicular and pedestrian traffic, with special routes reserved for the heaviest goods traffic. In regional planning matters it was he who, though still only a youth, first suggested the formation of a canal from Pisa to Florence, by means of certain changes to be effected on the river Arno.

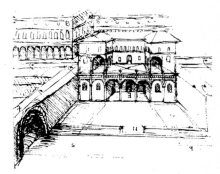

Figure 5.14 – Leonardo da Vinci, prophetic sketches for a multi-level city.

SCAMOZZI AND PALMA NOVA

Vincenzo Scamozzi (1552–1616) seems to have been exceptional among Italian Renaissance urban theorists in that his ideas were actually realised in practice. He is usually credited with building the small fortified town of Palma Nova which was started in 1593,

Figure 5.15 – Scamozzi, ideal city plan from his *L'Idea dell'Architettura Universale* (1615), notable for its use of the gridiron for internal layout, the hierarchy of squares and the introduction of a canal waterway system.

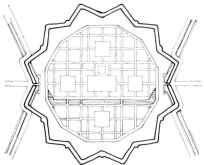

although some writers have queried his authorship of the plan. In 1615, the year before his death, he published in Venice a comprehensive ten-volume work, *L'Idea dell'Architettura Universale*, in which he recorded his architectural experiences. Nine chapters of the second book are concerned specifically with the subject of military fortifications based on a comprehensive study of outstanding western European examples. In his treatise Scamozzi includes a detailed plan of a theoretical fortified city which has features in common with Palma Nova, except for one basic difference – its street system is organised as a gridiron within the defensive perimeter (Fig. 5.15).

Figure 5.16 – Palma Nova (1593) the plan for which is generally attributed to Scamozzi. Adequate architectural detail is given in this reproduction for it to be seen that the regularity of the plan has not been complemented by standard building elevations.

The function of Palma Nova was to be a fortified garrison outpost of Venice's defences. Its perimeter is a nine-sided polygon and its central square a regular hexagon. These shapes are resolved into an integrated pattern by a complex arrangement of radial streets; six lead out from the centre to an angle of the wall, or, alternatively, to the centre of a side. Additionally twelve radial streets start from the innermost ring of three concentric streets. Main civic buildings are grouped around the central square. Six secondary squares are formed in the centres of house blocks. Palma Nova exists today as a quiet country town; fortunately it has retained the basis of its original plan, unobscured by subsequent developments.

Figure 5.17 – Palma Nova from the air, showing the great extent to which the town has retained its original plan and the comparatively vast area of the encircling fortification system. (See also the aerial photograph of Neuf Brisach, a Vauban fortress town of the late seventeenth and early eighteenth centuries, Figure 6.30.)

Florence

The city originated round about 200 BC in a new settlement established where the Via Cassia, extended north from Arezzo to Bologna, crossed the Arno. It was named Florentia and received brief status as a *municipium* in 90 BC before being completely destroyed by Sulla in the civil war of 82 BC. Florentia was rebuilt as a Roman colony a short distance downstream, occupying an area of 79.1 acres within the first of a sequence of defensive perimeters. (See page 70 for a description of the city's mediaeval town-building programme.)

Florence, for all its originating rôle during the early years of the Renaissance (see the opening section of this chapter) remained essentially a mediaeval city, its magnificent Renaissance *palazzi* unrelated, and in most instances, uncomplemented by suitable spatial settings. Of the city's two most important public spaces, one – the Piazza della Signoria (the civic centre for more than 600 years) – is a mediaeval creation, its spatial anomalies only partially resolved by Renaissance furnishing (Fig. 5.18). The Piazza Annunziata, on the other hand, is of great significance as a work of Renaissance urbanism.

Brunelleschi's Foundling Hospital of 1419–17, as completed, presented its beautiful arched arcade to the unresolved space in front of the Church of Santissima Annunziata, but it was to set the pattern for the eventual enclosure of the Piazza Annunziata – a space which had the dual function of providing an entrance forecourt to the church, and of terminating a long vista from the cathedral, on the axis linking cathedral with statue and church (Fig. 5.19).

Following the construction of the Foundling Hospital, Michelozzo in 1454 designed a one-bay entrance porch to the church in harmony with Brunelleschi's arcade. This porch was subsequently enlarged by Giovanni Caccini between 1601–04 into an entrance colonnade running the length of the north-western side of the square. A third arcaded side to the square, facing the Foundling Hospital, was designed by the architects Antonio da Sangallo the Elder and Baccio d'Agnola in 1516. These arcades serve to unify a number of disparate buildings into one spatial unity, in a manner reminiscent of the colonnades around the forum at Pompeii. Paul Zucker considers that in contrast to the mediaeval period, where an arcade belonged to an individual building, in the Renaissance arcades expanded the space of the square, integrating volume of structure and spatial void[36].

Edmund Bacon in an extremely important section of his *Design of Cities* bases his 'principle of the second man' on the Piazza Annunziata, stating that 'any really great work has within it seminal forces capable of influencing subsequent development around it, and often in ways unconceived by its creator. The great beauty and elegance of Brunelleschi's arcade of the Foundling Hospital . . . found expression elsewhere in the piazza, whether or not Brunelleschi intended this to be so.' The crucial decision, Bacon considers, was that of Sangallo 'to overcome his urge toward self-expression and follow, almost to the letter, the design of the then eighty-nine year-old building of Brunelleschi. This design set the form of the Piazza Annunziata and established, in the Renaissance train of thought, the concept of a space created by several buildings designed in relation to one another. From this the "principle of the second man" can be formulated : it is the second man who determines whether the creation of the first man will be carried forward or destroyed'[37].

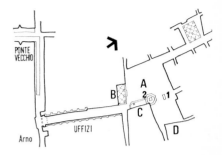

Figure 5.18 – Florence, the plan of the Piazza della Signoria related to the Uffizi and the river Arno and the Ponte Vecchio. Key: A, Piazza della Signoria; B, Loggia de Lanzi; C, Palazzo Vecchio; D, Palazzo della Tribunale di Mercanzia; 1, equestrian statue of Cosimo I; 2, statue of Neptune.

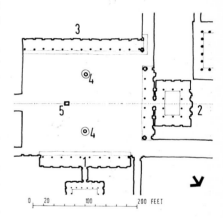

Figure 5.19 – Florence, plan of the Piazza Annunziata. Key: 1, the Foundling Hospital of 1419-24 (the first Renaissance building); 2, the Church of Santissima Annunziata; 3, Hall of the Servi di Santa Maria Brotherhood; 4, fountains; 5, equestrian statue of 1608 on the main central axis of the piazza.

36. Paul Zucker, *Town and Square.*

37. Edmund Bacon, *Design of Cities.*

I

Rome

DECLINE AND FALL

Norwood Young in his book *The Story of Rome*, on which this section relies to a considerable extent, considers that 'if the strictly mediaeval history of Rome closes with Boniface VIII in 1303 and the period of desertion and decay comes to an end on the arrival of Martin V in 1420, the era of new life, of renaissance, begins with Nicholas V in 1447'. Before concentrating on the planning achievements of the Renaissance popes during the century and a half from Nicholas V to Sixtus V, we must briefly take the history of the city through from its ancient zenith under the Caesars in the second century AD, to the deserted, desolated ruins which were the inheritance of the Renaissance.

Ancient Rome at the summit of its fortunes, in particular during the reign of the Emperor Trajan (AD 98–117) has been described in Chapter Three. From this time on, the fortunes of both the Roman Empire and its original capital city were on the wane. The unprecedented flooding of the city in AD 162 and the subsequent famine and plague seem to mark the beginning of the end. In AD 334 the first Christian emperor, Constantine, recognised this decline by moving the capital of the Empire from Rome to his new city of Constantinople. (See pages 61–62.)

The physical destruction of ancient Rome starts with the pillage of the city by the barbarians under Alaric the Visigoth in 410, after he had been bought off two years previously. Subsequent devastation followed the incursions of Genseric the Vandal in 476; he governed Italy from Ravenna whilst Rome was controlled only by a local prefect. A brief revival followed under Theodoric the Ostrogoth who took the city in 483, at the invitation of the Eastern Emperor, and repaired the aqueducts, the walls and many public buildings.

In 546 the Goths again besieged and captured Rome, this time under Totila who, lacking military strength sufficient to garrison the city whilst campaigning elsewhere in Italy, was determined to destroy the town entirely, to raze it to the ground, to make it a pasturage for cattle[38]. Totila was diverted from this extreme course, but as a secondary measure forced the entire population to abandon the city which even at this time was almost as magnificent as ever. Some temples and walls had been damaged and many statues taken away, but the town was still covered with immense marble buildings[39].

The first pope to be the practical lord of Rome in municipal affairs was Gregory I (590–604). 'In ecclesiastical matters he was undisputed head of Western Europe and in temporal matters a rival of the Eastern Emperor'[40]. In his first sermon in St Peter's he painted a dismal picture of the world laid waste and the devastation of the city of Rome. In 663, however, Constans II, the first Eastern Emperor to visit the city since the fall of the Western Empire, found it worth while removing from the roof of the Pantheon the bronze tiles and all the remaining bronze statues, with the exception of that of Marcus Aurelius which was thought to be of Constantine. (This is the statue which was used in 1538 as the focal point of Michelangelo's new Capitoline Piazza.)

From 800, as the generally acknowledged spiritual centre of the Holy Roman Empire, Rome again became for a while a great city and a centre of pilgrimage in Western Europe. Following further

Probably neither rebel generals nor barbarians on the frontier would have much endangered the Empire if it had not been steadily weakening within. Great nations break down more often from internal than external causes. That the resources of the Empire were wasted for centuries is only too clear. The pillage of the provinces in the last century of the Republic was shameless; and whatever recovery was made under the Empire, certain wounds cannot be healed. One Roman conqueror, a man of high character and repute, sold one hundred and fifty thousand inhabitants of Epirus as slaves. Sulla's furious vengeance on Asia will be recalled. The money that rolled up in masses to Rome was in large part wasted, as the wealth of Alexander's successors was. A mania for building huge villas, baths, arches, temples; a still more wasteful mania for beast-shows, in each of which the public slaughter of the animals (fetched with extreme cost from the ends of the earth); a universal desire to wear silk and to have spiced food – all these things and others wasted labour.

Lately the point has been well made that there was a new shortage of labour. For some two centuries, down to Actium, Eastern and Northern wars had meant a ceaseless supply of slaves in Italy. Agriculture and manufacture were carried on by slaves – a bad thing in itself, for slave labour is reluctant and careless labour, wasteful of material; there was no improvement in tools or methods (and improvement was needed); slaves generally left no offspring, and they crowded out free labour with its families. This contributed to decline in population, while land went out of cultivation. Italy began to repeat the experience of Greece.

(T. R. Glover. 'The Ancient World')

38, 39, 40. Norwood Young, *The Story of Rome.*

attacks, this time by the Saracens, Leo IV in 852 built the first fortifications of the Vatican quarter. The most destructive of all the sackings of Rome took place in 1084 when the Norman allies of Gregory VII set the city on fire with the results that the Field of Mars was swept nearly bare and the region between the Lateran and the Colosseum was utterly destroyed. The Caelian and Aventine Hills have never since returned to their former populous condition[41].

In 1065 the Turks captured Jerusalem and the ensuing crusades to liberate the Holy Land gave the popes their last chance to unite Christendom in one cause under their banners. The First Crusade, sponsored by Urban II and led by Godfrey de Bouillon, ended with the recapture of Jerusalem in 1099. Later crusades, including the two led by the French King Louis IX, for which he built the bastide port of Aigues-Mortes as a point of departure (see page 84), were progressively less successful. When the crusades came to an end with the fall of Acre in 1292 Boniface VIII hit upon the plan of using the Jubilee Year as a means of stimulating Christian enthusiasm and assisting papal finances by the sale of indulgences[42]. Previously indulgences – pardons for all sins against the Church – were granted to participants in the crusades and their financial supporters. The Jubilee of 1300 was an immense success. Norwood Young recounts that all Europe responded in a general contagion of religious zeal. The roads in the remotest parts of Germany, Hungary and Britain swarmed with pilgrims on the march to Rome. It was estimated that there was a traffic of 30,000 pilgrims in and out of the city daily, and that two million had entered Rome in the year. The offerings were gathered in at the altars with long rakes, the copper coins alone giving a value of 50,000 gold florins[43].

STRATEGIC REPLANNING

The jubilees were at first intended to mark the beginning of a new century but later were held every 25 years. To qualify for their indulgence, pilgrims to the city had to visit certain specified churches and from 1300 onwards the papal financial policy relied on the income from the pilgrims. Related papal plans for the rebuilding of Rome were to a considerable extent based on facilitating the movement of pilgrimage groups between the seven main churches. Providing suitable accommodation for them and policing the city for their safety were also primary considerations.

Important as it was to encourage the pilgrimage industry, Rome had of course a wider rôle to play in promoting the general authority of the Church. This policy was clearly reaffirmed by Nicholas V (1447–55) at the beginning of the Renaissance period in Rome. 'To create solid and stable convictions in the minds of the uncultured masses there must be something that appeals to the eye : a popular faith, sustained only by doctrines, will never be anything but feeble and vacillating. But if the authority of the Holy See were visibly displayed in majestic buildings, imperishable memorials and witnesses seemingly planted by the hand of God himself, belief would grow and strengthen like a tradition from one generation to another, and all the world would accept and revere it. Noble edifices combining taste and beauty with imposing proportions would immensely conduce to the exaltation of the chair of St Peter'[44].

In itself this was not original thinking. Several popes between Boniface VIII and Nicholas V had had visions of a revival of the

To a very large degree the first crusade owed its success to the spirit of the men who went on it. The common soldiers had been stirred in a way which would brook no halting; it was they who forced their commanders to lead them on to Jerusalem . . .

The Church had long been seeking to channel the vigour of such men into activities more pleasing to God than the endless feuding of the nobility. She had given her blessing to wars against the heathen, and especially had sought to organise soldiers for service in Spain against the Saracens. . . . Churchmen preached the crusade, they recorded the vows of the future crusaders, they collected and administered the alms of the faithful which helped to finance it. Acting through her diocesan bishops, the Church took into her special protection the lands and property of all who left for Palestine. Without the unitary papal system of administration behind it, the crusade could never have been organised as a large scale enterprise.

The crusade demonstrated, indeed, what a real unifying force in Christendom the Roman Church had become. To the canonists, the crusade became known as the 'Roman war', 'because Rome is the head and mother of our Faith'.

(Maurice Keen, 'A History of Medieval Europe')

41, 42, 43, 44. Norwood Young, *The Story of Rome*.

grandure that was Rome but such sweeping planning programmes presuppose a settled, ordered community. Instead, the period between the papal move to Avignon in 1309 and the end of the great schism with the election of Martin V in 1417 was a time of uncontrolled disorder in Rome; the city was a prey to anarchy[45]. Instead of being occupied with building the city of the future, all energies were consumed in continual struggles among the leading family groups, and between them and the papal authority. In 1329 an earthquake severely damaged many of the ancient buildings, adding to the desolation, and in 1347 the Black Death took its toll of the already greatly reduced population. The Jubilee of 1350 represented a brief interlude of prosperity with 1,200,000 pilgrims arriving in Rome between Christmas and Easter and 800,000 more at Whitsun. The condition of the city however was appalling. Petrarch was one of the visitors and he observed that the houses were overthrown, the walls come to the ground, the temples fallen, the sanctuaries perished, and the laws trodden underfoot. The Lateran lay on the ground, and the 'Mother of all Churches' stood without a roof, exposed to wind and rain[46].

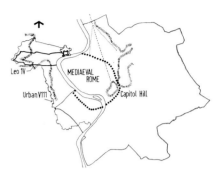

Figure 5.20 – Rome, approximate extent of the mediaeval city. Destruction or blockage of the aqueducts serving the healthier higher districts had long since rendered them uninhabitable: Rome's inhabitants, such as they were, were concentrated onto low-lying ground in the bend of the Tiber opposite St Peter's. Here for the most part they found shelter in the substantial remains of imperial monuments, continually subject to flooding and disease.

THE RETURN FROM AVIGNON

Gregory XI (1370–78) brought the papacy back to Rome from Avignon, after the 68 years of absence, returning to the hollow shell of a city in which perhaps only 17,000 occupied the area inside the Aurelian Wall where upwards of 1½ million had lived under the Caesars. Gregory's death in 1378 led to a yet greater schism in the church, between the elected Roman successor and the rival pope chosen by Naples, Savoy, France and Spain.

For the next 40 years Roman history is a chronicle of intrigue and revolution, ending only with the election of Martin V (1417–31); this re-established settled, orderly government for the first time since Boniface VIII. By this time Rome had reached the nadir of its fortunes. The Tiber river defences were broken down – in 1420 flood water lapped the high altar in the Pantheon – the drainage system was silted up, the aqueducts were long since destroyed. All of the inherent deficiencies of the site had re-asserted themselves and disease was rampant. The ancient Christian churches were dangerously decayed and from the account of Bracciolini, a Florentine visitor of 1420, it is evident that classical Rome had already been almost entirely destroyed[47].

Martin V achieved little in the way of the practical renewal of the city, other than starting to repair the churches, but his pontificate established the social and economic conditions essential for the work of future popes, although his immediate successor Eugenius IV (1431–47) was forced to leave the city in 1434 when a republic was once more established. During his reign the arrival of the Renaissance in Rome is marked by the new bronze gates for St Peter's, designed by Antonio Filarete.

Nicholas V, as recorded earlier, was determined to increase the prestige of the Church by the grandeur of a new Rome. The Jubilee of 1450 produced the revenue for a programme of church repairs and in addition the city's defences were reconstructed. There is little evidence of any general plan for rebuilding but key sites were made available for new buildings at nominal rent. Nicholas V also played an extremely important rôle in the development of the

45, 46. Norwood Young, *The Story of Rome.*
47. The same Poggio Bracciolini who had drawn attention to the Vitruvian manuscript in 1412–14. Norwood Young also quotes an English visitor to Rome of the same time exclaiming, 'O God, how pitiable is Rome! Once she was filled with great nobles and palaces; now with huts, thieves, wolves, beggars and vermin, with waste places, and the Romans themselves tear each other to pieces.'

Renaissance, in Rome and in Italy generally, in extending a generous hospitality to the émigré intelligentsia from Constantinople, particularly after it fell to the Turks in 1453.

At this time the inhabited part of Rome was concentrated largely on the low-lying Campus Martius, within the broad bend in the Tiber opposite the Castel Sant'Angelo; this latter served the popes as treasure house, prison and place of refuge in times of invasion or revolt (Fig. 5.20). Although of secondary importance to the later system of main streets linking the seven churches of Rome, from Nicholas V onwards, the bridgehead across from the castle was established as the focal point of a network of routes through the mediaeval city. Bufaldini's map of 1551 shows this bridgehead as the Forum Pontis – later to be renamed the Piazza di Ponte. Leading from it, five streets were pieced together out of the irregular lanes (Fig. 5.21); the most important, the Via Papalis, was subsequently widened and extended as the Corso Vittorio Emanuele. In an attempt to persuade people to move back on to the deserted higher parts of the city, Nicholas V in a Bull of March 1447 exempted the Quirinal, Viminal and Esquiline Hills from taxes, and reconstructed the Aqua Virgine to give the city a supply of 63,000 cubic metres of fresh water daily.

After Nicholas V three popes, Claistus III, Pius II and Paul II, contributed nothing of note and even failed to maintain settled conditions in the city. Sixtus IV (1471–84), however, took up the process of reconstruction and carried out many improvements both in preparation for the Jubilee of 1475 and, subsequently, with its proceeds. Before the arrival of the pilgrims he converted the old Ponte Rotto into the Ponte Sisto and, in order to avoid the recurrence of an earlier pedestrian crush in the narrow streets in which over 200 people had died, he introduced one-way routing; the crowd was made to use the Ponte Sant'Angelo in going to St Peter's and the Ponte Sisto for their return across the Tiber. Also in preparation for the jubilee, he rebuilt the great Santo Spirito Hospital, repaired the Aqua Virgine, and restored the Trevi Fountain. A direct network of main streets linking the city's major churches was also started and, in an edict of 1480, he commanded that all building projections and street obstructions be cleared away[48].

Sixtus IV was also an extremely able planning administrator, with views considerably in advance of his time in that he recognised that private interests should be subordinate to the public good. He insisted that although compensation for private loss must be fairly administered, there also existed on the other hand what became known later as 'betterment' and this ought to be also taken into account. A commission was established to consider the effect of property boundary adjustments brought about by the street improvements.

Alexander VI (1492–1503) restored the Castle of St Angelo and connected it to the Vatican by a new street, the Borgo Nuovo. His successor Julius II (1503–13) was mainly pre-occupied with the problem of the Basilica of St Peter and took the final decision to demolish the old church rather than attempt to repair its decayed fabric. In April 1506 the foundation stone was laid of the present church to the designs of Bramante, who lived only to see the completion of the four main piers and the arches under the dome. A succession of famous Renaissance artists subsequently worked on St Peter's before its completion in 1626, including Raphael and

Rome, Paris and London – the most important foci of Western Civilization – created the prototypes of the large cities of today. Rome's contribution came first. It was the work of the Popes of the sixteenth century, systematized and epitomized by Sixtus V. Under his initiative the limited, wall-girdled, star-shaped City of the Renaissance was converted into the City of Baroque, with those boldly drawn traffic lines which still form the warp and weft of the modern city.

Yet by the beginning of the Renaissance, Rome was a desolate city, at the end of a millenium of decline. When the Popes moved from the Lateran to the Vatican they preferred to build a new suburb, and so the Borgo Nuovo gradually grew round the Basilica of St Peter. Thus, about 1500, when the Popes began to rebuild medieval Rome in earnest, the Popes became the greatest builders in the world. Neither they nor their leading architects and planners were ever Roman by birth or upbringing. Julius II, a Rovere from Urbino, and Leo X, a Medici from Florence, called in their close compatriots – Bramante and Raphael from Urbino and Michelangelo from Florence – to carry out their grandiose schemes; and so it continued even in the time of Baroque Rome.

(Sigfried Giedion, 'Sixtus V and the Planning of Baroque Rome', 'Architectural Review', April 1952)

For Rome it was the century which transformed a relatively small medieval town of barely 20,000 inhabitants into a city of over 100,000, and the capital, not just of the Papal States, but of Catholic Christendom. It changed the name of the 'campo vaccino', the cow field, back to Forum Romanum, as an archaeological site and a tourist attraction. In 1526, just before Rome was sacked by the imperial armies, it had already 236 hotels and inns; at the end of the century, there were at least 360, plus innumerable furnished houses and rooms to let. Thus it was that during the jubilee year of 1600, Rome could accommodate over half a million pilgrims. Everything was geared to this: there was one wineshop for every 174 inhabitants; there were hundreds of tailors, goldsmiths, manufacturers of 'objets d'art' and religious souvenirs and, inevitably, street vendors. Yet all attempts to introduce a textile manufacturing industry into the city failed. Rome lived on the contributions of Catholic Europe, on the income of ecclesiastical offices and church lands, spent by their owners in the Eternal City; but, above all, it lived on its visitors: a city of beggars and prostitutes, of devoted clergy, pious pilgrims and indifferent tourists, of nobles and princes of the church, displaying their wealth and ruining their fortunes by sumptuous buildings and princely dowries to their daughters and nieces. Two things were necessary for success in Rome said St Carlo Borromeo, to love God and to own a carriage.

(H. G. Koenigsberger and George L. Mosse, 'Europe in the Sixteenth Century')

---

48. Sigfried Giedion, *Sixtus V and the Planning of Baroque Rome*, 'Architectural Review', April 1952.

Michelangelo, who built the magnificent dome and the supporting drum. But illustrative of the continuing disregard of the Romans for their ancient architectural heritage, Norwood Young comments that the new St Peter's was made entirely, even to the mortar, of materials taken from the ruins of classical monuments[49]. Julius II also laid out two new streets on either side of the Tiber – the Via Giulia on the left bank (downstream from the Piazza di Ponte) and the parallel Via Lungara on the right bank.

The next two popes, Leo X (1513–21) and Paul III (1534–49), were responsible respectively for the Via Ripetta and the Via Babuino, symmetrically laid out on either side of the Strada del Corso – the city's main approach from the north, by way of the Piazza del Popolo (see below and Fig. 5.26). Paul III also continued redevelopment around the Piazza di Ponte and laid out the line of the Via Trinitatis, extending a route from the piazza towards the church of Sta Trinita dei Monti. In 1561 Michelangelo built his magnificent Porta Pia in the old Aurelian Wall for Pius IV, who connected it back to the deserted Quirinal Hill by the Strada Pia (now the Via del Quirinal); he also built the Via XX Settembre, from 1555 to 1567.

SIXTUS V

Between the papacies of Sixtus IV and Sixtus V there is a period of almost exactly a century, during which the city was steadily improved. The major achievement of the Capitol Piazza was carried through and redevelopment of the Piazza del Popolo (see below) was commenced. But the final form of Renaissance Rome owes most to the five-year pontificate of Sixtus V (1585–90). In this relatively short time he carried out an extensive programme of works, mainly with the architect-planner Domenico Fontana as his executant adviser. This programme was based on three main objectives: first, to repopulate the hills of Rome by providing them with the direct water supply lacking since the cutting of the ancient aqueducts; second, to integrate into one main street system the various works of his predecessors by connecting the main churches and other key points in the city; lastly, to create an aesthetic unity out of the often disparate buildings forming the streets and public spaces. Sixtus V was 64 when elevated to the papal throne. He died of malaria, in his unfinished Quirinal Palace, just five years and four months later, during which time nowhere is his race with death more apparent than in the incredible rapidity with which he carried through his building programme; again and again Fontana remarks that nothing could be accomplished quickly enough to please his 'beloved lord'[50].

It is clear that before becoming pope Sixtus V had given considerable thought to Rome's planning problems, still major ones at this juncture. Immediately following his accession work was under way on the Aqua Felice; the Strada Felice, linking Santa Croce in Gerusalemme to Sta Trinita dei Monti, was commenced and completed during the first year; the obelisk, later to be erected in front of St Peter's, was transported to the site; the Lateran Palace and Basilica were under construction; and some 2,000 workers were put to draining the Pontine marshes.

Although other popes had restored water supplies to the lower parts of the city they had failed to do so for the hilly districts. To

*Sentence of death on the monuments of the Forum and of the Sacra Via was passed on July 22nd, 1540. By a brief of Paul III 'the privilege of excavating or giving permission to excavate is taken away from the Capitoline or Apostolic chambers, from the "magistrates of streets", from ecclesiastical dignitaries etc, and given exclusively to the "deputies" for the Fabbrica di S. Pietro. The pope gives them full liberty to search for ancient marbles wherever they please within and outside the walls, to remove them from antique buildings, to pull these buildings to pieces if necessary; he orders that no marbles can be sold by private owners without the consent of the Fabbrica, under the penalty of excommunication "latae senteniae", of the wrath of the pope, and of a fine of 1000 ducats.' No pen can describe the ravages committed by the Fabbrica in the course of the last sixty years of the sixteenth century. The excesses roused the execration of the citizens, but to no purpose; on May 17th, 1580, the 'conservatori' made an indignant protest to the town-council, when a portion of the palace of the Caesars had fallen in consequence of its having been undermined by the searchers for marble. A deputation was sent to Gregory XIII to ask for the revocation of all licences ('ad perquirendos lapides etiam pro usu fabricae Principis apostolorum'). We may imagine what answer was given to the protests of the city when we learn that by a brief of Clement VIII, dated July 23rd, 1598, the archaeological jurisdiction of the Fabbrica was extended over the remains of Ostia and Porto. The Forum Romanum was swept by a band of devastators from 1540 to 1549; they began by removing the marble steps and the marble coating of Faustina's temple (1540), then they attacked what was left standing of the arch of Fabius (1540). Between 1546 and 1547 the temple of Julius Caesar, the Regia, with the 'fasti consulares et triumphales', fell under their hammer. The steps and foundations of the temple of Castor and Pollux were next burnt into lime or given up to the stonecutters, together with the arch of Augustus. The temple of Vesta, the Augusteum, and the shrine of Vortumnus, at the corner of the Vicus Tuscus, met with the same fate in 1549.
(R. Lanciani, 'The Ruins and Excavations of Ancient Rome')*

---

49. See also Rodolfo Lanciani, *The Ruins and Excavations of Ancient Rome*.
50. Quoted by Sigfried Giedion, *Space, Time and Architecture*.

bring water to the Quirinal, Viminal and Esquiline Hills, Sixtus V constructed the Aqua Felice between 1585–89 (so called because Sixtus's name was originally Felice Peretti). This aqueduct was created in part from the ancient Aqua Marcia and Aqua Claudia; it was about 16 miles in length and because of a severely limited fall from its source involved seven miles of high aqueduct and seven miles of tunnel. It supplied over four million gallons a day.

THE ROMAN STREET SYSTEM

Once integrated by Sixtus V into a comprehensive movement system, the principal streets were, as one of their major functions, intended to link the seven pilgrimage churches of Rome – San Pietro in Vaticano (St Peter's); San Giovanni in Laterano; Santa Maria Maggiore; San Paolo fuori le Mura; and San Lorenzo fuori le Mura (the original five churches) and two accorded special veneration later – Santa Croce in Gerusalemme and San Sebastiano (Fig. 5.21). This realised the ambition of Boniface VIII, adumbrated some 300 years earlier, to make Rome a worthy capital of Christendom.

Sixtus V was not, however, only concerned to facilitate religious ceremonial. He was well aware of the rôle the new streets could play in generating growth in the largely uninhabited, although climatically propitious, eastern and south-eastern districts. In this respect his contribution to the reconstruction of Rome has been mis-represented by a number of urban historians. Sibyl Moholy-Nagy over-emphasises the religious function with her criticism that his nine processional routes through the sparsely built-up eastern section of town were designed for a blatantly anti-urban processional ritual of piety and penitence[51]; and Lewis Mumford uncharacteristically gets his facts wrong in stating that 'the three great avenues that radiate from the Piazza del Popolo – the conception of Sixtus V – were designed to make it easy for the pilgrim to find his way to the various churches and holy spots'[52]. (All three avenues were in existence before Sixtus's accession.) Sigfried Giedion, on the other hand, would seem to present a correct balance between religious and secular functions[53], as also does Edmund Bacon in a beautifully illustrated section of his *Design of Cities* in which he argues the powerful proposition that Sixtus V saw clearly the need to establish a basic overall design structure in the form of a movement system as an idea.

Before describing the basis of Rome's late Renaissance street system, it is appropriate to relate the achievements of Sixtus V to those of Napoleon III in Paris during the two decades between 1850 and 1870. Each has suffered historical distortion. Both were effec-tively absolute rulers. Sixtus had Fontana and Napoleon III his Haussmann (although Haussmann's rôle as Prefect of the Seine made him more the Emperor's agent than executive planner). Both rulers were responsible for giving their ancient cities incomparable main route structures, and both assumed power with already formulated proposals. Napoleon's rôle has been slighted in this latter respect; usually Haussmann alone has been credited with restructuring Paris. This record has been set right by David Pinkney, in his *Napoleon III and the Rebuilding of Paris*: 'When Georges Haussmann laboured as a little-known provincial prefect in the department of the Yonne, Louis Napoleon already had on paper his ideas for rebuilding the city and had been urging them on a reluctant prefect and

Only members of the nobility and the ruling houses of Italy were usually elected to the papal throne. There were, however, exceptions, even in a period such as the end of the sixteenth century, when the steadily increasing privileges of the nobility had usurped the mediaeval rights of the people. So it was possible for Sixtus V, a man from the lowest strata of society to be invested with the highest dignity of spiritual and temporal power to which a mortal could aspire. It says much for the inner strength, vitality and instinct of the Catholic Restauration that it had the courage – at this very dangerous moment – elevate a man such as Sixtus V to this office; a man whom regardless of his ancestry, was clearly born for action.

Sixtus V was the papal title chosen by the Franciscan mendicant friar, Felix Peretti, who had entered the order at the age of 12. His father, a small tenant farmer and gardener of Dalmatian stock, filled with visions of the future destiny of his son, had given him the name of Felix. This name Sixtus V – in contrast to other Popes – never laid entirely aside. He bestowed it upon the two projects that lay nearest his heart, and also nearest the place of his residence as a Cardinal, the Villa Montalto, north of Sta Maria Maggiore: the Strada Felice – Rome's grandiose, north-west south-east highway – and the Aqua Felice – the water system which brought life to the hills of the south-east.
(Sigfried Giedion, 'Sixtus V and the Planning of Baroque Rome', 'Architectural Review', April 1952)

Sixtus V is the patron saint of American city planners who credit him with the first urban renewal miracle. It is doubtful whether any saint has ever been canonized for less valid reasons. There is no evidence that Sixtus intended to change Rome from a maze of medieval slums into a planned orthogonal city by opening up linear communica-tions and designing effective 'reciprocal vistas'. From the available documents, it is abundantly clear that he hated the worldly Romans, who were disenchanted by the stern structures of the Counter Reformation, and that his nine processional routes through the sparsely built-up eastern section of town were designed for a blatantly anti-urban processional ritual of piety and penitence.
(Sibyl Moholy-Nagy, 'Matrix of Man')

---

51. Sibyl Moholy-Nagy, *Matrix of Man.*
52. Lewis Mumford, *The City in History.*
53. Sigfried Giedion, *Space, Time and Architecture.*

municipal council. On the day when Haussmann took the oath of office as the Prefect of the Seine, Napoleon handed to him a map of Paris on which he had drawn in four contrasting colours (the colours indicating the relative urgency he attached to each project) the streets that he proposed to build.' The reality of the Parisian situation is that emperor and prefect, and their professional advisers, together formed a near perfect team.

The record of achievement is however still further distorted. In the same way that the Parisian boulevards have been criticised as having only a strategic military rôle, directed at discouraging and suppressing civil disturbances, Rome's new streets have been seen only as religious routes. The Paris boulevards certainly were well suited to artillery and cavalry – generally rendered impotent in the ancient winding streets – but this was only one of their functions, and Rome's improvements also had quite complex purposes. (It is of additional interest to note that London, which has never 'enjoyed' the attentions of a despotic ruler, has also never been given a comprehensible main route structure.)

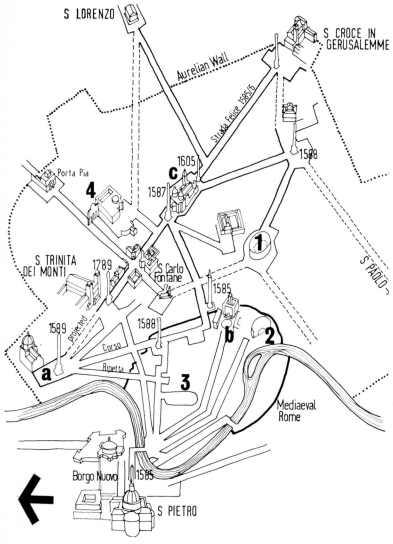

Figure 5.21 – Rome, showing the city's main street system related to the major churches, important ancient monuments and the extent of mediaeval Rome (as heavy outline). Key: 1, the Colosseum; 2, Theatre of Marcellus; 3, Piazza Navona; 4, ruins of the Baths of Diocletian; a, Piazza del Popolo; b, Capitol Piazza; c, S. Maria Maggiore.
Sixtus V's 'landmark' obelisks are located with dates of erection. The streets laid out to his instructions are shown in heavy line: his unrealised proposals are shown dotted.

It is important to distinguish between the work of Sixtus V and that of his predecessors. Fig. 5.21 serves as a general map of Renaissance Rome; it shows his routes in heavy line (broken for those which were to remain only projects). Earlier streets are credited individually. This map also locates the obelisks which were erected at key intersections and other important locations. Sixtus V based Rome's new movement system on his Strada Felice – the main route from south-east to north-west which was constructed in the first year of his papacy. This street was to have linked the isolated Santa Croce in Gerusalemme directly to the Piazza del Popolo, some $2\frac{1}{2}$ miles distant, by way of Santa Maria Maggiore. But although Fontana noted that 'so great a prince [Sixtus] has extended streets from one end of the city to the other, without concern for either the hills or the valleys which they crossed, but causing the former to be levelled and the latter filled, has reduced them to gentle inclines'[54], he was defeated by the steep slopes of the Aventine and was forced to terminate the Strada Felice in front of Santa Trinita dei Monti. From here a magnificent flight of steps – the Scala di Spagna – was built between 1721–25 down the hillside to the Piazza di Spagna, on the Strada del Babuino (Fig. 5.28). The obelisk in front of the church, terminating the Strada Felice, was erected in 1789.

Aware of Rome's immense planning problems, and his own limited time, Sixtus V devised a unique method of ensuring that his successors would be obliged to continue to implement his programme. 'Like a man with a divining rod [he] placed his obelisks at points where, during the coming centuries, the most important squares would develop'[55]. Sixtus V located four such obelisks: in the future Piazza del Popolo, at the intersection of the three routes; on the Strada Felice, immediately north-west of Santa Maria Maggiore; in front of San Giovanni in Laterano; and, most significantly in terms of its subsequent effect, in front of the still unfinished St Peter's. More obelisks were added by later popes.

During Sixtus's lifetime Santa Maria Maggiore was a typical asymmetrical Early Christian and mediaeval basilica. It occupied the key central position on the Strada Felice, and was connected to the San Giovanni in Laterano by the existing Via Gregoriana. Sixtus corrected the line of this street and also erected an obelisk at its southern terminal, in front of San Giovanni. North-west of Santa Maria Maggiore Sixtus's obelisk was to form the focal point of a new linear piazza when the church was remodelled by Rainaldi for Clement X between 1670–76. Connecting this space to the eastern edge of the old city, marked by Trajan's Column, Sixtus V laid out the Via Panisperna. San Lorenzo fuori le Mura was integrated into the processional system by a street running east from the Strada Felice, on the far side of Santa Maria. North from Santa Maria Maggiore the Strada Felice cut across Pope Pius IV's Strada Pia – linking the Piazza Quirinal to the Porta Pia and constituting a main route leading out to the south-east. This intersection was effected almost at right-angles, a situation which invariably creates architectural problems but which was resolved, in this instance, by Fontana's successful use of four fountains, fed by the Aqua Felice, at the corners. Views along the Strada Pia were also improved by correcting its level. Other street systems were projected by Sixtus but were never actually constructed (see Fig. 5.21). His death intervened to prevent completion of his building programme.

Figure 5.22 – Rome, a section of Nolli's plan of 1748, between the Tiber and the Piazza Navona (north at the top). This area of low-lying ground was part of the ancient Campus Martius, which is believed to have consisted of a number of formally planned, if unrelated, parts and to have included many of the city's latter day architectural monuments.

Haphazard conversion and rebuilding resulted in a typical mediaeval form; many ancient remains being incorporated into later buildings. The Piazza Navona, top centre, follows exactly the shape of the central area of the Emperor Domitian's stadium (AD 81-96) with seats and corridors incorporated into the foundations of the surrounding buildings (see page 131).

54, 55. Sigfried Giedion. *Sixtus V and the Planning of Baroque Rome*. 'Architectural Review,' April 1952.

ENVIRONMENTAL CONDITIONS

Sixtus V was also concerned to improve health conditions in the city. In addition to increasing the supply of pure water he introduced dust carts for the regular removal of household refuse, improved the drainage system, and constructed public wash-houses. Although his programme of public investment provided work for thousands of men it failed to solve Rome's chronic unemployment problem; accordingly in the last year of his reign he embarked on an ambitious scheme to convert the Colosseum into a wool-spinning mill, with manufacturing space on the ground floor and dwelling apartments in the upper storeys. At his death he had already begun to excavate the earth and to level the street, working with seventy wagons and a hundred labourers[56]. Had he lived only one more year, Giedion considers, the Colosseum would have become the first workers' settlement and large-scale unit of manufacture.

The work of rebuilding Rome did not end with Sixtus V; many important examples of urbanism in the city were carried out in later years. Moreover it should be noted that only in recent times has the city regained its ancient population level. Throughout the Renaissance centuries it was only a fraction of its former size, with approximate populations of 35,000 in 1458; 55,000 in 1526; 80,000 in 1580; and 124,000 in 1656[57].

It must be remembered that the examples of urbanism in Rome, described below, unlike those above, are essentially unrelated to each other, or, in several instances, to the main street structure. An important exception is the Piazza del Popolo which extends the structure through the north-western district. The illustrated sections of Nolli's 1748 map[58] clearly indicate the unplanned network of narrow winding streets and lanes still separating the city's Renaissance spaces, and the many ancient architectural remains restricting comprehensive redevelopment. Furthermore the examples described have to be seen in their correct historical perspective since, in several instances, they took centuries to complete.

THE CAPITOL PIAZZA

The Capitol Hill, the best known of the seven hills of Rome, was the seat of the Senate, the ancient Roman governing body, and the city's original religious sanctuary. Following the destruction of the ancient buildings between the eighth and twelfth centuries the market, and with it the seat of the prefect of the city, was transferred from the Forum Holiforium to the Capitol, so that the Capitol became the political centre of mediaeval Rome[59]. The Palace of the Capitol (later the Palazzo del Senatore) was known to exist on its present site in 1145 and was being rebuilt in 1299 and subsequent years in the form of 'a mediaeval town hall, a robber-baron stronghold, with corner turrets and parapets and a high central tower'[60]. In the early years of the fifteenth century the Capitoline Palace was so dilapidated that the municipal authorities, were forced to sit in the church of Sta Maria in Aracoeli, which had been built in 1290 some distance away to the north-east. In 1429 Nicholas V, as part of his programme of improvement, converted an existing building into the Palazzo dei Conservatori – an arcaded mediaeval design – immediately to the north of the Palazzo del Senatore. These two buildings formed a sharp angle at their nearest corners (Fig. 5.24). The Capitol however was just as disorderly as so many other places

Hence we went towards Mons Capitolinus, at the foot of which stands the arch of Septimus Severus, full and entire. save where the pedestal and some of the lower members are choked up with ruins and earth. This arch is exceedingly enriched with sculpture and trophies, with a large inscription. In the terrestrial and naval battles here graven, is seen the Roman Aries (the battering-ram); and this was the first triumphal arch set up in Rome. The Capitol. to which we climbed by very broad steps. is built about a square court, at the right hand of which, going up from Campo Vaccino, gushes a plentiful stream from the statue of Tiber, in porphyry, very antique, and another representing Rome; but. above all, is the admirable figure of Marforius, casting water into a most ample concha. The front of this court is crowned with an excellent fabric containing the Courts of Justice. and where the Criminal Notary sits, and others. In one of the halls they show the statues of Gregory XIII and Paul III, with several others. To this joins a handsome tower. the whole 'facciata' adorned with noble statues, bcth on the outside and on the battlements, ascended by a double pair of stairs. and a stately Posario.
In the centre of the court stands that incomparable horse bearing the Emperor Marcus Aurelius, as big as the life. of Corinthian metal, placed on a pedestal of marble, esteemed one of the noblest pieces of work now extant. antique and very rare.
(John Evelyn. 'Diary')

Figure 5.23 – Rome, location of the Capitol Piazza, related to the ancient Forum Romanum, showing how this outstanding example of Renaissance urbanism was orientated towards the mediaeval city area, turning its back on the centre of ancient Rome. Key: 1, modern monument to Victor Emmanuel; 2, north-eastern hemicycle of Trajan's Forum; 3, Via Sacra through the Forum Romanum; 4, Arch of Titus; 5, the Colosseum. (See Figures 3.10 and 3.12 for details of the centre of ancient Rome.)

56. Sigfried Giedion, *Sixtus V and the Planning of Baroque Rome.* 'Architectural Review,' April 1952.
57. Rodolfo Lanciani, *The Ruins and Excavations of Ancient Rome.*
58. Giovanni Battista Nolli, *Nuova Pianta di Roma.* 1748.
59. Thomas Ashby, *The Capitol, Rome.* 'Town Planning Review,' Vol XII, 1927.
60. S. E. Rasmussen, *Towns and Buildings.*

in Rome; the famous hill had no form, it had been ploughed up by horsemen, and bushes grew at random over the uneven terrain[64].

From 1471 onwards there started, under Sixtus IV, a policy of collecting the surviving antique marble statues in the city and displaying them on the Capitol. With the growing interest in classical sculpture it was realised that this would give an added attraction to the city but there was neither any consideration of their arrangement nor any plan for comprehensive redevelopment of the Capitol Hill. It was during the papacy of Paul III (1534–49) that plans were finally made for the creation of a monumental square on the Capitoline Hill and Michelangelo was commissioned in 1537.

Michelangelo is perhaps the most gifted of the many versatile artists of the Italian Renaissance. Painter, sculptor, poet, architect and urbanist, his achievements are unparalleled and much of his work, if equalled, never surpassed except, possibly, by Leonardo da Vinci. In 1538, as the focal point of his plan for the Capitol, the bronze statue of Marcus Aurelius (the only surviving equestrian statue of ancient Rome) was erected on a pedestal designed by Michelangelo. In 1550 his proposals for the new piazza were published but in his last years he was preoccupied with designing the dome of St Peter's and little progress had been made on the Capitol project before his death in 1564. Final completion, following the original scheme, was delayed until 1664.

Thomas Ashby, describing the Capitol, lists six basic objectives in Michelangelo's plan: (1) to refine and simplify the existing Palazzo del Senatore, eliminating the mediaeval angle towers and battlemented parapets, substituting in their place a new organised elevation; (2) to clear the whole area of shops, houses, other unsuitable uses and the many ruins; (3) to reconstruct the Palazzo dei Conservatori, eliminating all mediaeval character, creating an elevational design compatible with that of the Palazzo del Senatore; (4) to build a new palace balancing the Palazzo dei Conservatori about the axis through the centre and tower of the Palazzo del Senatore and the statue of Marcus Aurelius; (5) to construct new access stairs up to the piazza on the main axis; and (6) to use the statue of Marcus Aurelius as the focal point of the piazza[62].

In his use of a statue as the free-standing central focus of the piazza Michelangelo was breaking new ground. Previously '. . . sculpture was treated as part of a building, and if it stood alone it was placed as though under the protection of the building, close to its walls'[63]. As such the Capitoline Piazza is the first of the many 'monumental squares' which were built in all the countries of the Renaissance. The piazza is not a completely enclosed space. The three buildings form a trapezoid with the forth side open along the edge of the hill, up which the monumental approach flight of steps has been cut, slightly wider at the top than at the bottom. It is a small space, 181 feet across at its widest and 133 feet at its narrowest, between the flanking buildings. This effect of false perspective, forced on Michelangelo by the existing alignments, accentuates the importance of the Palazzo del Senatore. For Edmund Bacon, 'one of the greatest attributes of the Campidoglio [the Capitol Piazza] is the modulation of the land. Without the shape of the oval, and its two-dimensional star-shaped pattern, as well as its three-dimensional projection in the subtly designed steps that surround it, the unity and coherence of the design would not have been achieved'[64].

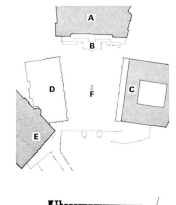

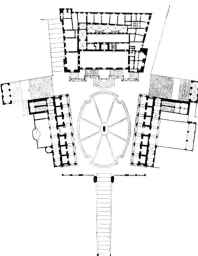

Figure 5.24 – Rome, the Capitol Piazza, before redevelopment of the area, showing the pre-existing buildings tinted (top); and after, with the detailed floor plans of the three buildings forming the new space (below). Key: A, the mediaeval Palazzo del Senatore built in part on the ruined Tabularium of the ancient Forum Romanum; B, the Renaissance extension and new north-west elevation; C, the Palazzo dei Conservatori, refaced as part of Michelangelo's design; D, the new building of the Capitoline Museum; E, the ancient church of Santa Maria in Aracoeli; F, statue of Marcus Aurelius.

61. S. E. Rasmussen, *Towns and Buildings*.
62. Thomas Ashby, *The Capitol, Rome*. 'Town Planning Review,' Vol XII, 1927.
63. S. E. Rasmussen, *Towns and Buildings*.
64. Edmund Bacon, *Design of Cities*.

PIAZZA DEL POPOLO

The Piazza del Popolo is situated on the northern side of the city
between the Tiber on the west and the steep slopes of Monte Pincio
on the east (Fig. 5.26). The main approach road from the north to
ancient Rome ran across this narrow area between the river and
the hill, passing through the Porta del Popolo, built in the Aurelian
Wall of AD 272, and continuing straight on through the city as the
Via Flaminia, up to the northern slopes of the Capitol Hill. The
Piazza del Popolo, immediately inside the gateway, was the main
entrance place to the city but little is known of its form during the
ancient Roman and mediaeval periods other than that the Via
Flaminia ran across it and the Via Ripetta started from it, aligned

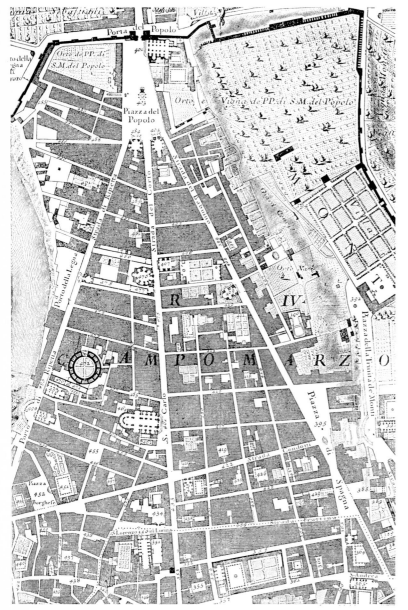

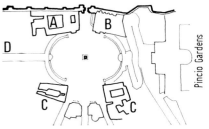

Figure 5.25 – Rome, the Piazza del Popolo as
finally completed in the nineteenth century to a
design by Guiseppe Valadier (1816–20). A new
church (A) repeating the design of Santa Maria del
Popolo (B), was built to the west of the Porta del
Popolo; new buildings (C) were added on either
side of the twin churches; a sweeping staircase and
ramp up to the Pincio Gardens integrated them into
the total design. At a still later date a street through
from the Tiber (D) was added to complete the
east-west cross axis.

Figure 5.26 – Rome, the Piazza del Popolo and the
three main routes south into the centre of the
city, from the Nolli plan of 1748 (north at the top and
left, the Tiber). This plan shows the piazza at an
interim stage in its development, before the remodel-
ling of 1816–20 under Pius VII.
The south-western corner of the plan shows part of
mediaeval Rome; the narrow formless streets are
in marked contrast to the formally laid-out, gridiron-
based, streets of the Renaissance district between the
Pincio ridge and the Tiber.
The Spanish Steps, shown as Figure 5.28, are
located to the bottom right, at the end of the
Strada Condotti.

at an angle which just skirted the Tiber. A less important third road ran along the foot of Monte Pincio[65].

The redevelopment of the Piazza del Popolo area, to make it a more impressive entrance to the city, started in 1516 under Leo X with the construction of a new third road, the Via Babuino, but the piazza was not completed in its present form until 300 years later (Fig. 5.25). The alignment of the new Via Babuino is such that it intersects with the line of the Via Flaminia at the same angle, and at the same point, as the existing Via Ripetta. In 1589 Fontana, for Sixtus V, erected a red granite obelisk at this focal point, in the centre of the piazza. (Many references to this incorrectly state that the obelisk was positioned *before* the Via Babuino was planned.) Earlier in 1586 Sixtus V had hoped to bring his Strada Felice into the piazza, to the east again of the Via Babuino, but this was prevented by the slopes of Monte Pincio[66]. The two twin-domed churches on the southern side of the piazza, in the angles formed by the three streets, were started in 1662 to the designs of Rainaldo and finished later by Bernini and Carlo Fontana. The other three sides of the piazza, completing its present form, were designed by the French architect-planner Valadier and date from 1816–20[67].

PIAZZA NAVONA

The houses, palaces and churches of the Piazza Navona follow precisely the layout of the stadium built by the Emperor Domitian (AD 81–96); indeed the well-preserved ruins of the seats and corridors are incorporated into the piazza's foundations (Fig. 5.22). The final spatial organisation of the piazza was carried out by Bernini between 1647–51, although one of his three sculptured fountains was not added until the nineteenth century. The long and narrow form of the space meant that all views had to be designed as oblique perspectives[68]. The piazza contains three richly modelled fountains whose cascading waters are enhanced by the neutral backcloth of the surrounding houses and the two churches of San Giacomo degli Spagnuoli (1450) and Sant'Agnese (1652–77).

PIAZZA OF ST PETER'S

The great church of St Peter's was built between 1506 and 1626 but it lacked an appropriate entrance forecourt until 1655–67 when Bernini carried out the two major sections of a three-part piazza complex (Fig. 5.27). These spaces are the *piazza retta*, directly in front of the church, and the vast *piazza obliqua* enclosed by the semi-circular colonnades[69]. The third section, the Piazza Rusticucci, has never been finally completed and is represented only in part by Mussolini's avenue linking St Peter's with the river Tiber. In preparing his layout, which was successful in competition with his leading contemporaries, Bernini had to incorporate the central obelisk erected in 1586 by Sixtus V, and fountains built by Maderna in 1613.

SPANISH STEPS

The 137 steps leading up from the Piazza di Spagna to the church of Santa Trinita dei Monti, were built by Alessandro Specchi and Francesco de' Santis between 1721–25. Paul Zucker considers that they represent the climax of stage effects in Roman city planning on a larger scale; here nature lent a helpful hand to the spatial vision of the planner with the staircase, the link between two topographic-

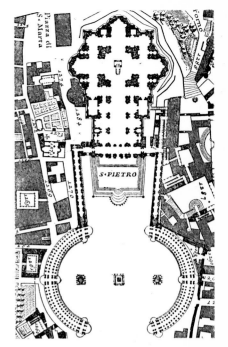

Figure 5.27 – Rome, the Piazza of St Peter's (north to the right). The Vatican City encloses St Peter's and extends east to the centre line of the oval *piazza obliqua*. The river Tiber is some 655 yards further east from the bottom of this plan extract, reached along the Via delle Conciliazione – the avenue which performs in part the internal functions of Bernini's Piazza Rusticucci. The scale of both the church and the spaces is vast: the *piazza retta* in front of the eastern elevation is 410 feet wide narrowing to 300 feet where it adjoins the *piazza obliqua*, and 320 feet deep; the *piazza obliqua* itself is not a true ellipse but consists of two semicircles of radius of approximately 260 feet, with a rectangle in between giving a total width of 650 feet.

65. Thomas Ashby and S. Rowland Pierce, *The Piazza del Popolo*, 'Town Planning Review,' Vol XI, 1924.

66. J. A. F. Orbaan, *How Pope Sixtus V lost a Road*, 'Town Planning Review,' Vol XIII, 1928.

67. See also Edmund Bacon, *Design of Cities*.

68, 69. See also Paul Zucker, *Town and Square*.

ally different levels becoming the square. He adds that the Scala di Spagna is the only example in the history of city planning where a staircase does not merely lead to a square in front of a monumental structure, but where the stairs themselves become the visual and spatial centre[70]. The steps lead up in curved flights from the piazza, a triangular space formed by the oblique-angled intersections of five streets. They are finely adjusted to the slope, with their axial directions subtly varied to incorporate into the design the obelisk set at the top in front of the church façade.

Venice

Venice, like the ancient city of Rome, has a mythical foundation date. The site – an easily defended group of islands in the north-west corner of the Adriatic – must, however, have attracted village settlement long before 'the 25th March, 421, at midday exactly'[71]. These islands on a lagoon were formed from sediment brought down by three ancient alpine rivers. Dominated at first by Ravenna and Byzantium, the Venetian Republic gradually developed into a major Mediterranean power able to exact full benefit from its strategic location on the most important trading routes. In his *Mediaeval Cities*, Henri Pirenne writes of Venice's debt to the Byzantium Empire: 'to it she not only owed the prosperity of her commerce, but from it she learned those higher forms of civilisation, that perfected technique, that business enterprise, and that political and administrative organisation which gave her a place in the Europe of the Middle Ages'.

Seeming deficiences in their archipelago location were turned to advantage by the Venetians in controlling their city's growth: individual islands were zoned for specific functions. Most of the islands gradually coalesced into a tight-knit group, traversed by the labyrinthine canal system, but a rigid oligarchic government continued to differentiate between land-uses.

In the twentieth century Venice is no longer an island. It is linked to the mainland by the rail causeway, 3,000 yards long and completed in 1846, and a motorway built in 1931. The former terminates in a modern railway station, whilst all vehicle traffic is allowed no further than the vast parking garage at the end of the motorway. As James Morris observes the lifestream of Venice arrives on wheels but most proceed by water or by foot[72]. Morris continues: 'There are said to be 177 canals with a total length of 28 miles. They follow old, natural water courses, and meander unpredictably through the city, now wide, fine and splendid, now indescribably tortuous. The Grand Canal – the central artery of Venice – is two miles long, it is seventy-six yards wide at its grandest point, and never less than forty; it has a mean depth of about 9 feet – 13 feet at the Rialto Bridge'. The Grand Canal divides the city into two parts. Following the line of the ancient river Alto it 'sweeps in three abrupt, but majestic curves, clean through the city; three bridges cross this tremendous waterway, 46 side canals enter it, 200 palaces line it, 48 alleys run down to it, ten churches stand upon its banks, the railway station stands gleaming at one end, St Mark's guards the other'[73].

On both sides of the Grand Canal, and on the separate Guidecca island, Venice is divided into six ancient segments – originally dis-

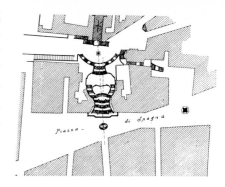

Figure 5.28 – Rome, the Spanish Steps, leading up the Pincio hillside from the Piazza di Spagna to the Church of S. Trinita dei Monti.

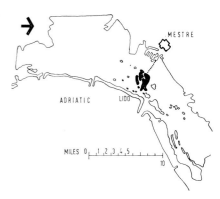

Figure 5.29 – Venice, the location of the city islands in the Lagoon; the access causeway from mainland Mestre is shown dotted.

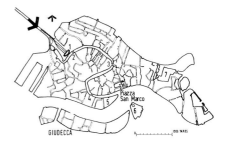

Figure 5.30 – Venice, general plan, showing the causeway from Mestre at top left. Key: 1, railway station; 2, Station Bridge over the Grand Canal; 3, Rialto Bridge; 4, Academia Bridge; 5, Santa Maria della Salute; 6, San Giorgio Maggiore; 7, the Arsenal. (The Grand Canal, the city's main traffic artery, takes the form of a reversed 'S' between the railway station and the Lagoon, just west of the Piazza of St Mark.)

70. Paul Zucker, *Town and Square*.
71, 72, 73. James Morris, *Venice*.

tinct islands in the archipelago but now unified into one continuous urban form (Fig. 5.30). In addition to the main square, the central Piazza San Marco, described below, each section has its own piazza. The Piazza San Marco in reality consists of two linked piazzas – the piazza proper in front of the Basilica of St Mark and the piazzetta which connects it to the edge of the lagoon. The detached Campanile of St Mark's is located in the relatively narrow space between the two piazzas and acts as a perfectly positioned hinge (Fig. 5.31). There is in addition a third, smaller piazza along the northern side of the basilica. The site of this overall design was originally occupied by a market place lying outside the walls of the embryonic Venetian settlement. It began to be the central focus of the city from AD 827 when the Chapel of St Mark (originally a private chapel of the Doge) was built as a sepulchre containing the body of St Mark (Fig. 5.33). The Doge's Palace, first constructed at the end of the eighth century as a fortress outside the walls, was rebuilt here between 1309 and 1424. The palace, together with the Basilica of St Mark, now forms the eastern side of the main piazza and the piazzetta.

During the early fifteenth century the piazza was still quite small and its surrounds consisted of uneven brick façade houses. Its present-day character dates from 1480–1517 when the Procuratie Vecchie was built on the north side. At this time the campanile –

Figures 5.31 and 5.32 – Venice, aerial photograph of the Piazza of St Mark from the south and key plan at the same orientation. Key: A, St Mark's Basilica; B, Doges' Palace; C, Procuratie Vecchie; D, Library; E, Procuratie Nuovo; F, Fabrica Nuova. The campanile and the small tempietto at its foot are shown as solid black, all other buildings are shown with their ground floor areas in heavy line. The aerial view shows a marked contrast between the carefully organised massing and architectural conformity of the piazza spaces, and the organic growth pattern of the surrounding buildings.

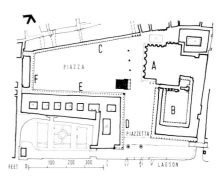

133

originally a timber construction dating from 888, but rebuilt in brick between 1329–1415 – was connected to the buildings on the southern side of the piazza. In redeveloping this side of the piazza, and the western side of the piazzetta, the width of the spaces was increased, isolating the campanile as a free-standing vertical element. The western side of the piazzetta is formed by the library building, designed in 1536 by Sansovino and completed by Scamozzi in 1484, after his death. The southern side of the main piazza was then formed by the Procuratie Nuove, designed in 1484 by Scamozzi and completed in 1640 by Longhena.

The final completion of the main piazza was not achieved until 1810 when the Fabrica Nuova was built across its western end. The three flagpoles in front of St Mark's, which play important secondary design rôles, were erected in 1505. The paving treatment, which constitutes a vital unifying element in the design, was carried out between 1722–35. The Campanile collapsed in 1902, destroying the small tempietto at its foot, but both have been successfully restored.

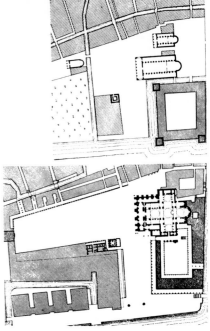

Figure 5.33 – Venice, two intermediate stages in the development of the Piazza of St Mark; its final, present-day form is shown in Figures 5.31 and 5.32. Top, the late twelfth century plan: a multi-purpose area in front of the old basilica served both as the main market and the city's public meeting space. The campanile, which dates from 888, was attached to the building in the south-west corner; the Doge's Palace was essentially a mediaeval castle in character, surrounded by canals in the form of a moat.
Below, the piazza in the early sixteenth century before reconstruction of the southern side, as the Procuratie Nuove, to a new building line, thereby giving the campanile its free-standing location. By this date the piazza occupied its final area, but the western end, the Fabrica Nuova, was only completed in 1810.

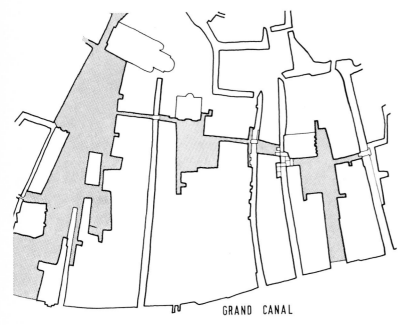

GRAND CANAL

Figure 5.34, Left – Venice, several of the minor squares and pedestrian route-spaces between the Piazza of St Mark (to the right) and the Academia Bridge on the northern side of the Grand Canal (see Figure 5.30 for their location).

6 — The Renaissance : France

The arrival of the Renaissance in France is marked by the work of Italian artists at the courts of Charles VIII (1483–98) and Louis XII (1498–1515). Because of the advent of printing the first books on architectural design and urbanism served as an early means of taking the new ideas from Italy to France and other European countries; reading about these revolutionary theories, however, had little impact compared to actually experiencing examples of their application.

Many individuals had made visits to Italy during the latter part of the fifteenth century, including both architects and their potential clients, but the first contact of lasting significance was made in 1494 when the French army under Charles VIII marched south through the country as far as Naples. The King and his court were faced, as Rasmussen puts it, with a style that made all they had known appear confused, crabbed and petty. At the same time these bold square palaces, these columns, balusters and round-headed arches, these garlands and laurel wreaths were so disconcertingly novel that it took even the most progressive many years to digest them[1].

The assimilation process took longest with architecture and urbanism but painters and sculptors could be commissioned immediately and a number of them returned to France with Charles VIII. Others followed, including Leonardo da Vinci who died at Amboise in the Loire Valley in 1519. Early Renaissance architectural activity was centred in this part of France, with the sequence of châteaux of the Loire constructed or rebuilt for the king and his courtiers, before Paris emerged as the undisputed national capital. At Blois, Renaissance details were introduced for Francis I; Chambord, in the heart of the forest, was started in 1519 with a vast symmetrical plan. The first phase of Chenonceaux (1515–22) and Azay-le-Rideau (1518–19) were other important early designs[2].

Under Francis I (1515–47) Paris became the capital of an effectively united French nation and scene of its brilliant royal court. The boundary of the city at that time was the defensive wall of 1367–83 and within this confined area the city displayed most of the characteristics of unplanned mediaeval urban form. The clarity of Lutetia's street pattern had been lost during the centuries after

The movement was more closely linked with the cultural programme of the rulers than in any other country. It was not the individual struggle of artists and scholars alone, as in Germany and the Netherlands, which brought about the discussion of the new achievements of the Italian Renaissance. It was more the planned activity of the sovereigns which opened new possibilities to artists and writers. French culture in the sixteenth century was not the culture of burghers as in Germany and the Netherlands, but a court culture – and thus far a continuation of the mediaeval order. King Francis I's patronage of the fine arts gave a decisive turn to the whole development. His sister Marguerite of Navarre fostered humanism and literature. Henry II reaped the fruits of what his predecessors had planted . . .

Francis I considered himself a connoisseur of painting, and he had the enthusiasm of a great collector. He saw his artistic ideal in the Italian Renaissance. When he was a young man, his expeditions and travels brought him into close contact with its sources. His agents in Italy tried to procure as many works of art as they could in order to transfer them to France. Francis even tried to transfer the masters themselves. Leonardo da Vinci spent the last years of his life in Cloux. Andreo del Sarto was in the service of the monarch for one year. A systematic colonization of France by Italian artists began in 1528, when the king rebuilt the old castle in the idyllic surroundings of the forests and ponds of Fontainebleau . . . They settled in the country, permeated it with a new artistic gospel, and at the same time assimilated themselves to its tradition. Thus an artistic culture of quite unique flavour arose, based on Italian Renaissance in form, on Latinism and Graecism in literary content, and on the French heritage in spirit.
(Otto Benesch, 'The Art of the Renaissance in Northern Europe')

---

1. S. E. Rasmussen, *Towns and Buildings.*
2. For an introduction to French Renaissance architecture the reader is referred to Nikolaus Pevsner, *An Outline of European Architecture;* and to Pierre Lavedan, *French Architecture.*

the Romans, when settlement contracted back on to the Ile de la Cité, and it was not re-established during the *laissez-faire* growth of the mediaeval city.

PRE-RENAISSANCE PARIS

As the Roman city of Lutetia, Paris was essentially a two-part settlement; the original Gallic inhabitants occupied the present-day Ile de la Cité – strategically a key crossing of the Seine – whilst the Romans themselves preferred the well-drained higher ground of the slopes and summit of mount Ste Geneviève, to the south (Fig. 6.1). Roman Lutetia was divided approximately in two by the line of the Rue St Jacques, which continued across the twin bridges of the arms of the Seine. (There was only a small, unimportant north bank bridgehead settlement.) Little is known of the detailed layout of Lutetia – a blank period in the city's history which it shares with London. The forum has been discovered between the Rue St Jacques and the Boulevard Saint Michel; the theatre and at least three bathing establishments have also been located on the right bank. Pierre Couperie, in his *Paris au fil du temps,* a beautifully meticulous sequence of maps showing the historical evolution of Paris, records that Lutetia occupied 480 acres, and had a population of around 10,000. The right-bank aqueduct delivered 2,000 m³ per day (compared with 75,000 m³ from its counterpart at the comparatively more important Roman city of Lyons). There is also the remarkably well preserved arena, entered today through an inauspicious doorway in the Rue Monge, east of the Rue St Jacques, and incorporated into the little-known, attractively laid out Place Capitan. On the Island, the palace of the governor occupied part of the site of the Palais de Justice, and the Temple of Jupiter had already established a religious focal point, later confirmed by the building of Notre Dame.

Lutetia at most could have been only lightly fortified and during barbarian invasions of Gaul between 253 and 280 the left-bank settlement was destroyed. When re-established the city, which has been known as Paris since about AD 360, was moved on to the Ile de la Cité where an encircling wall could augment the river defences. From this second island nucleus Paris continued to expand until the twentieth century on the basis of clearly defined concentric rings, each delineated by the successive defensive systems as shown on Figure 6.13.

First Renaissance towns in France

Renaissance town planning did not arrive in Paris itself until the early years of the seventeenth century, by which time several new towns had been constructed elsewhere in the country embodying Renaissance principles. Thus Vitry-le-François (Fig. 6.2) was built alongside the Marne for Francis I, from 1545, with a gridiron street structure set within symmetrical fortifications. It was notable for the fact that the four main cross-streets entered the central square at the mid-points of its sides: they did not run alongside the space, in the typical mediaeval bastide fashion. Navarrenx in the south of France followed in 1548, and Philippeville two years later; this latter example was in fact built by the Spanish King, Philip II, to help guard his Dutch frontier with France. Philippeville's central square within a five-pointed fortification system seems a straightforward

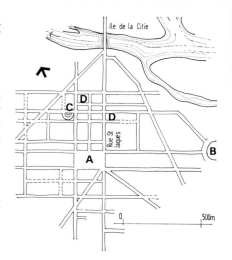

Figure 6.1 – Lutetia the largely conjectural street pattern of the left-bank Roman town. The line of the main north-south route (Rue St Jacques) has been maintained through to the present day. Key: A, the Forum; B, the Arena; C, Theatre; D, Baths.

Figure 6.2 – Vitry-le-François, general plan.

application of Italian 'ideal city' theories discussed on pages 113–8.

Nancy, which in the second half of the eighteenth century was to acquire a unique sequence of Renaissance spaces, was extended from 1588 by adding to the original mediaeval nucleus a regularly laid out *ville-neuve*, designed for Duke Charles III by an Italian architect-planner, Jerome Citoni. Several of the gridiron blocks were left open and half of one of them utilised for the Place d'Alliance. Paul Zucker notes of this square that the absolute regularity of its layout is still emphasised today by a quadrangle of regularly trimmed trees; the houses show identical façades and the parallel horizontals of their ledges, eaves and roof tops tie the area of the square, the streets at its four corners running into the square unconcealed[3]. The form of Nancy in 1645, with the area of the *ville-neuve* fully developed, is given in the view reproduced as Figure 6.20. Citoni's regular gridiron can be seen to be in direct contrast with the organic growth form of the old city. Details of the Renaissance defences of both parts of the city are also clearly illustrated.

The last of the early provincial examples is Charleville, constructed between 1608–20 (by which time the first Parisian urbanism was under way). Charleville is based on a gridiron incorporating a main central space – the Place Ducale – and, originally, six secondary squares (Fig. 6.4). The Place Ducale is considered by some authorities to be the predecessor of the Place Royale (Place des Vosges) in Paris – the prototype European residential precinct. There are aspects of the design of the two squares in common, eg, the arcaded two-storied houses, with their individual roofs, but the Place Ducale is basically a forecourt to the Palais Ducal (now the Hôtel de Ville) and the four streets entering it make it essentially a 'traffic-place' as opposed to the closed, balanced layout of the Place Royale. (As noted later, the Place du Champ à Seille, at Metz, probably had a greater influence on the design of the Place Royale.)

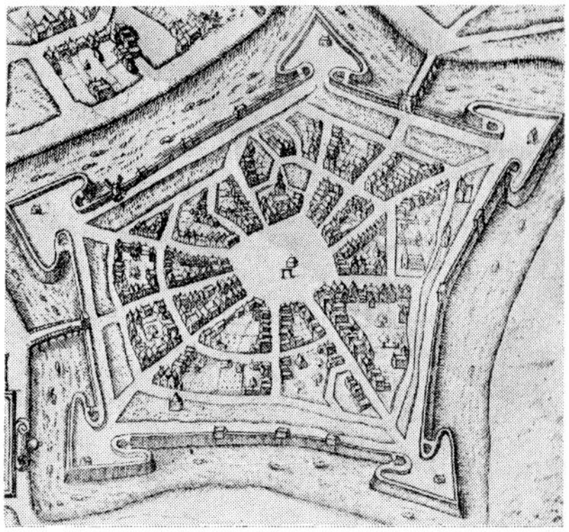

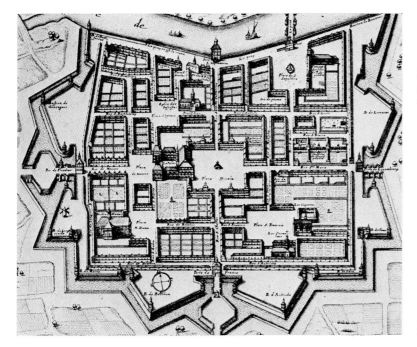

Figure 6.3 – Philippeville, general plan.

Figure 6.4 – Charleville, founded in 1608 on the Meuse in north-eastern France, by Charles of Gonzaga, Duke of Nevers and Mantua, where, according to John Reps, 'the principles of Alberti and particularly those of Palladio found expression in new town planning' *(The Making of Urban America)*. The Place Ducale, one of the influences on the layout of the later Place Royale in Paris, is in the centre of the town.

3. Paul Zucker, *Town and Square.*

Paris: Renaissance urbanism

In the Paris of Francis I there were no public urban spaces of major significance. Notre Dame was approached across a *parvis* far smaller in area than the present-day Place du Parvis Notre Dame. The ill-defined Place de Grève, now part of the Place de l'Hôtel de Ville, was the only other public space of any size. Views along the Seine from the three bridges – the Petit Pont from the southern (left) bank to the Ile de la Cité continued across to the northern bank as the Pont Notre Dame, and the Pont au Change across the northern branch only – were prevented by their being as continuously lined with buildings as the general street pattern. The banks of the Seine were also completely built-up[4].

This does not mean that the city must be thought of as a human ant-hill, quite deprived of light and air. If public open spaces were rare, private ones were many, particularly convent gardens. The town was still half rural. Pierre Lavedan wrote that 'poultry yards, rabbit hutches, stables and fields were close to the houses, and the agricultural calendars carved on the façades of the cathedrals did not represent an escape for the citizen, but an everyday reality'[5]. These open spaces and the often extensive private gardens gradually disappeared during the seventeenth and eighteenth centuries, on occasion as the result of complex property speculation.

Renaissance urbanism in Paris covers the period between Francis I and the end of the eighteenth century. During these two hundred and fifty years little was done to re-structure the mediaeval core and except for establishing the Champs Elysées axis westward and laying out the Grands Boulevards little of note was done which would predetermine the future form of the city. The work of Renaissance urbanists was essentially limited to creating isolated parts of the city, either on undeveloped land within and adjoining the city or by carving development out of the existing fabric. The most important examples of this work are the five royal 'statue' squares described individually later – so called because either a condition for their being constructed or the intention of the promoter required the creation of an appropriately dignified setting for an equestrian statue of the king. Henri IV was honoured once – outside the Place Dauphine; Louis XIII once – within the contemporary Place Royale (renamed later Place des Vosges); Louis XIV twice – the Place des Victoires and the Place Vendôme; and Louis XV once inauspiciously, for his successor was subsequently guillotined there in the Place Louis XV, now known as the Place de la Concorde.

The present-day pattern within the limits of the 1845 fortifications is itself the result of nineteenth century re-structuring. Napoleon I, whose ambition was to make his capital not only the loveliest town which ever had existed, but the loveliest that could exist[6], began the work which culminated in the achievements of the Napoleon III and Haussmann collaboration of the 1850s and 60s.

PONT NEUF AND PLACE DAUPHINE

From its earliest history Paris had only the one crossing over the Seine – the two separate bridges linking the central section of the Ile de la Cité to the north and south banks. During the mediaeval period both these bridges (and the later Pont au Change) were lined with buildings, in an identical manner to London Bridge and

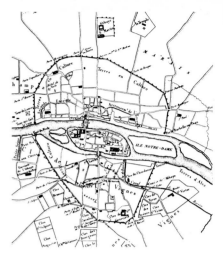

Figure 6.5 – Paris from 1180–1223. The line of the Roman crossing of the Seine has been broken, with a new bridge from the Ile de la Cité to the northern bank further downstream from the old bridge. It is clear from this map that there is a considerable area of land under cultivation within the wall; as the city expanded this land was progressively built over.

4. Construction of the quays alongside the Seine, as shown in Figure 6.6, was mainly carried out during the Renaissance period.

5, 6. Pierre Lavedan, *French Architecture*.

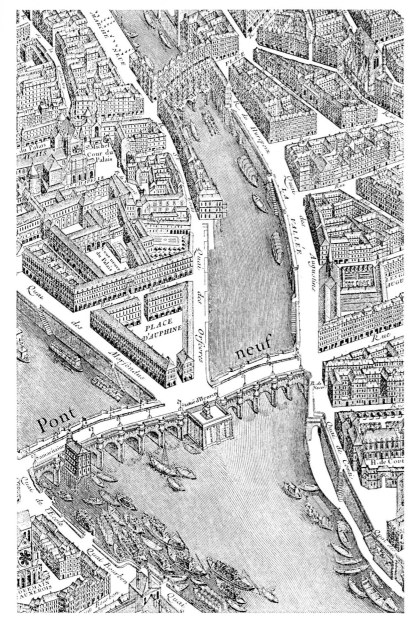

Figure 6.6 – The Place Dauphine and the Pont Neuf from the Turgot plan (1734-9). The old mediaeval bridge lined with buildings, at the top of the view, is in marked contrast to the open character of the Renaissance Pont Neuf. The Rue Dauphine, cut through the gardens of the Couvent des Grands Augustins, continues the line of the bridge to the right.

Figure 6.7 (below) – The 'before-development' counterpart of Figure 6.6, showing the undeveloped marshy islands at the downstream end of the Ile de la Cité which, following the construction of the Pont Neuf, were developed as the Place Dauphine and extensions to the Palais Royal. (From the Legrand map of 1380.)

the present-day Ponte Vecchio over the Arno in Florence. This crossing of the Seine had a national importance as a north-south route in addition to carrying city traffic. As Paris prospered, congestion on the bridges increased so that by the middle of the sixteenth century they were unable to cope. Under Henri III work started in 1578 on a second crossing – the two arms of the Pont Neuf – to connect the downstream end of the Ile de la Cité to the north and south banks. The Pont Neuf was constructed to the designs of Androuet du Cerceau and now belies its name as it is the oldest bridge in Paris, with the original structure still intact beneath restored surfaces. Progress was delayed between 1584 and 1598;

Henri IV finalised the design in 1602 to exclude any buildings on the bridge, apparently as much to provide views of the river as to facilitate traffic. Access to the new bridge from the north was provided by the Rue de la Monnaie, which had been widened under Henri III, but a new road was required on the southern bank. This was constructed as the Rue Dauphine, 11 yards in width across the gardens of the Couvent des Grands Augustins. Objections on the clerics' part were silenced by the king's comment that the money from rents would buy plenty of cabbages[7].

The bridge was finally completed in 1604, opening up the end of the island for development. Before then this area west of the royal palace (now part of the expanded Palais de Justice) consisted of gardens and a number of small islets (Fig. 6.7, taken from the Legrand map of 1380). This western end was given by Henri IV in 1607 to Achille de Harlay, the first president of the Parlement, who laid out on it a new residential *place* in honour of the six-year-old Dauphin, the future Louis XIII. The Place Dauphine was the first of a number of such residential precincts to be built in Paris during the Renaissance, but it was planned along unique lines. The essential difference between this *place* and later ones is not its shape, which tapers with the banks of the island, but the fact that the statue of the king – the erection of which was a condition of the development consent – is located outside the enclosed space. It is on its central axis but stands on the far side of the short length of road linking the two arms of the Pont Neuf. The statue undoubtedly belonged to the *place* and not the city at large, however; although occupying a most prominent site on the end of the island the king was facing the square and not the river[8]. In the middle of the *place's* wider end, facing the royal palace, there was one entrance into the Place Dauphine with the other at the narrow end leading out to the statue. The wider eastern end was demolished in 1874 to create space for an extension to the Palais de Justice, providing it with a new west front. Only the two skilfully restored houses at the apex, opposite the statue, show us the original pattern, but of the square as a whole we can have no idea except through engravings, particularly the fine plan of Paris attributed to Turgot (1734–9)[9].

PLACE DES VOSGES

The site of the Place Royale (renamed Place des Vosges after the Revolution) in the north-east corner of the city near the Charles V wall and close to the Bastille, was originally occupied by the buildings and gardens of the Hôtel des Tournelles, the town house of the Duc d'Orléans. After his assassination in 1407 the property was acquired by the Crown; Louis XII died there in 1515, and following the death of Henri II in a tournament in its grounds his widow, Catherine de Medici, caused the hotel to be demolished. The area remained derelict until Henri IV ceded half of it, temporarily, to Sully in 1594 as a horse market. In 1599 a M. Delisle put forward a proposal to build a *manufacture de velours* (velvet) which was eventually accepted in 1604. The king however had second thoughts and decided that the site was both too big and too important to be used merely as a factory. In the following year therefore a new civic square was formed in front of the completed factory to the south, by the addition of three matching residential terraces, possibly intended to house its operatives[10].

24 December 1643 – I went with some company to see some remarkable places without the city; as the Isle, and how it is encompassed by the river Seine and the Ouse. The city is divided into three parts, whereof the town is greatest. The city lies between it and the University in form of an island. Over the Seine is a stately bridge called Pont Neuf, begun by Henry III, in 1578, finished by Henry IV his successor. It is all of hewn free-stone found under the streets, but more plentifully at Montmartre, and consists of twelve arches, in the midst of which ends the point of an island, on which are built handsome artificers houses. There is one large passage for coaches, and two for foot-passengers three or four feet higher, and of convenient breadth for eight or ten to go a-breast. On the middle of this stately bridge, on one side stands the famous statue of Henry the Great on horseback, exceeding the natural proportion by much; and, on the four faces of a stately pedestal (which is composed of various sorts of polished marbles and rich mouldings), inscriptions of his victories and most signal actions are engraven in brass. The statue and horse are of copper, the work of the great John di Bologna, and sent from Florence by Ferdinand the First, and Cosmo the Second, uncle and cousin to Mary de Medicis, the wife of King Henry, whose statue it represents. The place where it is erected is inclosed with a strong and beautiful grate of iron, about which there are always mountebanks showing their feats to idle passengers. From hence is a rare prospect towards the Louvre and suburbs of St Germains, the Isle du Palais, and Notre Dame. At the foot of this bridge is a water-house, on the front whereof, at a great height, is the story of Our Saviour and the woman of Samaria pouring water out of a bucket. Above, is a very rare dial of several motions, with a chime, &c. The water is conveyed by huge wheels, pumps, and other engines, from the river beneath. The confluence of the people and multitude of coaches passing every moment over the bridge, to a new spectator is an agreeable diversion.
(John Evelyn, 'Diary')

---

7. Pierre Lavedan, *Histoire de l'urbanisme; Renaissance et temps modernes.*
8, 9. Pierre Lavedan, *French Architecture.*
10. Pierre Lavedan, *Histoire de l'urbanisme; Renaissance et temps modernes.*

The factory closed (or was closed) in 1606 and on its site an identical fourth, northern, side to the square was built. As finally completed in 1612 the Place Royale is of great significance in European urban history as the prototype of the residential square. In contrast to the previously generally accepted method of fronting houses on to multi-purpose traffic streets, the built-form is used in a residential square to enclose a space from which extraneous traffic is excluded, or at least discouraged. Not content with this revolutionary plan form, the royal urbanist also decreed that all the buildings facing into the space were to be of the same elevational design. Jean-Pierre Babelon[11] in his contribution to *L'Urbanisme de Paris et de l'Europe 1600–1680* considers it probable that the ordered, arcaded design of the mediaeval Place du Champ à Seille at Metz, which Henri IV visited in March 1603, influenced him in approving the design of the Place Royale.

The *place* was formed of 38 houses behind uniformly designed elevations. In the centre of the north and south sides, before the later roadway was brought in across the northern side, taller, dominant bays contained the only two arched entrances into the *place*. The entrance building on the southern side, the Pavillon du Roi, was intended by Henri IV for his own use but he died in 1610, two years before completion of the *place*. Above an arcaded ground floor, which gave sheltered entrance to the houses and provided a continuous under-cover connection between them, were two upper floors capped by steep slate-finished individual roofs containing a row of dormer windows.

Construction of the Place Royale may also have been of great social significance. Previously the nobility had lived in country châteaux or in hôtels in various parts of the city. The Place des Vosges, as Rasmussen says, can be regarded as a visible effort to bring the aristocracy under the control of an integrating idea, that of forming a background for the monarchy; instead of a galaxy of petty princes opposing each other and the King, they were now to become part of the pageantry of the court[12].

The centre of the *place*, between the buildings, was originally kept as a clear, gravelled space. Here the traditional use of the area as a tournament ground was continued for some years, with the upper floor windows of the houses providing direct views of the festivities. In 1639 Cardinal Richelieu, who lived at No. 21 for a period, presented an equestrian statue of Louis XIII for the central position and thereby superimposed on the residential function the character of a statue-square. With the addition to the central space of formal landscaping, based on fenced-in areas of lawn and symmetrically planted tree groupings, the character of the *place* was again modified, and the statue lost its dominant rôle. After an initial period when it was the focus of Parisian society, the fortunes of the Place des Vosges slowly declined; more modern residential areas arose, until it became no more than a feature in a slum housing district[13] – always however with the quality of the housing tempered by the attractively planted central open space, which has in recent years proved a main reason for the steady regeneration of the Place des Vosges. The current renewal programme for the whole of the Marais district could well further this renaissance of its fortunes and turn it once more into a fashionable residential district.

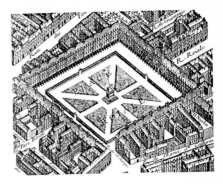

Figure 6.8 – The Place Royale (1605–12), renamed Place des Vosges after the Revolution, the prototype of the residential square from which extraneous traffic is excluded. The drawing shows the central space with the first stage of the landscaping work completed (the formal tree-planting is of a later date) and a new street access formed into the square at the bottom corner.

Within three years of Henri IV's death the treasury funds which had accumulated, amounting to nearly twenty million livres, were totally exhausted; during the same period expenditure rose by four million and revenues declined by five. The country was bankrupt. The collapse was disguised by exhibitions of pomp and circumstance which mesmerized contemporaries. One such display was organised to celebrate the engagement of Louis XIII in 1612. The Place Royale was just completed and its noble residents were able to sit at their windows and for three days at Easter enjoy the celebrations . . . the court, the nobility and fifty thousand people sat on scaffolds in the square to watch the gyrations of the nobly comparisoned houses. the fantastic floats drawn by reindeer and lions. the illuminations. fireworks and volleys of musketry and their ears were stunned by the salvoes overheard of one hundred cannon from the Bastille.
(D. P. O'Connell, 'Richelieu')

11. Jean-Pierre Babelon, *L'Urbanisme d'Henri IV et de Sully à Paris* contributed to *L'Urbanisme de Paris et de l'Europe 1600–1680*. edited by Pierre Francastel, Editions Klincksieck, Paris, 1969.
12. S. E. Rasmussen, *Towns and Buildings*.
13. See also the more extreme fate suffered by London's Covent Garden Piazza, work on which was commenced some 20 years after the Place Royale (page 186).

PLACE DES VICTOIRES

This circular *place* originated in a proposal by the Maréchal de la Feuillade to develop a site near the north-east corner of the Palais Royal gardens. The centre-piece of his scheme was a statue of Louis XIV, surrounded by four groups of lanterns, illuminated at night and therefore one of the earliest examples of street lighting. In 1687, when the King formally inaugurated the Place des Victoires, only a few of the houses were completed and the empty sites of the remainder had to be filled in with painted canvas screens.

Jules-Hardouin Mansart was responsible for the layout and design of the uniform façade around the circumference of the space. Originally there were six minor streets entering the *place*, only two of which constituted an axis across it, but, as part of extensive alterations it has suffered, the Rue Etienne Marcel was added in 1883 as a major traffic route. Only one sector of the building circumference has survived in anything like its original form.

In spite of its identical façades, Zucker observes that, 'the Place des Victoires does not achieve the impression of a closed square. Its openings to the surrounding streets (an anticipation of the typical *place percée* of the eighteenth century) are too numerous. It was in all likelihood just this connection between the square and its neighbourhood that made the Place des Victoires so much appreciated, especially by the theoreticians of the second part of the eighteenth century'[14].

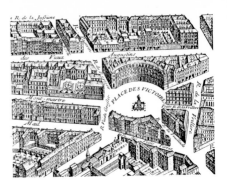

Figure 6.9 – The Place des Victoires (1687) designed by J.-H. Mansart. Although a carefully organised design in itself, there is clearly no considered relationship between the Renaissance space and the surrounding urban structure.

PLACE VENDÔME

The early history of this residential *place* north of the Tuileries Gardens beyond the Rue de Rivoli and the Rue St Honoré is a fascinating record of the problems which can face speculative property developers. As with many later schemes the initial idea was to realise the potential development value of land in an expanding urban area. The site was that of the impoverished Duc de Vendôme's town house and garden. After his death in 1670 these had to be set against his debts. Jules-Hardouin Mansart, a shrewd businessman as well as one of the leading French architects of the period, undertook, together with a number of financiers, to redevelop the site with leasable houses.

His first scheme soon ran into financial difficulties. Mansart subsequently put the project into the hands of Louvois, a wealthy courtier. But the Superintendent of Buildings meanwhile decided that instead of the proposed residential square the site should be used for a monumental statue-square dedicated to the glory of Louis XIV. Surrounding buildings were to include, among other prestige uses, various academies, a new national library, the Royal Mint and residences for foreign ambassadors. Louvois acquiesced in this; he was himself fired with an ambition to surpass the aspirations of the Duc de Feuillade, a rival courtier, to build his Place des Victoires. The site of the Hôtel Vendôme and its grounds, as well as the adjoining property of the Couvent des Capucines, was finally acquired in 1685. Shortly afterwards however the untimely death of Louvois removed the second of Mansart's clients and the scheme again fell into abeyance.

After further attempts to raise the necessary finances the land was ceded to the municipality of Paris in 1698. Mansart was able to maintain his professional involvement and finally in that year drew

Place Vendôme. Paris (previously Louis-le-Grand Square). Here the streams of architecture and town-planning have joined to form a lake of repose in the bristling town compressed within its military walls; an architectural fashion owing much to the interior decorator and the scenic designer flowered in the salons and the anterooms. Salons to the glory of kings and princes. A fashion that soon flourished in the provinces, abroad, wherever courts were held and courtiers dwelt.
(Le Corbusier, 'Concerning Town Planning')

14. Paul Zucker, *Town and Square.*

up outline plans of what was to become the present-day *place*. This was named the Place Louis XIV in honour of the King in 1699 and an immense equestrian statue was unveiled to his glory in the centre of the future *place*. There were, however, still no buildings and great difficulty in interesting potential tenants. Eventually, in desperation, the elevations surrounding the *place* were constructed in 1702 and the plots behind leased off over a period of years, in units of elevational bays as required by the different tenants. This unprecedented development procedure lasted until 1720.

The plan of the Place Vendôme constitutes a rectangle with its corners cut off, thus creating an octagonal effect. The enclosing buildings are of three storeys with an additional row of dormer windows in the uniform roofs. The total height was specifically limited so as to be lower than the 54 ft-high statue. In the centres of its shorter sides two relatively narrow streets lead from the *place*. Originally these outlets were only for minor traffic access and each terminated in vista-closing buildings short distances from the *place*. Later, however, they were both extended through to the main city network – as the Rue Castiglione and the Rue de la Paix. The centres of the two long sides of the *place* are emphasised by projecting pediments and columns and similar treatment is given to the four corners. The equestrian statue, perfectly scaled to suit the proportions of the *place*, was destroyed during the Revolution. Its replacement, the 144 ft-high Colonne d'Austerlitz, erected in 1810 by Napoleon, now seems obtrusive and out of scale.

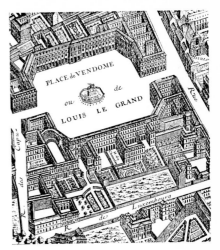

Figure 6.10 – The Place Vendôme (1670–1720) designed by J.-H. Mansart. The contrast between the ordered central space and the unco-ordinated buildings behind the elevations is typical of the way in which Renaissance examples of urban design exist as spatial 'islands' in otherwise uncontrolled growth contexts.

THE ILE ST LOUIS

At the beginning of the seventeenth century the area of the Ile St Louis was undeveloped and divided into two islets by a ditch which marked where the city wall continued across it. In 1609 a property group composed of a public works contractor, Christophe Marie, and two financiers, Le Regrattier and Poulletier, proposed to develop the islands. In return for constructing quays around the perimeter of the reunited halves of the Ile St Louis, and two new bridges, they were given the right to lease the building plots and to receive the rents for a period of sixty years. Royal assent to the scheme was given by Louis XIII in 1627 and by 1664 the work of preparing the island for housing purposes had been completed. It quickly became a desirable residential quarter with a distinctive character, which it still largely retains today.

CHAMPS ELYSEES

Catherine de Medici, widow of Henri II, tired of living in the cramped, enclosed courtyards of the Louvre, commissioned Philibert Delorme in 1563 to build a new palace outside the walls, with a spacious Italian style garden extending to the west. This was the Tuileries Palace, unfinished when Catherine died in 1568, and completed by Henri IV and Louis XIII. Henri linked the new palace to the Louvre by the Galerie du Bord de l'Eau. In the nineteenth century, under Napoleon I, the Grande Galerie du Nord was started along the south side of the Rue de Rivoli, thus creating an immense courtyard. This northern side was completed under Napoleon III between 1850 and 1857 but in 1871 the revolutionary Communards fired the Tuileries, leaving it a smouldering ruin. The Louvre itself was fortunate to escape; the damaged western ends of its north and

The Ile St Louis is what it always was: a piece of unified town-planning which happened to get built at one of the noblest moments in the evolution of French architecture; and as it has been relatively little altered it still presents, on every hand, a look of grand and simple amenity. If much of it is a little shabby, we are reminded of how Baudelaire, one of its admirer-citizens, used to rub his suits with emery-paper in order to remove that look of newness 'si cher au philistin'. as Gautier says, 'et si désagréable pour le vrai gentleman'.
Even ten years ago life on the Ile St Louis had still a note of discretion and retirement. The telephone alone seemed to link the island to the city proper: omnibus and Metro were excluded, dogs went to sleep in the middle of the main street, and if you chose to dream the day away by the water's edge nothing and nobody would disturb you. To-day this is not quite the case. The island has been 'discovered'. Tenants of long standing dread the day when easy money will outwit the law and send them packing from their apartments. The insides are being ripped out of old houses for the sake of an 'amusing' interior . . . Landlords cannot be blamed if they want to get something more than a peppercorn rent for some of the most delectable properties in Europe. Much of the Ile St Louis is in very bad condition and new money may prevent it from becoming. as it were. the Chioggia of Paris. And the island will in any case resist the attempt to 'hot it up': certain places simply cannot be vulgarised. and one of them is the Ile St Louis.
(John Russell. 'Paris')

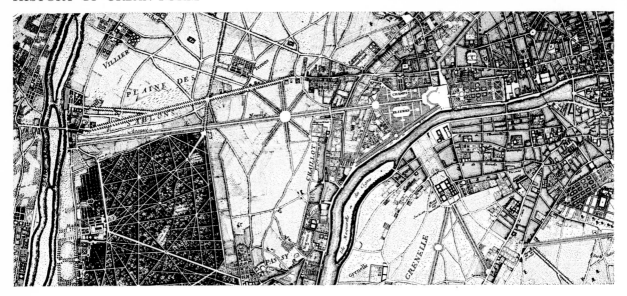

Figure 6.11 – Paris, a section of the beautifully engraved map of 1740 showing the extent of the urban area and the line of the westward axis of the Champs Elysées. (Refer to Figure 6.12 for identification of parts of the city.) The Bois de Boulogne bottom left, is shown with the formal landscaping layout, which was replaced by the present-day naturalistic design, under Haussmann, in the 1850s and 60s.

south wings were restored in 1873–78, giving the present-day open-ended courtyard form.

At the end of the sixteenth century the Tuileries Palace and Gardens, though self-contained, still had an essentially directionless layout; there was no hint of the dramatic westward thrust to follow. For the first time Parisian society could take attractive open-air recreation, enjoying the fountains, labyrinth and grotto.

But greater developments westward were to follow. Their first signs are seen in the Cours-la-Reine, created in 1616 for Marie de Medici. This did not extend the axis of the Tuileries Gardens west from the palace, however, but skirted the Seine as far as the site of the later Place d'Alma, at an angle to this axis. The Champs Elysées, with its dramatic perspective up the gentle slope of the Butte de Chaillot to the Place de l'Etoile, and the equally magnificent continuation down the far side to the bridge at Neuilly, and beyond, was begun by Le Nôtre, for Colbert in 1667 (Figs. 6.11 and 6.12).

The result of Le Nôtre's replanning are summarised by Edmund Bacon; the aim was 'to transform the whole nature of the Tuileries garden design from static to dynamic, with the thrust of the axis generated within the garden extended outward by the Avenue des Tuileries, now the Champs Elysées. Not yet present was the Place de la Concorde, which was later to occupy the open ground between the Tuileries garden wall and the planted area of the Champs Elysées and which connected the central Tuileries axis both with the area to the west and across the river Seine'[15]. Earlier in his perceptive analysis of the development of Paris Bacon observes that with this scheme 'an entirely new breadth and freedom have been introduced in the art of civic design. The outward thrust of the movement systems, generated from firm building masses, penetrates further and further into countryside. It simulates similar axial thrusts originating in the châteaux and palaces about Paris, which also extend and intertwine, creating in the late eighteenth and early nineteenth century a form of regional development unique in the history of city building'[16].

15, 16. Edmund Bacon, *Design of Cities*.

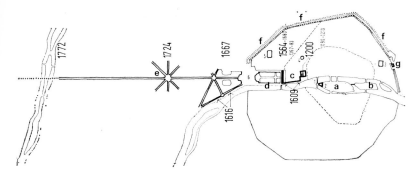

Figure 6.12 – A diagrammatic plan showing successive stages in the western expansion of Paris along the axis of the Champs Elysées to the bridge at Neuilly and beyond.
Key: a, Ile de la Cité; b, Ile St Louis; c, the Louvre; d, the Tuileries Gardens; e, the Arc de Triomphe location on the Butte de Chaillot; f, the line of the Grands Boulevards; g, the Bastille, 1, Pont Neuf; 2, Place Dauphine; 3, Place des Vosges; 4, Place des Victoires; 5, Place Vendôme; 6, site of the Place de la Concorde.

By 1709 extensive tree planting had matured sufficiently for the general area to become known as the 'Champs Elysées'. In 1724 the main axial avenue was extended as far as the top of the Butte de Chaillot, by the Duc d'Antin, director of the royal gardens. The further extension west down to the bridge at Neuilly by 1772 was the work of his successor, the Marquis de Marigny. The top of the Butte de Chaillot is shown on the 1740 map as a *rond-point* of eight avenues, set in the middle of an area of open fields (Fig. 6.11). In 1774 Soufflot lowered the height of the hill by five yards, to ease the gradient. The Arc de Triomphe, set in the centre of the Place de l'Etoile, was originally proposed by Napoleon I in 1806 and was completed in 1836 by Louis-Philippe. The present-day form of the Place de l'Etoile, with its twelve radiating streets, was created by Haussmann for Napoleon III from 1854 onwards: Hittorff was architect for the surrounding buildings[17].

GRANDS BOULEVARDS

By 1660 the fortifications around most of northern Paris, between the Bastille in the east and the present-day site of the Madeleine in the west, were in poor repair. Internal peace in France and military successes, culminating in the campaigns of Louis XIV, which established strong frontier defences, had reduced the need for complex city fortifications. This enabled those of Paris to be demolished.

Between the Bastille and the Porte St Denis there was a section of the wall first built by Charles V (1363–83). The western portion had been constructed under Louis XIII (1610–43) for an extension of the city which included the Tuileries Gardens. The ground occupied by the walls and earthworks was cleared and levelled to form a linear open space some 5½ km in length. Within this a central drive-way, wide enough for four lanes of carriages, was flanked by pedestrian *contre-allées*, each planted with double rows of trees. This work was completed in 1705 with a number of *arcs de triomphe*, including a new Porte St Denis (1672), marking the old entrances to the city. The term boulevard gradually became applied to this linear space as a corruption of, says Rasmussen, the nordic *bulvirke* (bulwark) which means a palisade – a mediaeval form of defence used before the employment of real walls and ramparts; the boulevard is the line of the fortifications itself but when these were converted into wide tree-lined streets the designation boulevard was kept and today the word means simply a broad tree-lined avenue[18].

Although not forming a physical barrier, the line of the boulevards continued to mark the limits of Paris; beyond them building was

*Under Louis XV, Paris, pushing outwards, had swallowed up the limits traced by Charles V in the fourteenth century and their western extension of 1631 under Louis XIII. The hated wall of the Farmers General, built in 1785 as a customs barrier with imposing monumental gates, took in a vast new area, stretching round the western and northern heights of Passy, Chaillot, Belleville, and Menilmontant, including – south of the river – the Faubourgs Saint-Victor, Saint-Marceau, Saint-Jacques, and Saint-Germain, and curving back round the vast Champ de Mars. At the end of the eighteenth century much of this new territory was not yet built up; within the barrier, beyond the Bastille and the Temple in the East, were fields and scattered houses with their gardens. In the west the Champs Elysées were woodlands crossed by roads and wandering paths, and the Champ de Mars a huge open space. Paris proper still huddled together within the boulevards that marked the site of its former fortifications, a solid agglomeration of high, closely-packed, terraced houses separated by winding, narrow streets and alleys, noisy with street cries, busy with passers-by, crowded and dangerous with carriages and wagons of all kinds, strewn with rubbish and filth lying about in heaps or carried along in the torrents of water pouring after a storm down the wide gutters, across which pedestrians could only pass dry-shod by little plank bridges.
(Alfred Cobban, 'A History of Modern France')*

17. See David H. Pinkney, *Napoleon III and the Rebuilding of Paris*, for a description of the detail planning of this perhaps best known Parisian *place* where, 'to assure the symmetry of the Place de l'Etoile the Prefect (Haussmann) located the radiating streets so that uniformly shaped building lots remained between every pair of streets. Eight of the lots were identical in size, and the four on the opposite sides of the Avenue Kléber and the Avenue de Wagram were double size. An imperial decree required that the buildings on these lots should have uniform stone facades set off by lawns and that the lawns be separated from the street by decorative iron fences, identical before all the buildings. To provide access to these houses, whose monumental fronts must not be marred by entrances, Haussmann built a circular street around the back of the lots. The Prefect was proud of his development of the Place de l'Etoile and considered it one of the most successful undertakings of his administration.'
18. S. E. Rasmussen, *Towns and Buildings*.

forbidden. The boulevards were put to no regular use until around 1750 when, probably as a result of the maturing of the landscaping, they became fashionable open-air recreation areas – the scene of the *promenade à la mode*. The main carriage-way was paved in 1778 and asphalt all-weather pavements were provided in 1838.

When the boulevards were built up, the western part became a fashionable housing district, in contrast to the eastern sections which retained their leisure functions, now embodied in innumerable cafés, restaurants and theatres. Under Haussmann many changes were made to the form of the boulevards. The Place de l'Opéra and the Place de la République were created and the eastern section completely reconstructed. Today the Grands Boulevards are divided into three distinct sections: to the west the Boulevards de la Madeleine, des Capucines, des Italiens and de Montmartre are lined with high-class shops, boutiques, cinemas, restaurants and cafés, and many prestige offices; east to the Place de la République all the uses are of a significantly lower quality with diminished tourist interest; whilst further east again towards the Place de la Bastille there are only residential and commercial uses.

Many other towns and cities on the continent of Europe, following the early example of Paris, have benefited from this reversion to peaceful purposes of their encircling fortification zones. Such resulting urban structures incorporate inner ring boulevards still able to provide invaluable traffic routes around the city centre, and serve in many instances as attractive open spaces. Vienna and Cologne are particularly clear examples of this radial-concentric growth which characterises continental European cities. Such a pattern is in marked contrast to the radial-ribbon – with infilling – tendencies that are the general rule in Great Britain, where urban defences were not required after the early Middle Ages. Where mediaeval town walls were retained in Britain to define city limits for one purpose or another the strip of land they occupied was normally too narrow to enable new roads and linear open spaces to take their place. Mediaeval walls in Britain dated from a period before the age of effective offensive artillery; they were not supplemented by the extensive earthworks needed in fortifications after the fifteenth century. Such mediaeval open fire-zones as had been maintained were comparatively small and were encroached upon to an extent not permitted on the continent[19].

Two further encircling walls were set around Paris. The first was the Wall of the Farmers General, 23 km in length, built under Louis XVI not for defensive purposes but rather to facilitate the collection of taxes on goods entering and leaving the city. The second was the last of the defensive systems constructed for the city: that by Thiers between 1840 and 1845. In turn both these rings were replaced by boulevards; those replacing the farmers general wall were mainly to the north of the Seine; those of the 1840–45 fortifications form a complete ring of *boulevards extérieurs* at an average distance of 5 km from the city centre[20].

PLACE DE LA CONCORDE

Originally named the Place Louis XV, this vast square at the eastern end of the Champs Elysées was built to the designs of Jacques-Ange Gabriel (1698–1782) between 1755 and 1775. A competition had been held to obtain plans for a suitable setting for an

Paris, at the end of the eighteenth century, was still in some respects a homogeneous city. Though there were faubourgs like Saint-Antoine and Saint-Marceau, inhabited mainly by small masters and their journeymen, and new wealthy quarters like the Faubourg Saint-Germain, in much of older Paris, the homes of the well-to-do, of the middling people and of the poor existed under the same roof. It might also be said that class stratification was vertical, the rich and the poor entering by the same door, the former to mount by a short and broad staircase to the impressive apartments of the first floor, the latter to climb high up by ever narrowing stairs till they reached the attics in the mansard roof. (Alfred Cobban, 'A History of Modern France')

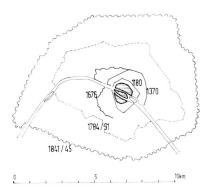

Figure 6.13 – Paris the successive rings of fortifications which determined the city's growth pattern from the twelfth to the nineteenth centuries. The wall of 1784–91 is the customs barrier of the Fermiers Généraux. (Compare with diagrams of London's growth pattern drawn to the same scale, as Figures 8.1 and 8.27)

19. See page 188 for John Stow's eye-witness account of the state of disrepair of London Wall in 1603.

20. The line of *boulevards exterieurs* – a natural 'plane of weakness' running through the structure of Paris – has been uncontroversially converted, to a great extent, into the city's ring motorway system. At the same time London's motorway box, which in contrast would run generally against the urban grain, has aroused vehement political opposition and may never be completed.

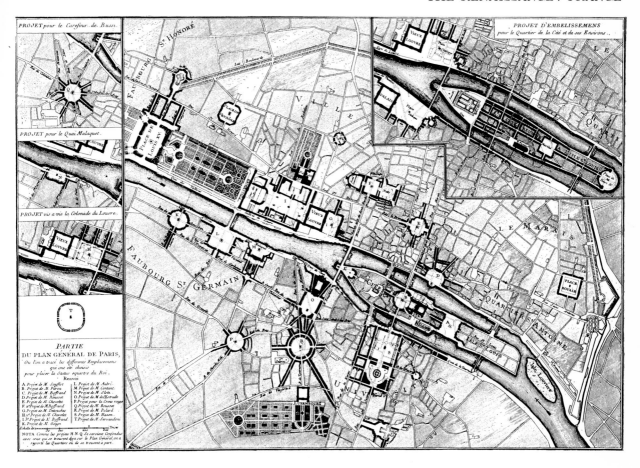

Figure 6.14 – Paris, competiton entries for the design of the 'statue-square' in honour of Louis XV plotted on a map of the city of 1765. The key at the bottom left identifies the locations proposed by individual architects; the inset top right shows a proposal to unify the Ile de la Cité and the Ile St Louis on the basis of a regularised street pattern with a symmetrical replica of the Louvre built on the left bank of the Seine. Neither this grandiose project, nor the proposal for the downstream end of the Ile de la Cité in the general map, shows any respect for the existing Place Dauphine. (Refer to Figure 6.12 for identification of parts of the city.)

equestrian statue of the king that had been commissioned by the city of Paris from the sculptor Bouchardon. Over sixty architects submitted their proposals for the location and treatment of the proposed statue-square. Their collected designs, published in 1765 in a volume of engravings, *Monuments érigés à la gloire de Louis XV,* present a fascinating record of contemporary urban thought. The extract from this book shows a number of the proposals plotted on to the map of the city (Fig. 6.14).

Gabriel was the winner of the competition. He chose as his location for the statue the extensive, abandoned terrace which lay between the Tuileries Gardens and the Champs Elysées. On the Turgot map of 1734–39 (the section reproduced as Fig. 6.16 on page 148), this area appears as an informally used transition-space. It had a typically organic path pattern unaffected, surprisingly, by continuation of either the main Champs Elysées axis or the secondary Cours-la-Reine.

The royal squares of the seventeenth century were essentially closed spaces : landscape elements, infrequently used, and then only in minor rôles, were dominated by the architectural built-form. During the eighteenth century, says Zucker, open space, in contrast to closed space, was the new ideal and its realisation was assured by the inclusion of nature; out of these sentiments the king presented the city of Paris with the open land adjacent to the Jardin

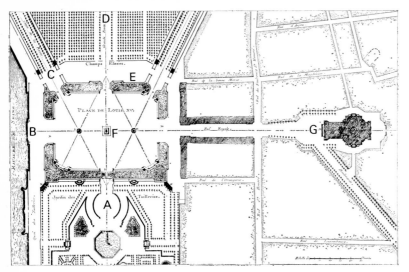

Figure 6.15 – The Place de la Concorde, originally the Place Louis XV, designed by Jacques-Ange Gabriel on the space between the Tuileries Gardens and the axis of the Champs Elysées. This plan is the 'after-development' counterpart of the land as shown in Figure 6.16. Key: A, Tuilieries Gardens; B, the future Pont de la Concorde; C, Cours-la-Reine; D, Champs Elysées axis; E, the sections of *fosse* with bridges over; F, statue of Louis XV (replaced by the present day obelisk); G, the Madeleine Church.

Figure 6.16 – Section of the Turgot plan (1734-9). At the top can be seen the Louvre; and the Tuileries Palace at right-angles to the river at the end of the Pont Royal. Below the Tuileries, destroyed in 1871 (to the west), the central section of the drawing shows the Tuileries Gardens, with the main axis leading further west to the Champs Elysées, across the derelict area later to become the Place de la Concorde.

des Tuileries, the river Seine and the Champs Elysées and the quarter around the projected church of the Madeleine. Thus the new square could expand on three sides into open space[21].

Gabriel's first problem was to define the *place* without separating it from the existing landscaped spaces to the west. His second problem was to organise a planned relationship of the four existing axes which crossed the site – those of the Tuileries Gardens/Champs Elysées and the Rue Royal (set out in 1732), and those of the Cours-la-Reine and its counterpart to the north of the Champs Elysées. In 1755 work started when the statue of Louis XV was erected at the intersection of the first two of these axes.

In the original plan landscape elements had played a more important space-defining rôle than buildings, which formed only the northern side of the *place*. The basis of Gabriel's layout was a 15 ft-deep fosse, or ditch, with a surrounding balustrade: this defined the main central space. The corners were cut off, creating an octagonal effect, similar in shape to the Place Vendôme. This 'angle' treatment was to provide entries into the *place* for the Cours-la-Reine and its counterpart in the north-west corner. With axial entrances in the centres of the four sides, these were taken across the ditch by a total of six bridges. The ditch was some 60 ft in width and grassed at the bottom. In 1854 it was filled in and the Place de la Concorde acquired its present-day appearance.

Along the northern side Gabriel built the Garde-Meubles between 1760 and 1765 – two identical buildings with elevations respecting those of Perrault's Louvre. These buildings are symmetrically planned on either side of the Rue Royale axis. To the east the *place* is separated from the Tuileries Gardens by an imposing terrace and balustrade. As at the Place Vendôme only the façades of the Garde-Meubles were built at first: completion of the buildings behind took many more years. This speculative process was repeated in 1805, when the Rue de Rivoli was formed to the east; the architects of Napoleon I, Percier and Fontaine, designed only the architectural part of the façades, whose acceptance and construction was binding upon the purchasers[22]. The statue of Louis XV was demolished in

21. Paul Zucker, *Town and Square*.
22. Pierre Lavedan, *French Architecture*.

1792 during the Revolution. Louis XVI went to the guillotine on 21 January 1793 in the north-west corner of his father's *place*, then renamed the Place de la Révolution.

The Madeleine Church was started in 1764. After a chequered early history, during which it was considered for a number of religious and secular functions, it survived proposals in 1837 to replace it by the first railway station in Paris and was consecrated in 1842. The imposing Pont de la Concorde across the Seine, on the Madeleine/Rue Royale/Place de la Concorde axis, was completed in 1790. The axial view is terminated by the dome of the Palais Bourbon (the Chamber of Deputies) on the left bank. The massive obelisk from Luxor, acquired from Egypt by Charles X, was erected in 1836 on what was earlier the site of the central statue. In 1854 Hittorff added two fountains, as originally had been proposed by Gabriel, on either side of the obelisk, at points where the axes of the Cours-la-Reine and its matching route in the north-west corner intersect with the Madeleine/Pont de la Concorde axis (Fig. 6.15).

Commencing with the palace and gardens for Catherine de Medici in 1563 the creation of this part of Paris took over 250 years. It has been shown that during this time successive clients, both royal and civic, employing a sequence of professional advisers, respected their inheritence from the past and contributed towards the eventual realisation of one of history's most magnificently organised urban achievements.

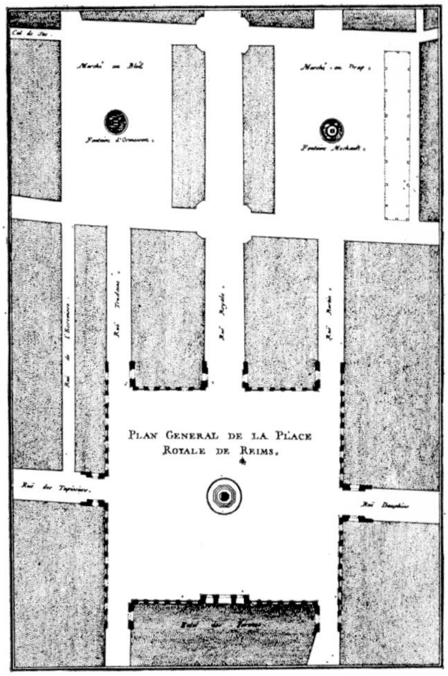

Provincial Renaissance urbanism

Statue squares were built in many of the leading provincial cities of France, and were proposed for others. Those examples in Rheims, Rouen, Nancy (together with the related sequence of eighteenth-century spaces), Bordeaux and Rennes are described below.

During the Renaissance, France had effectively no need for new, ordinary commercial-function towns, but a number of new towns were planned and constructed for other particular purposes. Included amongst these towns, and also described in this chapter, are two service-towns : Richelieu and Versailles (both of which represent something of a monument to the men who were the inspirational force behind their building – Richelieu and Louis XIV) and Neuf Brisach, one of the late seventeenth and early eighteenth century frontier fortresses built by Vauban, a man who could well be considered the outstanding engineer-urbanist of Renaissance Europe.

RHEIMS AND ROUEN

The Place Royale at Rheims (1756–60) originally contained a statue of Louis XV, and was designed as part of a plan to reconstruct a large area of the city centre. A new street, the Rue Royale (now the Rue Colbert) was created as the axial link between the existing square in front of the Hôtel de Ville and the Place Royale in front of the new Hôtel des Fermes. On either side of this axis are two smaller market squares (Fig. 6.17).

Patte's *Monuments* includes a project by Lecarpentier for a large statue-square to Louis XV in front of the Hôtel de Ville in Rouen, but this skilful proposal to regularise the entry points of streets in from the rest of the city was never realised (Fig. 6.18).

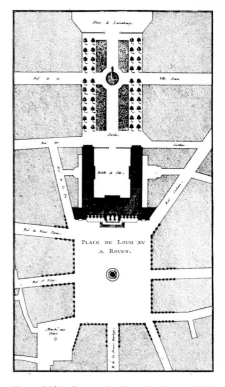

Figure 6.17 – Rheims, the Place Royale and the related streets and spaces in the centre of the city.

Figure 6.18 – Rouen, the Place Royale, a skilful theoretical exercise in planning an ordered relationship between existing streets and the new space.

NANCY

Nancy, the ancient capital of Lorraine, some 220 miles east of Paris on the main route to Strasbourg, was captured by the French in 1633. At that time the city was divided into two distinct parts, each with its own formidable defensive system. The old mediaeval town to the north, its street pattern typically formless and organic, constituted in effect the citadel; the ordered, gridiron-based Renaissance *ville-neuve* was to the south (Fig. 6.20). In 1697, before returning the city to the Dukes of Lorraine, Louis XIV ordered the defences to be completely demolished. Both parts thus became surrounded, and separated, by areas of derelict fortifications and open fire-zones.

Figure 6.19 – Nancy, an aerial view of the sequence of eighteenth century spaces seen from the west across the mediaeval city; the cathedral is in the foreground. The Place Stanislaus is to the top right.

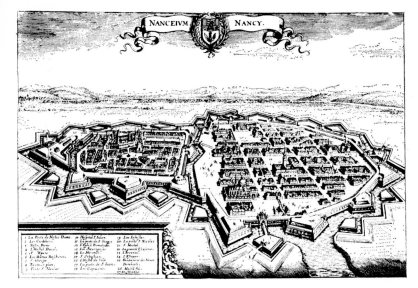

Figure 6.20 – Nancy in 1645, seen from the west, with the mediaeval city to the left. (This view has the reverse orientation from the general plan as Figure 6.21.)

In 1736, having again taken possession of the city, Louis XV gave Nancy to his son-in-law, Stanislaus Leczinski, ex-King of Poland. Stanislaus was to prove an enlightened ruler, aware of planning deficiencies of his city in the context of urban progress during the three preceding centuries. The problem was essentially that of uniting the two parts, mediaeval and Renaissance, into one integrated urban structure. Here Stanislaus was fortunate to find a gifted architect-planner, Héré de Corny (1705–63), as his executive collaborator. De Corny was commissioned in 1753 and developed a scheme in several parts (its outline is superimposed on the existing city in Fig. 6.21). A new statue-square to Louis XV – now the Place Stanislaus – is the meeting point of two axial developments. The first of these axes provided a new main east-west route across Nancy, just within the line of the fortifications in the *ville-neuve*. Running

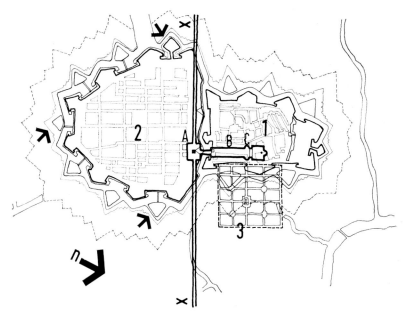

Figure 6.21 – General plan of Nancy showing the relationship of the eighteenth century redevelopment with the other parts of the city. The late sixteenth century Renaissance *ville-neuve* is to the left of the new east-west axis; the mediaeval city is to the right. This general plan and the detail arrangement of the eighteenth century spaces, as Figure 6.22, have the same orientation. Key: A, Place Royale; B, Place de la Carrière; C, the Hemicycle; 1, the mediaeval city; 2, the *ville-neuve* of the seventeenth century; 3, the later public park; X–X, the new main cross-axis.

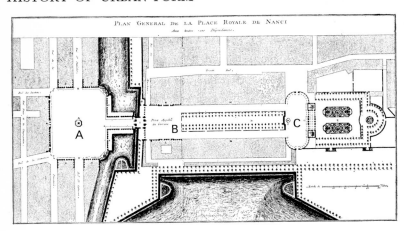

PLAN GENERAL DE LA PLACE ROYALE DE NANCI

Figure 6.22 – Nancy, the detail plan of the Place Royale (Place Stanislaus), and the related spaces planned by Héré de Corny. A part of the defensive moat is shown at the bottom of the plan. Key: A, Place Royale; B, Place de la Carrière; C, the Hemicycle (Patte).

north into the old mediaeval city, at right-angles to this first axis, a second development took the form of three inter-related spaces – the Place de la Carrière; the short length of the Rue Héré, which links it to the Place Royale: and the Hemicycle in front of the Provincial Government Palace, which forms the northern termination of this second axis. Between the Rue Héré and the Place de la Carrière there is an imposing triumphal arch.

The whole scheme, as illustrated in Patte's *Monuments*, shows how the plan has been skilfully organised to take account of the remains of the fortifications. In addition to these earthworks, de Corny's design had to incorporate an important existing building on the eastern side of the Place de la Carrière. This was the Hôtel de Beauvau Craon, the present-day Palais de Justice, designed in 1715 by Boffrand. Its elevation was repeated on the other side of this *place*, and its proportions became the basis of buildings framing the Place Royale. Houses on either side of the remainder of the Place de la Carrière were also given new unified elevations to accord with the overall design.

Nancy's Place Royale is notable for the magnificent curved wrought-iron screens which define its four corners. Those flanking the Hôtel de Ville, on the southern side, unfortunately have to admit traffic into the *place*, but those on the other corners provide controlled views out. The Rue Héré, leading from the Place Royale, was at first an open colonnade; later this was converted into two-storey shops, their elevations carefully related to these in the main *place*. The Place de la Carrière has two parts – the open paved space between the main buildings at its southern end and the long and narrow directional space leading to the Hemicycle. This directional character is emphasised by two rows of formally clipped trees on each side of the central axis. Finally in this marvellous sequence of spaces, there is the Hemicycle itself, in front of the Government Palace. It has semi-circular open colonnades around its narrow ends, through which access is gained into the mediaeval town to the west, and into a large park laid out during the nineteenth century to the east. This latter stands on part of the old fortified zone.

Edmund Bacon uses this scheme to demonstrate that great work can be done without destroying what is already there and says that 'here a new element is added, that of symbolically expressing in new structures the spirit of what has been associated with that particular

Rennes, devastated by fire in 1720, was largely re-built in the eighteenth century; in other towns, even without this adventitious advantage, the work of demolition and rebuilding went on apace. Who would have guessed, even before the Revolution, that in 1700 Bordeaux had still been a mediaeval city? While private individuals built their eternal mansions on earth, elegant, grand, but in their frequent repetition of the same themes ultimately a little boring, town planning and the creation of imposing set-pieces on a larger scale was the work of the royal intendants, who rivalled one another in the task of beautifying the seats of their authority. (Alfred Cobban, 'A History of Modern France')

Commercial prosperity and the growth of the state machinery inflated the size of the towns. Paris, in the middle of the century, had a population of half a million and was steadily increasing, Lyon had perhaps 160,000. Marseilles and Bordeaux were approaching 100,000. On the other hand, provincial capitals like Rennes, Dijon or Grenoble were towns of little more than 20,000. All told, by the end of the 'ancien régime' the urban population of France can hardly have exceeded two and a half million at most, which left a rural population of perhaps some 22 to 24 million. It is difficult to avoid the conclusion that France must have been suffering from intense and increasing rural over-population. (Alfred Cobban, 'A History of Modern France')

space in previous history. Thus the Arch of Triumph, built by Stanislaus, conveys the spirit of the fortified wall which divides the old mediaeval city from the new and recreates the feeling of the old bi-celled organic form'[23].

BORDEAUX

Bordeaux's Place Royale (Place de la Bourse) was designed by Gabriel the Elder (1667–1742) in 1729, and completed by his son Jacques-Ange Gabriel in 1743. It was designed as a statue-square around a monument to Louis XV (replaced in 1869 by a fountain). As the plan taken from Patte's *Monuments* (Fig. 6.23) illustrates, the main design problem was to relate the new space alongside the river Garonne to the city's unplanned street pattern. By cutting off the corners of the rectangle (following the example of the Place Vendôme and anticipating Gabriel's use of this motif in his Place de la Concorde design) entries into the *place* were limited to two, both from the land side with axes centred on the statue. Unified façades around the three built sides of the *place* frame the view out across the river, in a similar manner to John Wood the Younger's integration of built-form and open landscape at the Royal Crescent in Bath (1767–75). (See page 208.)

RENNES

Considered by Pierre Lavedan as the finest of the provincial squares dedicated to Louis XIV, the Place du Palais at Rennes was designed by Gabriel the Elder as part of the rebuilding of the town after the fire of 1721 (Fig. 6.24). This square provides a setting for the existing Palais de Justice (originally the Parliament of Brittany), designed by Salomon de Brosse, with the other three sides planned by Gabriel, with a great Ionic order over a high base; though it is almost unknown, it counts among the most perfect works of French architecture[24]. The statue of Louis XIV is now replaced by a fountain.

The Place du Palais is linked diagonally with the Place de la Mairie (originally the Place Louis XV) through a narrow passageway. As both of these squares contained statues, pains were taken to vary the position of the monument. Louis XIV stood, as always, in the centre of the square. Louis XV was set right against the façade of the Hôtel de Ville. The Place de la Mairie is divided in two by a cross street, with five parallel rows of trees balancing the volume of the town hall, one of the first examples of planting employed as an architectural element within the town[25].

RICHELIEU

In 1620 the Cardinal Richelieu decided to convert a small mediaeval château he had inherited into a vast new palace where he could entertain the king and his court retinue in the manner to which they were accustomed. He proposed to solve the problem of accommodating all the guests and their servants, in addition to his own enormous staff, by building a new town specially for the purpose. The palace has long since disappeared but the small town of Richelieu still exists, very much as it was in the cardinal's day, some 10 miles south of Chinon in the Loire Valley region.

The palace and town at Richelieu pre-date, by some 40 years, the similar and suitably more grandiose work for Louis XIV at Versailles. It is a tradition that Richelieu's project was intended to show

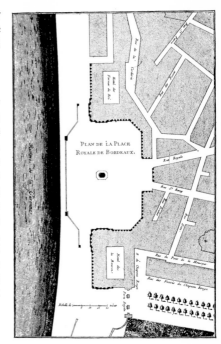

Figure 6.23– Bordeaux, the Place Royale (Place de la Bourse) created alongside the Garonne River by Jacques-Jules Gabriel and completed by his son.

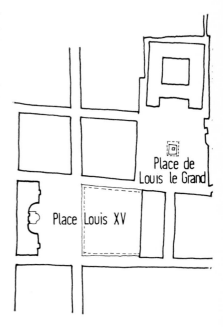

Figure 6.24 – Rennes, the Place de Louis-le-Grand (Place du Palais) in front of the Palais de Justice and the adjoining Place Louis XV (Place de la Mairie).

23. Edmund Bacon, *Design of Cities*.

24, 25. Pierre Lavedan, *French Architecture*.

Louis XIII how he might also live in fitting style if he could only bring himself to move from his cramped, obsolete accommodation in the Louvre.

Richelieu's palace was started in 1620 to the designs of Jacques Lemercier, the leading French architect of the day. In 1631 the town was laid out by Lemercier, who was also responsible for designing the public buildings and the most important houses. In 1631 the cardinal obtained from the king permission to hold a twice-weekly market in the town, in addition to four annual fairs. These valuable privileges should have guaranteed the commercial success of the town, but Richelieu was in a relatively isolated position, away from the main roads. As a further incentive the first citizens were excused all taxes until there were 100 houses in occupation. In addition to these persuasive measures, the cardinal, determined to make his property the premier centre of the district, proceeded to buy up adjoining estates so that he could dispossess their inhabitants[26]. Within a short time of starting, over 2,000 men were at work on the project.

By 1635 the palace had been completed. After three years the town was well advanced : the walls, church, college, law-court and most of the houses were finished, but there were still few inhabitants. Some years later, after the cardinal's death in 1642, the English diarist John Evelyn visited the town and observed that 'it consists of only one considerable street, the houses on both sides, as indeed throughout the town, built exactly uniform, after modern handsome design but it is thinly inhabited, standing so much out of the way and in place not well situated for health or pleasure'[27].

Richelieu is a small rectangular town, some 600 yards in length and 400 yards in width. The main street running the length of the town, exactly from north to south, originally constituted an axial link with the palace to the south. In this relationship the town was clearly subordinate to the palace : their respective axes intersected at right angles in the centre of the palace forecourt.

There are two *places* in the town, one at either end of the main street. Each is about 100 yards square. The southern one–the Place du Marché – has a distinctively designed church on its western side, facing the market hall. The Hôtel de Ville, originally the Palais de Justice, is also in this square. The Place des Religieuses at the northern end is less important now, lacking the theological college after which it was originally named.

The north-south Grande Rue is some 37 ft wide and comprises the 28 large houses alloted to principal members of the cardinal's retinue. These houses have a street frontage of about 70 ft each; an entrance gateway leads to a central courtyard in which there is the house door. The elevations of these houses were originally completely identical, with a cornice height of about 30 ft beneath steeply sloping individual slate roofs. Generally, within the town, house sites were granted free of charge, provided that Lemercier's standard elevations were completed within a stipulated period.

There is a marked contrast between the faded Renaissance elegance of these Grande Rue houses – now converted, unfortunately, in many instances, into shop fronts – and the poverty of the back lane 'cottages' which could well be part of some obscure declining agricultural village. Other than the buildings forming the squares and the main street there is every reason to suppose that the remainder of the dwellings were erected after the cardinal's interest in

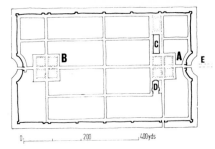

Figure 6.25 – Richelieu, general plan of the town as laid out by Jacques Lemercier in 1631. Key: A, Place du Marché; B, Place des Religieuses; C, the covered market; D, the church; E, the road leading, originally, to the château.

14 September 1644 – We took post for Richelieu, passing by l'Isle Bouchard. a village on the way. The next day, we arrived and went to see the Cardinal's palace. near it . The town is built in a low. marshy ground. having a narrow river cut by hand. very even and straight. capable of bringing up a small vessel. It consists of only one considerable street. the houses on both sides (as indeed throughout the town) built exactly in uniform, after a modern handsome design. It has a large goodly market-house and place. opposite to which is the church built of freestone. having two pyramids of stone, which stand hollow from the towers. The church is well-built and of a well-ordered architecture. within handsomely paved and adorned. To this place belongs an academy, where, besides, the exercise of the horse, arms, dancing, &c., all the sciences are taught in the vulgar French by professors stipendiated by the great Cardinal. who by this. the cheap living there, and divers privileges, not only designed the improvement of the vulgar language, but to draw people and strangers to the town; but since the Cardinal's death, it is thinly inhabited, standing so much out of the way, and in a place not well situated for health, or pleasure. He was allured to build by the name of the place. and an old house there belonging to his ancestors. This pretty town is handsomely walled about and moated. with a kind of slight fortification, two fair gates and draw-bridges. Before the gate, towards the palace, is a spacious circle, where the fair is annually kept. About a flight-shot from the town is the Cardinal's house. a princely pile. though on an old design. not altogether Gothic, but mixed. and environed by a clear moat.
(John Evelyn. 'Diary')

26. Martin S. Briggs, *Richelieu*, 'The Builder' 12 Jan, 1940.

27. John Evelyn, *Diary* (1644).

the town had ended. Richelieu has retained the complete circuit of its wall and gateways which probably had more of an aesthetic purpose than real military significance. The moat, originally about 70 ft in width and 10 ft deep, has been partially filled in.

With the death of its founder and the subsequent demolition of the palace, the *raison d'être* of Richelieu was removed. From an estimated maximum population of around 5,000 to 6,000 the town steadily declined in size and importance. Today it exists as a clear illustration of Renaissance planning principles, with only relatively small suburban accretions of recent years. Richelieu can thus be compared to mediaeval Winchelsea (as page 89), as the Renaiisance counterpart of that bastide port which failed to survive the silting up of its harbour.

THE WORK OF LE NÔTRE

The pre-eminent names in the history of landscape architecture are André Le Nôtre (1613–1700), whose greatest achievement was the layout of the park and town at Versailles, and Lancelot 'Capability' Brown (1716–83), perhaps best known for his work at Blenheim Palace[28]. Of the two Le Nôtre had by far the greatest impact on the related field of urbanism (although his output of work was very much less). Le Nôtre, however, had the unique advantage of working in seventeenth century France where profligate expenditure of national resources on personal aggrandisement finds few parallels in all history. Two all-powerful clients gave Le Nôtre the opportunities to design on an enormous scale, dwarfing the landscaping achievements of all his predecessors and hardly equalled by subsequent work. These two commissions were at Vaux-le-Vicomte, for Nicholas Fouquet, and his continuous involvement with Versailles for Louis XIV.

Le Nôtre belonged to a family of landscape gardeners and designers. His grandfather had been an under-gardener, and his father chief-gardener, at the Tuileries and in 1637 at the age of 24, he was promised the succession to his father's post. Eight years earlier, in 1629, his father had been employed laying out the park for Cardinal Richelieu's château adjoining his new town, and it was here that young André probably gained his first experience of large-scale landscape designing. In 1649 he is known to have been a salaried designer in the royal gardens before being appointed Controller-General of Royal Buildings in 1657.

Le Nôtre's first chance to create a landscape park was given by Fouquet at his ill-fated château – Vaux-le-Vicomte. Le Brun, the interior designer of the château itself, had been a painting student with Le Nôtre and recommended his friend for the work of creating a landscape setting for the building, and its related open-air social activities. The function of the landscape was 'not to be a spot in which a cultured man might take pleasure with his friends – the need which inspired the gardens of the Medicis; still less was its principal purpose to supply seclusion for repose or love; it was primarily to be a stupendous theatre for fêtes'[29]. The scale of operation, though less than at Versailles, presaged it. Three villages were demolished because they were in the way, and at times as many as 18,000 labourers were put to work.

It was at Vaux-le-Vicomte that Le Nôtre evolved his landscaping method. As summarised by Derek Clifford in his *History of Garden*

Two main routes traverse Poitou, one from Tours and the other from Saumur and they converge in the provincial capital, Poitiers. Between them on a tributary of the Vienne called the Mable is the little town of Richelieu. A regular quadrilateral with houses and two little squares of uniform style and elevation, it is the embodiment in stone of the spirit of Poitou, the province that almost simultaneously produced the master rationalist in philosophy, Descartes, and the master rationalist in politics, Armand-Jean de Plessis de Richelieu. It is, in fact, a village called into being by the Age of Reason, proclaiming its sense of order and authority . . . of the château itself nothing remains. It was confiscated at the time of the Revolution and sold early in the nineteenth century on condition that it would be demolished, and its only relics are a pavilion and the moats of its mediaeval ancestor in the midst of a great park. The Cardinal, ill and over-worked, at a time of war and national crisis, did not see his creation completed or even more than half-finished, but he gave no indicaton of any regret; for the château and the village existed, not to accommodate him, but to symbolise the entry of the family of Richelieu into the ranks of the great houses of France . . .
(D. P. O'Connell, 'Richelieu')

Long before Le Nôtre, the religion, philosophy and way of life of a people had been expressed in the form of a garden in China and Japan, and again in Persia and India. This had occurred in Italy, too, and was to happen again in England. In each of these countries many artists designed the gardens. But in France it was only one artist, André Le Nôtre, who expressed the civilisation of his time through the medium of his work, and did it so vividly, aptly and brilliantly that his gardens are the perfect symbol of his era.
(Helen M. Fox, 'André Le Nôtre: Garden Architect to Kings')

28. The reader is referred to Derek Clifford, *History of Garden Design*, as a general history cf landscape architecture; and to Dorothy Stroud, *Capability Brown*, and to Helen M. Fox, *André Le Nôtre: Garden Architect to Kings*, for detailed individual studies.

29. Derek Clifford, *History of Garden Design*.

Design, 'he seized on one great principle– that the whole extent of the enormous garden should be visible at a glance; accordingly whatever variety there might be within the parts, the parts themselves were to be subordinated to the whole. If the garden was to be seen at a glance it must be relatively narrow, but as it must be impressive by sheer size it had also to be long; the eye of a man on the uppermost terrace can look on and on, into the distance, but must not be asked to move from side to side'. The main vista, contained within densely planted flanking woods, is therefore arranged to be seen from the highest of a sequence of descending terraces. In addition to framing the vista these woods embrace secondary smaller gardens. Here groups of statues, pools and fountains provide alternative and more intimately scaled visual experiences to those of the dominant directional space.

VERSAILLES

In 1624 Louis XIII purchased an area of land near the small village of Versailles, some miles south-west of Paris. With plans attributed to Salomon de Brosse he built a royal hunting-box; this was a modest building of brick, with stone trim, and with a great slate roof such as could be seen at the time in Paris in the Place des Vosges[30]. The plan followed the standard French pattern; a main central block was flanked on either side by lower wings and these were joined at their ends by a low arcade to form an entrance courtyard on the Paris side. On the other side, a fraction of the extent of the present-day park, were small, formally laid-out gardens. Louis XIII frequently stayed at Versailles, both to hunt and to pursue his chaste love-affairs. The village gradually expanded to accommodate visitors' servants and all the increasing ancillary services and industries. But only in the France of the seventeenth and early eighteenth centuries could the subsequent developments have taken place. Over the years the modest hunting-box became inflated into history's grandest palace – more than one quarter of a mile in length – with decoratively planted gardens contained by sweeping landscaped perspectives of a suitably magnificent park. The village was expanded into a sizeable town, dependent on the palace for its livelihood, its three main streets constituting grand urban approaches and complementing the naturally formed spaces over the hill (Fig. 6.26). All this was possible only because of the absolute power enjoyed by the monarchy during the 72-year reign of Louis XIV (1643–1715). Versailles was 'the place he designed for his magnificence, in order to show by its adornment what a great king can do when he spares nothing to satisfy his wishes'[31].

Louis XIV had little altered his father's hunting-box when in 1661 he first set eyes on the magnificent combination of palace and landscaped park built by his finance minister, Nicholas Fouquet, at Vaux-le-Vicomte. Envious of this achievement, and suspicious as to how it had been paid for, Louis had Fouquet imprisoned and immediately requisitioned the services of his design team to create an even more magnificent scheme at Versailles. These designers were the architect, Le Vau, Le Brun, the interior designer, and André Le Nôtre. Le Nôtre was the first to see designs completed, replacing the earlier gardens with the vast park, the basic pattern of which, in spite of modification in detail, has never been altered. Lavedan describes it as 'a great vista flanked by two shrubberies and following

30. Pierre Lavedan, *French Architecture*.
31. Maurice Ashley, *Louis XIV and the Greatness of France*.

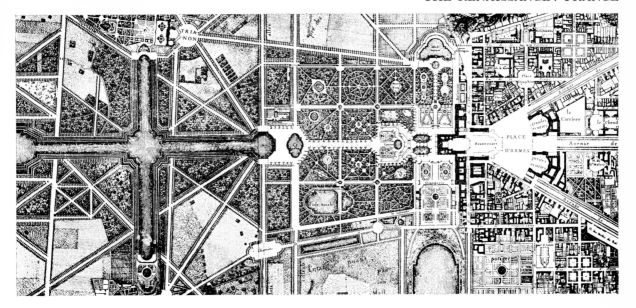

the central axis of the palace, with symmetrical arrangements of lawns and flowers on either side of this line; statues everywhere, the orangery built by Le Vau, and a menagerie for rare animals. This was the Versailles of Louis XIV's youth, where Molière came to act his plays, the Versailles of the king's love affair with Mlle de la Vallière'[32]. Vaux-le-Vicomte served as a tree nursery and it was Fouquet's plantings which graced the new orangery. Two grand fêtes in honour of the king's mistresses were staged in the gardens, in 1664 and in 1668, when over 3,000 guests were entertained on a lavish scale.

The scale of the original house was by now inappropriate for such a setting, and completely inadequate to meet the demands of court festivities. It was now the turn of Le Vau and Le Brun to create an architectural masterpiece complementing Le Nôtre's park. The king however would not tolerate demolition of his father's original building and eventually it was decided to extend around it on three sides leaving intact only the original elevation on to the eastern entrance court. Accordingly between 1668–71 Le Vau added extensions to the wings flanking the court – the Cour de Marbre – and constructed the immense central block of the present-day palace, facing the park. At the same time Le Brun completely remodelled the interiors.

Louis XIV had never felt at ease living in the Louvre in Paris; as an impressionable child he had experienced at first hand the latent power of the mob, which during the uprising known as the Fronde had proved so threatening that the boy king and his mother had been obliged to flee from the city. He therefore preferred to spend increasingly lengthy periods at Versailles and, around 1678, took the decision to expand still further the palace and town of Versailles, this time to a size where they could accommodate the entire court and government departments on a permanent basis. J-H. Mansart was the architect. He further extended the length of the palace by adding the south, or prince's, wing (1679–82) and the balancing north

Figure 6.26 – Versailles, detail plan of palace, park and town in 1746 (north at the top). The horizontal scale is vast indeed: from the west front of the palace to the near end of the cruciform-plan lake is 430 toises (900 m); from the palace to the central crossing of the lake is 750 toises (1,600 m); the cross-arms of the lake are 525 toises (1,000 m) across. However the visitor was not intended to experience the park on foot; the intended time and motion scale was 10–15 miles per hour – the leisurely speed of a horse-drawn carriage. To *walk* from the palace to the near end of the lake can be tiring, even eventually boring. To walk on from there, round the lake to the distant horizon through dusty all but deserted *allées* is a further $1\frac{3}{4}$ ml by the shortest route.

As Derek Clifford describes it, 'the main plan of the garden was as it still is. The area occupied by it was roughly rectangular, but the impression to the eye was of an enormous vista stretching from the facade for three-quarters of a mile to the beginning of the Grand Canal, which in turn diminished to the horizon, suppressing any desire to explore its remote distances. In the immediate neighbourhood of the palace the home terrace gave laterally on to *parterres*, so that to right and to left impressive pictures appear, one downward to the famous fountain of Neptune, the other across the enormous orangery to the lake that was dug by the Swiss Guards. To ensure that the effect of distance was not dissipated Le Nôtre repeated the device of flanking the central axis with groves as at Richelieu and Vaux, although here it was done on an even vaster scale with even more triumphant effect' *(A History of Garden Design)*.

32. Pierre Lavedan, *French Architecture*.

wing (after 1684). In 1682 this work was sufficiently far advanced for the Court to move out from Paris.

The work of laying out the town of Versailles had been proceeding concurrently with the palace expansions. The basis of the town plan is three broad avenues which are centred on the king's bedroom in the middle of what remained of the original Louis XIII block. Between the palace and the town there is the vast expanse of the Place d'Armes – a regular trapezium some 1,300 ft across by 600 ft deep. Facing the palace across this space in the angles formed by the three avenues, J-H. Mansart added the Royal Mews, barracks and other court offices. The horizontal scale is so vast as to make the whole composition meaningless, except when seen from the king's bedroom windows. Versailles received its charter in 1671 and had grown to about 30,000 population when Louis XIV died in 1715.

It is not known for certain who was responsible for the structure of the town but it is likely that Le Nôtre was significantly involved at some early stage. There is a direct connection between the use of the radiating routes motif in the town and much of the detail layout of the park; moreover, earlier in his career Le Nôtre had also been involved with similar radial axis planning of the Champs Elysées and the Cours-la-Reine, west of the Tuileries Gardens in Paris. This radial routes motif, which can be directly traced back to the plan of the Piazza del Popolo in Rome, also plays a key role in the layout of Washington DC, in the USA. (See pages 234–5.) It is highly significant that Pierre L'Enfant, the planner of Washington, spent his childhood in the park and town of Versailles.

THE WORK OF SEBASTIEN LE PRESTRE DE VAUBAN (1633–1707)

As a result of his lifetime's work in the service of Louis XIV, Vauban is recognised as the greatest military engineer in history. He is reputed to have taken part in nearly 150 battles, directed 53 sieges, fortified some 300 towns and built more than 30 new ones. His skill was such that it was acknowledged that 'a town beseiged by Vauban was a town captured and a town defended by Vauban was impregnable'[33]. In this history we are concerned primarily with his work in the development of the science of urban fortification, and its effect on continental European urbanism during his lifetime and in the eighteenth and nineteenth centuries. His interests however extended far beyond this work, leading Voltaire to regard him as 'a genius of the age'. Vauban's career involved him in many other aspects of national life, including establishment of the French internal waterways system, advocacy of methods of overseas territorial expansion[34] and army reforms – notably the invention of the bayonet which greatly increased the effectiveness of infantry. At the end of his life he also published a book concerned with radical reforms of the taxation system.

In 1651 the eighteen-year-old Vauban entered army service as a cadet, having a fair smattering of mathematics and fortification and being at the same time a passable draughtsman[35]. Four years later he received his commission as an engineer in ordinary to Louis XIV. The king had two main advisers – Louvois, responsible for war and the defence of the French frontiers, and Colbert, responsible for peace and the coasts and provinces. Vauban worked for Louvois beginning that ceaseless tour of the frontiers which lasted the whole of his life, and which attained an epic grandeur. 'From Antibes to

The King treated the presence of the greater nobles at Versailles and Fontainbleau as a parade, and if he found any were missing he enquired sharply about the reasons for their absence. But the function of the nobility was almost totally ornamental. They were strictly excluded from all ministerial duties and from the royal counsels, and they were not allowed to do honest work of any kind. The only thing they were permitted to do was to fight, and consequently the more energetic among them pressed the King to go to war at frequent intervals. At the same time, although they were exempt from taxation, the French nobles had expensive estates to keep up and many onerous ceremonial functions to fulfil. The King seems deliberately to have encouraged them to indulge in the most extravagant luxuries. Thus. unless they were lucky enough to make a rich marriage, many of them were in due course ruined. (Maurice Ashley, 'Louis XIV and the Greatness of France')

Through building an all-embracing palace and an artificial city on a wasteland and living and working in it, surrounded chiefly by servile ministers and idle courtiers, Louis XIV cut himself off from his people, and. like Philip II of Spain. was unable to compensate by hours of unremitting toil at his desk for lack of contact with the realities of the everyday life of his subjects. As that profound and witty French historian, M. Lavisse, observed: 'The great events of the reign are not always those which at once spring to the mind. The establishment at Versailles was more important and had graver consequences than any of Louis XIV's wars or all of his wars put together.' (Maurice Ashley, 'Louis XIV and the Greatness of France')

33. Reginald Blomfield, *Sébastien le Prestre de Vauban.*

34. Vauban's proposals for the development of North American colonies on an agricultural basis, receiving a continuous flow of emigrants, could well have seen France much more firmly established, and better able to withstand the British, than was the case.

35. Reginald Blomfield, *Sébastien le Preste de Vauban.*

Dunkirk he journeyed unceasingly, studying the lie of the land, working on every kind of terrain, the rocky shores of the Mediterranean, the sand dunes of the north, the Alpine escarpments and the inundated tracts of Flanders'[36].

At first he was mainly concerned with offensive military tactics for beseiging fortress towns, but was also soon involved in the creation of new, improved defences to replace those he had successfully destroyed. In 1667 he was with Louis XIV in the Netherlands organising successful assaults on Tournai, Douai and Lille, amongst several others. The subsequent reconstruction of the town and citadel at Lille in 1668–69 is considered by Sir Reginald Blomfield in his *Sébastien le Prestre de Vauban* as one of Vauban's most successful combinations of fortifications and urban planning.

Vauban himself regarded Maubeuge as one of his major achievements. His last important project was the building of Neuf Brisach; this small fortress town on the Rhine frontier is the clearest example of his methods as applied to a new site and is described separately later in this chapter. With Vauban military requirements dominated all others in the layout of towns and their defences and he was 'much more interested in giving shape to the varying polygonal outlines of his fortifications than he was in the inner structure of the town. When Vauban remodelled existing settlements, he did not change the old street system of the inner town but confined his work to the construction of its fortifications. In his newly built fortress-towns he took over the simplified gridiron scheme of the French mediaeval bastides with a quadrangular square in the centre, combining it with basic ideas of the Italian sixteenth-century theoreticians'[37].

VAUBAN AT VERSAILLES

One of Vauban's least successful tasks, in the sense that he failed to convince Louis XIV of the merits of his proposals, involved him in the ill-fated attempt to provide an adequate water supply for the gardens at Versailles. The idea of others had been to divert the river Eure to Versailles from a point some 80 kms south. By 1685 canals had been dug on both sides as far as the valley of the river Maintenon; the army, otherwise unoccupied during a period of peace, providing the massive labour force. The major problem was how to take the water across the valley and Vauban was assigned to this task in 1686. His was an original yet perfectly possible solution, based on the creation of an enormous siphon using cast-iron pipes. This however would have been far too unassuming visually for the king, who preferred a rival scheme for a gigantic aqueduct across the valley, surpassing the Pont du Gard and anything the Romans had built[38]. In 1686 work started on this aqueduct, which was to have been 5,000 yards in length. A division of 20,000 infantry encamped in the marshes to build it, but in these unhealthy conditions so many of the soldiers died that by the king's order nobody was allowed to speak of it[39]. Eventually a renewal of hostilities in 1688 brought an end to the project: only the lowest arcade had been completed, with 47 arches varying between 42 and 48 feet in height giving a length of 1,062 yards. The ruins of the aqueduct still stand in the valley of the Maintenon, and serve as a grim monument to the disastrous vanity and futility of Louis XIV.[40]

In 1687 Vauban invented a socket by which a bayonet could be attached to the musket without interfering with its firing. By this means pikemen could be abolished and the effectiveness of the infantry doubled . . . at the same time the artillery and engineers began to come into their own largely through the exertions of Vauban, who made use of them in siege warfare, which became the principal feature of the many Flanders campaigns. In conducting a siege Vauban's method was first to surround the fortress which was being attacked with parallel lines of entrenchments and then to launch from them mortar bombs, the range of which was calculated with mathematical accuracy, upon the enemy forces. The whole plan of a siege, with the prescribed entrenchments, sapping, and mortaring, was usually worked out in such precise detail that the date of the final assault and capitulation could be exactly estimated in advance. Ladies would be invited as witnesses of the last stages of a siege, and the final assault would take place to the accompaniment of violins. Louis XIV loved a good siege – the bigger the better – and would graciously accept the credit for all Vauban's hard work. (Maurice Ashley, 'Louis XIV and the Greatness of France')

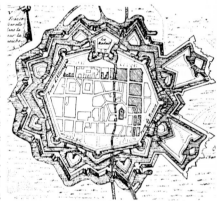

Figure 6.27 – Landau, an existing town, somewhat 'squared-up', within a typical Vauban fortification system.

36. Reginald Blomfield, *Sébastien le Prestre de Vauban*.

37. Paul Zucker, *Town and Square*.

38, 39, 40. Elie Halevy, *Vauban*.

NEUF BRISACH

In 1697 the Treaty of Ryswick finally forced France to withdraw from the line of frontier fortresses which she had established on the eastern bank of the Rhine during the half-century after the end of the Thirty Years War (1618–48). One of the most important of these fortresses was Alt Brisach, which controlled the principal river crossing on the long stretch of river between Strasbourg and the frontier with the Swiss Cantons above Basle. A replacement west-bank fortress was required as quickly as possible.

Vauban selected a site above the seasonal flood level, just out of range of the guns in Alt Brisach on higher ground, some four miles away to the north-east, across the river. The location was the meeting point of important roads to Strasbourg, Colmar and Basle, as well as the Rhine crossing leading to Freiburg in Germany. In 1700 the Rhine here was a multi-branched river; the crossing consisted of several short lengths of bridge linking together a number of islands. On the largest of these the French had built a regularly planned *ville-neuve* during their period of occupation. A condition of the treaty required this town to be demolished, and it subsequently served as a source of building materials for Neuf Brisach. The first and second plans prepared by Vauban were rejected by Louis XIV;

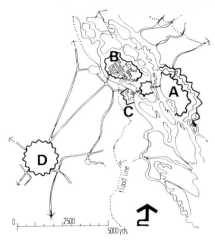

Figure 6.28 – Neuf Brisach, location of the Vauban fortress town related to the Rhine, which in the late seventeenth century had a considerably wider flood-plain than at the present day. Key: A, Alt Brisach; B, the French *ville-neuve*; C, left-bank bridgehead fortress; D, Neuf Brisach.

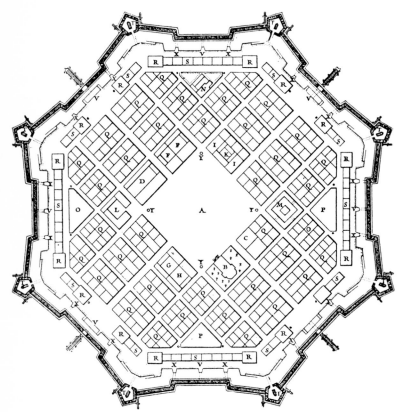

Figure 6.29 – General plan of Neuf Brisach, within the wall-proper of the defensive system. See the facing aerial view for the extent of the enveloping earthworks etc.

permission was given to proceed with a third in 1698. The military functions of Neuf Brisach were two-fold: it was to serve as a strongly fortified garrison town, from which forces could be deployed as required and its guns controlled the river crossing. In recognising the potential weakness of a civilian population in a military stronghold,

Figure 6.30 – Neuf Brisach and the surrounding countryside from the air (north at the top); the Rhine on the far right. This view also shows the strikingly contrasted form of several organic growth villages and the fascinating strip-farming patterns.

Vauban omitted it from his first plan but this was rejected as impractical[41]. The intricate system of fortifications was constructed by 1708, but the town within was not finished until 1772 when the church was completed. The quality of workmanship for the retaining wall section of the earthbanks was of a very high standard, and, with only a minimum of restoration in the past, the completed ring has survived through to the present day as probably the best remaining example of eighteenth-century military engineering. Although densely overgrown in parts the original form is clearly visible[42].

Within the defences the town was laid out to a typical engineer's grid of expediency. Nine streets in each direction, including the

41. Christopher Cooke, Clare Hennessey and David Wardlaw, *Neuf Brisach*, 'RIBA Journal', Feb 1965.

42. Neuf Brisach has retained a military garrison which, when visited at Easter 1969, was beneficially engaged in clearing the undergrowth from sections of the fortifications.

ring road inside the ramparts, form regular building blocks, around the central four-block Place d'Armes. This central space was primarily intended as the assembly area for the garrison: aesthetic considerations were discounted in its layout and the surrounding buildings are far too small in scale to be able to do more than define the extent of a bleak, somewhat anonymous, gravelled parade-ground. The town church is in the north-east corner of the square, and the market place and town hall form a separate, much more happily scaled public space off the south-east corner. The four main roads into the town are brought in through the fortifications to the centres of the Place d'Armes.

Parisian postscript

The history of Paris as a modern world city,' writes Anthony Sutcliffe in his book *The Autumn of Planning in Central Paris,* 'clearly begins with Napoleon III and Haussmann. But the seeds of the improvement policies which burgeoned then were planted long before in the reign of Louis XVI'. Thus although several aspects of Parisian urbanism of the late eighteenth and early nineteenth centuries could be seen as falling within the period of this book, consideration of these has been held over for inclusion in a proposed future volume. This urbanism, which includes legislation and planning proposals prepared under Louis XVI, during the Revolution (including the ambitious plan for Paris produced in 1793 by the Commission of Artists), and under Napoleon Bonaparte, would therefore constitute the immediate background for detailed assessment of the mid-nineteenth century programmes of Napoleon III and Haussmann.

By the turn of the century Paris had a population of some 550,000 – probably well over one quarter of the total French urban population which, to quote Cobban, 'must have been well under two millions. Probably some 95 per cent of France's 26 millions lived in isolated farms, hamlets, villages and small country towns' (*A History of Modern France: Volume Two 1799–1945*). In 1851, two years before Haussmann took up office as Prefect of the Seine, the city's population had almost doubled to 1,050,000. By far the greater part of the increase was accommodated in the new districts which rapidly filled the space between the Wall of the Farmers General (1784–91) and the line of the fortifications of 1840–45 (see Figure 6.13). During the second half of the nineteenth century, Paris progressively annexed suburban areas outside the fortifications and had attained a population of 2,715,000 by 1900.

The provincial cities were not important enough to receive much imperial attention, and there the eighteenth century largely survived, but considerable steps were taken towards the spoiling of Paris. Napoleon required a grandiose setting for the capital of his Empire, and of course a classical one. Triumphal arches – such as the Etoile and the Carrousel – were 'de rigueur'. For public buildings the correct thing was temples; so we have the temple of finance – the Bourse with its sixty-four Corinthian columns, the temple of religion – the Madeleine. the temple of the laws – the palais Bourbon, all heavy pastiches and all equally unsuited to the purposes for which they were intended. The proportions of the place Vendôme were ruined by sticking in its middle, in place of the destroyed royal statue, a monstrous column, in imitation of that of Trajan. To enable the Napoleonic monuments to be seen. the process of driving long straight roads through Paris, which was to be carried much further under the Second Empire, was begun. Unlike the lath and plaster erections of the Revolution, the buildings of the Empire were made to last – unfortunately, for they embody too well the Emperor's chief aesthetic rule: 'Ce qui est grand est toujours beau'.
(Alfred Cobban, 'A History of Modern France: Volume Two 1799–1945')

7 — The Renaissance: Europe in general

In European countries other than Italy, France and Britain, significant urbanism of the Renaissance period was either concentrated in the capital cities, which were undergoing extremely disproportionate growth relative to provincial urban centres, or, in a limited number of instances, took the form of new cities. To some extent the great majority of European cities and towns of any importance developed, or were redeveloped, according to Renaissance planning principles: new regularly planned districts were added, civic spaces were reformed, boulevard systems constructed and general restructuring organised. Rather than spread attention thinly over a large number of examples, with undue repetition, some city case-studies are described in detail in text and in captions to plans; others are illustrated by a plan, with only a brief description.

Amsterdam

Amsterdam is by far the most important example of that characteristic Dutch form of urban settlement: a river is dammed and its flow directed along alternative channels to the sea, the original downstream portion serving as an outer harbour and the upstream portion between the dam and the alternative channels as an inner harbour. As Gerald L. Burke, in his work *The Making of Dutch Towns*, goes on to state, the dikes constructed to define and contain the alternative channels provided the main circulation routes for land traffic and on their 'berms' were sited the buildings directly concerned with external trade, such as warehouses and offices. The dam itself constituted a valuable central space and was treated as such; it provided the setting for public buildings, like the town hall and weighing hall, and occasionally a church. Later in the seventeenth century, Amsterdam adopted a unique development plan which, implemented with compulsory purchase powers and strict building control legislation, ensured its growth, through its main period of expansion as a fine example of town planning[1].

The river Amstel was dammed in 1240, creating the Damrack and the Rodin as outer and inner harbours respectively. The dikes to the east and west, raised above flood level by the excavated soil from the new river channels, determined the lines of the two main

It was on a Sunday morning that I went to the Bourse, or Exchange, after their sermons were ended, to see the Dogmarket, which lasts till two in the afternoon, in this place of convention of merchants from all parts of the world. The building is not comparable to that of London, built by that worthy citizen, Sir Thomas Gresham, yet in one respect exceeding it, that vessels of considerable burthen ride at the very quay contiguous to it; and indeed it is by extra-ordinary industry that as well this city, as generally all the towns of Holland, are so accommodated with graffs, cuts, sluices, moles, and rivers, made by hand, that nothing is more frequent than to see whole navy, belonging to this mercantile people, riding at anchor before their very doors: and yet their streets even, straight, and well paved, the houses so uniform and planted with lime trees, as nothing can be more beautiful.

The Keizer's or Emperor's Graft, which is an ample and long street, appearing like a city in a forest; the lime trees planted just before each house, and at the margin of that goodly aqueduct so curiously wharfed with Klincard brick, which likewise paves the streets, than which nothing can be more useful and neat. This part of Amsterdam is built and gained upon the main sea, supported by piles at an immense charge, and fitted for the most busy concourse of traffickers and people of commerce beyond any place, or mart, in the world. Nor must I forget the port of entrance into an issue of this town, composed of very magnificent pieces of architecture, some of the ancient and best manner; as are divers churches.
(John Evelyn, 'Diary')

---

1. Lewis Mumford, *The City in History.*

streets of the original fishing village settlement – the Warmoesstraat (east) and the Nieuwendijk (west) (Fig. 7.1). Burke notes that their origin as dike streets is demonstrated by the fact that they are much higher than surrounding streets[2]. Thirteenth-century Amsterdam was only a small fishing village and Leyden, Delft and Haarlem were larger and more important Dutch towns.

During the fourteenth and fifteenth centuries the growth of Amsterdam as a trading centre was reflected in extensions of 1367, 1380 and 1450 which added a total of 350 acres to the original area of around 100 acres. This early expansion took a unique form, later also to be the basis of seventeenth-century development. New canals were excavated, in advance of building, at a more or less constant distance out from the existing urban perimeter. Eventually the ring of canals was to be complete to the west and south of the original nucleus, to the east it was modified by construction of larger basins and docks. The canals were used for direct barge access to the merchants' houses and warehouses – frequently combined in the same building – and at the time of their construction served as a defensive 'moat'. A first formal defensive system was begun in 1482 and marked the urban limits until the seventeenth century.

Extensive fires in 1451 and 1452 destroyed or damaged nearly all the buildings. In 1521 a law was introduced which required brick and tile construction in place of timber and thatch. In 1533 another ordinance, sought to improve public health in the city. Rapid increase of population had resulted in the occupation of single houses by two or more families, and there being no sanitary provisions on the upper floors, slops were disposed of by emptying buckets out of windows into the canal or street; the ordinance therefore obliged house owners to install sinks emptied by lead soil pipes and it also forbade the building of covered drains or sewers unless they were fitted at suitable intervals with detachable inspection covers[3]. Further legislation of 1565, which in part remained in force until the early nineteenth century, required approval of piled foundations by municipal inspectors, a privy for each plot, and the levying of charges for making up roads, pavements and canal embankments. Moreover this legislation was firmly enforced. In so doing the city created a respect for collective decisions – invaluable during implementation of the seventeenth century master plan.

In 1570 the Spanish destroyed Antwerp, the leading port in the Netherlands. This led to an immediate increase in the trade handled by Amsterdam: by 1600 it had taken over the dominant rôle of Antwerp. This rapid growth in trade and wealth during the last quarter of the sixteenth century could have resulted in urban expansion pressures beyond the control of the city authorities – as occurred, for example, in countless instances during the Industrial Revolution, when individual short-term commercial gain was considered before community interest. Amsterdam, however, was able to control its future development. Three main factors were responsible for this unique historical achievement – two of these were form-determinants derived from the function of the city, its site and the need for a defensive system; the third decisive factor was that Amsterdam was like a great and flourishing corporation in which each citizen owned shares[4]. Inevitably, as will be noted later, there were those who saw the possibilities of personal gain, but they were few and the collective spirit prevailed.

In 'The Making of Modern Holland', A. J. Barnouw writes: 'The Dutchman is by nature a rugged individualist. But rugged individualism does not make for civil liberty.' He explains that 'the Dutch, who for various reasons, physical, economic, or political, joined their individual lives into communal units, learned by bitter experience that their strength lay in co-operation, and that co-operation was feasible only if all agreed to limit their personal liberties by common obedience to self-made laws. By the end of the Middle Ages the majority of the Dutch people were living in urban centres. In 1500 Holland and Belgium number no fewer than 208 fortified towns and 150 large villages which, but for the lack of walls, might pass for towns.' Many of Holland's towns were built on the reclaimed floor of the sea. the so-called polders. To secure building land at all it was first necessary to dig canals, using the earth thus obtained to erect dikes around areas that had been filled up with sand brought there from long distances. And the erection of a house was no less toilsome. Piles had to be driven into the earth below ground-water. to procure a firm foundation. Then a constant water-level had to be provided. to secure the piles from rotting and all the houses from collapsing. The first communal institution these individualists had to agree upon was a water-level office. whose duty it was to keep the water of canals and sluices at a permanent level.
(S. E. Rasmussen, 'Towns and Buildings')

2, 3. Gerald Burke, *The Making of Dutch Towns.*
4. S. E. Rasmussen, *Towns and Buildings.*

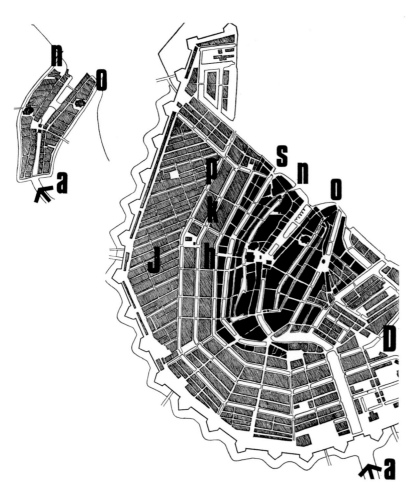

Figure 7.1, Far left – Amsterdam in about 1400; the original settlement was on the east bank dike of the Amstel with the old church on lower ground. Key: a, Amstel; o, Oudezijds Voorburgwal; n, Nieuwezijds Voorburgwal.

Left – Amsterdam at the beginning of the nineteenth century with the area laid out under the 'Plan of the Three Canals' fully developed. The extent of the city at the end of the fifteenth century, before the plan was adopted, is shown in solid black. Key (where different to above) : s, Singel Canal; h, Herengracht Canal; k, Keizersgracht Canal; p, Prinsengracht Canal; J, the Jordaan District; D, the main dock area. North at the top for both plans.

Control of development was strictest in the areas between the three great concentric canals. Here the plot sizes averaged 26 feet frontage and 180 feet depth, and the prescription of a minimum distance of 160 feet between the backs of buildings resulted in a minimum garden length of 80 feet for each plot. A maximum site coverage of 56 per cent was thus secured. A typical set of conditions of sale, published in 1663, stipulated that the following trades could not be carried on within the area: blacksmith, brewer, cooper, dyemaker, glassblower, gluemaker, soapboiler, stone-cutter, sugar manufacturer and similar noxious or noisy occupations. It is remarkable that these restrictions have remained in force there ever since. The 'Building Order' for the same district required, inter alia, that outside walls be constructed only in Lekse, Leytse, Vechtse or Rijnse bricks, and that only blue bricks or Bremen stone could be used for drains.

So rarely are buildings of less than three stories to be seen in this area that the existence of some form of municipal control to secure a minimum, as well as a maximum, height might be presumed. Investigation has so far yielded no evidence of such control, and it is unfortunate that most of the city's older records perished in three major fires; but land values along such important frontages doubtless induced developers to obtain the maximum return in lettable space.

(Gerald Burke, 'The Making of Dutch Towns')

PLAN OF THE THREE CANALS

Amsterdam developed from its late sixteenth century area of around 450 acres to an early nineteenth century total of nearly 1,800 acres, in accordance with the 'Plan of the Three Canals' (Fig. 7.1). Hendrik Jz Staets was responsible for this plan, adopted by the city council in 1607 but not without objections from certain speculators amongst the councillors who had bought up land in anticipation of development[5]. The layout of the new parts of the city was determined by the first two of the three factors referred to above. Amsterdam's trading function required direct water access to individual merchants' houses and warehouses. This was only possible through communal action in the construction of canals – linear expansion along existing waterfronts, for example, was precluded. Organised excavation of these canals required a plan, and the considerable investment needed for a defensive system imposed a limit on its extent.

The three canals of the 1607 plan are the Herengracht, the Keizersgracht and the Prinsengracht, named in sequence out from the centre. The Herengracht, 80 ft wide, had been excavated in 1585 and the Keizersgracht, 88 ft wide, in 1593. Both therefore predate the plan itself and were located in the city according to this

---

5. Gerald Burke, *The Making of Dutch Towns*.

uniquely controlled organic growth pattern of concentric canal systems. The third canal, the Prinsengracht, 80 ft wide, was excavated later, in 1622. The three main ring canals were linked by radial waterways and all had spacious quays and roadways on both sides. Outside the ring, to the west, there was the Jordaan, an area zoned for industry. Around the entire area and encompassing the harbour district in the south-east was constructed a 5-mile long defensive system with 26 bastions and seven gates.

It is easier to draw up a physical plan than to create the legislative framework to put it into practice. But in this latter respect Amsterdam obtained for itself the vital pre-requisite of compulsory land purchase powers in 1609 and, as Gerald Burke tells us, exercised them as it became necessary for the various parts of the scheme. Having acquired an area, the council prepared the land for building, divided it into plots of convenient size and shape and sold these in the open market subject to special conditions. Purchasers had to enter into covenants which bound their successors in title also, to the effect that the land would not be put to other than stipulated uses, that the plot coverage would be kept within prescribed limits, that the plot would not be sub-divided by lanes or alleyways, that the party wall connections would be afforded to developers of adjacent plots and that only certain types of brick would be used for external walls[6]. The civic administrator most responsible for implementing the scheme was surveyor-general Daniel Stalpaert (1615–76).

The planned growth of seventeenth century Amsterdam is a clear example of the rule that societies get the kind of cities they deserve. It is proof, if any is still required, that theoretical planning expertise is of little significance in the absence of community resolution. Without political direction, expressed in suitable legislation, plans are just so much paper.

Berlin

Berlin had its origins in two separate urban settlements: Colln, the oldest, located on an island in the river Spree, and Berlin proper, on the north bank of the river. Colln is first mentioned in 1237 and Berlin in 1244. The two towns concluded a treaty in 1307 which effectively united them as Berlin-Colln, although each retained its own council. During the fourteenth century Berlin-Colln became one of the most important towns in the German Mark with, effectively, the status of a free imperial town. This assumed independence brought Berlin-Colln into conflict with the interests of the all-powerful Hohenzollern family, who became Masters of the Mark in 1415. Unsuccessful opposition to Elector Frederick II (1440–70) resulted in the town twice being deprived of all its privileges, in 1442 and 1448, and a fortified castle was erected on the Spree between 1443–51 to keep the inhabitants under control. In 1448 each part of Berlin-Colln had about 6,000 population; throughout the sixteenth century and the first half of the seventeenth, however, the growth of Berlin-Colln was stunted, and the early suburbs which had grown up around the Altstadt of Berlin (Fig. 7.2) were destroyed during the Thirty Years War (1618–48). Although Berlin-Colln itself was spared, the economic situation was so bad that the citizens considered emigrating en masse and abandoning the town[7].

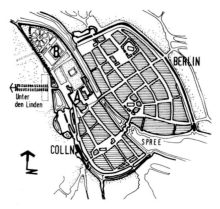

Figure. 7.2 – Plan of Berlin-Colln around 1650, before the re-fortification of 1658–85. Key: A, Royal Palace, with the Unter den Linden leading west from the entrance gateway into the open country; B, the formal gardens of the palace.

The town had been fortified under the Great Elector (1640–88), and foreign architects, foremost among them the Dutchman Nering. had erected some larger buildings. But the decisive development took place under the first King of Prussia. Friedrich I (1688–1713). who had not only commissioned Schluter for monumental tasks like the royal castle, palaces of nobility. and the monument to his predecessor. but had also added while new quarters like the Friedrichstadt. planned in a gridiron scheme. Under the following king. Friedrich Wilhelm I, three pedantically geometric squares were laid out: the Quarre (later the Pariser Platz) in the form of a regular quadrangle, the Rondell (later the Belle-Alliance Platz) based on a circular plan, and the Octagon (later the Leipziger Platz) laid out as an octagon; all of these were constructed between 1734 and 1737. No individual architects can be associated with the basic layouts of these squares since their designs were just another task of public administration for the king in his Spartan austerity. Originally they were planned as being surrounded by uniform houses, but the parsimony of the king did not allow their simultaneous erection and thus their spatial effect cannot be compared with other German squares of that time.
(Paul Zucker. 'Town and Square')

6. Gerald Burke, *The Making of Dutch Towns*.
7. E. A. Gutkind, *Urban Development in Central Europe*.

The city had been strongly fortified between 1658–83, incorporating the new district of Friedrichswerder within the defences. (These were designed by a Dutch engineer and involved the construction of 13 massive bastions.) Outside this zone two new housing districts were laid out to Renaissance gridiron pattern – Dorotheenstadt from 1674 (named after the elector's second wife), and Friedrichstadt from 1688. Both of these districts were linked back to the Altstadt by the line of the Unter den Linden. This was originally an avenue of lime trees giving access to the open country and forests on the west; it had gradually been built up on both sides as an impressive 198 ft wide street, about one mile in length between the Royal Palace and the Brandenburg Gate. It thus has striking parallels with the earlier establishment of the Champs Elysées in Paris – also originally a direct link between the royal palace and country districts beyond the city limits (page 144). Their existence helped to ensure that the western sides of both Berlin and Paris would become the most fashionable, expensive residential areas.

By the early eighteenth century Berlin had a population of around 60,000 and covered an area of 2 square miles. In 1737 a customs wall nine miles in length was built further out to protect the growing commercial and industrial interests of the city. This increased the city area to $5\frac{1}{4}$ square miles. At about this time the Dorotheenstadt and the Friedrichstadt were enlarged, the demolition of the defensive system was started, and new suburbs were added to the north and east. During the nineteenth century industrial expansion proceeded at a great pace, as evidenced by the population figures: 200,000 in 1820; 329,000 in 1840; 496,000 in 1860; 1 million in 1870; and $1\frac{1}{2}$ million in 1888. The customs wall was not demolished until 1850 when it was replaced by a ring-road system. The greater part of the population growth of the second half of the nineteenth century was accommodated in tenement housing districts between this line and the *Ringbahn* railway.

Budapest

The three separate urban nuclei which were to be consolidated by subsequent growth into the city of Budapest were still separate in the seventeenth century. Obuda on the western (right) bank of the Danube occupied part of the site of Aquincum, one of the most important legionary fortresses on the Roman Empire's eastern frontier. Buda was centred on a commanding hill downstream alongside the river some 3 km to the south. Pest, the youngest of the three nuclei, had developed on the extensive river plain stretching to the east of the river, downstream again from Buda. In Fig. 7.4 the extent of these three original centres is shown by vertical hatching.

The Royal Palace in Buda was built in 1247 and from then until 1526 this city was the capital of Hungary. Between 1526 and 1686 all three urban centres were held by the Turks. Pest was almost completely demolished and by 1710 had only regained a nominal population of 1,000. Maria Therese founded the university in Buda in 1777 (it was transferred to Pest in 1784); this marks the beginnings of the re-emergence of these urban centres and their transformation into an important European centre, in which Pest achieved dominance as the commercial and cultural core. The single municipality of Budapest was created in 1872.

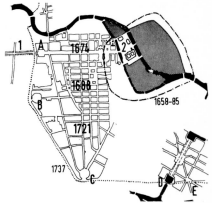

Figure 7.3 – Inner Berlin of the eighteenth century. The original Berlin-Colln area of Figure 7.2 is shown tinted, with the lines of the 1658–85 fortifications and the 1737 Customs Wall shown dotted. Key: 1, the Unter den Linden continuing west from the Brandenburger Tor (A) across the Tiergarten to the open country; 2, the Royal Palace facing onto Lustgarten Square. Gateways in the Customs Wall – A, Bradenburger Tor; B, Potsdamer Platz; C, Belle Alliance Platz; D, Thorbecken.

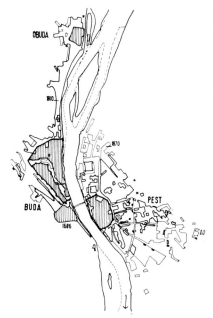

Figure 7.4 – Budapest, diagrammatic growth map (north at the top). The vertical hatched areas show the extent in 1685 of the twin cities of Buda and Pest, and the upstream settlement of Obuda (on the site of Roman Aquincum). The heavier outlined areas are those of 1810 – this includes the west bank river-front ribbon linking Buda and Obuda; the thin outlined areas show the extent of the city of Budapest in 1870.

M

The defences around Pest were demolished in 1808 to be replaced by the present-day inner ring boulevard. In the 1870s, when Budapest had a population of around 300,000, plans were drawn up for Pest's extension along similar lines to those adopted in Vienna, but only a small part of these proposals were put into practice.

Copenhagen

The first recorded reference to Copenhagen is as an insignificant fishing village, in 1043. But the existence here of one of the best natural harbours in northern Europe, conveniently located for both the Baltic-North Sea and European-Scandinavian mediaeval trading routes, was soon to lead to its growth as a major trading centre. At first the port area was situated between the original village settlement, on the mainland of Zeeland, and the island of Amager. In 1167 a castle was built on Strandholmen, a small island in the harbour. Copenhagen was acquired by the Danish Crown in 1417, and by the middle of the century had become a chartered royal borough. (The university was founded in 1479.) By the end of the fifteenth century the city had a population of around 5,000. In 1535 its plan was that of a mediaeval walled and moated mainland centre, with the castle on Strandholmen controlling the harbour (Fig. 7.5).

The introduction of Renaissance planning principles into Danish urbanism dates from the reign of Christian IV (1588–1648). During this time a number of small fortified towns were founded with regular gridiron plans incorporating numbers of squares. Christianstad (1614), Christiansand (1641) and Fredericia (completed by Christian IV's son) are typical examples[8]. Christian was also responsible in 1621 for the reconstruction of Christiana (present-day Oslo) in Norway.

Christian converted Copenhagen's defensive system to a typical Renaissance pattern between 1606 and 1624. Within its perimeter was included a new district to the north of the mediaeval core. Christianshavn, on the island of Amager, was constructed as a new separate fortified centre from 1617 to strengthen the harbour defences. Further works intended to safeguard the city's trading interests included the fortification of the harbour entrance begun in 1627 and the construction of a citadel on the mainland side. Strandholmen island, with its old castle, was joined to the mainland (Fig. 7.5). Under Christian V the defensive system around the central part of the city was extended to its furthermost extent, and in 1661, demarcation of the open fire zone was agreed. In 1662 a master plan for development of the city was produced but the citizens refused to accept the necessary land-use and architectural control measures. (A ring of outer fortifications around the suburbs was also proposed and never built.) The late seventeenth century population of the city was around 60,000.

Architecturally the most important example of Renaissance urbanism in the city is the Amalienborg Square development, started in 1749 under Frederik V (1746–66). This scheme was designed by a Danish architect, Nicolai Eigtved (1701–54), on the site of a royal park and an adjoining drill ground. 1749 was celebrated as the 300th anniversary of the House of Oldenberg; in recognition of this the king originally intended to create on this land a new com-

We cannot fail to admire the ability of the eighteenth century to build up an entire new quarter at one stroke. The plans of the Amalienborg district were first laid in 1749 and when Eigtved died in 1754 the whole of the extensive quarter with its beautiful palaces, a handsome hospital, and its many fine houses, was entirely laid out and many of the buildings completed. This was possible only because Eigtved fully mastered his art. In all his undertakings he worked with dimensions and shapes with which he was entirely familiar. He was able to combine them to form extraordinary compositions like the really quite extravagant church project. But he could also use them for purely functional buildings, such as Frederik's Hospital, in which the dimensions of the long wards are based on the size of hospital beds, and the wards located to obtain the best light. And there is the warehouse of the Asiatic Company, down by the harbour, in which the hoisting lofts are the dominating motif. In all his works, small as well as great, Eigtved demonstrated that it is the architect's problem to join the various elements of a building together in a clear and convincing manner, and to group them into inherent units.
(S. E. Rasmussen, 'Towns and Buildings')

---

8. See plans of these cities, with Oslo, page 177.

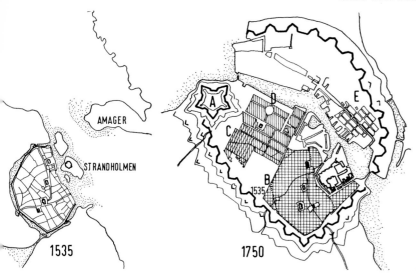

Figure 7.5, Far left – Copenhagen in 1535; the mainland defended town with the castle on Strandholmen.

Left – The city in 1750. The mediaeval nucleus is shown cross-hatched and the mainland Renaissance addition with vertical hatching. Christianshavn on the island of Amager is shown in outline. The castle, and the other small islands in the harbour, have been joined to the mainland, and the island of Amager is in progress of being extensively enlarged. Key: A, Citadel; B, mediaeval nucleus; C, Renaissance district; D, the Amalienborg Square development; E, Christianshavn.

mercial centre with a harbour frontage. The project was advertised as 'a very advantageous neighbourhood, due to the proximity of the harbour and the Customs House, which will greatly contribute to the facilitation and advancement of commerce'[9].

The freehold of building plots was to be given to applicants wishing to build houses: of these, timber merchants, with yards in the vicinity, were given priority in the choice of locations. Successful applicants were obliged to take up ownership immediately and required 'to build within five years and, in every detail, adhere to the plans approved by the king. Uniformity must be observed in every respect, and all buildings facing the street were to be constructed of brick with windows in horizontal rows'[10].

Rasmussen observes that from the first something more than an ordinary commercial centre must have been contemplated. On the original plan, which no longer exists, a great central space had been sketched in and the king expressly said that he would reserve the ground on which the four palaces were to be located which would form the central place. Four members of the Danish nobility were to be given the palace sites and their identical two-storied designs, with attics and high roofs became the basic structures of an octagonal square[11]. The other four sides were formed of two-storey pavilions, flanking the four streets entering the Amalienborg Square. The result is 'the unique motif of four palaces, each flanked by two pavilions, which together form the large unit of the octagonal place'[12]. The two streets which link the space to the surrounding district are the Amaliengade, running parallel to the waterfront, and the Fredericksgade, which connects the waterfront to the monumental Frederickskirke. This church was completed towards the end of the nineteenth century as a much less impressive version of Eigtved's original design. At the intersection of these axes, in the centre of the square, an equestrian statue was erected to Frederick V in 1771.

Paul Zucker considers that it is certainly no exaggeration to rank Amalienborg Square, although it is on a smaller scale, with the imperial fora, St Mark's Square and Piazzetta in Venice, St Peter's

Figure 7.6 – A section of a drawing of Amalienborg Square with the harbour to the right and the Marble Church to the top left.

9, 10. S. E. Rasmussen, *Towns and Buildings*.
11. Paul Zucker, *Town and Square*.
12. S. E. Rasmussen, *Towns and Buildings*.

Square in Rome, and Nancy, as one of the most perfect realisations of grouped squares[13]. Nicolai Eigtved was undoubtedly influenced by contemporary work in Paris. The competition for the statue-square for Louis XV which had been held in 1748, the year before the Amalienborg Square was started, would have been known to him and there is a close similarity between his plan and that of the Place de la Concorde – the winning scheme in the competition with a similar waterfront/statue/vista-closing church (the Madeleine) sequence[14]. Zucker considers that the regular alternation between the height of the four monumental palaces on the one hand, and of the smaller entrance pavilions on the other hand, creates a fluctuating rhythm which lends a certain visual freedom to the square; this freedom corresponds exactly to the French ideals of the eighteenth century when the compactness of the previous seventeenth century squares was criticised[15].

Development of the old fortified zone, largely for housing purposes, early in the second half of the nineteenth century, is similar in many ways to the Ringstrasse development in Vienna (page 175).

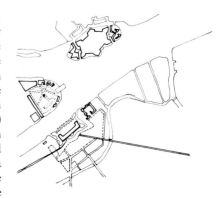

Figure 7.7 – St. Petersburg in 1750, after nearly a first half-century's growth (see below for location of parts).

St Petersburg

St Petersburg (now Leningrad) is the most important example of the application of fully developed Renaissance design principles to the planning of a complete new city. In contrast to conditions under which the great majority of Renaissance urbanists had to work – either having to add new districts to mediaeval cores, or carving space for their projects out of the existing urban fabric – the planners of St Petersburg had two major advantages. These were firstly, an empty site regulated only by topography; and secondly, the fact that by the time St Petersburg was founded in 1712 there were the examples of almost three centuries of European Renaissance urbanism to draw on.

During the seventeenth century Russia had grown into a unified expansive nation. But she was still without an outlet either to the Black Sea, controlled by the Turks, or to the Baltic, where Sweden had conquered the territory around the Gulf of Finland. Peter the Great (1688–1725) gave great strategic priority to the re-establishment of the Baltic outlet and successfully regained control of the Gulf of Finland during the Northern War of 1700–21. To consolidate the position along the line of the river Neva, the Russians began construction in May 1703 of the Peter and Paul Fortress on Zayachy Island, at the broadest point of the Neva estuary. By 1712, the fortress and associated naval base of St Petersburg had emerged to rival Moscow as the capital of Russia.

The first, temporary, earthworks of the fortress were converted into powerful brick fortifications between 1706–41. In 1712 the Cathedral of Peter and Paul was started as the first of a number of historic buildings within the fortress. Across the Neva the Admiralty Shipyard, also founded in 1703, was strongly fortified after 1705 and contained ten large covered slipways with ancillary storehouses and workshops. (Shipbuilding continued there until 1840. The present-day Admiralty Building, 1,340 ft in length, dates from 1806–23.) The increasing strength of the Russian navy and establishment of advanced frontier defences soon enabled St Petersburg itself to acquire a more peaceful character. On the left bank of the Neva,

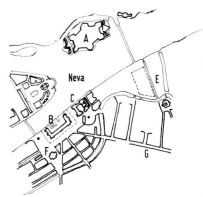

Figure 7.8 – Central St. Petersburg in 1850. Key: A, the Peter and Paul Fortress; B, the Admiralty; C, the Winter Palace (now the Hermitage Museum and Art Gallery); D, the Alexander Column in the centre of the Palace Square, as Figure 7.9; E, Summer Garden; F, St Isaacs Cathedral; G, Nevsky Prospect (terminated at its distant end by the Moscow Railway Station).

While working in the shipyards of Amsterdam and during his subsequent travels in the rest of Europe, Peter recruited a number of foreigners to return to Russia with him, mostly skilled craftsmen and shipbuilders, as well as other specialists and military and naval experts. He observed, and was impressed by, Dutch planning efficiency, a lesson which he later applied in the planning of St Petersburg. According to Peter's own words that city was to be laid out 'in the manner of the Dutch' with regular blocks and straight canals penetrating the territory of the city at right angles to each other.
(Y. A. Egcrov, 'The Architectural Planning of St Petersburg', translated by Eric Dluhosch)

13. Paul Zucker, *Town and Square.*
14. See Place de la Concorde, page 148.
15. Paul Zucker, *Town and Square.*

directly opposite the Peter and Paul Fortress, Peter laid out the Summer Garden (1704) where he dreamed of making a garden better than that of the French king at Versailles[16]. The Summer Palace was built between 1710 and 1714, to be followed by the Winter Palace (now the Hermitage Museum) of 1754–62. This latter was a rebuilding of an earlier and smaller fortified palace.

The most important element of the basic eighteenth- and nineteenth-century plan of St Petersburg is the centering of three main streets on the tower of the Admiralty. This gives to the immediate vicinity a combination of radial and gridiron streets which follows the example of the town area of Versailles (see pages 157–8), and presages the general use of this approach in L'Enfant's plan for Washington DC (see pages 234–7). The road from the east was an existing regional route and is now, as Nevsky Prospect, the main street in the city linking the centre to the Moscow railway station. The two other streets were completed by 1800.

The plan of Palace Square, in front of the Winter Palace (Fig. 7.9) is described by Edmund Bacon as an example of great design produced by accepting an existing plan and turning its problems into assets[17]. Until the beginning of the nineteenth century the space immediately to the south of the palace had an unresolved form. The western side was open to the Admiralty; facing the palace and forming an uncomfortable trapezoidal shape, were unimportant buildings, with some façades parallel to and others almost at right angles to Nevsky Prospect. It was decided to reorganise the elevations forming the square, to make it an appropriate setting for the palace. The properties on the southern and eastern sides were bought up and in March 1819 K. I. Rossie was commissioned to convert them into one building, known as the General Headquarters.

Work was finished in 1829 and the new elevation, some 640 yards in length, took the form shown by the heavy line on the plan. A magnificent triumphal arch on the central axis of the palace formed the new entrance into the square. An inspired touch linked this by curved sections to the retained south-western side and the new south-eastern side. New buildings closing the eastern side of the square, at right-angles to the palace, were added between 1840 and 1848, completing the design. Earlier in 1832, the 155 ft 6 in high, 600-ton triumphal column was erected in the centre of the square.

Thus the design of the Palace Square in St Petersburg, in its respect of the existing city form, can be compared with Michelangelo's plan for the Capitoline Piazza in Rome, where two mediaeval buildings determined the form of Renaissance urbanism (see page 129).

Mannheim

Although first recorded in AD 766, by the first decade of the seventeenth century Mannheim was still only a large fortified village settlement at the junction of the Rhine and Neckar rivers. For almost 1,000 years the strategic advantages of the site, alongside one of Europe's major natural waterways, had been offset by seasonal flood dangers. However by the seventeenth century the line of the Rhine had assumed renewed international boundary significance and in 1606 the Elector of the Palatinate, Frederick IV, started building a strongly defended citadel and town on the site of the village.

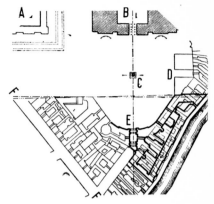

Figure 7.9 – St. Petersburg, the Palace Square in front of the Winter Palace (north of the top). Key : A, the Admiralty ; B, the Winter palace ; C, Alexander Column ; D, new buildings forming the eastern side of the square at right-angles to the palace elevation ; E, the new arched entrance into the square on the central axis of the palace ; F–F, Nevsky Prospect. The line of the pre-existing elevation across the south-eastern side of the square continued that of the linking street to Nevsky Prospect. The new building elevations of the General Headquarters (1819–29) are shown in heavy line.

The construction of the city commenced with the building of the Peter and Paul Fortress; a project which employed twenty thousand men. As the fortress rose amidst the marshes so did the city itself. Peter built himself a small house nearby and personally supervised the progress of the building. The conditions under which the labourers had to exist during the early years of St Petersburg's construction were terrible beyond belief. The climate was unhealthy, while the water was unfit for drinking. The Swedish prisoners of war and the thousands of conscripted labourers were so ravaged by dysentery and physical exhaustion that by 1710 Peter had to find additional labour. In that year he issued a ukase ordering the government of the interior to furnish 40,000 labourers, together with their most essential tools. These people drained the swamps, cut through the growth, dredged the river, dug canals, raised earthen dams and embankments, drove piles into the soft ground, and gradually accomplished the city of St Petersburg. Within three years the new city devoured an army of 150,000 workers.
(Y. A. Egorov, 'The Architectural Planning of Petersburg', translated by Eric Dluhosch)

16. Y. A. Egorov (translated, Eric Dluhosch), *The Architectural Planning of St Petersburg.*

17. Edmund Bacon, *Design of Cities.*

The star-shaped citadel of Friedrichsburg was about half as large as the town itself. This latter was laid out strictly according to the gridiron, within its own formidable defensive system. The citadel was destroyed for the first time in 1622. Vauban demolished the rebuilt defences in 1689, at which time Mannheim had a population of about 12,000. In the next reconstruction, which followed the Treaty of Ryswick (1697), both the citadel and the town were enclosed by one continuous defensive system. The last phase in the development of the plan of Renaissance Mannheim came with the final demolition of the citadel in 1720 to make way for the first stage of a monumental Baroque palace. This palace was extended between 1749–60.

Mannheim by 1799 represented a straightforward exercise in unimaginative drawing board design. The general gridiron street pattern was modified only by the slightly wider main axis-streets in front of the palace and by the broad cross avenue. Two of the street blocks were left open as, at most, only incidental public open space. The defensive system had so diminished in importance as to have only an aesthetic significance as marking the boundary of the urban area.

Camillo Sitte in his *City Planning According to Artistic Principles* is highly critical of both Mannheim and Renaissance grid planning in general. This much might be expected from the nineteenth century's strongest advocate of a return to the use of 'romantic' mediaeval urban form principles. Writing of the grid plan Camillo Sitte observes 'it was carried out already with an unrelenting thoroughness at Mannheim, whose plan looks like a chequerboard; there exists not a single exception to the arid rule that all streets intersect perpendicularly and that each one runs straight in both directions until it reaches the countryside beyond the town. The rectangular city block prevailed here to such a degree that even street names were considered superfluous, the city blocks being designated merely by numbers on one direction and by letters in the other. Thus the last vestiges of ancient tradition were eliminated and nothing remained for the play of imagination or fantasy'.

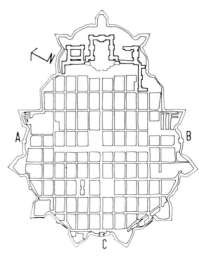

Figure 7.10 – Mannheim in 1799. The palace across the north-eastern end of the town occupies part of the former citadel area. The three gates into the town are marked as A, B, C. Paul Zucker has noted that 'this gridiron scheme, unique in Europe for such expansion, has often been mentioned as the prototype for the grids of eighteenth-century towns in the United States. Nor is it by chance that Mannheim is the only town in Europe where the streets are identified by numbers and letters instead of having individual names.' *(Town and Square)*

Prague

Prague developed at a strategically important location in the centre of the Bohemian plateau, where the river Vltava cuts deeply into the plateau and forms a dramatic escarpment on its left bank. At this point there was a ford across the river which constituted a focal point for east-west trading caravans. Two castles, with related civil towns, were built on high ground commanding the river banks and crossing. The more important was the Hradcany, built from the ninth century onwards on the left bank escarpment above the sweeping bend in the river. The second castle, Vysehrad, was erected on the opposite bank, about 2 miles upstream on a 160 ft high hill. Its northern approaches were protected by the steeply sloping valley of a tributary stream.

Town expansion in the second part of the thirteenth century added the Mala Strana civil town, south of the Hradcany on the left bank. The first permanent bridge across the Vltava was constructed in 1153, with the existing Charles Bridge dating from 1357. The Stare Mesto settlement on the right bank had grown up around

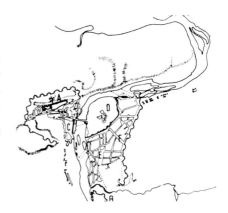

Figure 7.11 – Outline map of Prague in 1831 (north at top). Key: A, Hradcany Castle (the present-day national government centre); B, Vysehrad Castle; C, Mala Strana town, which grew up at the foot of Hradcany Castle hill; D, Stare Mesto (Old Town); E, Charles Square; F, Wenceslas Square. Both these squares form key parts of the mid-fourteenth century expansion of the city under Charles IV.

the approaches to the ford and, after completion of the bridge increased in size and importance as the stopping place of the caravans. As a legal entity the Stare Mesto dates from 1232 and the line of walls and moat, followed by the present-day inner ring street, was built from 1235. Within this ring, the Stare Mesto forms a typically organic, mediaeval plan-form centred on the beautiful Old Town Square and crossed from east to west by the winding Royal Road which leads across the bridge to the Hradcany (Fig. 7.12).

The northern part of the square and the entire north-western part of the Stare Mesto are however the unfortunate result of nineteenth-century 'improvements'. Parizska Avenue, which leads directly north out of the square, and as a vista street is in total contrast to the otherwise closed exits, is the worst aspect of this work.

The great period of urbanism in Prague is the reign of Charles IV (1346–78) during which time the city, as the capital of the Holy Roman Empire, was the most important urban centre in Europe. Charles IV founded Europe's oldest university in Prague in 1348 and laid out the area to the south and east of the Stare Mesto as a controlled extension to the city. This development was planned around three squares, two of which remain: Charles Square, intended as the centre of the new district and until recent times serving as cattle and general markets, and Wenceslas Square, in effect a widened street nearly half a mile in length and 200 feet wide, and now the modern business centre of the city.

Figure 7.12 – The upper-floor plan of the Ungeld block to the east of the Old Town Square (shown in solid black in Figure 7.13). From the eleventh century onwards this part of the Old Town had served as a customs and taxation district for merchants arriving in the city. Here they were assessed for duty, from which the name Ungeld was derived. Individual buildings surrounding the main courtyard and the subsidiary spaces immediately to the north are all of basically thirteenth and fourteenth century construction, but elevations have been remodelled since then.

Prague has an embarrassment of such historic buildings. There is a limit to the number that can be used for museums, or specialist offices, and rehabilitation for residential purposes is extremely expensive. In the case of the Ungeld block the proposal is to convert the old buildings for use as a hotel and a cultural meeting centre.

Charles
Bridge

B A C

Powder
Tower

D

Figure 7.13 – Prague, the detail plan of the Stare Mesto (north at the top). The Old Town Square is in the centre, with the Ungeld Hotel project behind the Tyn Church to the east (solid black on the plan). The river Vltava forms the western and northern sides of the Old Town; the defensive wall of 1235, with its moat, was demolished in 1760 to form the line of the present-day east-bank inner-ring boulevard. The age-of-buildings key shows clearly the extent of the oldest areas (shown in heavy outline) with their typical organic-growth structure, in contrast to the nineteenth-century redevelopment of the northern section (shown hatched) organised around the new Parizska Avenue.

Key: A, Old Town Square; B, Town Hall (northern wing destroyed in 1945); C, Tyn Church; D, northern end of Wenceslas Square.

Vienna

From the beginnings of European history the site of Vienna has been an important meeting place of trading routes. The river Danube was relatively passable at this point, using ferries to an island in the stream. The Romans recognised the strategic importance of the site, and in the first century AD they established a fortified camp on the southern bank of the river as a key part of their empire frontier defences. During the crusades, Vienna was an important military centre, trading interests following close behind. The first permanent bridge over the Danube was constructed between 1435 and 1440.

City defences were constantly improved during the fifteenth and sixteenth centuries and as a result Vienna was able to resist Turkish sieges in 1529 and 1683. The fortification system around the Altstadt, the old city of Vienna, followed the general pattern of Renaissance defensive works, combining formidable bastions and earthworks with a wide, cleared fire zone. An outer ring of suburbs grew up during the sixteenth and seventeenth centuries to provide for the 'overspill' population from the congested Altstadt and for houses with gardens for wealthier citizens. These suburbs, which were developed from the earlier village settlements around Vienna, were largely destroyed during the sieges, with their inhabitants sheltering within the Altstadt, but they were subsequently renewed.

After the 1683 Turkish invasion of central Europe, which was largely halted by Vienna's stubborn resistance, the cleared fire zone surrounding the defences was increased to a width of 1,700 ft involving the demolition of some 900 suburban houses. The Altstadt fortifications at that time consisted of twelve bastions, at first connected by earthen and later by stone walls, and of eleven outworks as an additional protection, the whole being surrounded by a wide moat[18].

After the 1683 siege the rebuilt suburbs represented sufficient capital investment to justify their own subsidiary outer defensive system. The legal boundary of the city was extended to include the suburbs and a Commission of Defences was set up, with Prince Eugene of Savoy as chief consultant to advise methods of protecting the new Greater Vienna area against attack. The outcome of this study was construction of the Linienwall of 1704 with its own 570 ft wide external zone supplemented by a 100 ft space along the inside of the walls. The Linienwall subsequently formed a customs barrier and was not completely demolished until 1893.

Throughout the eighteenth century Vienna developed on the basis of two distinct parts. Innermost was the congested Altstadt with narrow streets, tall houses, great old churches, the palaces of the aristocracy, and the Hofburg, the emperor's residence. Separated from it by a broad belt of defence works and open land lay outer Vienna in the form of extensive suburbs with gardens and spreading trees[19]. Napoleon captured Vienna in 1809 and rendered the city defenceless by demolishing the bastions and associated works.

From 1809 to the early 1850s the ruins of the fortifications remained untouched, with the broad space of the fire zone constituting an informally established park between the Altstadt and the suburbs. The ruins prevented any expansion of the Altstadt and the open space ring represented both a barrier separating the two parts of the city and an uneconomic use of land. In 1857, under the

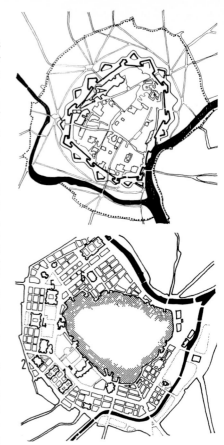

Figure 7.14, Top – Vienna in 1857, before the commencement of work on the Ringstrasse scheme. The defensive system around the Inner Altstadt was demolished in 1809 but remained in ruins and the fire-zone between it and the suburbs (outside the heavy dotted line) was used as an informally established park. Key: A, the Hofburg Palace; B, the Rathaus (Town Hall).

Above – The Ringstrasse Plan. The Altstadt is shown in outline only. Key: 1, Museum; 2, Palace of Justice; 3, Parliament House; 4, New Town Hall; 5, University; 6, Bourse.

---

18. E. A. Gutkind, *Urban Development in Central Europe.*

19. S. E. Rasmussen, *Towns and Buildings.*

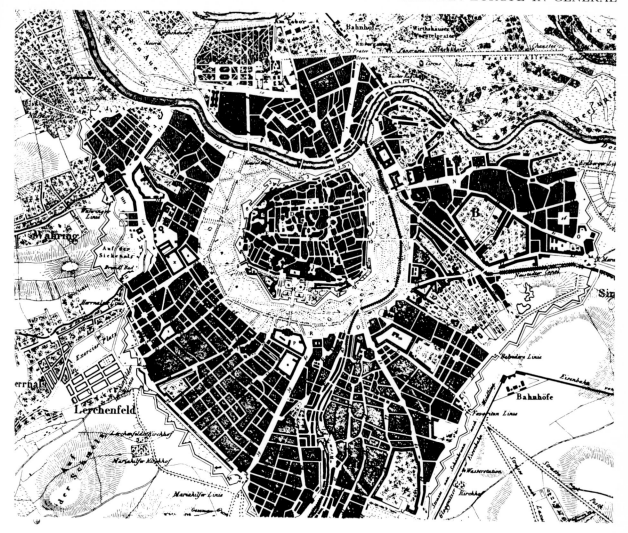

Figure 7.15 – Vienna in the early 1850s showing the extent of the suburbs, beyond the open space zone, enclosed within the Linienwall of 1704. The Danube canal passes across the northern side of the Altstadt; the main stream of the Danube is further to the north.

Emperor Franz Joseph, a competition was held for designs for the development of the derelict land. The competition conditions required that a large part of the area was to form residential sites, from the sale of which a building fund was to be created for financing the rest of the plan and erecting a number of large public buildings. In this respect the city was making maximum use of the fact that it owned all the previously fortified zone. Also required of competitors was the location of the given number of civic buildings, including the parliament building, *Rathaus*, university, museums, theatre and opera house. The winning design by Ludwig von Förster was approved in 1858 and carried out over the next decade. Its basis, as Fig. 7.14 shows, is a broad ring boulevard, the Ringstrasse, which is taken through the centre of the new area, circumscribing the Altstadt, with a linking quay along the bank of the Danube canal. The Ringstrasse is about 2 miles long and over 200 ft wide. It was laid out in the form of five straight sections each of which determined the alignment of five gridiron planned districts. Thus, says Rasmussen, the new districts were made up entirely of uniform building blocks except at the corner which would not come out right; the streets had no face, they were simply voids, empty spaces between the cubic blocks, not pleasant outdoor rooms as in old Vienna[20].

Vienna presents as clear a contrast as possible between the organic growth pattern of the mediaeval Altstadt and the formally planned Renaissance sections of the Ringstrasse. Much criticism of the visual aspects of the scheme – specially that of Camillo Sitte who makes constant reference to his native city in his *The Art of Building Cities* – is derived from this fact. Functionally, although the Ringstrasse project added the necessary public building, conveniently located to the old core, the new districts in turn formed a barrier between the centre and the suburbs with the problems of metropolitan traffic not recognised or understood.

Karlsruhe

The focal point of Karlsruhe – a palace, park and town example of autocratic planning second only to Versailles in Western Europe – was a forest hunting tower built in 1715 by the Margrave Karl Wilhelm, ruler of Baden Durlach. Although only modestly intended at first as a simple retreat, the tower soon became the centre of a total of 32 radiating routes, 23 of which served as forest rides and the remaining nine as the structure of a town which was laid out to the south. The tower was replaced by a grandiose palace between 1752–81 with flanking wings enclosing a formal forecourt. At the same time, the Langestrasse was laid out as a main cross axis through the town at right angles to that of the palace.

Early in the nineteenth century a formal western 'entrance' to the town was created by adding two streets at angles to the Langestrasse. Such drawing-board planning, whilst rigid and ingenious, nevertheless served as a perfect symbol of the 'l'Etat c'est moi' spirit of absolute rulers, whose considerable command of resources and power was both their strength and their weakness.

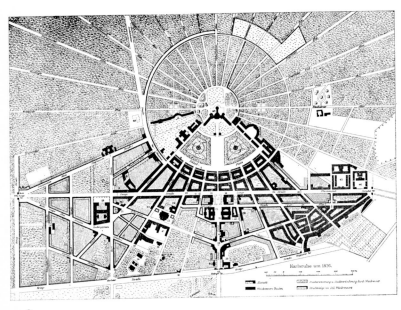

Figure 7.16 — Karlsruhe, palace park and town (north at the top).

20. S. E. Rasmussen, *Towns and Building*.

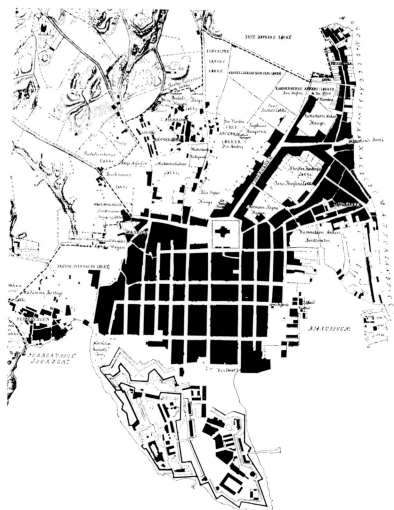

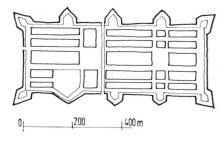

Figure 7.17 — Christiana (Oslo), showing the original blocks of Christiana as founded in 1624 alongside Akershus (north at the top).

Figure 7.18 — Christianstad, founded in 1614: a two-part plan with a canal as the dividing element. Like Fredericia (Fig. 7.19) this fortress-city was planned in the same era as Christiana (Oslo) and Gothenburg (Fig. 5.5).

Oslo

Oslo had its origins in a small fishing and trading settlement alongside the river Alna (modern Loevla) where it enters Oslo fjord some 80 miles from the Skagerack. Early in the fourteenth century Haakon V (1299–1319) made Oslo the capital of Norway ruling from the fortress of Akershus which was built on a rocky promontory. During the Middle Ages Akershus also served as a refuge for the civilian population; the town itself was not fortified. Apart from the main castle buildings, Oslo consisted of closely packed timber houses; the inevitable fires caused serious damage in 1352, 1523 and 1611 and were responsible for Oslo's slow mediaeval growth, until finally, in 1624, a three-day fire completely destroyed the town. As rebuilt by Christian IV on a new site alongside Akershus to the north-east, the town was renamed Christiana; a title which it kept until reverting to Oslo in 1924. This new town had a simple gridiron plan, and its spacious streets, combined with the compulsory use of stone, overcame the danger of further conflagrations. On this new basis Christiana grew steadily: all the original grid blocks were occupied by 1661,

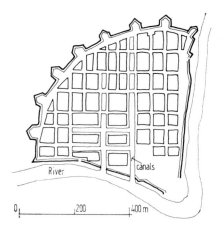

Figure 7.19 — Fredericia, founded in 1650: a plan notable for the penetration of canals into the defended area.

and with suburban additions the number of inhabitants had exceeded 5,000, and by 1704 a plan was drawn up controlling growth on the basis of new gridiron districts. Economic incentives for rapid growth were lacking however, and by the end of the eighteenth century the population of city and suburbs was little over 10,000.

Stockholm

Stockholm was founded in 1255 on Stadsholmen – an island in the narrow channel linking Sweden's extensive natural waterway system to the Baltic, by way of Lake Malaren. Thus it controlled shipping along key trading routes and the north-south land crossing by way of its two bridges, Norrbro and Soderbro.

Early expansion on Stadsholmen required made-ground, gained by filling in between harbour jetties, and consequently took the form of long narrow blocks between the old wall and the new quayside. By the late fifteenth century Stockholm had become established as Sweden's leading town; continued growth resulted in sizeable bridge-head settlements and during the period 1620 to 1650, when the number of inhabitants increased from less than 10,000 to aproximately 40,000, both Norrmalm and Sodermalm became extensively developed. Following the destruction by fire in 1697 of the old mediaeval palace, Tre Kronor, Nicodemus Tessin the Younger (1654–1728), architect to both the city and the royal court, designed the new palace of 1713 as part of a grandiose attempt to unite Stadsholmen visually and symbolically with Norrmalm. However as Kell Astrom relates, 'coming at a time of political and economic adversity, the whole project had to be kept secret, known only to the king and his closest associates'[21]. Some of Tessin's proposals were evidently implemented in the 1770s under Gustavus III. Development of the

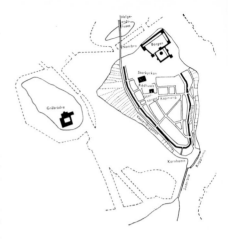

Figure 7.20 — Stockholm, the plan of Stadsholmen at the end of the thirteenth century. The present-day waterfront is shown dotted. The royal castle was located on the highest part of the island in the north-east corner.

NORRMALM 1640

Figure 7.21 — Stockholm, the plan of lower Norrmalm in 1640; the old city of Stadsholmen is at the bottom. Stockholm's continuing central area regeneration programme — one of the most ambitious in the world — covers most of this part of lower Norrmalm and its implementation has been considerably aided by the existence of a regular grid structure.

Figure 7.22 — Stockholm, the late nineteenth century plan showing the relationship of Stadsholmen to Norrmalm, and to Sodermalm, in effect a second island separated from the mainland by a partly artificial waterway.

21. Kell Astrom, *City Planning in Sweden*, 1967 (Swedish Institute for Cultural Relations with Foreign Countries).

mainland districts, especially Norrmalm and Kungsholmen further to the north-west, was such that by the beginning of the eighteenth century Stadsholmen had become an unfashionable backwater. The centre of Stockholm gradually moved across to Norrmalm leaving the island as the 'Old Town', with its shipping activities, warehouses and lower-class housing blocks.

The continuing story of Stockholm's mid-twentieth century ambitious, seemingly successful, central area conservation and renewal programme is outside the scope of this volume. Although history has favoured Stockholm's modern planners – providing a grid structure which facilitated renewal of the modern commercial centre of Norrmalm, and a uniquely preserved historic nucleus on Stadsholmen – it must be stressed once again that one of history's main lessons is that 'paper planning', however seductive its images, amounts to nothing without political support.

Warsaw

At the end of the thirteenth century town rights were granted to a small settlement which occupied the site of Warsaw's present Old Town. This was probably a rebuilding of an earlier town of Jazdow, burnt down in 1262. The site of the Old Town was on the edge of a steep embankment, some 70 ft high, on the wester side of the Vistula, which flowed in a flood plain some 12 km wide until it was contained from the eighteenth century onwards. The Old Town was strongly fortified by 1339, with a double wall on the land side and a single wall on the edge of the river embankment. Tributary streams formed natural moats to the north and south. Fourteenth century Warsaw was a small town covering only 40 acres; other Polish towns were much larger, notably Cracow and Poznan. Within roughly oval walls the Old Town comprised some 150 building plots, each about 30 ft wide and 115 to 130 ft long. The street pattern was based on the gridiron and the market place in the centre was around 310 by 230 ft in area. A ducal castle (rebuilt later as the Royal Palace) was constructed from 1289, immediately to the south of the Old Town.

Warsaw's favourable location at the meeting place of the main east-west, north-south central European trading routes resulted in steady growth, and by 1408, with the area within the walls fully developed, expansion was necessary and a 'New Town' was built immediately to the north. After the disastrous fire of 1431 the town council decreed that no more wooden dwellings to be permitted and Warsaw became a city of brick. The first permanent bridge dates from 1549 and in 1596 the capital was moved from Cracow to Warsaw thereby ensuring its continued growth as a major European city.

The 1830 Warsaw was occupied by troops of the Russian Tsar and a citadel was built immediately north of the Old Town. It was not finally removed until after 1945 and its presence meant that the city expanded in an unbalanced fashion, mainly south along the Vistula, and to the west.

The appalling record of the systematic destruction of Warsaw by the Nazi army in the last months of 1944, and the subsequent reconstruction achievements, is outside the period of this volume. For those who are interested in a description of this modern period, related to the general history of Warsaw, Adolf Ciborowski's book *Warsaw: a City Destroyed and Rebuilt* is recommended.

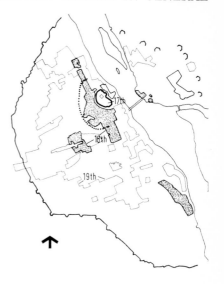

Figure 7.22 — Warsaw, a diagrammatic plan showing three growth stages of the seventeenth, eighteenth and nineteenth centuries. Nineteenth century expansion northwards along the western bank of the Vistula was prevented by the existence of the Tsarist Russian citadel.

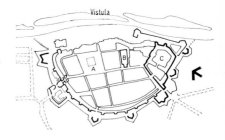

Figure 7.23 — Warsaw, the plan of the Old Town (Stare Mesto) in 1655, within its defensive perimeter. Key: A, the Old Town Square; B, St John's Cathedral; C, the Castle.

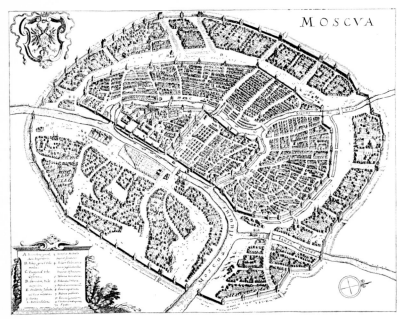

MOSCVA

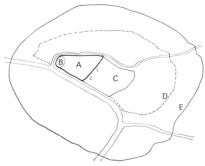

Figure 7.24 — Moscow in 1606, one of the clearest European examples of concentric-ring growth within successive defensive perimeters. The key diagram (below) identifies the following: A, the Kremlin; B, assumed extent of original settlement; C, Kitay Gorod; D and E, sixteenth century perimeters; 1, site of Red Square; 2, St Basil's Cathedral.

At this period the city's growth was contained within the sixteenth century perimeters (D and E). The first of these rings was placed approximately 2 km out from the Kremlin, on the north bank only, and forms the line of a modern park boulevard system. The second perimeter, 15 km in circumference, was centred precisely on the belfry of the Cathedral of Ivan the Great in the Kremlin and today forms a continuous inner-ring motorway system including multi-level intersections with the main radial streets. Following the loss of the city's governmental functions to St Petersburg in the eighteenth century, Moscow devoted itself increasingly to trade and industry. Two-thirds of the city was destroyed by fire during Napoleon's brief occupation in 1812, but vigorous rebuilding under Alexander I saw reconstruction completed in 1825. From a population of about 100,000 in 1520 the city reached 350,000 by 1863, and had exceeded one million by 1897.

Moscow

The earliest known reference to Moscow is of 1147 although it seems most likely that the attraction of the site – a prominent ridge alongside and commanding the Moskva river – would have encouraged earlier occupations. In 1147 Yuri Dolgoruki, Prince of Suzdal, constructed a fortress on the northern, left-bank of the Moskva on high ground some 130 feet above the river, in the angle formed by the main stream and a tributary, the Neglinnaia. Within an oaken palisade of 1156–8 the first settlement occupied an area of about 10 acres at the western end of the ridge. After two centuries of steady expansion eastwards along the ridge – the area of the present-day Kremlin – approximately 75 acres had been occupied. (*Kreml*, meaning 'high town', is analagous to burg.) The first Kremlin wall of masonry was constructed from 1367; the immensely impressive present-day wall was built between 1485 and 1508. This wall was crenellated, after the Italian fashion, and was strengthened by 20 towers.

From the fourteenth century the Kremlin consolidated its rôle as a city within a city, the political and administrative citadel of a ruling élite. Further to the east, beyond a moat cut across the ridge and the market place, later to become Red Square, a merchant's town, known as Kitay Gorod, became established from this time. (Although this name translates literally as 'China Town' its true derivation is from the Tartar word 'fortress'.) Kitay Gorod was walled between 1535–8.

8 — The Renaissance: Britain

In Britain the first Renaissance urbanism was Covent Garden Piazza in London – developed from 1630 onwards. In this country, as in Western Europe generally, the Renaissance in the plastic arts – painting, sculpture, architecture and urbanism – was preceded by the creation of a favourable intellectual climate based on the growth of literacy and scientific humanism, as outlined in Chapter Five. The Renaissance had similar origins in both France and England; painters and sculptors were brought in from Italy to work at the royal courts in the new style; the dates are around 1500 in France and during the reign of Henry VIII (1509–47) in England.

The significant delay between the more or less simultaneous advent of Renaissance art in both countries, and the first urbanism (dating from 1545 in provincial France with the planning of Vitry-le-François, 1607 in Paris and the 1630s in London) is mainly accounted for by the firm hold retained by Gothic architecture in its concluding phases. Italy, on the other hand, had never fully accepted the essentially northern Gothic style and when the first Renaissance building was started in Florence in 1419 architecture in England was still vigorously developing its late Perpendicular masterpieces – notably the chapels of King's College, Cambridge (1446 onwards), St George's at Windsor (1481 onwards) and Henry VII's at Westminster Abbey (1503–19). It was only towards the end of the sixteenth century that English architecture saw the gradual introduction of Renaissance details on otherwise Gothic buildings, and it is not until 1621 that the first essentially Renaissance building was completed – the Banqueting Hall in Whitehall – to be followed within a decade by the first urbanism in London[1].

London

PRE-SEVENTEENTH CENTURY GROWTH

Following the withdrawal of the Roman legions from Britain in the fifth century, London was sacked on a number of occasions, but the strategic importance of the site, which controlled the lowest possible crossing of the Thames[2], always encouraged its reoccupation, at least in part. Alfred the Great repaired the defences and consolidated London 'as a fortified garrison town which served the interests of

It is probable that the population of England and Wales at the end of the Queen's reign (Elizabeth I) had passed four millions, about a tenth of its present size. More than four fifths lived in the rural parts; but of these a fair proportion were engaged in industry, supplying nearly all the manufactures required by the village, or, like the clothiers, miners, and quarrymen, working for a more general market. The bulk of the population cultivated the land or tended sheep.

Of the minority who inhabited towns, many were engaged, at least for part of their time, in agriculture. A provincial town of average size contained 5,000 inhabitants. The towns were not overcrowded, and had many pleasant gardens, orchards, and farmsteads mingled with the rows of shops. Some smaller towns and ports were in process of decay. The recession of the sea, the silting up of rivers (which gradually put Chester on the Dee out of action as a port), the increase in the size of ships demanding larger harbours, the continued migration of the cloth and other manufactures in rural villages and hamlets, were all causes of the decline of some of the older centres of industry or commerce.

Yet the town population was on the increase in the island taken as a whole. York, the capital of the north; Norwich, a great centre of the cloth trade, welcoming skilled refugees from Alva's Netherlands; Bristol with mercantile and inland trade of its own wholly independent of London – these three were in a class by themselves, with perhaps 20,000 inhabitants each. And the new oceanic conditions of trade favoured other port towns in the west, like Bideford.

But, above all, London, absorbing more and more of the home and foreign commerce of the country at the expense of many smaller towns, was already a portent for size in England and even in Europe. When Mary Tudor died it may have had nearly 100,000 inhabitants; when Elizabeth died it may already have touched 200,000.

(G. M. Trevelyan, 'Illustrated English Social History')

---

1. For a general introduction to Renaissance architecture in Britain the reader is referred to Nikolaus Pevsner, *An Introduction to European Architecture*, and Peter Kidson, Peter Murray and Paul Thompson, *A History of English Architecture*.

2. For the history of Roman London and the origin of settlement on the site, see page 58.

the king by maintaining its own independence'[3]. Although not yet the national capital, London was by far the most important commercial centre.

Early in the eleventh century the kings moved their residence from Winchester to Westminster – some miles upstream from the City of London – where a royal precinct was established on Thorney Island, consisting of church, monastery and palace. William the Conqueror confirmed the existence of the independent royal and commercial cities of Westminster and London. These twin centres were linked by Whitehall and the Strand, the land between this route and the river being mainly used for the town palaces of noble families. As early as 1175 the cities were joined by a ribbon of development and it was inevitable that the first stage in the expansion of the capital was their unification into one continuous urban area, with each, however, still zealously guarding its political independence.

By 1605 London's estimated population was 225,000, of which total '75,000 lived in the City, 115,000 in the liberties (which included such precincts as St Martins-le-Grand, Blackfriars, Whitefriars, Duke's Place Aldgate, and the areas between the gates and outer bars, ie the suburbs), and 35,000 in the out-parishes'[4]. The population of the City in 1530 had been around 35,000 with the figure for the whole London area about 50,000. Only a small proportion of this increase was due to natural population growth; by far the greater part represented population movement into the capital, both from other parts of the country and from abroad. The internal migration was brought about by a number of factors, in particular the effect of the land enclosures. These had created more efficient sheep-farming conditions for wool production, but deprived many countrymen of their living and sent them to the towns in search of employment. Immigration from the Continent was also influenced by the growing textile industry, with many weavers, among others, coming to settle around London.

Parliament, the Crown, and the City of London authorities were all united in their resolve to arrest the drift to the capital. This policy, which proved to be markedly unsuccessful, was the result of a number of inter-related pressures, each involving the interests of the City merchants. First there was the political danger of revolutionary action by a large unemployed urban mob. This, by its existence, enabled wages to be kept at an extremely low level: a degree of unemployment was to the City's advantage. But by the second half of the sixteenth century the situation was dangerously out of control. The problem was increased still further after the dissolution of the monasteries, with 'the friars who formerly had relieved the poor, now added to their numbers themselve.'[5]. A second consideration was a dawning awareness of the connection between urban overcrowding and disease; the sequence of plagues, culminating in the visitation of 1665 which killed an estimated 90,000 people in the London area, represented a constant threat to the development of foreign trade. The third and most immediate challenge to the City's commercial interests, however, was the growth of suburban workshops operating outside the control of the long-established guilds, set up in many instances by unqualified apprentices in direct competition with their erstwhile masters.

Queen Elizabeth's famous proclamation of 1580 which 'doth

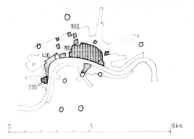

Figure 8.1 – Three stages in the early growth of London showing the unification of the Cities of London and Westminster along the line of the Strand, on the north bank of the Thames. Subsequent expansion east and north-east took the usual British form of radial-route ribbon-development, followed by infilling of the back land. West and north-west of the City of London development was partly planned – eg Covent Garden, and Lincoln's Inn, and partly unplanned. (For the extent of the eighteenth and nineteenth century planned districts further west and north see Figure 8.17.) South of the river the original bridgehead settlement grew slowly by comparison, mainly as a waterfront ribbon along the Thames.

The rising importance of parliament enhanced the capital's popularity and it was the home of busy tradesmen and merchants, of poets and painters, of beautiful women and witty and intelligent men. It was by far the largest port in the country and provided much employment; at the same time it contained poverty and disease and there were numerous slums. Though it was a gay city, above all when decorated by the full pageantry of the Court, it was also incredibly dirty and smelly. Hackney and Stepney were overcrowded and insanitary, while our modern suburbs such as Kensington and Hampstead were still country villages.
(Maurice Ashley. 'England in the Seventeenth Century')

3. S. E. Rasmussen, *London, the Unique City.*
4. Nikolaus Pevsner, *London – the Cities of London and Westminster.*
5. S. E. Rasmussen, *London, the Unique City.*

charge and strictly command all manner of persons, of what quality soever they be, to desist and forbear from any new buildings of any house or tenement within three miles from any of the gates of the City of London'[6], was based on 'the good and deliberate advice of her Council, and the considerate opinions of the Lord Mayor, Aldermen, and other grave wise men in and about the City'[7]. This proclamation, which was embodied in an Act of Parliament in 1592, is a clear recognition of the fact that the government of the realm was economically dependent on London and London meant, to Elizabeth, the government of the City that is to say the rich masters who governed as Lord Mayor and Aldermen.

It is essential to recognise the extent to which London dominated England's international trade. From 50 per cent of customs revenues in 1500, the proportion had increased to 66 per cent during Henry VIII's reign, and by 1581–82 it was over 86 per cent[8]. Rasmussen remarked that 'Elizabeth, who knew how to keep on the right side of the merchants, never called on the City in vain in time of need'[9].

Retaining favour with the merchants inevitably resulted in one law for the rich and another for those who could not afford to buy 'planning' consents. An early law of 1588 prohibited building around London (and other towns) unless the house was to be built on four acres of ground, and the Crown was always prepared to waive the restrictions on receipt of suitable 'dispensation'. Legislation imposing the 3-mile limit was re-enacted in 1602; the distance was reduced to 2 miles in 1607 but increased again, to 7 miles, in 1615. Nikolaus Pevsner has noted that a 7-mile radius would have drawn this *cordon sanitaire* as far as Tottenham and Chiswick, and it must have been clear from the beginning that no such restriction could be enforced[10]. The 1580 proclamation and the subsequent legislation were also concerned to prevent multiple occupation of existing buildings. Penalties for contravention were severe but the results of bought permissions and lax administration meant a continuing increase in the extent and population of the capital.

In England in the sixteenth and seventeenth centuries, for example, plague epidemics were common in the large towns like London, Norwich and Bristol, and each major outbreak brought a very severe toll of life. In London in 1603 at least 33,000 people died of the plague and 10,000 of other causes making a total of 43,000; in the plague of 1625 41,000 (63,000); in the Great Plague of 1665 (the last major English outbreak) 69,000 (97,000). These figures are based on the Bills of Mortality and are minima; the true figures must have been higher and may have been very much higher. In between the big outbreaks there were many years in which plague deaths could be measured by the thousand. During the period 1600 to 1660 the population of London grew from about 200,000 to about 450,000. In plague years therefore between a sixth and a quarter of the population of a great city might die even in the seventeenth century.
(E. A. Wrigley, 'Population and History')

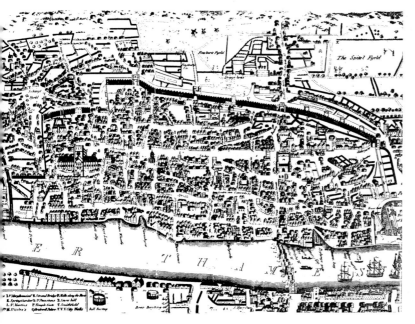

Figure 8.2 – Part of a map of the City of London before the Fire of 1666, showing the line of the mediaeval wall and ditch (already being built over to the west); Old St Pauls Cathedral; and Old London Bridge as lined with buildings.

6, 7. S. E. Rasmussen, *London, the Unique City*.
8. G. W. Southgate, *English Economic History*.
9. S. E. Rasmussen, *London, the Unique City*.
10. Nikolaus Pevsner, *London – the Cities of London and Westminster*.

The new districts were concentrated east and west of the City of London (Fig. 8.1). To the north development was not taken far beyond the old mediaeval wall. Eastwards, Stow writing in 1598 records 'half a mile of bad cottages in Whitechapel' and the existence of Wapping as 'a continual street or filthy passage'[11]. Expansion westwards at first covered the area between the Cities of London and Westminster and it is here, north of the Strand, that the Covent Garden development introduced Renaissance urbanism into the country.

COVENT GARDEN

This land, on seven acres of which the original Covent Garden development was carried out[12], was the first estate to be owned by the powerful Russell family. It was granted by Edward VI to the first Earl of Bedford in 1553, having been acquired by the Crown from the Abbey of Westminster in 1536. The name Covent Garden is derived from its previous use as part of the produce gardens of a convent. The Bedford Estate at first leased the land for grazing purposes – in 1559 the Earl is recorded as letting 28 acres on a 21-year lease for this purpose. Part of the Strand frontage was used for the Bedfords' town house in about 1560, with an enclosed and formally planted garden immediately behind, to the north. Unplanned, generally illegally-constructed, groups of houses were built in the open fields north of this garden from 1603 onwards, as part of the uncontrolled growth of London. The Covent Garden district was clearly 'ripe for development' and the fourth Earl of Bedford, 'very intelligent in a practical business-like way'[13] as Sir John Summerson has described him, recognised its potential value. Summerson records that developments along Drury Lane and Long Acre were already bringing in £500 a year when the earl succeeded to the property[14].

Obtaining the seventeenth-century equivalent of planning permission for an extensive upper-class housing development, as opposed to the tolerated process of gradual suburban accretion, proved difficult at first. Eventually, in return for a consideration of £2,000, a licence to build was made out, on the king's own instructions, in 1630[15]. It was not however unconditional consent; the earl was required to carry out his speculative building on such a scale and in such a manner as to provide a distinguished ornament and not merely an extension to the capital[16]. He was also required to use Inigo Jones (1573–1652) as architect.

INIGO JONES

As Summerson has said, it is essential to think of Jones, from first to last, as a Court architect imposing foreign formulae which were neither comprehensible nor particularly welcome to the ordinary Englishman[17]. In 1615, when he was 42 and recently returned from a second study tour in Italy, Inigo Jones was appointed Surveyor to the King (James I: 1603–25). He had previously been in great demand in court circles. His flair with the design of scenery for masques, in the now increasingly fashionable Italian Renaissance style, was incomparable. His post was one of great influence and personal opportunity. In London he was soon designing the Queen's House at Greenwich, built between 1618 and 1635 (now part of the National Maritime Museum), and the Whitehall Banqueting House

... sometime the Bishoppe of Carliles Inne, which now belongeth to the Earl of Bedford, and is called Russell or Bedford House. It stretcheth from the Hospitall of Savoy, west to Ivie bridge, where sir Robert Cecill, principall Secretary to her Majestie, hath lately raysed a large and stately house of brick and timber as also leviled and paved the highway neare adjoining, to the great beautifying of that street and commoditie of passengers. Richard the 2, in the 8. of his raigne, granted license to pave with stone the highway called Strand street from Temple barre to the Savoy. and tole to be taken towards the charges and the like was granted in the 24. of H. the 6.
(John Stow, 'A Survey of London', 1603)

11. John Stow, *A Survey of London. 1603.*
12. At the time of writing, the definitive proposals for redeveloping the whole of the Covent Garden area (following the market's move to a site at Nine Elms) are still unpublished. See Ralph Rookwood, *A New Covent Garden*, 'Official Architecture and Planning', May 1969, for an interim policy statement.
13, 14. John Summerson *Georgian London.*
15. *Le Début de l'Urbanisme anglais, l'Urbanisme de Paris et l'Europe 1600–1680*, edited Pierre Francastel, Editions Klincksieck, Paris, 1969. John Summerson, *Covent Garden.*
16. John Summerson, *Georgian London.*
17. John Summerson, *Inigo Jones.*

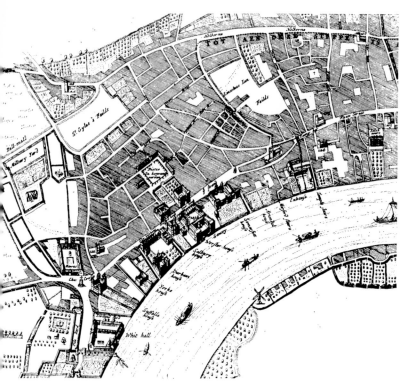

Figure 8.3 – A section of a map of London produced around 1667 showing the built-up area joining the City of London (to the right) and the City of Westminster (bottom left). A number of the mansions between the Strand and the Thames can be seen; Covent Garden Piazza is located left of centre, immediately north of the garden of the Duke of Bedford's mansion on the north side of the Strand. Lincoln's Inn Fields has yet to be formally developed (Kingsway, the present day main north/south route to its west dates only from the early years of the twentieth century). Trafalgar Square at the south-western end of the Strand was the work of Nash in the 1820s.

The undeveloped southern (right) bank of the Thames is in total contrast to the already densely built-up northern district. The Thames served as a main highway for commercial and private movement; it was the most convenient way to travel between the two cities and the numerous landing stages along the northern bank.

of 1619–21, which was intended to form part of a grandiose Palace of Whitehall[18]. He was the first English architect thoroughly to understand the principles of Renaissance design, and the originator of Renaissance urbanism in England.

In 1625 Charles I came to the throne with definite and autocratic ideas about the improvement of his 'rather squalid and untidy metropolis'[19]. One of the king's first actions was to establish a commission for buildings as an attempt to control the development and form of London through enforcement of existing legislation, imposition of limits on new building and regulation of methods of construction. Inigo Jones was one of its members, but the powers of the commission were limited, with Parliament resolved that Charles was not to be allowed to play with his capital as if it was a royal pleasance[20].

The Covent Garden Piazza took the form of a rectangle located immediately north of the Bedford House garden (Fig. 8.3). Its northern and eastern sides were uniformly designed terraces; identical houses flanking the church of St Paul formed the western side. The southern side was kept open, maintaining the views northwards from the house and garden to the hills of Highgate and Hampstead, and reducing loss of privacy to a minimum. Two streets entered the piazza in the centres of the eastern and northern sides. In designing his piazza, Inigo Jones was undoubtedly aware of continental precedents, notably the first of the residential squares in Paris, the Place Royale, built by Henry IV in 1605–12[21].

Covent Garden was at first an extremely fashionable residential district. But the demolition of Bedford House in 1703 and its replacement by poorer quality housing, together with the completion

How Inigo Jones, the King's Surveyor, came to be employed on the work is not obvious from the documents but inferences can be drawn. The Proclamation of 2 May 1625 was in the nature of an absolute prohibition of any building whatever, except on old foundations. The commissioners appointed to implement the Proclamation, however, were given some latitude. Nothing was said about building on old foundations and authority was given to any four commissioners, of whom the King's Surveyor of Works was to be one, to allot ground for the rebuilding of houses in such a way as to achieve 'Uniformitie and Decency'. This still did not allow for any increase in the number of houses but it did facilitate planned redistribution and, more significantly, established the principle that any new shaping of London's streets should come under the eye of the King's Surveyor – in other words Inigo Jones.
(John Summerson, 'Inigo Jones')

18. The Palace of Whitehall, as proposed, would have rivalled Versailles for size but the English monarchy lacked the absolute authority to build on such a scale. Charles I was executed in front of the Banqueting Hall – the only completed part of his intended palace.

19, 20. John Summerson *Georgian London*.

21. See page 140.

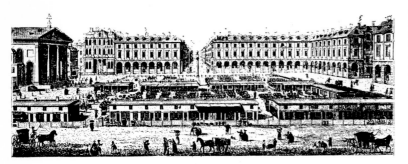

Figure 8.4 – Covent Garden in 1751. The market in the central space has already assumed a permanent character, consolidating temporary stalls present since the 1670s. This view is looking north, as from across the garden of Bedford House. Modern James Street is the central street running north out of the piazza; the corner bays to the west (left in view) have been reconstructed as a replica of the original design, all the other residences have long since been demolished although the outline of the piazza can still be clearly traced. St Paul, Covent Garden (left), was rebuilt after fire in 1795. The entrance to the Playhouse, later rebuilt as Covent Garden Opera House, was through the arcade in the top right-hand corner of the piazza.

of new attractive squares further west, accelerated the decline in its fortunes. As early as 1671 the new Duke of Bedford was granted the right to have a daily vegetable market in Covent Garden[22]. At first this was an open-air market; later, in 1828–31[23], informal permanent stalls were replaced by the earliest of the buildings still existing in 1972. Following the establishment of the market, and marking the decline, a number of the Covent Garden buildings came to be used for some of London's earliest coffee houses, with the arcades around the northern and eastern sides making attractive and sheltered meeting places.

One of the coffee houses became the venue of the theatrical fraternity and in 1731 John Rich, previously manager of the playhouse in Lincoln's Inn Fields, where *The Beggar's Opera* was first performed, leased the ground on which the present-day opera house stands. He also acquired the house of Dr Douglas on the north-east corner of the piazza, to make the principal entrance from there; the frontage to Bow Street contained only the approaches to the stage door[24]. Covent Garden Playhouse opened in 1732. By then 'the neighbourhood had ceased to be a fashionable place of residence; apart from Lord Archer, all the aristocratic inhabitants had moved to the newly developed West End. Covent Garden became the centre of London's night life; here were taverns, bagnios and houses of ill-fame, patronised alike by noblemen and persons of the lowest class throughout the night'[25]. Part of the eastern side was demolished in 1769 and the remainder in 1880 and 1890. The western corner of James Street, on the northern side of the piazza, was reconstructed along the original lines and gives an impression of the character of the design. St Paul's Church was burnt in 1795 but subsequently restored.

LINCOLN'S INN FIELDS

A first attempt to develop the fields adjoining Lincoln's Inn to the west was made in 1613. The king was petitioned for a building licence but strong opposition from the Society of Lincoln's Inn, who wanted the area to remain a public recreation space, influenced the application's rejection. Five years later, following pressure from local inhabitants, the king instructed Inigo Jones to prepare a plan for landscaping the fields with tree-lined walks after the pattern of Moorfields, a long established and popular open space to the north of the City. In 1638 William Newton acquired the lease of the fields and was quick to point out to the king that in its undeveloped state the land was worth only £5 6s 8d to the Crown in annual rental. His application to build 32 houses was granted before the Society

The south side of Covent Garden Square lieth open to Bedford Garden, where there is a small growth of trees, most pleasant in the summer season; and on this side there is kept a market for fruits, herbs, roots and flowers every Tuesday. Thursday and Saturday, which is grown to a considerable account, and well served with choice goods, which make it much resorted to.
(John Strype. 1720 revision of Stow's 'A Survey of London')

22. Donald J. Olsen, *Town Planning in London – the Eighteenth and Nineteenth Centuries.*
23. Nikolaus Pevsner, *London – the Cities of London and Westminster.*
24, 25. Hugh Phillips, *Mid-Georgian London.*

of Lincoln's Inn could object, but as Rasmussen notes, Newton 'made the agreement with them that the walks should remain an open square'[26].

By August 1641 the houses forming the southern and most of the western sides had been completed. At this point the society, changing its tactics, petitioned Parliament for an order preventing further building. This was granted and despite Newton's lobbying he was unable to get it rescinded before his death in 1643. The next owners persuaded the society to agree that the new buildings on the north side should have the same proportions as to height and breadth as those already built on the south side, so that the whole formed a regular square[27]. Before it could be completed the society was to change its mind once more, obtaining an order from Cromwell, preventing building, in 1656. Finally, in 1657, the society and the developers reached agreement whereby Lincoln's Inn Fields was given its present-day form. There were to be continuous terraces on three sides – south, west and north – the garden wall of the inn itself making the east side. The whole was to be a large tree-planted square, which was opened to the public in 1894.

Preceding the developments of Lincoln's Inn Fields and forming a western extension of its northern side Great Queen Street had been built in about 1635-40. The elevational designs of both the square and the street were assiduously controlled by the Commissioners on Buildings, for in every case the houses were fronted 'in the Italian taste'[28]. Tradition associates Inigo Jones with their detailed design but as Summerson observes, 'his rôle in getting such things done was probably far more that of a civil servant than a professional architect'[29]. Great Queen Street is generally regarded as the first regular street in London and was to serve as the pattern for the integrated architectural design approach of the succeeding two centuries – an approach which was reinforced by the statutory legislation introduced after the Fire of 1666. Great Queen Street's buildings have long since been demolished and the street itself is now separated from Lincoln's Inn Fields by Kingsway, which was cut through a slum area between 1889 and 1906.

LONDON BEFORE THE FIRE

Between June and December 1665 an estimated total of 90,000 persons in the London area died in the outbreak of the plague. In four days at the beginning of September in the following year the Fire of London destroyed a total area of 437 acres – 373 acres within the city walls and 64 acres outside. Only about 75 acres remained undamaged within the city walls, the ruin being so complete that the Thames could be seen from Cheapside[30]. G. M. Trevelyan has observed that the fire was a unique event; the plague was merely the last, and not perhaps the worst, of a series of outbreaks covering three centuries[31]. This quotation must be qualified. The fire of 1666 was unique because of its extent, which far surpassed all previous outbreaks, but both disease and fire were ever present hazards to life and property in an urban agglomeration the size of London, and far from unknown in towns in general.

London in 1666 was a typical mediaeval city with narrow, meandering streets and lanes. Most of the buildings were of timber construction, often with thatched roofs and corbelled out over the streets to obtain as much floor space as possible on their several

In 1650 London was already a city of about 350,000. In spite of the immense loss of life in the plague of 1665 and the disruption brought about by the Great Fire in the following year, London was the biggest city in Europe by 1700 with a population of about 550,000. By 1800 the figure had reached 900,000 and London was about twice the size of Paris, her nearest rival. Already in 1650 about 7 per cent of England's population lived in London; a hundred years later 11 per cent (Paris contained about 2 per cent of the total French population at the later date). Some of the cities of the classical world, though much smaller, had a malign effect upon local economies and could with reason be termed parasitic. In the case of London, however, its growth brought great benefit to the economy and provided much of the impetus to the general transformation of English society.
(E. A. Wrigley, 'Population and History')

26, 27. S. E. Rasmussen, *London, the Unique City.*
28, 29. John Summerson, *Georgian London.*
30. C. H. Holden and William Holford, *The City of London – A Record of Destruction and Survival.*
31. G. M. Trevelyan, *England under the Stuarts.*

upper floors. The monasteries and many of the merchants' mansions had been divided up into tenements and their gardens densely developed. The skyline was a romantic grouping of towers and spires: there were 109 churches in the City, dominated by the Gothic mass of St Paul's Cathedral. The fabric of the cathedral was, however, in an extreme state of disrepair – a condition reflecting that of the City in general. The street system was as obsolete as the buildings, which had gradually encroached on to the thoroughfares. It was totally unsuited to London's newly assumed rôle as a leader of world trade. The narrow, tortuous lanes leading down to the wharfs had already failed to accommodate packhorse traffic and could not possibly deal with the growth of cart and dray transport. As early as 1598 John Stow 'had been moved to describe carts and drays as one of the two great plagues of London, and in the intervening years their numbers had grown fast'[32]. Attempts were made to control this traffic by a system of licensing, broad wheels were made compulsory, and the number of horses was limited.

John Evelyn, the social commentator whose diaries give such a vivid picture of city life, had strongly condemned a number of its failings, notably the general use of soft coal which kept a pall of smoke continually obstructing the sun. Evelyn's general observation that the buildings and surroundings in London were as deformed as the minds and confusions of the people aptly summarises the situation in the London of 1666.

THE FIRE OF LONDON

The fire started in a baker's shop in Pudding Lane near London Bridge in the early hours of Sunday 2 September 1666. From being just another blaze of local interest this outbreak soon gathered force and, fanned by a strong north-east wind, spread from its origin just north of the bridge down to the warehouses and wharfs on the river. Before it was checked four days later the fire had destroyed 13,200 houses, the Royal Exchange, the Custom House and the halls of 44 of the city companies, Guildhall and nearly all the City buildings, St Paul's itself and 87 of the parish churches, besides furniture and commodities valued at over three and a half million pounds. In all the bill was reckoned at more than ten million[33].

About 80,000 people were made homeless by the fire. Tents were provided by the king, and the city authorities granted permission for temporary buildings on available open spaces. Royal proclamations ordered neighbouring parishes to provide lodgings, appointed new markets and instructed magistrates in the Home Counties to organise supplies. More important still Charles II broke down for the refugees the privileges of the corporate towns, commanding that all cities and towns whatsoever should without any contradiction receive the distressed persons and permit them the free exercise of their manual trades[34]. Of the 13,200 houses destroyed a large proportion represented both the homes and the work-places, warehouses and shops of the city merchants and craftsmen. Already suffering from the counter attractions of rapidly developing suburban centres, the City's commercial interests had to start rebuilding as soon as possible. In addition, the City's own property was largely destroyed and its rental income effectively cut off.

Charles II was not a Londoner and 'its patent disadvantages were not dimmed for him by a kindly veil of familiarity'[35]. He had

John Evelyn, the diarist, was walking one day in the well kept grounds of Whitehall Palace when a cloud of smoke came up in the direction of London, which so invaded the Court that all the rooms, galleries and places about it were filled and infected. Men could hardly discern one another for the cloud and none could suffer it without choking. Indignant he wrote his 'Fumifugium; or the Inconvenience of the Aer and Smoak of London Dissipated,' proposing remedies.

'It is horrid smoke', writes Evelyn. 'which obscures our churches and makes our palaces look old, which fouls our clothes and corrupts the waters. so that the very rain and refreshing dews which fall in the several seasons precipitate this impure vapour, which with its black and tenacious quality spots and contaminates whatever is exposed to it'. He bitterly complains that the gardens around London no longer bare fruit, instancing especially Lord Bridgwater's orchard at Barbican and the Marquis of Hertford's in the Strand.

(W. G. Bell, 'The Great Fire of London in 1666')

16th July 1665 – There died of the plague in London this week 1100; and in the week following, above 2000. Two houses were shut up in our parish.

2nd August. A solemn fast through England to deprecate God's displeasure against the land by pestilence and war; our Doctor preaching on 26 Levit. v. 41, 42, that the means to obtain remission of punishment was not to repine at it; but humbly to submit to it.

8th I waited on the Duke of Albemarle. who was resolved to stay at the Cock-pit, in St James's Park. Died this week in London, 4000.

15th There perished this week 5000.

28th The contagion still increasing, and growing now all about us, I sent my wife and whole family (two or three necessary servants excepted) to my brother's at Wootton, being resolved to stay at my house myself, and to look after my charge. trusting in the providence and goodness of God.

7th Sept. Home. there perishing near 10,000 poor creatures weekly; however, I went all along the city and suburbs from Kent Street to St James's, a dismal passage, and dangerous to see so many coffins exposed in the streets, now thin of people; the shops shut up, and all in mournful silence. not knowing whose turn it might be next.

(John Evelyn. 'Diary')

32. John Stow, *A Survey of London. 1603.*
33, 34, 35. T. F. Reddaway, *The Rebuilding of London after the Great Fire.*

already endorsed Evelyn's 1661 criticisms of its failings with 'encouragement to press on to find remedies'[36]. He had been aware of fire hazards and the need for wide streets to accommodate growth of trade with its traffic, and he must have known of the proposals to improve the Paris of Louis XIV. The king was therefore sympathetic to the concept of a completely replanned City of London, as embodied in the several designs prepared for his consideration. But he recognised, and acted upon, the need to minimise delay in starting the reconstruction process. 'In this he was at one with the City'[37].

On 13 September the king published a proclamation, in which he set out 'the decisions for the immediate present and his intentions for the future; the first step had been taken, and men could feel that the rebuilding was under control'[38]. Although only an interim step, the proclamation contained several of the measures later embodied in rebuilding legislation. Fire-resisting external building materials had to be used and important streets widened to constitute fire-breaks. The network of inconvenient and unhygienic lanes was to be replaced by wider streets; and, as a specific recommendation, there was to be a new quay along the bank of the Thames, maintaining the continuous contact between City and river revealed by the fire. The king undertook to rebuild the Custom House as soon as possible and to relinquish Crown property where it would be for common benefit. As the basis of financial provision for the rebuilding, the Crown promised to turn over all the coal tax revenue for seven years. The proclamation also instructed the City to prepare a survey of the devastated area, showing the existing land ownerships 'that provision may be made, that though every man must not be suffered to erect what buildings and where he pleases, he shall not in any degree be debarred from receiving the reasonable benefit of what ought to accrue to him'[39]. The time needed for the survey was to be utilised to agree a general plan for the rebuilding. In the interim a strict embargo was placed on unauthorised buildings. Those proven owners who wished to make an earlier start could do so if they conformed to the general plan.

By the end of September, realistic assessment of the complex obstacles in the way of complete replanning had led to general agreement that the existing street lines and property boundaries must be accepted. The property boundary survey, later to be abandoned, was already proving extremely difficult; ordinarily available revenue could not begin to pay for the land acquisition involved and the compulsory purchase legislation for street widening could not have been extended to comprehensive acquisition and redistribution of land, even if the political necessity to rebuild had been less urgent.

Because the fire occurred in September, it was possible to organise large-scale reconstruction. If the City had been devastated earlier in the year, the pressures to rebuild before the winter could have been irresistible. But by the time the ruins had been cleared, a particularly severe winter had set in and had prevented any further work until spring. At the beginning of October six commissioners were appointed, nominally to supervise the survey but in effect to control all technical aspects of the rebuilding work. The king nominated three commissioners – Wren, Hugh May and Roger Pratt. The City's representatives, styled surveyors, were Robert Hooke, Edward Jerman and Peter Mills. 'A better equipped body could hardly have been found . . . it had to be improvised and as an improvisation the six nominated

But tho' by the new buildings after the fire, much ground was given up, and left unbuilt, to inlarge the streets, yet 'tis to be observed, that the older houses stood severally upon more ground, were much larger upon the flat, and in many places, gardens and large yards about them, all which, in the new buildings, are, at least, contracted, and the ground generally built up into other houses so that notwithstanding all the ground given up for beautifying the streets, yet there are many more houses built than stood before upon the same ground; so that taking the whole city together, there are more inhabitants in the same compass, than there was before. To explain this more fully, I shall give some particular instances, to which I refer, which there are living witnesses able to confirm.

For example, Swithen's Alleys by the Royal Exchange, were all, before the Fire, taken up with one single merchant's house, and inhabited by one Mr Swithin; whereas, upon the same ground where the house stood, stands now about twenty-two or twenty-four houses, which belong to his posterity to this day.

Copt-Hall-Court in Throckmorton-street, was, before the Fire, also a single house, inhabited by a Dutch merchant; also three more courts in the same streets, were single houses, two on the same side of the way, and one on the other.

The several alleys behind St Christopher's Church, which are now vulgarly, but erroneously, call'd St Christopher's-Churchyard, were, before the Fire, one great house, or, at least, a house and ware-houses belonging to it, in which the famous Mr Kendrick lived, whose monument now stands in St Christopher's Church, and whose dwelling, also, took up almost all the ground, on which now a street of houses is erected, called Prince's-street, going through into Lothbury, no such street being known before the Fire.

Kings-Arms-Yard in Coleman-street, now built into fine large houses, and inhabited by principal merchants, was, before the fire, a stable-yard for horses and an inn, at the sign of the King's Arms.

I might fill up my account with many such instances, but 'tis enough to explain the thing, viz. That so many great houses were converted into streets and courts, alleys and buildings, that there are, by estimation, almost 4000 houses now standing on the ground which the Fire left desolate, more than stood on the same ground before.

(Defoe, 'A Tour through the whole Island of Great Britain')

36, 37, 38. T. F. Reddaway, *The Rebuilding of London after the Great Fire.*

39. W. de G. Birch, *The Historical Charters and Constitutional Documents of the City of London,* 1897.

could not have been bettered'[40]. Wren, Pratt and May were architects though Wren was not much more than a student. Hooke was a mathematician and scientist, as Wren also was by training. Jerman and Mills, the City Surveyor, had practical building background and an extensive understanding of the City's requirements.

Dr Christopher Wren – he was not knighted until 1674 – submitted the first rebuilding plan to the king on 11 September. John Evelyn followed with his proposals two days later. Robert Hooke's plan was shown to the Royal Society on 19 September; 'the court of the Lord Mayor and aldermen had approved of it and, greatly preferring it to that of the city surveyor Peter Mills, desired that it might be shown to his Majesty'[41]. The surveyor's plan has not survived but three others have – two versions by Richard Newcourt (see page 224 for influence on the plan of Philadelphia) and one by a Captain Valentine Knight. With the exception of Wren's plan, which must be assessed at greater length, notes on the designers and their proposals are given as captions to the plans.

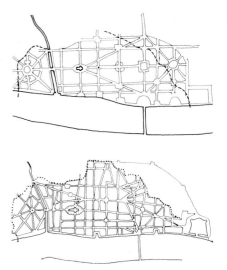

SIR CHRISTOPHER WREN (1632–1723)

In 1666 Wren, at the age of 34, was Professor of Astronomy at Oxford and an outstandingly gifted member of the Royal Society. He had put forward numerous scientific inventions and theories, many of which 'aimed right at the central problems of astronomy, physics and engineering'[42]. He had only two buildings to his credit – the Sheldonian Theatre at Oxford, designed in 1664, and Pembroke College Chapel, Cambridge, 1663–66. Sir Reginald Blomfield, 'while describing himself as not the least of Wren's admirers has to admit that between 1660 and 1670 he was the merest amateur in architecture and that his appointment had in it more of influence than of justice'[43]. Nikolaus Pevsner dismisses the two first buildings as 'evidently the work of a man with little designing experience'[44].

Figures 8.5 and 8.6 – Two of the three plans produced by John Evelyn, 'a typically wealthy, well-educated nobleman, who could live entirely for his hobbies and who divided his time equally between aesthetic and practical subjects' (S E. Rasmussen, *London, the Unique City*). Both plans are similar in many respects to Wren's plan, notably the section west of the Fleet.

Wren, however, had excellent connections. As early as 1661 he had been offered an appointment surveying and directing harbour works at Tangier[45], and he was involved with the work of the royal commission (set up in 1663) on the state of St Paul's. From July 1665 to March 1666 he was in France studying architecture. No doubt he had the repair of the cathedral very much in mind, because a few weeks after his return he submitted a report with suggestions for its restoration. Wren was closely connected with John Evelyn and Eduard Sekler is no doubt right in assuming that both men had pretty much the same views on the ideals to be pursued in town planning[46]. Certainly their respective plans for the City have much in common.

The history of urbanism has created a number of myths, centred around personalities ancient and modern. Totally fictional claims are made for Hippodamus as the father of town planning and the inventor of the gridiron, and even his planning of Miletus could only have involved a small part of the city. The Emperor Augustus may well have found Rome a city of brick, but he could only have left it partially a city of marble. In recent years more than one planner has achieved a reputation that will certainly be undermined, if not demolished, sooner or later.

Wren has been accorded mythical significance on several inter-related counts. He has been described as an exceptionally gifted town planner, whose brilliant proposals for rebuilding the City

Figure 8.7 – 'Brilliant, cantankerous, secretive, always in ill-health, Robert Hooke was Curator of Experiments to the Royal Society, Professor of Geometry at Gresham College and already well known for the experiments which were later to bring him enduring fame' (T. F. Reddaway, *The Rebuilding of London after the Great Fire*). Hooke's plan has been lost, but a small drawing of a plan included in Doornick's *View of the Fire* may be of his proposals. The regular gridiron structure contains a range of civic spaces and a spacious quay along the Thames.

40, 41. T. F. Reddaway, *The Rebuilding of London after the Great Fire*.

42. Nikolaus Pevsner, *An Outline of European Architecture*.

43. Reginald Blomfield, *English Architecture in the Seventeenth and Eighteenth Centuries*.

44. Nikolaus Pevsner, *An Outline of European Architecture*.

45, 46. Eduard Sekler, *Wren and his place in European Architecture*.

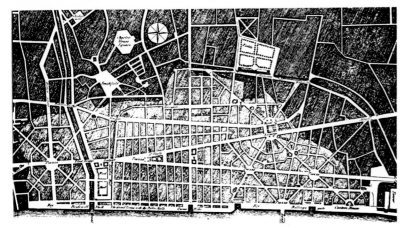

Figure 8.8 – Wren's plan for the rebuilding of London, as redrawn by John Gwynn in 1749 and presented for the 'consideration of the Lord Mayor, Aldermen, and Common Council of the City of London' under the totally misleading heading, 'Designed by that great architect Sir Christopher Wren and approved of by King and Parliament, but unhappily defeated by faction'. This claim by Gwynn (who was using Wren's plan as an example of what could be done, in his campaign for planning improvements in London) is a main source of the myth of Wren's plan. Later, in 1766, Gwynn wrote of '. . . the unaccountable treatment the noble plan of Sir Christopher Wren met with from the interested views of ignorant, obstinate, designing men, (notwithstanding it had the sanction of the King and Parliament) who by rejecting it did an irreparable injury to the city of London . . . .' (John Gwynn, *London and Westminster Improved*. London 1766. Republished in 1969 by Gregg International Publishers Limited.)

were 'unhappily defeated by faction'[47]. These were the words of his apologist, the architect Gwynn, written in 1749, an observation restated by Lewis Mumford, who described the proposals as being foiled by tenacious mercantile habits and jealous property rights[48]. It has also been said that the rejection of his proposals and the rebuilding of the City as before, without improvements, was the greatest missed opportunity in urban history.

That Wren's plan was totally irrelevant to the needs of the City has already been established. As such it was neither more nor less invalid than all the other plans. Criticism on this count is therefore less of Wren himself than of his advocates. Also we do not know how seriously Wren regarded his proposals. It is recorded that he was greatly concerned to get in first with his plan, but perhaps this was the policy of an ambitious embryo architect seeking to establish his claim to a major share of the rebuilding commissions. Such pre-empting activity has not been unknown in more recent times, and it can be argued that his plan was the means to the end of being appointed Surveyor-General in 1669 and acquiring the commission to design the new St Paul's and 66 city churches, in addition to almost all the other worthwhile architectural work of the period.

On the other hand, his proposals could have had serious intent, and the plan therefore needs to be examined in greater detail. Steen Rasmussen regards them as the work of 'a mathematician who, starting from certain definite postules, has solved... an interesting geometrical problem. To him [Wren] it was a given thing (1) that the entrances to the town were its gates and its bridges; (2) that a town is composed of rectangular houses; (3) that all street corners should preferably be rectangular; (4) that the entrances should give easy access to the different parts of the town; and (5) that the centre of commerce, the Stock Exchange, and the religious centre, St Paul's, should have a dominating position. The problem was the plexus of streets. This he solved by means of the common form ideals of those days'[49].

The Wren plan, in common with the others, would certainly have improved the street system, particularly the east-west routes, and it is competently related to the streets giving access to the City. But it would have suffered from the usual defects of a plan that imposes radial streets on a basic grid pattern, as in Washington DC. Moreover

Figure 8.9 – Captain Valentine Knight, an army officer, devised a plan that laid greater emphasis on the regular re-organisation of building plots, in contrast with the plans of Wren and Evelyn, who put the street system first. Main streets 60 ft wide form a 'super-grid', which is broken down by 30 ft-wide secondary streets, parallel to the river, into building plots of around 500 ft by 70 ft, which would allow two rows of buildings separated by a central back alley. Pavements were to be as arcades beneath the buildings (as at Covent Garden) and a 30 ft canal was to run around the central section of the new City from the Fleet, at Holborn Bridge, to Billingsgate – an interesting idea but topographically impossible at other than great expense.

47. John Gwynn, *London and Westminster Improved, 1766* (Republished 1969). Appendix A of Reddaway's *The Rebuilding of London after the Great Fire* deals most thoroughly with sources of the myth that Wren's plan was first accepted only to be discarded as a result of commercial pressures.

48. Lewis Mumford, *The City in History*.

49. S. E. Rasmussen, *London, the Unique City*.

there are also two inherent major counts on which it can be seriously faulted, the first being that it is not related to the site. This is not flat, but undulating, with the two hills which rise on either side of the valley of the Walbrook, more steeply sloping in 1666 than in modern times (Fig. 8.10). The same conditions existed on both sides of the Fleet and the slopes down to the Thames. Superimposition of a grid on undulating ground results in visual effects contrary to the basic objectives of Renaissance urbanism – that of creating a unified, ordered architectural entity. Because of the nature of the land Wren's main avenues, notably those flanking his new St Paul's, would have had vertically staggered cornice lines to accommodate the slope; the magnificent perspective vistas that seem to be created on Wren's two-dimensional diagram could never have existed in reality on the ground. The second main criticism is of the arbitrary divisions of his city into three parts, each of which is given a basically different structure. From east to west there is first an unresolved radial system; then a central, relatively straightforward grid section crossed by the two main avenues; finally, mainly west of the Fleet, there is a section arranged around a large traffic area.

It is surely not possible to see Wren's plan as more than an over-night exercise based on the use of undigested continental Renaissance plan-motifs. On balance, allowing for all that has happened since 1666, London as rebuilt to an improved version of its old plan is to be preferred. If a new plan had been adopted, it would appear from evidence from the USA, where the gridiron seems flexible enough to accommodate radical change[50], that a simple rectilinear network would have had most to offer – if adjusted to the topography.

The rest of the myth – that his plan was ignored and the City reconstructed without improvements to the existing form – is best refuted by describing the rebuilding process.

RECONSTRUCTION OF THE CITY

Statutory provision for the reconstruction was given by the first and second Rebuilding Acts of February 1667 and April 1670. The first Act generally followed the lines of the royal proclamation and incorporated the work of the commissioners. The three most significant improvements – the streets, the buildings and the Fleet Canal project – are described later in this chapter. Proposals for the Thames Quay were omitted from the first Act but included in the second.

The first Act implemented the king's proclamation by granting a duty of one shilling per ton on coal brought into the port of London for ten years – a sum which Professor Reddaway describes as so niggardly that the City might almost have appealed in vain. Reddaway shows that over the ten years it would have raised around £150,000 and that 'the land required for the quay ... alone would have taken approximately that figure'[51]. In addition to paying for riverside land purchases, the duty was intended for road widening acquisitions and the rebuilding of the city prisons.

The second Act recognised the financial shortcomings of the first and increased the coal duty to three shillings per ton, effective until 1687 – ten and a quarter years after the end of the original period. The City was granted one quarter of the increase, giving it one shilling and sixpence per ton to pay for land purchases, work on the Fleet Canal and improvements to several public buildings. The remainder of the increased duty was for the rebuilding of the city

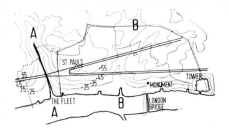

Figure 8.10 – The topography of the City of London today. The site is undulating, with the two hills on either side of the valley of the Walbrook (B–B) more steeply sloping in 1666 than in modern times. The same condition existed on both sides of the Fleet (A–A) and the slopes down to the Thames. The rise and fall along the lengths of Wren's main east-west streets are clearly shown.

The familiar story of Wren's rapid production of a plan for rebuilding the City after the Fire of 1666, and the fate that befell it, needs no recital here. The merits of the plan were considerable, substituting method, broad streets, and generous spaces for cramped building congestion and tortuous lanes that had long given encouragement to pestilence and fire. Adoption of the plan would have vastly affected for good the future of the city, so needlessly stifled within its wall, and the greater metropolis that was soon to stretch out indefinitely beyond it. Not to take advantage of the exodus of population, that followed plague and fire, to carry out radical reforms must now be regarded as lack of foresight carried to the point of folly. At the same time it must be acknowledged that the position created was a very difficult one, and the impatience of the displaced citizens to return to their homes quite understand-able ... Wren's reasoned scheme of replanning was, accordingly, set aside in favour of the status quo, or largely so, and the opportunity for generous roads and spaces, and much hygienic gain, was neglected. What was even worse was that this major misfortune revealed a complete lack of any effective centralised control over town development, which was to continue as a drag on urban reform and civic administration throughout the whole country.
(Frederick R. Hiorns, 'Town-Building in History')

---

50. See Chapter 9.
51. T. F. Reddaway, *The Rebuilding of London after the Great Fire.*

churches – one quarter of it for St Paul's. This income from coal tax and its ability to raise loans on security enabled the City to finance the rebuilding as fast as the availability of labour and materials allowed.

At a meeting on 11 October 1666 the commissioners determined the street widths of the new city as : 'Key, 100 ft; high streets, 75 ft; some other streets 50 ft and others 42 ft; the least streets 30 ft or 25 ft; alleys, if any, 16 ft'[52]. Although the Thames Quay was never started and the street widths were subsequently modified to range from 50 ft down to 14 ft, the new provisions nevertheless were an enormous improvement on previous dimensions[53]. The post-1666 street pattern was essentially a reinstatement of the old system, with its capacity greatly increased; of the very few new routes created the most important was 'the formation of King Street and the transformation of an ancient lane into Queen Street, the combined thoroughfares giving direct access from Guildhall to the Thames'[54].

In addition to standardising street widths the commissioners also insisted on having standard house types. Sir John Summerson has described how the whole of the houses were divided into four classes, for better regulation, uniformity and gracefulness. In the high and principal streets (six only were classified as such) houses were to be neither more nor less than four storeys in height; in the streets and lanes of note three storeys was the rule; while in by-lanes two storeys were prescribed. A fourth class was reserved for houses of the greatest bigness, which did not front the street but which lay behind, with their courtyards and gardens. Their height was limited to four storeys[55] (Fig. 8.11). Building construction was standardised; thicknesses of the walls at various heights and the sizes of floor and roof timbers were rigidly controlled. To ensure conformity with regulations 'knowing and intelligent persons in buildings' were appointed.

The only materials permitted for the elevations were brick and stone. There was not, in effect, a free choice. Stone had high carriage surcharges on it and was in relatively short supply, whereas London was surrounded by large areas of readily accessible brick-earth. The new city was therefore predominantly of brickwork, with stone reserved for the civic buildings and the churches and St Paul's. An invaluable encouragement to rebuilding was the introduction of party-wall legislation; this required common boundary walls to be set out equally on both sites, with the first owner erecting the entire wall and the second owner paying half the cost, plus 6 per cent interest for the intervening period.

THE FLEET CANAL AND THAMES QUAY

By the middle of the seventeenth century the Fleet river, which had been navigable from the Thames up to Holborn Bridge, had gradually deteriorated into a shallow and evil-smelling sewer[56]. The second Act included proposals for the redevelopment of the valley of the Fleet. Reddaway says that this, if successful, would both have eliminated the troubles within the area of the city and have made a valuable addition to the wharves and storage accommodation of the port; a dangerous nuisance would have been disposed of, much needed facilities provided, and the streets serving the older wharves relieved of their overgreat burden of traffic[57]. The scheme was to canalise the Fleet, making it 40 feet in width for its nearly half-mile course below Holborn Bridge. Both banks were to provide 30-foot wide wharves,

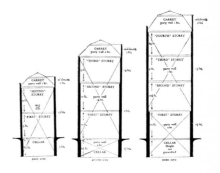

Figure 8.11 – Sections through the three main types of building authorised by the Rebuilding Act of 1667. The four-storey type was to front the 'high and principal streets', the three-storey type was for the 'streets and lanes of note and the River Thames', and the two-storey version was for 'by-streets and lanes'.

52. T. F. Reddaway, *The Rebuilding of London after the Great Fire*.

53. C. H. Holden and William Holford, *The City of London – A Record of Destruction and Survival*.

54, 55. John Summerson, *Georgian London*.

56. John Stow, *A Survey of London*, 1603, notes that, '. . . in the yeare 1502, the 17. of Henrie the 7. the whole course of Fleete dike, then so called, was scowred (I say) downe to the Thames, so that boats with fish and fewel were rowed to Fleete bridge and to Oldburne bridge, as they of olde time had been accustomed, which was a great commoditie to all the inhabitants in that part of the citie. In the year of 1589 was granted a fifteene, by a common Councell of the citie, for the cleansing of this Brooke or dike: the money amounting to a thousand marks was collected and it was undertaken, that by drawing diverse springs about Hampstead heath, into one head and course, both the citie should be served of fresh water in all places of want and also that by such a follower as men call it, this brooke should be scowred into the river of Thames, but much mony being spent, ye effect fayled, so that the Brooke by meanes of continuall in crochments upon the banks getting over the water, and casting of soylage into the streame, is now becoming woorse cloyed and choken than ever it was before.'

57. T. F. Reddaway, *The Rebuilding of London after the Great Fire*.

built over underground warehouses, with second-category houses fronting on to them. The City aldermen approved the plan drawn up by Wren and others on 9 March 1670. Early in April statutory provision for the work was given with the passing of the second Rebuilding Act and on 23 April the lines of the canal and the wharves were set out on site.

After a slow start to the actual work, largely resulting from the need to accumulate capital and to acquire the land, and in the face of considerable difficulties, the Fleet Canal was completed in 1674 for the sum of £51,307 6s 2d.[58] It was not a commercial success. Few tenants were found for the warehouses and the canal dues did not pay the necessary dredging and maintenance costs. The open wharves slowly degenerated into general storage areas and, reflecting London's change from water to land transport, became increasingly used by carts and carriages as a direct north-south route. In 1733 the canal was arched over between Holborn and Fleet bridges, with the southern section similarly treated in 1766. Blackfriars Bridge was opened to cross-river traffic in 1769, at the southern end of the still existent culverted Fleet.

In contrast to the Fleet Canal project, proposals for a new quay along the north bank of the Thames failed so completely that today no trace of it remains, and even its history is confused. For decades, however the need for improvements was discussed, there was general agreement that the city's waterfront was in a disgraceful condition. Public landing places serving London's predominantly water-orientated east-west transport routes shared the river front with many contrasting commercial users and refuse dumps. Reddaway describes how the whole area, landing places, lay-stalls and wharves, was approached by an inconvenient network of lanes so narrow that the drays in their passage endangered houses and pedestrians and so steep that the drays themselves were endangered every time a horse stumbled[59].

All the rebuilding proposals, official and unofficial, took advantage of the opportunity to create a new riverfront with a quay extending between the Tower and the Temple. There was complete accord between the 'city beautiful' party and the commercial interests, who anticipated improved port facilities at minimum cost. The proclamation of 13 September included the construction of a 'fair key or wharf' and the commissioners gave it a width of 100 feet at their 11 October meeting, later reducing it to 80 feet.

The subsequent history of the Thames Quay is that of a universally agreed improvement which failed, for a combination of reasons, to get built. It was omitted from the first Rebuilding Act, although redevelopment was prohibited within 40 feet of the riverside in order not to compromise its future construction. The second Act made statutory provision for the quay but although several attempts were made to get it started it has remained only a planners' dream.

THE LONDON SQUARES

Before describing a number of the more important late seventeenth-century and eighteenth-century squares the general background to their development must be established. The plague of 1665 and the fire of 1666 gave impetus to a trend on the part of the nobility and other wealthy families to leave the City of London and move to new houses in the country immediately to the west, within easy carriage distance of both cities. In addition to this local population move-

*The canal or river, called Fleet-ditch, was a work of great magnificence and expense; but not answering the design and being now very much neglected, and out of repair, is not much spoken of, yet it has three fine bridges over it, and a fourth not so fine, yet useful as the rest, and the tide flowing up to the last; the canal is very useful for bringing of coals and timber, and other heavy goods; but the warehouses intended under the streets, on either side, to lay up such goods in, are not made use of, and the wharfs in many places are decay'd and fallen in, which make it all look ruinous.
(Daniel Defoe, 'A Tour through the whole Island of Great Britain')*

*The typical English residential square — and the vast majority of all English squares are residential squares – may be defined as a green framed by architecture, just as the French park and formal garden have been characterised as architecture built of greenery. But it had not always been like that; when the first squares were established in London they were not yet planted. Only in the eighteenth century did the adulation of nature by the English become so strong that they felt almost a moral obligation to plant every free area.
(Paul Zucker, 'Town and Square')*

58, 59. T. F. Reddaway, *The Rebuilding of London after the Great Fire.*

Figure 8.12 – The western section of John Roque's 1769 map of London (north at the top), showing the completed development of the estates south of Oxford Street through to Park Lane (the eastern boundary of Hyde Park) and the work in progress north of Oxford Street. The line of the New Road, constructed in 1756 as a direct link between Paddington in the west round to the City of London, by-passing the congested existing streets especially Oxford Street, is at the top of the map. Forty years later the fields north of the New Road at Marylebone were being developed to John Nash's plan as the Crown Estates Regent's Park scheme. (See Figure 8.16) John Nash's early nineteenth century Regent Street, linking the new park to the St James's area, follows approximately the line of Swallow Street north to Oxford Street.

Lincoln's Inn is on the right-hand edge of the map; St James's Park, in front of the Queen's Palace (Buckingham Palace), is shown with the formal layout which was changed early in the nineteenth century to the present day 'naturalistic' design; south of the river, growth by 1769 was still comparatively very slow, but, stimulated by the construction of Westminster Bridge in 1738–49, the fields shown by Roque were soon being built over.

ment, large general migration to the capital from other parts of the country included a considerable proportion of noble and wealthy families attracted by the flourishing social life. At first the pattern in the western fields was a scattering of mansions and large houses and ancillary service buildings, within their own spacious parks and gardens. As Rasmussen describes it, 'the arrival of each noble family increased the population not only by the family itself and its many servants and their relatives, but also by merchants, artisans and others who lived on the aristocracy. Besides London, the town of producers, the capital of world-trade and industry, there arose another London, the town of consumers, the town of the court, of the nobility, of the retired capitalists. Where a little room was left between the big mansions the middle classes settled in groups of smaller houses, which sprang up as best they could'[60].

London expanded during the seventeenth and eighteenth centuries on the basis of clearly defined social-class districts. Upper-class and middle-class families established a respectability for the West End, conveniently situated for the relatively short journeys east to the commercial City of London and south to the Court and increasing

60. S. E. Rasmussen, *London, the Unique City.*

central administration activities of the City of Westminster. As new squares and streets were created further out, pockets of working-class housing developed around, and eventually in a number of the original squares. Principal working-class districts were to the north and east of the City of London, where the commercial and industrial activities of the capital were rapidly taking hold. In marked contrast to the spacious character of the West End, the East End was densely built up in all stages of its expansion.

Rasmussen observes that 'when an earl or a duke did turn his property to account, he wanted to determine what neighbours he got. The great landlord and the speculative builder found each other, and together they created the London square with its character of unity, surrounded as it is by dignified houses, all alike'[61]. Sir John Summerson establishes three clear principles of these squares' development. First, the principle of an aristocratic lead – the presence of the land-owner's own house in his square. Second, the principle of a complete unit of development, comprising square, secondary streets, markets and perhaps church. Third, the principle of the speculative builder, operating as a middle-man and building the houses[62].

The great estates to the west of London were generally developed by granting building leases, a system peculiar to this country. The first building leases were granted in 1661 for the properties fronting Bloomsbury Square and set the pattern whereby the great land-owners retained both ownership of the land and control of buildings erected on it. Under such leases the tenant paid a low ground rent on the understanding that the lessee built at his own expense a house, or houses, of substantial character, which house, or houses, at the end of the lease, became the property of the ground landlord. Summerson observes that this system represents a convenient device by which land can be rendered profitable over and over again[63]. This was an essential consideration for such estates, which were generally entailed in a family, or which were held in trust, and which required an Act of Parliament before they could be sold.

The squares and their surrounding streets were given extremely simple layouts, invariably based on the gridiron principle. A number of squares followed the example set by Covent Garden, with the development of the gardens on the northern side of the landowner's house. The southern side was generally left open, until the house itself was redeveloped. Frequently a wide street out of the centre of the northern side was stipulated in order to preserve the highly-esteemed views of Hampstead and Highgate Hills.

Bloomsbury Square – Following the example set by Lord Bedford, Lord Southampton in about 1636 applied for permission to build on his Bloomsbury Manor estate. This was refused. By the late 1650s he had negotiated consent, however, for the erection of a mansion for himself and an associated residential square planned to front it on the south. The square originally consisted of two rows of houses – Allington Row and Seymour Row – west and east respectively of the Southampton House (later Bedford House) axis. The house was pulled down in about 1800 and terraces were added along the north side to complete the square. At about the same time the gardens in the square were laid out by Humphry Repton, who also laid out Russell Square on the site of the Southampton House gardens and thus gave London the largest square it had had down to that time.

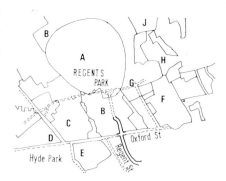

Figure 8.13 – London showing the extent of the major north-western estates in the eighteenth and early nineteenth centuries. Key: A, Crown (Regent's Park as developed in the early nineteenth century; see Figures 8.16 and 8.17); B, Portland; C. Portman; D, Bishop of London; E, Grosvenor; F, Bedford; G. Southampton; H, Somers (developed as Somerstown); J, Camden (developed as Camden Town).

Any town planner would envy the power the great landowner of London had within the boundaries of their own estates . . . What has given the ground landlords of London and other cities in the British Isles their particular power and responsibility has been the enormous size of their buildings. The freeholder of two or three lots. or even two or three streets, may have some discretion as to the sort of houses his lessees erect; but he can hardly aspire to anything worthy of the name of planning. The Duke of Westminster. in contrast, had the whole of northern Mayfair together with what is now Belgravia and Pimlico to work with. Lord Portman and the Duke of Portland had nearly the whole of Marylebone between them. The Duke of Bedford had Bloomsbury and Covent Garden. The Marquis of Northampton had Clerkenwell and Islington. The whole character – social. architectural and economic – of a neighbourhood could be determined by the kind of street plan the landlord chose to impose. the kind of leases he chose to grant and the kind of control he chose to exercise over his tenants.
(Donald J. Olsen, 'Town Planning in London – the Eighteenth and Nineteenth Centuries')

61. S. E. Rasmussen, *London, the Unique City.*
62, 63. John Summerson, *Georgian London.*

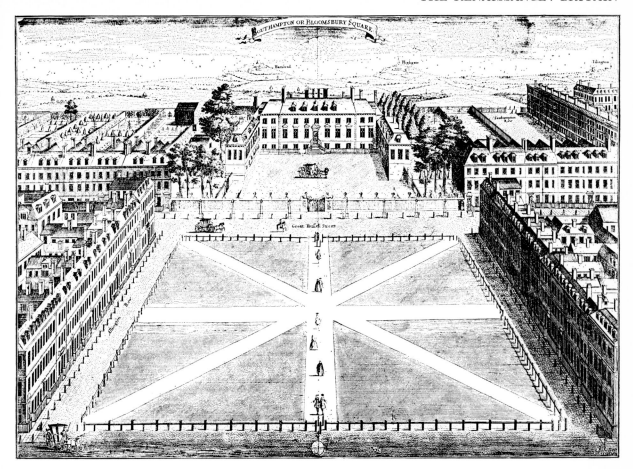

St James's Square – The first proposals for St James's Square date from 1662 when Lord St Albans obtained as a favour from the king a 60-year lease of an area of land near St. James's Palace[64], which he proposed to develop as 'a square consisting entirely of really large mansions – only three or four on each side – to be built and occupied by the very best families, including his own'[65]. Market research revealed a reluctance to build such expensive houses on leasehold sites. St Albans then successfully asked, in 1665, for the freehold of the land to be given to him and the king's wish to have suitable near-neighbours undoubtedly prompted him to acquiesce. The concept of an exclusive enclave was dropped in favour of a scheme which closely paralleled Bloomsbury Square, with a total of 22 plots let to wealthy individuals for their own houses and to professional speculators. Also following the lead of Bloomsbury Square, St Albans built a market and reserved a site for a church on the central axis of his square – St James's built by Wren between 1776 and 1784 alongside Piccadilly.

Soho Square – This was laid out as a speculative development in 1681 by an architect, Gregory King, after whom it was originally named. It was built immediately to the north of Monmouth House, which, set back behind its forecourt, provided an impressive central building on the southern side. Soho Square was initially a highly favoured address – the rate books record four dukes and a total of at

Figure 8.14 – Bloomsbury (Southampton) Square, from the south, in 1731, looking towards Lord Southampton's London mansion, and beyond to the twin hills of Hampstead and Highgate – a highly thought-of view. The square is shown with the usual unlandscaped, open character of the seventeenth and eighteenth century London squares – Bloomsbury Square's magnificent plane trees (still surviving) are the result of later planting. The eastern (right-hand) terrace has been replaced by a monstrous commercial development; the western side has retained its original scale, as also has the northern side with the later terraces on either side of the street which replaced the mansion in about 1800. Russell Square, of which Southampton Row (right, top) formed the southern side, was not laid out until the 1830s.

64. St James's Palace was the royal residence until the end of the eighteenth century.
65. John Summerson, *Georgian London.*

least 24 earls and barons among its residents[66]. The diarist Evelyn wrote in 1689 that he went to London with the family to winter at Soho in the great square[67]. Extensive sub-letting was a feature of Soho Square. Thus Hugh Phillips, in his detailed study *Mid-Georgian London*, quotes an advertisement in the General Advertiser of 10 May 1740: 'To be lett in Soho Square, a convenient house, ready furnished with clean Furniture, free from Bugs. With Coach House and stables for a middling family'.

Red Lion Square – Nicholas Barbon, 'speculative builder and bogus doctor'[68], carried out property developments between about 1670 and 1698, the year of his death, on an unequalled scale. Sir John Summerson notes that he was active all over London, building here a square, here a market, here a few streets or chambers for lawyers; he completely grasped the advantages accruing from standardisation and mass-production in housing; it was not worth his while to deal little, he said – that a bricklayer could do[69]. In 1684 he laid out Red Lion Square on fields to the west of Gray's Inn Walk. His workmen had to resist physical assaults by the Gentlemen of Gray's Inn endeavouring to protect the open space; Wren protested against the project and the Middlesex Justices issued warrants. But Barbon was not to be thwarted, and the square was completed.

The Mayfair squares – John Roque's great plan of London of 1769 is reproduced in part as Fig. 8.12. The great estates south of Oxford Street had been completely developed through to Tyburn Lane (Park Lane) by that date, the eastern boundary of the Royal Hyde Park followed about 1800. Hanover Square and adjoining streets were built between 1717 and 1721. Grosvenor Square was started in 1725, with 32 houses on the northern side and 15 on the southern side completed by the following year. With an area of six acres Grosvenor is the largest Mayfair square. Berkeley Square was laid out on the gardens to the north of Berkeley House (built in 1664 and demolished in 1733 to make way for Devonshire House) from 1739. The streets around the gardens had been constructed earlier, however – in 1675.

Of the Mayfair streets, Old Bond Street, running north from Piccadilly, was started in 1686. Its northern extension through to Oxford Street, New Bond Street, was delayed until 1721. Swallow Street, later to be widened into Regent Street by John Nash, was the main north-south link between Piccadilly and Oxford Street. Until 1719 residents on the west side of Swallow Street had been able to look out from their back windows across meadows as far as Park Lane, where a magnificent avenue of walnut trees stretched from Oxford Street to Piccadilly on its western side[70].

DEVELOPMENT NORTH OF OXFORD STREET

The year 1769 saw development of estates as far as the New Road well under way. The New Road had been built in 1756 as a direct route into the City of London from Paddington in the west, initially through fields still clear of development to the north of the new residential districts, before turning south into the City of Moorgate. Later renamed Marylebone, Euston, Pentonville and City Roads, in sequence from the west, this route formed a northern limit of development until the early nineteenth century and subsequently marked the southern termini of the main railway lines from the north.

Georgian London was a city made up almost entirely of these long narrow plots with their tall narrow houses and long narrow gardens or courts. Practically the whole population lived in one version or another of such houses. A handful of aristocrats had their isolated palaces; and the unemployable and criminal classes had their centuries-old rookeries; but the remainder, from earls to artisans, had their narrow slices of building, now called for no very good reason, 'terrace-houses'.
(John Summerson, 'Georgian London')

As for the plan of the house itself, nothing could be simpler. There is one room at the back and one at the front on each floor, with a passage and staircase at one side. On a site as narrow as 24 feet hardly any other arrangement is possible; in broader sites it is still a perfectly satisfactory and economical arrangement. There is no escape from it. Mariners' humble cottages in the East End have this plan; and so have the great houses in Carlton House Terrace.
(John Summerson, 'Georgian London')

In other words, the concept of these squares represents the greatest imaginable contrast to contemporaneous French squares and continental squares under French influence. There, representative display, and, if possible, monumentality were the artistic aim, based on integration of the area into the total structure of the city, as exemplified by Patte's plan of Paris. In London the aim was privacy, the privacy of the pedestrian, residential comfort, and seclusion from the life of the surrounding neighbourhood. There can be no doubt that architecturally, and also emotionally, the basic concept of these squares was rooted in the collegiate of the Middle Ages.
(Paul Zucker, 'Town and Square')

66. Hugh Phillips, *Mid-Georgian London*.
67. John Evelyn, *Diary*, 27 November 1689.
68. Nikolaus Pevsner, *London – the Cities of London and Westminster*.
69. John Summerson, *Georgian London*.
70. Hugh Phillips, *Mid-Georgian London*.

The first of the squares to be started north of Oxford Street was Cavendish Square. This was an initial phase of an ambitious plan to develop the Cavendish-Harley estate. From 1717 the square, the surrounding streets, a market (still known as Market Place) and a church (St Peter, Vere Street) were under construction. In spite of publicity stressing its relative nearness to Westminster, Cavendish Square was not a great success, and its completion had to await the building boom of the 1770s. Portman Square was laid out around 1761 and partly completed by 1769. The extensive Queen Anne Square projected for north of Foley House and shown in outline on Roque's plan was not built. Other squares in this district include Manchester Square, 1776, and Bryanston and Montagu Squares, both 1811.

The most important street architecture of this period is Portland Place, planned in 1774 by the Adam Brothers as the widest street in London to preserve the view north from Foley House. Portland Place was later incorporated into John Nash's *via triumphalis* between Regent's Park and Carlton House. Fitzroy Square was another Adam project, commenced in 1793–98 but not completed until 1827–35. East of Tottenham Court Road, the map of 1769 shows no development north of the buildings fronting Great Russell Street, the two most important of which were Montagu House, which had contained the British Museum since 1759, and Bedford House, in front of which was Bloomsbury Square. By 1769 plans for Bedford Square had been discussed, and construction was started in 1776. Sir Nikolaus Pevsner considers that it remains without any doubt the most handsome of the London squares, partly because it is preserved completely on all sides[71]. Gower Street, which runs north-south across the eastern end of Bedford Square, dates from 1790 but the general development of the Bloomsbury squares is a nineteenth-century enterprise.

Duke's New Road and Queen Square – Southampton Row and its northern extension, Woburn Place, are shown on Roque's map as the Duke of Bedford's New Road, leading out across Lamb's Conduit Fields to the New Road proper. East of the Duke's New Road much of the land between it and Gray's Inn Lane was owned by the Foundling Hospital, which in 1790 instructed its architect, Samuel Pepys Cockerell, to report on its development potential. Cockerell recommended the creation of two new squares, with related streets, one to the west and one to the east of the hospital buildings. These were later named, respectively, Brunswick and Mecklenburg Squares. This project was not completed until about 1810, by which time development further north, reaching to the New Road, was under way.

Queen Square, south-west of the Foundling Hospital, when completed by 1720, 'was unique in having three sides and a view – the beautiful prospect of the hills, ever verdant, ever smiling, of Hampstead and Highgate'[72]. The northern side of Queen Square remained open until finally built over as part of the Foundling Hospital development. This took place, despite vigorous protests and legal action by the residents to retain their visual amenity. Within 20 years Queen Square had lost its fashionable appeal. Hugh Phillips quotes a resident saying, around 1820: 'When I came to the Square I was the only lady who did not keep a carriage. Before I left I was the only one who did'[73].

Farther west, in the same line, is Southampton great square, called Bloomsbury, with King-street on the east side of it, and all the numberless streets west of the square, to the market place, and all through Great-Russel-street by Montague House, quite into the Hampstead road, all which buildings, except the old building of Southampton House and some of the square, has been formed from the open fields, since the time above-mentioned, and must contain several thousand of houses; here is also a market, and a very handsome church new built.

From hence, let us view the two great parishes of St Giles's and St Martin's in the Fields, the last so increased, as to be above thirty years ago, formed into three parishes, and the other about now to be divided also.

The increase of the buildings here, is really a kind of prodigy; all the buildings north of Long Acre, up to the Seven Dials, all the streets, from Leicester-Fields and St Martin's-Lane, both north and west to the Hay-Market and Soho, and from the Hay-Market to St James's-Street inclusive, and to the park wall; then all the buildings on the north side of the street, called Piccadilly, and the road to Knight's-Bridge, and between that and the south side of Tyburn Road, including Soho-Square, Golden-Square, and now Hanover-Square, and that new city on the north side of Tyburn Road, called Cavendish-Square, and all the streets about it.

(Daniel Defoe, 'A Tour through the whole Island of Great Britain')

71. Nikolaus Pevsner, *London – The Cities of London and Westminster.*

72. Hugh Phillips, *Mid-Georgian London.*

73. Hugh Phillips, *Mid-Georgian London.*

JOHN NASH (1752–1835)

John Nash is undoubtedly one of the most important and fascinating personalities in the history of urbanism. Coming from obscure origins he acquired a knowledge of architecture in Robert Taylor's office, was bankrupt at 31 (losing a legacy in his first property venture) and subsequently self-exiled to Wales before returning to London. A prosperous period in partnership with Humphry Repton, the leading landscape architect of the day, established Nash in high society and led to him becoming a protegé of the Prince of Wales at the turn of the century. In 1798 Nash exhibited at the Royal Academy a drawing of a conservatory he had designed for the prince. At the end of that year he married, and if one believes the rumours that his wife had a relationship with the prince which was still continuing, the mystery concerning Nash's sudden rise to fame and favour is explicable. The key to his future success was to be his appointment in 1806 as architect to the Department of Woods and Forests. This was a comparatively obscure post but Sir John Summerson is in no doubt that Nash 'must have guessed, or was perhaps persuaded, that his humble appointment would lead somewhere'[74].

'In the eighteenth century', says Summerson, 'the Crown lands were loosely and uneconomically managed, with assets neglected and liabilities nursed, and a commission, set up on George III's suggestion in 1786, found itself faced with much difficult research'. As a result of the commission's investigation the post of Surveyor-General of His Majesty's Land Revenue was established, and John Fordyce was appointed in 1793. Summerson recognises that 'London owes much to Fordyce. It was he who guided the development of Marylebone Park on to farsighted lines, who first propounded as an urgent necessity the need for a great street from Marylebone to Charing Cross, and who forcibly stated to the Government of his day the superiority of comprehensive planning over piecemeal alteration'. In September 1793 Fordyce raised the question of Marylebone Park, an extensive area of Crown land 'over which it is probable that on the return of peace the town may be extended'[75]. Fordyce was authorised by the Treasury to hold a competition for proposals for developing the park. At the time of his death in 1809 little interest had been shown in the competition, and there was still no plan. No successor to Fordyce was appointed, and the Office of Land Revenue was combined with that of Woods and Forests, under the direction of three commissioners. With less than two years remaining before the reversion of the lease the competition was abandoned, and the official architects of each of the two departments – Nash and Leverton, his Land Revenue counterpart – were instructed in October 1810 to prepare their proposals for the area ostensibly in competition. The two reports were submitted in July 1811. It is unlikely that the result of the competition was other than predetermined for Nash, with his rivals very likely used simply as a check on his proposals and estimates. Very little is known of the rôle that Nash's patron, the Prince Regent, played in all this, but he is quoted in October 1811 as being 'so pleased with this magnificent plan (which) will quite eclipse Napoleon'[76]. Nash's proposals were duly recommended to the Treasury. His Land Revenue rivals, Leverton (designer in 1785 of Bedford Square) and his partner Chawner, avoided the problem of the new street and based their uninspired scheme on a straightforward extension northwards of the existing gridiron structure south of the

74, 75. 76, 77. John Summerson, *John Nash, Architect to King George IV*.

New Road, punctuated by 'bigger and better Bedford Squares'[77]. The Nash report is unquestionably the work of a very special kind of genius, that of great creative ability wedded to the political expertise required to realise ideas in practice. In his report he dealt thoroughly with all aspects of the problems of developing the park and providing the new residences with a suitably imposing connection with the St James's and Westminster district.

Regent Street, as this new route south from the park was to be known, has been erroneously attributed by several town-planning historians to the Prince Regent's desire to link his Carlton House (which occupied a site at the St James's Park end of Lower Regent

Figure 8.15 – Regent's Park seen beyond the line of the New Road of 1756 (as Figure 8.12), 'A–A' from right to left (east to west). Portland Place is the wide street running north from the British Broadcasting Corporation's building at the bottom of the photograph (the spire of All Souls, Langham Place is just visible in the centre of the bottom edge); the crossing of Portland Place and the New Road (Marylebone Road) was effected with Park Crescent and Park Square (as Figure 8.17); and the line of Portland Place is shown continued through into the park by the avenue of trees. The regular gridiron structure of this part of northern Mayfair is clearly shown; Harley Street and Wimpole Street are the two routes parallel to and west of Portland Place.

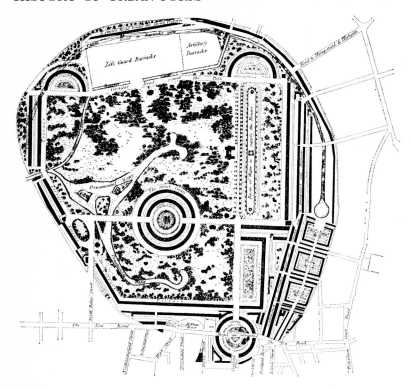

Figure 8.16 – John Nash's 1811 proposals for Regent's Park; compare with Figure 8.17, opposite, which shows the layout as actually constructed. In most respects change was for the better: the proposed circus at the crossing of the New Road (Marylebone Road), for example, would have provided a far less satisfactory extension of Portland Place, as the main entrance into the park, than the combination, as built, of semi-circular Park Crescent and Park Square, further extended as an avenue of trees. In addition it would seem that Nash's real-estate instincts had at first led him to provide for too many residences within the park – both as detached villas and in the grandiose Great Circus. (The site for the Life Guards and Artillery Barracks, across the northern side of the park, is that occupied in part by London Zoo.)

Street) to the new Royal Park. This was, it is true, a secondary benefit resulting from the line of the street, but its main function was determined by real-estate commonsense. Nash also redesigned the landscaping of St James's Park and proposed for it a peripheral development which would repeat the terrace motif adopted for Regent's Park. Both the park and the street must therefore be seen in this wider context.

REGENT'S PARK

The 1811 report contained proposals for the layout of the park which, although subsequently modified in some respects, were to form the basis of the final plan. Sir Nikolaus Pevsner has aptly summarised the basic concept as 'the combination of palatial façades with a landscaped park. The terraces are urban but their setting is countrified. Tenants paid the price for a three-windowed terrace house and obtained the illusion of living in a vast mansion in its own grounds. The scheme catered for the genuine love of the English for a life away from the town, and also clearly for snobbery'[78]. Humphry Repton's influence is clearly apparent in most aspects of the design, from the basic Reptonian strategy of 'apparent extent' down to the detailed use of trees and water.

The point of entry into the park from the south was from the top end of the existing Portland Place, which had been built by the Adam Brothers from 1774, and which was taken by Nash as the determining line of the northern section of his street proposals. The New Road was crossed through a large circus, with the stipulated church in its centre. A second double-circus was located on high ground near the centre of the park, with the required 'Valhalla' in the middle. The long lines of the residential terraces are stiffly laid

The Regent's Park, above all, is a scene of enchantment, where we might fancy ourselves surrounded by the quiet charms of a smiling landscape, or in the delightful gardens of a magnificent country house, if we did not see on every side a countless number of mansions adorned with colonnades, portices. pediments. and statues, which transport us back to London; but London is not here, as it is on the banks of the Thames. the gloomy commercial city. Its appearance has entirely changed; purified from its smoke and dirt, and decked with costly splendour, it has become the performed abode of the aristocracy. No artisans' dwellings are to be seen here; nothing less than the habitations of princes.
(Charles d'Arlincourt, 'The Three Kingdoms', 1844)

78. Nikolaus Pevsner, London – The Cities of London and Westminster.

Figure 8.17 – Part of North London, mapped in 1832 (north at the top), showing Regent's Park as originally completed with Portland Place integrated into John Nash's new route south to St James's and Westminster. (See Figure 8.19 for the detail treatment of the junction with Oxford Street.) Immediately to the east of the park, across Albany Street, there are the three squares intended as markets for the new development – York Square, Clarence Gardens and Cumberland Market. Cumberland Basin, on a branch of the Regent's Canal, has now been filled in (1942–3). Further north, beyond the Horse Barracks, on both sides of the canal, Nash laid out his two Park Villages – East and West – as detached and semi-detached villa developments. In these estates embryonic twentieth century suburbia can be discerned. This map also shows the western Bloomsbury squares and streets, including Bedford Square; the first London University building in Gower Street (present day University College); Euston Square, and the mainly working class housing streets to the north through which the railway was brought to the station in 1836.

out, surrounding the open space in which Nash proposed the location of between 40 and 50 villas, on sites ranging from four to 20 acres in area. This original Nash plan for the park (Fig. 8.16) was approved in August 1811 and in October, moving with commendable speed, the Treasury authorised preliminary works, including a drive-way around the park and the planting of young trees to ensure an attractive landscape setting by the time houses were completed.

The southern half of the entrance circus was started in 1812, but the original lessee, Charles Mayor, was bankrupt before the end of the year; work was suspended until 1815 and completion of the south-eastern quadrant was delayed until 1822. In that year the two quadrants north of the New Road were deleted from the design and replaced by the eastern and western sides of Park Square (1823–25). The canal was removed from the interior of the park to a less conspicuous perimeter route in 1812. The number of villas was drastically reduced to eight and the double-circus with its 'Valhalla' was omitted in order to enhance the illusion of a rural park.

The section of an 1832 map of London reproduced as Fig. 8.17, shows the arrangement of terraces as built. The first to be started was Cornwall Terrace in 1821 and all the others were under way by 1826. York Terrace is about 1,080 ft long, in two equal sections on either side of York Gate; the parish church of Marylebone is axially

Mr Nash is a better layer-out of grounds than architect. and the public have reason to thank him for what he has done for Regent's Park. Our gratitude on that point induces us to say as little as we can of the houses there. with their toppling statues, and other ornamental efforts to escape from the barrack style. One or two rows of the buildings are really not without handsome proportions, those with the statues among them; and so thankful are we for any diversity in this land of insipid building. where it does not absolutely mortify the taste, that we accept even the bumpkins of Sussex Place as a refreshment . . . we have reason to be thankful that the Regent's Park has saved us from worse places in the same quarter; for it is at all events a park and has trees and grass and is a breathing space between town and country. It has prevented Harley and Wimpole-streets from going further; has checked. in that quarter at least, the monstrous brick cancer that was extending its arms in every direction.
(Leigh Hunt, 'The Townsman')

located at the end, on the southern side of the New Road. Individual residences comprising the various parts of York Terrace were all entered via porches in the service road at the rear. Avoidance of a succession of front doors in the park elevations meant that the palace illusion was preserved on one side at least. In general Nash controlled only the basic elevational designs of the terraces, working drawings and supervision of construction was delegated to others, who were by no means as careful as they should have been. Many of the sections of terrace spared by Second World War bombing have required reconstruction in recent years, care being taken to preserve or, in the cases where this was no longer possible, to reconstruct the original elevations.

REGENT STREET

The Roque 1769 map of London, reproduced in part as Fig. 8.12, shows most of the existing urban fabric through which John Fordyce stipulated the driving of the new main street south from the park. Incomplete for Roque's survey, Portland Place, the 'grandest street in London', ended just short of the line of the New Road and seemed to Nash to form the obvious northern section of the new route. The southern end was determined by the position of Carlton House, on the south side of Pall Mall, and the new street would both connect the Prince Regent's house to the park and provide it with a suitably impressive approach. The problem now was to create an axial route north from Carlton House to Portland Place.

Nash's flair for separating the essential problem from all the conflicting overlying issues revealed that along a certain line the town abruptly changed character; the mean streets of Soho stopped and the spacious criss-cross West End began. In Nash's own words from his 1811 report the new street should constitute 'a boundary and complete separation between the streets and squares occupied by the nobility and gentry, and the narrow streets and meaner houses occupied by mechanics and the trading part of the community'[79]. The central section of the street was therefore pencilled in along a line drawn north-south across the eastern ends of the Mayfair streets, roughly following the existing north and south parts of Swallow Street.

The next problem was how to relate this central section to the southern and northern ends. Here the plan contained in the report differs from what was built and, to a great extent, from the present-day layout of the intersection with Piccadilly (construction of Shaftesbury Avenue from 1870 required demolition of the north-eastern corner of the junction). In building Piccadilly Circus Nash abandoned his initial thoughts for a grand square crossed diagonally by the line of the street, with a secondary circus at the Piccadilly intersection, and evolved his famous quadrant, swinging west and north from a small square adjoining the circus as one unbroken curved section of street.

From Oxford Street to Portland Place the line was determined by the need to keep a respectful distance from the Cavendish Square houses, and the 1811 plan shows a grand circus at Oxford Street enabling a simple change of direction to be made. Objections on the part of the Cavendish Square residents forced the line still further east. Additional complications posed by the presence of Foley House, on the axis of Portland Place, provided Nash with an opportunity to

Figure 8.18—Detail plan at the southern end (Lower Regent Street) of Nash's *via triumphalis*, with Carlton House at its terminal point, showing the arrangement of Piccadilly Circus where Regent Street curves away to the west and north. Nash's proposals for Trafalgar Square are also shown, to the bottom right.

Looking at old prints of Regent Street we are apt to think of it as a series of quasi-classical blocks making up a fairly balanced 'Regency' thoroughfare with the Quadrant as its most spectacular element. In fact it was nothing of the sort; the blocks, ionic, corinthian, astylar, elaborate or plain, provided a progress of great variety and were sometimes interspersed by a church, an assembly hall, an hotel or other non-terraced buildings.
(Terence Davis, 'John Nash: The Prince Regent's Architect')

79. Quoted by John Summerson in *John Nash, Architect to King George IV*.

achieve a second brilliantly contrived change of direction at the circular-spired vestibule of All Souls Church which 'is made to do its work in the larger scheme of things so well that it still conducts the movement around the difficult turn in Regent Street with power and grace'[80]. In 1813 Parliament passed, by a substantial majority, the Act 'for making a more convenient communication from Marylebone Park and the northern parts of the metropolis ... and for making a more convenient sewage for the same'. In addition to its primary purpose the Act also provided for the widening and eastern extension of Pall Mall, and creation of what is today Trafalgar Square, and the provision of a 'more commodious access from the Houses of Parliament ... to the British Museum'. The shape of Trafalgar Square was regularised by Nash, but his proposals to surround the new space by an imposing sequence of buildings, with the Royal Academy in its centre, were not carried out. Neither was his plan for the new street from the square to the British Museum. (Shaftesbury Avenue, which today only indirectly serves this purpose, was built later in the nineteenth century.)

Bath

RALPH ALLEN AND WOOD THE ELDER

Three men are usually associated with the rise to fame of eighteenth-century Bath : Beau Nash, Ralph Allen and John Wood the Elder. Bath's social pre-eminence seems to have dated from Queen Anne's visits to the city in 1702 and 1703. Beau Nash was appointed Master of Ceremonies in 1704 : before that Bath was a place visited for reasons of health only but Nash made it into a social centre and with the help of dictatorially enforced rules taught it elegance[81]. Ralph Allen was Bath's richest citizen; whilst the city's postmaster he had re-organised the national postal system – to his own considerable financial benefit. In 1727 he acquired Combe Down quarries and the chance to exploit their stone products is generally accepted as one of Allen's reasons for introducing John Wood the Elder to Bath. The Woods, father and son, are by far the most important of the eighteenth-century architect/planners who worked in the city.

By the 1720s the context in which the Woods were to operate had been established. The city was on the point of rapid expansion : money was starting to flow into Bath and much more was on the way. The city itself had to expand over fairly hilly ground – a factor brilliantly exploited by the younger Wood with his design of the Royal Crescent. A further factor of great importance is that Bath is essentially a single-material city – local stone used for almost all the buildings giving a rare architectural unity; the eighteenth century additions to Bath were also almost all designed in the same architectural style.

John Wood the Elder (c 1700–54) moved to Bath in 1727, the year in which his son and successor, John Wood the Younger, was born. Little is known of the father's early life or where and in what form he received his architectural training. It is generally assumed that while he was engaged in Yorkshire as a road surveyor he met Ralph Allen and was either persuaded to move to Bath or, having heard of the prospects, 'was independently attracted'[82]. Having first checked on the city's development potential Wood notes, in his own account, 'I procured a plan of the town, which was sent me into Yorkshire, in

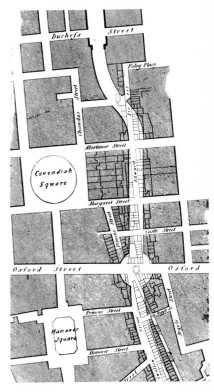

Figure 8.19 – Regent Street at the crossing of Oxford Street, showing the displacement to the east required to avoid disturbance to Grosvenor Square properties, and the return curve needed to join with the existing line of Portland Place (at the top of the plan).

There is one thing very observable here, which tho' it brings abundance of company to the Bath, more than ever us'd to be there before; yet it seems to have quite inverted the use and virtue of the waters (viz.) that whereas for seventeen hundred or two thousand years, if you believe King Bladud, the medicinal virtue of these waters had been useful to the diseased people by bathing in them, now they are found to be useful also, taken into the body; and there are many more come to drink the waters, than to bathe in them; nor are the cures they perform this way, less valuable than the outward application; especially in colicks, ill digestion, and scorbutick distempers.

This discovery they say, is not yet about fifty years old, and is said to be owing to the famous Dr Radcliff, but I think it must be older, for I have myself drank the waters of the Bath above fifty years ago: But be it so, 'tis certain, 'tis a modern discovery, compar'd to the former use of these waters.

(Defoe, 'A Tour through the whole Island of Great Britain')

80. Edmund Bacon, *Design of Cities*.
81. Nikolaus Pevsner, *North Somerset and Bristol* (Buildings of England series).
82. Walter Ison, *The Georgian Buildings of Bath*.

the summer of the year 1725, where I, at my leisure hours, formed one design for the ground at the north-west corner of the city, and another for the land on the north-side of the town and river'[83]. Wood returned to London with his designs, which he discussed with the owners of the land involved – first with a Mr Gray and second, in March 1726, with the Earl of Essex. Gray's land north-west of the existing mediaeval city limits was considered most suitable for development, both by reason of its altitude and immediate proximity, and this was acquired.

A 99-year lease of land was obtained from Gray sufficient for the east side of what was to become Queen Square, the first of the sequence of spaces which have gained for Bath and the Woods a unique place in the history of urbanism. With Queen Square, John Wood was in control of all aspects of the development process: he was at one and the same time architect, contractor and estate agent. Between November 1728 and October 1734 Wood took up further leases as building progress required and in seven years Queen Square was built.

QUEEN SQUARE

As it was originally planned, Wood intended Queen Square to be dominated by the palatial composition of the northern elevation – a single unified architectural ensemble, with the eastern and western sides of the square forming a 'palace' forecourt. The eastern side was started in January 1729 and was completed according to plan, with Wood sub-letting parcels of land 'to such persons as were willing to build in direct or near conformity with his designs'[84]. There are six houses on the east side, with those at the ends having their entrances from side streets. The houses are stepped down in accordance with the sloping ground. Wood had intended to level the site, but he saved some £4,000 by omitting this work. Queen Square is dominated by the magnificent northern elevation, comprising seven large houses organised with great skill into a symmetrical composition. The southern side is noted by Walter Ison as being merely a pale echo of its splendid opposite number[85]. The western side shows the main departure from the plan: the repeat of the eastern elevation is abandoned in favour of a design based on a large central mansion set back from the street line and flanked by buildings forming an entrance court. The central garden was enclosed within a low balustraded wall, with imposing entrance gates in the centre of each side. This space was crossed by gravel walks, with four formally planted parterres at its corners. In the centre a water-basin of a diameter of 44 feet, provided the setting for the obelisk (69 feet in height) which was erected in 1738 in honour of Frederick, Prince of Wales.

Queen Square was built as a speculative development. Wood's great achievement was to create an ordered architectural composition out of the varying requirements of his tenants. Walter Ison describes his working method as follows: 'Wood devised houses of different size and degree conforming to six definite standards, which he classed as first-rate to sixth-rate, in that ascending order of magnitude ... Having first designed the elevation he sub-leased sites for individual houses to builders or building tradesmen, giving them full liberty to plan the interiors to suit their prospective tenants, but demanding strict adherence to his exterior design'[86].

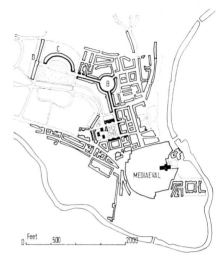

Figure 8.20 – Bath (north at the top), showing the relationship of the Renaissance spaces and streets to the north and west of the mediaeval nucleus. Key: A, Queen Square; B, the King's Circus; C, the Royal Crescent; D, Marlborough Buildings.

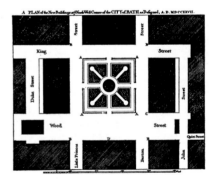

Figure 8.21 – Queen Square, the original plan of John Wood the Elder (north at the top).

83. John Wood the Elder, *An Essay towards the Description of Bath*, 1742.

84, 85, 86. Walter Ison, *The Georgian Buildings of Bath*.

THE KING'S CIRCUS AND ROYAL CRESCENT

The continuation northwards of the southern side of Queen Square – Gay Street, started by John Wood the Elder and finished by his son in 1760 – leads into the circus (originally the King's Circus) as one of its three radial connections. The building of the circus started in February 1754. In the following May John Wood died, and his design was completed by his son. The circus is 315 ft in diameter, with a total of 33 houses forming three equal-length segmental elevations of 11, 12 and 10 houses respectively. Although the plans vary considerably, each house consists of three principal floors with a basement and an attic, giving a uniform height of 42½ ft. Pevsner, in the Bristol and Somerset volumn of *Buildings of England*, describes

Figure 8.22 – An aerial view of the sequence of spaces in Renaissance Bath, looking north. (This view and the general layout, Figure 8.20, have the same orientation.) The ground rises fairly steeply from bottom to top of this view. Key: A, Queen Square; B, the King's Circus; C, the Royal Crescent; D, Lansdown Crescent.

207

it as the most monumental of the elder Wood's works, even more so if one remembers that the old plane trees which are now so much more splendid than the buildings did not exist and were not projected. The centre was paved-stone and had no greenery[87].

John Wood the Elder's plan for the circus provided for short lengths of street leading out to the north-west and north-east, each terminated by a suitably imposing building. Continued demand for houses resulted in his son changing the plan for the street radiating to the north-west (Brock Street). This he made a link to yet another residential development, the Royal Crescent, built between 1767 and 1774, and a work of true genius. With its integration of built form and natural landscape it is in complete contrast to his father's equally outstanding approach. Brock Street (1767–68) leads directly out of the circus, with continuous building frontages, and was designed as an architecturally subdued approach to the magnificent curve of the Royal Crescent. The 30 houses that make up the crescent follow the practice of the earlier developments. They have a strictly controlled elevational design, within which there are different plans. The basic form is that of half an ellipse, with a major axis of 170 yards, built around a sloping lawn on the side of the hill; the southern side was open to the magnificent view of then unspoilt natural landscape. The ground floor of the houses is plainly designed and serves as a base for the range of giant Ionic columns, 22 ft high, spaced generally at 8 ft centres, framing one window on each of the two upper floors. Set back behind the cornice line there is an attic floor. The view out to the north-west across the Royal Crescent is stopped by Marlborough Buildings (c1790) where, as Pevsner observes, urban Bath comes as abruptly to an end now as it did 150 years ago[88].

Edinburgh

Until early in the second half of the eighteenth century Edinburgh retained a characteristic mediaeval form: there were only tentative development ribbons leading away from the historic single-street city which ran along the ridge eastwards from the castle to the Palace of Holyroodhouse. From 1765 a Renaissance extension – known after its architect-planner as Craig's New Town – was developed. This, with its extremely simple gridiron-based plan in total contrast to the organic structure of the old city, makes Edinburgh the clearest example with which to compare the two types of urban development. Many cities show similar contrasts in form between mediaeval cores and Renaissance additions: Berlin (page 166) and Nancy (page 150), are notable examples. But neither of these cities, nor any other, has such a clear cut division of the two sections as Edinburgh.

A pamphlet entitled *Proposals for carrying on certain Public Works in the City of Edinburgh* was published in 1752 as a first move in a sustained campaign to improve the city. In very favourably comparing London to Edinburgh, the author noted as the latter's failings that 'Placed upon a ridge of a hill, it admits but of one good street and even this is tolerably accessible only from one quarter. The narrow lanes leading to the north and south, by reason of their steepness, narrowness and dirtiness, can only be considered as so many unavoidable nuisances. Confined by the small compass of the walls, and the narrow limits of the royalty, which scarcely extends beyond the walls, the houses stand more crowded than in any other town in

Here, in three spinal extensions, Gay Street, the Circle, and the Royal Crescent, with the adjacent Queen Square at the south end of Queen Street, one had, in miniature, the new order of planning at its captivating best. Even now, after a century and a half of change, the heart of Bath has qualities of design that even the best examples in Paris, Nancy, London, or Edinburgh do not surpass. The excellence of Bath shows the advantage of a strict discipline, when it is supple enough to adapt itself to challenging realities, geographic and historic. The placing of the Royal Crescent on a height that commands the whole valley, protected by the park that spreads below, shows that it was no mere application of an arbitrary geometric figure; and while nothing in the rest of the eighteenth century reaches this level of planning, the further building of Bath, right through the Regency, never fell too short of its standard. Not less notable than the preservation of the park-like environs was the generous allotment for gardens in the rear: gardens visible through their iron gates, spacious and richly textured, as shown in the plan of 1786, and still often handsomely kept up today. This is a superior example of open planning, combined with a close urban relationship of the buildings, which are treated as elements in a continuous composition. In short, Bath's eighteenth-century town planning was as stimulating and as restorative as the waters, and the money invested has brought far higher returns in life, health, and even income than similar amounts sunk into more sordid quarters.
(Lewis Mumford, 'The City in History')

Edinburgh indeed was an extreme example of the French type of town, kept within its ancient limits for reasons of safety and defence, and therefore forced to find room for growth by pushing its tenement flats high in air – in contrast to the ground plan of the easy-going peaceful towns of England, that sprawled out in suburbs ever expanding, to give each family its own house and if possible its own garden. French influence and the disturbed condition of Scotland in the past had confined the capital within its walls and pushed its growth up aloft.
(G. M. Trevelyan, 'English Social History')

87, 88. Nikolaus Pevsner, *North Somerset and Bristol* (Buildings of England series).

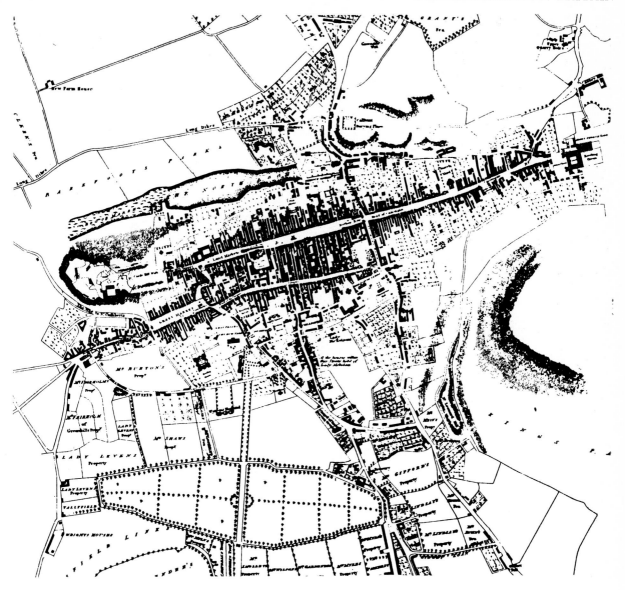

Figure 8.23 – Edinburgh in the first half of the eighteenth century before the addition of Craig's New Town on the fields to the north of the North Loch. The castle (at left) and Holyroodhouse (at right) terminate, respectively, the High Street and Canongate.

Europe, and are built to a height that is almost incredible ... The principal street is encumbered with the herb market, the fruit-market, and several others; the shambles are placed along what was the side of the North Loch, rendering what was originally an ornament of the town a most unsufferable nuisance'[89]. The pamphlet stressed that there were powerful motives prompting the improvement of Edinburgh and that the time was right, with several of the principal parts of the town now lying in ruins. Many of the old houses were decayed, several had already been pulled down, and probably more would soon be in the same condition. The most important of the several detailed proposals put forward advocated an Act of Parliament for extending the royalty to enlarge and beautify the town by opening new streets to the north and south, removing the markets and shambles, and making the North Loch a canal, with walks and terraces on each side.

89. *Proposals for carrying out certain Public Works in the City of Edinburgh.*

209

In March 1766 it was announced that the land to the north of the city had been surveyed, and in April notice was given inviting architects and others to submit plans of a new town, making out streets of proper breadth, and by-lanes, and the best situation for a reservoir, and any other public buildings which might be thought necessary[90]. Six plans were submitted. In August 1766 James Craig's proposals were selected, and after discussion and revision his design was finally adopted in July 1767.

Craig's plan is extremely simple – three long east-west streets, run the length of the ridge and seven shorter streets cross them at right angles; the central long street links two squares, one at each end of the ridge (Fig. 8.25). A total of eight large building blocks is formed by this gridiron structure, each divided into two parts by a service road giving access to mews. Four smaller blocks, also served by mews, form the remaining sides of the two squares.

Neither Craig nor the Town Council seem to have seriously considered the possibility or desirability of designing 'standard' unified elevations to which individual buildings would have to conform, as was the rule for example in London and Bath. It was accepted that, with a limited housing market, this might risk alienating possible tenants. The council did however take special steps to control building, initially with an Act of July 1767 and later with stricter legislation of 1782 and 1785. The first controls laid down continuity of building lines, established pavements as 10 ft wide and made provision for a sewer in George Street. Youngson records that no one in Edinburgh had adequate knowledge of this subject and that Craig himself was paid thirty guineas to carry out the necessary research in London. By 1782 St Andrew's Square was completed

Figure 8.24 – Edinburgh, aerial view looking past the castle, at the western end of the old ridge, across the North Loch towards Craig's New Town. Beyond the line of trees forming its northern boundary is the nineteenth century sequence of circuses and squares planned by Reid and others. Princes Street forms the southern, near side of the New Town. The layout of the buildings on the Mound, linking the old and new parts of the city, across the North Loch, dates from the early 1830s; this is seen to the right of the photograph.

90. A. J. Youngson, *The Making of Classical Edinburgh*

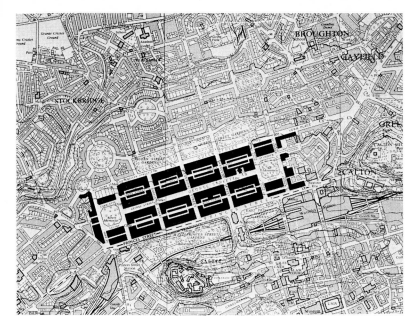

Figure 8.25 – Edinburgh, a section of the Ordnance Survey map of the centre of the city (north at the top), reproduced at the scale of 3 inches to one mile, showing the relationship of Craig's New Town, in solid block, to the old ridge city. The subsequent housing developments immediately to the north of Queen Street, the northern boundary of Craig's New Town, also have spacious, civilised qualities: compare however with the mean later nineteenth century by-law streets of working-class terraces in the north-western corner of the map.

and work was under way as far west as Hanover Street. The new legislation of that year was much more specific in content and included the following provisions :

(1) That no feus shall be granted in the principal streets of the extended royalty for houses above three storeys high, exclusive of a garret and sunk storeys, and that the whole height of side-walls from floor of sunk storey shall not exceed 48 feet.

(2) That the Meus Lane shall be solely appropriated for purposes of building stables, coach houses or other offices, and these shall in no case be built on any of the other streets of the extended Royalty.

(3) That the casing of roofs shall run along the side-walls immediately above the windows of the upper-storey, and no storm or other windows to be allowed in the front of the roof, except skylights, and that the pitch of the roof shall not be more than one-third of the breadth or span over the walls.

A. J. Youngson in his detailed study of *The Making of Classical Edinburgh* has this to say regarding the qualities of the plan: 'The New Town owes its superiority partly to situation, partly to the whole being built to conform to a regular and beautiful plan. But in the Dictionary of National Biography the same plan is damned as utterly destitute of any inventive ingenuity or any regard for the natural features of the ground. The truth is that the plan is entirely sensible and almost painfully orthodox'. Sensible yes, but certainly not painfully orthodox. Working at almost exactly the same time that John Wood the Younger was creating his Royal Crescent, Craig also adopted the revolutionary, but right and obvious, response to his own ridge-top site. His two bounding side streets, Princes Street (on the old city side) and Queen Street were designed with houses forming the inner side only, and aspects outwards across the street, in the one case over the low ground towards the castle and High Street, in the other down the slope towards the Firth of Forth and the distant hills of Fife.

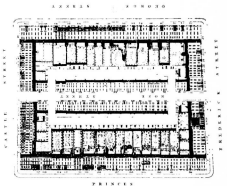

Figure 8.26 – Edinburgh, a typical gridiron block on the southern side of Craig's New Town, between Princes Street, George Street and Castle Street, to the right and Frederick Street to the left. Also shown is the arrangement of the rear service mews and the minor internal terraces fronting the secondary cross-street. Building elevations generally conformed to parapet-line uniformity so that, although there were minor variations of detail, the overall effect would have been one of pleasant unity. (It is not clear why the line of Frederick Street is not parallel to Hanover and Castle Streets and is thus a non-conforming element in an otherwise rigidly rectilinear plan.)

HISTORY OF URBAN FORM

Epilogue

In addition to London, Bath and Edinburgh, the three principal centres of Renaissance urbanism in Britain, the majority of cities and towns of appreciable standing included in their eighteenth and early nineteenth century expansion at least one carefully laid-out residential district or estate, frequently embodying one or more unpretentious, landscaped Georgian square. However these attractive developments catered exclusively for the rising ranks of the moneyed middle and upper classes: less fortunate urban families lived at rapidly increasing densities and under steadily deteriorating standards, either in older parts of town or in new working class areas which spread around factories in the early industrial centres.

Britain's Industrial Revolution has been exhaustively chronicled, perhaps best through the eyes of a Frenchman, Paul Mantoux. Readers are referred to his admirable book, *The Industrial Revolution in the Eighteenth Century*, for a background to nineteenth century urban development in Britain. It is also intended that this period will form part of a successor volume to this present work.

Industrialisation goes hand in hand with urbanisation. From its origins in England around the middle of the eighteenth century, the Industrial Revolution effected a gradual but inexhorable reverse of the proportion of people living in rural and urban areas. In 1750 probably fewer than twenty per cent of England's population lived in towns; by 1900 fewer than twenty per cent remained in the country.

The last major works of the Renaissance in Britain must therefore be seen against the sombre background of the uncontrolled expansion of the industrial towns. Figure 8.28 shows the nineteenth century rate of growth of eight major industrial centres from the first census of 1801. Industrial urban growth usually progressed through distinct phases, commencing with a thickening-up of the original organic-growth, mediaeval nucleus. This was followed by small, expediency-grid, residential developments interspersed with factories, as the tempo increased around the turn of the century. But, contrary to a general impression, these did not develop into the seemingly limitless expanse of two storey by-law housing – Britain's particular urban nadir – until legislation in the second half of the century imposed some minimum standards for hygiene and for the provision of light and air. M. W. Flinn in his introduction to the 1965 edition of Edwin Chadwick's famous *Report on the Sanitary Condition of the Labouring Population of Great Britain* (first published in 1842) aptly observes that 'some towns expanded during the early nineteenth century at rates that would bring cold sweat to the brows of twentieth century housing committees', and that as a result of the appalling living conditions 'the history of British towns in the first half of the nineteenth century is, to a considerable degree, the history of typhus and consumption'. For further reading on this subject reference should be made to Chadwick's *Report* and to Friedrich Engels' *The Condition of the Working Class in England,* which is much more coldly factual than might be imagined.

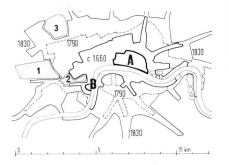

Figure 8.27 – The growth of London showing three stages (1660, 1790 and 1830) related to the City ot London (A) and the Whitehall area of the City of Westminster (B). Three royal parks are shown: 1, Hyde Park; 2, Green Park and St James's Park; 3, Regent's Park.

This map is drawn to the same scale as Figure 8.1, showing the extent of London at the earlier dates of 1100, 1400 and 1650. This map is also at the same scale as Figure 6.13 which shows Parisian growth stages within successive rings of fortifications: a pattern which is in total contrast to London's militarily unconstrained, main-route ribbon and infilling development. In 1830 the major constraint determining London's physical expansion was the lack of public transport, a factor which was overcome from the early years of the railway age.

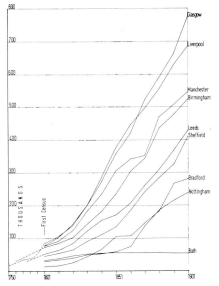

Figure 8.28 – Nineteenth century urban growth represented by example cities in England and Scotland. (Bath has been included as a non-industrial 'control' example.)

9 — Urban USA

On August 3, 1492, Christopher Columbus set out from Palos, in southern Spain in his ship *Santa Maria*, accompanied by two smaller vessels, to find not a New World, but a new way to get at the oldest part of the Old World – the Indies[1]. A direct ocean route to these fabulously wealthy countries could avoid having to pay out tolls to 'a horde of caravan conductors, camel jockeys, junk sailors, Oriental brigands and miscellaneous middlemen'[2]. Curiosity and greed, the twin pressures behind trans-Atlantic exploration, were encouraged by the scientific improvements of the late fifteenth and sixteenth centuries, which made navigation from an act of faith into a science[3]. Map-making gave a basis of fact and improvements in ship building provided vessels capable of long distance voyages.

The voyage of the *Santa Maria* needs no retelling. What is not generally known is that 'when, in December 1492, Christopher Columbus built a crude fortress from the timber of the wrecked *Santa Maria* on the northern coast of the island of Espanola, he began an era of city planning in the Americas'. This quotation from John Reps' *The Making of Urban America* is not intended to confer urban status on a pile of secondhand timber, but rather to record the first European 'settlement' in the continuing history of American urbanism. La Navidad, with its 39 occupants, failed to survive the winter and Columbus, returning in the following year after reporting back to his Spanish employers, established the town of Isabella some 75 miles to the east. This too was a short-lived venture and it was not until 1496 that a lasting urban settlement was created at Santo Domingo on the southern coast of Espanola. In 1501 this city was rebuilt across its river, to the west, as the oldest existing city founded by Europeans in America[4].

Spain, moving northwards, was the first nation systematically to establish urban settlements on the North American continent. France followed next, initially spreading down from the north. The English, ultimately the dominant colonisers, entered the scene later still, in company with a number of minor nations, notably the Dutch. Portugal, the only effective rival to Spain in the first phase of European world expansion, was preoccupied (apart from interests in Brazil) with exploiting colonies in the Orient following the voyages of Vasco da Gama. For the next half-century Spain was effectively unchallenged in the Western Hemisphere.

Recent estimates by Alfred L. Kroeber, James Mooney and Herbert J. Spinden lead to the conclusion that about 125,000 Indians were resident along the Atlantic seaboard from the St Lawrence River to Florida at the opening of the seventeenth century. According to Spinden, for example, the Indian population of the Northeast – that is, the area now included in New England, New York, Pennsylvania, and New Jersey – was 55,600, while 52,500 lived along the sea-board from Maryland to Georgia. Estimates of the native population of the Canadian maritime region at a comparable time vary from 25,000 to 50,000. The over-all density of population was about one person to 4 square miles, but there were great variations from place to place. Density of Indian population reached its maximum in the Chesapeake Bay region and was least in the interior. Southern New England perhaps ranked next in aboriginal population; according to Charles C. Willoughby, this region had a total population of 24,000 at the beginning of the seventeenth century despite the plague which had swept through the villages just before the arrival of Europeans. Kroeber's analysis of tribal data 'leaves little doubt that as a whole the population density in the farming parts of the Atlantic and Gulf region was perhaps twice as heavy on the coast, including habitats on tidewater or within a day's travel of salt water, as immediately inland thereof.'
(Ralph H. Brown, 'Historical Geography of the United States')

1,2.   S. E. Morrison, *Oxford History of the American People.*
3.   R. B. Nye and J. E. Morpurgo, *History of the United States.*
4.   J. W. Reps, *The Making of Urban America*, Princeton University Press, 1965.

Mexico was conquered in 1519–21, after which Spain's main emphasis was on plundering the wealth of the southern continent. This was partly because of the disappointing findings of a number of reconnaissance parties which had penetrated deep into North America in search of gold or the mythical passage to India. (The Grand Canyon was reached in 1540 and the Mississippi explored up to Memphis by 1541.) When Spain did eventually found the first permanent settlement on what is now the territory of the USA, she did so more to keep out the French than for her own aggrandisement. In 1565 St Augustine in Florida was established as a Spanish base for operations against the French in Fort Caroline, which had been set up in the previous year. The French were overwhelmed, and in order to secure their victory Spain studded the coastline as far north as the Carolinas with forts and missions[5].

Spanish settlements

Spanish settlement took three basic forms: *presidios*, which were primarily military bases; *pueblos* for trade and as centres of farming activities; and missions, which were religious foundations for conversion of the Indians. Although Spanish influence in the east was usurped by the New England colonies from the early seventeenth century onwards, Spain remained the dominant European power in the south and west until well into the 1800s.

Santa Fé was founded in 1609 – the same year that Jamestown began to be established as the first British settlement. San Diego dates from 1769, when in the east Florida was being ceded to the British[6]. Albuquerque, New Mexico in 1706, San Francisco in 1776 and Los Angeles in 1781 are other prominent cities of Spanish origin. Having stumbled into North America with no clear idea as to why they were there, it took the Spanish authorities some time to draw up a settlement policy. Once formulated this policy, as embodied in the *Laws of the Indies* of 1573, was rigidly applied and the structure of hundreds of settlements was determined by its rulings. (Earlier, in 1513, directions to one colonist had noted that 'one of the most important things to observe is that the places chosen for settlement be healthy and not swampy, good for unloading goods, if inland to be on a river if possible; good water and air, close to arable land'[7]. The directive on water transport is a key one and will be returned to later.)

The regulations of 1573 can be regarded as the first American planning code. Many aspects of urban planning are included, starting with site selection and dealing at length with urban form. The plan of the place, with its squares, streets and building lots, was to be outlined by means of measuring by cord and ruler, beginning with the main square from which streets were to run to the gates and principal roads and leaving sufficient open space so that even if the town grew it could always spread in a symmetrical manner[8]. Without specifically defining a gridiron street structure it is obvious that this is what the code required: the most characteristic aspect of American urbanism is thus already being introduced.

The location and proportions of the main public plaza are detailed at length in the *Laws* and one significant instruction, adherence to which could only have improved the present day urban scene, required settlers to endeavour, as far as possible, to make all structures uniform for the sake of the beauty of the town[9].

Figure 9.1 – Los Angeles, based on Neve's plan of 1781, showing the principal buildings grouped around a plaza. Los Angeles, founded comparatively late in the history of urban America, has been included early in this chapter, out of sequence, to illustrate the inauspicious nature of its origins – a feature of many other major American cities.

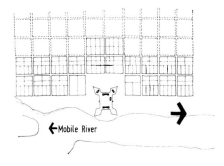

Figure 9.2 – Mobile (Alabama), founded by the French in 1711.

5. S. E. Morrison, *Oxford History of the American People*.
6. R. H. Brown, *Historical Geography of the United States*.
7, 8, 9. J. W. Reps, *The Making of Urban America*.

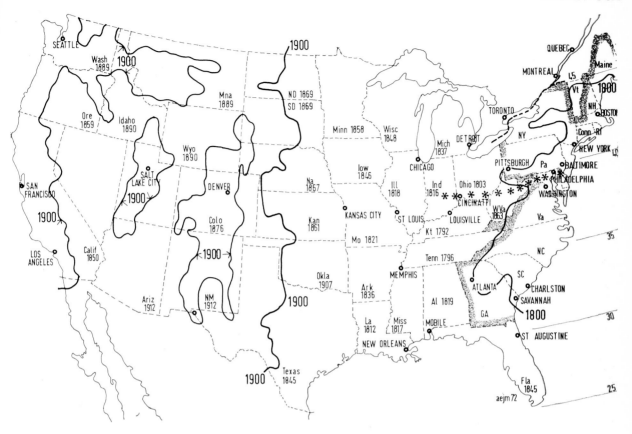

French settlements

France entered the New World over 100 years later than Spain, having failed to follow up the explorations of Jacques Cartier between 1534 and 1542. From 1604 onwards French settlements were established along the Canadian coastline and up the St Lawrence River, commencing with Sainte Croix on the island of Douchet in what is now Maine. Quebec dates from 1608 and Montreal from 1642. Louisburg, founded on Cape Breton Island in 1712 was originally intended as the main French fortress in Canada but after capture by the British in 1758 it was completely destroyed. With the St Lawrence as their baseline and water transport the only effective means of movement, the French were able to move south and create a widely distributed network of trading posts at a time when the British colonists in New England were still struggling through the forests a few miles inland from their coastal origins. Detroit was founded in 1701 by Antoine de la Mothe Cadillac to control the key Detroit River link between the Erie and St Clair Lakes, and Fort Duquesne of 1724 (renamed Pittsburgh after capture by the British in 1758) had a similar strategic rôle where the Allegheny and Monongahela Rivers unite to form the Ohio, the main waterway to the west and south. St Louis on the Mississippi was founded in 1762 and marks the end of French urban settlement. At the southern extremity of their vast inland territory Mobile had been founded in 1711 and New Orleans in 1722.

Figure 9.3 – General map of the United States. The extent of the first colonies is indicated by the shaded boundary; the limits of the settled areas in 1800 and 1900 are marked by heavy lines. The asterisks across eastern states show the western movement of the centre of population at the end of each decade from 1790 to 1890.

Figure 9.4 – St Louis (Missouri) in 1796. The city was founded in 1762 and named in honour of Louis XV and his canonised ancestor.

P

English settlements

Henry VII had missed the opportunity to sponsor Columbus but made amends by authorising one of his countrymen, Giovanni Gaboto – known as John Cabot – to seek out new unknown lands and to claim them for the English Crown. This Cabot did during a short voyage in the summer of 1497, the details of which are lost to history except that he is known to have made a brief landing on Cape Breton Island[10]. Cabot's landing was invaluable as the basis of the 1583 English claim to all of America north of Cape Florida, whereby, as S. E. Morrison put it, England set aside the Pope, Spain and Portugal and used convenient, if almost imaginary, history to give authority to the fulfilment of national desires. England had no intention of recognising Spanish monopoly in the Americas[11].

In 1584 Sir Walter Raleigh was commissioned to find a suitable site for a colony and despatched an expedition fleet for that purpose. On its return with optimistic reports, Queen Elizabeth permitted Raleigh to name the new lands Virginia. The first English settlement followed in 1585, when Raleigh sent out seven ships with 108 men on board – hardly a balanced emigrant party, which probably meant that a military base was the real objective. This party established a small fort on Roanoke Island, in North Carolina, but Ralph Lane, its commander, 'seems to have contrived to turn the Indians from friendly and curious neighbours into violent and treacherous enemies'[12]. Luckily Sir Francis Drake arrived in time to rescue them. The next move was to despatch three ships with 117 settlers, including this time 17 women and nine children, to re-establish Roanoke. Unfortunately open war with Spain intervened, culminating in the 1588 defeat of the Armada, and it was not until 1589 that a fresh expedition was sent. This found Roanoke deserted, with no sign of its inhabitants[13]. Thus the sixteenth century ended with no permanent English foothold in America.

During the seventeenth century English colonisation was reorganised on a new basis, passing from individual adventuring to corporate enterprise through the medium of royal-chartered joint-stock companies. The first of these date from 1606 with the Virginia Company of London and the Virginia Company of Plymouth authorised to settle lands roughly between the 34th and 45th parallels, from Cape Fear River in North Carolina to the coast of Maine. The London Company kept to the south and the Plymouth Company to the north.

Three ships with about 120 settlers were sent out by the London Company in December 1606 and after exploring the lower James River a site was finally agreed about 30 miles from the coast where they founded Jamestown in May 1607. This first English settlement was triangular in shape, with one side along the riverfront of 400 feet and the others each of 300 feet. The area within the fortified palisade was about one acre and contained the church, storehouses and probably a double row of houses flanking a single street. The original settlement was later destroyed by flooding of the James River. John Reps observes that there was little here reflecting the status of civic design in the Europe of that era. Not even the bastide towns of the late Middle Ages in France, Spain and England were so modest in scale and primitive in character. If the first settlers had ever believed that they could at once create an English village in the New World, this illusion was quickly dispelled[14].

It resteth I speak a word or two of the natural inhabitants, their natures and manners, leaving large discourse thereof until time more convenient hereafter. Now only so far forth as that you may know how that they, in respect of troubling our inhabiting and planting, are not to be feared; but that they shall have cause both to fear and love us, that shall inhabit with them.

They are a people clothed with loose mantles made of deerskin & aprons of the same round about their middles; all else naked; of such a difference of stature only as we in England. Having no edge tools or weapons of iron or steel to offend us withal, neither know they how to make any. Those weapons that they have are only bows made of witch hazel & arrows of reeds; flat-edged truncheons, also of wood, about a yard long. Neither have they anything to defend themselves but targets made of barks and some armours made of sticks wickered together with thread.

Their towns are but small, & near the sea-coast but few, some containing but 10 or 12 houses, some 2. The greatest that we have seen have been but of 30 houses. If they be walled, it is only done with barks of trees made fast to stakes, or else with poles only fixed upright and close one by another. Their houses are made of small poles made fast at the tops in round form after the manner as is used in many arbories in our gardens of England; in most towns covered with barks, and in some with artificial mats made of long rushes, from the tops of the houses down to the ground. The length of them is commonly double to the breadth. In some places they are but 12 and 16 yards long, and in other some we have seen of four and twenty.

(Thomas Hariot, 'A Brief and True Report of the New Found Land of Virginia', 1588; as quoted in Wright & Fowler's 'English Colonization of North America')

10. R. B. Nye and J. E. Morpurgo, *History of the United States.*

11. S. E. Morrison, *Oxford History of the American People.*

12. R. B. Nye and J. E. Morpurgo, *History of the United States.*

13. Roanoke might have become permanently established if, like the later Jamestown, it had been supported from England. However, as Morrison observes, 'it was the wrong time to look for help from home. A Spanish armada was being prepared to invade England, where nobody could spare the effort to succor a tiny outpost in Virginia.' *(Oxford History of the American People)*

14. J. W. Reps, *The Making of Urban America.*

The early history of the English colonies proved in reality to be a ceaseless struggle to maintain a subsidence agricultural economy. The first great improvement in their fortunes came with the discovery that a cross between West Indian and local Virginia tobaccos produced a smooth smoke which captured the English market. Virginia went tobacco mad; it was even grown in the streets of Jamestown[15]. By 1619, with tobacco plantations extending some 20 miles along the James River, the colony had a population of about 1,000. Over 50,000 lbs of leaf were exported to England during the previous year. The early disadvantages of this single-crop economy – including the need to import food from England and the unsympathetic local Indians – were overcome: by the mid-1620s Virginia had entered a prosperous consolidation era.

Early urban growth

From well before 1600 fishermen had been familiar with the coastline of the future New England but a first attempt by the Northern Virginian Company to establish a trading post on the Kennebec River failed after precariously surviving only the winter of 1607–8. The history of permanent settlement in New England starts in the autumn of 1620 after the arrival of the Pilgrim Fathers in the *Mayflower*. With their first rudimentary huts they were to establish the settlement of Plymouth in the December of that year. Although no plan of Plymouth has survived, John Reps is able to quote a visitor's observations of the late 1620s, from which he infers that the neat regularity of this little village plan reflected the tight social and economic organisation of the Pilgrim group[16].

Plymouth did not attain urban status in time to become the dominant city in New England. The Massachusetts Bay Company was created in 1629 with Charlestown, on a peninsular between the Charles and Mystic Rivers, intended as the colony's capital. Almost immediately this site proved unsuitable. As an alternative location a hilly peninsular, barely connected to the mainland by a low, marshy narrow neck of land, was selected across the Charles River to the south. The new town was named Boston, and its establishment was carried out with great energy: within four years it had become the centre of the plantations, where the monthly courts were kept. By 1722, the date of John Bonner's map reproduced as Figure 9.6, Boston had a population of around 15,000, making it the largest English colonial settlement.

Boston, however, suffered a major setback during the War of Independence, although as Blake McKelvey notes in his *The City in American History*, 'the King's apparent expectation in the 1770s that he could subdue the colonies by occupying the rebellious ports proved false'. The Patriots were driven inland and the major effect of British occupation of Boston, New York and Philadelphia was to reduce their populations to an estimated 3,500, 5,000 and 20,000 respectively. Subsequently neither Boston nor Philadelphia fully recovered their former dominance.

The foundation and early growth of Boston coincided with the 'great migration' of the Puritans. In 1630 alone well over 1,000 settlers arrived in the Massachusetts Bay Colony[17]. In the way these successive waves of Puritan immigrants established themselves in New England there is a fascinating instance of history repeating itself.

The New England town of the seventeenth century was a village community settled for purposes of good neighbourhood and defence. Its most characteristic features resulted from the topography of the country, and from the ideas of the nature of a town which the colonists brought from England. Forced by the geographical features of New England and by the necessity of protection, the colonists, already acquainted, settled in groups, and at once began organizing their settlements in accordance with the type familiar to them – the old English manor. Between this and the New England town many analogies may be drawn, showing the Germanic origin, not only of the government with its democratic features, but of the form of settlement – a compact town with outlying fields – and of the land system, with 'the houses and home lots fenced in and owned in severalty, with common fields outside the town, and with a surrounding track of absolutely common and undivided land used for pasturage and woodland under communal regulations'.
(Anne Bush Maclear, 'Early New England Towns')

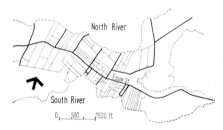

Figure 9.5 – Salem, the oldest of the Massachusetts Bay villages. This plan shows the home lots in 1670 with the line of present-day Essex Street along the high ground between the North and South Rivers.

15. S. E. Morrison, *Oxford History of the American People*.
16. J. W. Reps, *The Making of Urban America*.
17. G. M. Trevelyan has observed that, 'both patriotic and religious motives inspired many of those who supplied the funds, the ships and the equipment for the enterprise. Between 1630 and 1643 £200,000 was spent in conveying 20,000 men, women and children to New England in 200 ships: in the same period 40,000 more emigrants were conveyed to Virginia and other colonies.' (*English Social History*)

Figure 9.6 – Boston in 1722, as drawn by Capt John Bonner. Boston and New York City are the most important by far of those American urban settlements which developed initially without a plan, along organic growth lines. The description, bottom left, lists eight 'Great Fires' in the years 1653–1711 and six 'General Small Pox' epidemics in 1649–1721. In 1722 there were nearly 3,000 houses (1,000 of brick) on 42 streets, 36 lanes and 22 alleys. There were nearly 15,000 people. John Reps observes that 'the location of the rocky banks, the marshes, the low and muddy sinks of the virgin site was never recorded. The odds are, however, that these minor topographic variations shaped the early street pattern that has so persistently remained to plague the modern driver.' (The Making of Urban America)

The Anglo-Saxon and other settlers of the fourth to tenth centuries in England had also either observed the territorial rights of earlier arrivals and moved on, or created new settlements with overspill population drawn from the existing villages. In both the old and new countries the effect was the same – a steady expansion of the settled area, but whereas in England the process must have been based as much on the rule of strength as respect for the rights of others, in New England the rule of law prevailed from the start.

The original settlements had neither the resources nor, in most instances, the inclination to take in newcomers, most of whom, with sturdy independence, were determined to make their own way. As with the early seventeenth-century villages in England, which provided the majority of the settlers, agriculture was the basis of the New England communities who were only one crop removed from starvation[18]. Given the same economic base, the physical form of these communities also closely followed that of the contemporary English village. Each settler received a 'home lot', generally as one of the number which comprised a village, and a share of the surrounding common fields – frequently in the form of long and narrow strips[19]. The total extent of the built nucleus, its immediate home lots and the common fields, was called a town or township, a term which applied later, as one example, to the six-miles-square units of the 1786 sale of the first seven ranges of townships west of the Ohio River (see page 220).

The 1620s and 1630s along Massachusetts Bay and this first incursion into the mid-west after the War of Independence resulted, however, in totally different land-ownership patterns, which over the years have each in turn led to the development of contrasting urban forms. Whereas the New England pattern is best defined as controlled organic growth – with the planned field and street layouts determined by natural, topographical boundaries – by 1786 in the mid-west the inflexible surveyors' gridiron, which essentially ignores topography, had long been accepted as the only practical method of controlling

Though there are in all the provinces of New England large towns which drive a considerable trade, the only one which can deserve to be much insisted upon in a design like ours. is Boston; the capital of Massachusetts bay, the first city in New England, and of all North America. This city is situated on a peninsula, at the bottom of a fine capacious and safe harbour, which is defended from the outrages of the sea, by a number of islands, and rocks which appear above water. It is entered but by one safe passage; and that is narrow, and covered by the cannon of a regular and very strong fortress. The harbour is more than sufficient for the great number of vessels, which carry on the extensive trade of Boston. At the bottom of the bay is a noble pier, near two thousand feet in length, along which on the north side extends a row of warehouses. The head of this pier joins the principal street of the town, which is. like most of the others, spacious and well built. The town lies at the bottom of the harbour, and forms a very agreeable view. It has a town house, where the courts meet, and the exchange is kept, large, and of a very tolerable taste of architecture. Round the exchange, are a great number of well furnished booksellers shops, which find employment for five printing presses. There are ten churches within this town; and it contains at least twenty thousand inhabitants.
(From Edmund Burke, 'An Account of the European Settlements in America', Fourth Edition. Dublin 1762; quoted in Blake McKelvey's 'The City in American History')

18. J. W. Reps, The Making of Urban America.
19. For a description of the settlement of New England villages – notably Salem, Dorchester, Watertown, Roxbury and Cambridge – see Anne Bush Maclear, Early New England Towns.

the growth of the nation. New England therefore contains almost all of the USA's historic non-grid urban cores, notably Boston and, further south, New York[20].

Meanwhile, on the eastern sea-board, the Dutch had established New Netherland, at one time comprising the entire Hudson Valley and the shores of Delaware Bay and Long Island[21], with Albany (Fort Orange) founded in 1624 and New York City (New Amsterdam) of two years later as their main trading posts. The French were active further north and by establishing Quebec in 1608 and Montreal in 1620 Champlain put his king in possession of the one great river valley that led from the heart of North America to the east coast[22].

The end of this eventful seventeenth century nevertheless saw only a 50-mile wide fringe of country settled inland from navigable water. From Maine to North Carolina the development was fairly continuous, but from there to South Carolina there was a gap of 250 miles where the Indians were still undisturbed[23]. The future of North America as an English-speaking continent, however, was by now ensured. Although the British had come last into the New World they created from the outset the basis for their ultimate supremacy by sustaining the flow of emigrants – accepted regardless of nationality and capital into agriculturally-based communities. This was in direct contrast to the exploitative mineral and fur trading posts of Spain and France[24].

EIGHTEENTH CENTURY EXPANSION

In 1763, with the War of Independence of 1776 already inevitable, Morrison notes that the settled area included about 1½ million people, a total which was in excess of 2¼ million by 1775. 'The bulk of the population was involved in agriculture, but visiting Europeans regarded the country as a wilderness because over 90 per cent of it was still forested. Only near the Atlantic, in sections cultivated for over a century, could one have found anything resembling the farming areas of Iowa, Illinois or Nebraska today. Elsewhere and especially in the south, farms and plantations lay miles apart, separated by forest'[25].

Of the 1½ million people in 1763 almost one-third were slaves. This social situation had its origins in the earliest years of the European colonisation and is today the most demanding of urban America's problems[26]. Within 20 years of Columbus reaching the New World, African negroes transported by Spanish, Dutch and Portuguese traders were arriving in the Caribbean Islands. The first negroes were landed in colonial America at Jamestown in 1619. By the beginning of the Revolution there were 500,000 slaves – 20 per cent of the population with three-quarters of them in the south where they amounted to 40 per cent of the total. In Virginia in 1756 there were about 120,000 negroes out of a total of around 293,000; and in the tidewater counties they outnumbered whites by at least two to one.

The New England colonies also had their slave populations: Massachusetts had the most – 5,250 out of 224,000 in 1746 – but Rhode Island with 3,000 out of 31,500 in 1749 had by far the largest proportion. At the outbreak of the Civil War in 1861, largely fought over the issue of slavery, the south had 4 million slaves out of a total of 12 million. Although of immense continuing social significance, slavery and the resultant minority ethnic group problem had little direct effect on the pattern of urban settlement in the emergent United States.

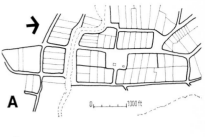

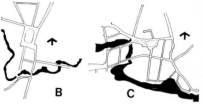

Figure 9.7 – Three organic growth New England urban nuclei: A, Hartford, Connecticut; B, Fairhaven, Vermont; C, Ipswich, Massachusetts.

But the King's apparent expectation in the 1770s that he could subdue the colonies by occupying the rebellious ports proved false. New towns had appeared in the interior and together with the older ports they developed a system of communications sufficient to carry on the struggle. The major effect of the British occupation of Boston, New York, and Philadelphia was to drive the Patriots inland, reducing the populations of these cities to an estimated 3,500, 5,000, and 20,000 respectively and leaving ample space to house the troops. Norfolk escaped that fate when its Patriot defenders, unable to withstand a siege, burned it to the ground to deny facilities to the British.
(Blake McKelvey. 'The City in American History')

20. See *The Making of Urban America* for the plans of a number of other, smaller organic growth towns, notably Exeter, New Hampshire, in 1802; Woodstock, Vermont, in 1869; Lebanon, New Hampshire, in 1884; Fairhaven, Vermont, in 1869; Ipswich, Mass., in 1872.

21. In 1621 the Dutch East India Company received exclusive trading rights from the Dutch Government for New Netherland. Morrison records how in return for New Amsterdam (New York), the British renounced claims in parts of the East Indies, in favour of the Dutch.

22, 23. S. E. Morrison, *Oxford History of the American People*.

24. See Chapter 6, page 158, for reference to French policy in North America.

25. S. E. Morrison, *Oxford History of the American People*.

26. *Urban USA: Population Growth and Movement*, 'Official Architecture and Planning', December 1968.

Factors affecting development

Before describing the establishment, layout and early development of key cities before the early years of the nineteenth century, we must consider briefly several determining factors, with eighteenth century origins, which influenced the expansion of urban USA.

The extent of the settled areas of the United States in 1800 is shown in Fig. 9.3. The population was around 4 million, of whom only some 170,000 were settled west of the Alleghenies. The conclusion of the War of Independence freed restraints which had limited further western expansion and heralded the beginnings of the inexorable drive west which ended only in 1906 when the United States were finally constituted as today.

THE GREAT AMERICAN GRID

One of the most controversial issues which had to be resolved in framing the Articles of Confederation was the question of the undeveloped western lands. Seven states were claiming western projections of their boundaries and only in 1802 did Congress gain full control of the situation. A national land policy was required and the Land Ordinance of 1785 represented the results of compromise between the Government's desire to raise public funds from the sale of land and mounting pressure from the countless thousands who wanted enough land, preferably as a grant, for a farm.

The law required that the territory to be sold should be laid out in rectangular townships, 6 miles square. Each township was to be divided into 36 square sections of 1 square mile or 640 acres. Half the land was to be sold by townships, the other half by sections[27]. This rectilinear survey basis obviously disregarded topography, with many anomalous results, but it was easy to locate a purchase in the wilderness and to avoid boundary disputes[28].

The first seven ranges of townships were surveyed by 1786, immediately west of the Ohio River (Fig. 9.8). Given the speed of western expansion, there was no alternative to general adoption of these regional grids-of-expediency, and their existence as property boundaries reinforced the preference for gridiron urban structuring. Section boundaries proved natural rural road lines and villages either established themselves at junctions, or were laid out and promoted by property speculators. Section 16 in each township was reserved for the support of schools.

TRANSPORT

A formidable deterrent to prospective western settlers had been the lack of transport facilities to get farm produce from the Ohio region to the urban markets of the east. Originally the United States was settled on the basis of water transport. To be distant from the sea or navigable rivers meant effective isolation. Roads were non-existent. Goods haulage was by horse and cart or pack animals, both inefficient and costly. Personal movement was only possible by horseback for most of the year.

One of the earliest political incentives to provide improved communications resulted from the admission of Ohio as a state of the Union in 1803. Because of its relative isolation behind the mountains there had been fears that the newly organising territory might turn further west and seek allegiance with Spain, so as to gain use of the

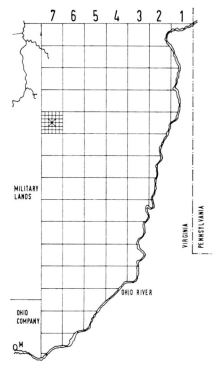

Figure 9.8 – The first seven ranges of townships, as surveyed by 1786, west of the Ohio (numbered 1 to 7 from east to west). An example township, in the seventh range, is shown as divided into its thirty-six one square mile sections each of 640 acres. Key: M, in south-western corner – the town of Marietta platted in 1788.

'Today', writes John Reps, 'as one flies over the last mountain ridges from the east, one sees stretching ahead to the horizon a vast chequer board of fields and roads. With military precision, modified only on occasion by some severe topographic break, or some earlier system of land distribution, this rectangular grid persists to the shores of the Pacific.' (The Making of Urban America)

27. J. W. Reps, The Making of Urban America.
28. E. C. Kirkland, A History of American Economic Life.

Mississippi trade routes. To ensure the entry of Ohio the Government promised a new road to the east across the Alleghenies. This 'National Road' was authorised in 1806 and opened in 1818 between Cumberland on the upper Potomac and Wheeling on the Ohio River – a distance of 130 miles. It served primarily to connect navigable waterways. Before its provision, to transport 100 lbs of freight from Philadelphia to Pittsburgh cost from 7 to 10 dollars; afterwards the cost was under 3 dollars[29]. British expertise in new road construction had earlier been used to build the Philadelphia – Lancaster road.

New York business interests were well aware that the National Road would take western trade to Baltimore. A long-discussed canal project to link the Hudson River with Lake Erie became an economic necessity and was started in 1817. By 1824 it was completed to Buffalo, 363 miles from the Hudson. At once the charge for transporting one ton of freight from Buffalo to New York dropped from 100 to 10 dollars[30]. In 1825 Buffalo, previously an obscure village, built over 3,400 houses and reached over 18,000 inhabitants by 1840. Rochester, Syracuse and Utica, all with canal-side locations grew rapidly into prosperous cities. As hoped, the greatest effect of all was on New York, which grew from 152,000 in 1820 to 391,000 in 1840, achieving unchallenged eastern seaboard dominance. In its first part-year of operation the Erie Canal recouped one-seventh of its cost in tolls and gave impetus to many other projects[31].

The first steamship service in the USA was started in 1790 between Philadelphia and Trenton, 40 miles away up the Delaware. Robert Fulton's 'Clermont'[32] inaugurated a New York to Albany service in 1807 and in 1809 the Ohio and Mississippi Rivers were surveyed for steamboat possibilities. Both rivers had long been used for bulk transport, but in effect only in the downstream direction with freight floated on dispensible rafts. In 1811 the first steamboat built west of the Alleghenies was launched at Pittsburgh, with a Boulton & Watt engine imported from England. She was named the 'New Orleans' and duly reached that port after a triumphant passage down river. This inaugurated the river-boat era of American internal transport, which in turn resulted in the rapid development of riverside settlements.

The Baltimore and Ohio, chartered in 1827, was the first commercial railway in the USA[33], and had the intention of competing with the Erie Canal. By 1830 the economic advantages of rail transport were such that all established urban centres were engaged in railway promotion. The effect of railway construction on the location, form and functions of urban America cannot be over-emphasised. For an established settlement it meant certain growth. The existence of the lines themselves led to inevitable track-side development. To be by-passed meant stagnation, if not effective commercial death.

INDUSTRY AND URBANISATION

Before the War of Independence the British government had attempted to minimise industrial activity in the colonies, hoping to maintain them as markets for the developing home industries. In 1765 legislation barred emigration of skilled operatives from Great Britain. This was reinforced in 1774 when the export of machinery was prohibited. These factors, however, played only a small part in the slow development of American engineering industry before 1860, until which year the emphasis was on food and clothing, with the

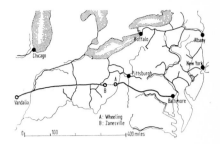

Figure 9.9 – Canals in the north-eastern states as completed by 1850, in heavy line; related rivers in lighter line. Also shown is the line of the 'National Road', the first section of which was opened between Cumberland, on the Potomac, and Wheeling, on the Ohio, in 1818. Later extensions linked Baltimore with Vandalia.

Figure 9.10 – The Railway system in 1840 (heavy line) and 1850 (lighter line extensions). Completed mileages as:

	1830	1840	1850	1860
New England States	–	517	2,508	3,660
Middle States	30	1,566	3,105	6,354
Trans-Mississippi	–	40	80	2,906
Southeast	10	522	1,717	5,351
Old Southwest	–	74	336	3,392
Old Northwest	–	111	1,276	9,583
Total U.S.	40	2,818	9,022	31,246

(From E. C. Kirkland, *A History of American Economic Life*)

29, 30. E. C. Kirkland, *A History of American Economic Life*.

31. 'In the first year of operation the Erie Canal carried 13,111 boats and 40,000 persons west.' (R. B. Nye and J. E. Morpurgo, *A History of the United States*, Volume Two.)

32, 33. F. M. Reck, *The Romance of American Transportation*.

most compulsive of the new demands coming from transportation – for steam engines, for locomotives, and for iron rails[34].

The Industrial Revolution in the United States followed that in Britain. The years from 1815 to 1830 were sometimes remembered in New England as 'the period when attention shifted from the wharf to the waterfall; from foreign trade to local manufacturing'[35]. It took the next century, through the First World War, for the labour force in manufacturing to exceed that in agriculture, and not until the census of 1920 did the enumerators discover that slightly more than half the American people lived in urban communities, if those with as little as 2,500 could be esteemed as such[36].

The established urban areas of the eastern states, with their excellent water transport and power facilities, were the natural locations of industry during the first half of the nineteenth century. From about 1820 the iron industry was concentrating around Pittsburgh. This western shift in industrial location was accelerated after 1870 with the triangle contained by Pittsburgh, Cleveland and Chicago forming the centre of heavy industry. Pig-iron production, an excellent index with which to relate urban growth, totalled 54,000 tons in 1810. Although this had increased to around 540,000 tons in 1850, the USA was importing about twice this amount. Subsequent growth was such that the USA surpassed British production in 1894 and the combined British and German totals in 1906. Coal production is a second valuable index; in 1860 the USA mined 14,610,000 tons as against nearly thirty times that figure in 1914. Only one person in ten had lived in a town of more than 1,000 inhabitants in 1800. In 1790 the first census had found no city exceeding 50,000 (although Philadelphia was almost there); by 1860 there were sixteen cities with this total; by 1900 seventy-eight; by 1920 one hundred and forty-four; by 1940 one hundred and ninety-nine. Moreover, by the beginning of the twentieth century there were thirty-eight cities of over 100,000 population.

City examples

PHILADELPHIA

Until the early years of the seventeenth century the valley of the Delaware was heavily forested and sparsely populated, the domain only of the Leni Lenape tribe, a branch of the great Iroquois people. 1609 saw the first European contact with this region when Henry Hudson's 'Half Moon', chartered by the Dutch, entered Delaware Bay. The first settlement on the Delaware was under Swedish auspices, although led by Peter Minuit of earlier 'Manhattan Purchase' fame. This was in 1638 at the mouth of Christina Creek, now part of present day Wilmington. The Dutch captured this settlement in 1655, before in turn giving way to the English in 1664. These activities set the historical context for the founding in 1682, by William Penn, of the city of Philadelphia.

William Penn (1644–1718) inherited on his father's death in 1670 a substantial estate, including a 'sizeable but uncertain' asset of £16,000 in the form of a debt owed by Charles II[37]. Penn had been an active participant in developing the New England colonies in both East and West Jersey from 1670; and, in return for cancellation of the debt, Charles II granted him a charter in 1681 establishing his authority as governor and proprietor of Pennsylvania.

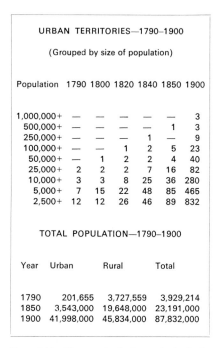

URBAN TERRITORIES—1790–1900

(Grouped by size of population)

Population	1790	1800	1820	1840	1850	1900
1,000,000+	—	—	—	—	—	3
500,000+	—	—	—	—	1	3
250,000+	—	—	—	1	—	9
100,000+	—	—	1	2	5	23
50,000+	—	1	2	2	4	40
25,000+	2	2	2	7	16	82
10,000+	3	3	8	25	36	280
5,000+	7	15	22	48	85	465
2,500+	12	12	26	46	89	832

TOTAL POPULATION—1790–1900

Year	Urban	Rural	Total
1790	201,655	3,727,559	3,929,214
1850	3,543,000	19,648,000	23,191,000
1900	41,998,000	45,834,000	87,832,000

Figure 9.11 – The growth of urban territories in the nineteenth century.

34. E. C. Kirkland, *A History of American Economic Life.*
35. Jean Gottmann, *Megalopolis.*
36. E. C. Kirkland, *A History of American Economic Life.*
37. J. W. Reps, *The Making of Urban America.*

In July of that year Penn published his general scheme of colonisation including in the first paragraph the statement that 'so soon as it pleaseth God a certain quantity of land or ground plat shall be laid out for a large town or city and every purchaser and adventurer shall, by lot, have so much land therein as will answer to the proportion which he hath bought or taken up upon rent'[38]. Three commissioners were selected to lead the first group of settlers and Penn, who was not intending to leave London until the following year, drew up a detailed brief for them in September 1681, shortly before their departure. John Reps aptly sums up these instructions as specific, practical and to the point – the work of a man to whom planning was no longer a novelty[39]. For the location of the new city Penn directed that 'the rivers and creeks be sounded on my side of the Delaware River and be sure to make your choice where it is most navigable, high, dry and healthy, that is where most ships may best ride, of deepest draught of water, if possible to load or unload at the bank or key side, without boating or lightening of it. Such a place being found out, for navigation, healthy situation and good soil for provision, lay out ten thousand acres contiguous to it in the best manner you can, as the bounds and extent of the liberties of the said town'[40].

The Surveyor-General for the new colony was Captain Thomas Holme, whose arrival on the Delaware in June 1682 was probably too late for him to be involved in the siting of Philadelphia. He did, however, lay out the first section of the city so that a drawing of lots for town plots could be held on 9 September. In this work Holme and the commissioners had received further precise instructions from Penn 'to settle the figure of the town so as that the streets hereafter may be uniform down to the water from the country bounds; let the place for the store-house be on the middle of the key, which will yet serve for markets and statehouses too. This may be ordered when I come, only let the houses built be in a line, or upon a line'[41]. Penn himself arrived at Philadelphia in October 1682 to find the city located as he had directed, on the neck of the peninsular between the Delaware and Schuylkill. Here the Delaware has scoured a deep channel forming a steep bluff on its western bank, permitting inshore mooring of large ships. There was also a small creek, called the Dock, penetrating inland to provide shelter for small boats. The site met all Penn's requirements. It was high, free from flooding, well-wooded, provided with fresh water and reasonably flat.

Holme's Philadelphia plan, of which there is no surviving copy, extended only about half way across to the Schuylkill. One of Penn's first actions was to extend the city over the peninsular to give it a frontage to both rivers. The combined Holme-Penn plan for Philadelphia was drawn up in 1683 and used as the basis for advertising the colony in London (Fig. 9.12). In Holme's words 'the city consists of a large Front-Street to each River, and a High-Street (near the middle) from Front (or River) to Front, of one hundred foot broad, and a Broad-Street in the middle of the city from side to side of the like breadth. In the centre of the city is a square of ten acres; at each angle are to be houses for Public Affairs, as a Meeting House, Assembly or State House, Market-House, School-House, and several other buildings for Public Concerns. There are also in each quarter of the city of eight acres, to be for the like uses, as the Moore-fields in London; and eight Streets (besides the High-Street), that run from Front to Front, and twenty Streets (besides the Broad-Street) that

Philadelphia. the Expectation of those that are concerned in this Province, is at last laid out to the great Content of those here. that are any wayes Interested therein; The situation is a Neck of Land, and lieth between two Navigable Rivers, Delaware and Skulkill. whereby it hath two Fronts upon the Waters. each a Mile, and two from River to River. Delaware is a glorious River, but the Skulkill being an hundred Mile Boatable above the Falls. and its Course North-East towards the Fountain of Susquahannah (that tends to the Heart of the Province, and both sides our town) it is like to be a great part of the Settlement of this Age . . . It is advanced within less than a Year to about four Score Houses and Cottages. such as they are, where Merchants and Handicrafts. are following their Vocations as fast as they can, while the Countrymen are close at their Farms; Some of them got a little Winter-Corn in the Ground last Season, and the generality have had a handsom Summer-Crop, and are preparing for their Winter-Corn. They reaped their Barley this Year in the Moneth called May; the Wheat in the Moneth following; so that there is time in these parts for another Crop of divers Things before the Winter-Season. We are daily in hopes of Shipping to add to our Number; for blessed be God, here is both Room and Accommodation for them. (From William Penn's Letter to the Society of Traders. 16 August, 1683; quoted in Blake McKelvey's 'The City in American History')

---

38. Extract from *Certain Conditions and Concessions Agreed upon by William Penn*, 1681, as included in Samuel Hazard's *Annals of Pennsylvania*, 1850. (Quoted by Reps.)

39. J. W. Reps, *The Making of Urban America*.

40, 41. Samual Hazard, *Annals of Pennsylvania*.

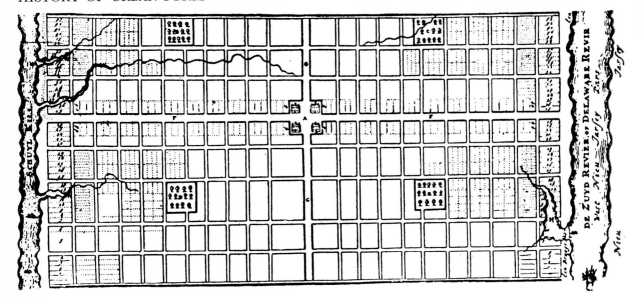

run across the city, from side to side; all these streets are of Fifty-Foot breadth'[42].

In the plan of Philadelphia in Fig. 9.12 the gridiron is clearly being used as a means to an end. Both the drawing and Holme's description refer to a closed urban programme which is in total contrast to the open-end uses of the gridiron as an end in itself, as generally employed across the American continent by later city 'planners' (including also subsequent expansions of Philadelphia itself).

Two distinct influences determining the Philadelphia plan can be traced back to English precedents. The first of these is a general one, and is embodied as such in Penn's original briefing; the second is specific and relates to post-1666 plans for the rebuilding of London after the fire. (Penn himself had been in London during both the great plague and the fire. His detail instructions included the advice that 'every house be placed, if the person pleases, in the middle of its plot, as to the breadth way of it, so that there may be ground on each side for gardens, or orchards, or fields, that it may be a green country town, which will never be burnt, and always be wholesome'[43].

In 1665 Penn had been living in Lincoln's Inn. As has been noted, this was then the centre of extensive building operations involving the creation of regular-façade, residential squares. Covent Garden was still almost the latest fashion, as yet unspoilt by market activities and the Bloomsbury squares were taking shape. Holme's direct reference to Moorfields in London is of great significance: this open space was available to all rather than only to those people actually living in a square.

The second influence is not directly acknowledged by Penn or Holme, but it is probable that both were familiar with the plans produced for the city of London after the fire (see pages 189–190). The plan drawn up by Richard Newcourt, with its main central square and four smaller corner ones (Fig. 9.13) bears a close resemblance to that of Philadelphia.

After three years of development there were some 600 houses in the city: this had increased to more than 2,000 by the turn of the

Figure 9.12 – Philadelphia, Penn and Holmes's plan of 1683 (north at the top). The city was approximately two miles in length, from the Delaware in the east to the Schuylkill in the west, by one mile in width. The two main cross streets were 100 feet wide; the eight east-west and twenty north-south minor streets were 50 feet wide. The grid blocks were 425 feet by 675 feet and 425 feet by 500 feet. The main central square was of 10 acres, the four minor squares were each of 8 acres. The 'Dock', off the main stream of the Delaware, was the first harbour.

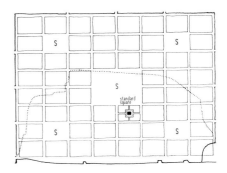

Figure 9.13 – Richard Newcourt's plan for re-building London after the fire of 1666. The grid blocks were 855 feet by 570 feet, each with a church in the centre. (See also page 230 for possible relationship between Newcourt's London plan and the layout of Savannah.)

42. *A Short Advertisement upon the Situation and Extent of the City of Philadelphia and the ensuing Plat-form thereof, by the Surveyor General*, London, 1683.

43. Samuel Hazard, *Annals of Pennsylvania*.

44. Gabriel Thomas, *An Historical and Geographical Account of Pennsylvania and West New-Jersey*, 1698.

With continued growth in the eighteenth century, all the colonial ports assumed additional responsibilities. Muddy streets were improved and extended; Boston by 1720 had a street system that excelled any in the colonies and, as Bridenbaugh has shown, rivalled all but London's in England. Its drainage sewers and its new public market, a gift by Peter Faneuil in 1742, were likewise outstanding. But a move by the selectmen, endorsed by the town meeting, for a bridge over the Charles River failed to secure the approval of the Governor's council. In similar fashion, inadequate powers and limited resources often checked the efforts of the officials in other towns to expand their services. Householders in each place had to sweep the streets in front of their properties, dispose of their garbage and night-soil, and hang lanterns over their doors if they wanted street lights. Philadelphia was the first in 1750 to secure authorization for a public system of street lamps and won acclaim two years later as the best lighted city in the Empire. Each such accomplishment added to the self-confidence of the colonial ports.

(Blake McKelvey. 'The City in American History')

Figure 9.14 – Philadelphia, eighteenth-century waterfront activity.

century, most of them stately and of brick, generally three stories high, after the mode in London, and as many as several families in each[44]. The Delaware had great advantages over the Schuylkill for shipping and it was soon apparent that Penn's concept of equal river-front growth was unrealistic. Development formed a crescent, centred on High or Market Street and extending up and down the Delaware for about a mile in each direction. By 1755 an additional street between Front Street and the river – Water Street – had en-

Figure 9.15 – Philadelphia, an eighteenth-century waterfront view. The contrast between the rigid orthogonal geometry of the ground plan (Figure 9.12) and the totally uncontrolled three-dimensional form was a general characteristic of American townscape which is discussed further in the conclusion to this chapter.

couraged commerce to concentrate along the waterfront. A detailed map of 1762 shows this intrusion, together with other minor streets added to break down the size of the original building blocks.

Philadelphia with its commercial, maritime and civic activities based on the central section of the waterfront became the busiest port in America. Civic buildings were built where sites were available, as and when the need for them arose. The master plan had provided for them around the central square but despite the city's prosperity it was not until well into the nineteenth century that it had expanded so far. As a result Philadelphia's historic civic buildings are scattered around the eastern quarter of the city, in an area which is currently undergoing comprehensive redevelopment[45].

Thus only towards the end of the nineteenth century did Philadelphia reflect the original intentions to have its focus around Centre Square. A new city hall was eventually completed there in 1890. This new 'central business district' attracted legal, financial and commercial enterprises away from the waterfront, at a time when ocean shipping requirements were determining a move away from the old restricted wharf district. These factors, together with the growth of the railways, resulted in gradual decay of the original port area and the earliest residential districts immediately behind[46].

NEW YORK

In contrast to Philadelphia, its great eastern seaboard rival, New York started without a plan and it was only after almost a century and a half of organic growth that the first contiguous gridiron districts were laid out. The foundation of the city by the Dutch in 1624 as New Amsterdam and the real estate 'bargain' Peter Minuit negotiated in 1626 needs no further recounting. The original settlement took the form of a small fortified village located at the extreme southern end of Manhattan Island, between the broad Hudson River to the west, and the East River.

When the British captured the city in 1664, renaming it New York, the population was around 1,500. Present-day Wall Street, the line of a 1633 defensive system, marked its extent. Chambers Street was reached by 1775, when the population was 23,000. By 1767 growing demand for housing land had already brought about a change from small-scale, sporadic, uncontrolled individual-street development to the laying out of extensive new districts, based inevitably on the gridiron. The Ratzen Plan shows the proposed development of Delancey property including the city's first planned public open space – the Great Square (see Figure 9.17). Unfortunately the War of Independence intervened; subsequently the land, which had become city property, was sold off piecemeal and the Great Square concept was abandoned. (British occupation during the war, and two disastrous fires, reduced the population to an estimated 5,000.) Around 1820, with the Erie Canal having its effect, 150,000 was passed; 300,000 in 1840; 515,000 in 1850 and 942,000 in 1870 show the rate of development. To cater for just such a rapid growth, the city in 1807 was authorised by New York State to appoint commissioners to lay out the undeveloped main part of Manhattan Island, north of Washington Square.

By this date the gridiron had been used for some additions to the city, but only for unrelated sites. The commissioners' plan of 1811 imposed a completely uniform grid over the island, based on twelve

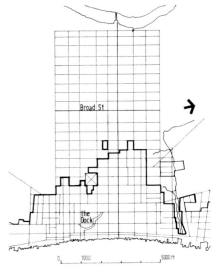

Figure 9.16 – Philadelphia, the central part of the city, between the Delaware and Schuylkill Rivers, showing the extent of the built-up area in 1794. The general form of Philadelphia in 1794 was triangular: the base formed by the Delaware water front; the other two sides running inland, intersecting on High Street, somewhat less than half way across the city and still well short of Broad Street, the main cross axis. Only one of the four residential squares – that in the south-east corner – is shown on this 1794 plan. The main central square at the intersection of High Street and Broad Street is also not marked as such in any way.

Figure 9.17 – New York City in 1767 (based on the Ratzen Plan). The line of Wall Street across Manhattan Island – marking the defensive wall of 1633 – is shown by asterisks at its Hudson and East River ends. Key: C, the Great Square.

45. Edmund Bacon, *Design of Cities*.
46. *Urban USA: Redeveloping the Waterfront. Penn's Landing.* 'Official Architecture and Planning', December 1969.

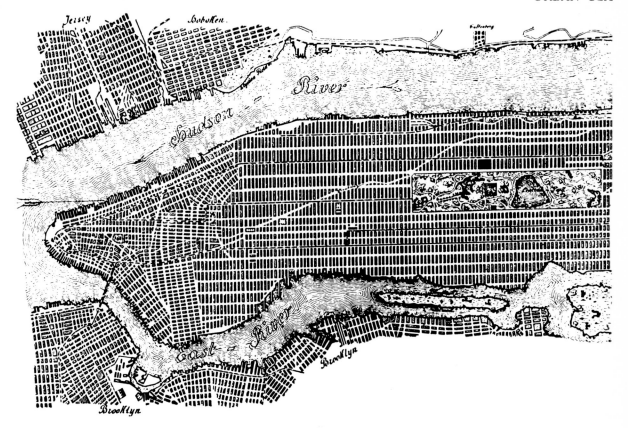

100-ft wide north-south avenues, and 155 east-west streets, 60 ft in width between the rivers. The rocky topography of Manhattan was ignored by the plan; it also allowed for inadequate open space and had other faults which have been revealed by time. In its favour it can be said to have been farsighted, by extending much further north than was originally considered necessary, and it did provide the means to control the extremely rapid nineteenth-century expansion. John Reps nevertheless regards the plan as an unequalled opportunity for speculators, with the commissioners motivated mainly by narrow considerations of economic gain[47]. 42nd Street was the northern limit in 1850 and the entire island was covered by about 1890. In 1898 the present day five-borough City of New York was constituted with Brooklyn, the Bronx, Queens and Staten Island added to Manhattan. The inexorable process of filling empty spaces in the commissioners' grid had reached 42nd Street by 1850 without any provision having been made for major public open spaces. A campaign for a park had been launched in 1844 by William Cullen Bryant, editor of the New York Evening Post, but as an issue it lacked political support until 1851 when it was taken up by newly elected Mayor Kingsland. Real estate interests failed to block a project for a large park and by mid-1856 some 810 acres had been acquired, for nearly eight million dollars, between 59th and 106th Streets and Fifth and Eighth Avenues. (A further land purchase extended the area north to 110th St.) In April 1858 Frederick Law Olmsted and Calvert Vaux won the competition for the design of Central Park and construction work on America's first major public park began[48].

Figure 9.18 – New York City, the southern two-thirds of Manhattan Island as developed according to the Commissioners' Plan of 1811 (north to the right; the approximate scale of this plan is one inch to a mile). The extent of the city in 1811 is clearly seen towards the southern (lefthand) end of the island, marked by the uneven junction of the irregular grid districts and the totally regularised grid of 1811. Central Park (right) is shown at its final extent.

Manhattan Island developed from the south on the basis of three forms of growth, each of which can be clearly discerned on the map: first, organic growth; second, unrelated, distinct, gridiron – planned estates; third, the commissioners' gridiron.

Commenting on the commissioners' Plan, Sibyl Moholy-Nagy writes, 'It ignored all topographical features and the aesthetic-recreational value of a continuous waterfront. Yet, when all criticism has been levelled, the question remains: what else could anyone have done with a shelf in the ocean, two and one-half miles wide and eighteen miles long, whose population was determined to concentrate the economic affairs of the world market on one spot?' (Matrix of Man)

47. J. W. Reps, The Making of Urban America.
48. Consideration of the design of Central Park is outside the scope of this present volume. Readers are referred to J. W. Reps, The Making of Urban America, and Theodora Kimball, Frederick Law Olmsted, for further details.

CHARLESTON AND SAVANNAH

In 1660, when Charles II succeeded to the throne, there were no
formally organised white settlements between Virginia and Spanish
Florida. Three years later, Carolina territory was established as a
proprietary colony and after a false start in April 1670, on an unhealthy site near the mouth of the river Ashley, Charleston was
founded in 1672 further inland on the peninsular between the Ashley
and the Cooper. The original layout of Charleston consisted of eight
irregular grid blocks within a fortified perimeter. By 1717 its population had reached 1500 and the danger of Indian attack had receded
enabling the town to expand beyond the wall. Figure 9.19 shows the
extent of Charleston in 1739, with the fortifications of 1672
apparently still retained.

Planning for growth was limited to merely projecting outwards
into the countryside the lines of the original gridiron streets, suitably
straightened out in one or two instances. At the intersection of the
two main streets there was an open square: this space and the
attractive harbour promenades would have given the grid some
distinction, but 'so little attention was given over the years to pre-
serving the square as an open plaza that one corner was occupied
by the market as early as 1739, a church was constructed in another
corner in 1761, and in 1780 and 1788 the remaining two corners
furnished the sites for an arsenal and the courthouse'[49]. Such 'colonial'
neglect of inherited civic space should not give British readers any
sense of superiority – a strikingly similar process had already despoiled
London's Covent Garden Piazza by the mid-eighteenth century. And
what is more, this was encouraged by the landlords, the Dukes of
Bedford, who were supposed to know better. John Reps observes that
'when compared to New Haven or Philadelphia, the Charleston plan
comes off distinctly second best. The Lords Proprietor were never
known for particularly lavish expenditures on behalf of the well-
being of the colony, and one is forced to conclude that they carried
over this niggardly attitude when they decided on the plan of their
capital city. In fact they might well have copied the plan of
Londonderry, doubled the scale, added an extra tier of blocks all
around, and laid it off in their delta site in the Carolinas'[50].

The southern part of Carolina territory was conveyed by George
II to a new group of trustees, in 1732, with the object of founding
the colony of Georgia. James Oglethorpe, Member of Parliament and
a leading prison reformer, undertook to establish the first settlements
and he sailed with the first group of 114 colonists in November
1732. The following February, after calling in at Charleston,
Oglethorpe's pioneering party was at work among the pine trees on
the southern bank of the river Savannah, clearing a site for the first
houses of the future town of that name. An engraving of 1734, shown
as Figure 9.21, 'dramatises the pioneer hardships and portrays the
underlying ordering of the ground'[51].

In two letters of February 1733, Oglethorpe informed the trustees
back in London of his intentions: '. . . I fixed upon a healthy situation
about ten miles from the sea. The river here forms a half-moon, along
the south side of which the banks are about forty feet high, and on
the top flat . . . the plain high ground extends into the country five
or six miles, and along the riverside about a mile. Ships that
draw twelve foot of water can ride within ten yards of the bank.
Upon the riverside in the centre of this plain I have laid out the

Figure 9.19 – Charleston, South Carolina, in 1739.
The defensive perimeter of the original settlement is
shown dotted and the beginnings of the extension
of the grid outwards into the surrounding countryside
can also be seen.

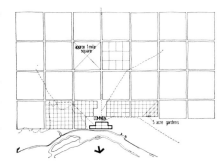

Figure 9.20 – Savannah, the city and land-sub-
division in the surrounding countryside at the
beginning of the nineteenth century. The original
city blocks are in black; the garden and farm lots are
in outline.

49. Frederick R. Stevenson and Carl Feiss,
Charleston and Savannah, 'Journal of the Society
of Architectural Historians', December 1951.

50. J. W. Reps, *The Making of Urban America*.

51. Edmund Bacon, *Design of Cities*.

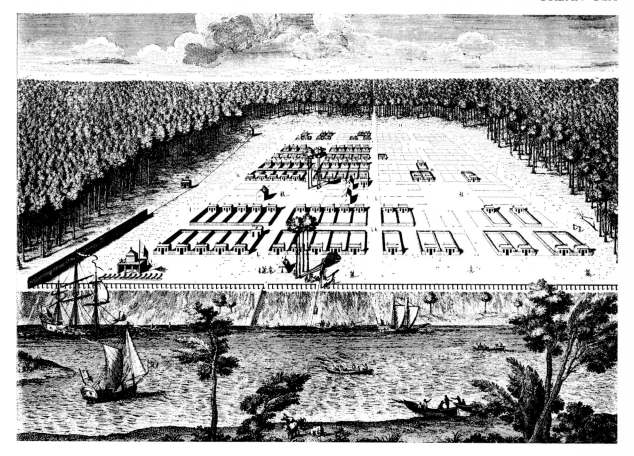

Figure 9.21 – Savannah, a view of 1734. In the most advanced, bottom left hand ward, three of the central public building sites are shown occupied. The uniformity of house building (cabins more likely) may be artistic licence but could also reflect standardisation in order to minimise construction time.

town . . . I chose the situation for the town upon an high ground, forty feet perpendicular above high water mark; the soil dry and sandy, the water of the river fresh, springs coming out from the sides of the hill. I pitched upon this place not only for the pleasantness of the situation, but because from the above mentioned and other signs I thought it healthy; for it is sheltered from the western and southern winds (the worst in the country), by vast woods of pine trees, many of which are an hundred and few under seventy feet high'[52].

Oglethorpe's plan for Savannah extended far beyond the immediate limits of its urban nucleus. As shown in Figure 9.20, three kinds of land allocation were provided for: each settler received a house plot in the town, 60 feet wide by 90 feet long; a garden plot of 5 acres near the town; and farmland further out, making a total area outside the town of 50 acres. It was stipulated that a house must be completed within eighteen months; ten years was the time allowed to clear at least ten acres of the farmland and to put it into production. Wholly reasonable requirements which contributed greatly to the successful consolidation of the British colonies, and which closely follow those accompanying mediaeval bastide land grants[53].

Few American cities used the gridiron as more than an equitable expedient: Savannah is probably the most important exception and the orthogonal geometry of the urban mid-west might well have been less monotonously debasing under its influence had it not been isolated

52. Oglethorpe's letters quoted by Reps, from Georgia Historical Society, *Collections, 1 and 2*, Savannah 1840 and 1842.
53. See Chapter 4, page 84.

from the immigrant tide in a southern backwater. John Reps sees this as 'one of the great misfortunes of American town planning'[54]. Savannah was different because it was laid out on the basis of finite cellular units and not as an infinitely extensible grid. The units, called wards, contained 40 house plots and had an identical layout: four groups each of ten house plots and four plots reserved for public buildings enclosed a public square, as shown in Figure 9.22. Four wards were laid out at first, providing for a total of 160 houses (Fig. 9.21). The route structure which organised the cells into an urban entity clearly differentiated between types of traffic on a hierarchical basis. Main streets were 75 feet wide, minor streets half that width, and the back access service lanes (reminiscent again of bastide planning) were 22½ feet wide. The widest street ran through the wards, across the central squares, but Edmund Bacon's diagrams illustrating the way in which Savannah developed, and his description of its modern central city situation[55], show that through traffic was limited to the streets between wards. Tree-lined boulevards parallel to the river, replacing ordinary streets at intervals, and the creation of an axis at right-angles, through the centres of five wards and continued by a large late nineteenth century park, ensured that Savannah's unique growth by cellular repetition did not lose coherence with size.

American urban historians have been greatly concerned to trace back the origins of Oglethorpe's plan. Clearly, as in the case of Philadelphia, the London squares were an immediate source of ideas, more so for Oglethorpe than for Penn and Holme; by the 1730s Mayfair had demonstrated their use, combined with grid streets, over a large new part of the city, as noted on page 196. Reps establishes that Oglethorpe was fully aware of the planning of Londonderry as an English plantation in Ulster[56]. But he strangely omits pointing out the similarity between Newcourt's plan for London after the Fire of 1666 and Savannah, although as described earlier in this chapter Reps argues an influence by Newcourt on Philadelphia (Fig. 9.13). By comparison Savannah owes much more to Newcourt than does Philadelphia. Turpin C. Bannister writing in the *Journal of the Society of Architectural Historians* puts forward the argument that Renaissance ideal city planning was the most probable source of the Savannah plan, in particular a design of 1598 by one Robert Barret[57]. Bacon takes a similar approach and cites a plan by Pietro di Giacomo Cataneo included in his *L'Architettura* published in Venice in 1567 (Fig. 5.12).

Whatever its origins and whoever assisted him, Oglethorpe's name coupled with that of Savannah merits a far higher position in urban history than hitherto accorded. Great credit is also due to those anonymous city fathers who refused, long after their planner's death, to allow the design to be compromised.

LOUISVILLE AND JEFFERSONVILLE

As established earlier, points of trans-shipment from one means of transport to another were an almost certain location of urban settlement. A survey of 1824, on which Fig. 9.24 is based, shows that five such settlements had been established alongside the Ohio, each of which claimed to be the future metropolis of the falls area and engaged in the typical antics of town promotion[58]. Clarksville and Louisville were first on the scene, followed by Jeffersonville, Shippings-

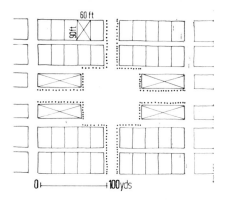

Figure 9.22 – Savannah, the basic ward unit, comprising forty house plots and four reserved public building sites.

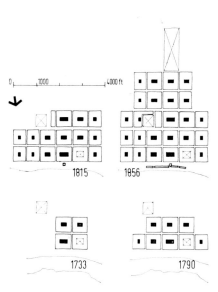

Figure 9.23 – Savannah, four growth stages of 1733, 1790, 1815, 1856. The standard ward unit (Figure 9.22) is in outline with the central open squares in black. Not all the ward units were the same size.

54. J. W. Reps, *The Making of Urban America*.

55. Edmund Bacon observes that 'when one is within any of these squares one feels entirely removed from the rushing traffic of the surrounding streets, which crosses but does not parallel the lines of sight... traffic has been allowed to park only on the square which was originally the market.' *(Design of Cities)*

56. For Londonderry, founded 1611, see Chapter 4, page 94.

57. Turpin C. Bannister, *Oglethorpe's Sources for the Savannah Plan*, 'Journal of the Society of Architectural Historians', May 1961.

58. J. W. Reps, *The Making of Urban America*.

port and Portland as river traffic increased and the possibilities of canals by-passing the Falls were discussed. Later a sixth city, New Albany, was founded on the north bank of the Ohio.

Clarksville was founded in 1783 on the northern, Indiana bank, but benefited little from the developing trade which became monopolised by the southern, Kentucky-side cities. Louisville, eventually the dominant city, was founded on 24 April 1779 when, 'the intended citizens of the Town of Louisville' met to draw lots of half-acre sites in the township. The new owners undertook to clear off the undergrowth and begin to cultivate part of the lot by 10 June and to build a good covered house 16 by 20 ft by December 25[59]. These first citizens formed a part of a small military force which had arrived at the Falls of the Ohio, many with their families, early the previous summer. Their first fortified encampment was on Corn Island. A previous attempt (1773) to found a town in the vicinity on 2,000 acres of land granted to a Doctor John Connolly for military services had been abandoned during the war.

Louisville was named in honour of the French king and the plan, attributed to George Rogers Clark, the military commander, comprised 'a number of lots, not exceeding 200 for the present, to be laid off, to contain half an acre each, 35 yards by 70, where the ground will admit of it, with some public lots and streets'[60]. This plan was notable for the reservation of the area between Main Street and the river, together with the row of plots along the southern boundary, as public land (Fig. 9.25). Reps mentions a local tale which credits Clark with the intention of repeating this strip of common land every third street to the south. In reality, however, Louisville had to dispose of this potentially invaluable asset very early on in order to meet debts of Connolly's, for which, as the result of political manoeuvres it was held responsible. On a city plan of 1836 there is evidence of an attempt to revive this feature which would have been as attractive and functional as it would have been unique[61] but such community amenities were disregarded in later growth.

By 1797 Louisville is recorded as having some 200 houses, whilst Clarksville was a village of about 20 houses. Shippingsport, downstream from Louisville at the foot of the Falls, was platted in 1803 and by 1806 had become the favoured port for upstream traffic, thus complementing Louisville. Further downstream Portland was platted in 1814, in anticipation of the construction of the canal around the Falls. This was completed on the southern side in 1830, after years of vicious wrangling between rival Kentucky and Indiana business, interests, each determined to capture the future toll income.

Jeffersonville on the Indiana shore was first established in 1802; its novel layout is shown in Fig. 9.26. The commercial intention was to hive off Louisville's trade. President Jefferson was notable for a keen interest in urbanism; he had been closely involved in the planning of Washington, supplying L'Enfant with details of contemporary European design, and he had been concerned with drafting the 1785 Land Ordinance. Jefferson had observed the ease with which yellow fever epidemics were spreading through American cities and recommended a more open form of planning than their built-up grids. Using the chequer board as an example he proposed that the black squares only be building squares, and the white ones be left open, in turf and trees; every square of houses would be surrounded by four open squares, and every house would front an open square[62].

Figure 9.24 – Towns at the Falls of the Ohio: Louisville, 1779; Clarksville, 1783; Jeffersonville, 1802; Shippingsport, 1803; Portland, 1814. (The Ohio flows from right to left.)

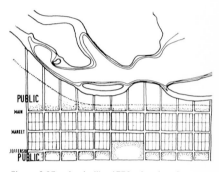

Figure 9.25 – Louisville, 1779, showing the open strips of common land on each side of the original two rows of grid blocks.

Figure 9.26 – Jeffersonville, 1802, showing the original chequer-board pattern of open and built squares and the diagonal street system.

59. R. H. Brown, *Historical Geography of the United States.*
60. J. W. Reps, *The Making of Urban America.*
61. John Reps writes that 'for 3,300 dollars the town disposed of its lands'.
62. J. W. Reps, *The Making of Urban America.*

Unfortunately, the executive planner, John Gwathmey, 'fancied himself something of a L'Enfant' and combined a diagonal street pattern with the building grid (Fig. 9.26). The town proprietors opposed the plan with its 'wasteful' use of space. In this they were prompted by the demand for lots in a likely candidate for the metropolis of the Falls region, and they petitioned Congress for 'an Act to change the Plan of the Town of Jeffersonville'. This was passed in 1816 and under the new plan only one of the open squares survived.

Louisville profited greatly from the increase in river traffic following the introduction of steamboats in 1840 and the completion of the Kentucky-Ohio Canal. There were the usual doubting businessmen, frightened as to the possible damaging effects of the canal on the city's trade, but they were silenced by Henry McMurtrie's question 'do the gentlemen really believe that Louisville draws her importance solely from the obstruction to the navigation of the river, or do they pretend to assert that a canal or river has ever deducted from the population, wealth or business of a town through which it has passed'[63]. Before the canal was built through-traffic in the city was very heavy, but as industries established themselves an increasing proportion of the river-borne freight remained to be processed in Louisville. Nevertheless the city today has neither the prosperity it desired nor the unique plan it did not appreciate.

WASHINGTON DC

From the outset the new United States government intended to create a federal capital, so that national administration could be conducted free from local political pressures, and without favouring any one State with its presence[64]. The first president, George Washington, was authorised by the Residence Act of 1790 to select a site, not more than 10 miles square, on the Potomac River between the mouth of its Eastern Branch and the Connogocheague. He was to appoint three commissioners to supervise the survey, and have the new city ready for its national functions by the first Monday in December 1800. (During this period Philadelphia was to be capital.)

Possible sites were investigated during the autumn of 1790, and in January 1791 the President announced the choice of the southern end of the authorised territory. The selected area had the well-established small town of Georgetown on the Potomac to the west, and included two other platted settlements, Hamburgh and Carrollsburg, neither of which, however, contained many buildings. Two independent advisers were responsible for surveying the site: Andrew Ellicott, a professional surveyor, was appointed in February 1791 to determine the boundaries, followed one month later by Major Pierre Charles L'Enfant, later to be responsible for planning the new capital city but with an initial commission providing only for the internal site survey.

L'Enfant (1754–1825) was born in Paris and spent his childhood in and around the palace and park of Versailles. The son of a gifted painter he studied at the Académie Royale de Peinture et de Sculpture before emigrating to America in early 1777, to take up a commission in the revolutionary army. He was first mentioned in the *Journal of Congress* as being present at the siege of Savannah in the autumn and during the later stages of the war he served under Washington as a military engineer. After the war, L'Enfant settled for a while in

Louisville, at the falls of the Ohio, is about the size of Lexington, or perhaps, at this time, more populous. From a commercial point of view, it is by far the most important town in the state. The main street is nearly a mile in length, and is as noble, as compact. and has as much the air of a maritime town, as any street in the western country. It is situated on an extensive sloping plain, below the mouth of Beargrass, about a quarter of a mile above the principal declivity of the falls. The three principal streets run parallel with the river, and command fine views of the villages and the beautiful country on the opposite shore. It has several churches, among them churches for the presbyterians, baptists and Roman catholics. The mouth of Beargrass affords an admirable harbour for the steam boats. and river craft. The public buildings are not numerous, but respectable; and the people are more noted for commercial enterprise. than for works of public utility.
(From Timothy Flint, 'A Condensed Geography and History of the Western States, or the Mississippi Valley', Cincinnati, 1828; quoted in Blake McKelvey's 'The City in American History')

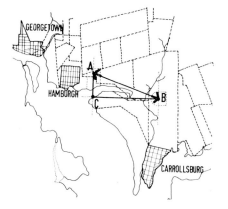

Figure 9.27 — Washington, the site of the national capital in 1791 showing the three existing platted towns — Georgetown, substantially developed and able to entertain the president when he visited the locality; and Hamburgh and Carrollsburg which were essentially 'paper towns' with few houses. This map also shows the property boundaries in dotted line, and superimposed in heavy line, the Federal Triangle (ABC), from which the plan of the city was developed.
Key: A, the President's House (White House); B, the Capitol (Jenkin's Hill); C, location for a memorial (the Washington Memorial).

63. R. H. Brown, *Historical Geography of the United States.*
64. Washington is therefore one of a number of Federal Capitals which have been created; others with significant urban form importance include Brazilia (the idea for which predates that for Washington) and Canberra.

New York City where, in practice as an architect, his work included alterations to Federal Hall in January 1785 to accommodate Congress. On 11 September 1789, Paul Caemmerer records that 'while yet the idea of having a capital city was still unsettled, L'Enfant wrote to President Washington asking to be employed to design the capital of this vast Empire'[65].

Figure 9.28 — Washington, the L'Enfant plan, a copy of the original manuscript drawing, made in 1887. (See Figure 9.31 for details of the central section of the city as given by Ellicott's version of 1792.) The manuscript contained numerous marginal notes, giving an indication of L'Enfant's detailed planning intentions. Unfortunately these notes cannot be reproduced in their original (as copied) handwritten form, but they include the following points, keyed on the related sketch plan below.

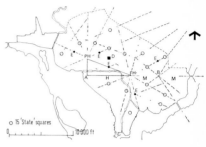

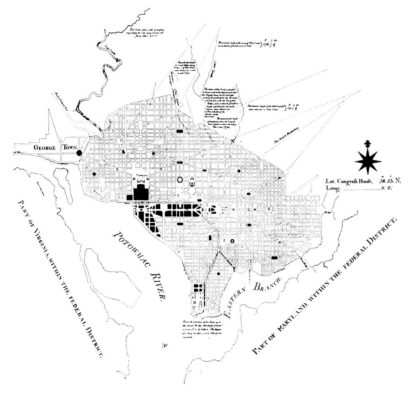

References (see sketch plan above):

A, The equestrian figure of George Washington, a monument voted in 1783 by the late Continental Congress.

B, An historic column . . . from whose station (a mile from the Federal House) all distances of places through the Continent are to be calculated.

D, This Church is intended for national purposes . . . and assigned to the special use of no particular sect or denomination . . .

E, Five grand fountains intended with a constant spout of water NB: there are within the limits of the City above 25 good springs of excellent water abundantly supplied in the driest season of the year . . .

Squares . . . being fifteen in number are proposed to be divided among the various States in the Union, for each of them to improve, or subscribe a sum additional to the value of the land for that purpose, and the improvements around the Square to be completed in a limited time . . .

Every house within the City will stand square upon the streets, and every lot, even those on the divergent Avenues, will run square with their fronts, which on the most acute angle will not measure less than 56 feet and many will be above 140 feet.

H, Grand Avenue, 400 feet in breadth and about a mile in length, bordered with gardens ending in a slope from the houses on each side . . .

M, Avenue from the two bridges to the Federal House, the pavement on each side will pass under an arched way under whose cover shops will be most agreeably situated. This Street is 160 feet in breadth and a mile long.

By the end of March 1791, when delimitation of the federal district and compensation of landowners were agreed, L'Enfant was further commissioned to plan the city itself. In his site analysis report he identified Jenkin's Hill – now Capitol Hill – as the best location for public buildings, and he stressed the need for a plan which would '. . . render the place commodious and agreeable to the first settlers while it may be capable of being enlarged by progressive improvement . . . which should be foreseen in the first delineation in a grand plan of the whole city'[66]. Working with commendable speed L'Enfant presented his final plan to the president in August 1791. (The reproduction in Figure 9.28 is from a copy of the damaged original made in 1887.) L'Enfant did not enjoy a smooth relationship with the commissioners during the design phase, but his obvious planning expertise made him indispensable; added to which he had the president's whole-hearted support. But as soon as the implementation phase was under way, L'Enfant's position quickly became much less secure. He had his own site development ideas, based on establishing the main streets and public buildings first, before selling to the public a proportion only of the 15,000 or so lots. He argued that the better situated land would then realise its potential, higher value. However,

65. Paul Caemmerer, *The Life of Pierre Charles L'Enfant.* New York, 1970.

66. L'Enfant's complete initial site report is included in Elizabeth Skite, *L'Enfant and Washington 1791–92* (1929). (Quoted by Reps.)

for neither the first nor last time in urban history pressing political considerations made essential as rapid a start as possible. An anti-federal-capital campaign was gathering momentum and Philadelphia's claims in particularly made any delays inexpedient. The commissioners therefore instructed L'Enfant to have 10,000 copies of his plan prepared for the public land auction of 17 October 1791.

Not only did L'Enfant fail to produce the copies – blaming engraving difficulties – but he also refused to allow his original plan to be exhibited at the auction which was held, rather unsatisfactorily, on the basis of the plats of individual blocks. Earlier, in August, L'Enfant had directed the demolition of a new house not in conformity with his plan, without consulting the commissioners. In December there was further friction over instructions to contractors. Still L'Enfant enjoyed the president's confidence and survived, but his days were numbered. He continued to obstruct publication of the plan, so much so that early in 1792 the president was forced to direct Ellicott to carry out the necessary engraving and printing work. L'Enfant refused him access to his master copy and Ellicott was forced to reconstruct the design on the basis of his own survey information, incorporating, it would seem, modifications put forward by various people, including Jefferson. (The central section of the Ellicott plan is given in Figure 9.31.) The changes, although not of great consequence, provoked L'Enfant to write to the president alleging that his plan was 'most unmercifully spoiled and altered . . . to a degree indeed evidently tending to disgrace me and ridicule the very undertaking'[67]. Whether by design or accident L'Enfant's name had also been omitted from the printed version. In late February, after he had spurned the final offer of continued involvement, made on the condition that he accepted the authority of the commissioners, L'Enfant's stubbornness gave the president no alternative but to end his appointment. Of L'Enfant's brief eleven-month career as capital city planner[68], well under half the time – about 144 days in all – had sufficed to produce the fully developed design. This was remarkably fast work. Even allowing for the fact that L'Enfant was known to have been determining the basis of the plan whilst occupied with his earlier survey work – giving him six months at the outside – it would clearly have been impossible for anyone less a genius than L'Enfant, or less familiar with the design idioms that make up this vast essay in civic development[69]. Judged on his plan L'Enfant in all probability was a genius and apparently one of the most uncompromising kind. Inspired adaptation of existing ideas to a site, rather than significant innovation was his forte but, as discussed below, widely differing views are held as to the merits of his work.

Three particular influences can be traced in L'Enfant's plan : first, his French family background; second contemporary late eighteenth century European urbanism; third, proposals for Washington put forward by Jefferson. The significance of L'Enfant's childhood at Versailles has already been established; he would have been familiar with the combination of grid and superimposed diagonal streets which in Versailles, lead up to the palace and which is the basis of Washington's plan. He was also a student in Paris where he would have appreciated the carefully arranged 'use of monuments or important buildings as terminal vistas to close street views'[70]. It is possible that the Place de la Concorde's fusion of architectural and landscape elements found an echo in his treatment of the Mall and the setting

. . . a territory not exceeding 10 miles square (or, I presume. 100. square miles in any form) to be located by metes and bounds.

3 commissioners to be appointed
I suppose them not entitled to any salary.

> *(if they live near the place they may, in some instances. be influenced by self interest. & partialities: but they will push the work with zeal. if they are from a distance. & northwardly. they will be more impartial, but may affect delays.)*

the Commissioners to purchase or accept 'such quantity of land on the E. side of the river as the President shall deem proper for the U.S.' viz. for the federal Capitol. the offices, the President's house & gardens. the town house. Market house, publick walks, hospital. for the President's house. offices & gardens, I should think 2. squares should be consolidated. for the Capitol & offices one square. for the Market one square. for the Public walks 9. squares consolidated.

the expression 'such quantity of land as the President shall deem proper for the U.S.' is vague. it may therefore be extended to the acceptance or purchase of land enough for the town: and I have no doubt it is the wish, & perhaps expectation. in that case it will be laid out in lots & streets. I should propose these to be at right angles as in Philadelphia, & that no street be narrower than 100. feet. with foot-ways of 15. feet. where a street is long & level, it might be 120. feet wide. I should prefer squares of at least 200. yards every way. which will be of about 8. acres each.

The Commissioners should have some taste in architecture because they may have to decide between different plans . . .

In locating the town. will it not be best to give it double the extent on the eastern branch of what it has on the river? the former will be for persons in commerce, the latter for those connected with the Government.

Will it not be best to lay out the long streets parallel with the creek, and the other crossing them at right angles, so as to leave no oblique angled lots but the single row which shall be on the river?

(Thomas Jefferson. as quoted by Saul K. Padover in 'Thomas Jefferson and the National Capital' Washington: United States Government Printing Office. 1946)

---

67. L'Enfant in a letter to Tobias Lear, Secretary to the President, dated Philadelphia, 17 February 1792. Beginning 'Dear Sir, Apprehending there may be some misconstruction of my late conduct and views' L'Enfant seeks to blame Ellicott for delays etc. Paul Caemmerer, *The Life of Pierre Charles L'Enfant.*

68. L'Enfant was appointed shortly before arriving on the site of future Washington on 9 March 1771 ; he was dismissed formally in a letter of 27 February 1792. Immediately after his Washington commission was terminated, L'Enfant was engaged in planning Patterson in New Jersey, as a city that would '. . . far surpass anything yet seen in this country' (L'Enfant quoted by Paul Caemmerer). It is not clear exactly what he achieved but this second involvement was also short-lived. In 1794 L'Enfant was the architect for Robert Morris's proposed mansion in Philadelphia ; on account of its cost, this became known as 'Morris's Folly'.

69, 70. J. W. Reps, *The Making of Urban America.*

for the President's House. His proposal (unfortunately never realised) to line main streets in Washington with arcaded shops has a precedent in the shops under construction near the Palais Royal when L'Enfant revisited Paris in the winter of 1783–4[71].

Thomas Jefferson, the second president, whose urban planning interests have been described earlier in this chapter, generously passed on to L'Enfant a collection of some twelve European city plans, including Paris, Karlsruhe, Milan and Amsterdam, after hearing that

Figure 9.29 – Washington, aerial view looking west from a point just north of the axis Capitol Hill (A) to the Washington Memorial (C). The White House (B) completes the Federal Triangle, connected to the Capitol by Pennsylvania Avenue. The Pentagon, on the Virginia bank of the Potomac, is keyed D. Georgetown is at the top right.

71. J. W. Reps, *Monumental Washington*, Princeton University Press, 1967.

his own hopes of planning Washington were not to be realised. Jefferson in fact produced what were most probably the original sketch plans for the new city, firstly for the area covering the site of Carollsburg and secondly for for the central section of the land subsequently taken for the city by L'Enfant (Fig. 9.30). The latter's debt was essentially to this second sketch; this located the President's House in more or less its final position and related it eastwards to the Capitol by a riverside walk along the northern bank of Tyber Creek. The Capitol, however, was only about half-way between the President's House and Jenkin's Hill (its eventual location) giving Jefferson's plan, with its simple gridiron structure, only a modest uninspired scale, which would most probably have proved unsuited to Washington's future role. Jefferson was an advocate of the gridiron and looked no further than Philadelphia for his inspiration but his Washington, although given a certain individuality by its waterside location, must surely have been just another expediency-grid city had it expanded on that base without later, distinctive, re-structuring elements.

THE L'ENFANT PLAN

Because of its modest extent Jefferson's plan – if it had been implemented – could quickly have attained an urban character and might perhaps have grown by the controlled addition of new blocks along the lines of Savannah. L'Enfant's plan meant that there was to be about a century of sporadic urban development at Washington; but the plan was fulfilled in the long term. It proved able to cope with unforeseeable future requirements, functional and symbolic, rather than mere short-term practicalities. Indeed, as noted below, the unsatisfactory and sporadic implementation of his plan may well also have been avoided had L'Enfant's development proposals been adopted. His plan has detailed failings, both inherent and imposed, but above all else it has ensured a magnificently scaled setting for the government of a dominant world power.

The apparent complexity of the layout was developed from a simple base: that of the right-angled triangle formed by the Capitol, the President's House and, at the intersection of their respective east-west and north-south axes, the Washington Memorial (Fig. 9.31). These axes were also those of a regular gridiron – the essential basis of land sub-division. The third side of the triangle cut across the grid as a direct link between the Capitol and President's House. This is

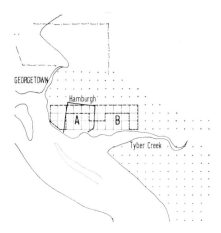

Figure 9.30 – Washington, Thomas Jefferson's plan of 1791 for the capital city, located between Georgetown and Tyber Creek and comprising a total of only 33 grid blocks, 14 of which were earmarked for the President's House (A), the Capitol (B), and the connecting Public Walk along the northern bank of Tyber Creek.

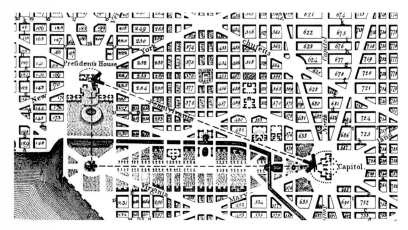

Figure 9.31 – Washington, detail plan of the centre of the city, taken from Ellicott's version of the L'Enfant plan; the Federal Triangle has been added by the author. The approximate scale of this extract is 1 : 36,000; from the President's House to the Capitol is just over 1½ miles.

Reciprocity of views between the three most important of L'Enfant's 'objects' – President's House, Capitol and the Washington Memorial (denoted by an asterisk) – has not been retained; the US Treasury building blocks the view along Pennsylvania Avenue (see Figure 9.37, a plan of Lafayette Square, 1857), and the Washington Memorial, eventually built from the mid-nineteenth century as a 580 foot high obelisk, was located some 300 feet east of its intended position at the intersection of grid axes through the White House and Capitol, because more expensive foundations would have been necessary for it to have been placed in the correct place.

Pennsylvania Avenue, ostensibly the nation's most important street, and it symbolises the distinct but mutual relationship between legislature and executive. Based on the diagonal line of Pennsylvania Avenue, a system of symmetrically arranged main routes was superimposed on the grid to connect other key internal locations and to relate to important regional roads.

Implementation of the plan starting slowly, Washington still deserved the various epithets that were coined, such as 'the city of magnificent distances' and 'the city of magnificent intentions'. Reps quotes Francis Bailey, an English visitor of 1796, as writing : 'there are about twenty or thirty houses built near the point as well as a few in South Capitol Street and about twenty others scattered over in other places : in all I suppose about two hundred : and these constitute the great city of Washington. The truth is, that not much more that one half of the city is cleared : the rest is in woods; and most of the streets which are laid out are cut through these woods, and have a much more pleasing effect now than I think when they shall be built; for now they appear like broad avenues in a park, bounded on each side by thick woods; and there being so many of them, and proceeding in so many directions, they have a certain wild, yet uniform and regular appearance, which they will lose when confined on each side by brick walls[72]. Little did Bailey know how true his observation was to be : how beautiful those distant views must have seemed but how ugly they were to become when transposed into undisciplined bricks and mortar.

Although as assessed below, Pennsylvania Avenue's non-existent street architecture has deserved all the criticism it has received, Jefferson, immediately following L'Enfant's dismissal, did ensure that the physical and symbolic link between the President's House and the Capitol would at least be defined by planned tree planting. Accordingly he invested one-third of the limited funds that were available in a landscaping programme that subdivided L'Enfant's route into a roadway flanked by footpaths and reservations.

However, the raising of money for the construction of federal buildings through sale of lots reserved for the purpose, and by lotteries, proceeded very slowly. As also the population which, from an estimated 3,000 in 1800, had only attained 23,000 by 1846 when Congress ceded back to Virginia that part of the Federal District lying across the Potomac. In the second half of the century, Washington grew much more rapidly : 61,000 in 1860 had become nearly 110,000 ten years later, under the stimulus of the Civil War. Only then were the extensive open spaces revealed on a detail map of 1854 even beginning to be occupied[73]. Washington's magnificent intentions had long since been abandoned; by mid-century it had resolved itself into 'a plan without a city'. The late nineteenth and twentieth century proposals to resolve the worst of the two-dimensional anomalies and to create, at least for the major avenues, a suitable street architecture are outside the period of this present work and will form part of the proposed succeeding volume[74].

This chapter, establishing significant aspects of the origins of urban America, is concluded with a brief mention of a further seven city examples, and a summary of reasons for the characteristic total contrast between the two-dimensional order of urban plans, and the consequent three-dimensional anarchy, embodied in visual poverty, which resulted when these plans were put into practice.

Philadelphia April 10. 1791

To Major L'Enfant
Sir
I am favoured with your letter of the 4 instant, and in compliance with your request I have examined my papers and found the plans of Frankfort on the Mayne, Carlsruhe, Amsterdam, Strasburg, Paris. Orleans. Bordeaux. Montpelier, Marseilles, Turin, and Milan, which I send in a roll by this Post. They are on large and accurate scales, having been procured by me while in those respective cities myself. And they are connected with the notes I made in my travels and often necessary to explain them to myself. I will beg your care of them and to return them when no longer useful to you, leaving you absolutely free to keep them as long as useful. I am happy that the President has left the planning of the Town in such good hands, and have no doubt it will be done to general satisfaction ... Whenever it is proposed to prepare plans for the Capitol. I should prefer the adoption of some one of the models of antiquity. which have had the approbation of thousands of years, and for the President's House I should prefer the celebrated fronts of modern buildings, which have already received the approbation of all good judges. Such are the Galerie du Louvre, the Gardens meubles, and two fronts of the Hotel de Salm. But of this it is yet time enough to consider, in the mean time I am with great esteem Sir &c

TH. Jefferson
(From 'The Writings of Thomas Jefferson', H. A. Washington. 1859; quoted in Blake McKelvey's 'The City in American History')

72. Francis Bailey, *Journal of a Tour in Unsettled Parts of North America in 1796 and 1797* (London, 1856).

73. For this magnificent map of 1854 (prepared by the US Coast Guard and Geodetic Survey) which plots every building in existence at that time, see *Of Plans and People.* a study of the plan of Washington prepared by the Washington-Metropolitan Chapter of the American Institute of Architects, May 1950.

74. For the later history of Washington, readers are referred to the following sources: J. W. Reps, *The Making of Urban America; Of Plans and People; The Grand Design.* an exhibition catalogue tracing the evolution of the L'Enfant plan and subsequent plans for developing Pennsylvania Avenue and the Mall area, organised jointly by the Library of Congress and the President's Temporary Commission on Pennsylvania Avenue (The Library of Congress, Washington, 1967) ; and a summary of proposals for the redevelopment of Pennsylvania Avenue and the creation of a new square at its White House end, based on the author's discussions in 1968 with planning staff of the president's commission ('Official Architecture and Planning'. January 1969).

DETROIT

Detroit was established in 1701 by Antoine de la Mothe Cadillac to control the Detroit River for the French, between Lakes Erie and St Clair. The original fortified settlement was about 600 by 400 ft in extent and strongly reminiscent of a mediaeval French bastide. In June 1805 fire destroyed the fort and some 300 dwellings in the adjoining civil town, but earlier that year Detroit had been designated as the capital of the new Michigan Territory of the USA. One of the three judges appointed to administer the Territory was Augustus Woodward. Judge Woodward, only thirty-one years old, was the man 'shortly to focus his numerous talents on the exciting task of creating a metropolis in the west'[75]. He had already been an experienced property speculator in his native Washington, where he knew both L'Enfant and Jefferson.

Arriving in Detroit some three weeks after the fire, Woodward was in time to prevent the citizens from redeveloping their old sites, and managed to have himself appointed 'a committee of one to lay out the new town'. Under an Act of Congress of 1806, 'To Provide for the Adjustment of Title of Land', the city area was surveyed and its new layout approved. This design, (shown in Figure 9.32), was based on a combination of rectilinear and diagonal streets, with a variety of open spaces, and was clearly influenced by the plan for Washington (see Figure 9.31).

LOS ANGELES

Los Angeles, founded in 1781, was Spain's last surviving *pueblo* (civil settlement) in the area of the United States. Philippe de Neve, Governor of Upper California, was responsible for the original plan of the city (see Figure 9.1); his instructions included the requirement that 'the plaza ought to be 200 ft wide by 300 ft long, from said plaza four main streets shall extend, two on each side, and besides these two, other streets shall run by each other... for the purpose of building there shall be marked out as many building lots as there may be agricultural plots susceptible of irrigation. Also a tract of land 600 ft wide between the planting lands and the *pueblo* shall be left vacant... every building lot shall measure 60 ft wide by 120 ft long. The front of the plaza looking towards the east shall be reserved to erect at the proper time the church and government buildings'.

By 1850 Los Angeles had slowly grown to a population of around 5,000. It was the centre of a rich agricultural district, specialising in vineyards, and the town itself retained the sombre cast of a Spanish *pueblo*, relieved, as it were, by the innovations of American comforts. The Southern Pacific Railway of 1876, and its rival the Santa Fé of 1887, with fares through from Kansas City falling as low as one dollar, provided the stimulus for a widespread urban growth, later to pass through further dramatic stages.

SAN FRANCISCO

San Francisco was established in 1776 as one of four *presidios* (military bases) created by the Spaniards in California during their last urban settlement phase in what is now the United States. (The others were San Diego, 1769; Monteray, 1770; and Santa Barbara, 1782.) In 1839 the small village of Yerba Buena, which had grown up about two miles from the original San Francisco

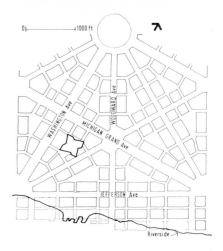

Figure 9.32 – Detroit, a part of the 1807 Woodward plan for the centre of the city, with the Grand Circus of 5½ acres at the top. The problems of implementing such an involved plan had direct parallels with the situation in London after 1666, and, perhaps inevitably, a similar outcome: within months it was largely rejected in favour of a conventional gridiron pattern. Half of the Grand Circus was however constructed, and between it and the riverfront the downtown central business area has retained some of the main diagonals in combination with more or less rectilinear building blocks.

75. J. W. Reps, *The Making of Urban America*.

presidio, alongside the natural harbour on the bay, was planned as a community of perhaps a dozen houses and some fifty residents. In 1846 the Americans took possession of San Francisco and in January 1848, when gold was first discovered in California, its population had not exceeded a thousand. By 1849 it had passed five thousand and 91,415 passenger arrivals in the port were recorded. With few exceptions these newcomers were heading for the diggings, 40 miles away, but San Francisco served as an outfitting base and suffered the full impact of the boom. The modest area of Yerba Buena was soon submerged beneath the urban extensions required to cope with the immigrants who stayed in the city and swelled its population to around 35,000 by 1850. New gridiron districts were plotted in 1849 and again in 1856. Although the hilly topography might be thought ill-suited to such a rectilinear layout, this surveyors' expediency offered the only way of ensuring a degree of control over such rapid growth. Visually the result can be superb: San Francisco, alone amongst major American cities, literally rises above the limitations of the grid.

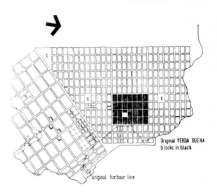

Figure 9.33 – San Francisco, the plan of 1849, showing the original Yerba Buena grid blocks filled in solid black and the original shoreline dotted.

CHICAGO

Fort Dearborn was built in 1803, on the site of the present-day city centre, to command the portage between the Ohio-Mississippi Basin and the Great Lakes. A canal had been proposed here as early as 1673 and eventually in 1826 Congress authorised federal aid for the project. This took the form of a land grant, to the State of Illinois, of alternate sections on each side of the canal for five miles. To pay expenses a town was laid out in 1830 in Section 9, Township 39, Range 14. This was the site of Chicago, hitherto consisting of the fort and a small village.

Although the canal was not operating until 1848, the promise of the trade it would bring served to create the city's first land boom. By the summer of 1833 Chicago had a population of about 350 and its harbour entrance was being improved. In 1837 Chicago, with a population of 4,170, was chartered as a city, and surviving the 1837 crisis the population stood around 20,000 when the canal opened. The first two railways reached the city from the east in 1852–3 and within years these and eight other lines made Chicago the undisputed railroad centre of middle west. Industry developed rapidly, stimulated by the Civil War, such that the population figures for 1865 were around 180,000. This figure increased fourfold over the following two decades.

Figure 9.34 – Chicago in 1834. The space between the eastern side of the platted area and Lake Michigan was reserved in federal ownership, subsequently much of it became railway land. 'S' denotes blocks reserved for schools, one of which, Reps records, was sold for 38,000 dollars in 1833 and valued at nearly $1\frac{1}{4}$ million dollars three years later, during the city's short-lived land boom.

MEMPHIS

Memphis originated around 1820 as one of a large number of towns which were established along the Mississippi after the general introduction of steamboat transport on the river in the years following the first successful Pittsburgh-New Orleans journey of 1811. By 1827 its population had grown to about 500 and Memphis was incorporated as a town. Competition for the river trade was intense with Memphis being rivalled by Raleigh and Randolph which lay some 25 miles upstream. Its eventual dominance as the regional centre was only assured when the railways chose Memphis as their western terminus, on the east bank of the river; and at the end of the nineteenth century, in spite of recurring yellow fever epidemics, the population had exceeded 100,000.

ATLANTA

In March 1838 construction work started on the newly authorised Western and Atlantic Railway. The route was planned to run from the Tennessee state border to some point on the south-eastern bank of the Chattahoochee River. The site selected for this southern terminus and the future junction for lines to be built to other cities in Georgia was known simply as Land Lot 78 in what was then Dekalb County. A small village called Terminus grew up around the end of the line, but the question of a permanent base for the railway remained unresolved until 1842, when land in the vicinity was purchased for depot buildings. This location, later that of Union Station, determined the precise centre of Atlanta, between Pryor and Central

Population breakdown – 1700 and 1790

	1700	1790
New England		
New Hampshire	10,000	141,885
Massachusetts Bay	80,000	378,000
Rhode Island	10,000	68,825
Connecticut	30,000	237,946
Total	130,000	727,443
Middle Colonies		
New York	30,000	340,000
New Jersey	15,000	184,139
Pennsylvania and Delaware	20,000	434,373*
Total	65,000	958,632
Chesapeke Colonies		
Maryland	32,258	319,728
Virginia	55,000	691,737
Total	87,258	1,001,465
The Carolinas		
North Carolina	5,000	393,751
South Carolina	7,000	249,073
Total	12,000	642,824

This figure is for Pennsylvania only, not Delaware.

(Samuel Morrison, 'Oxford History of the American People')

Figure 9.35 – Atlanta, plan of the central part of the city in 1847 within a circle of a radius of one mile. The plan shows how the early unrelated gridiron districts of the first railway settlement were subsequently resolved into a standard north-south, east-west orientated pattern.

Streets. Around the depot the new town, still known as Terminus, was laid out on the basis of 17 land lots, its layout largely determined by the railway tracks and the existing footpaths (Fig. 9.35).

Terminus was renamed Marthasville in 1843 and was chartered by the Georgia General Assembly, with a council composed of five commissioners. Early attempts on their part to restructure the town with a uniform, convenient, gridiron street pattern were frustrated by a general reluctance to assume this expense. It was felt that Marthasville would not survive the completion of the railway's construction programme; early growth therefore took place without an overall plan. By 1845, however, the Georgia Railway was brought to the Western and Atlantic's terminus and the first passenger train linked Marthasville to Augusta. Later in the same year the W & A Railway was in full operation as far as Marietta, and the commercial advantages of the key junction point were quickly recognised.

Marthasville was renamed Atlanta in honour of its lifeline on 26 December 1845. Its future assured, the town grew rapidly, achieving city status in 1847 with a charter giving it 'authority and jurisdiction extending one mile from the State (Railway) depot in all directions'. One of the council's first actions was to appoint a surveyor to plat the city within the one-mile radius circle. With a population of 6,000 by 1853, Atlanta successfully petitioned for the creation of a new county, Fulton County, with itself as the centre of government.

The Civil War at first boosted Atlanta's importance as a key industrial and transportation centre by December 1864 saw its burning by the Union forces, under General Sherman, immortalised in the epic *Gone with the Wind*, after months of near siege. From 1865 the rebuilding process was under way, with an enlarged three-mile diameter boundary of 1866 and a new, stronger charter of 1874.

Conclusion

Within a necessarily small compass this chapter has been concerned with establishing the origins of urban settlement in the USA and to trace the early development of a number of significant city examples through to the second half of the nineteenth century. In effect this is a summary of the history of urban America before the advent of mass production, factory-system industry which, although originating on a small scale before the Civil War (1861–65), consequently came to an awesome fruition. The extent to which American cities were subsequently submerged under the rising tide of national urbanisation, and a consideration of those underlying social, economic and political currents that, one hundred years later, continue to shape their form will form a major section of the proposed succeeding volume. However, several causes of the American urban malaise are deep-rooted and are best considered in the context of the present chapter. In particular, it is necessary to explain how it was that, from seemingly auspicious origins as *planned* settlements, American cities came to exhibit many of the least desirable characteristics of *laissez-faire* growth, offset only by the quality of small, isolated residential enclaves and a few individual centre-city architectural groups.

Much of what is wrong with urban America can be attributed to the gridiron although, almost as if history has for once relented, its ubiquitous presence today provides a simple, logical framework for restructured renewal which is the envy of many European planners. Without the all-American grid the situation today, given the growth rates that pertained, would have been inconceivably worse. Nevertheless it can be argued that, because the grid gave a semblance of planning, it pre-empted any further controls once growth had extinguished the few isolated civic pretensions. Frontier towns had neither the political unity enjoyed by long-established European communities when rebuilding or expanding (as in the case of London's development after the Fire, Amsterdam's Plan of the Three Canals and

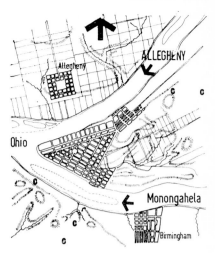

Figure 9.36 – Pittsburgh, Pennsylvania, the plan of about 1815. The original foundation was French and dated from the construction in 1724 of Fort Duquesne at the confluence of the Allegheny and Monongahela Rivers. After capturing it in 1758, the British renamed it Fort Pitt. Ten years later, along with an extensive territory in western Pennsylvania, the small but strategically and commercially well-located settlement became the property of heirs of William Penn (of Philadelphia fame). In 1784 the triangular area between the rivers was platted to give a waterfront grid alinement on both sides. The neat little settlement of Allegheny around its central square, across the river of that name, dated from 1784–8.

As long as a single proprietor or builder carried out the planning and building of a new quarter within a limited time it might have great consistency and elegance: witness Bath, Nancy and Potsdam. But when the plan existed only in patches, as in London, or when the execution of a good part of it was left for future action, as in Washington, the result might be a disorder that could hardly be distinguished from what would have existed without the plan: witness the sordid slum that is still Pennsylvania Avenue.
(Lewis Mumford, 'Culture of Cities')

Edinburgh's New Town), nor the despotic control to carry through extensive, coordinated building programmes. Neither the American West, nor for that matter the East, was settled by people who would tolerate more than a basic minimum of interference with their rights to do what they wished with their land. The fact that some pattern of land uses emerged fairly early in the post-frontier urban growth phases was only the result of natural commercial concentration.

To understand the current problems of American cities, it is important to appreciate that, compared to many of their European counterparts, they generally missed out on one vital stage in their development. With the exception of the original historic nucleus, the first main buildings would have been primarily residential but with expanding groundfloor shop and small workshop industry uses. In those European cities that acquired a consistent street architecture, these first houses around the original historic nucleus were replaced during the nineteenth and early twentieth centuries by more or less uniformly designed commercial and appartment buildings of, say, four to ten storeys. Paris is a clear example of this process, subsequently the breakdown of architectural conformity and high-rise opportunism have occurred, to varying extents, under planning controls. In addition, comparatively slower-moving European economics have delayed replacement of 'monumental' street façades.

In the average American city the intermediate phase did not occur. Replacement of the first domestic-scale buildings took place in a planning vacuum, generally after the development of high-rise techniques and a variety of styles, and after mass and private transit innovations started to break down the dominance of the original core. The result has been visual anarchy. Th most modern skyscrapers may either have dilapidated two-storey neighbours or be virtually surrounded by vacant parking areas, in turn awaiting renewal. This has been the case with Pennsylvania Avenue in Washington, where much of the south-western side has been built up with various grandiose federal buildings, whereas the other side is a sequence of buildings of all ages, sizes, styles and conditions, interspersed with a number of vacant lots. This then is the end result of Jefferson's dream of a regulated classical architecture. However there are indications that perhaps by 1992, for its bicentenary celebrations, L'Enfant's avenue may have been made more worthy of its place in the national history.

It is tempting to anticipate further this later period in the history or urban America, but it must be sufficient to leave it around the middle of the nineteenth century, its ubiquitous grids energetically going places, though without any clear aim in view.

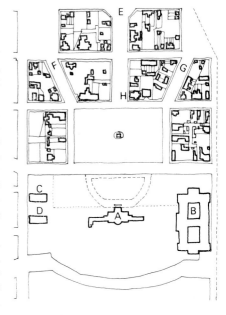

Figure 9.37 – Lafayette Square, Washington DC, at the middle of the nineteenth century. Key: A, the White House; B, US Treasury; C, War Department; D, Navy Department; E, 16th Street NW; F, Connecticut Avenue; G, Vermont Avenue; H, St John's Church.

In addition to the absence of street architecture, the United States also had hardly any historic urban spaces worthy of consideration and the few exceptions were mostly informally domestic in character, including Lafayette Square. It had been intended as a forecourt to L'Enfant's designated 'Palace', but by around 1850 all that had developed was an unrelated and above all unplanned collection of individual private houses, admittedly those of important people, known as 'the lobby of the White House'. Jefferson's ideal of a regulated classical architecture, complementing the plan, was so irrelevant to the needs of society that it failed even to create a uniform square to provide an adequate setting for the President's House.

Appendix A—China

'Chinese civilisation, and with it Chinese architecture,' writes Andrew Boyd, 'are less remarkable for their antiquity than for their continuity'[1]. Archaeological knowledge of ancient China is very recent; the first Neolithic village settlement at Yang Shao in Honan, was not identified until 1921. Daniel notes that the earliest date for these villages seems to be somewhere in the middle or at the end of the third millenium BC, and emphasises that, 'this is of course very much later than the date of incipient agriculture and the date of the first settled peasant farmers in the ancient Near East'[2]. Considered opinion now believes that agriculture had an independent origin in northern China and was not introduced from outside, as previously postulated. Figure A.1 gives the location of the first, Shang, Chinese civilisation on the river plains of the Yellow River. Its chronology, as presently accepted, is dated as: Proto-Shang (Neolithic), 2500 to 2100 BC; Early Shang, 2100 to 1750 BC; Middle Shang (Early Dynastic Period), 1750 to 1400 BC; Late Shang, 1400 to 1100 BC.

Little is known of Shang urban centres. Anyang was founded as a capital by King P'an Keng and is dated to 1384 BC but it arose late in the period[3] and there would have been earlier cities. Shang society was rigidly stratified: an urban warrior élite, based on walled cities, held absolute control over the peasant masses, a situation which only the present regime has been concerned to change. Such conditions are not favourable to widespread urban settlement and it is possible that Shang centres were few and far between. The Shang dynasty, traditionally dated 1776–1122 BC, was succeeded by the Chou dynasty (1122–255 BC) – one of the great periods, notable for the writings of Confucius and other philosophers. The second half of the third century BC, however, was a period of political turmoil; internal power struggles encouraged barbarian incursions until, under Shih Huang-ti – the first emperor of the Ch'in dynasty (221–206 BC) – reunification of northern China was possible within the Great Wall, which he commenced building around 220 BC. Eventually extending for more than 1,500 miles in length, and between 20 and 30 feet high and 12 feet wide at the top, it still defines much of the northern boundary of China.

The foundation of Ch'ang-an as a capital of China dates from the

Figure A.1 – Map showing the origins of the Shang civilisation in the valley of the Yellow River in northern China.

1. Andrew Boyd, *Chinese Architecture and Town Planning 1500BC–AD1911.*

2, 3. Glyn Daniel, *The First Civilisations.*

early years of the Han dynasty (206 BC – 220 AD). At first, as Boyd explains, 'it was a makeshift capital; enclosing two pleasure palaces from the conquered Ch'in house, the city was not a rectangular one, it lacked both the north-west and south-east corners because of irregular terrain ... this was in the early years of the new dynasty while military campaigns in many areas of the country were still going on'[4]. The Han dynasty eventually disintegrated and was followed by nearly five centuries of renewed political instability, before the Sui dynasty (581–618 AD) could effect Chinese reunification. This was based on a new city of Ch'ang-an, located some distance southeast of the old Han city. The new Ch'ang-an, known at first as Tahsing, was planned before the end of the sixth century and became during the T'ang dynasty (618–907) 'the largest, richest and grandest city in the world of that time'[5].

The seventh-century plan of Ch'ang-an is given in Figure A.2. Nelson Wu notes that, 'if it deviated from the ancient canons in many ways, it set new standards for both its size (5.7 by 5.28 miles) and its rigidity – eleven north-south streets and fourteen east-west streets – the former an odd number to privide a north-south axis'[6]. The royal place was built at the northern end of the axis, traditionally facing south, with the administrative city adjoining it to the south. The design provided for two market places, one to the east and the other west of the central axis. 'As the great capital of Tahsing was taking shape, villages were levelled, avenues laid out, and rows of trees were planted. According to legend there was one old locust tree that was not in line. It had been held over from the old landscape because, underneath it, the architect-general had often sat to watch the progress of construction, and a special order from the emperor in honour of his meritorious official spared it from being felled. Thus, except for this tree, the total superimposition of man's order on natural terrain was complete'[7].

Masuda notes in *Living Architecture: Japanese:* 'the allotment of the living quarters was quite rational. The *bo* grid blocks in Ch'ang-an, with the exception of the Imperial court and the Administrative City which were square, were all rectangular, with the long axis pointing east-west. Even the square *bo* had a single smaller road running through them from east to west making oblong building lots. The rectangular *bo* were subdivided by smaller crossing roads into four similar oblong blocks, and as a result it was possible to arrange every house facing the sun, and with a courtyard garden.'

Peking and Rome, the world's oldest major capital cities, have both experienced extremes of urban fortune. Peking is known to have been the site of a Neolithic village around 2400 BC. Later as Boyd notes, 'it was the capital of Yen (one of the "Warring States") in the third and fourth centuries BC. A provincial town in Han times, it was lost to the northern invaders during the fourth to sixth centuries AD, and recovered by T'ang. In the tenth to twelfth centuries it was held by various nomadic peoples and from 1153–1215 became Chung-tu, the capital of the kingdom of the Golden Tartars to whom the Sung emperors paid subsidies after their removal to Hangchow'[8]. Figure A.3 shows the extent of Peking as the capital of the Ch'in (265–420 AD), and Yuan (1279–1368) dynasties; and that of the Ming (1368–1644) and Ch'ing (1644–1911) dynasties. This latter area forms the historic nucleus of what is now modern Peking.

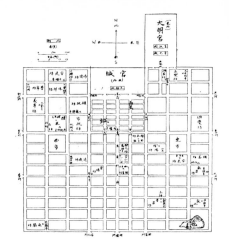

Figure A.2 – Ch'ang-an, general plan. The rectangular area added north of the original city was the Ta-ming Kung, the Pleasure Palace of the Great Luminosity. In the centre of the northern part of the city, the Imperial Palace of the Sui and T'ang dynasties occupied an area some 1½ miles long by ¾ mile wide, immediately north of the administrative city which was planned on the basis of 24 smaller grid blocks.

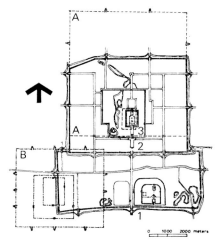

Figure A.3 – Peking, showing the extent of the Yuan dynasty capital (A) and that of the Ch'in dynasty (B). Also keyed are the Outer City (1), the Inner City (2) and the Imperial City (3). The area of the city during the Ming and Ch'ing dynasties, which forms the historic nucleus of modern Peking, is in heavy outline.

4, 5. Andrew Boyd, *Chinese Architecture and Town Planning 1500BC–AD1911.*

6, 7. Nelson I. Wu, *Chinese and Indian Architecture.*

8. Andrew Boyd, *Chinese Architecture and Town Planning 1500BC–AD1911.*

Appendix B—Japan

This brief summary of the orgins of urban settlement in Japan and the development of several key city-examples down to the Mejii Restoration of 1868 – after which Japan's industrial revolution can be said to have begun – is based mainly on two sources: *Social Change and the City in Japan*, by Takeo Yazaki (Professor of Sociology, Keio University) and *Living Architecture: Japanese*, by Tomoya Masuda.

In its pre-urban history Japan passed through similar food-gathering and agricultural-village economies to those which have been described in Chapter One and for China in Appendix A. The comparison however ends there. Although by the latter half of the third century AD the Emperor Sujin (known as 'the Emperor who opened and ruled the country') had effected unification of almost all of present-day Japan, excluding Hokkaido, 'the Japanese, unlike the Chinese, had no experience with urban life before the institution of the capital was imported from the continent (China).[9]' Masuda continues that, 'because of the small scale of the topography, and the agricultural livelihood of rice-cultivation in primarily swampy land, large settlements engaged in collective production were not necessary, and settlements rarely numbered more than one family (clan). This lack of urban experience made the capital merely a symbol of political authority and it scarcely functioned as a collective urban society. Most of the inhabitants were government officers, often single men who had left their families in the provinces'[10]. (Even when the capital later acquired unmistakable urban status this demographic instability persisted[11].)

There are fascinating parallels with ancient Egypt; in Japan it was also customary for each emperor to build for himself a new imperial residence and government accordingly moved from place to place, latterly in the central Yamato region. Since Japan was relatively isolated from the Asian mainland, as well as being racially homogeneous and politically stable, resource investment in urban defensive systems was also unnecessary during this period. *Miyako*, the modern Japanese word for capital city, originally meant the location of the imperial residence. Before the seventh century this was more a symbolic centre of association of clans, rather than the nucleus of the central government's administrative machinery required to supervise the political, military, economic and religious life of a unified country. As in ancient Egypt, virtually all the population lived in self-sufficient agricultural villages with only the one quasi-urban centre[12].

Inevitably, bureaucratic concentration did develop; the *miyako* assumed modern administrative characteristics and, 'though still shaped by the clan system, life in the capital no longer had its former flavour of an agricultural society with its small-scale system of intricate face-to-face relationships. While the ordinary people's lives advanced little beyond the primitive condition of earlier ways of the pit-dwellings, the nobility now occupied new continental homes with elevated floors, dressed stylishly in the new continental modes, and surrounded themselves with the splendid products of the fine arts and crafts of Chinese origin. The distinction between rural and urban ways of life was greatly intensified'[13]. It is hardly surprising that

Figure B.1 – Japan, outline map locating major cities including the historic ones mentioned in this brief summary of Japanese urbanism. The country is mountainous and the proportion of flat and moderately sloping land is 24 per cent.

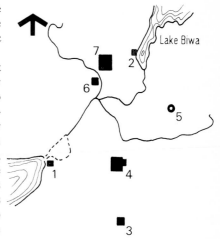

Figure B.2 – Detail map of the Yamato region, locating the following keyed ancient capitals of Japan: 1, Naniwa (Osaka); 2, Otsu; 3, Fujiwara; 4, Heijokyo (Nara); 5, Shigaraki; 6, Nagaoka; 7, Heinakyo (Kyoto).

9, 10. Tomoya Masuda, *Living Architecture: Japanese*.

11. Estimates of population in Edo in 1721 (excluding warriors and priests) give figures for men, 323,000 and women, 178,000; and in Kurume in 1699 – men, 5,143 and women 3,621.

12. See page 12 for a discussion of a comparable situation in ancient Egypt.

13. Takeo Yazaki, *Social Change and the City of Japan*.

Chinese influence extended to supplying, in 645, the plan of Ch'ang-an as the model for the first Japanese capital city.

From about 590 the *miyako* had been located in the Asuka region where a complex of palaces, temples and shrines and government offices comprised a loosely formed city. Consolidation of central authority throughout western Japan required a much larger, formally structured capital and in 645 the Emperor Kotoku instigated a move to Naniwa, now part of modern Osaka. This site controlled the mouths of the Yamatogawa and Yodogawa rivers, and major regional roads. It was also the port for trading and diplomatic contacts with the T'ang court on the Chinese continent. A planner named Aratai-no-Hirabu was responsible for laying out the new city of Naniwa as a replica of the gridiron structure of the Chinese capital of Chang'an (see Figure A.2). Yazaki notes that, 'in addition to the buildings for the top administrative organ, the *Dajokan*, there were also constructed offices for the eight major ministries, *sho*, and hundreds of subsidiary offices. Residential lots were allocated according to the stratification of nobility and commoners, with accompanying differences in sizes and shapes of houses. Reform measures included an imperial edict appointing a responsible head for each city block, *bo*, and supervisors, *rei*, for every four *bo*, who were responsible for peace and order throughout the city'[14]. Naniwa was shortlived : unable to rely on adequate support from religious leaders and nobility from the Asuka district, the emperor was forced to return there, to a new palace south of Nara (Figure B.2).

Similarly in 667 the Emperor Tenchi was thwarted in his efforts to move from Asuka to a location between Mount Osaka and Lake Biwa. Unable to break free from the powerful local clans, the imperial family recognised its limitations and in 694 the Empress Jito built Fujiwara as her capital city in the south-eastern corner of the Yamato plain. Again Chang'an served as the model. Fujiwara was accepted by religious and political leaders but, hemmed in by mountains, it was unable to expand in response to continuous growth of centralised bureaucratic activity. Furthermore its communications with Japanese provinces and China were increasingly inadequate.

The next move was to Heijokyo – the famous Nara site – where in 710 the Emperor Genmei founded a capital city that eventually served seven Emperors over a period of some seventy years before in turn being superceded by Heiankyo (modern Kyoto). Heijokyo was given a well-chosen compromise location, not far enough from the Asuka district to antagonise long-established religious and political factions, yet admirably situated for communications within the northern part of the Yamato plain. 'The conciliatory approach to the Heijokyo,' writes Yazaki, 'resulted in many Asuka temples being moved to the new city . . . in re-establishing these temples in Heijokyo steps were taken to leave the main temples in Asuka standing to pacify the feelings of the people in the old city who were dissatisfied with the transfer of the capital to Nara'[15].

The plan of Heijokyo (Fig. B.3) was also based on the Chang'an model. Its gridiron structure provided a total of 72 *bo*, each of which was subdivided into 16 equal-size minor blocks called *cho*. The city was eight *bo* in width from east to west (4,817 yards) and nine *bo* in length (6,667 yards). After the capital was moved to Heiankyo in the ninth century, a further twelve *bo* were laid out on the eastern side. These blocks comprise the central nucleus of modern Nara.

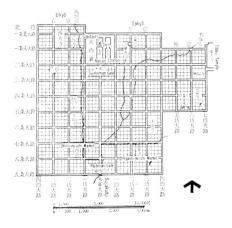

Figure B.3 – Heijokyo (Nara), general plan. The twelve grid blocks that were added to the eastern side of the plan in the early years of the city's history form the area of modern Nara. Somewhat confusingly for modern visitors, the city's modern axis runs west-east, away from the proposed area of the ancient capital which, it is believed, was only partially occupied and which lies in open country today.

Masuda notes that although 'the city blocks of Fujiwara-kyo, Heijokyo and Heiankyo were laid out on the model of Ch'ang-an . . . the shape of the blocks was influenced by the existing system of land division for rice cultivation, the *jori* system. One block in Ch'ang-an, called a *bo*, was a rectangle with its long axis lying east-west, but in Japan the *bo* were generally square. The provincial capitals, like Dazaifu in northern Kyushu ; Suho, in Hiroshima Prefecture ; and Izumo, in Shimane Prefecture, were planned so that the existing *jori* land division grid coincided with the city grid . . . the planners probably imagined this to be the only structural pattern for a city.'

Similarly extensions to the existing organic growth nuclei, either villages or castle towns, notably Edo (Tokyo), usually entailed building over areas of paddy fields whose modular orthogonal patterns determined the new street structure. Gridiron planning also facilitated maintenance and development of Japan's rigidly structured, hereditary social system with its standardised hierarchy of building plot sizes.

14, 15.   Takeo Yazaki, *Social Change and the City of Japan*.

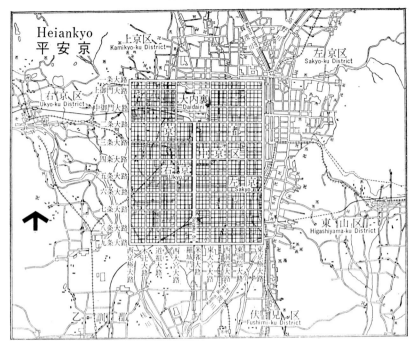

Figure B.4 – Heiankyo (Kyoto), the plan of the ancient city superimposed on the layout of modern Kyoto.

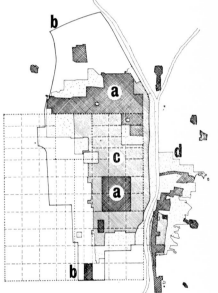

Figure B.5 – Heiankyo, showing the area occupied by the city at various stages in its history, related to the original master plan (north at the top).
Key: a, the city in the late fifteenth century; b, the 'Odoi', an earthern rampart some 15 ml in length, constructed at the end of the sixteenth century; c, the extent of the city at the beginning of the seventeenth century; d, additions of the seventeenth and eighteenth centuries (stippled); 1, Kinkaku-ji Temple (Golden Temple); 2, Daitoku-ji Monastery; 3, Shimogamo Shinto Shrine; 4, Ginkaku-ji Temple; 5, river Kamo; 7, Kiyomize-dera Temple; 8, To-ji Temple.

'Residential land grants for noblemen and officials were made for life ... nobles holding the third rank or above were allocated I *cho* (2.45 acres), fourth and fifth rank holders $\frac{1}{2}$ *cho*, and lower ranks only $\frac{1}{4}$ *cho*. Nobles of the first group were allowed frontage on the main street of the city ... commoners' lots of 1/16 or sometimes only 1/32 *cho*, allowed only about I *tsubo* (3.95 sq yds) per head'[16]. Heijokyo soon became a major religious centre with the imperial government providing generous subsidies for the construction of temples and related buildings. Todaiji became the centre of state Buddhism and its massive wooden hall, the Daibutsuden, although reconstructed on several occasions after fire, remains one of Japan's most important historic buildings. The original area of ancient Heijokyo has been deserted for upwards of one thousand years and there are no visible signs of occupation, other than a number of temple complexes located in agricultural surroundings or modern suburbs of Nara[17].

Short-lived early moves from Heijokyo were made in 741, 744 (to Naniwa), 745 and 749 (to Nagaoka, south-west of modern Kyoto). Finally in 794 the Emperor Kammu resolved to move his palace and capital to an entirely new site where no contending power had any claim and where the emperor's position would be neutral with respect to the rival families. The chosen location was in the Kuzuno district, in the northern corner of the Yamato plain, surrounded by mountains on three sides, open to the south and traversed by the river Kamo. In his edict announcing the move the emperor stated that 'the rivers and mountains of the imperial site in Kuzuno are beautiful to behold, may our subjects from all over the country come to see them'. It was, and remains to this day, a most beautiful location for a city, well situated for communications and imperial political strategy.

For the early establishment and construction of Heiankyo a special government agency, the *zoeishi*, was set up with a staff of some 150

16. By European standards Japanese homes have remained generally very small: eg in 1965 the average area of nearly 40,000 rented dwellings in the Arakawa ward in Tokyo was 22.67 sq metres at an average of 1.6 rooms per dwelling and 1.75 persons per room. (See Japan issue of 'Official Architecture and Planning', August 1970.)

17. See the Japan volume of the Nagel Travel Guide Series.

R

officers empowered to determine land and building distribution and to requisition labour and materials. The plan (Fig. B.4) was essentially a larger version of Heijokyo : its eight east-west *bo* gave a width of approximately 5,100 yards, and with an extra half *bo* at the northern end it was around 6,150 yards in length. Heiankyo was divided into eastern and western halves, each with its own market, but as with Philadelphia the process of filling in the spaces in the grid was essentially a case where natural growth failed to conform to the preconceptions of planners. The western half of Heiankyo, Ukyo, was low-lying and damp compared to the higher and dryer parts of Sakyo, to the east. Figure B.5 shows how Ukyo remained undeveloped whilst the majority of the Sakyo blocks were densely built up, except for the southern area. Development east of the Kamo was partly to take advantage of the beautiful scenery and partly to escape the severe restrictions imposed on building within the city.

Heiankyo remained as the nominal *miyako* until the Mejii Restoration of 1868 but from the middle of the ninth century the 'effete court aristocracy gradually lost its political dominance and the *miyako* degenerated into a symbolic front of authority with no true power'[18]. Power from then on was firmly in the hands of the military class and in 1192 Minamoto Yoritomo, who had received the title *Seii-tai-Shogun* (generalissimo) from the thirteen-year-old puppet emperor, devised the *bakufu* form of military government, initially based on Kamakura. Heiankyo slowly acquired commercial functions but they could not make up for the loss of the bureaucrats and even the establishment of a new *bakufu* in the city in 1366 failed to promote a lasting revival. Nevertheless, as a mainly commercial city with residual imperial functions, Keiankyo survived numerous vicissitudes (fire, earthquake and military devastation) and by the seventeenth century it had a population of between 400–500,000. But this was halved when the imperial residence moved to Edo in 1869.

Renamed Tokyo after the Mejii Restoration of 1868, Edo was originally established as a small castle town towards the end of the twelfth century. The first castle was constructed by Edo Shigenaga, the newly appointed governor of Musashi province which included the immensely fertile plain of Kanto. Edo was centrally located at the head of a bay to control land and coastal traffic and occupied part of the area of the present-day Imperial Palace. Originally named Edojuku, it enjoyed comparative prosperity but did not attain significant size until after Ota Dokan rebuilt the castle in the years following 1456. He gave it moats of a total length of around 50 *cho* (3.4 miles) and there were three lines of defence entered through 25 stone gateways. The Hirakawa river flowed through the town and promoted a thriving coastal traffic. However Edo had not yet achieved total dominance of the Kanto plain and in 1486 its development was set back when it came under the control of its main rival, Odawara. When in 1591, following the defeat of Odawara by Tokyugawa Ieyasu, the victor transferred his residence to Edo, 'there remained only a greatly diminished Edojuku at the mouth of the Hirakawa river with only a handful of merchants and craftsmen. Only humble cottages with simple stone fences could be seen in the village called Hirakawa-mara surrounding the Edojuku nucleus... the central, intermediary and tertiary fortresses had fallen into decay; embankments were poor earth and wood structures... entrances consisted of four or five wooden gates... at one place the floor of the castle was nothing

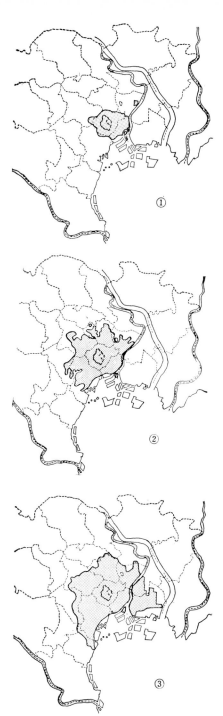

Figure B.6 – Three stages in the growth of Edo (Tokyo) : 1, 1624–43; 2, 1652–55; 3, 1673–80. (A fourth map in Yazaki's *Social Change and the City of Japan* shows the area of the city in 1840–43, effectively the same as that of the third map.)

18. Takeo Yazaki, *Social Change and the City of Japan.*

248

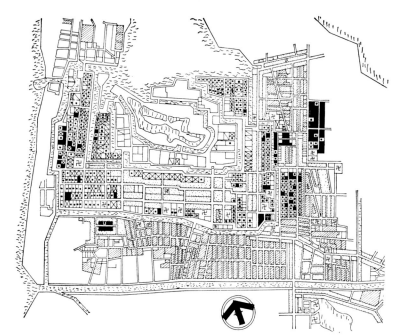

Figure B.7 – A typical castle town, after Yazaki, who observes that 'wherever the castle town was located the castle was central, and the structure of the town was schematically determined through the exercise of power in consideration of defence needs and status . . . the upper military class was close to the castle, while the lower military class was located on the town's periphery. The artisans and merchants were settled in definite sections.'

卍	Temples and Shrines
▦	Townsmen (artisans and merchants)
▨	Lower class warriors
▰	50 koku
▱	100 koku
⊠	300 koku
�	500 koku
▭	1000 koku
⦂	streams and moats
⊓	hills and dirt embankments

warrior classes by ranks as indicated by yearly rice stipend (1 koku equals 4.96 bu)

more than planks salvaged from old boats'[19]. Ieyasu's ambitious rebuilding and expansion programme moved slowly until his appointment as *shogun* in 1603 made him the effective ruler of Japan and his city the centre of *bakufu* military government[20]. The next few years ensured the dominance of Edo.

Edo's rapid growth into a very large city – probably the largest in the world in the early seventeenth century with an estimated total population certainly exceeding one million – was a result of Ieyasu's enforcement of the *sankin-kotai* system requiring the *daimyo* to be resident for alternate years in Edo. 'This kept the families of the lords in Edo permanently, and brought great numbers of retainers and warriors regularly to the capital'[21]. In addition to the 260 or so *daimyo* and 50,000 standard-bearers, there were possibly in excess of 500,000 warriors resident in the city. If to this figure is added the assumed total of 500–600,000 townsmen, shrine and temple communities and untabulated non-citizens, the grand total at that time would have been nearer 1.4 million. Yazaki gives the proportional areas as: military class 9,549 acres; temples and shrines 2,174 acres; and townsmen 2,201 acres[22]. Compared to the gross overall density of 55 to 60 persons per acre in the military class, there would have been a comparable density of approximately 250 persons per acre in the townsmen class.

In contrast to the gridiron clarity and simplicity of Heijokyo and Heiankyo, Edo at first followed the organic growth pattern of a castle town with its deliberately complex structure around the castle nucleus. The layout included both organic growth and planned districts, the former generally occupying regained marshy areas, whereas the development of the planned districts was determined by an earlier paddy-field pattern. Because of its seismic zone location, the reliance on charcoal braziers for cooking and heating, and the invariable use of lightweight timber and thatch for all but the most important buildings, Edo was particularly susceptible to fire and consequently did not lack opportunities for extensive rebuilding. As a result, the areas of gridiron development gradually extended until,

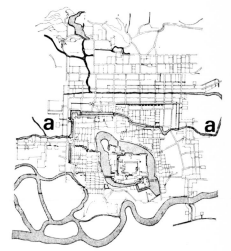

Figure B.8 – Takata, the seventeenth century plan of this castle town in Niigata Prefecture (north at the top). The military quarter around the castle is south of the line a-a; the townsmen's quarter is north of that line.

19. Tomoya Masuda, *Living Architecture: Japanese.*

20. By 1639 Edo castle, built by Ieyasu, was the largest in Japanese history.

21, 22. Takeo Yazaki, *Social Change and the City of Japan.*

249

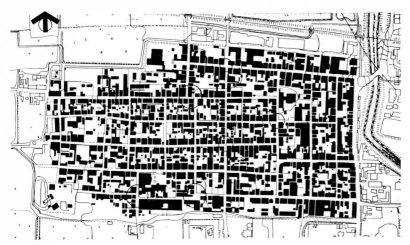

Figure B.9 – Imai, a small mid-sixteenth century town in Nara Prefecture. The use of cranked inter-sections, whereby hardly any streets are continuous, is primarily to facilitate defence and is characteristic of Japanese gridiron layouts.

by the early eighteenth century, most of the centre of the city had been regularly laid out. 1657 saw a particularly devastating fire. Over 50,000 people died, more than 50 miles of street were burnt out, and over 500 *daimyo* mansions were destroyed with those of 770 standard-bearers. The major buildings of Edo castle were burnt to the ground. Subsequent measures for fire prevention included the widening of most streets and lanes, and the formation of fire-break moats and earthen walls.

The rapid growth of Edo from the middle of the seventeenth century raised its consumer demands far beyond the productive capabilities of the Kanto district and required a very high level of imports. Most of this trade came through Osaka, an ancient centre of the commodity economy, which quickly consolidated its position as Edo's supply base and attained a population of 350,000 at the end of the seventeenth century. Since transport by road was very difficult, most of the trade was on the basis of coastal traffic.

Appendix C—Mexico: the Aztecs

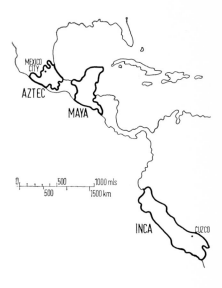

'The Aztecs', writes G. C. Vaillant, 'were a concentrated population of independent groups living in the Valley of Mexico and later welded into an empire, whose authority reached out to dominate much of southern and central Mexico'[23]. They were the last of a series of civilisations in Mexico, flourished from the fifteenth century, and were preceded by other cultures with significant urban activities including the Zapotec capital of Monte Alban and the Olmec ceremonial centre of Teotihuacan (Fig. C.1).

The earliest permanent village settlements in the valley date from about 1500 BC. It was a propitious environment for eventual synoecism : '7,000 feet above sea-level, high mountain chains walled in a fertile valley in which lay a great salt lake, Texcoco, fed at the south by two sweet water lagoons, at the north-west by two more, and at the north-east by a sluggish stream which drained the fertile Valley of Teotihuacan. The lakes were shallow and their marshy shores, thick with reeds, attracted a teeming abundance of wild fowl. On the wooded mountain slopes deer abounded. During the rainy season thick alluvial deposits, ideal for primitive agriculture, were washed down along the lake shore'[24].

Tenochtitlan was established in 1325 AD by the Aztecs as a modest mud-hut village on an island in Lake Texcoco, some $3\frac{1}{2}$ miles from its south-western shore and about one mile south of a second small island, Tlatelolco, which had been occupied since about 1200 AD. The two islands gradually coalesced into the complex of islands separated by numerous canals, that formed the city of Tenochtitlan, present-day Mexico City. Two factors determined this development : first, the gradual drying out of the lake; and second, the formation of intensively cultivated *chinampas*, or floating islands, out of the extremely fertile soil dredged up from the lake bed (a technique still employed on the outskirts of the modern city, according to Hardoy[25]). During the reign of Montezuma I (1440–68) the Aztec state greatly extended its boundaries and Tenochititlan rapidly developed as the political, military, religious and cultural capital. An aqueduct was built to bring in pure water; a dike some 10 miles in length was

Appendices C, D and E summarise significant aspects of the three major Central and South American urban civilisations, those of the Aztec, Maya and Inca. Their locations are shown on the map above.

It must be stressed that these civilisations had all been through lengthy formative periods, and indeed were in a state of decline, by the time of the Spanish Conquest.

These three appendices are based on one general source, Jorge Hardoy's 'Urban Planning in Pre-Columbian America' (a well illustrated but not very orderly book) and three specialist works, G. C. Vaillant's 'Aztecs of Mexico', Michael D. Coe's 'The Maya' and J. Alden Mason's 'The Ancient Civilisations of Peru'.

Figure C.1 – Teotihuacan, detail map of the central part of the city. This immensely important archaeological site is located some 25 miles north-east of Mexico City (Tenochtitlan). In the 1520s, when the Conquistadors arrived in the Valley of Mexico, it was about 8 miles from the shore of Lake Texcoco, across from Tenochtitlan.

Hardoy notes that, 'from the very last centuries of the first millenium BC, Teotihuacan was the residence of a large and permanent population occupied in government duties, services, trade and handicrafts without the necessity to leave the city to earn their living'.

Whilst the structure of Teotihuacan includes parts that are recognisably gridiron-based, it is preferable to regard this plan in general as consisting of a large number of various sized square and rectangular precincts and buildings, organised according to the same orientation. The general layout dates from the first three or four centuries AD and takes the form of groups of buildings arranged on either side of the main north-south axis. This main street, called the Street of the Dead, was some 145 ft in width and led up to the impressive Pyramid of the Moon running from the south for about $3\frac{3}{4}$ miles.

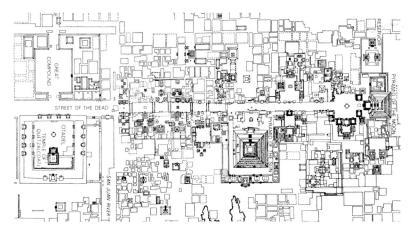

23, 24. G. C. Vaillant, *Aztecs of Mexico*.

25. Jorge Hardoy, *Urban Planning in Pre-Columbian America*.

constructed to prevent flooding and to obviate effects of increasing salinity on the cultivated *chinampas*; and architects were brought in to design suitably impressive buildings. The cruciform basis of the city's plan was probably determined by the preceding Aztec king, Itzcoatl, (1428–40), who built the three causeways linking the islands to the mainland. A reconstruction of the plan of Tenochtitlan as it existed in 1519, when Cortes and his four hundred men first landed, is given in Figure C.2.

In his *Aztecs of Mexico*, Vaillant includes as one chapter a 'Glimpse of Tenochtitlan: what the Spaniards saw when they entered this great Aztec Capital'. He quotes Bernard Diaz del Castillo, one of Cortes' men, who after first seeing the city 'did not know what to say or whether what appeared before us was real, for on one side in the land were great cities and in the lake ever so many more, and the lake itself was crowded with canoes, and in the causeway were many bridges at intervals, and in front of us stood the great City of Mexico'. Tenochtitlan was the Venice of pre-Columbian America; apart from the main causeways there were few streets, and transport was either on the backs of bearers or by boat. The city had two magnificent architectural complexes: one in the centre of Tenochtitlan, comprising the sacred enclosure with its 25 temples, the most impressive of which had been completed only in 1487, the royal palace of Montezuma, and a public plaza; and the other in Tlaltelolco with its great temple to the war god, Huitzilopochtli. Tlaltelolco also included the city's main market place. The city was divide into twenty tribal divisions or 'wards', each of which enjoyed local government autonomy. Estimates of the population of Tenochtitlan give 60,000 households and a total of about 300,000 people.

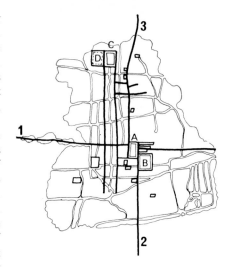

Figure C.2 – Tenochtitlan (Mexico City), reconstruction of the plan of the 1520s when Cortes entered the city. It occupied a large number of islands which comprise an urban unit with very few streets, the most important of which are in thick line. Key: 1, causeway to the western shore of Lake Texcoco, a distance of some 1½ miles in 1520; 2, causeway to the south, 4 miles in length; 3, causeway leading from Tlatelolco, the northern of the city's twin nuclei, to the northern shore of the bay in which Tenochtitlan was located; A, the Great Temple of Tenochtitlan; B, the palace of Montezuma II; C, the Great Temple of Tlatelolco; D, the market place of Tlatelolco.

Appendix D—Central America: the Mayas

The Conquistadors found the Maya living in decline in the tropical forests and mountainous areas of Guatemala, Honduras and Yucatan in southern Mexico. Daniel states that 'they have been called the Greeks of the New World, and in their achievements they certainly outstripped other American pre-Columbian high cultures'[26]. However, although they had considerable knowledge of mathematics and astronomy (their calendar had leap year corrections almost as accurate as those of the present day), they had no metal technology except that which produced a few gold and copper ornaments. Their magnificent stone buildings were fashioned with stone implements. Their agricultural methods were also rudimentary being based on the technique of 'slash and burn' clearance of small fields in the jungle, the *milpas*, which had a fertile life of only a few years. When the soil was exhausted an area further into the forest had to be cleared and the process started all over again. Obviously this was not a very productive method of cultivation and when the added problem of the encroaching forest is considered, one realises the difficulties facing the Mayan civilisation. Finally it succumbed, though whether on account of agricultural collapse, or because of disease or earthquakes, has not yet been established.

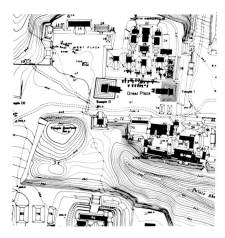

Figue D.1 – Tikal, layout of the central part of the site, north at the top. The area in this map is 0.9 ml wide by just over 1.25 ml long.

26. Glyn Daniel, *The First Civilisations*.

The generally agreed periods in Maya history comprise : the Formative (1500 BC – 150 AD), during which time village settlements were established in all Maya areas; a short Proto-Classic (150–300 AD); the Classic (300–900); and the Post-Classic phases which lasted until the Spanish Conquest of the 1520s. Maya civilisation reached its peak of achievement during the Classic period, notably in the lowlands. Subsequently it went through a series of retrogressive phases and was effectively a dead culture by the time of the Spanish invasion.

Michael Coe states that 'the great culture of the Maya lowlands during the Late Classic period is one of the "lost" civilisations of the world, its hundreds of ceremonial centres buried under an almost unbroken canopy of tropical forest'[27]. Opinions differ as to whether or not these centres amounted to 'cities'. Coe is in no doubt that 'none of the great sites...were anything of the sort'. Other authorities accord them full urban status. Hardoy is not certain, observing that 'in every Mayan settlement a clear differentiation has to be made between (1) the central complex; (2) an intermediate sector; and (3) the agricultural countryside. Because of their higher concentration of buildings and superior architecture the central complex and the intermediate sector may be qualified as urban by comparison with the countryside, although they had neither the density, nor the layout, nor the visual characteristics of what would be considered as urban today, or even then, among other Middle American cultures'[28].

Densities in the *milpas* areas of Mayan settlement were comparatively low, perhaps two to three persons per hectare, living in scattered, unplanned groups of generally less than five houses. In the intermediate zone the density of houses and *milpas* was markedly higher and temples and palaces also appear. A description of a typical central complex is given by Coe as consisting 'of a series of stepped platforms topped by masonry superstructures, arranged around broad plazas or courtyards. In the really large sites like Tikal there may be a number of building complexes interconnected by causeways. Towering above all are the mighty temple pyramids built from limestone blocks over a rubble core...the bulk of the construction however is taken up by the palaces, single-storied structures...containing plastered rooms, sometimes up to several dozen in the same building'[29]. The central area of the ruins at Tikal, a meticulously mapped site of around 900 AD, is illustrated in Figure D.1.

Appendix E—Peru: the Incas

The empire of the Incas ultimately extended along the Pacific coast of South America for some 2,500 miles, from Ecuador in the north to midway down the coast of Chile in the south. It included the narrow seaboard plains but was essentially a highland civilisation centred on the valleys and plateaux of the Andean range. The Incas had no form of writing but could keep arithmetic records by means of knotted strings called *quipus*. 'Technologically speaking,' Daniel tells us, 'the Incas were in a full Bronze Age when discovered by the Spaniards. Their craftsmen made knives, chisels, axes of a mixture of copper and tin, but these tools were [often] not hard enough to cut rock...'[30].

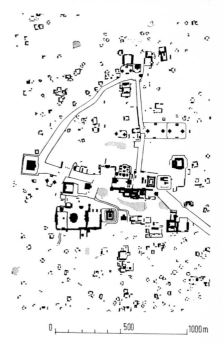

Figure D.2 – Tikal, enlarged plan of the western part of the centre. Coe notes that 'within a little over six square miles there were about 3,000 structures, ranging from lofty temple pyramids and massive palaces to tiny household units of thatch-roofed huts'.

Figure E.1 – Cuzco, plan of the city at the end of the nineteenth century, showing the extent of the Inca square and the way in which it was broken up by subsequent Spanish redevelopment.

27, 28, 29.   Michael D. Coe, *The Maya.*
30.   Glyn Daniel, *The First Civilisations.*

Although it is believed that indigenous plant domestication had reached its maturity by the third millenium BC, and that agriculture along the Peruvian coastline was rapidly advanced following the introduction of maize corn from Mexico around 1500 BC, little is known of pre-Inca urban cultures during the first millenium AD. One location which has been partially investigated is the valley of Tiahuanaco, 'the last place in the world to expect a great stupendous archaeological site,' writes J. Alden Mason[31]. The valley is 13 miles south-east of Lake Titicaca and some 13,000 feet above sea level. It is a bleak, chilly, practically treeless *puna*, too high for intensive agriculture. How then to explain the existence of several extensive masonry structures and human statuary? Mason leaves the question open, but notes a considerable superficial likeness to Carnac, in Brittany, and suggests that Tiahuanaco may also have been an important, infrequently visited ceremonial centre. No accurate dates are available; estimates range from 150–360 AD to 800–1000 AD.

The period 1000–1400 is known as the 'urbanist period' in Peruvian history, during which many 'city states', the results of protracted synoecism, struggled for local mastery before gradually being drawn into the one Inca empire. Chimu, on the fertile northern coastal strip, was probably the most important of these kingdoms and was able to retain considerable political and cultural autonomy under Inca rule. Most valleys supported their own urban nucleus, with a capital city at Chan-Chan, alongside the Pacific near modern Trujillo. Mason describes it as a 'stupendous site – and sight. The ruins cover about six square miles, filled, the major part at least, with great tall boundary walls, smaller house walls, streets, reservoirs, pyramids and other edifices and features expected of a great metropolitan centre'[32] (Fig. E.2).

The 'urbanist period' was followed by the 'imperialist period' from 1440 to 1432: this is the only Inca period whose history is known to the average reader. Inca history was traditional and was based on royal reigns, commencing in about 1200 AD with eight undated and generally insignificant emperors followed by five rulers of the Inca empire proper. The first of these was Pachacuti (the ninth in succession) whose reign lasted from 1438–71. Pachacuti was both a great military leader and, apparently a skilled urbanist. From their capital Cuzco, he and his son, Topa Inca (1471–93), extended imperial power for some 2,500 miles along the coast and over an area of about 350,000 square miles.

Inca history credits Pachacuti with the basic form of Cuzco. Amongst many other works he is reputed to have greatly increased the size of the city, and to have demolished all the villages for six miles around to increase its agricultural land. The plan of Cuzco in the second half of the nineteenth century, on which Figure E.1 is based, suggests that the Inca city had a rectilinear base, modified most probably by the terrain.

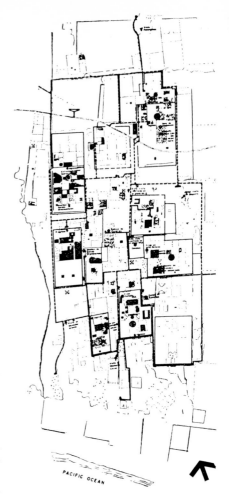

Figure E.2 – Chan-Chan, general arrangement of the citadels.

31, 32. J. Alden Mason, *The Ancient Civilisations of Peru*.

Appendix F—Indian mandalas

This brief summary of the rôle of the mandala in Indian town planning is based on 'City and Temple Layout: The Vision of a Cosmic Plan', in Andreas Volwahsen's *Living Architecture: Indian*.

An ancient Indian text records: 'A long time ago something existed that was not defined by name or known in its form. It blocked the sky and the earth. When the gods saw it they seized it and pressed it upon the ground, face downwards. In throwing it to the ground, the gods held on to it. Brahma had it occupied by the gods and called it *vastu-purusha.*'

Volwahsen explains that 'the name given to form is mandala. Thus the so-called *vastu-purusha* mandala is the form assumed by existence, by the phenomenal world ... the *vastu-purusha* mandala is an image of the laws governing the cosmos, to which men are just as subject as is the earth on which they build. In their activities as builders men order their environment in the same way as once in the past Brahma forced the undefined *purusha* into a geometric form ... building is an act of bringing disordered existence into conformity with the basic laws that govern it. This can only be achieved by making each monument, from the hermit's retreat to the layout of a city, follow exactly the magic diagram of the *vastu-purusha* mandala.'

The *vastu-shastras* (general manuals on architecture) define thirty-two ways in which the *vastu-purusha* mandala can be formed. The basic mandala is a square; the remainder consist of this square divided into 4, 9, 16, 25, and up to 1,024 smaller squares, called *padas*. Scale is immaterial 'so far as its magic efficacy is concerned. In a plan for a large area it can regulate the disposition of the various buildings, and in the plan of a temple it can define the rhythm of the architectural members or the proportion between the thickness of the wall and the size of the interior.'

The manuals determined all aspects of town planning: the selection of the site, the choice of a suitable mandala, its subdivision according to a rigid caste system, the mystical procedures for setting out, and the detail design of important buildings. In choosing the mandala, the priest-astrologer was concerned to reconcile astrological auguries with the requirement that there should be as many *padas* as residential quarters. Volwahsen notes that mandalas with 64 and 81 *padas* were particularly popular (Fig. F.1).

Early in the eighteenth century the ancient city of Jaipur was replanned by its ruler, Jai Singh II, according to the rules of the *vastu-shastras*. Discounting irregularities in the plan (Fig. F.3) – the extension to the east and the incomplete north-western corner – Volwahsen describes the plan as follows: 'a splendid avenue running from east to west, an incomplete street parallel to it, and the two main streets which run from north to south divide the city (which was originally rectilinear in plan) into nine parts. The central area of the Brahma-sthana is reserved for the palace of the Maharaja; the other blocks are subdivided more or less regularly by side streets and unpaved footpaths ... individual professional groups were allotted certain quarters of the town, wholly in accordance with *vastu-vidya*. If one wants to go to a cloth-merchant, one must go to a particular street reserved for such persons ... even bicycle shops are grouped together.'

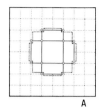
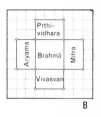

Figure F.1 – Two north Indian mandalas: A, the *manduka-mandala*, containing 8 by 8 *padas*. Around the central Brahma-sthana (4 units) are the *padas* of the inner gods (2 units) and the ring of the outer gods (1 unit). The points of intersection (*marmas*) must not be interrupted by the lines of the ground plan (shown here by thick lines). The *paramasayika-mandala*, keyed as B, contains 9 by 9 *padas*.

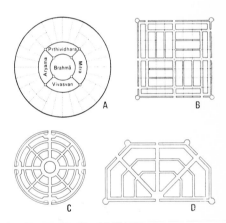

Figure F.2 – Four mandala variants: A, a circular *manduka-mandala*; B, a swastika-form city plan; C, an ideal city plan based on A; D, a *kheta* city for Shudras, low caste inhabitants, without a proper centre.

Figure F.3 – Jaipur, general plan.

S

Appendix G—Jane Jacobs' New Obsidian Theory

Jane Jacobs' assertion in her *Economy of Cities* that 'agriculture and husbandry arose in cities', rather than as an essential rural pre-requisite for the creation of cities (as the accepted traditional view has always held) was introduced but not challenged in Chapter One.

New Obsidian was imagined by Mrs Jacobs to be a 'pre-agricultural city of hunters' in which 'grain culture and domestication of animals could have emerged'. It was 'the centre of a large trade in obsidian, the tough, black, natural glass produced by some volcanoes. The city is located on the Anatolian plateau of Turkey.' Two reasons are given for her choice of New Obsidian: first, 'the ruins of a city, Çatal Hüyük, that might well have been the successor to my imaginary New Obsidian, have been found by a British archaeologist, James Mellaart, and are beautifully described and illustrated in his book, *Çatal Hüyük*' (see Figure G.1 and caption description); second, 'obsidian was the most important industrial material traded in the part of the world where scholars believe wheat and barley culture first arose ... thus a city in which obsidian trade centred is a logical choice as a pre-agricultural metropolis'.

'In 8500 BC, New Obsidian's population numbers about two thousand persons. It is an amalgam of the original people of the settlement and of the obsidian-owning tribes, much of whose population is now settled within the city because of the trade and the various kinds of work connected with it ... the people of the city are wonderfully skilled at crafts and will become still more so because of the opportunity to specialise ... The system of trade that prevails runs this way: the initiative is taken by the people who want to buy something. Travelling salesmen have not yet appeared on the scene; the traders, rather, regard themselves, and are regarded as, travelling purchasing agents. Undoubtedly, they take trade goods of their own to the place of purchase, but this is used like money to buy whatever it is they came for ... for the most part the barter goods they bring consist of the ordinary produce of their hunting territories.'

Thus, as Mrs Jacobs asserts at the crucial stage in her argument, 'the food of the New Obsidian is derived in two ways: part of it comes from the old hunting and gathering territory—which is still hunted, foraged and patrolled as diligently as it was formerly when the people were solely hunters and gatherers—and from territories of the volcano-owning groups whose headquarters are now also at New Obsidian. But a large proportion of the food is imported from foreign hunting territories. This is food that is traded at the barter square for obsidian and for other exports of the city. Food is the customary goods brought by customers who do not pay in copper, shells, pigments or other unusual treasures. Wild food of the right kind commands a good exchange. In effect, New Obsidian has thus enormously enlarged its hunting territory by drawing, through trade, upon the produce of scores of hunting territories. The right kind of food to bring to the barter square is non-perishable. Except in times of great shortage and unusual hunger when anything is welcome, only non-perishable food is accepted. There are two reasons for this. First unless the customers are from territories nearby, non-perishable foods stand the trip to the city best. Second, and more important, the people of

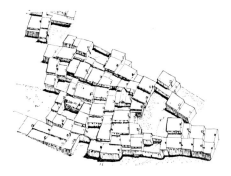

Figure G.1 — Çatal Hüyük, reconstruction of a sector of the town showing the arrangement of houses, characteristically entered by ladder from the roof, and grouped around a public square.

Mellaart's excavations of the site of Çatal Hüyük, with its fifty-foot deposit of Neolithic remains, yielded twelve successive building levels, representing twelve different cities, not phases or repairs of original buildings. He numbered them from the top as levels 0 to X (there were found to be two different building levels in VI–VIA and VIB). Radio-carbon dating has established an estimate of c 6500 BC for the oldest of the twelve levels, and c 5600 BC for levels I to 0. After 5600 BC the old mound of Çatal Hüyük was abandoned and a new settlement established to the west. In his book *Çatal Hüyük* Mellaart observes that 'the need for defense may be the original reason for the peculiar way in which the people of Çatal Hüyük constructed dwellings without doorways, and with sole entry through the roof. Villages of this type are still found in central and eastern Anatolia ... a solid outer wall built of stone is the alternative, but stone was not available on the plain ... moreover the city of Çatal Hüyük was extensive and would need considerable manpower to man the entire circuit against enemy attack. Once the wall was breached an enemy would have been able to break into the city. The solution adopted was a different one: the planners did not build a solid wall but surrounded the site with an unbroken row of houses and storerooms, accessible only from the roof.'

New Obsidian like to store the food and mete it out rationally rather than gorge upon it and perhaps go hungry later. Thus the imported food consists overwhelmingly of live animals and hard seeds.'

Mrs Jacobs develops the basis of New Obsidian's trading activity at considerable length but we need consider her argument no further : already at least three vital questions have arisen which require answers that are not in fact forthcoming. First, a total catchment area of 2,000 square miles would have been needed to provide foodstuffs for New Obsidian's population of 2,000. This figure is based on the highest population density estimates for comparable gathering economies, quoted on page 3 : France, one person per square mile (average 0.1 to 0.2); North America, 0.11 persons per square miles; Australia, 0.03 persons per square mile. But the figure for New Obsidian is based on the exceptionally favourable food resources enjoyed by the Magdalenian culture in France, and a catchment area assessed on an average density of 0.1 persons per square mile seems an entirely reasonable basis on which to calculate New Obsidian's territory as measuring 20,000 square miles in area, without making allowances for the food requirements of those tribesmen trading with the city. At least 20,000 square miles gives a circle of a radius of approximately 80 miles. How would the seeds, nuts, berries etc have been transported in quantities into New Obsidian over such distances? Wheeled transport was still 5,000 years in the future; utilisation of pack-animal power also came much later. (Mellaart, moreover, confirms that New Obsidian in 8500 BC would have been Pre-Pottery Neolithic. The storage of non-perishable foodstuffs raises yet another question.) Secondly, it must be seriously doubted as to whether any significant number of wild animals could have been caught and driven to New Obsidian. Huntsmen made kills and, in the absence of curing techniques, were obliged to eat as much as they themselves could, as quickly as possible. (Mellaart mentions domestication of sheep around 8900 BC. This however is no aid to Mrs Jacobs' argument : such domestication was practically certain to be the work of hunters and not city dwellers.) Thirdly, it is surely reasonable to expect that all this trading activity and meting out of stores required some kind of permanent recording system? Yet, as far as is known, the earliest forms of writing originated several millenia later.

The credibility of New Obsidian is not vital to *Economy of Cities* which is otherwise a valuable work, although when doubt is cast on some of the author's typically dogmatic claims, the main body of the work must inevitably come under very careful scrutiny. It would seem that Jane Jacobs was over-ambitious in seeking to extend her basic thesis to take in Mellaart's intriguing finds at Çatal Hüyük – findings which pose many questions, but which at present are best taken as showing that, under certain favourable conditions, permanent concentrations of people could be established as early as 8500 BC. The 'dogma of agricultural primacy' is not seriously challenged by New Obsidian.

Figure G.2 – Plan of building level VII (c 6050–6200 BC). In writing of the town plan of Çatal Hüyük, Mellaart is in no doubt that 'its builders were well aware of the necessity of planning an orderly settlement, far removed from the disorderly and random agglomeration of free-standing huts and hovels characteristic of the Protoneolithic period in Palestine, the only region where settlements of this period have been explored *in extenso*.'

This is of course a challenging statement of great import. If Çatal Hüyük *was* planned as a whole then radical revision of the history of town planning is required, for it would predate even the Harappan cities by some three thousand or more years. However, Mellaart was able to excavate only an area of about one acre (about one-thirtieth of the evident *tell*) and he seems mistaken in assuming that renewal of a part of a city comprising a number of more or less rectangular cells, or the addition of a similar unit, can be seen as representing deliberate town planning. Rather, it is a form of controlled organic growth.

Appendix H—Comparative plans of cities

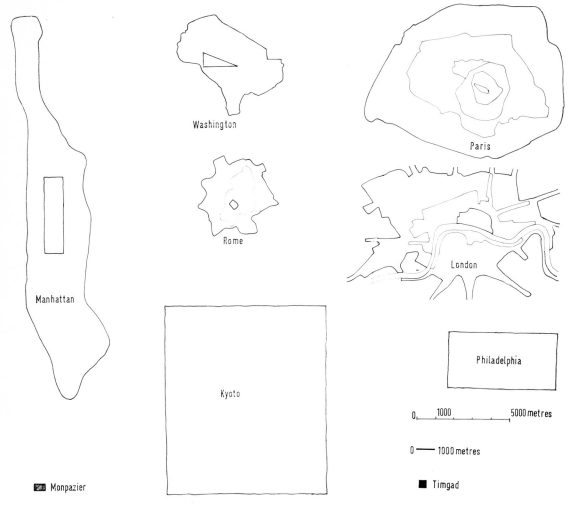

Washington

Paris

Rome

London

Manhattan

Philadelphia

Kyoto

0   1000   5000 metres

0 —— 1000 metres

Monpazier

Timgad

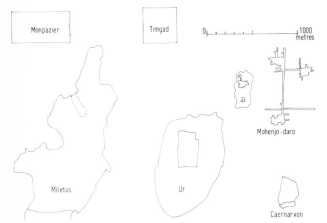

Monpazier

Timgad

0   1000 metres

Mohenjo-daro

Miletus

Ur

Caernarvon

Outline plans of important examples of urban areas drawn to the same scales. Above are seven important cities; on the left are six much smaller ones at one-fifth of the scale of the large ones. For direct size comparison, Monpazier and Timgad have been drawn to both scales and shown in the upper group as solid black, for meaningful illustration. An immediate value of this comparative presentation of areas is to show how small ancient cities were.

For comparison see also Manhattan Island of New York City, including Central Park in outline (Fig. 9.18); Washington DC, including the Federal Triangle, and showing the extent of L' Enfant's plan (Fig. 9.28); Rome, with three growth stages down to 280 AD (Fig. 3.6) Paris, with its successive rings of fortifications down to 1841 (Fig. 6.13); London growth down to 1830 (Fig. 8.27); Philadelphia as originally planned (Fig. 9.12); Kyoto-Heiankyo as originally planned (Fig. B.5); Monpazier (Fig. 4.26); Miletus (Fig. 2.8); Ur of Chaldees (Fig. 1.8); Mohenjo-daro (Fig. 1.21); and Caernarvon as in the Middle Ages (Fig. 4.31).

Select bibliography

Of the vast number of sources on urban history I have listed those works which have been of great assistance in the preparation of this book and which are strongly recommended for further reading. Others are referred to in the footnotes to the main text.

THE EARLY CITIES

Prehistory and the Beginnings of Civilisation. Jacquetta Hawkes and Sir Leonard Woolley. George Allen & Unwin. 1963
Technology in the Ancient World. Henry Hodges. Allen Lane Press, Penguin Books. 1970
The First Civilisations: The Archaeology of their Origins. Glyn Daniel. Thames and Hudson. 1968 (Penguin paperback 1971)
What Happened in History. V. Gordon Childe. Penguin Books. 1964
World Prehistory: A New Outline. Grahame Clark. Cambridge University Press. 2nd edition 1969

GREEK CITY STATES

Greek Town Building. Anthony Kriesis. National Technical University of Athens. Athens. 1965
How the Greeks built Cities. R. E. Wycherley. Macmillan. 2nd edition 1962
L'Urbanisme dans la Grèce antique. Roland Martin. A. and J. Picard. Paris. 1956
The Architecture of Ancient Greece. W. B. Dinsmoor. Batsford. 3rd edition 1950
The Greeks. H. D. F. Kitto. Penguin Books. 1951

ROME AND THE EMPIRE

Daily Life in Ancient Rome. Jerome Carcopino. Penguin Books. 1956
Roman Britain. I. A. Richmond. Penguin Books. 1955
Roman Britain and English Settlements. Oxford History of England Book I. R. G. Collingwood and J. N. L. Myres. Oxford University Press. 1937
The Romans. R. H. Barrow. Penguin Books. 1970
The Ruins and Excavations of Ancient Rome. Rodolfo Lanciani. Macmillan. 1897
Town and Country in Roman Britain. A. L. F. Rivet. Hutchinson. 1964

MEDIAEVAL TOWNS

An Historical Geography of Western Europe before 1800. C. T. Smith. Longman. 1967
Mediaeval Cities. Henri Pirenne. Princeton University Press. Princeton. 1925
Mediaeval England: An Aerial Survey. M. W. Beresford and J. K. S. St Joseph. Cambridge University Press. 1958
Mediaeval Town Planning. T. F. Tout. Manchester University Press. 1968
New Towns of the Middle Ages. M. W. Beresford. Lutterworth Press. 1967
The Italian City Republics. Daniel Waley. Weidenfeld & Nicolson. 1969
The Making of the English Landscape. W. G. Hoskins. Hodder & Stoughton. 1970 (Penguin paperback 1970)

continued on page 260

THE RENAISSANCE: ITALY SETS A PATTERN

International History of Urban Development in Southern Europe: Italy and Greece. E. A. Gutkind. Free Press of Glencoe. New York. 1969
The Story of Rome. Norwood Young. J. M. Dent. 1901
Venice. James Morris. Faber. 1960

THE RENAISSANCE: FRANCE

French Architecture. Pierre Lavedan. Penguin Books. 1956
Histoire de l'urbanisme: Renaissance et temps modernes. Pierre Lavedan. Laurens. Paris. 1941
Paris through the Ages. Pierre Couperie. Barrie & Jenkins. 1970
Sébastien le Prestre de Vauban, 1633–1707. Reginald Blomfield. Methuen. 1971

THE RENAISSANCE: EUROPE IN GENERAL

International History of Urban Development in Central Europe. E. A. Gutkind. Free Press of Glencoe. New York. 1964
The Architectural Planning of St Petersburg. Y. A. Egorov. Ohio University Press. Athens, Ohio. 1969
The Making of Dutch Towns. Gerald L. Burke. Cleaver-Hume Press. 1956

THE RENAISSANCE: BRITAIN

Georgian London. John Summerson. Barrie & Jenkins. 1970 (Penguin paperback 1969)
London, the Unique City. S. E. Rasmussen. Jonathan Cape. 1948
Mid-Georgian London. Hugh Phillips. Collins. 1964
The Georgian Buildings of Bath from 1730 to 1830. Walter Ison. Kingsmead Reprints. Bath. 1969
The Making of Classical Edinburgh. A. J. Youngson. Edinburgh University Press. 1966
The Rebuilding of London after the Great Fire. T. F. Reddaway. E. Arnold. 1951

URBAN USA

A History of American Economic Life. Edward Chase Kirkland. Appleton-Century-Crofts. New York. 3rd edition 1951
A History of the United States. R. B. Nye and J. E. Morpurgo. Penguin Books. 1955
The Making of Urban America. J. W. Reps. Princeton University Press. Princeton. 1965

GENERAL REFERENCE

A Prospect of Cities. Cecil Stewart. Longman. 1965 (3,6)
Design of Cities. Edmund Bacon. Thames and Hudson. 1967 (3,5,8)
Matrix of Man. Sibyl Moholy-Nagy. Pall Mall Press. 1969
Space, Time and Architecture. Sigfried Giedion. Oxford University Press. 5th edition 1967 (5)
The City in History. Lewis Mumford. Secker & Warburg. 1961
Town and Country Planning. Patrick Abercrombie. Oxford University Press. 3rd edition 1959 (5)
Town and Square. Paul Zucker. Columbia University Press. New York. 1959
Town and Buildings. S. E. Rasmussen. MIT Press. 1969 (6,7,8)

Relevance to particular chapters is noted in brackets

Index of place names

Figures in italics indicate illustrations

General Index